Issues in Feminism

Issues in Feminism

A First Course in Women's Studies

SHEILA RUTH

SOUTHERN ILLINOIS UNIVERSITY, EDWARDSVILLE

FOREWORD BY SHEILA TOBIAS

Houghton Mifflin Company   Boston

Dallas   Geneva, Illinois   Hopewell, New Jersey   Palo Alto   London

To my father, George Sack,
whose values and dreams formed mine

To Amity, my daughter,
who gives so much and is so much

To Michael, for Technicolor

Chapter-opening drawings by Michael Crawford.

"Femininity" reprinted from *New Introductory Lectures on Psychoanalysis* by Sigmund Freud, translated and edited by James Strachey. By permission of W. W. Norton & Company, Inc. Copyright 1933 by Sigmund Freud. Copyright renewed 1961 by W. J. H. Sprott. Copyright © 1965, 1964 by James Strachey.

The lines from "Snapshots of a Daughter-in-Law" are reprinted from *Snapshots of a Daughter-in-Law, Poems 1954–1962* by Adrienne Rich, with the permission of W. W. Norton & Company, Inc. Copyright © 1956, 1957, 1958, 1959, 1960, 1961, 1962, 1963, 1967.

Selection from Chapter One is reprinted from *The Feminine Mystique* by Betty Friedan, with the permission of W. W. Norton & Company, Inc. Copyright © 1974, 1963 by Betty Friedan.

Printed in the U.S.A.

Library of Congress Catalog Card Number: 79-88795

ISBN: 0-395-28691-3

Contents

Foreword

Ten years ago, when individual scholars, teachers, and students began to work in what has become the field of Women's Studies, there was precious little material available in any compact form and, except for a few seminal works such as those of Simone de Beauvoir, Margaret Mead, and Betty Friedan, even less analysis.

At the outset, the priorities centered on the need to make up for deficiencies in information about women: what women did and what happened to them (history); which, if any, of the characteristics taken to be universally true about the female personality were innate, and which were learned through a process of socialization (psychology, sociology, and anthropology); what was the nature of the relationship between women and patriarchy (cultural studies, literary studies, economics, and politics); and what were the possibilities for change.

Catherine Stimpson, then professor of English at Barnard College and now, in addition, editor of *Signs,* noted in the early 1970s that in regard to women there are three kinds of problems in the curriculum: there are omissions, distortions, and trivializations.

The ensuing ten years of scholarship and the development of courses and programs in Women's Studies have gone far to correct many of the misconceptions and to fill many of the gaps in knowledge about women and female culture. Courses ranging in scope from "The Images of Women in Russian Literature" to "Sex Roles and Public Policy" abound. To educate professors, the lay public, and students, hundreds of new monographs, anthologies, and much thoughtful criticism have been published. As Professor Ruth expresses it in her first chapter, a large segment of the research community is involved in a "serious examination of women's world and its implications for all humanity."

What we have in this volume is both a text, usable in a Women's Studies course, and a systematic examination of the sources and the implications of "woman's place." A teacher and a philosopher, Professor Ruth has brought her considerable knowledge of the history of thought and her skills as an analyst and a logician to bear on what might appear at first to be a disparate group of materials about women. Mindful as any philosopher must be that together myth and language shape our way of thinking about things, she begins her book with a discussion of "masculinity" and the "male-identified woman." Central to woman's feeling of "otherness," as de Beauvoir put it twenty years ago, is that she does not name herself. She is told who she is and who she might become, during a systematic process of growing up. Thus the images of woman and the categories they represent — angel, mother, witch, child — are not mere emblems of a male-dominated culture; they are psychological events in the female child's experience and powerful barriers to self-exploration and self-trust.

It is this level of definition that permits the author to link in a single section housework and sexuality, and it explains why rape

— and especially the web of laws and usages that have grown up about rape — are not marginal issues for womankind (even though rape itself might be perpetrated by marginal men). It is also why politics, religion, and even Science itself are part of the problem.

This volume is not value-free. Professor Ruth believes that sex roles put a limit on human choice and that what she quotes one writer as calling "degenderization" of society and culture is both possible and desirable. Still, she includes in her selections many who disagree with these principles and others who would achieve degenderization in ways more or less radical than she would espouse.

What distinguishes this book from other collections of material on women and patriarchy is the full commentary that the author provides in her own chapters and in the headnotes to the selections. Here, the links among ideas and events are forged and assistance is offered in making sense of the excerpts themselves and their connection with one another.

Women's Studies has earned its place in the curriculum, but in many places it is seen as a "special interest" field. A book such as this demonstrates powerfully that Women's Studies must be considered central to the liberal arts. In the process of working through sometimes dense and not always comparable material, Professor Ruth shows that by focusing on one case — such as the condition of women — students can learn much about culture and society in general, especially the intersection of the disciplines and the empowering tools that logic and analysis provide.

Sheila Tobias
WASHINGTON, D.C., JULY 1979

Preface

Women's Studies was born out of the Women's Movement, which was born out of the concrete experience, realities, and possibilities of women's lives. No matter how much a part of the traditional, "respectable" university the research, faculty, or students of Women's Studies become, we never lose sight of our beginnings or continuing rootedness in Women's Liberation, because it is the rootedness in its issues that gives impetus and meaning to our work.

Those of us engaged in what is currently called Women's Studies (research and learning in a feminist context) have come along different routes, yet almost without exception each of us is here because at some time in our personal history we have specifically experienced events or ideas that have propelled us into a reappraisal of our lives as women. Generally it was the power of those experiences and the shock of the appraisal that created in us the desire and the commitment to know more about women, womanhood, and the consequences of gender definition.

This book is designed for beginners in Women's Studies and feminist perspective, for those who have not yet had the experience of recognition and the drive to reappraisal, or who have had it only in the most inchoate way. The text and readings included here not only impart information but seek as their foremost goal to precipitate in the reader the awareness of self versus gender definition that gives rise to the questions that must be answered. This is a primer in the most exact sense: it is directed at the prime, the spring, the source, the level of consciousness wherein

is occasioned the need to know and the decision to find out. It aims to engage the student's interest and concern by revealing to her/him the ongoing issues imbedded in the facets of life with which she/he is most familiar — family relationships, work, education. That is why the ideas presented here comprise a *first* course in Women's Studies, first both logically and existentially. They must generally happen in one first, in order to make sense of and give rise to more advanced and perhaps more ordered analysis. Instructors and students in a variety of disciplines may refer to the section entitled For Further Reading at the end of the book as a source for more detailed research that is currently being done within the different fields related to Women's Studies.

The experiences we have, the awarenesses we develop, and the manner in which we develop them are rarely ordered along the patterns of academic disciplines. Reality, after all, is not disciplinary. Neither is this book, since it attempts, at least in part, to present ideas as life might. The readings are interdisciplinary, ranging across many fields of study and chosen to reveal certain problems and issues in their interrelatedness. I have not necessarily selected the most recent pieces, the most erudite, or even the most reputable. I have brought together statements, judgments, and arguments from past and present that are representative of the prevailing notions that have had terrific impact on the lives of women (and hence of men) and still do, although sometimes in a different form. These readings, diverse as they are, go together.

They have been selected in concert for their collective power to provide a picture of the pattern of ideas about women, to present the questions and answers, attitudes, practices, and beliefs that make up the complete jigsaw puzzle of notions affecting our lives. The readings are meant to educate in the broadest sense: not only to bring students face to face with their experience now, but to provide them with a context, the sources of current beliefs in the ideas of the distant and not-so-distant past.

The theme of this book, expressed in both text and readings, is twofold. First, in order to understand ourselves and our world we must be aware of and comprehend all the notions regarding women, from the academic to the popular, from the scientific to the pseudo-scientific, from the complex to the simplistic, and from the thoughtful to the downright silly. Second, truth can emerge from critical evaluation and analysis only if it is ultimately grounded in and verified through a sensitivity to even the homeliest events of our day-to-day lives.

After a short discussion of the nature of Women's Studies, we begin with an explication of the major themes of sex-role arrangements — the images of male and female ideals, the roles and expectations of gender as they have been expressed in various aspects of our culture. We begin with these images, the Mars and Venus ideals, because they are at the root of social beliefs and attitudes toward the sexes. They have great explanatory value, both for the traditionalist, as justification for current behaviors, and for the feminist, as the schema to be explored. Then, following the presentation of some classic theories of why gender bifurcation and asymmetry exist, the images of ideal masculinity and femininity are traced through their appearance in such pertinent and affecting aspects of life as family, sexuality, education, work, and politics. Here, in the parts of our lives we feel most deeply, the images are revealed in all their distortion and power. It is hoped that if the student can recognize the destructive potential of the traditional images and stereotypes in her/his own life, she/he will seek alternatives.

If there is a discipline involved in the book, it is Philosophy. Its process is to pose questions, articulate varying responses, assess them, set the stage for further questions, and so on — the Socratic approach, all in the quest for knowledge. Its consequence is growth in wisdom and spirit.

There were moments in the making of this book when my energy and spirits foundered. Certain people, at just the right times, gave me the encouragement or good advice I needed to go on with it, among them Sheila Tobias and Lee Raffel. From and with Julia Mahoney I learned more about feminism and human excellence than she realizes, and she has my enduring affection and respect. Chris Shannon and Peg Simons read my manuscript at a crucial time and gave me the perspective I needed to see where I was going.

At Southern Illinois University, Edwardsville, the Graduate School and the School of Humanities supported me generously with time and funds, and Carol Keene, my friend and Dean of Humanities, led me as gently as she could through the rituals of rules and procedures. The people of the stenographic pool deserve medals. Foremost among my benefactors here were my students who, in word and deed, taught me what I needed to know.

Finally, special thanks go to those closest to me for sustaining me in the most important way: to Linda and Gary Houck, who listened sympathetically so many an afternoon or evening; to Amity, who was incredibly patient and kind; and to Michael, who inspired both the work and the author.

Sheila Ruth

I

An Introduction
to Women's Studies

What Is "Women's Studies"?

In the middle to late 1960s a scattering of courses focusing on feminist issues began to appear on college campuses; in 1970 the term *Women's Studies* or *Feminist Studies* was first used to refer to them.[1] Against strong resistance from traditional academic structures, two or three courses developed into thousands of courses, into programs, into a whole new educational and intellectual enterprise.

According to a study by Florence Howe, in 1974 nearly 3,000 faculty were teaching more than 4,600 such courses in 885 institutions in the country. Programs existed on all levels of study from the undergraduate minor to the doctorate. We can judge the extent and size of Women's Studies to be much greater if we consider the thousands of noncredit courses offered through extension and continuing education programs, those offered in other countries, and those developed since 1974, which were not included in Howe's study.[2]

By 1977, the number of people involved in feminist research had grown so large and their interests so diverse that it became necessary to establish some formal means of communication and support. In January of that year, delegates from institutions all over the country participated in the founding of the National Women's Studies Association.

For contemporary university education and for some high schools Women's Studies is a fact of life. But what is the nature of this new enterprise? What precisely does it do?

It is difficult to suggest an absolute definition. Women's Studies is very young, just beginning to articulate and explain the challenging new insights and methods that are developing within it. Typically on the boundaries of what is considered intellectually respectable or academically acceptable, Women's Studies is a field that has few if any dependable models; it quite regularly rejects traditional forms of inquiry, concepts, and explanatory systems; and it has not yet developed traditions and authorities of its own. Although such a situation may seem chaotic in contrast to the formal structures of traditional disciplines, those who work in Women's Studies also point to its creativity, authenticity, and productiveness.

You will learn in this chapter how feminist researchers are discovering that the historically accepted theories and explanations, even the methods of pursuing knowledge, are rife with prejudice and misunderstandings about women in particular and humanity in general. Sensitive to our own resultant confusion, we, as feminist thinkers, ourselves are extremely hesitant to impose limits on the work of others who seek to restore balance and find clarification.

Feminists place a high value on freedom and self-determination. Ideologically, and often temperamentally, we are suspicious of hierarchies and structures of control, whether in social relations or in intellectual pursuits. Self-disciplined freedom and cooperative efforts, we believe, are more apt to produce constructive results in most endeavors. We therefore tend to be supportive and open to ideas and approaches very different from our own.

For all these reasons — the newness of feminist research, the hesitancy to embrace standards that may be constricting, and the unusually strong predilection for tolerance and experimentation — the ideas, methods, curricula, and theories of Women's Studies exhibit great diversity and resist easy definition. Those now working in Women's Studies

[1] Florence Howe, "Introduction," *Who's Who and Where in Women's Studies,* ed. Tamar Berkowitz, Jean Mangi, and Jane Williamson (Old Westbury, N.Y.: Feminist Press, 1974), p. vi.

[2] Ibid., pp. viii–ix.

have called it variously a process, a field of inquiry, a critical perspective, a center for social action, and/or the academic arm of the women's movement. It is all of these and more.

The "Study of Women"

For centuries, women have been "studied." We were studied by Aristotle, who concluded that we were "misbegotten males," conceived instead of men when the winds were not propitious; studied by Aquinas, who decided that since women were at least necessary for procreation, God had not after all made some terrible mistake in creating us. Freud studied women extensively and determined the vengeful, castrating, penis-envying character of us all, and the philosopher Karl Stern theorized about our "nonreflective," cosmically tied life of nature.[3]

Such high points in the study of women reflect the nature of most of these studies: until very recently they were carried on almost exclusively by men working together in institutions and disciplines absolutely closed to women. An examination of the many traditional works on women reveals certain characteristics:

• Women are generally looked *at*; we rarely do our own looking and still more rarely are asked for our opinions or expressions concerning our own experience. Those expressions that women have offered have tended to be ignored or debunked unless they reinforced existing beliefs.

• Women are generally "studied" in a separate section or subsection of a work, as though we were some kind of extra appendage or anomaly, not readily understood within the general context of the inquiry. In Aristotle's *Politics,* for example, following a discussion of human excellence, there is a separate section asking whether women as well as men might have "excellence," and if so, in what it might consist.[4] (He decided, by the way, that women are admirable when we are obedient and silent.)

• Professional and academic studies of women reflect the prejudices and attitudes that exist in the wider culture. Without women's own perspectives and statements to balance and uncover the historical fund of ignorance and superstition surrounding our lives, conventional (misogynist) wisdom has been carried into research by so-called authorities on the subject, has hardened into accepted theories, and has ultimately become Science. As Science, the myths have been used to justify all sorts of oppression, from witch hunts to clitoridectomy.

The accepted studies of women from primitive times to the present have examined women as if we were senseless, semihuman creatures, unable to speak for ourselves; we have been prodded, dissected, categorized and filed, researched and resolved. It is no wonder that the products of the "study of women" are distorted and counterproductive.

That such an approach to understanding women's lives would necessarily produce poor information is readily seen if we turn the tables on the situation, reverse the process, and see what happens. For example, consider the implications of a history of Westward expansion containing a chapter on the pioneer husband or the pioneer male. Consider the utility of an analysis of masculine attitudes to impotence that was researched and written entirely by women on their observations alone and with no input by men.

[3] In Karl Stern, *The Flight from Woman* (New York: Farrar, Straus & Giroux, 1965), pp. 21–22.

[4] Book I, Ch. 13, 1259b–1260a.

Women's Studies and Feminism

What transforms the "study of women" into Women's Studies is reflected in the terms themselves: in the *"study of women,"* women are objects; in *Women's Studies,* we are subjects.

Women's Studies has a feminist base. Feminists do not agree among themselves on one all-inclusive and universally acceptable definition of the term *feminism*. Depending on one's political or sociological observations and goals, one's individual aspirations for womanhood and for humanity, one's understanding or interpretation of the word *woman,* and several other factors, the term *feminism* can mean different things and have a variety of functions. We shall see later that there are several different theories of feminism, and there is much discussion centering on what it means to be a feminist, what goals feminism should have, and how feminists should behave. Feminism may be a perspective, a world view, a political theory, a spiritual focus, or a kind of activism. Actually, one learns best what feminism means by listening to the statements of women who perceive themselves to be feminists and by understanding how they respond to events and conditions.

Yet there are certain beliefs, values, and attitudes common to all feminists. These might be articulated as follows, to set a context within which to comprehend the rich variety of feminist thought:

• *Feminism* means, derivatively, "womanism." As feminists we value women, not in the hypocritical fashion of centuries of male-dominated cultures, in which women were valued for the work they could produce, the price they could bring, or the services they could render; nor do we value women provided they behave according to some externally imposed set of requirements. We value women in and of themselves, as ends in themselves, and for themselves.

• As feminists we value and prize the fact of being women as highly as we value the fact of being human. We do not accept the cultural images of women as incompetent, petty, irresponsible, or weak. Rather, we affirm our capacities to be strong, capable, intelligent, successful, ethical human beings. Many of us believe that our history and special forms of experience have set the conditions for making us particularly "excellent" human beings.

• As feminists we value autonomy, for ourselves as individuals and for women as a group. We mean to develop in ourselves and in our environment the conditions that will enable us to control our own political, social, economic, and personal destinies.

• As feminists we reject attitudes that regard the traditionally masculine characteristics of aggression, power, and competition as good and desirable and the traditionally feminine characteristics of compassion, tenderness, and compromise as weak and ridiculous. We tend to reject both the practice of separating human qualities into two categories — one of them for men and one for women — and the valuing of one of those categories above the other. Rather we recognize that all such characteristics may appear in either sex, and we evaluate each of them on its own merit, relative to its effect on the quality of life.

• As feminists we understand that the majority of beliefs and attitudes regarding women both in our own culture and in most other cultures are false or wrong-headed, based on myth, ignorance, and fear. We believe that it is necessary to replace myth with reality, ignorance with knowledge created by women about women, first for women and finally for all people.

• As feminists we point out that for centuries we have been denied our rights as citizens and as human beings. The right to vote, the right to earn a substantive living commensurate with effort, the freedom to determine whether to bear children — the denial of these and other freedoms constitutes the concrete instances of oppression. Yet we recognize, as well, women's persistent strength and spirit in the face of such oppression and are optimistic about the possibilities of change. We recognize that many of the qualities developed by women in the face of denial are precious and unique.

It is this feminist base — on the one hand, a realization that women's reality has been distorted; on the other, a positive and affirming stance toward women and womanhood — that transforms the "study of women" into Women's Studies. Women's Studies might have been called Feminist Studies, and it is in some institutions; but some feminist educators have argued that the use of that term is strategically unwise, since it evokes resistance from entrenched and powerful antifemale forces within institutions.

Women's programs, both academic and nonacademic, are often met with derision or intolerance, if not outright hostility. The same forces that limit the freedom, status, and power of women in the wider society limit women within academe. For reasons we shall explore in this book, a pro-woman stance is very threatening to traditional attitudes and structures. The very word *feminism* carries fearful connotations for many people and evokes a defensive response.

Remarks that the student of Women's Studies may encounter express that defensive posture.

- "Are you taking that stuff?! What are you, a *libber*?"
- "Women's Studies? What good is that going to do you?"
- "Since you've been reading that stuff, you've

been hard to get along with. I don't want to hear any more about it."

Faculty hear the same kind of comments, cast a little differently.

- "Feminism is biased. How do you expect to teach a course like that fairly? You can't be objective."
- "You were hired to teach political science, not 'women's lib.' Women in Politics is just too esoteric a course for this department to waste time on."
- "Women's Studies! Are you kidding? When are we going to get a Men's Studies program?"

Although women constitute more than half the human population, serious examination of women's world and its implications for all humanity is simply not perceived to be meaningful and important from a male-centered perspective. Feminist contentions that both women and the wider society are being deprived of female power are not seen as valid; the argument is dismissed just as women are often dismissed.

Feminism and Feminology

There is yet another argument for avoiding the term *Feminist Studies*. Some researchers have contended that certain areas of investigation directly relevant to women's lives may be pursued without a political perspective or a sex-theoretical stance: the female endocrine system, for example, or human reproduction. Such subjects, it is argued, are simply factual; it matters not whether they are pursued by feminists or nonfeminists, and their content, being neutral in this respect, might be considered Women's Studies, but not Feminist Studies. A European term for the politically neutral investigation of women is *Feminology*.[5]

Feminist theoreticians in every field, however, are becoming convinced that there are no purely factual studies, that even the way knowledge has been ordered, the methods of asking and answering questions that have evolved, and the constructs used to understand data have developed within a framework of male bias. Even an apparently true statement like the following becomes problematic from a feminist perspective: *the Renaissance took place during the fourteenth, fifteenth, and sixteenth centuries.* The reminiscence of a feminist historian illustrates the effect of a woman-oriented perspective on this traditionally accepted, so-called historical truth.

A young specialist in the Renaissance spoke to the obvious but unasked question, "Did women have a renaissance?" Her response was a jolt, for she suggested that the bourgeoisification of Italian society deprived women of power, created a patriarchal culture, and, in general, set women back in their quest for human liberty and autonomy. So what "renaissance" can be considered? What is progress, after all, if the transformation to a modern social order is achieved at the expense of half a population?

Such questions would never have been asked within the context of traditional political and economic history, nor would they emerge in ordinary considerations of intellectual "revolutions." The Renaissance becomes problematic only as a question of social history, and it is precisely that field with which the women's movement has merged to create a wholly new way to regard the human past.[6]

[5] The only time I have seen this term in print was in a report by Barbara Rubin on a Dutch/Scandinavian symposium on woman's position in society. See Barbara Rubin, "International Feminology Conference," *Feminist Press,* 4, No. 2 (Spring 1976), 3.

[6] Bari Watkins, "Women and History," in *Women on Campus: The Unfinished Liberation,* ed. Change Magazine Editors (New York: Change Magazine, 1975).

It is still a matter of argument whether there may be investigations truly neutral with respect to sex orientation. Perhaps there is a continuum of neutrality/non-neutrality. Our developing conceptual tools will resolve this question. Whatever the resolution, it remains that Women's Studies as a whole, the framework of the enterprise itself, must be feminist.

Bias in Academe

It is ironic that the enterprise of Women's Studies should be charged with bias. *Bias,* which means prejudice, the absence of objectivity, derives from a term that means oblique, slanted, not standard or true, off-center. Bias implies some kind of distortion, usually unconscious.

When it is argued that feminist thinkers and Women's Studies are biased, at least two things are being said: (1) that feminists hold a set of beliefs that is somehow off-center, askew from "the truth"; and (2) that either we are unaware of having a distorted perspective, or we are deliberate in an intent to impose slanted views on unsuspecting and vulnerable minds.

Feminism is perceived as a skewing of reality. Feminists would argue, however, that it is the traditional male-controlled image of reality that is skewed.

Centuries ago, discerning thinkers in science, theology, and philosophy recognized the fallacy of mistaking the part for the whole. In philosophy and theology, it was perceived that to mistake human values and perspectives for universal ones was to be misled in analyses of God and reality. This mistake was called *anthropocentrism,* and cautious thinkers learned to avoid it. More recently, social scientists have become aware of the conceptual dangers of *ethnocentrism,* the practice of imposing the standards of one's own culture on another. *Egocentrism,* too, whether conceptual (as when an individual assumes that others see reality as he or she does) or ethical, distorts understanding. The error lies in assuming that one's own special perspective or world view is the true and only one, applicable everywhere to everyone or everything. Universally acknowledged to be fallacious, all such isms are guarded against by careful thinkers — all, that is, except the most pervasive and distorting ism of all: *masculine-ism* or *masculism* (sometimes called *androcentrism*).

Masculism, the form of sexism practiced in our culture, has many facets, and we shall explore them in Chapter 2. Here we need only say that masculism is in part the mistaking of male perspectives, beliefs, attitudes, standards, values, and perceptions for all human perceptions. Both the cause and result of women's social and intellectual disfranchisement, masculism is pervasive in our culture except for feminist challenge, and it is most frequently unconscious.

In almost every culture, including our own, the tools and conditions necessary for learning and analysis, the means of communication, and the forms of legitimization of knowledge have been jealously and effectively kept from women. In some societies, the artifacts of history, the symbols of religious significance, and the activities of power are all secreted in a special hut, the men's hut, taboo to women. In other cultures, men speak a private language that the women of the tribe are forbidden to utter; in that language, the policies of the tribe are decided. In our own culture, disfranchisement was effected in an analogous way. It was argued that reading and studying were dangerous for women, conducive to discontent and rebellion against our "natural" roles as wives and helpmates. Too much learning, it was said, would drain the energies necessary for us to produce children. Mathematics and science were particularly dangerous since they might

rob women of a meek and gentle loveliness. Politics was an arena for which women were supposed to have neither the stomach nor the wit. Such views have functioned as justifications for denying women the education, tools, and power to sustain ourselves and direct society.

In effect, women have been barred from the possibility of contributing all we could to the acknowledged intellectual and scientific world view. That has been reserved for men, who, after all, control the academic disciplines, the universities, the learned societies, the presses, and the research foundations. As a result of the virtual exclusion of women from the intellectual power centers, the (male) minority opinion has been fallaciously equated with all that could be said; the part has been mistaken for the whole. In essence, the male establishment has appropriated reality for itself. As men have dominated the wider society, as their needs and goals have become official social goals, so in the realm of learning, male thought has become official thought; the male stance has become the official human stance.

Consider,[7] for example, the following analysis of the concept of respect by Joel Feinberg, a contemporary philosopher (italics mine):

In olden days, when power and authority went hand in hand ... the scale of respect was one with the scales of power and status. This was the background against which the earliest moralists could begin demanding that respect be shown to various classes of the *deserving weak*, too. Hence our rude and unimpressed ancestors were urged to "show respect" for women, for the aged, for the clergy.... Christianity gave dignity even to

[7] Some of the following discussion is included in my paper, "Methodocracy, Misogyny, and Bad Faith: Sexism in the Philosophic Establishment," *Metaphilosophy* (January, 1979).

the *meek and humble*. Respect could then be extended to the aged, to women, to the clergy....

. . .

To see a woman as having dignity now is to see her as in a moral position to make claims against *our* conduct, even though she may lack physical or political power over *us*. Certain minimal forms of consideration are her due, something she has coming, and can rightfully claim, even when she is in no position to make demands in the gunman sense. Insofar as *we* think of her that way *we* have respect for her ... and insofar as she shares this image of herself she has self-respect.[8]

As I read this argument from my woman's perspective, I think: Indeed! And would any *man* in such a position — weak, meek, humble, and without power — perceive himself with self-respect? Who is this author to speak for me? And who are the *we (us, our)* of whom Feinberg speaks? A club he belongs to? He is a philosopher addressing philosophers. But he could not mean that only philosophers grant respect in this fashion. (Besides, I am a philosopher.) No, Feinberg is analyzing the concept of respect as it is used, given, and granted in society, among people. Which people? Society surely must include women. Do women grant respect that way? Am I part of that *we, us?* I certainly do not perceive women and our worthiness that way. Generic *we?* Rather not. This is a mental involution impossible for me to make without self-alienation.

Feinberg's essay and his use of *we (us, our)* in juxtaposition to the term *women* is only one example among many of a world view that constitutes humanity as male and relegates women to the status of out-group. Comfortable and confident that "we boys"

are "we everyone," Feinberg exhibits the masculist usurpation of universality. The usurpation is conveniently masked by the linguistic device of generic *man,* and is so generally accepted that it has become invisible to the naked (that is, nonfeminist) eye. A film entitled *Why Man Creates* (1968), produced for the Kaiser Corporation and ostensibly an inquiry into the nature and motivation of *human* creativity, is composed of sequences in which scientists, artists, inventors, and symbols are all male and women appear only as wives, foils, or subjects of art. *The Uncommitted: Alienated Youth in Modern American Society* (1960), a sociopsychological study by Kenneth Keniston based on profiles of alienated young people, contained not one female profile, yet purported to be a study of alienated *youth*. The jacket of the book stated that "Mr. Keniston starts from an intensive study of alienated *youth,* asking why a group of talented and privileged young *men* should reject ..." (italics mine). An advertisement describes a work entitled *The States of Human Life: A Biography of Entire Man* (1974) as follows: "In this study of the career of *the individual,* the age-grades are considered as escarpments.... The perspective of *the individual* ... shifts radically as *he* grows from infancy to young *manhood,* and from maturity to old age" (italics mine). A modern logic textbook asks the supposedly general reader, "She won't give you a date?" The Constitution of the United States had declared, "We the people," although women had been totally disfranchised. The examples are endless.

The conceptual confusing of *human* and *male* historically and in the present in all disciplines and inquiries is so pervasive as to be the rule rather than the exception, and it is becoming glaringly apparent as feminist analysts turn their increasingly acute sensitivities on it. Feminist criticism is revealing male bias, not creating a female one, as

[8] Joel Feinberg, "Some Conjectures About the Concept of Respect," *Journal of Social Philosophy,* 3, No. 2 (April 1973), 1–3.

charged. Women's Studies seeks to be the prophylactic of bias, not the cause.

The Goals of Women's Studies

Among the goals of Women's Studies is the uncovering of masculist bias in the history of knowledge as well as the creation of new knowledge through positive research into women's experience. Women's Studies seeks, as a result of this

* to change women's sense of ourselves, our self-image, our sense of worth and rights, our presence in the world
* to change women's aspirations, based on an increased sense of self-confidence and self-love, to allow women to create for ourselves new options in our own personal goals as well as in our commitments and/or contributions to society
* to alter the relations between women and men, to create true friendship and respect between the sexes in place of "the war between the sexes"
* to give all people, women and men, a renewed sense of human worth, to restore to the center of human endeavors a love for beauty, kindness, justice, and quality in living
* to reaffirm in society the quest for harmony, peace, and humane compassion

Such goals may appear presumptuous or at least not obviously related to the study of women's lives. But feminists have found that the movement that began in the concrete events of women's daily lives has implications that reach to the very foundations and structure of all human living.

The Enfranchisement of Women

Earlier, in the discussion of bias, reference was made to the exclusion of women from all the powerful policy-making institutions of our society and culture. That women should have been denied the vote until 1920 is an indication of our powerlessness in other arenas. Until the end of the nineteenth century, except for the lowest paid, lowest status jobs, most women in the Western world had little access to economic independence. Within the family, they had small power over their possessions, their work, or their reproductive capacities. Legally they were at the mercy of male judges, lawyers, jurors, and laws. Women of any race or class found the doors of institutions of higher education barred to them. Oberlin was the first American college to admit women, in 1833, but its earliest programs for women were largely composed of home economics, religion, and other "female" subjects.

Today it is illegal to bar women from admission to any public institution on the basis of sex, and we are entering universities and professional schools in increasing numbers. One would think, therefore, that women's lives, priorities, and values would be significantly enhanced, and that the institutions, too, would manifest the results of our particular input. But there are strong forces, both within women and within the institutions, that impel women to be absorbed into the male world view rather than to create a new one. The masculine perspective in education; the preponderance of male faculty, administrators, textbooks, and curricular materials; the pressures of husband care and child care; the conflicts between women's family roles and educational needs; the general contempt for women's views all conspire to allow women on campus only a physical presence, not an intellectual/spiritual influence or full participation.

Certainly it is a major goal of Women's Studies to reverse discriminatory conditions in the educational system, and campus feminists engage in a number of activities to accomplish that end. Besides increasing the university community's awareness of the conceptual issues, we are often involved in activities directed toward changing policies in administration that have direct bearing on women's abilities to attend school — policies regarding admissions, financial assistance, health facilities, child-care programs, part-time attendance, scheduling, and more. Feminist faculty, in or outside of Women's Studies, move for fairer decisions on salaries, promotion, and hiring, and we work toward increasing women's participation in decision making by seeking important administrative or committee appointments. All in all, the intent is to restore balance and to eradicate the historical accumulation of masculist control.

The Restoration of Humane Commitments

As human beings and citizens, women have the right to full educational and professional opportunity, and this is the primary reason for ending university discrimination. But there is another reason as well, also profound and far-reaching.

It has already been pointed out that education and learning have historically been the private preserve of men; that today, as in the past, knowledge and the formation of knowledge are largely in the hands of men; and that masculism distorts conceptualization. But as we shall see in Chapter 2, masculism goes well beyond conceptual bias, beyond the universalization of male perspectives in thought, to a universalization of male perspectives and attitudes in values and behavior.

Masculism is not only the cause of misinterpretations of women's nature, it is also the reflection, the expression of an almost universal abhorrence for women themselves and for a whole set of characteristics histori-

cally ascribed to women in Western culture: sensitivity, acquiescence, compassion, compromise, aesthetic sensibility. These qualities, though officially regarded with respect, are actually considered appropriate only in women. In men, except in special circumstances and in measured amounts, they are generally regarded with contempt. The complementary qualities have been prescribed for and encouraged in men — strength, competitiveness, power, emotional reserve, the warrior virtues — and these are the qualities that are truly respected, truly expected in the public sphere. In any environment that has been historically dominated by men, the warrior virtues are likely to prevail. The university is no exception.

For the last decade, educators have been decrying a growing dehumanization in universities, a waning of aesthetic and ethical commitment. Students and faculty alike question the university's moral mission; we feel our absorption into the wider technocracy, shudder at the presence of war research and the "cash mentality" among us. There are those who speak of a moral crisis or a failure of standards.

Of course something *is* wrong, and we can look to many factors involved — increased democratization of higher learning, economic conditions, or social upheaval. But as Adrienne Rich has pointed out,[9] the androcentric university is a microcosm of the wider society and its character defects reflect those of society.

Universities, like other social institutions, are products of the cultures that provide the individuals who people them and the ideas that govern them. In turn, by contributing to society the leaders of government, industry, art, and communication, by bequeathing to

---

[9] Adrienne Rich, "Toward a Woman-Centered University," in *Women and the Power to Change,* ed. Florence Howe (New York: McGraw-Hill, 1975), pp. 15–46.

society scientific and social theories or inventions and discoveries, the universities help to mold and direct cultural attitudes and consciousness. There is an exchange of authority between society and the halls of knowledge.

It can be easy to lose sight of the tremendous impact of much that is said and done in academe. What researchers and professors have learned and created in their institutions is passed to their students, who in turn pass it to others through their work — in business, in government, in every phase of social life. The theories and arguments developed in lunchrooms and offices become tomorrow's "science," the "truths" that ultimately govern legal policy, psychotherapeutic techniques, media expression, and finally social behavior. If the truths of academe, developed in a masculist environment, seem to reflect and reinforce the warrior qualities, it is small wonder.

Consider the tone of university experience. It is not difficult to see that human compassion and caring, personal sensitivity, authenticity, love, and openness are not highly prized in formal education. In fact, talk of such things tends to embarrass people, to make them uneasy. Academic language is distant, cold, rife with jargon. Instructional faculty combat with administrators. Professors bore and bombard their students with disconnected facts not clearly relevant to life experience. Students are wary of participation in class or intimacy with one another. Courses and programs die and are born and die again, fitting students (however poorly) to meet the requirements of industry or government but rarely giving them the tools to live well. Academe is not typically a loving, caring environment.

It is, however, competitive, sometimes ruthless. Students learn to be "successful." Faculty spar at intellectual gatherings, guard their positions, compete for salary, status, or power. We are all reluctant to reveal our feelings and admit vulnerability. The warrior

virtues prevail in contemporary education, blotting out the humane, a condition becoming increasingly obvious, as Rich describes:

Until the 1960s, the university continued to be seen as a privileged enclave, somehow more defensible than other privileged enclaves, criticized if at all for being too idealistic, too little in touch with the uses and abuses of power; and romanticized as a place where knowledge is loved for its own sake, every opinion has an open-minded hearing, "the dwelling place of permanent values ... of beauty, of righteousness, of freedom," as the Brandeis University bulletin intones. The radical student critique — black and white — of the sixties readily put its finger on the facts underlying this fiction: the racism of the academy and its curriculum, its responsiveness to pressures of vested interest, political, economic and military; the use of the academy as a base for research into weapons and social control and as a machinery for perpetuating the power of white, middle-class men. Today the question is no longer whether women (or nonwhites) are intellectually and "by nature" equipped for higher education, but whether this male-created, male-dominated structure is really capable of serving the humanism and freedom it professes.[10]

Arguing that women's drive for true equality in the university will require and imply a whole shift of values, actions, and effects for the entire system, she concludes:

Whatever the forms it may take, the process of women's repossession of ourselves is irreversible. Within and without academe, the rise in women's expectations has gone far beyond the middle-class and has released an incalculable new energy — not merely for

[10] Ibid., p. 22. Used with permission. Copyright © 1975 by The Carnegie Foundation for the Advancement of Teaching.

changing institutions but for human redefinition; not merely for equal rights but for a new kind of being.[11]

Human Redefinition and Social Values

Rich's discussion closes on the notion that women's reclamation of ourselves and our power may bring about a whole new way of being, a redefinition of human values. I agree, but point out that such an idea must be based on a belief that is much debated among feminists — the idea that women are somehow in a special position with regard to value, better able to make ethical or humane judgments than most or many men.

For centuries, culminating in the Victorian period, a certain kind of woman — one removed from or rising above her carnal nature — was thought to be especially sacred, especially like the Virgin Mary, a Mother of the Generations, a keeper of morality. In the nineteenth century, enshrined within the family, middle-class women were charged with the responsibility of maintaining human morality by keeping their own lives "pure," by investing the young with a love for virtue, and by creating a home where it could flourish. Women were to furnish society with a place and experience apart from the harsh realities of work and government.

The image of woman as keeper of morality was, however, double-edged. As we shall see in Chapter 3, it was based on all kinds of myths and misconceptions; and it placed impossible burdens on women, denying them their own freedom and requiring them to maintain public morality when they had no power to do so. Feminists quite rightly reject this image.

That women may be especially predisposed to human virtue carries yet another assumption that is problematic — that women and men really are by nature different, at least in this respect. The contention that women and men are constitutionally different has been used as the main justification for rigid role distinctions and female subordination for centuries, and feminists have taken great pains to gather evidence against it.

Yet the belief that women may be in a special position with regard to value, better able to make humane judgments, is not necessarily based on the concepts described above. Rather it may be based on one or more of the following arguments: (1) in our culture women are trained and encouraged to develop the caring or nurturing values and aesthetic sensibilities; (2) women's position outside the realms of power has also kept us from being fully absorbed in the psychodynamics of power and the warrior values; (3) women's history of oppression and denial makes us especially sensitive to the abuses of power and domination; (4) the concrete realities of women's lives — the creation of life, the intimate connection with rites of passage, the maintenance of the necessities of living — give us different perspectives on what is valuable and important in existence.

From infancy onward, women's lives are suffused with the affective (that is, feeling, experiential, noncognitive) aspects of living. Considerations of beauty, tenderness, warmth, compassion, and love have been prescribed to be the special province of women. No doubt society's motivation was *not* to make women especially humane, but to make us excellent servants. Nonetheless, our intimate relationship with the nonwarrior (or antiwarrior) virtues, our inculcated avoidance of domination together with our intact intellectual capacities may indeed render women especially insightful in matters of human value.

Women, particularly feminist women,

[11] Ibid., p. 44.

hold a key to new perspectives on society. If new goals, values, and visions are to be infused into society, we must win for women access to all the centers of power and policy, from science and industry to art and communication. This is a major goal of Women's Studies.

Changes in Lifestyles and Self-Concepts

Nothing goes deeper in one's personal awareness, carries more weight in the self-image, or has more far-reaching implications for the whole of one's existence than her or his sexual identity. This accounts in part for the great resistance to feminism; it also accounts for the impact feminist learning and consciousness-raising have on students. Propelled into self-examination by the intensity of the search and the research, women and men alike report changes in attitudes and lifestyles that represent tremendous emotional, intellectual, spiritual, and professional growth.

Consciousness-raising means what it says: it raises the level of consciousness, of awareness one has about the feelings, behaviors, and experiences surrounding sex roles. The woman who learns how much of her personal being emanates from her social and political status as a woman must ask herself how much of that being she wants to keep, how much she wants to change, to what she might want to change, and how she plans to do it. She experiences bewilderment, surprise, pain, joy, anger, love, and all the feelings that accompany growth.

Feminist instructors and students alike have been chided about the element of consciousness-raising in Women's Studies courses. It has been argued that consciousness-raising (1) makes the courses "soft," (2) belongs in the women's movement, not in school, (3) is not a legitimate part of formal university

education, (4) is brainwashing, and (5) sometimes causes great anguish with which some students are unable to cope.

You will discover as you read the selections in this book and pursue their subject matter that Women's Studies is anything but soft. You will find that consciousness-raising occurs as a result of new insights and innovative ideas, an event that should occur in any high-quality course. Rather than brain-*washing,* raised consciousness comes as a result of brain-*opening.*

You will discover that consciousness-raising can be painful. Yet pain is not in itself something always to be avoided, for there are two kinds of pain — destructive pain and constructive pain. Destructive pain is suffered in a no-win situation. Embedded in the status quo, it leads to no benefits, no improvements. It just hurts. Such pain is better avoided. Constructive pain is very different. It is like the physical distress we feel when we decide to get our bodies in shape after some disuse. Our muscles ache; we strain and groan, but we grow stronger. Much the same thing happens when we grow emotionally or spiritually. Our insights, memories, and feelings, not accustomed to such use, may cause us pain. Our new sense of autonomy and freedom, its attendant responsibility, may make us anxious. We hurt, but we grow stronger. Just as physical strength and health are necessary to well-being, so is emotional and spiritual strength.

Consider some of the comments taken from the journals of students in an introductory course in Women's Studies, much like the one you are now taking.

• "I feel like a ton of bricks has been lifted off my shoulders. I finally found me. For the first time in my life I really looked at myself and said 'I like you!' I decided that there is only one companion that you can count on all through your life — yourself. If I don't like me, who will? I took a full survey of myself and decided what I liked and what *I* would like to change, not because I wanted to look good in someone else's eyes, but because I wanted to look good in *my* own eyes. I feel so free, happy; like I could lick the world. This is the way I want to stay — this is the way I always want to feel. And I will because I like me."

• "I have more pride; I am more confident in myself as a woman. I used to wonder if my womanhood would be a slight handicap. I now realize it is my strongest asset!"

• "While we were talking about fear and pain being all a part of growing, I found a great deal of consolation because I had felt both.... It took a while, but I now realize that all the things I learned and have become aware of will not allow me to keep silent. Also, those feelings of understanding and support will never really be left behind because I'll carry those feelings inside of me forever."

The Terms and Techniques of Women's Studies

Women's Studies must be pursued on its own terms if it is to maintain its integrity. Although the integration of feminist perspectives and insights into the regular curriculum is an ultimate goal of feminist educators, the absorption of Women's Studies into the masculist domain is not sought. That might imply a loss of the unique configuration of methods and approaches we have developed. In ways that can be difficult to articulate, the feminist classroom typically differs from others, and feminist research bears the mark of its status outside the mainstream.

Feminist Pedagogy

Feminist faculty, like any others, gather information and ideas and impart them to stu-

dents. Often they do this in traditional ways: they lecture, lead group discussions, show films, assign term papers, and give exams. Just as often, however, they opt for other procedures, sometimes unorthodox.

Feminist faculty frequently diverge from their colleagues in attitudes, experience, or methods. Many of us have come to academe from the learning laboratories of social action outside the university — from counterculture organizations, from consciousness-raising groups and feminist groups, from political parties and equal rights agencies. Out of these experiences we have learned the strength of the entrenched power structures. Others of us, having lived within the established system and having tried its regular channels and found them resistant, have learned the same lesson in another way. Having lived, as philosopher Mary Daly puts it, "on the boundaries of patriarchal space,"[12] we have developed modes often in juxtaposition to traditional academic etiquette.

As yet, there are no formal credentials in Women's Studies. One enters this field as thinkers entered any field centuries ago — through experience and self-directed research. We have no models after which to style our activities. The criterion for our methods is productivity.

The result of these factors and others is a highly innovative, spontaneous, and authentic modus operandi. In a feminist classroom, one is apt to find group projects, small group discussions, self-directed or student-directed study, credit for social change activities or for life experience, contracts or self-grading, diaries and journals, even meditation or ritual. Noticeable in a feminist classroom are two factors not typical in college classrooms: an acceptance of, and even emphasis on, the

---

[12] Mary Daly, *Beyond God the Father* (Boston: Beacon Press, 1973).

personal/affective element in learning; and a warm, human relationship among persons in the class, students and teacher. Having rejected the commitment to inappropriate or unnecessary reserve, feminist teachers are no longer at pains to maintain the manly aura of distance — from their work or from one another. Recognizing too that hierarchical structures belie the commonality of female experience as well as the commonality of human purpose, feminist faculty often seek alternatives to the traditional student/teacher dichotomy.

The Interdisciplinary Nature of Women's Studies

Almost all Women's Studies programs, curricula, and analyses are interdisciplinary. For the most part, the programs have avoided separating into discrete departments. Although this has raised some serious practical problems — of funding, staffing, and scheduling, for example — it serves important purposes. Some of the purposes are pragmatic, having to do with survival in the institution, professional flexibility for instructors, and the like; but the important reasons for the interdisciplinary structure of Women's Studies are philosophical.

Feminist theorists have found that insights into the elements of women's lives and their effects on the progress of humanity do not sensibly divide into the traditional packets of learning we call academic disciplines; they cut across all modes of inquiry. Understanding, for example, how the concept *human nature* is distorted by the omission of women from the subject requires sophisticated knowledge of history, sociology, psychology, linguistics, philosophy, and other fields. Feminist analysis requires global knowledge.

Sensitized by our own investigations, many feminists have gone on to challenge the entire departmental or disciplinary structure as it exists today. Some of us suggest that the division of knowledge into neat little areas with boundaries that ought not to be crossed is analogous to (and possibly derived from) the warrior behavior of separating land into territories that then must be justified and guarded. Intellectual boundaries, we may argue, are not only artificial; they are destructive.

Feminist theoreticians, then, recognizing the importance of global knowledge and not typically given to territorial competition, are at least interdisciplinary — I tend to think of us as counterdisciplinary. Elizabeth Janeway, feminist educator, comments:

> Women have both history and reality on their side. Our knowledge of the world as it is is really quite formidable, broadly based, aware of detail, and not afraid to make connections between areas which the traditionally minded see as separate. Our experience makes us interdisciplinary. Well, this is a most useful and needed ability in a fragmented society, and particularly in an educational system where the trend for years has been to know more and more about less and less. Research is valuable — if it is used; and to be used, it must be allowed to connect with other research and, even more, with everyday life.[13]

The Scope of Women's Studies

Given what has been said about the global nature of feminist research, you can see how broad a scope Women's Studies must have. It ranges across history, psychology, art, economics, literature, philosophy, sociology, political science, biology, mathematics, law, and on through every area called an academic

[13] Elizabeth Janeway, "Women on Campus: The Unfinished Liberation," in *Women on Campus,* ed. Change Magazine Editors, p. 27.

discipline. Of course, no one can be conversant with the details of all fields, but the study of women's experience requires some sophistication in each.

The Women's Studies investigators must be multifaceted in perspectives; yet there is specialization as well. A feminist psychologist is a psychologist with a woman-orientation. She pursues her work with a feminist perspective, challenges the sexist bias and beliefs in her field, often, though not always, focusing on issues most pertinent to women. As a feminist philosopher, I have the traditional interests in metaphysics, ethics, and epistemology, but I add to their study my special feminist awareness. I might, for example, challenge the validity of Hobbes's argument that life is "a war of all against all," wondering whether this may be so for men (warriors?) but perhaps not so for women. I question the traditionally accepted basic assumptions of philosophy, its definition of *objectivity,* for example, and its relationship to male reserve. But beyond a feminist analysis of traditional questions, I am involved in raising other questions, crucial for women, and not usually raised: What does the term *matriarchy* imply for utopian visions? How does a notion of God as female change theology? What does my woman's understanding of the dehumanizing effect of rape tell me about the ethical implications of physical integrity?

Some Basic Concepts

This book is primarily about women, their experience, history, present situation, and future. It is about men too, but only insofar as men's lives affect women. When we say that we are going to talk about women and men, when we use the words *woman, man, female, male, feminine, masculine,* what do we mean? What is a woman or a man?

What possible different meanings do the terms *feminine* or *masculine* involve?

Perhaps the questions seem odd, their answers obvious. Yet it will become increasingly clear that such words as *woman, man, female,* or *male* are used in a variety of ways; they connote all sorts of meanings, and therefore have wide-ranging implications — psychological, political, social, and so on. Unless this is understood, one is apt to encounter a great deal of confusion in the analyses of sex roles.

To inquire into what it is to be a woman or a man, one must understand that there are various contexts in which to formulate definitions and make analyses, and though these may impinge on one another, their viewpoints are not the same. For example, the fact that females bear offspring (a biological aspect of womanhood) may be partly responsible for the kind of work a woman engages in (a cultural aspect), and that may have tremendous bearing on her status (political and social aspects). Furthermore, to understand that arrangements of these variables change from culture to culture (an anthropological aspect), it is necessary to know what economic and historical factors affect the others, and how.

Before we continue, there are some terms and concepts that should be clearly understood, because they are essential tools of our analysis. These are: *sex, gender, role, stereotype,* and *ideal.*

Sex is a term used by social scientists and biologists to refer to certain biological categories, female and male. In the human species as in others, identification of sex is based on a variety of factors including chromosomal patterns, hormonal make-up, and genital structure. The determination of sex is considerably more complex than is generally understood, but it is the least ambiguous of the five concepts we are considering.

Gender, on the other hand, is a social, not

a physiological, concept. *Femininity* and *masculinity,* the terms that denote one's gender, refer to a complex set of characteristics and behaviors prescribed for a particular sex by society and learned through the socialization experience. For example, femininity (female gender) for certain groups of women in our culture requires passivity, fragility, and proclivities for nurturance. A little girl, given dolls to play with, prohibited from engaging in wild play, dressed in frilly or constricting clothing, and rebuked for so-called unladylike behavior, is reinforced in those behavior patterns here called feminine, and learns to be passive, fragile, nurturing.

The exact relation between sex and gender is controversial. Some argue that sexual characteristics are fixed in nature and account for gender and role arrangements; others sharply disagree. (This is part of what is called the "nature/nurture controversy.") Lionel Tiger,[14] for example, argues that "leadership" or "dominance" is a characteristically male trait in animal as well as in human communities. He contends that the trait is inheritable, therefore biological, and thus accounts for the dominance of men over women in human society. In other words, dominance/submission is a biological (sexual) characteristic that accounts for the gender prescription of passivity in women and aggressiveness in men. Tiger is challenged by those who point to the tremendous variation of behavior and arrangements both in the animal kingdom and in different societies. These antagonists argue that the observed malleability and diversity of behavior imply a loose association between sex and gender.[15]

Gender is composed of a set of socially defined character traits. *Role* is composed of a pattern of behaviors prescribed for individuals playing a certain part in the drama of life. The sociologist Theodore R. Sarbin defined role as "the organized actions of a person in a given position."[16] For example, the role of teacher in our society requires such actions as imparting knowledge to the student, attending classes, counseling, or grading papers; it might include as well certain attitudes, values, and even appearance.

In almost every society, females and males on the basis of their sex are assigned separate and specific roles, the sex roles. Varying from culture to culture, and within a culture by a variety of factors (class, religion, race, age, and so on), the sex roles are made up of a set of expected behaviors with accompanying gender traits. The role of a middle-class white female in our society includes playing with dolls, helping mother, getting married, having children, doing housekeeping, being sexy, typing, and so on. Many of these behaviors in their turn form other role configurations. Marrying, for example, requires that one be a wife, which then entails another whole set of behaviors. The role of a woman, then, includes a series of subroles such as daughter, wife, mother, office worker, and so on. In this book, we shall be largely concerned with analyses of sex roles, their nature, composition, effects, and implications.

Stereotype is a concept related to role, yet distinct. Defined by one author as a "picture in our heads,"[17] a stereotype is a composite image of traits and expectations pertaining to some group (such as teachers, police officers, Jews, hippies, or women) — an image that is persistent in the social mind though it is

---

[14] Lionel Tiger, *Men in Groups* (New York: Random House, 1969).

[15] See, for example, Margaret Mead, *Sex and Temperament in Three Primitive Societies* (New York: Morrow, 1935).

[16] Theodore R. Sarbin, "Role Theory," in *Handbook of Social Psychology,* ed. Gardner Lindzey (Reading, Mass.: Addison-Wesley, 1954), I, 225.

[17] Walter Lippmann, *Public Opinion* (New York: Harcourt, Brace, 1922).

somehow off-center or inaccurate. Typically, the stereotype is an overgeneralization of characteristics that may or may not have been observed in fact. Often containing a kernel of truth that is partial and thus misleading, the stereotype need not be self-consistent, and it has a remarkable resistance to change by new information; to wit, Lippmann's following remark:

> If the experience contradicts the stereotype, one of two things happens. If the man is no longer plastic, or if some powerful interest makes it highly inconvenient to rearrange his stereotypes, he pooh-poohs the contradiction as an exception that proves the rule, discredits the witness, finds a flaw somewhere, and manages to forget it. But if he is still curious and open-minded, the novelty is taken into the picture, and allowed to modify it. Sometimes, if the incident is striking enough, and if he has felt a general discomfort with his established scheme, he may be shaken to such an extent as to distrust all accepted ways of looking at life, and to expect that normally a thing will not be what it is generally supposed to be.[18]

Not all stereotypes are pejorative, but many are. One stereotypic image of a "libber" is a woman incapable of fulfilling the traditional role requirements for femininity, incapable of "catching a man," homely, dirty, aggressive, strident, shrill, sexually promiscuous (or frigid, or a lesbian, or all three), unkempt, ill-clothed, middle or upper middle class, childish, making speeches, carrying banners, and burning underwear. It is this image that is meant when clearly feminist women demur, "Now, I'm no libber, but ..." and

when newspaper accounts chortle at "the strident extremists." That many feminists are not middle class or white or college educated, that feminists wear a variety of costumes and have differing sexual codes and identities are pieces of information that do little to change the image. Stereotypes, often born and maintained in ignorance and fear, can have wide-ranging effects on both the stereotyped group and those with whom the members of the group interact. Stereotypes can and do direct behavior.

An *ideal* is much like a stereotype. It too is a "picture in our heads"; it is resistant to change, frequently inconsistent, frequently based on false information. But the ideal contains only desirable traits. It functions as a standard and a goal.

All of these concepts are involved in the analyses of women's experience. Feminist investigators ask: What are the biological, physiological, and anatomical characteristics that distinguish women from men, and what are their implications? How are the sexes inherently different in make-up and behavior? What are the major psychological factors in women's lives; which, if any, are based on femaleness per se, and which come as a consequence of women's role in this and other societies? Since women's lives are apt to be markedly different across economic, educational, or racial lines, what traits or qualities, if any, can be said to characterize the category of women in general? How and why do they operate? How is the perceived female ideal different from the perceived stereotypes? What is their origin? How do they affect the daily lives of women in particular and people in general? In the following chapters, we shall be using the concepts of sex, gender, role, stereotype, and ideal to explore such questions as these.

[18] Ibid., p. 100.

Selections

THE MYTH OF THE MALE ORGASM

Bette-Jane Raphael, a writer who has been senior editor for *Viva* magazine and for *Working Woman,* here presents with humor the absurdity of research and theories based on myth, false assumptions, and misplaced objectivity. Parodying Freud and other "experts" who presume to explain and describe the female sexual experience from their armchairs, so to speak, she shows with great hilarity what nonsense might have been produced if the tables had been turned and all that we knew about male sexuality (or, for that matter, male *anything*) had been created by women looking at men.

Is there such a thing as male orgasm? For decades, scientists have argued about it, written tracts about it, philosophized about it, and, in more recent years, conducted countless studies. But as Dr. Mary Jane Grunge, president of SMOS (the Society for Male Orgasmic Studies), said in her opening statement of the society's ninth annual cook-out: "We still don't know."

But do we? Recent findings by Dr. Fern Herpes and her colleague, Dr. Lavinia Shoot, indicate that the mystery is at last on the brink of being unmasked. Working under a grant from NASA, which was disturbed by the cleaning bills for its last Apollo mission, Dr. Herpes and Dr. Shoot conducted a study of 300 middle-class men between the ages of 14 and 23. Their findings seem to indicate

that not only is there a male orgasm, there may actually be two distinct kinds!

While 43 percent of the men in the Herpes/Shoot study were found to have trouble attaining orgasm consistently, or did not attain orgasm at all, and while another $4\frac{1}{2}$ percent had no opinion, a whopping $50\frac{1}{2}$ percent (four men fell asleep during their interviews, which accounts for the other two percent) admitted they had two distinctly different kinds of orgasms. After careful questioning, psychological testing, and physical examinations, Dr. Herpes came to the following conclusion (Dr. Shoot came to a different conclusion and left in a huff): there are two types of male orgasm. For purposes of clarification, Dr. Herpes called these penile orgasm and the spherical orgasm.

Of the two orgasms, Dr. Herpes hypothesizes that the spherical orgasm is the more mature. "Men who are enamored of their penises, who see their penises as the seat

Reprinted by permission of *The Village Voice.* Copyright © The Village Voice, Inc., 1973.

of all sexual pleasure, are just a bunch of babies. I hate them. Only the spherically oriented male can be thought of as mature because he can identify with the female to a much greater extent than the penile-oriented male. Thus the former's identification with his balls, which are the closest thing he has to female breasts."

Dr. Shoot, who consented to speak in rebuttal to Dr. Herpes, had this to say: "That woman is crazy. Men don't have two types of orgasm. They just think they do. My own findings reveal that they don't even have one kind of orgasm. Actually, there is no such thing as the male orgasm. What passes for orgasm in the male is really a mild form of St. Vitus dance. This afflicts more than 55 percent of the male population in this country, and if Herpes wasn't so hipped on orgasm she'd admit she's wrong. But as far as she's concerned, *everything* is orgasm!"

It should be noted that Dr. Amelia Leviathan is in close agreement with Dr. Shoot. She too believes that what passes for male orgasm is actually a disease. But contrary to Dr. Shoot, she believes the affliction is actually a form of epilepsy localized in the groin. She feels she proved this in her much publicized recent study of 100 male rats, 50 of whom had epilepsy. The epileptic rats, Dr. Leviathan found, could mate with the female rats, even if the female rats didn't want to. The nonepileptic rats just sat around exposing themselves.

Confusing the question of male orgasm even further is Dr. Jennifer Anis, who conducted a study of nearly 700 married males in their late 20s and 30s. According to the results of her study, the issue of male orgasmic or nonorgasmic capacity is clouded by the fact that many men simulate orgasm in order to please their partners. Nearly 25 percent of the men in the Anis group admitted they had at some time in their marriage faked orgasm either because they were tired, or because they knew their partners would be hurt if they didn't climax, or because they had headaches.

Nearly half the men in the Anis study had mild to severe orgasmic difficulties. (It was this group, incidentally, whose psychological profiles appeared in Dr. Anis's widely acclaimed paper, "The Prostate, the Penis, and You-oo," wherein it was revealed that all the orgasmically troubled men shared a common fear of their mothers' cuticles, a hatred of Speedwriting ads in subways, and a horror of certain kinds of peaked golf hats.) What has not been revealed until now, however, is that a great many of these men lead perfectly satisfactory sex lives *without* orgasm, a finding which would seem to put to rest the theory that men must achieve orgasm in order to enjoy sex.

Well, if men can enjoy sex without orgasm, can they also become fathers without achieving climax? Here again the answer is by no means clear. Dr. Herpes and Dr. Shoot, of course, disagree. Dr. Shoot says yes, they can, if they think they can. Dr. Herpes says no, not unless they have either a penile or a spherical orgasm. Dr. Anis believes they can fake it.

Lastly there is the question of the multiple orgasm. Do men have them? Unfortunately, here we are still very much in the dark. The only person ever to do research in this area was Dr. Helen Hager-Bamf, in 1971. From January through April of that year Dr. Hager-Bamf personally tested more than 3,000 randomly selected men for duration and number of orgasms. Tragically dead at the age of 28, she never recorded her findings.

So where do we stand? Is there such a thing as male orgasm? Can men enjoy sex without it? Is a low orgasmic capacity psychologically or physiologically induced? To quote Dr. Grunge at her recent press conference, "Who knows?"

Perhaps the answers are not as important as the fact that the questions are finally being taken seriously. So that, someday, the boy who sells shoes, the young fellow in upholstery, and the man who sews alligators on shirts will no longer have to walk around in perplexity, confused and unnerved by the myth of the male orgasm.

When that day arrives, perhaps male sexuality will come out of the bathroom and into the bedroom where it belongs.

BEYOND INTELLECTUAL SEXISM

JOAN I. ROBERTS

Joan I. Roberts, born in the United States in 1935, is a social psychologist whose interests focus primarily on the effects of racial and ethnic influences on people. She is a member of NOW and of the American Psychological Association, the American Sociological Association, and the American Anthropological Association, and has been active in the formation of Women's Studies curricula and research.

In the discussion that follows, Joan Roberts reveals the far-reaching consequences of feminist analysis for knowledge itself. In describing her own development in Women's Studies from a concern for role expansion to the arduous task of rethinking all the concepts inherited from men, Roberts retraces the odyssey so many of us make — from the examination of our own social roles through a re-examination of social theories, to a reassessment of knowledge about women, to a challenge of all knowledge, its forms, its basic assumptions, its methods, and its utility.

Illustrating how social beliefs and institutions imbed themselves in the scientific world view, Roberts draws the important parallels between bias in the social realm and bias in the intellectual realm. She details the nearly impregnable distortions such a situation creates. Yet, in her experience, the radically altered, unconventional perspectives and methods of woman-oriented scholarship are breaking the hold of the masculist monolith. Feminist thinkers are building a new reality.

The Meaning of Women's Studies

The meaning of our work in women's studies has, for at least some of us, changed substantially over the last few years. When I first commenced my work in this area, I conceived of the study of women as essentially concerned with role reinterpretation and role expansion based on the documentation of, and subsequent change in, social inequities. The basic task was to discover and present the full facts of sex discrimination, to add new knowledge to that which already existed, and to formulate new directions that would reduce inequities by a redefinition and an expansion of roles for men and women.

I soon began to realize that the task was going to be considerably more difficult than that proposed in this original definition of the problem. It was going to be, eventually, a daring and difficult reassessment of social reality, bringing us inevitably into intellectual confrontation with many major paradigms current in the literature of several disciplines. After beginning the search for relevant facts and concepts, some of us came to realize that neither facts nor concepts about females existed in critical scholarly areas. In still other areas, ideas, presumed to pertain to both sexes, were in actuality based on the study of males and extended to females. When females were studied, the paucity of fact and prevalence of opinion were painfully apparent. Thus, the challenging and arduous task before us was to rethink the concepts inherited from men — about them, about us, and, therefore, about humanity.

Some women have mistakenly assumed that we can study existing models and theories in each of our disciplines and modify them without questioning their origins. One social psychologist, speaking to women at a research conference, attempted to make female "passivity," as detailed in the psychological literature, the basis for heightened reflectiveness which could lead to greater creativity.[1] Such logic can stand only if the basic concept stands, and "passivity" is a concept that is riddled with masculist biases.[2] Clearly, then, we must begin our investigation of the concepts themselves. The study of women will engage us in a reassessment of the nature of knowledge, first, through reconceptualization, and then through the construction of new explanatory systems.

Even the modes of inquiry are being subjected to careful scrutiny. In our search for knowledge of ourselves, we find repeatedly that the "scientific" methods are essentially reasserting, with new terminological "weightiness," the same biases against women. Strangely, the "objectivity" of science has sustained a subjective bias that maintains, against the woman's experience of her own life, the myths of female inferiority. Thus, some of us have begun to question the propriety of a social science that remains several steps removed from the "subjects" studied. We have begun to question the findings from natural science that are propounded far from the field of the natural habitats of each species. And we question the humanities where the criticism of intellectual work is too often more important than the creation of that which is to be critiqued. Many of us wonder why institutions look backward, constantly reiterating the glories of previous male thinkers whose ideas have sustained grossly distorted theories of female existence.

If the masculist God of religious belief is dead, as publicly proclaimed, why are women subjected to a new masculist God of science from whom they obtain no greater justice? The male-defined essence of existence remains thoroughly alive. In fact, the old male cosmogony is clearly reflected in a recent pronouncement by a leading religious official: "Satan and his cohorts are using scientific arguments and nefarious propaganda to lure women away from their primary responsibilities as wives, mothers and homemakers. . . . Satan is determined to destroy you. You cannot compromise with him." [3] Despite such pronouncements, Satan is not leading women astray; women are leading one another away from a cosmogony that assumes male leadership in religion or in science. As women *themselves* change the nature of both religious *and* scientific knowledge, our understanding of social reality will change, too. In this way, some of us have come to see that the creation of new social being is the ultimate objective of the study of women.

For those of us who teach courses in this area, the new reality is constantly being created in the students with whom we work. The women, and those few men who dare to face women honestly, are daily engaging in the creation of a social reality that, for many of them, goes far beyond simple role innovation. They face the historical and current facts of sexism with shock, and out of that shock an initial impetus to achieve equality emerges. But as this occurs, a more important transformation engages them in a new sense of self and a new feeling for future possibilities. Listen to three older women, of the more than four hundred students I have known in my courses, they they reflect on these new possibilities:

> For a while I thought that what I was doing was totally nihilistic. I was the one who was crazy enough or foolhardy enough to say shit to the whole thing: I won't accommodate the paternalistic system. But I have begun to see that it isn't nihilism. Maybe there's a reality to what I'm doing that is totally positive. In opting out entirely, or as entirely as I dare, I'm reaching a new plane of validity or honesty or clarity.

> Clarity isn't the word I'm seeking. It's a new integration — an intuitive integration. If I try to pull it together logically right now, it isn't going to work.

> We're returning to the same thing. It's called intuitive because women haven't expressed, in words, their own reality. We call it intuitive because we've no language to clarify it.

The problem for women thinkers now is to conceptualize that new reality. The women students who come to us feeling inauthentic, uncertain, even crazy, are afraid but ex-hilarated with a fuzzy but sharp sense of new being. Our problem is not only to help them create and live that new being, but also to clarify and conceptualize it intellectually.

To do this, some of us have to begin with the historical development of knowledge in each discipline in order to grasp the existential and social factors that invade basic concepts and distort explanations about women and, therefore, about humanity. Underlying knowledge in all disciplines is an ontological set of assumptions about the nature of being or existence. These ontologies, whether derived from religion or science, are subject to the cultural conditions of the particular historical period in which they arose. Basic to our own cultural ontology is the sexual caste system, ordained by religion and in part sustained by science. Essentially, as de Beauvoir stated it, we are "the other" whose meaning for existence is defined as nonbeing or, at best, as peripheral or contingent being.[4]

As women openly reject this idea, we become self-determined ontological exiles who are confronting and changing the symbols and values basic to the thought systems of our culture. Our exclusion from decision-making parallels our exclusion from the creation of explanatory schemata. Those of us whom Germaine Greer labels "intellectual escapees" have too often denied our own experience and accepted only the ideas and procedures defined by the men's thought systems. As Mary Daly suggests, those of us who have perceived the reality of sexual oppression have exhausted ourselves in breaking through the barriers surrounding us, leaving little time or space or energy for our own interpretation of existence. But this interpretation is exactly what is necessary: "What is required of women at this point in history is a radical refusal to limit our perspectives, our questioning, our creativity to any of the preconceived patterns of male-dominated culture." [5] As Daly puts it, we have had the power of naming stolen from us. We must reclaim the right to speak — to name the self, the world, the meaning of our own existence.

As we destroy the images that maintain unequal social arrangements and sustain a façade of change through tokenism, we find ourselves living in a new space, centered in the lives of women, located in the interstices between institutions. As Daly expresses it, "The new space has a kind of invisibility to those who have not entered it . . . it is experienced both as power of presence and power of absence . . . it is participation in the power of being . . . an experience of becoming whole." [6] Women studies courses, although seen by many men as trivial, are the core of these experiences. The possibility of experiencing, even vicariously, both the absence and presence of women in their new space may come as a threatening shock to some men.[7]

It may be even more surprising that women are also entering a new time dimension, rejecting linear time and, in particular, refusing to be caught in the past.[8] Women feel acutely the complex problem of living in the presently felt experience of being a woman while dealing with the demands of a masculist past. Speaking about one major theorist in sociology, a graduate student put it succinctly: "He slammed the door in my face fifty years ago. Why should I bother with him now? He said nothing to women then and he has nothing to say to me about me now." The serious study of women brings us into abrupt confrontation with institutions that live in the historical past. For women living on the boundaries of new time, few adequate models from the past may exist. In fact, we are now reversing the academician's usual approach based on the slow accretion of new knowledge built on previous models. Instead, women break the models that repeatedly demean their existence or degrade their being.

The Sociology of Knowledge

As women define their own ontological meaning within new dimensions of time and space, we will probably use only those segments of explanatory systems that can be adapted to our problems. One useful set of ideas is embodied in the sociology of knowledge first suggested by Karl Marx and later articulated by Karl Mannheim.[9] For Marx human consciousness is determined by social being. Because he avoided the sexual caste system as the precursor of social class, Marx conceived of ideology as false consciousness abstracted from material conditions and used to mask social-class differences. Mannheim extended the idea by including a variety of social groups — occupational, geographical, national — that shape human consciousness. Like Marx, he overlooked the most basic social grouping by sex.

Nevertheless, Mannheim's basic assumptions about the sociology of knowledge are useful since he showed that any system of thought is in part a product of the social conditions in which it is produced. Systems of thought so blatantly distort women that in consciousness-raising groups today they return to their daily lives and earliest experiences to begin the difficult reevaluation of the nature of their existence. Similarly women scholars, when faced with concepts that either exclude or distort women, often begin our analyses at the fundamental level of cultural and existential intrusions into the perceptions of female, and thus, human reality.

The ideology about women consists of

either intentional or unintentional deceptions or distortions that present females in accordance with the socially accepted power distribution by sex in our society. These sexual politics are so accepted as the "natural order" that distortions about women are often not open to the thinker's own conscious intent. The perspective of the thinker, the whole mode of conceiving of women, is in large part determined by the historical and social setting, only a portion of which may appear in conscious thought. In this way, sexist assumptions come to pervade "empirical" theories of women.

Social factors penetrate not only the content but also the forms of knowledge about women. Ideas about women cannot, therefore, be understood on the level of ideas. Every formulation is possible only in relation to previous experience with women; every choice of problem is a selection from many possible options; every analysis will be completed within the context of a sexual caste system. For these reasons, as Mannheim states, the genesis, form, content, scope, and intensity of expression will all be influenced by social conditions.

The social position of the thinker is first established in the earliest social groups — girls or boys — with which children identify. If male, identification with a presumed "masculine" superiority creates a pervasive and subtle perspective which, although unknown at times to the person, will influence the way he views women, what he perceives in them, and how he construes them in his thinking. The sexist perspective can be observed in the total absence of certain concepts about women, in the refusal to deal with selected life problems of women, in the exaggerated presence of concepts about women in highly limited areas, in the dichotomized nature of the structure of categories used, and in the simplistic level of abstractions developed.

The dominant modes of thought used to order experience about and with women intrudes, not only into thought systems, but even into the model of how fruitful thinking can be carried out. Historically, the most obvious bias is that fruitful thinking cannot be undertaken by women at all. In recent versions, women are relegated to limited spheres of productive thought. Less obvious are the intrusions related to early and largely artificial dichotomization and polarization of the world learned by male children which come to be associated with a pseudo sense of superiority. How polarization and dichotomization affect thought systems is still open to much consideration. The "we and they," the "foe and friend," the "reward and punishment" — the ubiquitous and fallacious paired opposites are obvious. What is unclear is the extent to which social sex polarization provides the basis for such dualistic thinking.

Without careful scrutiny of the underlying assumptions that form the social perspective of the thinker, attempts to change the conditions of women and men will probably fail. As both sexes try to equalize their different social groups, agreements and disagreements will focus more on opinions than differences in the total outlooks underlying these opinions. Witness, for example, the recent debate on quotas. But it is the social perspectives, the matrices of assumptions, that we must look at if we are to determine the sources of differences.

Increasingly, a detached perspective, to use Mannheim's term, is occurring among women as we leave traditional social positions, as large groups of us shift away from historically accepted norms and institutions, and as we clash with men's interpretations of us. But out of these conflicts, critical analysis may make the underlying assumptions that intrude into knowledge visible to both groups.

To sum up, in women studies we are beginning to make clearly visible the social factors that condition every product of thought about women. To do this, we will eventually take as our problem the total mental structure underlying the assertions — the perspective of the thinker, her or his whole mode of conceiving of women as determined by the historical and social setting.

Notes

1. Elizabeth Douvan, "Higher Education and Feminine Socialization" (Wingspread Conference on Women's Higher Education convened by the National Coalition for Research on Women's Higher Education and Development, March 1972).
2. Julia Sherman, *On the Psychology of Women: A Survey of Empirical Studies* (Springfield, Ill.: Charles C Thomas, 1971).
3. "Mormons Warned: Satan at Work in Women's Lib," *Capital Times*, 1973.
4. Simone de Beauvoir, *The Second Sex* (New York: Alfred A. Knopf, 1952).
5. Mary Daly, "Theology after the Demise of God the Father: A Call for Castration of Sexist Religion," in *Women and Religion: 1972. Proceedings of the Working Group of Women and Religion,* ed. Judith Plaskow Goldenberg (Waterloo, Ontario: American Academy of Religion, CRS Executive Office, Waterloo Lutheran University, 1973), p. 10. I am indebted to Dr. Daly for her excellent theoretical discourse.
6. Ibid., pp. 11–13.
7. George Gilder, *The Suicide of the Sexes* (New York: Quadrangle Press, 1973).
8. Dorothy Lee, "Autonomous Motivation," in *Anthropology and Education* (Philadelphia: University of Pennsylvania Press, 1961), pp. 103–21.
9. Karl Mannheim, *Ideology and Utopia,* trans. Louis Wirth and Edward Shils (New York: Harvest Books, 1936), pp. 264–90.

WOMEN

JESSIE BERNARD

Sociologist Jessie Bernard was born in 1903, received her Ph.D. at Washington University in St. Louis in 1935, and has written widely on the sociology of marriage, family, motherhood, and gender. Author of *Academic Women* (1974), *The Future of Marriage* (1972), *The Future of Motherhood* (1974), and many other books, she has been widely recognized as an authority and scholar.

In the following selection, Bernard makes it clear that the terms *woman* and *man* are not simple concepts; each in its turn denotes groups of people often tremendously different from some members of their own category and yet similar to members of the other. In her explanations of the meaning and applications of sex, gender, and role with regard to the definition of the word *woman,* Bernard articulates the difficulties in developing adequate categorizations and types for analysis, describes the errors and pitfalls that have characterized such work in the past, and shows how stereotypic expectations have imbedded themselves in social scientific research.

Female and male are to some extent ambiguous categories; feminine and masculine are much more so. An abundance of evidence from anthropology, sociology, and other fields attests to the variability of gender definition within and across cultures. Traits expected of women in one culture (passivity or obesity, perhaps) may be repugnant in others. Men of the Middle East are expected to be openly affectionate with one another; American men on the other hand are required to be reserved. What all this implies, of course, is that manhood and womanhood, femininity and masculinity, are not absolute, cosmically ordained realities, unchanging and unchangeable; they are at least in part if not in toto socially defined patterns and arrangements, hence open to critique on many grounds including utility, productiveness, justice, and esthetics.

The Mark of Eve

Despite universal recognition of differences among women, whatever their causes, women as everyone knows, are women.[1] Still, Ruth Useem, a sociologist, once commented on the inadequacy of the single mark she had to make on all documents asking for "sex." All she could do was check the F box. But she knew that this "mark of Eve" told the reader very little about her. There were so many kinds of F: $F_1, F_2, \ldots F_n$, and yet there was no way to let the reader know which one she was.[2]

Her comment was by no means trivial, facetious, or irrelevant to policy, for the "mark of Eve" a woman makes in the F box ascribes a status to her that is quite independent of her qualities as an individual. Every other mark she makes on that or any other documents will be evaluated in terms of that mark. Assumptions will be made about her on the basis of it. Privileges, responsibilities, prerogatives, obligations will be assigned on the basis of it also. Policy will rest on it. A great deal rides on that one mark, for it refers to the most fundamental differentiation among human beings. But it leaves out differences among the Fs themselves, as important as the similarities. Yet, though there are few bodies of lore and literature more extensive than that on the na-

ture of differences between men and women, there are few less extensive than those on the nature of differences among women themselves.

The Visibility Gap

In the age of innocence, moving picture producers made it very clear to us at the very outset of a picture who were the good guys and who the bad. The good guys wore white hats. In nineteenth-century melodramas the villain wore an identifying mustache so that we knew he was going to foreclose the mortgage unless the beautiful daughter capitulated to his advances. In Greek drama there were appropriate masks to inform us about the characters.

Despite our dependence on visual cues, however, there is always a visibility gap. The outer mark does not tell us all there is to know about the person inside. The same mark stamps a wide variety of people. Not all the farmers who bore the mark of Cain killed grazers and herders. A wide variety of men bore that mark. A wide variety of people inhabit the bodies of women (as also, of course, the bodies of men as well). For women are not interchangeable parts.

$F_1, F_2, \ldots F_n$

Whatever the differences may be between M and F, and whatever the origin of these differences may be, they are matched and in some cases exceeded by differences among women themselves. A woman may in many ways be more like the average man than she is like another woman. A very considerable research literature undergirds the fact that there are extensive differences among women in such sociologically relevant variables as interests, values, and goals. These differences have to be taken into account when dealing with programs or policies involving women.

Two polar types turn up with singular consistency in the research literature on women, whether the point of view is sociological or psychological.[3] Alice Rossi assigned the terms "pioneer" and "housewife" to these types, using the term "traditional" for those who fell in between (Rossi, 1965, pp. 79–80). Another team of researchers called the polar types "homemaking-oriented" and "career-oriented" (Hoyt and Kennedy, 1958). Another researcher spoke of "creative intellectual" when referring to a type that corresponded to pioneer or career-oriented (Drews, 1965). Eli Ginzberg and his associates found women they called "supportive," who corresponded roughly to the housewife or home-oriented subjects in the other studies, and "influential" women who resembled the pioneer type (Ginzberg, 1966). The existence of such types can scarcely be challenged.

The exact numerical population size of these several types is not important, for it doubtless changes over time and is certainly changing today. In the recent past, however, one of the striking facts that emerged from the studies was the agreement they showed with respect to the incidence of the several types in different samples. At the high school senior level, 7 to 8 per cent of the "creative intellectuals" had the drive to achieve the life style they desired. Among college freshmen, 8 per cent

fell into the career-oriented category. Among college graduates, 7 per cent were pioneers. Among women who had done graduate work, 10 per cent were living an influential life style. At Cornell, 8 per cent of a sample of women in 1950 and 6 per cent of a sample in 1952 showed high career orientation (Goldsen, 1960, p. 136). At Vassar, however, also in the 1950's, two-thirds answered "true" to the statement "I would like a career" (Freedman, 1967, p. 136). In context, this answer was interpreted by Caroline Bird to mean "career" in a secondary sense. Perhaps more indicative of a pioneer orientation was the answer to the statement "I enjoy children," which elicited a negative in 8 per cent of the women. That the Vassar women were changing rapidly was suggested by Caroline Bird, who noted that the classes of 1964 to 1966 voted for "career with as little time out for family as possible" and that there was even a notable rise in the number of girls who said they were pursuing a "career period" (Bird, 1968, p. 184). The proportion in all the samples who fell into the housewife or homemaking or supportive category was consistently about a fifth or a fourth. It is interesting to compare this figure with the proportion, about 18 per cent, of college women who, a generation ago, were reported by Lewis M. Terman to be greatly interested in the domestic arts (Terman and Miles, 1936, pp. 209–210).

It would require considerably more focused research to pinpoint with greater accuracy and precision the relative incidence of the several types and the reasons that explain these proportions. Equally important would be research to document trends in such incidence. My own reading of current trends is that one of the most drastic shake-ups in the social order today is the breaking up of old blocs and their re-forming into new configurations. Yesterday's data no longer reflect the current scene. In 1969 a national sample of youth showed 10 per cent of the young women to be radical reformers and 17.1 per cent moderate reformers (Yankelovich, 1969).

The characterization of the pioneer (or career-oriented or creative intellectual or influential) type varied with the interests of the researchers; but here, too, there was notable convergence. Among the high-school girls, the creative intellectuals tended to be more receptive than other girls to the new, to growth, and to change; they were less conventional and conforming. Among college students, those who fell into the pioneer or career-oriented category tended to show up in all the studies as different from other college women. The Kansas State career-oriented freshmen were higher on "endurance" and "achievement" than the homemaking-oriented women and lower on "succorance" and "heterosexuality" — in the sense of being interested in attracting young men, not as contrasted with homosexuality (Hoyt and Kennedy, 1968). Rossi's housewives characterized themselves as dependent; they showed strong nurturance toward the young; they were socially rather than occupationally competitive. In contrast, the pioneers were less dependent, less nurturant, more egalitarian; they valued the world of ideas more. They characterized themselves as dominant and occupationally competitive (the married less so than the single). Ginzberg's women with the influential life style were characterized by a striving for autonomy; they found their major sources of gratification in the social significance of their work and the personal relations involved in it. In both the Rossi and the Ginzberg samples, the women in the pioneer or influential category were far more likely to be working (70 per cent in both samples) and less likely to be married; the reverse was true for the housewives and supportive women. At Cornell, it was found that the

career-oriented women were more likely than the family-oriented women to be non-conformists with "a certain irreverence for rules and conventions" (Freedman, 1967, p. 140). At Vassar, years of careful research yielded this picture of career-oriented students:

> Students who say "true" to "I would like a career" are somewhat more intellectual, unconventional, independent (perhaps rebellious), and flexible in thinking and outlook. They are also somewhat more alienated or isolated socially. [At Cornell, career women engaged in just as many extracurricular activities as other women and were just as likely to associate with men (Goldsen, 1960, p. 54).] It is interesting to observe that these differences are most pronounced [among seniors]. Results for the Ethnocentrism Scale . . . are in line with findings of other studies which demonstrate that attitudes toward the role and behavior of women are likely to accord with attitudes toward members of outgroups or "underprivileged" groups. Individuals, including women themselves, who hold somewhat stereotyped views of Negroes or foreigners, for example, are likely to adhere to traditional or rather fixed notions of what is appropriate activity for women (Freedman, 1967, p. 140).

The explanations of such differences among women also vary according to the researchers' predilections. One team of psychologists is satisfied by a pattern of "needs." Career-oriented women, they believe, are motivated by one or more of four such needs: to establish one's worth through competitive behavior or achievement, to know intellectually and understand ("intraception"), to accomplish concrete goals (endurance), and to avoid relations with men (heterosexuality). The homemaking women are motivated by needs of affection and acceptance (succorance) (Hoyt and Kennedy, 1958). But another psychologist is quite agnostic: "Psychology has nothing to say about what women are really like, what they need and what they want, essentially, because psychology does not know" (Weisstein, 1969, p. 78). Sociologists and social psychologists tend to look to socialization variables to interpret the differences. Since career orientation may change with age and experience, it is hazardous to put too much credence in any analysis that makes it depend on personality variables, which are presumably quite stable. Such an approach, in any event, still leaves the genesis of the needs themselves to be explained.

Whatever the incidence and whatever the explanation, telescoping all these women into the single F box blots out a great deal of sociologically important diversity. In many situations F_1 may have more in common with M_1 than with any of the other Fs. Rank, for example, is more important than sex in many situations. A princess has more in common with a prince than with a domestic; a professional woman often has more in common with a colleague than with a cleaning woman; an heiress with an heir than with a woman receiving welfare payments. Sometimes F_i and F_j have not only different but opposing points of view, each seeing the other as a threat either to a vested interest or to opportunity for achievement. The wife of a workingman may not agree with the woman worker on the principle of equal pay for equal work; she believes her husband should get more because he has to support his family. (Perhaps the only thing that all Fs have in common as yet is the concern that adequate gynecological, obstetrical, and pediatric services be widely available, and that public toilet facilities be supplied with emergency equipment.)

It would, then, be more in line with the facts of life if, instead of compressing all women into the single F category, the diversity among them could be recognized by allowing for F_1, F_2, ... F_n. Thus the woman who says she is content to devote her life to the traditional pattern of homemaking could be differentiated from the woman who is willing to settle for nothing less than the complete gamut — marriage, children, and a career. . . .

Sex

If both the layman and the scientist have underplayed the differences among women, they have tended to overplay the differences between females and males. A great deal of the work of running the world rests on making simple classificatory decisions. Into which category does X fall? Y? or Z? Which rules apply? Anything, therefore, that simplifies this process by predecision is welcomed by administrators and executives and copers in general. Sex is such a predecision-maker. F goes here, M there: so much easier than having to study each case individually to decide on its merits where it belongs, which rule to apply. It is such a simple, straightforward, ineffable, easily applied criterion that it has rarely been challenged.

But new research issuing from clinic and laboratory is beginning to shake our old naiveté about sex. We now know that, far from being a simple, straightforward, genetically determined phenomenon, sex has at least three components — chromosomal, hormonal, anatomical — and conceivably more. Although for most people these three components are matched to produce a clear-cut male or female individual, such is not always the case. There can be mistakes. These "errors of the body" have alerted us to some of the anomalies possible in the sphere of sexuality. When all goes normally, as it usually does, the M and F boxes fit very well to distinguish males and females. They can accommodate almost everyone. But things do not always go normally. Sometimes a genetic F is masculinized hormonally *in utero* with the result that anatomical anomalies confuse gender assignment at birth; or a genetic M is not masculinized *in utero,* making gender equivocal. Such errors are rare and turn up so infrequently that relatively little is yet known about them; they are so rare that, once they are recognized, we can disregard them in any analysis of large-scale sociological phenomena.[4] Their major relevance for our discussion here is the lesson they teach with respect to the relative contribution of biological, social, cultural, and sociological factors to gender.

With the exception of those who are victims of "errors of the body" there is no overlap between male and female populations. They are categorically different (Figure 1). Still it is interesting to note that, different though the equipment at their disposal may be, they respond quite similarly to the same stimuli. Estrogens and androgens, for example, have the same effect on both sexes, making for greater or less sexual motivation, greater or less aggressiveness (Hamber and Lunde, 1966). This suggests that the two sexes also respond about the same way to other kinds of stimuli — psychological and social. What is important are the kinds of stimuli they are subjected to. Interesting also is the finding that creative personalities, whether housed in female or in male bodies, have similar personality characteristics.

Gender

Gender refers to the complex of traits that determine whether one checks the M or the F box. It is, to be sure, inextricably related to sex, but "the two realms, sex and gender, are not at all inevitably bound in anything like a one-to-one relationship, but each may go in its quite independent way" (Stoller,

Figure 1 The sexes are categorically different.

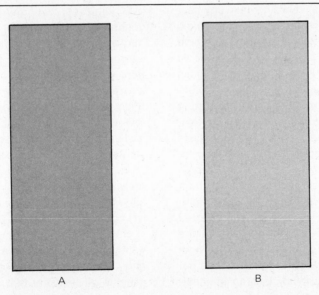

A   B

1968, pp. vii–ix). Sex is a biological fact; gender, though based on biology, is a social-cultural-sociological-psychological fact. Gender consists of gender identity and gender role (Stoller, 1968, p. 92): the first a social and psychological phenomenon; the second, a cultural and sociological and interactional one.

Gender identity begins in the hospital delivery room. As soon as an infant is born it is, on the basis of anatomical cues, assigned a gender which is well established by age two. The infant's life course is almost sealed by that act; for it is primarily this gender assignment rather than anatomy, or even heredity, that, in Freud's terminology, is destiny. Almost every decision made by the outside world about this child is going to take this assignment into account. Every structured relationship will be defined in terms of it, and the child will accept it in most cases.

Gender Identity

Scarcely a woman alive would have any hesitation about marking the proper F or M box. A woman knows she is a female. The whole matter of gender identity would probably never have occurred to a woman; it looks to her like a man-made problem manufactured by male psychoanalysts, illustrating the sexism that modern women are protesting against. This sexism of psychoanalysts is nowhere better portrayed than in their inability to understand how women could possibly have any sense of femaleness without something like a phallus to prove to themselves that they were women. An inverted phallus or vagina was invoked to solve the riddle. It has been a major contribution of recent gender research to show it does not take a vagina, notoriously lacking in sensitivity, to confer gender identity on females.

Breasts and menstruation serve quite adequately to remind them that they are female, strange as it may seem to a breastless non-menstruating individual. To psychoanalysts, the muscle that daily (and, in youth, hourly) reminds males of their sex seemed the sine qua non of gender identity; a creature lacking it must be only a defective male. The results of this thinking showed up in therapy; "It is possible that the analyst's view of a successful analysis may be skewed if he feels he has reached the core of a woman's femininity when he has been able to get her to share with equanimity his belief that she is really an inferior form of male" (Stoller, 1968, p. 63).

Actually a woman's gender identity is firm, even, in some cases, if her heredity or anatomy is not. In Table 1 for example, three women are discussed who would unhesitatingly mark the F box; they have female gender identity (numbers 2, 3, and 5). But both their heredities and their anatomies differ. One (number 3) has female heredity and external anatomy but no vagina. One (number 2) has female heredity but, as a result of masculinization *in utero,* male-appearing genitalia; female gender was assigned to her at birth and despite the anatomical anomaly she finds the F box acceptable. A third woman (number 5) has neuter heredity and anomalous anatomy; but, assigned female gender at birth, she, too, has no problem with the F box. Such women may be unhappy about their inadequate or flawed sexuality, but their gender identity is unimpaired; they feel like women and unequivocally check the F box. All are F even though either their heredity or their anatomy does not conform to F specifications.

Such cases show the independence of gender identity from either heredity or anatomy. They illustrate its social nature: "those aspects of sexuality that are called gender are ... learned postnatally" (Stoller, 1968,

Table 1 Deviances illustrating the equivocal relation of gender identity to heredity and anatomy

Genetic sex	Internal anatomy	External anatomy	Gender assignment	Gender identity
1. Female	Female	Equivocal	Male	Male
2. Female	Female	Equivocal	Female	Female
3. Female	Defective	Female	Female	Female
4. Female	Female	Female	Female	Male
5. Neuter (XO)	Defective	Female	Female	Female
6. Equivocal (XXY)	Female	Male	Male	Female
7. Male	Male	Equivocal	Female	Male
8. Male	Male	Equivocal	Male	Female

Source: Data from Robert J. Stoller, *Sex and Gender, on the Development of Masculinity and Femininity* (Science House, New York, 1968).

1. "Money and the Hampsons ... describe two children masculinized *in utero* by excessive adrenal androgens, both biologically normal females, genetically and in their internal sexual anatomy and physiology, but with masculinized external genitalia. The proper diagnosis having been made, one child was raised unequivocally as a female ... ; she turned out to be as feminine as other little girls" (p. 57).

2. "The other, not recognized to be female, was raised without question as a male ... and became an unremarkably masculine little boy" (p. 57).

3. "The patient is a 17-year-old, feminine, attractive, intelligent girl who appeared anatomically completely normal at birth, but behind whose external genitalia there was no vagina or uterus. Her parents, having no doubts, raised her as a girl, and female and feminine is what she feels she is" (p. 56).

4. "These people, living permanently as unremarkably masculine men, are biologically normal females and were so recognized as children ... Among those I know one is an expert machine tool operator, another an engineering draftsman, another a research chemist. Their jobs are quiet, steady, and unspectacular; their work records as men are excellent. They are sociable, not recluses, and have friendships with both men and women. Neither their friends nor their colleagues at work know they are biologically female. They are not clinically psychotic" (pp. 194, 196).

5. "[She] is a person as biologically neuter as a human can be, chromosomally XO ... And yet when she was first seen at age 18 ... she was quite unremarkably feminine in her behavior, dress, social and sexual desires, and fantasies, indistinguishable in these regards from other girls ... Her gender identity is not based on some simple biological given, such as endocrine state. It comes from the fact that she looked like a girl ... Given the anatomical prerequisites to the development of her femininity, it set in motion the complicated process that results in gender identity" (p. 22).

6. "... born an apparently normal male, ... the boy's body became feminized" (p. 77).

7. "A child ... at birth was found to be an apparently normal female and so was brought up as a girl for fourteen years ... A physical examination [at adolescence] raised doubts shortly to be confirmed. ... The inquiry ... revealed that although the external genitalia looked the same as those of a normal girl of her age, she was in fact a chromosomally normal male" (pp. 67, 69).

8. "This patient ... was male in anatomical appearance. However, as far back as memory goes, he was extremely feminine. ... Hospitalized as a result of hepatitis, he was discovered to be genetically and anatomically male" (p. 75).

p. xiii) primarily from the mother but also from the father, siblings, and friends.

Cases number 1 and 2 also illustrate the social nature of gender identity or the acceptance of the gender assigned at birth. In both cases the infants were genetically females but in both cases the external genitalia, according to which gender is assigned, had been masculinized *in utero* and were therefore anomalous. In the case of one of the children (number 2), the diagnosis of sex was correct and the child was assigned female gender and reared as a female. In the other (number 1), the diagnosis was incorrect and the child was assigned male gender and reared as a male. The first became as feminine as other little girls, the other a masculine little boy. Same sex heredity, same prenatal "error," but different gender assignment and hence different gender identity.

Gender is so thoroughly bred into the infant by the world around it and becomes so much a part of its identity that even if the assignment is later discovered to be an error, it is almost impossible to change. Despite the discovery that the individual is genetically a male, he continues to have female gender identity.

All these findings warn us against taking the M and F boxes too much for granted. Gender identity does not apparently always just come naturally. It has to be learned. And there is no one-to-one relationship between it and sex.

The emphasis on the social and acquired nature of gender identity does not rule out a biological component, for "if the first main finding of [recent research] is that gender identity is primarily learned, the second is that there are biological forces that contribute to this" (Stoller, 1968, p. xiii). Sometimes, for reasons not yet clear, gender assignment does not "take," as in cases 4, 6, 7, and 8. The resulting phenomena curb any dogmatism we may show with respect to our knowledge of sex and gender. The nature of the biological component involved in gender is still an open question. Beach calls it an unresolved issue (Beach, 1965, p. 565) and Stoller confesses that the evidence is equivocal, "so we must leave this subject without any sense of its having been settled" (Stoller, 1968, p. 85). For this reason as well as for the reason that sexual anomalies are so rare, the strictly biological factors in gender are given no further attention here. Although they teach us a great deal about the normal aspects of sex and gender, they cannot be invoked in sociological analyses. Further

discussion would distort the picture by over-emphasizing rare exceptions.

Although the etiological contribution of biological factors to gender identity may be equivocal and often irrelevant, the indirect or derivative contribution of biological factors cannot be denied. In the crucial years when both F and M are working out their mature identities, they are producing different reactions in one another. She produces an erection in him; another boy does not. His touch on her breasts thrills her; another girl's does not. She wants him to caress her; she does not want another girl to. Being reacted to by others as F is different from being reacted to by them as M. And the reaction to F is different from the reaction to M. She can receive him, he cannot receive her. It does not take a sophisticated analysis in terms of symbolic interactionism to see that the different effect each has *on* the other and the different reaction each has *to* the other will produce different conceptions of the self in both M and F. These differences are ultimately biological but, like the functional basis for differences (to be discussed later), in a derived rather than in a direct sense.

Gender Role

Along with gender assignment goes a constellation of traits suitable for characterizing the gender. When illustrating or demonstrating the gender identity of patients, Stoller gives such evidence of feminine gender identity as wanting babies and having a great interest in clothes, cooking, sewing, make-up, ornamentation, and the like (Stoller, 1968, pp. 21–22). These are clearly not all the product of heredity nor of anatomy. They are traits that our society labels feminine.

Some of the specific contents or traits that constitute masculine or feminine gender may vary from place to place and time to time. In Iran, for example, some of the traits that we develop as parts of feminine gender are included in the pattern for masculine gender and vice versa:

In Iran...men are expected to show their emotions.... If they don't, Iranians suspect they are lacking a vital human trait and are not dependable. Iranian men read poetry; they are sensitive and have well-developed intuition and in many cases are not expected to be too logical. They are often seen embracing and holding hands. Women, on the other hand, are considered to be coldly practical. They exhibit many of the characteristics we associate with men in the United States. A very perceptive Foreign Service officer who had spent a number of years in Iran once observed, "If you think of the emotional and intellectual sex roles reversed from ours, you will do much better out here." ...Fundamental beliefs like our concepts of masculinity and femininity are shown to vary widely from one culture to the next (Hall, 1963, p. 10).[5]

The specific contents of masculinity and femininity vary with time also; people worry over the "masculinization of women" and the "feminization of men." The Victorian contents of feminine gender included weakness, helplessness, fragility, delicacy, and even ill health. Clark Vincent has pointed out how ill-fitting the traditional contents of gender roles are today for both F and M. On tradition-oriented tests, modern middle-class women tend to test low; middle-class men, on the other hand, "tend to score high on femininity when items are included which formerly described the more dependent, intuitive, sensitive, 'peacemaking' role of the female in a tradition-oriented society" (Vincent, 1966, p. 199).

Gender specifications vary not only with time and place but also with the researcher or scientist who reports them. One survey of the literature on the feminine character concluded that "there is hardly any common basis to the different views. The difficulty is not only that there is disagreement on specific characteristics [of feminine gender] and their origin, but that even when there is agreement the emphasis is laid on absolutely different attributes" (Klein, 1946, p. 164).

The most widely recurrent traits attributed to women in western societies have been passivity, emotionality, lack of abstract interests, greater intensity of personal relationships, and an instinctive tenderness for babies (Klein, 1946, p. 164). The test of masculinity-femininity includes such items as passivity, disinclination for physical violence, sensitivity to personal slights and to interpersonal relations, lack of concern for abstractions, and a positive attitude toward culturally defined esthetic experience.

If femaleness and maleness are categorical, nonoverlapping, the same cannot be said with respect to femininity and masculinity. Here the overlap can be considerable (Figure 2). Traits denominated as feminine show up in men and those denominated as masculine show up in women.[6] Here the distinction between *typical* and *characteristic* is important. The typical is the average or the modal. And for many traits, where the overlap is great, the average woman and the average man may not be very different. But when women and men do differ, they differ in characteristic ways, women "characteristically" in one direction, men in another. By and large, women tend to differ in the direction of passivity, nurturance, nonviolence, and men in the direction of aggression, dominance, and violence. The tendency of most societies is to pull women in one direction

Figure 2 Masculine and feminine gender traits overlap.

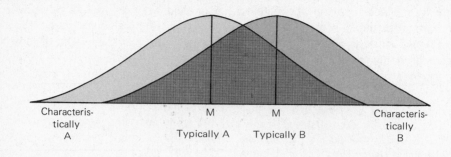

Characteris-
tically
A

M

Typically A

M

Typically B

Characteris-
tically
B

Figure 2a The range of overlap between A and B can vary widely.

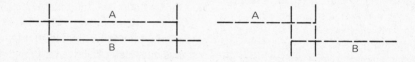

and men in the other, so that very often the distributions are skewed (Figure 3). For the convenience of managers and copers, it would be ideal if femininity and masculinity were as categorically clear-cut as female-ness and maleness; it would save them a great deal of trouble if all females were characteristically feminine and all males were characteristically masculine. But the fact is that they aren't. The important thing is not, therefore, whether or not "women" are z-er than "men," or "men" v-er than "women," but whether Mary is z-er than John, or John v-er than Mary.

Viola Klein has traced the conceptualiza-tion of sex differences through three stages, beginning with Aristotle's category of femi-nine traits which led him to conclude that femininity was a "kind of natural defective-ness." According to this conceptualization, women are underdeveloped beings with the external attributes of human beings but

lacking individuality, intellectual ability, or character. A second stage granted that women were not inferior men but simply dif-ferent, complementary, inverse. This point of view flourished at the end of the nineteenth and beginning of the twentieth centuries. The third, current, conceptualization sees personality traits as products of functional roles (Klein, 1946, pp. 169–170).

Despite the enormous amount of ink that has been spilled in clearly specifying the na-ture of psychological gender differences, the conclusion seems to be that it is not so much *what* is defined as masculine or femi-nine as that such distinctions are made at all. It makes no difference whether pink is for girls and blue for boys, emotionality for girls and rationality for boys, or the other way round. What does make a difference is that a difference is made. It is not the ex-planations offered for the existence of dif-ferences (inherent, acquired, functional,

Figure 3 Skewed distributions of gender traits. *The socialization process has pulled A and B in different directions, so that the distributions are skewed in a desired direction.*

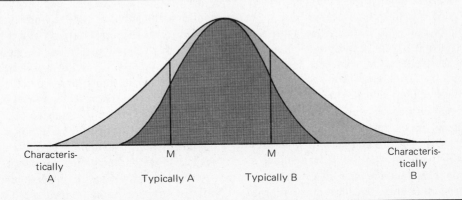

Characteris-
tically
A

M

Typically A

M

Typically B

Characteris-
tically
B

structural) but the fact that there is something to explain. It is the bifurcation by sex that is the fundamental fact. The traits, functions, and work assigned to each part of the bifurcation are secondary; the bifurcation itself is what is primary.

Sex has inevitable structural concomitants and consequences. The structural components that operate differentially on the sexes are both horizontal and vertical; the world women live in tends to be different, and it is usually secondary to the world of men.

The Sphere of Women

Once an individual has been assigned a gender, he (or she) is thereafter relegated to the world or sphere designed for those with his (or her) gender. Even when the work of both women and men was in the home, they lived in different worlds: there was a sphere for men and a sphere for women. Even today there is a woman's world recognized by almost everyone and thoroughly exploited by the mass media. It has quite a different structure from the world of men.

These worlds can be described in terms of several dimensions or variables that those sociologists who follow Talcott Parsons have found useful in describing social systems. Five such dimensions have been encapsulated in terms of five pairs of variables. A community can, first of all, make one's position rest on what one *does* or on what one *is;* it can be the result of achievement or of ascription. Second, the expectations that parties in any relationship share may be specific or diffuse. Duties, obligations, and responsibilities may be defined specifically and contractually or they may be left unspecified. If they are specified, each party knows precisely what is expected of him and of others; nothing more can be demanded than what is specified and nothing less can be supplied. The accountant may not be asked to run the computer, the lawyer to run the elevator. If they are left diffuse, there is a rather amorphous, blurred set of expectations that leave precise limits undefined. A friend may be expected to lend money, arrange a date, or share a record collection. Third, a community can require that all relationships be governed by general universalistic principles or it can permit them to be governed by particularistic personal loyalties and obligations tailored to the particular individuals involved. Fourth, it can permit behavior to be oriented toward furthering one's own interests or it can require that actions be oriented toward a larger group or the collectivity as a whole, regardless of individual wishes. Finally, the community can admit a wide range of relationships in which there is a minimum of affect or emotional gratification (in which relationships are neutral) or it can allow a wide range of relationships in which affectivity or emotional gratification plays a large part. It is clear that a society in which the first of each of these five pairs of variables prevails will be quite different from one in which the second of each does.

These dimensions or ways of patterning the variables have been used to describe communities or societies of different kinds. For example, ascription, diffuseness, particularism, collectivity-orientation, and affectivity have been used to describe preliterate societies. The first three pairs of dimensions have been used to characterize developing countries as contrasted with modern ones; the degree to which they approached achievement, specificity, and universalistic characteristics has been taken as a measure of modernization (Hoselitz, 1964).

It is not too fanciful to view the gender world or sphere in which women live as characterized, like a preliterate society, by ascription, diffuseness, particularism, collectivity-orientation, and affectivity. In effect, to view women as inhabiting an underdeveloped, if not a primitive, world.

The first step has been taken when feminine gender is ascribed to the female infant. A lifelong train of consequences then ensues. She is thereafter dealt with on the basis of what she is — a woman — rather than on what she does, on her (feminine)

qualities rather than on her performance, just as reported for preliterate cultures.

Once this assignment and consequent ascription have been made, a woman is consigned to a world or "sphere" in which her relationships are diffuse rather than specific or contractual. Even in a work situation where, presumably relations are contractual and specific, the secretary has diffuse expectations to live up to, such as the variegated services expected of an "office wife" or "girl Friday." The sphere of women is expected to be characterized by particularistic morality more than by universalistic morality, by intense personal loyalty more than by principles. Women are to protect their children even when the children are delinquents or criminals, to do everything they can for those near and dear to them rather than be blindly just or impartial. On the job, women, as part of their supportive function, are expected to be more loyal to their employers than are men. One reads from time to time that men have reported wrongdoing on the part of their employers, one rarely reads that women have. The "developed" country that men inhabit almost forces them to undercut one another to get ahead. In the women's sphere, women are expected to be oriented toward the larger group or the collectivity and to make sacrifices for it. We know that in marriage it is wives who make more of the adjustments; it is taken for granted that mothers make sacrifices for their children; it is expectable that if necessary, the daughter rather than the son will sacrifice marriage to take care of elderly parents. Yet the pursuit of self-interest is almost a virtue in the world men inhabit.

In using this form of "pattern-variable" it is essential to make perfectly clear that the personal characteristics of the individuals involved are not the focus of attention; it is rather the shared expectations built into the situation. A social system leads to certain kinds of behavior on the part of its members regardless of their personal qualities or traits. We tend thereafter to attribute to the individuals the qualities expected in them by the system. For example, Freud tells us that the superego of women "is never as inexorable, as impersonal, as independent of its emotional origins as we require it to be in men [affectivity]. Character-traits which critics of every epoch have brought up against women — that they show less sense of justice than men . . . that they are more often influenced in their judgments by their feelings of affection or hostility [particularism] — all these would be amply accounted for by the modification in the formation of their super-ego" (Freud, 1925, pp. 257–258). In terms of the pattern-variable frame of reference, Freud is saying that in women's world affectivity rather than affective neutrality is the expectation, and particularistic rather than universalistic morality. The expectation of this particular pattern in the world of women imposes it on them.

Spock offers specific examples of how such expectations are realized in the modal personality types of men and women. Women, he tells us, become indignant when legal logic results in an unfair decision. "Her husband says, 'Don't you see that the law *has* to take this position, even if it occasionally causes injustice?'" (Spock, 1970). The feminine modal personality type does not. That is not the logic of her (particularistic) world. Her perch is in a particularistic world, his in a universalistic one. They do not see the same things.

There are those who bemoan the passing of the ascriptive, diffusely defined, particularistic, collectivity-oriented, and affective pattern, who believe that a great loss was suffered when it gave way to an achievement-oriented, contractual, specifically defined, universalistic, and affectively neutral pattern. This judgment may have some validity. Still, so long as half of the population inhabits a world patterned one way and the other half another world, the first is at a disadvantage. . . .

Notes

1. There is, interestingly, less consensus with respect to the term *lady*. In Victorian times a lady was a special kind of person, refined, circumspect, noble, virtuous, sexless, well behaved, and well mannered. Both the term and the concept went out of fashion in the twentieth century. Modern women did not want to be ladies; to be called "ladylike" came to be something to be resented. It has been with some surprise, therefore, that I have noted a return to the use of this term, even by fellow social scientists in research conferences. They speak of research subjects as "ladies," as though at a loss of what else to call women.

2. In my book, *The Sex Game,* I used the concept of subsexes as a ploy to emphasize the importance of such intrasex differences among both women and men.

3. It is important always to note the date of any research on women. The era of the feminine mystique, from the end of the war through the 1950's, exerted a powerful influence on what women thought and felt.

4. Female anomalies are especially rare, being only one-third to one-eighth as common as male anomalies (Stoller, 1968, p. 197).

5. Margaret Mead also made a great deal of the cultural contents of gender, which she labeled *temperament* (Mead, 1925).

6. In a sample of 604 men and 696 women in the general population Terman found both men and women in the range of scores on masculinity-femininity from −80 to +60; but above 60 there were no women and below −99 there were no men (Terman, 1936, p. 72).

References

Adler, Alfred, *The Practice and Theory of Individual Psychology* (London: Kegan Paul, 1924).

Beach, Frank, "Retrospect and Prospect," *Sex and Behavior* (New York: Wiley, 1965).

Bernard, Jessie, "Observation and Generalization in Cultural Anthropology," *American Journal of Sociology,* 50 (1945), pp. 284–291.

————. *The Sex Game* (Englewood Cliffs, N.J.: Prentice-Hall, 1968).

Bird, Caroline, *Born Female: The High Cost of Keeping Women Down* (New York: McKay, 1968).

Drews, Elizabeth Monroe, "Counseling for Self-Actualization in Gifted Girls and Young Women," *Journal of Counseling Psychology,* 12 (Summer 1965), pp. 167 ff.

Eells, John S., Jr., "Women in Honors Programs: Winthrop College," in Philip I. Mitterling (ed.), *Needed Research on Able Women in Honors Programs, College, and Society* (New York: Columbia University Press, 1964).

Freedman, Mervin, *The College Experience* (San Francisco: Jossey-Bass, 1967).

Freud, Sigmund, "Some Psychological Consequences of the Anatomical Distinction between the Sexes," *Collected Works,* Standard edition, Vol. 19 (London: Hogarth Press, 1961). This paper was originally published in 1925.

Ginzberg, Eli, et al., *Life Styles of Educated Women* (New York: Columbia University Press, 1966).

Goldsen, Rose K., et al., *What College Students Think* (New York: Van Nostrand, 1960).

Hacker, Helen, "Women as a Minority Group," *Social Forces,* 30 (Sept. 1951), pp. 60–66.

Hall, Edward T., *The Silent Language* (Greenwich: Premier Books, 1963).

Hamberg, David A., and Donald T. Lunde, "Sex Hormones in the Development of Sex Differences in Human Behavior," in Maccoby, Eleanor (ed.), *The Development of Sex Differences* (Stanford, Calif.: Stanford University Press, 1966), Chapter 1.

Hoselitz, Bert F., "Social Stratification and Economic Development," *International Social Science Journal,* 16 (2) (1964); also "Social Structure and Economic Growth," *Economia Internationale,* 6 (Aug. 1953).

Hoyt, Donald P., and Carroll E. Kennedy, "Interest and Personality Correlates of Career-Motivated and Homemaking-Motivated College Women," *Journal of Counseling Psychology,* 5 (Spring 1958), 44–49.

Klein, Viola, *The Feminine Character* (New York: International Universities Press, 1946).

Mead, Margaret, *Sex and Temperament in Three Primitive Societies* (New York: Morrow, 1935).

Riesman, David, "Introduction," in Jessie Bernard, *Academic Women* (University Park: Pennsylvania State University Press, 1964).

Rossi, Alice, "Who Wants Women in the Scientific Professions?" in Jacqueline A. Mattfeld and Carol G. Van Aken (eds.), *Women and the Scientific Professions* (Cambridge: M. I. T. Press, 1965).

Spock, Benjamin, "Decent and Indecent" (*McCall,* 1970). This citation from *Washington Post,* Feb. 5, 1970.

Stoller, Robert J., *Sex and Gender* (New York: Science House, 1968).

Terman, Lewis M., and C. C. Miles, *Sex and Personality: Studies in Masculinity and Femininity* (New York: McGraw-Hill, 1936).

Vaerting, Mathilde, and Mathias Vaerting, *The Dominant Sex, A Study in the Sociology of Sex Differences* (London: Allen and Unwin, 1923).

Vincent, Clark, "Implications of Change in Male-Female Role Expectations for Interpreting M-F Scores," *Journal of Marriage and the Family,* 28 (May 1966), 196–199.

Weisstein, Naomi, "Kinder, Kuche, Kirche as Scientific Law: Psychology Constructs the Female," *Motive,* 19 (March-April 1969), 78–85.

Yankelovich, Daniel, *Generations Apart* (Columbia Broadcasting Company, 1969).

I

Consciousness: Concepts,
Images, and Visions

"Men know a lot about dying, but they don't know enough about living."

— MARGARET MEAD, speech before the Fourth Plenary Session, First National Women's Conference, International Women's Year, Houston, November 20, 1977

As we explore the topics in this book, we will consider womanhood in all its perspectives — including the biological, social, political, and philosophical. We begin in Part I with what I term *sexual consciousness* — the abstract, symbolic, sometimes prelingual elements of our sexual reality. Meanings, associations, expectations, images, stereotypes, and ideals of both sexes form the framework, the underpinnings, the motivational pool, the consciousness or "head set" of sexual reality, which, I believe, directs and determines in large part our social-sexual behavior and arrangements. *We* begin here because much of *it* begins here.

We will examine first in Chapter 2 the dynamics of patriarchy, the male-identified, male-governed, masculist society in which we live. It is both the setting in which traditional (male-identified) images of womanhood were created and the foil against which new (woman-identified) ideals are being forged. In Chapters 3 and 4 we will explore images of women, patriarchal stereotypes and ideals as well as feminist affirmations. The discussion of consciousness will close in Chapter 5 with an analysis of some of the theories and explanations for the asymmetrical relations of the sexes.

2

The Dynamics of Patriarchy

Conceptions of Patriarchy

The terms *patriarchy* and *matriarchy* may have a variety of meanings. Since the suffix *-archy* literally means "the rule of," patriarchy means literally *the rule of the fathers* and matriarchy, *the rule of the mothers*. The traditional use of the terms in social science, particularly anthropology, has intended a meaning close to the literal sense: in this context a patriarchy is a society in which formal power over public decision and policy making is held by men; a matriarchy is then a society in which policy is made by women.

Many contemporary anthropologists argue that although there have been, and still are, societies that are matrilineal (in which descent is traced through the females) and matrilocal (in which domicile after marriage is with the wife's family), there is little if any evidence that true matriarchies (gynocracies), societies ruled by women, ever existed. Yet the concept of matriarchy, typically juxtaposed to patriarchy, flourishes in feminist theory.

Such a circumstance can be confusing unless it is realized that the terms *patriarchy* and *matriarchy* can be used by feminists in various ways. Depending on context, the terms may be scientific (as above), political, philosophic, or even poetic. In feminist thought, matriarchy can mean not only the rule of women (any women), but also the rule of what historically has been taken to be the female principle, or the rule of feminist ideals. Patriarchy, then, would refer not simply to a society where men hold power, but rather to a society ruled by a certain kind of men wielding a certain kind of power — a society that reflects the underlying values of the traditional male ideal. Thus feminists frequently use *patriarchy* to denote a culture whose driving ethos is an embodiment of masculist ideals and practices.

Feminists argue that we in contemporary Western culture inhabit a patriarchy, both in the anthropological and in the philosophical (that is, political, feminist) sense. Patriarchy, then, has determined in very large part the nature and quality of our society, its value and priorities, the place and image of women within it, and the relation between the sexes. Therefore, to comprehend our lives and experiences, we must understand the dynamics of patriarchy — what it is and how it works. We must ask the following questions:

- Since patriarchy is an embodiment of the masculist ideal, what is that ideal; how is it derived from the traditional picture of ideal masculinity?
- What is the structure and underlying theme of that ideal; how and why does it function in reality?
- What is the effect of the ideal — on men, on women, and on society in general?

Let us begin with a discussion of the nature of the male ideal, its content and imperatives. We can then burrow deeper, examining its underlying dynamic, to reveal the hidden realities and prescriptions of contemporary masculinity, its implications and effects.

The Male Ideal

We must begin with a caution that we are examining masculinity and the male ideal, and not the concept of human excellence. Because historically our masculist society has perceived men to be the only fully and primarily human creatures, and because, as we saw in Chapter 1, the concepts *human* and *male* have frequently been confused, the concept of the human ideal has been similarly confused with that of the masculine. This blurring of concepts has caused a good deal of misunderstanding and mischief.

The "Human" and the "Male": A Preliminary Distinction

When I have asked students (women and men alike) to suggest people who they believed represented human ideals, they have named Mahatma Gandhi, Abraham Lincoln, Martin Luther King, Jesus, and other great-hearted individuals. When I have asked them to suggest "ideal men," they have again listed Gandhi, Lincoln, King, and Jesus, but the same lists have also included such names as James Bond, John Wayne, and Joe Namath. Even the students were perplexed by the range and disparity of their choices. What, they asked, accounts for this confusion?

The students were confused by the ambiguity surrounding the term *man,* which can mean by usage either *human* or *male.* Such usage, feminists point out, derives from the traditional though covert masculist belief that humanity and masculinity are coextensive if not identical categories, and that excellence in humanity is therefore the same as excellence in masculinity. By such reasoning, if a man enhances his masculine qualities, so must he be enhancing his "human" qualities; and as he develops excellence in human character, so must he be, as well, more "manly." Recognizing that ambiguity, we can understand why the terms *male ideal* and *ideal man* might not be distinguished, and why Joe Namath and Mahatma Gandhi might appear on the same list.

Very little consideration had been given in research to the masculine dynamic, distinct from the human, until feminists crystalized the problem in their polemic. But once the simple fact is realized that *human* and *masculine* are not the same, it is evident that masculine and human ideals are different too, and that no sense can be made of either until they are separated and compared.

The intellectual community has spent considerable energy on identifying the qualities of human excellence. Classical antiquity included intelligence, independence, temperance, honesty, courage, responsibility, altruism, justice, and rationality in the vision. Modern authors have added more characteristics, particularly the affective traits, such as humor, compassion, and sensibility. Now, to fully comprehend the male ideal, we must ask how these qualities of human excellence are related to the imperatives of masculinity. Which of them are retained and which discarded? How are they adapted to the masculine image, and how are they changed? In a conflict between masculine and human ideals, which takes precedence for most men? Under what conditions? These are questions that must be explored if we are to understand more than superficially what contemporary images of masculinity mean and require.

The Masculine Ideal

Consider the men, real or fanciful, who have come to be known as masculine heroes in our culture. Figures like Paul Newman, Clark Gable, Tarzan, 007, John Wayne, Joe Namath, Superfly, Speed Racer, the Lone Ranger, Kojak, and Dr. Ben Casey — giants all — are the personalities that have had enduring appeal to audiences of both sexes.

An examination of these images begins to reveal the qualities of today's ideal male. Typically, our hero exhibits many of the classical traits of human excellence, adapted though they may be to contemporary circumstances: He is intelligent, competent, courageous, honest (at least with the "right" people), healthy, and strong. Responsible and persevering, he pursues right as he sees it and lets no one deter him from his course: That is, he has spirit or backbone. Thus from the shores of Iwo Jima to the hills of Montana, soldier or cowboy or rugged ex-fighter-come-home,

John Wayne gets the job done. Not an intellectual, nonetheless natively intelligent, he always knows just how to make things come out right. Fearless in the face of danger, he speaks truth to his adversaries — Indians, captors, crooks, townspeople — and always triumphs.

It becomes apparent that our image of the ideal male is not fully drawn by expression of the classical qualities of intelligence, honesty, courage, and so on. There are added dimensions that transform the contemporary ideal from the merely human to the masculine: the contemporary hero is (1) sexual and (2) tough, that is, violent in a socially approved way. (As we shall see later on, these two factors — sex and violence — coalesce.)

For the most part, the masculine heroes in our culture can be grouped into just a few categories: soldiers (warriors), cops and detectives (warriors against crime), cowboys (pioneer warriors against bad guys, Indians, or the untamed environment), tough doctors (warriors against disease, ignorance, or the hospital administration), and rough but basically good crooks (warriors against . . . fill in the blanks). Our hero may be handsome or rugged, young or graying or bald, a good guy or a good bad guy, a learned professional or a street-educated bum, but one thing is certain — he is tough in a special and desirable way; he isn't afraid of pain; he doesn't shun a "necessary" fight; he can't be pushed; he perseveres in his will; he wins. Taciturn or talkative, he doesn't mince (words or movement), and whether he be covered with a lab coat or a three-piece suit, he communicates the untamed animal within, under control but operative.

The Warrior Imperative

Masculinity, manhood, is symbolized by the astrological symbol ♂ , which represents Mars, the ancient god of war. That is no accident, for the heart and essence of the masculine ideal is the warrior image. The true male, the "man's man," the virile, exciting hero is a warrior, regardless of what he battles. Without the aura of the fighter, a man may be important or powerful, or even humanly excellent, but he will not be masculine in the traditional sense. Ben Casey, the neurosurgeon of 1960s television, was represented as intelligent, successful, probably wealthy, certainly competent, but so were the other doctors with whom he worked. What characterized Casey's personality and behavior and set him apart as a sex image was primarily his resistance to conformity and authority. He argued with his more conservative older mentor, battled the administration when necessary, and gruffed at his patients for their own good. Cool Hand Luke, the perfect antihero, a criminal, powerless and in jail, the bad boy par excellence, was yet an ideal, for he fought until the end, never gave in, never gave up.

John Wayne, Tarzan, Superman, 007, or the Green Berets, all the male heroes are fighters. Aggressive, sometimes downright truculent, even violent, they epitomize the ideal of the primal warrior, the prototype of pure masculinity. In the words of Marc Feigen Fasteau, a lawyer and feminist, ". . . men are brought up with the idea that there *ought* to be some part of them, under control until released by necessity, that thrives on [violence]. This capacity, even affinity, for violence, lurking beneath the surface of every real man, is supposed to represent the primal, untamed base of masculinity."[1]

But a proclivity for violence, though necessary, is not in itself sufficient characterization of the warrior-hero. Within the ideal lies a further, hidden prescription. It is the reverse

[1] Marc Feigen Fasteau, *The Male Machine* (New York: McGraw-Hill, 1974), p. 144.

side of the coin: the "real" man must never exhibit the complementary characteristics, those qualities that would render him unfit for battle — delicacy, sensitivity, fastidiousness, pity, emotionality, fearfulness, need, tenderness toward other men, and certain other humane traits — exactly those qualities reserved for women, expected and required of women, symbolized by ♀, the sign of Venus, Goddess of Life. The masculine ideal is *all* "man," *all* Mars, *none* of Venus. Ultimately, it comes to this: The warrior virtues together with the negation of their complement (the affective qualities) compose the patriarchal ideal of masculinity.

Patriarchal Ideal of Masculinity

Warrior Virtues	Not (Venus Qualities)
aggressiveness	sensitivity
courage	delicacy
physical strength and health	fastidiousness fragility
self-control	needfulness or
emotional reserve	dependence
perseverance and endurance	emotionality timidity
competence and rationality	tenderness pity
independence	fancifulness
self-reliance	sensuality
individuality	
sexual potency	

The ideal patriarchal male must be not only brave, but never-timid; not only independent, but never-needful; not only strong, but never-weak. Committed to victory in battle, his first priority, he is a man of constraint and restraint, for violent emotions of any kind might deter him from his rationally designed course or strategy. For this man, control over himself and his needs or feelings is perceived to be the key to control over events. It is little wonder that Fasteau refers to him

as "the male machine." It is not an uncommon typology.

Though a machine, the contemporary superhero is supersexed; yet with all the emphasis on potency (as a sign of strength and power), the version of sex presented by the masculist imperative is a bastardized one, for it is a sexuality devoid of sensuality. According to the precepts of Mars, the warrior must not involve himself with commitments other than success; nor can he allow himself the luxury of compliance, of shared control or surrender—to himself or to his partner. If feeling must be denied, if sensitivity, delicacy, and needfulness are prohibited, then surely an experience as profoundly emotional and affective as full sensuality must be denied as well. Instead of yielding to the affective self, as implied by sensuality, the warrior hero must fight another battle, treating sex as war (between the sexes), making conquests, gaining victories. Even the contemporary vision of the sexual expert is more a matter of a "job-well-done" than of shared delight. James Bond, we can all see, drives women mad with his dangerous chic and secret techniques, yet we can see as well that his own involvement is less than complete, is distant, controlled, and businesslike.

James Bond is actually an interesting character, for he represents a bridge between the formal image of ideal masculinity (so perfectly represented by John Wayne) and another of its aspects, culturally subliminal, slightly illicit, and only grudgingly acknowledged. The official portrait, à la Wayne, depicts a man accomplished and successful, a warrior, a fighter in socially approved arenas, strong, powerful, and dominating, fully controlled, emotionally detached, logical, orderly, duty-bound, and committed to the "right" side, a hero. Bond, on the other hand, strays just a bit: He beats women (though only enemy women), he kills with his bare hands, and he thrives on violence. He is "b-a-a-a-d."

This other, darker aspect of maleness is captured in Marlon Brando's characterizations in *The Wild Ones* and *A Streetcar Named Desire,* in a pop song of the 1950s titled "Leader of the Pack," and in characters like Hud. It is an alliance of violence, sexuality, a certain baseness, and mischief, pointedly manifest in events like the one described here:

> According to Seymour Hersh, some of the GIs who conducted the My Lai massacre raped women before they shot them. The day after that "mission," an entire platoon raped a woman caught fleeing a burning hut. And a couple of days later a helicopter door gunner spotted the body of a woman in a field. She was spread-eagled, with an Eleventh Brigade patch between her legs. Like a "badge of honor," reported the gunner. "It was obviously there so people would know the Eleventh Brigade had been there." [2]

Machismo: Bad Is Good

Under the gloss of the classic heroic ideal there is a hidden agenda, a group of themes and imperatives spawned by the warrior ideal and containing the underlying realities of patriarchal manliness. They take precedence over, or transform the classical values, and they constitute the concrete fleshing out of the abstract formal ideal. There is a word for this aspect of masculinity: *machismo.*

Machismo is the Latin-American word for the mystique of "manliness." It denotes a configuration of attitudes, values, and behaviors clearly though symbolically articulated by an advertisement for men's cologne: "Macho!" It's "b-a-a-a-d (and that's good)," a scent for men in a bottle obviously shaped like the

male genitalia. All the associations are made: masculinity, genitalia, bad . . . desirable.

The machismo element of masculinity is that of the bad boy, of mischief that can and sometimes does slip into downright evil. The configuration is not an aberration, peripheral to masculinity. It is essential. Encouraged by parents ("Trouble, trouble, trouble; isn't he *all* boy?"), tolerated in school, and enhanced by sports, military traditions, and many rites of passage — the bachelor dinner, for example, Friday night with the boys, or "sowing wild oats" — machismo is real and present. Although its expression may vary with class, race, or location, it forms an important part of the male world view, for its alternative is the sissy/goody-two-shoes, an object of ridicule and rejection.

The expression and the intensity of mischief vary, but the components are relatively stable:

GENERAL NAUGHTINESS; BREAKING THE RULES Perhaps this behavior should come under the general heading of disobedience; el Macho does what he chooses, often the opposite of what is required. Christian society requires certain attitudes of temperance; el Macho drinks too much, spends too much, gambles, and engages in excessive and/or illicit sex. In extreme, he may steal or kill; in polite society, he swears and fools around. The point of the behavior is in the fact of breaking the rules; too much concern for submission is clearly effeminate.

VIOLENCE El Macho thrives on it. Not mere fighting satisfies this requirement, but blood-and-guts confrontations, or at least a willingness to accept them. Cockfighting, boxing, and hand-to-hand infantry combat are perceived as male pursuits. El Macho Minor plays football, brawls with the guys in the tavern, tells war stories, or initiates fraternity

[2] Lucy Komisar, "Violence and the Masculine Mystique," *Washington Monthly,* 2, No. 5 (July 1970), 45.

brothers with a paddle. El Macho Major carries a switchblade and is not afraid to use it.

SEXUAL POTENCY Machismo is a cultural image, a human type, but it is a sexual identity as well. Potency — defined as the ability to have sex often and as rapidly as possible, to impregnate with ease — is tightly integrated into the other components described. Violence and sexuality are *not* juxtaposed in this context. Instead, they are different facets of the same thing. El Macho uses his sex like a weapon. In street language you "deck 'em and dick 'em," you "tear off a piece" or "bang 'em" or "hit 'er" — all very violent metaphors. In extreme, one rapes, one gang-bangs; ordinarily, one simply exploits.

CONTEMPT FOR WOMEN Since masculinity requires a commitment to Mars and an aversion to Venus, it is hardly surprising that el Macho should be contemptuous of Venus's earthly manifestations: women. The official macho attitude requires that women, in their delicacy, dependence, timidity, gullibility, and softness, are to be used and enjoyed, like a peach plucked ripe from a tree and discarded just as easily. A young man told me that his father advised him to practice the four *f*'s: "Find 'em, feel 'em, fuck 'em, and forget 'em." Contempt blossoms into hatred: women are stupid, dangerous, wheedling. The only exceptions are those who cannot be contemplated as sexual partners — mothers and sisters, for example, or nuns.

The women's movement reserves the word *macho* for behavior and attitudes expressive of these values wherever they appear, even in women. He who even jokingly brags of his macho orientation (and there are those who do) either misunderstands what he says or deserves the misapprobation he receives, for it is this aspect of the masculine imperative that transforms an inadequate lifestyle (the Martial hero) into a destructive one.

The Male Role in the Twentieth Century

In a recent book that includes a variety of writings on the male role,[3] Deborah S. David and Robert Brannon have translated these concepts into the concrete imperatives of masculinity for the contemporary Western man. They contend that four major themes underlie the required behavior for men and boys. These themes appear very early in life, function powerfully in the socialization process, and pervade the masculine conceptual environment.

1. "No sissy stuff" — the rejection of any of the characteristics reserved for femininity, either in the male's own behavior or in others. This includes the fear of being labeled a sissy and the discomfort in female environments, the rejection of vulnerability, and the flight from close male friendships.
2. "The Big Wheel" — the quest for wealth, fame, success, and signs of importance.
3. "The Sturdy Oak" — the aura of confidence, reliability, unshakable strength and toughness. "I can handle it."
4. "Give 'em hell" — the enjoyment and expression of aggression, violence, and daring.[4]

The Effects of Patriarchy

I have described a two-part image of masculinity in our culture: on the one hand, the warrior hero, a compilation of classical ideals and warrior qualities; on the other hand, the machismo syndrome, the undercurrent of mischief, composed of a predilection for violence, intemperate and exploitative sex, and recklessness.

[3] Deborah S. David and Robert Brannon, eds., *The Forty-Nine Percent Majority: The Male Sex Role* (Reading, Mass.: Addison-Wesley, 1976).
[4] Ibid., pp. 13–35.

The commandments of Mars are:

Dominate and control — people, events, objects.

Succeed at any cost. Corollary: Never admit defeat or error.

Control your emotions. Avoid strong feelings.

Strive for distance — from others and from self.

Banish needfulness (called "weakness"). Be contemptuous of needfulness in others.

Guard against the female within and without.

Protect your image (or ego).

Add the machismo orientation:

Exhibit a kind of reckless unconcern for rules.

Embrace violence.

Place sexuality in a power context.

Such are the imperatives of the masculine ideal in our patriarchy.

As we observe the imperatives of the masculine mystique, it is essential to remember that we are dealing with an image, an ideal, or a stereotype. The image functions as a standard; it does not represent any individual, or even a group of individuals. Although a man may strive to meet the requirements of the image, he cannot become the image in reality, any more than a woman can become in reality all that is implied by the title "Playmate of the Year."

The sexual stereotypes, in this case the masculine ideal, function as social norms and mores in the culture. These are, as the sociologist William G. Sumner showed,[5] values and attitudes that begin dimly somewhere in the past, become so habitualized that they take on an aura of cosmic validity, and ulti-

mately become so imbedded in the social fabric that they cannot allow for deviation or rejection. They are usually perceived not as social rules but as enduring truths and realities. Learned through the process of socialization, mores, including sex-role prescriptions, are internalized by individuals and become extremely powerful determinants of behavior. As David and Brannon's discussion points out, the young boy learns truculence as a value for men the same way he learns that Americans eat beef but not horse meat. The picture of ideal manhood is presented to him as a required model, not as a choice.

Yet a variety of factors impinge on a male's response to the model — how strongly it is presented to him, the successes (or failures) he has within it, the values that are juxtaposed to it, the alternative lifestyle he learns and tries, and many more. One way or another, by adoption, rejection, or adaptation, each male must reckon with these idealized images of masculinity. Insofar as he internalizes the masculine imperatives, he will exhibit its characteristics, will control with them, and will be controlled by them.

The sex-role prescriptions function in this way: although they are male expressions, they are in large part independent of individual men; although men may benefit from them, use them, and have a stake in maintaining them, nevertheless as social beings men are subject to them, as are women.

Men Under Patriarchy

Men are not the greatest victims of patriarchy (as I have heard it said), but they are victimized. If the sex roles, both female and male, are destructive, as feminists believe they are, then men as well as women are afflicted by them.

One might hypothesize that any externally imposed role model would present difficulties.

[5] William G. Sumner, *Folkways* (Boston: Ginn and Co., Publishers, 1907).

After all, any prescriptive set of behaviors and values will contain elements contrary to existing patterns and "natural" inclinations. What makes the sex roles particularly difficult and conflictive, however, is their tremendous scope, the intensity of feelings surrounding them, their inflexibility, and the aspects of one's identity that they affect.

A role model for a pop musician, let us say, requires certain standards of competence with music and with instruments. It also prescribes other activities and values related to the work, such as mobility and a willingness to hustle for engagements. Going a little deeper, one expects as well a particular personal style. If the pop musician fails to meet these expectations, the penalty for deviation may adversely affect his or her musical career but is unlikely to be extreme beyond that point. That is, it is unlikely to imply diminution of the player's very being and human worth.

Deviation from the sex roles, however, has just that effect. In our culture, and possibly for all people, the sense of one's sexual identity and of one's sexual desirability are powerful components of the sense of self and self-worth. Accordingly, deviation from sexual norms incurs severe penalties and misapprobation, not only from others but often from oneself as well. In other words, the inability or even the refusal to meet sex-role prescriptions, for whatever reason, creates serious conflicts for the individual. Whether in terms of adapting to the culture and the society, or in terms of resolving inner confusion, the person who deviates from gender expectations experiences a good deal of difficulty.

In a very real way, then, and in several respects, men in patriarchy[6] are presented with a painful situation. Certainly, should a man fail to adopt the masculine role expectations, either by default (because he cannot meet them) or by choice (because he rejects them on principle), he must confront and resolve both the social traumas and the conflicts within himself. People will punish him for his deviation — through rejection, ostracism, ridicule, or more formidable signs of hostility. Because he is not a "man's man," a "real" man, or what have you, he is apt to find himself ill received both in traditional male environments and among many traditional women. Male students not in the mold have described their surprise at being rejected not only by men (as they expected) but by women, who consider them unmanly or unattractive as sexual partners.

If the pain of rejection from without is hard to bear, so is the pain of rejection from within. From our childhood, from our membership in the culture, we carry with us beliefs and attitudes extremely difficult to change. Even after we have deliberately altered our opinions and behaviors, in the light of a better considered and more rationally chosen set of ideals, the old value judgments internalized earlier continue in force, thwarting our resolve through doubt and self-contention, raising anxieties and emotional turmoil. Breaking habits is hard; breaking these ancient and heavily prescribed habits of thought, feeling, and action is *very* hard. While part of the person opts for a new style, the other part rejects it. The result is inner war.

The problems entailed in rejecting traditional gender ideals are obvious; they are much the same problems involved in the rejection of any highly valued cultural norm. The problems that follow on *accepting* the patriarchal image are far less obvious, because they are so fully integrated into the culture, but they are considerably more severe in their effects. The supermale image of masculinity is not a human image; machismo is

---

[6] In Chapter 3 you will see that women face many of the same problems, cast differently, that men face in dealing with their sex roles.

not human. The masculine mystique is actually at odds with a good portion of the classical and Christian ideals of human excellence; it is at odds with many of the known components of mental health; and it is at odds with many of the elements that both philosophers and social scientists believe to be essential to human happiness.

The classical ideal, although inadequate because it fails to treat the affective qualities of human life, is yet an ideal that includes a certain tranquillity of spirit born of temperance, a strong commitment to the rights and needs of other individuals through social order, and thoughtful ethical awareness and responsibility. It is an ideal of intelligent, rational behavior, and although it contains a goodly element of physical strength, courage, and spirit, it is not given to violence per se, pugnacity as an end in itself.

The Christian ideal, too, is one of temperance and tranquillity. With greater emphasis on peace and gentleness, it is yet disciplined and highly concerned with law.

But the masculine mystique, particularly the machismo component, values violence, recklessness, intemperance, exploitativeness, and aggressive pursuit of success at all costs. Surely the man raised under the imperatives of both the classical and the Martial visions must suffer a considerable amount of conflict. Since our society officially teaches him the traditional, or classical, virtues and at the same time requires the Martial, he is asked to exhibit incompatible qualities and behaviors; to love his neighbor or brother but carry a bayonet; to be charitable and loving but succeed in business; to be a responsible father and husband but prove his potency through untrammeled sex. To be tossed between contradictory values and requirements is not unusual in our changeable, diverse society. In fact, some social commentators suggest that the most important capacity for people in the coming era will be the capacity to change

and adapt. But the Martial imperative is such that it denies men the means to adapt in a substantive, meaningful, integrative way.

Adaptation and growth, change at the spiritual and emotional level, requires a great deal of reflection, introspection, self-awareness, self-criticism, and emotional integrity. To flourish under these conditions, one must be capable of understanding one's feelings and accepting them, of seeking and using assistance, of nurturing an enduring internal sense of self. But these are the very capacities denied by the masculist male ideal. The proper warrior has neither the time nor the patience for reflection and introspection. His imperative is direct action. He perceives thinking as effete and equates it with indecisiveness.

And feelings? We know that big boys don't cry. They also don't get scared and don't need anyone to help them. Although the Martial virtue of emotional reserve refers primarily to feelings not convenient for a warrior — such as fear, anguish, grief, and hurt — the truly "manly" man is expected to exhibit reserve in the full array of feelings. Anger and lust might be acceptable, but even these ought never to operate spontaneously, independent of plan, for they must not interfere with success. Even the so-called positive emotions — humor, love, joy — must be controlled lest they interfere with duty. (Have we not been regaled with tales of foolish men who forsook their commitments for love and were dashed into dishonor? Think of *Antony and Cleopatra, Of Human Bondage,* or *The Blue Angel.*) Young boys are trained early not to feel — to "take it like a man" and to "keep a stiff upper lip."

The key word is *distance* — from the self, from one's feelings and needs, from other men, and from women. The perfect warrior trusts no one and has one loyalty: the battle and its success. He succeeds, or he is worthless. In business, in science or argumentation, in relationships or encounters, or in sex, a man under patriarchy must win or set himself to winning. That is why weakness is contemptible — the weak (the needful or the feeling or the tender) do not win (that is, dominate, control, overwhelm). A man must push, strive, never let up, and loathe himself if he fails.

Where Mars triumphs, men are shorn of their affective elements, impelled toward distance and truculence, and robbed of some of the most precious experiences of life and self. They are consigned to an arena of striving, pressure, anxiety, and threat. They must content themselves with the prescribed fruits of patriarchal success — status, power, and public praise. In such a context even pleasure is transitory and shallow. Not a happy prospect. But happiness, in terms that Aristotle or Plato or Buddha or even contemporaries like Marcuse or Maslow might understand — an ongoing, profound experience — is not the issue for the warrior. He has no time for that kind of experience. He is too busy winning.

This is not a wholesome picture, to be sure. Men are indeed robbed of a good deal in life, yet we must not be blind to a harsh reality: They do have a tremendous advantage in power, privilege, and position. And because men have the presiding power in society, their perspectives and values, including the Martial ideal, permeate our culture. These have become, in fact, the guiding ethos of social behavior. That is why, feminists argue, we inhabit a patriarchy.

Social Priorities in Patriarchy

It has been shown that the essential element of the masculine ideal is warrior aggressiveness. The rationale is as follows: "Since this is a violent world, the man of the world must be violent." It is rarely proposed that the world is violent because the man of the world

is violent. Feminists, however, both female and male, have suggested just that.

Shulamith Firestone, Andrea Dworkin, Kate Millett, Gloria Steinem, Marc Feigen Fasteau, Mary Daly, and countless others have commented on the principle of violence in our patriarchal culture. Some argue that this element of masculism is the root of all the other destructive forces that plague us: war, racism, rape, and environmental abuse. Mary Daly, a feminist theologian, philosopher, and educator, argues that all of these problems are manifestations of the "phallocentric" commitment to power and domination (of people, events, and things). The configuration of power through violence she calls "phallic morality," expressed through "The Most Unholy Trinity: Rape, Genocide, and War."[7] If Daly's language seems extreme or exceptional, her thesis is not.

Sexism, Masculism, and Patriarchy

Before we go on, let us pause briefly to review and order some important concepts. Sexism, masculism, and patriarchy are related, as we have seen, but the terms may not always be used interchangeably.

Sexism is a way of seeing the world in which differences between males and females, actual or alleged, are perceived as profoundly relevant to important political, economic, and social arrangements and behavior. To understand more readily the base meaning of the term *sexism*, consider some human factor not typically perceived as relevant to such arrangements and substitute it for sex differences — for example, hair color: Hairism is a way of seeing the world in which differences

---

[7] Mary Daly, *Beyond God the Father* (Boston: Beacon Press, 1973), ch. 4.

in hair color are perceived as profoundly relevant to important political, economic, and social arrangements and behavior. In that case, ego identities, social roles, work assignments, rights and obligations, and human relationships would all be determined in large measure by the color of one's hair. It seems absurd, doesn't it? After all, the color of one's hair has nothing to do with one's functioning in society. Hair color as a sociopolitically relevant trait is recognized as absurd because in our culture there are no claims that it is related in any way to other traits that *are* important to social function, such as intelligence, character, competence, maturity, and responsibility.

Now sexism is of this class of concepts. Claims are made that functionally relevant traits (character, competence, and the rest) are related to, in fact determined by, one's biological sexual identity: Males are intelligent, responsible, courageous; females are emotional, dependent, and flighty; thus males rather than females are suited to authority.

Of course, the maintenance of such claims does not fully constitute the meaning of sexism. For if that were the case, sexism would simply be a logistic for ordering social functions, evaluatively neutral. Men and women would be perceived as different, therefore having different things to do, but they and their activities would still be held to be of equal worth and consideration. The argument would be much like this: Bananas and apples are different, and respectively go better with certain foods, but neither fruit is judged superior to the other. In fact, many sexists claim that this is precisely what they do believe about sexual arrangements. However, the claim is false.

The essence of sexism (and of racism, nativism, and similar prejudices) is its evaluative element. The term *sexism* may appear to be neutral, and there are those who maintain that women too may be sexist (that is,

female chauvinistic), but that is not the way sexism functions in our society. "Separate but equal" is a lie between the races; "complementary but equal" is a lie between the sexes, for functioning sexists believe, maintain, require, and insist that men are superior to women in every way that matters. Both a dichotomy of sexual characteristics and a negative judgment about women (misogyny) are essential features of our culture's brand of sexism, *masculism*.

Masculism (sometimes called *androcentrism*) is the elevation of the masculine, conceptually and physically, to the level of the universal and the ideal. It is a valuing of men above women. It is, as well, an honoring of a male principle (conceived of as Mars, a warring configuration of qualities) above the female (conceived of as Venus, a serving and nurturing configuration). Some feminists have referred to this honoring of the male and the male principle as phallic worship or *phallocentrism*. Political phallocentrism is *patriarchy*.

Women Under Patriarchy

A consideration of the condition of women under patriarchy will fill the remainder of this book, but some general remarks are appropriate here, because the misogynist, patriarchal treatment of women and womanhood is the quintessence of masculism, its culmination and fullest expression.

If masculism is at heart the worship of Mars and the embracing of phallic morality to the exclusion of its complement, then the rejection of Venus, the rejection of the traits symbolized by her — love, beauty, tenderness, or acquiescence — and the rejection of woman, her earthly manifestation, is logical and predictable. No "real man" may tolerate — within himself, at least — the tender qualities. He must deny himself any tendency toward them, any personal experience of them. Instead, these traits must be projected outward; the complement of his masculine character is settled on his sexual complement, woman: "I am man; she is woman. I am strong; she is weak. I am tough; she is tender. I am self-sufficient; she is needful."

Woman serves this important function in patriarchy: As the negative image of man, his complement, she is the receptacle of all the traits he cannot accept in himself, yet cannot, as a *human* being, live without. The image of Woman contains that element of humanity ripped from Man — an element she keeps for him, still in the world, available when and where needed, but sufficiently distant to avoid interfering with business. Yet even as negation, woman's place is not safe. As man must flee from the Venus principle within himself, as he must hold that configuration in contempt, so he must hold woman in contempt as well, for under patriarchy she is the incarnation of Venus, and nothing else. The outcome of the arrangement for man is ambivalence. He is both drawn to and repelled by

woman. Although she is love, tenderness, compassion, nurturance, passion, beauty, and pleasure, she is also, fashioned by him, the composite of all the reasons why these traits were banned for men: She is weak, emotional, dependent, imprudent, incompetent, fearful, and undependable.

Woman's place, then, as we shall see in detail in Chapter 3, is precarious and unstable. She is the object of love and hate, fascination and horror. As Venus she carries traits that are at once beautiful and terrible, seductive and dangerous; hence she may be held and tolerated by men, but only so long as she serves and is controlled, like feelings within. Adored and reviled, worshiped and enslaved, the image of woman as well as her "place" is the natural outcome of masculist values and needs. More than a convenience (which it is), the subordination of women is a necessity in patriarchy. Economically, politically, biologically, and psychologically, it is the foundation on which the entire structure rests.

Selections

THE MASCULINE VALUE SYSTEM: MEN DEFINING REALITY

WARREN FARRELL

Warren Farrell, a sociologist, is the author of the best-selling book in the United States on "men's liberation," from which this selection is taken. He has been active in developing consciousness-raising groups for men and has pioneered a great deal of the research now being done on the male sex role. Three times a member of the NOW board of directors, he has written for *Ms.* and other popular magazines and learned journals; has taught at Rutgers, Georgetown, American University, and Brooklyn College; and in 1965 was chosen by President Johnson as one of the country's outstanding young educators. Farrell has described "changing on the personal level" as the most difficult challenge for him, and he considers the following selection the most important segment of his book. In this discussion Farrell describes the highest values of masculinity (hence masculism) and shows how they infiltrate the social fabric and become universalized, distorting the lives of both sexes.

The masculine value system is a series of characteristics and behaviors which men more than women in our society are *socialized* to adopt, especially outside of the home environment. Men are not born with masculine values. They are taught them by both men and women. But one lesson derived from the teaching is that it is more permissible for a man to lead and dominate than a woman. Since the dominant group in a society generally has its values adopted by the majority, masculine values have become the society's values in the public sphere. As they become society's most rewarded values, it is easy for both men and women to assume that masculine values (and therefore most men) are superior to traditionally feminine values (and therefore most women)....

Assumptions of Superiority

What are some of these masculine (now societal) values which we assume to be superior to traditional feminine values?

- a good talker and articulator *rather than a good listener*
- logic *as opposed to emotion*
- visible conflict and adventure *rather than behind-the-scenes incremental growth*
- self-confidence *in place of humility*
- quick decision-making *rather than thoughtful pondering*
- charisma and dynamism *more than long-term credibility*
- an active striving for power *rather than a general desire to achieve even if power*

does not accompany the achievement
- politics or business as an end in itself *rather than a human concern as an end*
- a hard, tough and aggressive approach *instead of a soft, persuasive approach*
- a responsiveness to concrete results and to external and tangible rewards (money, trophies, votes) *rather than less concrete, more internal satisfactions, as the rewards of learning, of communicating, or of a good family life*
- sexuality *rather than sensuality*

There are some characteristics associated with men, such as sexual conquest and stoicism, which are not considered superior to feminine characteristics, but are still developed by men as a consequence of the other expectations of masculinity....

In the real world, a man's world, the best of the feminine values, which are more humane values, are considered nice but unrealistic. Many of the traditional female values, though, are just the qualities politics and management are now discovering are missing. Politicians and business people have learned to talk their way in and out of anything, but thousands of companies are discovering that some of the salespersons who do best are the ones who listen. A customer will often have a need for something in the back of tes* mind, but it is not drawn out by the aggressive man in sales who is too ready just to sell his preplanned package. Research by Wyer, Weatherly and Terrell indicates that while aggressiveness is considered an important quality in the hiring of salespersons, when actual performance is measured, equally successful results are frequently achieved by persons of directly *opposite* personality traits.[1]

Once we are trained to look for one characteristic it takes considerable awareness to prevent ignoring others. Sheila Tobias,

who heads the Women's Studies Program at formerly all-male Wesleyan University, says, "I never cease to be astounded at how readily male students will talk in class and how long it takes women students to respond.... A woman's questions are more subtle, her appreciations more complex. She digests a lecture slowly, referring to it or the reading weeks later." If Ms. Tobias had just assumed that those who responded immediately were her sharpest students (and many women who adopt the male or societal values make this assumption as readily as men), she would be discounting perceptive students and missing important contributions. The quick response of the men is rewarded over slow deliberation: an aggressive approach is praised more than a considered approach which seeks out subtleties.

Masculine Values As Reality: The "News"

If Ms. Tobias gives her aggressive talker a higher grade and if the employer does hire a salesperson on the basis of aggressiveness, then the male system of values becomes the masculine system of realities. In almost every occupation realism is used as an excuse to fulfill masculine values. News reporting in the papers and on TV and radio is a prime example. News reporters contend they must report crimes to the extent they do because "crime is reality — to ignore it would be unrealistic." Yet reality is ignored all the time — the reality of *growth,* constructive and incremental growth. In education, for example, reporting reality would be reporting how students best learn or how effective teachers teach, not just how a few male union leaders conduct a strike once every two years. Yet the latter makes the front pages more than all the former put together. The strike is conflict and combat. Normal education is growth. The strike is

Te = he or she; *tes* = his or her; *tir* = him or her.

male-conducted. Normal education is fe-male-conducted.*

News reporters do not report reality because it is uneventful and doesn't sell papers to men or women. The public and the news reporters, both operating within the masculine value system, assume reality is found in the conflict that surfaces rather than within the events and nonevents beneath the surface. "Stories" mean conflict, and conflict gets "covered." *Goods news is no news. So we hear more about Watts during the few days it burst into flames than in the fifty years preceding this and the nine years since.* The masculine value system in news coverage reinforces the male socialization to create conflict by making it the only way to capture the attention necessary to create change. It also forces women who want change into the masculine value system. The Equal Rights Amendment, for example, sat in a House Committee for almost fifty years with millions of quiet supporters, but it took a women's liberation movement, with its concomitant sit-ins and demonstrations, to provide the atmosphere for its increased coverage. Careful arguments documenting injustices did not warrant coverage until the conflict atmosphere preceded it.

The masculine value system also limits news reporting by its focus on active decision-making, rather than the decisions which grow incrementally, that may in fact never be consciously made. For example, fascinating and crucial news such as how our everyday investments in Latin America force the U.S. government to support dictators are seldom reported until a situation erupts into conflict. The conflict can be tossed off

as the product of rebels because the background events are seldom reported. The masculine value system, then, focuses on the biases which erupt into conflict, but rarely on the biases clouded in consensus or incremental growth.

Female-conducted conflict, the crises of romance magazines and soap operas, are not considered "news" worthy of coverage on the front pages of newspapers or by the Cronkites and Grimsbys of the media world. In fact, they are not worthy of front-page coverage. But neither is most of the male-conducted conflict which receives the coverage.

Journalists balk at the suggestion that crimes be listed in small type, as are obituaries; that an obituary page and a crime page be at the back of the paper. The protest goes "but obituaries do make the front page when an outstanding person dies." Crimes, though, make the front page when *any* person commits them, as long as the adventure, violence and blood are outstanding. The inherent value of crime is that very conflict and violence. With white-collar crimes, the participants must be important or the conflict value great before it is covered extensively. Watergate possessed both important participants and conflict value and was therefore covered extensively. With crimes of violence, though, the participants can be insignificant. Men's upbringing treats conflict and combat as the all-important processes of life. This is their reality. Women's upbringing treats growth as all-important. The humane value is clearly growth.

Masculine Values As Reality: Business

In business, men's attitudes and values force women to play the game by men's rules —

* Education becomes less female-conducted the more the status and income increase. Status and income are external rewards which men have learned to associate with their masculine role as breadwinner.

unless they are willing to take "women's jobs." The woman is forced to take on a double load of the masculine value of aggressiveness to overcome the special barriers to success which are placed in her way. She then fulfills the male prophecy that "those women who make it are worse bitches than the men — what they really need is a good roll in the hay." If she continues to act aggressively, she provokes fear; if she returns to feminine values, she provokes laughter. She finds herself saddled with a burden of "proving herself" which is worse than any man's. In the meantime, the corporation and the men in it forfeit any of the human qualities women might otherwise have brought into the system.

When women do employ some of men's tactics, in addition to their "own," their effectiveness is often overlooked. For example, the direct power which men exert in business situations blinds them to the contributions of indirect power which women have traditionally made. In an article in the *Harvard Business Review,* Orth and Jacobs estimate that "in almost every company there is an informal power group of women that everyone knows about but no one overtly recognizes. The president's secretary eats lunch each day with a group of other senior women, and as a result, the group knows more about what is really happening in the company than do most of the senior officers." [2]

In my interviews with employers, I found many managers readily admitting, "I could not do my job without my secretary. She's invaluable, and actually, I'll tell you, she's highly competent." The "I'll tell you" is often said with an inclination of the head and a quick glance with the eyes to make sure no one is looking; and in a confiding manner which signals a "Now, don't tell anyone." Ironically, no one does tell anyone, and as

Orth and Jacobs point out, even those women who do recognize their own competence and resent its lack of formal recognition hide their resentment and continue to channel their competence toward making the men feel good. While the managers are benefiting from their secretaries' luncheon discussions, they will often gaze benignly at the secretaries gathered at a table and consider their discussion "gossip." Their own gossip, though, is considered "realistic," "a broadening of my information base" or "a deepening of the understanding of the way the company really works — its corporate politics."

Women operating in a masculine value system are often overlooked for their effectiveness because their effectiveness just piles up credit for the men they are supporting. The indirect power of women has another limitation — its minimal scope. The woman is usually limited to influencing one man. She must choose to influence in the areas which he chooses to have influence, according to his timetable (or that of more influential men), his priorities, but most importantly, his talents — meaning that her talents seldom get recognized in their most unique form. (Gloria Steinem might have been a talented assistant to a president, but not until she defined her own talents as editor, speaker and writer did she stand out in a way she could not have by doing someone else's bidding.) In business and in marriage the man recognizes "the invaluable help" he receives. Her true effectiveness, though, can never blossom as long as the focus is on his career and his ideas. On the job, in the home and in the bed she helps *him*. She is like a jockstrap — always supporting but never seen.

The validity of the argument that woman's focus is on the man should not cloud the lack of freedom which confronts the man.

He also has little choice in the decisions he makes. He is caged by limitations imposed by his position within the corporation or factory and by the limited focus of the corporation itself. Yet the threatened man often complains about "those women's lib ladies," instead of looking to the source of his own unhappiness — male-imposed corporate goals and bureaucratic power-seeking. Nor does he see how, when his own attaché* is sharing the responsibility for breadwinning, he becomes freer to question these goals, since if his questioning results in his being fired, his attaché provides a cushion of financial support, offering him the freedom to seek another position without panicking.

Masculine Values As Reality: Politics

In politics the integration of the more human-oriented of the traditional female values is most effectively repressed. Internal approval, satisfaction with one's self, and self-improvement for its own sake are sacrificed in politics for the masculine values of external approval and success depending upon another's failure. The politician's very existence is dependent on external approval. This is almost the definition of electoral politics. Internal satisfaction with seeking the truth is irrelevant unless it can be translated into external approval terms, and as most politicians know all too well, "The truth never catches up with the lie (during the campaign)." Success for the politician is dependent on the *failure* of everyone else. The politician cannot win unless all tes opponents lose. The politician cannot succeed unless everyone else fails *if* the politician

defines success as obtaining office. The masculine value system has defined success that way; many women politicians also define success that way. Few seek the internal satisfactions of communicating or the rewards of the learning experience, or are satisfied with alternative paths of influence or the influence involved in the campaigning process itself.† It is not that winning office is inherently wrong. It is that society gives so much positive feedback for concrete success — and so little for a person losing with 49 percent of the vote — that only an exceptionally strong person can count the blessings of a loss.

The need to win is reinforced by the American winner-take-all political system, in which there is only one winner — the one with the most votes. This contrasts with the political system of many of the countries of Western Europe — the proportional representation system, in which, say, ten delegates will represent a larger area, with a party that receives only 20 percent of the vote still sending two of the ten delegates to represent that party in office. In addition, the fact that the focus is on the *party's* percentage of the total votes, rather than the individual's, means there is less personal ego at stake from an electoral loss. It means as well that the internal value of seeking the truth as one sees it, although it may only be convincing to 20 percent of the electorate, is still rewarded externally, thereby making the seeking of internal rewards a more realistic goal.‡

The masculine value system of success in politics is reinforced by the definition of success in capitalism. The competitiveness

---

* *Attaché* = a person's "mate" — male or female, hetero- or homosexual.

† Two exceptions are Shirley Chisholm and Harold Hughes.

‡ The proportional representation system has many more advantages and disadvantages, but the purpose here is only to illustrate how the U.S. system reinforces the male value system.

of business tends to make the electorate itself not only insensitive to the development of internal values but disdainful of them as not pragmatic in the "real world." The real world of the capitalist does conflict with the development of an inward-turning personality. The success of the salesperson (the backbone of business), like the success of the politician, is dependent on external rewards — the very definition of commission. External rewards such as money, power, votes and titles are the essence of business and politics. Most persons unconsciously evaluate themselves on the basis of their ability to outdo others in the accumulation of these rewards. Competition for success is so important that I have witnessed persons who, upon hearing of a friend's failure, react with a suppressed smile.

Masculine Values As Reality:
The Bedroom

Playgirl is perhaps the perfect example of masculine values defining women's reality in bed.[3] It is produced by a man who views the bedroom as the domain of sexuality rather than sensuality. So *Playgirl* pictures a male nude — women "coming up to" men's standards of *sexuality.* If an attempt had been made to appreciate the feminine value system, the editors would have seen the focus in "women's magazines" on the senses — the smells of body oils and perfumes, the tastes of foods and spices, the touch of embroidered materials and fabrics. They might have translated this into close-ups of men's lips, earlobes, body hair; toe-touching, tongue-caressing, or men and women eating foods together in novel and sensuous ways. Of the Best Films of the New York Erotic Film Festival only one was made by a woman. It was an incredibly erotic film of the sectioning and peeling, the

touching and eating, the squeezing, tormenting and fingering of an *orange* — done photographically so close up that it appeared as if it were the most intimate body part.

Men's magazines, though, view the bedroom as almost entirely sex-oriented and woman-oriented. If men are pictured, it is never being sensuous. The exceptions are so few they stand out. For example, the wrestling scene between two men in the film version of D. H. Lawrence's *Women in Love* was portrayed with great sensitivity. But it still contained all the male symbols of dark wood, trophies, thick red velvet, deep fireplaces and, of course, the wrestling.

The advertisements in men's magazines also deal with the power and status symbols associated with sex — sleek sports and racing cars, the Marlboro Man on horseback, ties, and gadgets from digital clocks to stereo systems.

Men learn to be more "thing"-oriented — be it a gadget or a penis; women more total body- and sense-oriented. When men deal in senses — the taste of wine, Scotch, beer or gin — it's always surrounded in status. Finding the "right wine," a status Scotch, a man's beer, an extra-dry martini. In the masculine value system, sensuality is distorted with the reinforcement of men's insecurities about their sexuality.

The assumption in the producing of *Playgirl* is that women will come up to men's concern with power, status and things — that they will be concerned with *sex* and *men* rather than sensual experiences with men, women, themselves or nature.

Her Place for Her Values

The masculine value system is like an exclusive WASP Wall Street brokerage firm which, upon admitting its first Jew, examines tir microscopically for any unrefined sign of greed. The masculine value system does this with women who attempt entry. The slightest lack of refinement brings accusations of "karate types" or "Lesbians"; women are accused of flaunting their nudity as a way of showing their liberation. As one writer points out, "It was all right when the girl in the *Playboy* centerfold was photographed naked, since that event was *arranged by and for men*. But let a woman initiate nudity, especially if it is for her own pleasure, and immediately men see the apocalypse upon us." [4]

The masculine value system has another dimension — the assumption that certain general values, like creativity, are applied by men in ways that count, but are applied by women only in roles assigned to them. For example, men will compliment a woman for being creative in decorating, but will stop short of imagining how that creativity could also work in an employment situation. They will give a woman credit for being a disciplined student, but will never offer her the chance to apply this discipline in a bureaucratic setting, where constant distractions require such discipline. They praise women for their patience with children, but do not realize that the same patience could be applied gainfully to adults. Appreciation is shown for women's human concern as teachers, mothers and social workers, without recognizing that the same ability could be effective with customers.

If women were to twist their value system to eliminate men from certain areas, their argument might look like this:

Why We Oppose Votes for Men

1. Because man's place is in the army.
2. Because no really manly man wants to settle any question otherwise than by fighting about it.
3. Because if men should adopt peaceable methods women will no longer look up to them.
4. Because men will lose their charm if they step out of their natural sphere and interest themselves in other matters than feats of arms, uniforms, and drums.
5. Because men are too emotional to vote. Their conduct at baseball games and political conventions shows this, while their innate tendency to appeal to force renders them particularly unfit for the task of government.

— Alice Duer Miller, 1915

Notes

1. Robert S. Wyer, Donald Weatherly, and Glenn Terrell, "Social Role, Aggression, and Academic Achievement," *Journal of Personality and Social Psychology*, Vol. 1, No. 6 (June 1965), pp. 645–648.
2. Charles D. Orth and Frederic Jacobs, "Women in Management: Pattern for Change," *Harvard Business Review*, July-August 1971, p. 141.
3. Credit for this idea to Mimi Lobell, co-author of *John and Mimi* (New York: Bantam paperback, 1972).
4. Elizabeth Pochoda, "Even the Sympathetic Ones Are Maddeningly Patronizing — It's Separatism or Complete Re-education, Says a Radical in Women's Lib — So Where Do Men Fit In?" *Glamour*, July 1970, p. 142.

VIETNAM AND THE CULT OF TOUGHNESS
IN FOREIGN POLICY

MARC FEIGEN FASTEAU

Born in Washington, D.C., in 1942, and graduated from Harvard College and Harvard Law School, Marc Feigen Fasteau is an attorney and author who has written for *Ms.* magazine and practices law with his wife, feminist Brenda Feigen Fasteau. His book, *The Male Machine,* was one of the earlier introspective inquiries into the nature and consequences of the male sex role. Having served as a member of the staff of the Joint Economic Committee of Congress, as assistant in foreign affairs to Senator Mike Mansfield, and as a research fellow at the Kennedy Institute of Politics, he has moved within the halls of political power and is qualified to consider the issue that follows.

In the passage presented here, Fasteau, through the concrete case of the Vietnam War, gives flesh to his argument that "the fact that a capacity, almost a readiness, for violence is an accepted part of the personal image of the ideal male also makes men resort to it faster as a tool of public policy." In doing so, he lends support to the thesis of many feminists that masculist/Martial ideals do not end with personal behavior and relationships, but underlie much of the landscape of political and public policy, and hence are universally destructive.

The Vietnam war has been for me, as it has been for many other Americans, a central influence in the evolution of my political beliefs and personal values. One of my most sustained intellectual endeavors has been the effort in the early years to decide whether the war made sense and then the longer and more difficult attempt, once it became clear to me that it was a pointless and futile undertaking, to understand what it was that kept the United States in the war. The process began in 1963, when I graduated from college and went to work as a member of Senator Mike Mansfield's staff, where my responsibilities led me to try to articulate and examine the underlying premises and rationale of our involvement. They did not stand up under scrutiny: Vietnam was not another Munich and there was no empirical or solid theoretical support for the "domino theory." In fact, the explanations were so clearly weak, that I could never quite understand how so many obviously intelligent men could believe them. Six years later, when everyone in his or her right mind knew the war was a disaster and still we couldn't get out, this nagging question connected up with an embryonic awareness of the masculine stereotype.

The precipitating event for me in making the connection was the publication of the Pentagon Papers. Here, at last, was the inside story — a good chunk of it at least — a twenty-year-long view of the policymaking process, free of political if not bureaucratic posturing. I scoured the Papers eagerly for the analysis and motivation behind our involvement. But the most striking revelation of the Papers was not what they did say but what they did not say. Even at the highest and most private levels of our government, the rationale and supporting analysis for the American objective of winning in Vietnam had been incredibly flimsy. Secretary of Defense Robert S. McNamara wrote to President Johnson in March 1964:

> Unless we can achieve [an independent non-Communist South Vietnam], almost all of Southeast Asia will probably fall under Communist domination (all of Vietnam, Laos and Cambodia), accommodate to Communism so as to remove effective U.S. and anti-Communist influence (Burma) or fall under the dominance of force not now explicitly Communist but likely to become so (Indonesia taking over Malaysia). Thailand might hold for a period with our help, but would be under grave pressure. Even the Philippines would become shaky, and the threat to India to the west, Australia and New Zealand to the south and Taiwan, Korea and Japan to the north and east would be greatly increased.[1]

This is the fullest supporting discussion of the "domino theory" in the Papers. Even in memoranda discussing the broad outlines of United States policy, only an introductory paragraph (usually the shortest) is devoted to a discussion of our national interest in Vietnam. The only lengthy and careful examinations of this question in the Papers were produced by Undersecretary of State George Ball and by the CIA in response to a question from President Johnson. The CIA concluded that

> with the possible exception of Cambodia it is likely that no nation in the area would succumb to Communism as a result of the fall of Laos and South Vietnam. Furthermore, a continuation of the spread of Communism in the area would not be inexorable, and any spread which did occur would take time — time in which the total situation might change in a number of ways unfavorable to the Communist cause.[2]

Ball's memo examining the likely effect of U.S. withdrawal from Vietnam on a country-by-country, area-by-area basis concluded that only in Southeast Asia proper would there be an adverse effect and that this would be short-lived.[3] Both analyses were dismissed by the Administration without a response on their merits.

Why was there so little serious analysis or rethinking of United States objectives in South Vietnam by the men holding power? Not because their achievement was thought to be cheap. Fairly early in the Johnson Administration, the President and his advisers were far more pessimistic in private than in public about the actual results of past war efforts and the forecasts about the results of each new escalation. CIA analyses consistently predicted the failure of escalation in the air and on the ground. Each new escalation was undertaken because the Administration did not know what else to do — getting out was (except at one point for Robert Kennedy) unthinkable. A partial explanation for this attitude is that Presidents Kennedy and Johnson and their advisers misapplied the lessons of history.

In the spring of 1965 Johnson said privately to columnist James Wechsler, as he was to say to others: "I don't want to escalate this war, I want nothing more than to get our boys home. . . . But I can't run and pull a Chamberlain at Munich." This analogy was often drawn.[4] But it rested on a number of very doubtful assumptions: that Communist China created and controlled the Viet Cong in the South and could produce similar insurgencies elsewhere; or that North Vietnam itself had imperialist ambitions and the capacity to carry them out on a scale which would threaten the security interests of the United States; that a Communist regime would be worse for the people of South Vietnam than the government they had; that even if China did not create the insurgency in South Vietnam, the struggle there was still "a test case" — despite Vietnam's unique character as a divided country and a history which made the Communists the heirs of nationalist sentiment; that Indochina was strategically vital to U.S. security; that China would somehow be able to force national Communist regimes in Indochina into actions furthering Chinese ambitions but not their own; and, finally, that if the United States won in South Vietnam, Communist parties in other underdeveloped countries would roll over and die.

These propositions can be debated, although they do not stand up under careful review. The shocking fact, however, is that nowhere in the Papers do our policymakers even articulate any of these underlying propositions, much less examine them critically. The process by which United States defeat in South Vietnam would lead to catastrophe is described only in the conclusory terms of the McNamara memo quoted above.

I made this discovery in a more impressionistic way myself in 1965 by cornering William Bundy, then Assistant Secretary of State for East Asian and Pacific Affairs, at a cocktail party, and asking him to spell out how the loss of South Vietnam to the Communists would injure the security interests of the United States. He couldn't do it. Coldly calculating, realist to the core, rational examiner of all sides of every policy issue set before him, ostensibly a believer in the systems-analysis article of faith that if effect follows cause the steps in between can and should be articulated, he hadn't even thought about it, hadn't even stated for himself the assumptions underlying the conclusion. Among other things, that conversation ended for me the lingering faith that the insiders "knew" more than those of us outside the situation-room circuit.

This incredible lacuna suggests that the "domino theory" was primarily a rationale supporting a policy chosen for other, not

fully conscious, motivations. Major decisions are not made on such a transparently thin basis unless another, unstated rationale and set of values are at work. No other reasons are spelled out in the Pentagon Papers, but the feeling that the United States must at all costs avoid "the humiliation of defeat" is the unarticulated major premise of nearly every document. For example, John McNaughton, Assistant Secretary of Defense, McNamara's right-hand man and head of International Security Affairs at the Pentagon, described United States aims in South Vietnam, March 1965, as

> 70% — to avoid a humiliating United States defeat (to our reputation as a guarantor). 20% — to keep South Vietnam (and the adjacent territory) from Chinese hands. 10% — to permit the people of South Vietnam to enjoy a better, freer way of life.[5]

The Task Force on Vietnam, created by President Kennedy the day after the collapse of the Bay of Pigs invasion of Cuba and headed by Roswell Gilpatric, Deputy Secretary of Defense, reported that allied efforts should impress friends and foes alike that "come what may, the U.S. intends to *win* this battle." [6] President Johnson said on many occasions that he would not be the first American President to lose a war. For Nixon, "peace with honor" — meaning "peace without losing" — was a goal worth any sacrifice which could be sold to the American public. And the repeated admonitions of Secretary of State Henry Kissinger that it mattered "how" the United States disengaged from Vietnam, as we shall see, amount in the end to the same thing.

Statements like those quoted, consistent discounting of reports that the adverse consequences of losing in Vietnam would not be substantial, and the absence throughout the twelve years of active United States involvement of any serious analysis of the specific effects of defeat suggest that the Kennedy, Johnson, and Nixon Administrations have been emotionally committed to winning, or at least not losing, in Vietnam, regardless of actual consequences. It does matter sometimes whether a nation wins or loses, but whether it matters depends on the particular circumstances and on the specific consequences that flow from the defeat or victory. Avoiding the "humiliation of defeat," per se, is not automatically an important national objective. But for our Presidents and policymakers, being tough, or at least looking tough, has been a primary goal in and of itself.

The connection between the war and the cult of toughness has not been prominent in the flood of writings about Vietnam, but the evidence is there, subtler in the Kennedy Administration and more blatant under Johnson and Nixon.

There was the Kennedy emphasis on personal toughness. An excessive desire to prove this quality had taken early root in John Kennedy and showed itself first through wild recklessness in sports that led to frequent injuries.[7] This need was demonstrated again in the famous PT-boat incident during his Navy career. Kennedy's bravery in rescuing a shipmate after his boat was rammed and bringing the survivors to safety is well known. But during this rescue, some of his actions appear to reveal the same straining after heroics:

Trying to signal American PT boats which patrolled a nearby channel at night, Kennedy swam alone into the dangerous passage and was almost carried out to sea by the current. There was no need for such foolishness, which endangered not only Jack but the rescue of his crew. He had eight uninjured men with him, plus a plank, lifejackets, and the island growth from which to make some sort of float or raft (as recommended by Navy survival doctrine in the South Pacific at that time) on which Kennedy and another man could have put to sea.[8]

Later, sharing his brother's values but being more outspoken, one of the first things Robert Kennedy would want to know about someone being considered as a Kennedy adviser or appointee was whether he was tough.[9] If he was — on to other questions; if not, he lost all credibility.

This attitude was reflected in the counterinsurgency fad that so captivated the Kennedy Administration. Americans, excellent specimens both physically and mentally, would be trained to be the Renaissance men of the twentieth century. They would be able to slit throats in Asian jungles, teach the natives in their own language how to use democracy and modern technology to improve their lives, and would quote Thucydides in their reports. President Kennedy once had the entire White House press corps flown to Fort Bragg, South Carolina, to watch an all-day demonstration of ambushes, counter-ambushes, and snake-meat eating.[10] The Special Forces epitomized, much more clearly than any civilian engaged in the messier business of politics, the ideals of the Kennedys. They were knowledgeable, they were progressive, up-to-date, they would do good, but above all they were tough, ready to use power and unaffected by sentiment.

Closely allied to the concern about toughness was the Kennedy drive to win at all costs. We have seen the efforts made by Joe, Sr. to drill this precept into the Kennedy sons. By all accounts he succeeded. Eunice Kennedy Shriver said of her brother:

Jack hates to lose. He learned how to play golf, and he hates to lose at that. He hates to lose at anything. *That's the only thing Jack really gets emotional about* — when he loses. Sometimes, he even gets cross.[11]

Throughout his adult life, Kennedy's affable and deceptively casual manner concealed, as a friendly biographer commented, a "keyed-up, almost compulsive, competitiveness." [12]

Kennedy's actions in Vietnam can be understood only against the background of these values, which he brought with him into the Presidency and which strongly colored the interpretation he placed on certain events that occurred in his Administration: the Bay of Pigs fiasco, his Vienna meeting with Khrushchev, and, closely tied to the summit meeting, the confrontation with the Soviet Union over Berlin.

He came into office looking for challenge in his chosen field of interest: foreign relations. In his inaugural address (which never once mentioned the domestic scene) he declared America ready to defend "freedom in its hour of maximum danger," willing to "pay any price, bear any burden, meet any hardship, support any friend, oppose any foe to assure the survival and success of liberty." David Halberstam has written,

> Almost at the same moment that the Kennedy Administration was coming into office, Khrushchev had given a major speech giving legitimacy to wars of national liberation. The Kennedy Administration immediately interpreted this as a challenge (years later very high Soviet officials would tell their counterparts in the Kennedy Administration that it was all a mistake, the speech had been aimed not at the Americans, but at the Chinese), and suddenly the stopping of guerrilla war became a great fad.[13]

Questions about the Soviet Union's or China's actual *capacity* to produce or control insurgencies around the globe, and about whether the success of a few nation-ally oriented Communist insurgencies would in fact affect the security of the United States were not asked. For Kennedy and his men, it was enough that they had been challenged. They believed that relaxation of tensions could come only after they had proved their toughness.[14]

The first Kennedy response — to a challenge his own Administration had created — was the Bay of Pigs invasion, an unqualified fiasco which added, as we saw in the Gilpatric Task Force Report, more fuel to the feeling that the United States had to win the next one, no matter what.[15]

The next challenge, as Kennedy saw it, was over Berlin. The division of Berlin was the remaining unresolved issue of World War II, primarily because the Allies, pressured by West Germany, refused to give up occupation rights and sign a peace treaty recognizing East Germany. Until the U-2 affair ended plans for a summit meeting with Khrushchev, Eisenhower had been moving slowly toward negotiations on the subject. In 1961, the Soviet Union was under strong pressure to close off West Berlin as an escape route for East Germans and was pressing for negotiations on a treaty which would allow them to do this.

Kennedy's staff divided on the issue. Dean Acheson, the hard-liner appointed by Kennedy to study the problem, wanted to respond to any Russian demands with an immediate show of force. As Arthur Schlesinger observed, "For Acheson the test of will seemed almost an end in itself rather than a means to a political end." [16] Kennedy's experienced experts on Russia, including Ambassador Llewellyn Thompson and Averell Harriman, disagreed. They believed that Russian aims were defensive, an attempt to consolidate and prevent the erosion of their position in Europe rather than a preliminary to an aggressive takeover of Europe. Kennedy was much closer to Acheson's position than to that of his more realistic advisers. Nancy Gager Clinch, quoting Louise Fitz-Simons' careful, but critical study of Kennedy foreign policy, wrote:

President Kennedy had assumed in preparing for the summit that to fail to adhere firmly to the Western powers' occupation rights in Berlin would be to show weakness. Crisis planning in Washington was already under way and a series of military steps were under consideration to demonstrate the American will to risk war over Berlin.... Any Russian requests at this time seemed to be viewed as encroachment [on the Free World] by Kennedy and his most influential advisers.[17]

Harriman, the American with the longest experience and demonstrably the best judgment in dealing with the Russians, an early dove on Vietnam, and a man long past concern with proving his own toughness, advised Kennedy not to view the meetings with Khrushchev as a personal confrontation. He told him,

Don't be too serious, have some fun, get to know him a little, don't let him rattle you, he'll try to rattle you and frighten you, but don't pay any attention to that. Turn him aside, gently. And don't try for too much. Remember that he's just as scared as you are.... Laugh about it, don't get into a fight. Rise above it. Have some fun.[18]

When Khrushchev, true to form, blustered and threatened in pursuit of his objectives, Kennedy disregarded Harriman's advice and retaliated in kind. After their last meeting, Kennedy met privately with James Reston of *The New York Times*. As reported by Halberstam, he told Reston of Khrushchev's attacks:

"I think he did it because of the Bay of Pigs, I think he thought that anyone who was so young and inexperienced as to get into that mess could be taken, and anyone who got into it, and didn't see it through, had no guts. ...So I've got a terrible problem. If he thinks I'm inexperienced and have no guts, until we remove those ideas we won't get anywhere with him. So we have to act." Then he told Reston that he would increase the military budget and send another division to Germany. He turned to Reston and said that the only place in the world where there was a real challenge was in Vietnam, and "now we have a problem in trying to make our power credible and Vietnam looks like the place."[19]

Shortly after his return to the United States, he requested 3.25 billion dollars more in defense funds, large increases in the armed forces, a doubling then tripling of the draft, authority to call up 150,000 reservists, and a vastly enlarged bomb-shelter program. Certainly a large measure of this apocalyptic response was based on a personal reaction to an unpleasant confrontation.

Khrushchev was not so stupid as to risk all-out nuclear war over Berlin. He had threatened several times before to sign a separate peace treaty with East Germany, but had never done so.[20] If he did, it was uncertain whether the East Germans would have tried to cut the access routes to West Berlin. And if they took such actions, there were, as in 1947, many gradations of diplomatic and economic pressure that could be applied before an overt military response was threatened. Nevertheless, Kennedy leaped to describe the problem in cataclysmic terms. "West Berlin," he told the American public in July 1961, "...above all, has now become — as never before — the great testing place of Western courage and will, a focal point where our solemn commitments stretching back over the years to 1945, and Soviet ambitions now meet in basic confrontation...."[21]

In October 1961, when it became clear that the Viet Cong were winning, Kennedy felt he had no choice. Vietnam was the place to prove his Administration's toughness. He sent two of his key advisers, Walt Rostow and General Maxwell Taylor, to Vietnam. Although the mission was said to be designed to give the President a first-hand, objective view of the facts, its composition reveals otherwise. Rostow and Taylor, as Kennedy well knew, were both hard-liners and leaders of the counterinsurgency movement. In particular, Rostow's eagerness to demonstrate the accuracy of his theories of guerrilla warfare was well known.[22] The mission included no one with countervailing views. The President had stacked the deck. No one would — and no one did, in the White House on their return — consider the option of doing nothing, or of removing the economic-aid mission then in place in South Vietnam. Although rejecting direct involvement of American troops (he had been burned once at the Bay of Pigs), Kennedy did accept the Rostow-Taylor recommendation to send combat support units, air-combat and helicopter teams, military advisers and instructors and Green Beret teams, an American involvement which had grown to more than 15,000 men by the end of 1963. The fact that a special national intelligence estimate prepared by U.S. agencies reported that "80–90 percent of the estimated 17,000 Viet Cong guerrillas had been locally recruited, and that there was little evidence that they relied on external supplies,"[23] thereby belying the "Communist monolith" theory of the war, was ignored by Kennedy (as Johnson would ignore, at great cost, other intelligence reports that pointed away from involvement). To "win the next one" Kennedy had taken the key step of committing American soldiers to the war, thereby giving the military a foot in the door and drawing press and national attention to the conflict and his Administration's commitment.

By the fall of 1963, when reports in the press that Viet Cong were doing very well against the South Vietnamese army and their American advisers could no longer be denied, Kennedy himself was unhappy with the commitment and — with Attorney General Robert Kennedy, his closest adviser — may have been looking for an opening to move away from it. By then the President was able to allow his natural skepticism somewhat freer rein. His handling of the Cuban missile crisis was considered at the time to be a great success* and he had gone a long way toward demonstrating not only to the public but to himself that he was tough and in command. It did for him — at the risk of Armageddon — what a career as a general in the army had done for Dwight Eisenhower: put his toughness and manhood beyond doubt.

There is also some indication that by 1963 Robert Kennedy too was changing. According to Halberstam, he began to shed his simplistic, hard-line view of the world, and to develop "a capacity...to see world events not so much in terms of a great global chess game, but in human terms." He *felt* things, despite a conflicting attempt to maintain his cool. Virtually alone among the President's advisers, "his questions at meetings always centered around the people of Vietnam: What is all this doing to the people? Do you think those people really want us there? Maybe we're trying to do the wrong thing?"[25] And that fall, he was the first high official of the Administration to suggest that it was time to consider withdrawing from Vietnam.

Against these factors one must weigh President Kennedy's fear of domestic political reaction to a "pullout" — he foresaw a resurgence of the "soft on communism"

---

* Recently, however, historians taking a second look have considered Kennedy's handling of the Cuban missile crisis to be a case of reckless, unnecessary heroics.[24]

charges hurled at the Democrats by Senator Joseph McCarthy during the fifties — and its effect on the impending Presidential election of 1964. Taken together with his personal emotional commitment to counterinsurgency and victory, and the growth of the American effort under his aegis up to November 1963, it seems unlikely that Kennedy would have quickly ended United States involvement.[26]

But if there was at least a chance that the Kennedys were growing away from the view that they had to win in Vietnam, President Johnson and the advisers he inherited from Kennedy were not. McGeorge Bundy and Walt Rostow, academicians who became, under Johnson, the key White House advisers on Vietnam, were believers in the ultrarealism school of government. "Its proponents believed that they were tough, that they knew what the world was really like, and that force must be accepted as a basic element of diplomacy. . . . Bundy would tell antiwar gadfly John Kenneth Galbraith with a certain element of disappointment, 'Ken, you always advise against the use of force — do you realize that?' "[27] Bundy also had an impulse toward action. Enormously confident, both in himself and in the power of the United States, he gloried in the challenge of taking a problem apart and mastering it. His instinct was always to try something. And, of course, power accrued to the "can-do" men, men whose mastery took the form of visible action, not those who expressed doubts and attacked the proposals of others. To answer, "Nothing," to the question, "What can be done about disagreeable development X?" was passive, the mark of a loser and a weakling.[28]

The tough, no-nonsense posture, common among professors of government and history in the late 1950s and 1960s, was also a kind of protection. University intellectuals have always been suspected in America of being a little soft; exclusive devotion to intellectual matters has been thought of as not quite manly. It's legitimate to attend the university to gather knowledge and technique and even to improve oneself, but after that the real man goes out into the harsh world of action and conflict and gets things done. A tough line in foreign affairs made one sound like a man of action — even if the action was all on paper.

Johnson's single most influential adviser on Vietnam, Secretary of Defense Robert McNamara, had shown that he could get things done before he got to Washington by serving as president of the Ford Motor Company. But there was a split in his personality. His neighbors in Ann Arbor, where he had lived while at Ford, and his social friends in Washington knew him as a warm man of deep and humane feeling. But during the working day he was a different person, cold and machinelike, all emotion ruled out as antithetical to the task to be accomplished. His chief passion was rationality, a quintessentially masculine and, finally, narrow rationality based on the premise that anything worth knowing can and ought to be reduced to numbers and statistics.

> One was always aware of his time; speak quickly and be gone, make your point, in and out, keep the schedule, lunch from 1:50 to, say, expansively 2 P.M., and above all, do not engage in any philosophical discussions, *Well, Bob,* my view of *history is . . .* No one was going to abuse his time. Do not, he told his aides, let people brief me orally. If they are going to make a presentation, find out in advance and make them put it on paper. "Why?" an aide asked. A cold look. "Because I can read faster than they can talk." [29]

This total distrust of feeling, of intuition, of nuance which can be conveyed only in personal contact was costly for McNamara. On his frequent early trips to South Vietnam, it led him to ignore the unquantifiable but real signs that the war was not going well, signs that, behind the body count and barrage of statistics about villages secured, the political structure of South Vietnam was falling apart. It led him to disregard the repeated warnings from the CIA that things were not what the numbers made them seem, that the bombing would not, in the phrase of the day, "break Hanoi's will to resist."

Most important, McNamara kept his professional life separate from the "unmasculine" values and impulses that would have led him to question the assumption that the United States had to win in Vietnam: compassion for our soldiers and the people of Vietnam; doubt about his mandate and ability to impose his view of the world on others; and the willingness to feel, through an act of empathy, what the other side is feeling and so understand that their "logic" might be different from his own. This schism made it impossible for him to challenge the objective of victory. Basic policy objectives, the starting point for strategic and tactical analysis, always grow out of underlying personal values. And values are closely linked to — in fact are the organized expression of — the emotions we consider legitimate and allow ourselves to express.

McNamara was not alone in his attempt to cut the "soft," "subjective" element out of his professional life. Secretary of State Dean Rusk cabled his ambassadors to stop using the word "feel" in their dispatches.[30] He and Rostow were not torn by the war. They were true believers. Rusk's career had been built on the cold-war dogmas of the late forties and fifties and he thought them eternal verities. They felt no conflict and, later, no remorse over the war.

McNamara's role, on the other hand, was tragic. He had great drive, an incredibly organized intelligence, and a strong commitment to public service. And he had deeply humane and liberal impulses — and what goes with them, a strongly held ethical framework. But this side of his personality was compartmentalized, walled off from his professional life. In this tension, he exemplified the *best* in American public men and, in the end, the war tore him apart. He could not bring the humane side of himself to bear in thinking about the war. Instead, the cult of toughness went unchallenged as the unarticulated major premise of all the systems analysis, war gaming, and policymaking. For all his other sensitivities, he was as much a victim of it as the others. His spontaneous response in a hostile confrontation with a group of students after a speech at Harvard in November 1966 was to shout at them that he was tougher than they were — although that had nothing to do with the issue in dispute.

In Lyndon Johnson there was no foil, no wellspring of opposing values and perspectives that would have allowed him to understand the limitations of these men. He was more openly insecure about his masculinity than John Kennedy and often made explicit the connection between these doubts and his decisions of state. No one has captured this better than Halberstam in his discussion of Johnson's decision to begin the bombing of North Vietnam:

> He had always been haunted by the idea that he would be judged as being insufficiently manly for the job, that he would lack courage at a crucial moment. More than a little insecure himself, he wanted very much to be seen as a man; it was a conscious thing.... [H]e wanted the respect of men who were tough, real men, and they would turn out to be the hawks. He had unconsciously divided people around him between men and boys. Men were activists, doers, who conquered business empires, who acted instead of talked, who made it in the world of other men and had the

respect of other men. Boys were the talkers and the writers and the intellectuals, who sat around thinking and criticizing and doubting instead of doing. . . .

. . .

As Johnson weighed the advice he was getting on Vietnam, it was the boys who were most skeptical, and the men who were most sure and confident and hawkish and who had Johnson's respect. Hearing that one member of his Administration was becoming a dove on Vietnam, Johnson said, "Hell, he has to squat to piss." The *men* had, after all, done things in their lifetimes, and they had the respect of other men. Doubt itself, he thought, was almost a feminine quality, doubts were for women; once, on another issue, when Lady Bird raised her doubts, Johnson had said of course she was doubtful, it was like a woman to be uncertain.[31]

Others played on Johnson's fear of not being manly enough. In late 1964 and 1965, Joseph Alsop, a prowar Washington columnist, wrote a series of columns which suggested that the President might be too weak to take the necessary steps, weaker than his predecessor was during the Cuban missile crisis. The columns hit Johnson's rawest nerve. He was very angry about them, but not unaffected. Bill Moyers, one of his closest aides, recalled that the President told him, after a National Security Council meeting, of his fear that, if he got out of Vietnam, McNamara and the other ex-Kennedy men would think him "less of a man" than Kennedy, would call up Alsop and tell him so, and that Alsop would write it up in his column. In dealing with a man with these anxieties, the military always had the advantage. "In decision making," Halberstam put it, "they proposed the manhood positions, their opponents the softer, or sissy, positions."[32]

Johnson was more open than the other men in his Administration about the connection between his views about the war and his preoccupation with aggressive masculinity and sexuality. The day after ordering the bombing of North Vietnam PT-boat bases and oil depots, the first act of war against North Vietnam, Johnson buoyantly told a reporter, "I didn't just screw Ho Chi Minh. I cut his pecker off."[33] Speaking of Johnson's psychological stake in the war, Moyers has said,

> It was as if there had been a transfer of personal interest and prestige to the war, and to our fortunes there. It was almost like a frontier test, as if he were saying, "By God, I'm not going to let those puny brown people push me around."

The tragedy of Vietnam for Lyndon Johnson was that he fought the war in part to protect the political capital he needed to push through his Great Society programs at home, and in the end it was the war that destroyed his credibility and brought the Great Society to a dead halt. Unlike John Kennedy and the men of the Eastern Establishment he brought into the government to run the country's foreign affairs, Johnson's real interest lay in the domestic sphere. He cared deeply about civil rights, education, and poverty; the place in history he wanted would come from progress on these fronts, not through the execution of grand designs in the international arena. But he thought he had to be tough in dealing with Vietnam or, even after his landslide victory in 1964, the Congress, sensing "weakness," would turn on him as he thought they had turned on Truman for "losing China."[34] But even his reading of domestic political history, like Kennedy's before him and Richard Nixon's later, was biased by his preoccupation with toughness.

Just as they did not examine carefully the question, "What exactly is the U.S. interest in Vietnam?", Kennedy and Johnson and their experts did not look to see if their fears about a reaction from the right were supported by the facts. If they had, the McCarthyite storm clouds would not have appeared so near and so dark. During the years that our Vietnam policy was shaped, 1954–1965, public awareness of and interest in Vietnam was low. Presidents Eisenhower, Kennedy, and, until 1965, Johnson, were not acting under pressure of aroused public opinion, even from the right.[35] Their Administrations *made* Vietnam into news, by treating events there as significant, by making predictions of victory which did not come true, and, ultimately, by sending in United States forces and their inevitable companions, the television and writing press.

Even after Vietnam was forced into the headlines, our Presidents have consistently dragged public opinion behind them. Support for United States policy has risen after dramatic military moves or initiatives which promised peace, and then trailed off as the war continued. In fact, a key concern which runs consistently through the Pentagon Papers is how to create and maintain public support for the war. Somehow it never struck Johnson, and later Nixon, as paradoxical that they should have to strain so hard to justify the war — preserving American honor; saving democracy in Southeast Asia; keeping our word; stopping the spread of communism — and at the same time fear a strong political reaction from the right if they withdrew.

In the 1940s and 1950s a powerful and vocal group of Americans naively believed that we had a special relationship with China which could be "lost." There were no comparable myths about South Vietnam. Joe McCarthy's appeals took root during the Korean war and during a period of adjustment to the fact that victory in World War II was followed by the cold war instead of the tranquility we expected. The real lessons of the era — that Eisenhower was elected in large part to end the Korean war, and that the end of that war, even on the ambiguous terms of the armistice, decreased rather than increased McCarthy's influence — seem to have been ignored. Finally, political scientists examining the results of the 1952 elections have shown that, contrary to myth, McCarthy's charges of being "soft on communism" did not translate into votes. Democrats lost the 1952 election generally, but Democrats whom McCarthy had attacked did no worse than the others. Senator William Benton of Connecticut, who was attacked by McCarthy and whose defeat was widely attributed to McCarthy's political clout, for example, lost no more support in the Eisenhower landslide than other Democratic candidates in Connecticut.

In short, Presidents Kennedy, Johnson, and Nixon and their advisers drew an analogy between the politics of the fifties and the politics of the sixties without examining the realities of either. This failure of analysis and the readiness to believe that the right, which might accuse them of being too soft and weak if they withdrew from Vietnam, had great political power, was in large part the result of their personal preoccupation with toughness and the projection of that preoccupation onto the voting public.

Another rebuttal to the suggestion that the cult of toughness directly influenced our policymakers is to suggest that individuals did not feel personally threatened by the idea of backing down in Vietnam but, rather, realistically recognized that advocating withdrawal would discredit them within the decision-making bureaucracy. As Richard Barnett has pointed out, one can be a "hawk," have one's advice rejected, and still maintain credibility in Washington, while unsuccessful advocacy of a "dovish" position is permanently discrediting. But this explanation only proves the point. What created the climate in which the "soft" position is riskier than the "hard" position? It grows out of the fears of the powerful individual members of the bureaucracy that they themselves will appear soft.

The cult of toughness has also biased the Vietnam policies of President Nixon and Henry Kissinger, his chief foreign-policy adviser, but in a subtler and, in some ways, purer form than in previous administrations. Richard Nixon turned out not to be the rigidly doctrinaire anti-Communist we believed him to be. The *détente* with China and his willingness to deal with the Soviet Union on a broad range of issues from arms control to trade made that clear. There is no question that he is aware of the depth of the split between the Soviet Union and China and that the Communist nations of the world do not now, if they ever did, constitute a monolith with a coordinated foreign policy aimed at subverting the non-Communist world. Henry Kissinger, his chief White House adviser and then Secretary of State, has an extraordinarily sophisticated view of foreign affairs.

Kissinger became convinced in 1967–1968, as the result of his analysis of the political forces at work in Vietnam, that the United States could not win there in the sense of keeping a non-Communist government in power indefinitely.[36] And despite Nixon's public pronouncements, there is strong evidence that he shared this belief. Richard Whalen, a Nixon adviser and speechwriter during the 1968 campaign, quoted Nixon as saying in March of that year, "I've come to the conclusion that there's no way to win the war. But we can't say that, of course. In fact, we have to seem to say the opposite, just to keep some degree of bargaining leverage."[37] And, at least privately, Kissinger explained that a genuine victory was not a vital United States objective. What he and Nixon did believe

was critical — critical enough to justify four more years of war, ten thousand American casualties, countless Vietnamese killed, maimed, and homeless, endangerment of the Arms Limitation Agreement with the Soviet Union, and social and political upheaval at home — was that the United States avoid the *appearance* of losing. It was vital, in Kissinger's off-the-record words, that there be "a decent interval" between United States withdrawal and the collapse of the Saigon government, a period of time which would allow the Communist takeover of the South to appear to be the result of political forces within the country rather than the failure of United States assistance.[38] Again the rationale was that this was necessary to prevent a right-wing McCarthyite backlash at home as well as to preserve American "credibility" — a favorite Kissinger term — abroad. Kissinger wrote, in January 1969, that

the commitment of five hundred thousand Americans has settled the issue of the importance of Vietnam. For what is involved now is confidence in American promises. However fashionable it is to ridicule the terms "credibility" or "prestige," they are not empty phrases; other nations can gear their actions to ours only if they can count on our steadiness.... In many parts of the world — the Middle East, Europe, Latin America, even Japan — stability depends on confidence in American promises. Unilateral withdrawal or a settlement which, even unintentionally, amounts to it could therefore lead to the erosion of restraints and to an even more dangerous international situation.[39]

The principal audience for the demonstration of credibility is the Soviet leadership and it is their restraint that is the focus of the Nixon-Kissinger foreign policy. So far so good; it is hard to argue with the premise that the United States has some responsibility for restraining the Soviet Union from efforts, however unlikely, to overrun Western Europe, from sending their own forces to fight in a "war of national liberation," or threatening Japan with nuclear weapons, or decisively shifting the military balance in the Middle East. Such actions are less likely if the Soviet Union, and this nation's friends, believe that the United States will respond, to the point of meeting force with force if necessary. But the other key premises of the Kissinger-Nixon foreign policy are more leaps of faith than applications of logic. "Credibility" is made into an absolute virtue, independent of the context in which it is demonstrated and the situations to which, like accumulated savings, it is later to be applied. Responding to a "challenge" where we have nothing at stake except credibility itself is considered just as important in maintaining this elusive virtue as responding firmly where national security is directly and immediately threatened; maybe, in the Nixon-Kissinger calculus it is even more important — if Americans are willing to fight over tiny, remote South Vietnam, maybe the other side will believe that we are ready to fight over anything. As Nixon wrote in *Six Crises,*

> we should stand ready to call international Communism's bluff on any plot, large or small. If we let them know that we will defend freedom when the stakes are small, the Soviets are not encouraged to threaten freedom when the stakes are higher. That is why . . . all the . . . peripheral areas are so important in the poker game of world politics.[40]

This is a very high-risk strategy, since it is based on the assumption that the Soviet Union will follow a "weaker" policy of *not* turning every confrontation with the United States into a test of its own credibility. In 1961, for example, Kissinger wanted our forces to invade East Berlin and tear down the Berlin Wall to maintain United States credibility, although he recognized the essentially nonaggressive motivation of the Soviet Union.[41] The second key premise of the Nixon foreign policy is "linkage," the idea that

> all the world's trouble spots exist on a single continuum which connects the Soviet Union and the United States. In this context, the resolution of individual issues depends not so much on the merits of the specific issues as on the overall balance of power between the two sides. And the underlying assumption of linkage is that the settlement of a crisis in one area of the world can be predetermined by the strength and degree of resolution which one or both of the contending parties have shown in other areas.[42]

As applied by Kissinger to Vietnam, this meant that if the United States appeared to fail there, the enemies of our allies elsewhere would feel less constrained in resorting to force; and even where our allies were not the object of armed attack, some might feel coerced into one or another form of voluntary submission.[43] It is indisputable that many international developments are in fact linked, or at least — in the phrase of James C. Thompson, Jr. — have "ripple" effects on each other depending on the geographical and conceptual distances between them.[44] But, as David Landau — writing in 1972, before our "peace with honor" exit from the Vietnam war and before the October war in the Middle East — prophetically suggested:

> At a certain remove linkage becomes unjustified; it is silly to think that Soviet assistance to the Arab nations in the Mideast is in any way comparable to, or closer to a solution by virtue of, America's prosecution of a full-scale Indochina war. And it is even less reasonable to suppose that America's steadfastness in

Southeast Asia measurably affects Washington's credibility in the European theatre, with the Soviet Union, or even with the West European Allies; from Europe's vantage point, the war is an exercise not in credibility, but in irrational and absurd theatricality.[45]

. . .

Nixon and Kissinger cannot satisfactorily demonstrate to themselves or to anyone else that a high degree of "resolution" in one area will have the desired effect in other areas. From a detached outsider's view, it seems as plausible to say that this approach builds tension by encouraging Soviet toughness as to claim that it relaxes hostility by forcing Moscow to be more reasonable.[46]

In short, the search for "peace with honor" in Vietnam, after Kissinger's sophisticated intellectual gloss and skilled diplomatic tactics are stripped away, was shaped and governed by the same tired, dangerous, arbitrary, and "masculine" first principles: one must never back away once a line is drawn in the dust; every battle must be won; and, if one fails to observe the first two injunctions and by some fluke the rest of the world doesn't care, the domestic right — the "real men" — will get you for being too soft.

Kissinger is too subtle and private a person for these underlying personal imperatives to be seen directly in what is known of his character and work. But the same is not true of Nixon.

Nixon's particular variant of the cult of toughness is, in Garry Wills' phrase, the "cult of crisis." The ultimate embodiment of the self-made man, he is always remaking and testing himself, watching from some disembodied vantage point to make sure his machinery is working. And the test that counts, the action that separates the men from the boys, that allows him to parade his efforts and virtue, and to experience his

worth in the marketplace of competition most vividly, is the crisis. This can be seen in "his eagerness, always, to be 'in the arena,' his praise of others for being cool under pressure, for being 'tested in the fires.' "[47] The title and format of Nixon's book, *Six Crises,* also reflects this preoccupation. Each chapter describes a problem he faced, his efforts to deal with it, and the lessons he learned, mainly about his own reactions to pressure. Some of these lessons are quite revealing.

The most difficult part of any crisis, he wrote, "is the period of indecision — *whether to fight or run away.*"[48] But the choice, as he poses it, is not a real choice at all. What self-respecting man, let alone a President of the United States, can choose to "run away"? Even within the limited range of options he posits, he could have used other words — "walk away," "avoid the issue," for example — which encompass the possibility that retreat can be rational and dignified. "Run away" permits none of these overtones; it sounds just plain cowardly. More important, the *substance* of the issue, what is actually at stake (apart from honor and "credibility"), has dropped from sight. The emphasis is not on the problem at hand, not on trying to determine what objective is worth pursuing at what cost, but on *himself* — on his courage or lack thereof. In his October 26, 1973, press conference, for example, he said of himself in answer to a question about Watergate, "the tougher it gets the cooler I get"; he responded to another question about the Middle East conflict with "when I have to face an international crisis I have what it takes."[49]

During Nixon's 1958 tour through South America, he was told that violent anti-American demonstrations were likely at a planned visit to San Marcos University in Lima. There was real danger of physical injury. The decision: should he cancel the visit or go through with it? Here's how he saw it in *Six Crises:*

> The purpose of my tour was to present a symbol of the United States as a free, democratic, and powerful friend of our South American neighbors. In this context, my decision became clear. If I chose not to go to San Marcos, I would have failed at least in Peru. But if I did go, I would have a chance to demonstrate that the United States does not shrink from its responsibilities or flee in the face of threats. . . .
>
> . . .
>
> But the case for not going was also compelling. I would be risking injury, not only to myself but to others. If someone was hurt, I would be blamed. And if I took the easier and safer course of canceling the visit to San Marcos and going to Catholic University I might well be able to put the blame on both the Peruvian officials and the Communists.
>
> . . .
>
> But my intuition, backed by considerable experience, was that I should go. . . . [If I did not go, it] would not be simply a case of Nixon being bluffed out by a group of students, but of the United States itself putting its tail between its legs and running away from a bunch of Communist thugs.[50]

Two things stand out: first his view of the challenge to him — which was, after all, only a small, transitory, and propagandistic piece of the mosaic of relations with Latin America — as affecting the long-term realities of this country's fortunes; and, second, his tendency, like Kennedy and Johnson, to sweep away all complexities in a conflict and reduce the issue to the question of whether to stand up to the schoolyard bully. (In Caracas, another stop, Nixon's car was stoned by demonstrators and he was also physically threatened. Every year Nixon celebrates the anniversary of that brush with danger with a small party.)

In his meeting with Khrushchev while Vice-President, also described in *Six Crises,* he took the same approach, even in private sessions where propaganda was not involved. Khrushchev blustered away, boasting about the strength of the Soviet military. In that forum, Nixon said, "I could answer him and counterattack, point by point, and I proceeded to do so. It was cold steel between us all afternoon." His account of the meeting and his tactics read like a debating manual, Nixon describing how he countered this point with that, got the Premier off balance or was momentarily thrown off balance himself. Again, what is striking is the extent to which Nixon, like Kennedy in Vienna, identified the fate of the United States with his "showing" in the meeting and his ready assumption that the most important aspect in the meeting was to demonstrate, while not seeming belligerent, that he could not be pushed around.

Outstanding among Nixon's unacknowledged feelings, Bruce Mazlish pointed out in his psychohistorical study, *In Search of Nixon,* is his fear of passivity:

> He is afraid of being acted upon, of being inactive, of being soft, of being thought impotent, and of being dependent on anyone else. . . . He is constantly talking about an enemy [the Soviet Union used to be the chief villain; these days it is "those who would use the smokescreen of Watergate. . ."] probing for soft spots in him (and thus America). To defend us or himself, Nixon must deny he is "soft" on communism, or Castro, or anything else.[51]

He compensates with an inordinate preoccupation with strength and fighting. The apparent ability to "hang tough" or "tough it out" appears to be the main conscious criterion in his choice of key advisers. A President needs, Mazlish recorded him as saying, "people who aren't panicking . . .

somebody who brings serenity, calmness or strength into the room." [52]

In 1969, long after it became clear that "international communism" as a working entity did not exist and that the North Vietnamese could not create or control revolutionary movements in other countries, Nixon's rhetoric focused even more explicitly on credibility and face. Speaking to the nation after the invasion of Cambodia by American troops he declared, "It is not our power but our will and character that are being tested tonight." (Sounds like Kennedy's description of West Berlin as "the great testing place of Western courage and will.") And deeply moved by the vision of the United States acting like "a pitiful, helpless giant," he vowed that he would not see the country become a "second-rate power" and "accept the first defeat in its proud 190-year history." Mazlish noted,

In the first two short paragraphs of that speech, . . . the pronoun "I" is used six times. The speech as a whole is filled with "I have concluded," "I shall describe," "this is my decision," and other similar phrases. We also have "we will not be humiliated," "we will not be defeated," and the repetitive threat that if the enemy's attacks continue to "humiliate and defeat us," we shall react accordingly.[53]

Vice-President Agnew, doing Nixon's gut work during the 1968–1972 Administration, compared then-Senator Charles Goodell to Christine Jorgensen, a man surgically changed into a woman, literally an emasculated man, in describing Goodell's shift from hawk to dove.

Foreign affairs is an ideal area into which to project the need to be tough and aggressive. There are fewer constraints in that sphere than in domestic affairs. Domestic affairs are characterized by wide dissemination of information and fast political response which tends to check the transformation of psychological needs into policy. Basic objectives in foreign affairs are necessarily stated in highly abstract terms — "a world safe for diversity" — and are achievable, if at all, only in the long term, making strategy and programs difficult to evaluate. How, for example, could it be proven that progess toward the objective of an economically strong, politically liberal Latin America did or did not result from United States intervention in the Dominican Republic in 1965? In foreign affairs, one can more easily get away with labeling the other side in a confrontation as thoroughly evil, a description which justifies complete victory and makes a defeat less acceptable. There is less pressure to deal with the enemy up close, as human beings rather than abstractions. And only in foreign affairs can the President's advisers gather in the White House communications center at three in the morning to read freshly decoded cables describing battles in progress and use their analytical skills to map out "scenarios" involving aircraft carriers, generals and troops and real guns to "break the will of the enemy." For the foreign-policy intellectuals of the Kennedy and Johnson Administrations the Vietnam conflict was an opportunity to exercise overt, direct power usually denied to scholars and foundation executives. It was their chance to play in the big leagues.

The arms race is another area in which judgments have been distorted by male values. Two mistakes have characterized United States policy. First, our government has assumed that the Soviet Union would build as many and as advanced planes or missiles as was economically and technically possible — known among defense planners as "worst-case analysis." The illusory missile gap of 1959–1961 is an example. If American men are brought up to believe that they should be constantly aggressive and dominant, it is only natural that they assume their opponents will act the same way, regardless of the objective evidence. Second, despite strong indications that additional missiles are not necessary or particularly helpful as a deterrent, we have frequently made arms policy as though the key objective were to maintain a force larger in numbers or megatons of deliverable bombs than the Russians'. The United States rushed into equipping its missiles with multiple independently targeted warheads (MIRVs) while arms limitation talks were in progress. The rationale was that MIRVs were needed to establish a strong bargaining position. Since the United States was in fact in a position of strength before the MIRV program started, this suggests a commitment to competition for the sake of competition, the influence of the psychological need to feel bigger and more powerful than opponents regardless of actual national security needs. The result, predictably, was to make it inevitable that the Russians push ahead with their own MIRV program.

Not every male policymaker is driven by the masculine ideal, but most are significantly moved by it. Even among men who are subject to its pressures, however, decisions are the result of a complex set of influences, some of which, for particular individuals in particular areas, tip the balance away from the masculinist imperatives. Former Undersecretary of State George Ball, for example, who advised President Johnson against escalation, had a long history of diplomatic involvement with Europe and the idea of an American-European political and economic union. This helps explain why, of all President Johnson's senior advisers, he was most predisposed to play down the importance of conflict in Southeast Asia in favor of an emphasis on Europe. I do not

mean to denigrate in any way the value of Ball's courageous and clear-headed opposition to the Vietnam war, I am simply suggesting that a confrontation between the United States and the Soviet Union in Europe would have posed a greater test of objectivity for someone with his professional history.

It is fair to ask whether the need to dominate and win in every confrontation situation isn't likely to be characteristic of anyone, male or female, who climbs to the highest ranks of government in our competitive society. The answer is a complicated no. Most women are not as personally threatened as most men by the suggestion that they are not tough enough. As Daniel Ellsberg pointed out, "In almost every case the wives of [the] major officials [directing the United States' participation in the Vietnam war] *did* manage to see both the impossibility of what their husbands were trying to achieve and the brutality of it and immorality of it." [54] The comprehensive Harris poll of American women's opinion conducted in 1970 supports Ellsberg's observation. Seven out of ten women and eight out of ten men are willing to go to war to defend the continental United States. But women are much less willing than men to go to war over actions that do not threaten the United States directly: invasion of Canada (78% of women willing compared to 84% of men willing); Communist invasion of Western Europe (42% to 60%); Russian takeover of West Berlin (37% to 50%); Communist invasion of Australia (37% to 54%); Communist takeover of South Vietnam (33% to 43%); takeover of South American country by Castro (31% to 43%); imminent Israeli loss in a war with the Arabs (17% to 28%). Significantly more women than men felt that the pace of Nixon's withdrawal of American forces from Vietnam was "too slow." Two out of three women but only 49% of men say they would become upset upon hearing "that a young draftee has been killed in Vietnam." [55]

Women have also been brought up to shy away from rigorous intellectual pursuits and vigorous initiative and leadership, so it *is* more difficult for a woman in this culture to maintain the self-confidence and drive needed to achieve a position of responsibility in government or elsewhere.

In the past women who did make it were able to do so only by adopting male values; it seems unlikely that these women would have done a better job on Vietnam, or the arms race. But, in the last five years under the influence of feminism, substantial numbers of women have broken away from the traditional female self-images and roles without adopting the compulsive toughness of the male stereotype. These women, and the smaller number of men who have begun to question the validity of the traditional male sex-stereotype, have the self-confidence to achieve positions of responsibility and power without feeling a personal need to respond to every challenge. Female or male, this kind of human being might well have kept us out of Vietnam.

The reasoning of this chapter will sound strange and illegitimate to many readers. American foreign policy is almost never analyzed in terms of the psychology of its makers. By unwritten consensus, this influence on public policy has been regarded as too personal and too subjective to be reliable. In fact, the taboo exists because the men who make the policy and analyze it are often uncomfortable with and ill-equipped to understand the role that their personal feelings and values play in decisions of state. As a result, men tend to be not only unwilling to focus on the role that their own psychology plays in their decisions but also only dimly aware that they have distinct psychological biases. Feeling that way about themselves, government officials and their male critics are more comfortable dealing exclusively with the "objective" elements of public policy, despite a growing awareness that analyses of military strength, political support, and cost-benefit ratios often involve leaps of subjective intuition.

Armchair psychoanalysis of public figures is unreliable. Conclusions are usually drawn about personality characteristics and problems unique to the individual on the basis of inadequate evidence and, for that reason, are useful neither to the individual involved nor to society at large. But analyses of the influence of widely shared psychological biases which are created by common conditioning steers clear of these pitfalls. As psychohistorian Mazlish wrote,

[The] "style" of politics may be vastly different among political leaders — for example, John F. Kennedy and Richard Nixon — while the substance of personality may be greatly alike. From different backgrounds and different life experiences, political figures may arrive at the same character traits of competitiveness, fear of softness, and so forth. The reason must be sought in the fact that they all emerge from the same mold of American values; in short, from the constant corresponding processes and the basic "character" of the American people as it has been up to now.[56]

Analyses of this kind will not alone fully explain complex governmental decisionmaking. Along with the failures of judgment examined here, our nation's long involvement in Vietnam was grounded on our World War II role as defender of the Free World; our attempt in the early fifties to barter aid to the French in Indochina for France's membership in a projected European Defense Community; Cardinal Spellman's lobbying, during the Eisenhower Administration, for United States support of Diem, a devout

Catholic; and the bureaucratic inertia created once officials staked their careers on recommendations that we intervene. But these other causes, like the "objective" arguments for and against United States involvement, have been exhaustively and repeatedly analyzed over the last decade. And all those articles, war games, area studies, and systems analyses — the accepted tools for exploring public issues — have not dented the basic attitudes of men like Richard Nixon who, as late as 1968, could describe the Vietnam war as "one of America's finest hours." Nixon got our troops out of Vietnam, but only because their withdrawal was required for his political survival and because he was able to avoid, at least in his eyes, the appearance of losing.

We may even avoid exact, carbon-copy Vietnams of the future. But the lesson of enduring value — the lesson that our policy is in danger of being pushed in stupid, costly, and dangerous directions by the cult of toughness — has not and will not be learned from public debate which does not focus critically on the existence and influence of the biases created by the masculine ideal. A decade of traditional dialogue and interpretation of the Vietnam experience did not stop Nixon from continuing to support the prosecution of the war – at a cost of two billion dollars a year and a million new refugees; it didn't stop him from bombing Cambodia; it didn't stop him from believing that our prestige required an SST which was a disaster from every other point of view;* and it didn't stop him from adding MIRVs to the nation's existing nuclear overkill capacity.

To learn the real lessons of Vietnam for our foreign policy, we need desperately to broaden the scope of public debate. Let us make mistakes at the outset if we must, but let us begin to talk about what is really going on in the minds of the men who spend our blood and our treasure to save their sacred honor.

Notes

1. *The New York Times* (ed.), *The Pentagon Papers* ([Quadrangle: 1971] Bantam ed.: 1971), p. 278.
2. CIA Memorandum, June 9, 1967, reprinted in *The Pentagon Papers, op. cit.,* p. 254.
3. *The Pentagon Papers, op. cit.,* pp. 449–54.
4. See the author's article, "Munich and Vietnam: A Valid Analogy?" *Bulletin of the Atomic Scientists* (September 1966), p. 22, for a full statement and critical discussion of this analogy.
5. *The Pentagon Papers, op. cit.,* p. 432.
6. *Ibid.,* p. 89.
7. Nancy Gager Clinch, *The Kennedy Neurosis* (Grosset & Dunlap: 1973), p. 100.
8. *Ibid.,* p. 114.
9. David Halberstam, *The Best and the Brightest* (Random House: 1972): p. 273.
10. *Ibid.,* p. 124.
11. Clinch, *op. cit.,* p. 98 (emphasis added).
12. Joe McCarthy, *The Remarkable Kennedys* (Dial: 1960), p. 30, quoted in Clinch, *op. cit.,* p. 131.
13. Halberstam, *op. cit.,* p. 122.
14. *Ibid.,* p. 151.
15. See also Halberstam, *op. cit.,* p. 72.
16. Arthur M. Schlesinger, Jr., *A Thousand Days* (Houghton Mifflin: 1965), pp. 380–81.
17. Louise FitzSimons, *The Kennedy Doctrine* (Random House: 1972), pp. 97–98, quoted in Clinch, *op. cit.,* p. 192.
18. Halberstam, *op. cit.,* p. 75.
19. *Ibid.,* p. 76.
20. Clinch, *op. cit.,* p. 194.
21. *Ibid.,* p. 195.
22. Halberstam, *op. cit.,* pp. 156–62.
23. *The Pentagon Papers, op. cit.,* p. 98.

---

* Vice-President Ford, Nixon's choice, said, arguing in Congress for the SST, that the vote would determine whether each Congressman was "a man or a mouse." [57]

24. Richard J. Walton, *Cold War and Counter-revolution* (Viking: 1972); Louis Heren, *No Hail, No Farewell* (Harper & Row: 1970); Fitz-Simons, *op. cit.;* Sidney Lens, *The Military Industrial Complex* (Pilgrim Press: 1970).
25. Halberstam, *op. cit.,* p. 274.
26. Clinch, *op. cit.,* pp. 219–21.
27. Halberstam, *op. cit.,* p. 56.
28. *Ibid.,* p. 63.
29. *Ibid.,* p. 215.
30. *Ibid.,* p. 312.
31. *Ibid.,* pp. 531–32.
32. *Ibid.,* p. 178.
33. *Ibid.,* p. 414.
34. *Ibid.,* p. 425.
35. Charles Yost, *The Conduct and Misconduct of Foreign Affairs* (Random House: 1972), pp. 39–40.
36. David Landau, *Kissinger: The Uses of Power* (Houghton Mifflin: 1972), pp. 155–58.
37. Richard Whalen, *Catch the Falling Flag: A Republican's Challenge to His Party* (Houghton Mifflin: 1972), p. 137.
38. Landau, *op. cit.,* pp. 158, 180–82.
39. Kissinger, *American Foreign Policy* (W. W. Norton: 1969), p. 112, quoted in Landau, *op. cit.,* pp. 186–87.
40. Richard M. Nixon, *Six Crises* (Doubleday: 1962), p. 273.
41. Landau, *op. cit.,* p. 71.
42. *Ibid.,* pp. 118–19.
43. *Ibid.,* p. 158.
44. *Ibid.,* p. 120.
45. *Ibid.,* pp. 119–20.
46. *Ibid.,* p. 125.
47. Garry Wills, *Nixon Agonistes* (Houghton Mifflin: 1970), p. 166.
48. Nixon, *op. cit.,* p. xv (emphasis added).
49. *The New York Times,* October 27, 1973, p. 14.
50. Nixon, *op. cit.,* p. 199.
51. Bruce Mazlish, *In Search of Nixon* (Basic Books: 1972), p. 116.
52. *Ibid.*
53. *Ibid.,* p. 177.
54. *New York Post,* June 22, 1971, p. 67.
55. Virginia Slims American Women's Opinion Poll, Louis Harris and Associates (1970), pp. 74–77.
56. Mazlish, *op. cit.,* p. 170.
57. *Boston Globe,* March 19, 1972, p. 2.

3

Images of Women in Patriarchy: The Male-Identified Woman

The "Naming" of Women

...It is necessary to grasp the fundamental fact that women have had the power of *naming* stolen from us. We have not been free to use our own power to name ourselves, the world, or God. The old naming was not the product of dialogue — a fact inadvertently admitted in the Genesis story of Adam's naming the animals and the women. Women are now realizing that the universal imposing of names by men has been false because partial. That is, inadequate words have been taken as adequate....

To exist humanly is to name the self, the world, and God....[1]

In a society where men have controlled the conceptual arena and have determined social values and the structure of institutions, it is not surprising that women should have lost the power of *naming,* of explaining and defining for ourselves the realities of our own experience. In a patriarchal culture, men define (explain, analyze, describe, direct) the female as they define nearly everything else. The issue is not only that men perceive women from masculine perspectives, but that given the nature of socialization, all members of society, including women, perceive the female from the prevailing masculine perspective.

The Male Identification of Women

It is argued by some feminists,[2] and properly so, that women, sometimes directly, often indirectly, have had considerable impact on the structure and quality of society. In primitive times women were very likely the inventors of pottery, food preservation, and other "domestic" technology, hence they were probably the originators of early forms of social organization. As teachers of the young, women have always done much to form the individual attitudes and values within the community, and our personal influence on one another and on men has long been recognized (although often maligned). But informal networks and personal power are not social power, and many feminists, myself included, point out that the influence that women do wield is frequently deflected and counterbalanced, often distorted, by the subordinate and peripheral place we have been assigned in society. The attitudes and values we teach, the influences we mean to effect are often alien to us, originating not in our own perspectives and insights, but in sources we have inherited and internalized. We learn our roles and their attendant behaviors from mothers who were bent to the yoke as we are meant to be. We attend male-dominated schools and universities. We read books, manuals, and bibles written by men for male ends. We learn about and care for our bodies through male physicians, institutions, and medical societies. We are exhorted and chastised by male priests. We model ourselves after images presented in media controlled almost entirely by men, who publish the newspapers and magazines, manage the advertising agencies, produce and direct films, and determine fashion trends in the great couture houses of Europe. Finally, through societally cultivated dependency, we place ourselves in the position of bartering our self-definition for "protection."

The naming of women has been effected by men primarily through control of the social institutions that determine behavior and attitudes. As social beings subject to those

---

[1] Mary Daly, *Beyond God the Father* (Boston: Beacon Press, 1973), p. 8.

[2] See, for example, Mary R. Beard, *Woman as Force in History* (New York: Macmillan, 1946). Some contemporary feminists make this argument from a cross-cultural perspective, pointing out that "power" is a highly complex notion that varies within and across social groups.

institutions, we have most frequently (although not without exception) adopted the images wrought by that naming, most often unaware that the ideals and visions by which we live are not our own creation. From our first breath — from our entry into a world of pink and white ruffles; of dolls and docility; of behaving like a lady; of loving strokes for submission, quiet, and gentility; of cutout dolls in wedding gowns and Barbie dolls that develop breasts; of cheering on the sidelines; of applause for being picked; of frowns for "tomboy" activities, assertiveness, intelligence, and independence — from that very earliest time before we can question, we inhale an environment that teaches us a vision of femininity so pervasive and complete that it appears real; it appears to be our own. By the time we are old enough, wise enough, and angry enough to discard it, the seed planted in our infancy and constantly tended has so taken root, becomes so much a part of us, that to reject it has almost the force of rejecting ourselves. Such is the meaning of saying that it is easier to fight an external enemy than one who has "outposts in your head." [3]

The alien definition of women, even more extreme than it first appears, goes beyond merely the production and imposition of foreign images, beyond women's accepting these images as our own; it proceeds all the way to our accepting the status of not only less-than-standard humanity, but of less-than-standard *being*, of "otherness." [4] "Otherness," in existentialist terms is a social/moral as well as a personal/psychological assignment of women to the role of a less than primary, less than completely worthy human being. Otherness defines women as the "other half" of humanity, the half that helps, that *assists* in the work of society whether by staying out of the way, by relieving the primary beings of chores that would impede them in their work, or by procreating. Otherness defines woman as satellite, as adjunct, as alter to man, but not as an end in herself. It accounts for woman being tuned to a servant consciousness, to *care for* before being *cared for*, to keep to the background in a place of her own, to yield to man's will, which is valued in itself directly *for* the world whereas she is only *in* the world. It accounts for women being told not to take jobs away from men, as if the jobs were somehow cosmically ordained the property of men. It accounts for wanting sons and deeming daughters less valuable.

Woman Identification Versus Male Identification: The Alternatives

The woman created in and by the male perspective is called by the women's movement the *male-identified woman*. The alternative, the woman-identified woman, is surely a feminist vision. She is a person who indeed understands herself to be subject (self), not object (other); she respects both her womanhood and her humanity; she takes her direction and definition from values that are her own, born of her own self-perceived qualities and goals as well as those of other women; she contributes to society that which she takes to be meaningful, and does so in her own way.

Now, such a woman is only evolving. In a patriarchal environment, hostile as it is to assertive, self-defined women, the processes of woman identification and of growth toward

---

[3] Sally Kempton's terminology in "Cutting Loose," *Esquire,* July 1970, p. 57.

[4] The treatment of "otherness" relative to women is most typically associated with the French existentialist philosopher Simone de Beauvoir, who developed the concept in her landmark work, *The Second Sex* ed. and trans. H. M. Parshley (New York: Knopf, 1953).

that new identity are perplexing, confusing, and arduous. The new images that feminists are laboring to draw are necessarily influenced by the struggle in which we are engaged.

What we shall see, then, in this chapter and the next, is a contest of visions: on the one hand, the male-identified ideals and masculist stereotypes; on the other, feminist responses and affirmations. The pictures created, primarily of women, but affecting all humanity, are intricately interwoven by circumstance, yet they are so different as to entail *two* separate realities: patriarchal perspective and feminist consciousness.

Ideals and Images: The Masculist Definition

It is an extraordinary fact of women's lives that for centuries, across space and time, from culture to culture, women have been consistently treated with ambivalence, misogyny, and subordination.[5] These constant themes in the naming of women by patriarchal societies may find different expressions and may vary in intensity and effect, but they almost universally recur.

Although various hypotheses have been formulated, ranging from the scientific to the religious and from the accepting to the vehemently opposed, the origins and causes of women's subordination have never been definitively explained. Certain things are clear, however. The masculist images of women and the roles that these images support are constructed so as to create a situation in

many ways very convenient for men. The patriarchal definitions of femininity provide the masculist with excellent rationales for the uses to which women have been put as well as potent sociopsychological advantages. The female role of helpmeet, for example, follows "naturally" from the patriarchal definition of women's nature, and it provides men with tremendous privilege, power, and pleasure. Women are expected to serve men physically, taking care of their homes, property, clothing, or persons; economically, doing countless jobs for which women are ill paid or not paid at all; sexually, as wives, mistresses, or prostitutes; and reproductively, assuring men of paternity through female chastity. Because women do the "shitwork" of society (as the movement refers to all the work men do not wish to do), men are freed to spend their time on socially valued activities for which they receive all kinds of material and psychological rewards. From the use of women, men accrue extra time, energy, and power.

The image of woman as man's complement offers an extremely effective support mechanism for the masculist self-image: The softer, weaker, and more dependent the woman is, the stronger and more powerful the man appears; the more a servant the woman, the more a master the man. And the more the woman withdraws into home and gentility, the more the arenas of government and industry are left to the iron grasp of warriors and warrior values.

The misogynist picture of women as substandard, not quite human, incompetent, petty, evil, and lacking in responsibility and moral aptitude stands as clear justification to the masculist for our subordination and suffering. After all, since we cause all the trouble in the world and instigate misfortune and disaster (Eve taking the apple, Pandora opening the box), it is natural and fitting that we should be punished for our deeds and controlled, lest we do further harm.

---

[5] There is a school of feminists who question the thesis of the universal subordination of women within patriarchal culture. They contend that women's power in some societies is different but real; hence subordination is a term not universally applicable. I am not of this opinion.

"...in sorrow thou shalt bring forth children; and thy desire shall be to thy husband, and he shall rule over thee." (Genesis 3:16)

Surely, patriarchal society has been well served by these masculist images; it behooves us to understand them. Although the origin or cause of these images cannot definitively be traced, feminists have proposed some rather cogent conjectures that help to clarify the issue.

Ambivalence: An Undercurrent

The images of women in our culture are fraught with contradiction: Woman is the sublime, the perfect, the beautiful; she is the awful, the stupid, and the contemptible. She is the Mother of God as well as the Traitor of the Garden. She is the tender young creature man marries and protects as well as the treacherous, manipulative sneak who tricked him into a union he never sought. Keeper of virtue, she is yet a base and petty creature, incapable of rational moral judgment, cosmically wise, concretely stupid. Explicitly or implicitly, women are represented as having dual natures, of being all that is desirable, fascinating, and wonderful, yet extremely destructive and dangerous. Ambivalence toward a whole range of real and alleged female powers (birth, menstruation, seduction, intuition) expresses itself in a subliminal patriarchal belief that women have a great deal of "big magic," very much worth having, but destined to go awry if not controlled and subdued.

This bifurcation of images is called the Mary/Eve dichotomy: woman is represented as being at once a manifestation of the divine and an incarnation of evil.

There are, no doubt, a variety of sources of such attitudes, but, feminists argue, they all must be understood in this important context: In patriarchy, images of women, like other conceptualizations, have been male created. The stereotypes of women, contradictory and conflicting, are male projections, and as such they must be understood as outward expressions of male attitudes. The dichotomy in the representation of women, therefore, is a strong indication of extreme ambivalence on the part of men.

In literature, psychology, philosophy, or religion, one comes face to face, again and again, with the ambivalence of men toward women. They seek her, the eternal feminine, they want and desire her; but oh, so much the worse for them! Men are exhorted by the stronger and more stoic among them to beware the lures and entrapments of females. In the first century A.D., Paul proclaimed the dangers of sin, sex, and uncontrolled women (all related). Centuries later, in language altered for "science" yet reminiscent of primitive mythology — toothed vaginas and grasping spiders — Freud did the same.

Students of many disciplines have developed hypotheses to account for the origin and cause of these attitudes. Some sociologists have pointed out that ambivalence is typical of feelings experienced by any dominant group toward those it colonializes or exploits — mixed feelings of need and contempt, guilt, anger, and fear.

Many anthropologists, tracing a long history of male fear of women, place great emphasis on attitudes toward female regenerative powers and organs, so magical, so powerfully important and stirring, yet so utterly female, so mysterious and alien to men. Such anthropologists as H. R. Hays, Wolfgang Lederer, and Joseph Campbell point to the frequency of myths crediting the *first* birth to a man (like Adam); they point to menstrual taboos and blood magic, and postulate strong envy on the part of men for a power that men can never have themselves.

Psychologists, from classical times to the

present, have pointed to male fears surrounding the sex act — fear of impotence, of detumescence, of vaginal containment, and of other, more abstract matters, such as absorption by the partner, possession, or even castration. That the act of intercourse[6] is simultaneously perceived as a most desirable experience and also a fearful or dangerous one may account for male ambivalence, in the view of many psychologists.[7]

That all these factors contribute to ambivalence is very likely so, yet I, as well as many other feminists, am more apt to seek the major source of masculist attitudes to women or womanhood in the intricate, primal dimensions of men's own gender identity, in the values and imperatives of the Martial ideal.

Masculinity as defined in patriarchy, you remember, requires men to repudiate in themselves most of the affective components of human experience: It is imprudent to feel. It is very difficult, however, not to acknowledge feeling, and therefore at least two major facets of life are thrown into severe conflict for men — sex and an entire configuration of experience we may call *the tender*. These conflicts have direct bearing on male attitudes toward women.

Although it is surely true that the sex act is surrounded with certain fears and danger, I contend that it is not sex itself that provides the greatest conflict, but rather what sex represents. It is not the mechanical act of sex, intercourse, that has usually been presented as the great source of "sin," but rather the *enjoyment* of sex, the surrender to sex; it is

sensuality and its attendant implications — fun, caprice, relaxation, nonstriving. Whether the language be religious (Paul warning against sin and damnation) or psychological (Freud fretting about the id and sublimation), sensuality and pleasure have been consistently presented as the foe of duty, the primary value of the Martial ideal. The message is always the same: A man has a choice between duty (manhood) and indulgence (sensuality, pleasure, and self). If he chooses the former, he gains pride, identity, praise, and worthiness; if he chooses the latter, all he may expect is dissipation and disgrace.

For the masculist, *woman* and *sex* are nearly synonymous terms. The rejection of sensuality necessitates, then, a rejection of the object and instigator of sensuality — woman. If sex evokes mixed feelings — of approach and avoidance — most certainly woman must evoke the same feelings.

But the problem does not end here. The ambivalence goes further. Besides sensuality and pleasure, the warrior must also expunge from his character the parts of himself that either express vulnerability or render him vulnerable — fear, sensitivity, need, desire, grief, hurt, trust, and all the other traits, qualities, and feelings that are part of the tender. Because the tender is not allowable in men but is impossible to live without, patriarchy splits this element off from men and invests it instead in women, where it may be more safely enjoyed. Yet even in this externalized form, the tender remains a danger that each man must guard against, because he knows, though he would deny it, how easily he might yield to it, how much he wishes to yield.

In this light, contempt for women's "emotionalism" may be understood as a rejection of emotions within; ridicule of female timidity as flight from timidity within; hatred of the woman without as fear of the woman within. The ambivalence, then, that men feel

---

[6] For an interesting analysis of the meaning of the relation of carnality and femaleness for men, see Beauvoir, *The Second Sex*, chap. IX.

[7] Whether there are oedipal components to male fear of sex I hesitate to conjecture, although others have. Certainly it ought to be considered, but in another, wider study of this problem.

toward women may be understood, at least in part, as a displaced expression of an inner conflict so frustrating and frightening that it cannot be contained, but must instead be projected outward, onto women.

That we should be the recipients of all these "bad" feelings is not surprising; it is common for minorities or out-groups to serve as scapegoats for the masters. But that we should function as the object of this particular displaced ambivalence is even more to be expected: We are, after all, the male-identified symbols of the entire configuration the male is required to excise.

Man has ordained woman the carrier of all he dare not entertain in himself — and he hates her for it. It is as if mankind has said to woman: "Woman — be tenderness, be nurture, be vulnerability, be laughter, play, and fun for me, because I cannot be these things myself"; but "You are all the things the great Mars has deemed evil and dangerous; and therefore you are evil and dangerous."

Misogyny: The Expression

Attitude is easily converted into judgment: *woman is desirable* is transformed into *woman is good; woman is frightening* becomes *woman is bad*.

Misogyny is an integral part of masculism and patriarchy. Veiled by chivalry or a mythic masking of female roles, it is nonetheless a potent force in the relations of men and women, and readily apparent should the veil or mask be rent even a little. It is misogyny that underlies not only rape, invective, and abuse, but also beauty contests, work segregation, menstrual taboos, mother-in-law jokes, old bag myths and themes, patronizing etiquette, and current sexual mores.

Misogyny includes the beliefs that women are stupid, petty, manipulative, dishonest, silly, gossipy, irrational, incompetent, unde-

pendable, narcissistic, castrating, dirty, over-emotional, unable to make altruistic or moral judgments, oversexed, undersexed, and a host of other rather ugly things. Such beliefs culminate in attitudes that demean our bodies, our abilities, our characters, and our efforts, and imply that we must be controlled, dominated, subdued, abused, and used, not only for male benefit but for our own. St. Jerome, Freud, the Rolling Stones, and numerous others have all agreed that when it comes to punishment women need it and love it.

The image of woman as victim is nowhere more acutely portrayed than in *Story of O*,[8] a rather notorious little book, originally published in France and described by reviewers variously as "pornographic," "political,"[9] or "mystical."[10] It is undoubtedly all three. The plot is simple: O is a young woman subjected by her lover and his comrades to continual sado-sexual torture and humiliation unto death, all of which (vividly portrayed in erotic images) both O and her lover willingly, consciously, even joyfully accept as proof of O's love as well as punishment for her "wantonness" (any little bits of self-assertion). During the course of the book, O is transformed from an individual to a totally degraded, totally pliant, totally selfless (in the worst sense) creature — a sexual garbage pail, for "love."

Many feminists have pointed out that what is important about the book is not the plot, but the theme, as it is interpreted and responded to by its commentators. Jean Paulhan, in a prefacing essay significantly titled "Happiness in Slavery," describes the "mystical" theme in these familiar terms:

[8] Pauline Reage, *Story of O*, trans. Sabine d'Estrée (New York: Grove Press, 1965).

[9] Andrea Dworkin, *Woman Hating* (New York: Dutton, 1974), pp. 55–63.

[10] André Pieyre de Mandiargues, "A Note on *Story of O*," in Reage, *Story of O*, p. xvi.

At last a woman who admits it![11] Who admits what? Something that women have always refused till now to admit (and today more than ever before). Something that men have always reproached them with: that they never cease obeying their nature, the call of their blood, that everything in them, even their minds, is sex. That they have constantly to be nourished, constantly washed and made up, constantly beaten. That all they need is a good master, one who is not too lax or kind: for the moment we make any show of tenderness they draw upon it, turning all the zest, joy, and character at their command to make others love them. In short, that we must, when we go to see them, take a whip along.[12]

Paulhan praises woman's uniqueness, her greater "understanding" born of childlikeness, her more primitive decency, requiring "nothing less than hands tied behind the back … the knees spread apart and bodies spread-eagled, than sweat and tears."[13] The other "official" commentator, Mandiargues, proposes that the theme is "the tragic flowering of a woman."[14]

Such talk is important. It is not simply an aberration, but rather the expression of a vital and common principle of masculism: that woman is most adored, most exquisite, most revered when she is sufficiently selfless to be martyred. In O, self-effacement that would be repulsive in men, inimical to all the classical values of human excellence, is deemed mystically beautiful, fulfilling, and sacrificial. The Sacred Principle of Victimization[15] means that women are more conveniently exploitable and indeed more sexually exciting when they are stripped not only of clothing but of power, strength, assertiveness, and sense of self. Should one doubt the relevance today and here of such an attitude, consider how titillating to men are the newspaper stories of rape, the torture-murders of *True Detective Magazine*, the bent-over beauties in *Hustler* magazine, and the tough sex of 007 and *The Clockwork Orange*. Because women are bad, they must be-punished. Misogyny earns women torture of one kind or another.[16]

Stereotypes: Good Women and Bad

The ultimate ambivalence expresses itself finally in the ultimate bifurcation — good women and bad. The judgments of good and bad, like the images themselves, are male projections, resting not only on the extent to which any woman meets the specifications of her role requirements or adheres to the standards set for her, but on a particular male's needs and his attitudes toward that role configuration at some moment in time. That is, an image may be judged good at one time, bad at another, depending on its serviceability to the man making the judgment. As the image is judged, so is the woman incarnating that image. Meeting the complex im-

---

[11] It is a sport among the readers and commentators of *Story of O* to guess at the sex of its author (who uses a pen name). Actually it matters little whether it was written by a man or a woman; the book is the expression of one fully steeped in the perspectives and values of masculism, and, as I have pointed out, that is not gender specific.

[12] Jean Paulhan, "Happiness in Slavery" in Reage, *Story of O,* p. xxv.

[13] Ibid., p. xxviii.

[14] Mandiargues, "A Note," ibid., p. vii.

[15] The idea that victimization per se is an essential principle of female excellence in patriarchy appeared in Andrea Dworkin's *Woman Hating.*

[16] Some of this discussion appeared in S. Ruth, "Sexism, Patriarchy, and Feminism: Toward an Understanding of Terms" (Paper delivered at Pioneers for Century III Conference, Cincinnati, Ohio, March 1976) and published in D. V. Hiller and R. A. Sheets, eds., *Women and Men: The Consequences of Power* (Cincinnati: University of Cincinnati, Office of Women's Studies, 1977).

peratives of femininity is a tenuous affair at best.

All male-identified ideals of women rest on one basic presupposition: that women are and ought to be completely defined and understood within their biological capacities, sexual or reproductive. These capacities determine our "place" in the world, and we are only "good," one way or another, when we are (willingly or unwillingly) in that place. Should we instead stray, particularly through our own assertiveness, but even by accident, then we are bad women and can be redeemed only if we are returned to our proper sphere.

In patriarchy, for women "anatomy is destiny,"[17] and our physical capacities enjoin us two separate and often conflicting roles — that of Procreator/Mother and that of Sexual Partner. The "good" woman, then, each in a different sense, is she who serves, either in the capacity of excellent mother or of excellent mistress, or both.

Mother: The Primary Ideal

The Marian image, Mother, nurture incarnate, is woman's most positive image in patriarchy. This lady, charged ostensibly with the care of the young, is the complement of male power — she is tenderness, fragility, love, charity, loyalty, submission, and sacrifice. Carrier of man's seed, she is the essence of purity, totally absorbed in the activities and qualities of caring. Serene and satisfied within her role, placing the needs of her charges above her own, she busies herself with feeding them, watching over them, making them happy. Intuitively knowing and cosmically linked with lunar cycles, she has special powers and little need for rationality.

Just as in sexual physiology the female principle is one of receiving, keeping and nourishing — woman's *specific* form of creativeness, that of motherhood, is tied up with the life of nature, with a *non-reflective bios*. . . . Indeed, the four-week cycle of ovulation, the rhythmically alternating tides of fertility . . . the nine months of gestation . . . ties woman deeply to the life of nature, to the pulse beat of the cosmos.[18]

I think, perhaps, that insofar as insight — the seeing into, the throwing of light into darkness, the intellectual illumination — aims at greater self-awareness and a more conscious functioning, it belongs into the mode or sphere of male development. The eternal feminine, static, perfect in itself, does not and need not develop. What any given woman does not know about it, insight therapy cannot ever teach her. Insight therapy, even in women, can only address itself to the masculine aspect. A given woman, through insight, can become more aware and more conscious, but not more feminine — although the balance of male and female within her may at times be shifted through insight which enables her to place less stress on male modes of functioning; in that case a covered-up femininity may emerge: but only as much of it as was there in the first place. One *is* a woman, one *learns* to be a man. Therapeutic theories stressing insight deal primarily with men because only men — and the masculine aspects of women — can be approached by and can utilize insight.[19]

Womanhood, it would seem then, is closer to nature than manhood, more compelling,

---

[17] "Anatomy is destiny," argued Sigmund Freud. For the female, he contended, the body, its make-up and potential, determines personality and character in a far more definitive way than is true for men.

[18] Karl Stern, *The Flight from Woman* (New York: Farrar, Straus & Giroux, 1964), pp. 21–22.
[19] Wolfgang Lederer, *The Fear of Women* (New York: Grune & Stratton, 1968), pp. 269–270.

more disastrous if denied. One might wonder (and feminists do) how anything so "natural" and "instinctive" could be denied. Yet according to theory it sometimes is, and then not only do women themselves suffer, but the whole world goes topsy-turvy; it is askew, even in danger. Men lose their manhood, children become psychotic, society dissolves, and the natural order is disturbed!

In the language of the women's movement, the mothering role is mystified, covered over with a whole set of myths, fantasies, and images that hide many of the realities of the role and the person who lives it.

Playmate: The Illicit Ideal

Mother is the *official* good woman of the Western world. But there is another kind of "good" woman, good in a different sense, good in a less-than-socially-acceptable, elbow-in-the-rib kind of way, slightly déclassé — a sexy, naughty, fun-loving lady: the Playmate.

The Marian image, the classic model of femininity in the West, born out of the fear and loathing of sex and sensuality rampant in the early Christian church, is pointedly asexual: pure, chaste, and virginal, despite marriage, wifehood, and childbirth. Mother, the good woman in this image, is an asexual or even antisexual ideal, too pure for carnality. Sex is beneath her. She is patient, enduring, dutiful, submissive, and nurturing, *and she doesn't play around*. She's not supposed to, and she doesn't want to, not even with her husband. Hence her converse, the Playmate.

For the Playmate, playing around is a raison d'être. She is built "to take it" and to give it. You can tell by the seductive, compliant look in her eyes, the parted lips, the knowing smile, the receptive, open posture of her opulent young body. But the Playmate is no ordinary whore. She is interesting (bright enough to be companionable, but not too bright to be uncooperative or threatening). She is independent (able to take care of herself, but needful enough to succumb to male power). She is choosy (nobody wants something that anyone can have). She is even a little aggressive, a little dangerous — enough to make her a worthy trophy.

"There are two kinds of girls," a saying goes, "the kind you bring home to Mother and the kind you bring home to Father." Each has an attendant schema of responses and rewards. The Playmate is for playing, for fun, not for seriousness and heavy obligation. She has waived her claims to adulation from afar. She isn't chaste, so one need not hide "baser" motivations and appetites. Since she's not timid or naive, one needn't be solicitous or protective. She's worldly-wise — no need for protocol, courtship, and protestations of love. Having opted out of "purity" and the category of the primary ideal, she has abandoned the status and prerogatives of the "official" good woman. Mother and Playmate, lady and tramp, Mary and Eve — the dichotomy is a familiar one in novels, movies, and sermons, and the tension it causes puts women in a bind.

The Wife

It should be obvious by now that the two female ideals, perfect mother and perfect mistress, are incompatible. No one can be chaste, submissive, timid, needful, innocent, loyal, tender, and serene and *at the same time* sexually wise, perky, naughty, independent, and so on. Yet that is exactly the position into which middle-class American patriarchy places women, for to be both Mary and Playmate is the prescribed role and image of the ideal woman — girlfriend, roommate, date, or wife. Like the "hell of a woman" in Mac Davis's popular song lyric, she is supposed to be all things to her hell of a man: not just *act* all things, but *be* them — "woman, baby, witch, lady." It's a difficult game, for even if she wins, she loses — her identity, her self-concept, her sense of autonomy, cohesion, and direction. It is schizophrenic.

The Dichotomy Dichotomizes: The Misogynist Flip

All that effort, and as often as not, it doesn't even work. Each of us may indeed choose between a life modeled on Mary or a life modeled on Playmate, settling for the rewards of the role. We may even manage to negotiate the tricks and turns of playing both, yet even that cannot guarantee us undying love.

There are circumstances over which none may have control and in which Mary, the Playmate, or even Helluvawoman may become a pain in the neck, an object of contempt, a creature to be avoided. Reflected visions, after all, are dependent on the minds of those who reflect, and the extent to which any of these roles is prized (and the woman playing it praised) depends on how well it serves the function for which it was created and how long that function endures. Mary is desirable to one seeking nurture, understanding, and mothering (for himself or his children). She becomes a nuisance when that same man sets out to find exuberant or illicit sex. The Playmate is fun when playing is what he wants, but she is unsuitable at the company dinner.

Each ideal is subject to a "serviceability" factor: The status of the role itself, its value and meaning, and even the language used to refer to it can shift radically as its utility shifts or as its context changes. She who is "the little woman" in church becomes "the old lady" at the bar; she who was seen as "a good old girl" in graduate school may be seen as "a slut" when he joins the Club.

In the space of one moment, depending on changing attitudes or interests, the image may shift — good becomes bad, bad becomes good. The nurturing Mary becomes the Old Ball and Chain, and very easily her innocence becomes stupidity; her chastity, frigidity, her nurture, suffocation; her loyalty, imprisonment; her beauty, vanity; her earthiness, carnality; her children, obligation. The Playmate becomes Eve, the Traitor of the Garden; she who is trouble. Contempt becomes hatred.

> And I have found a woman more bitter than death, who is the hunter's snare, and her heart is a net, and her hands are bonds. . . .
> More bitter than death, again, because that is natural and destroys only the body; but the sin which arose from woman destroys the soul . . . bodily death is an open and terrible enemy, but woman is a wheedling and secret enemy.[20]

Even less a function of a woman's actual behavior than the images that allege to portray her, the serviceability factor in women's role manifests more clearly than all the rest that in patriarchy women's lives are meant to be lived not for themselves, but for men's needs, and our cultural images are defined by that fact. The major factor in the flip from good to bad (that is, serviceable to not serviceable) is the matter of intrusiveness into male affairs; it has to do with self-assertion, self-direction, and will. It is important to have Mary; it is fun to have Playmates — as long as they don't get in the way. When women move toward their own needs, get "pushy," or stand in the way of *his* wishes, at that point Mary becomes the Ball and

20 K. Kramer and J. Sprenger, *Malleus Maleficarum,* trans. M. Summers (London: Arrow Books, 1971), p. 112.

Chain (alias the Wif'nkids), and the Playmate becomes the Bitch.

As you look at the chart below, remember that any or all of these images may be perceived or expected in any one woman, sometimes all at the same time.

Variations on the Theme:
Ethnic Overlay

Since the men who make up and direct the patriarchy in which we live are, for the most part, white, Christian, and middle class, it is not surprising that the primary models of womanhood in our society are markedly WASP. Across racial, ethnic, and class lines, one composite image prevails. The fragile, pale-skinned Madonna and the saucily tanned Playmate with flowing blond hair are clearly white, Christian images not even marginally attainable for the very large segment of the female population who are members of racial or ethnic subgroups. Yet, viable or not, these images continue to function as models, held up to us either as ideals we must strain to copy in whatever meager way possible or as evidence of our inferiority.

The WASP quality of the cultural ideal puts minority women — black, Chicana, Jew, or other — in a double bind. Not only are we

Basic Female Stereotypes

	Nonsexual	Sexual
	The Virgin Mary/Mother-Wife	*The Playmate/Lover*
Serviceable	chaste, pure, innocent, good proper-looking, conservative nurturing, selfless, loving, gentle, "mother of his children" submissive, pliable, receptive compromising, tactful, loyal fragile, needful, dependent feeling, nonrational, aesthetic, spiritual understanding, supportive	sensuous, sexually wise, experienced sexy, "built" satisfying, eager, earthy, mysterious, slightly dangerous sexually receptive, agreeable, "game" challenging, exciting independent, carefree, "laid back" bright, fun-loving, playful responsive, ego-building
	The Old Ball and Chain/Wif'nkids	*Eve/The Witch-Bitch Temptress*
Nonserviceable	frigid, sexually uninteresting frumpy or slatternly cloying, suffocating, obligating incapable of decision, changeable, scatterbrained, dumb, passive nagging, shrewish, harping helpless, burdensome over-emotional, irrational, unreasonable shrewd, manipulative, sneaky	promiscuous, bad coarse, vulgar, trampy tempting, leads one into sin and evil undiscriminating; she's "anybody's" bitchy, demanding, selfish; she "asks for it" immoral, makes trouble thoughtless, sinful, evil immodest, unladylike

subject to all the usual contradictions of the bifurcated female image — sexual/nonsexual, good/bad — but we must deal as well with a second set of problems compounded and enlarged by our particular ethnic status and circumstances. Oppressed as women, oppressed as minorities, we are expected to choose between loyalties, between liberations. Caught between minority men's anger at WASP behavior and their unconscious acceptance of WASP ideals, minority women "cannot win for losing": If we strain to meet prevailing standards, we are selling out; if we do not, we are unattractive.

Whichever way we choose to go, however we resolve the cultural loyalties, there is in addition the issue of our own self-image. The traditional minority woman, as any other, seeks desirability as a mate, seeks the whole range of social approbation that comes of being thought "beautiful," of meeting the current standards of beauty. Should those standards be even farther removed from her real self than they are from other women, she must either work harder to meet them, risking proportionately deeper self-alienation, or she must accept defeat and wrestle with an intense sense of inferiority.

I vividly remember, as an adolescent Jewish girl of the 1950s — hooked on Marilyn Monroe and Ava Gardner, Debbie Reynolds and Liz Taylor — how I fretted at my unfashionably curly hair, trying tirelessly to straighten its resilient black locks. I remember, too, staring enviously at my *shiksa* girlfriends' straight noses. Anything, I thought, even being fat, would be better than having this awful bumpy nose. At nineteen, I had it "fixed."

For the Jewish women who fix their noses, for the black women who straighten their hair, for the millions of us who attempt "corrections" to body and character that must ever remain inadequate, there must always be a severe sense of either deceit or defeat.

The experience is more than self-diminishing; it is crushing.

Although ideals and models vary very little from one group to another, the pejorative stereotypes, born of particular history and circumstance, admit of a good deal of variation and adjustment. For example, the Jewish woman, as a woman, may still function as the old Ball and Chain or the Bitch Temptress; but she may, as well, be placed within some other disparaging categories, exotic variations on the traditional themes. The young Jewish woman ethnically identifiable and hence acceptable to the community (and therefore *less* acceptable to her male compatriots for the reasons pointed out above) is known as "the nice Jewish girl" — the NJG. Her more chic, less ethnically identifiable counterpart, the Jewish American Princess (the JAP) is disparaged precisely because she avoids the social pitfalls of ethnic identification and strives so diligently to meet the WASP model. In either case, the mythology will turn both women ultimately into the Jewish Mother — aggressive, brassy, domineering, suffocating, unwholesomely self-inclined. If she cares too little, she's a shrew; if she cares too much, she's sick. Ultimately, any Jewish woman may be typed as the "pushy Jewish broad," characterizing in her female person all the worst traits of the Jewish stereotype — a classic example of an image created by an external dominant group and internalized within the group, that is to say, by the men of the group and ultimately by the women themselves.

Similarly but more intensely caught in the dilemma of ethnic identification is the black woman, bound on the one hand by white images of black women and on the other by black images of white women. For men, black or white, who adopt the traditional WASP models, the black woman functions both as a symbol of racial difference and as the usual receptacle of misogyny. Her pejorative images are intensifications of the traditional dichotomies.

In the black context, the Mother/Nurturer gone wrong is not only the frigid nuisance, the nag of white society; she is also the destroyer of the race — the Matriarch of the Moynihan Report,[21] who controls the family, castrates the black man by displacing him as head of the household, and thereby contributes to the destruction of black manhood, the family unit, and black pride. The strength, resiliency, and independence developed in the black woman through centuries of hardship, rather than being prized and lauded, are in true masculist style deflected and turned against her.

The same traits of strength and assertiveness are the very ones that mark the black adaptation of Eve. Eve, the Playmate gone awry, is still Eve in the black context, only worse. Here we have the Hot Black Bitch, an image obviously constructed by the white overlord, yet at least partially reflected in the black community as well. Whereas the white Playmate is naughty, her stereotypic black counterpart is depicted as without morals, without limits, sexually voracious, undiscriminating, and hard as nails, her behavior and character placing her completely outside the bounds of chivalry and masculine protection.

Whatever the ethnic, racial, and class variations, however the images are adapted and reflected, they all have this in common: They are born of masculist experience and serve masculist needs. They have little to do with women's undistorted natures, but reduce *all*

---

[21] Daniel Patrick Moynihan, *The Negro Family: The Case for National Action,* U.S. Department of Labor, Office of Policy Planning and Research, 1965. Moynihan wrote this analysis of black needs and problems for the president of the United States, thereby launching many of the economic programs of the sixties. Moynihan argued that "In essence, the Negro community has been forced into a matriarchal structure, which . . . imposes a crushing burden on the Negro male, and in consequence on a great many Negro women as well." (p. 29).

women to the same thing: sisters in service to the patriarchy.

Effects of the Stereotype

The patriarchal images of women, whether sexual or nonsexual, working class or middle class, black or white, have a common denominator. They all say that women as human beings are substandard: less intelligent; less moral; less competent; less able physically, psychologically, and spiritually; small of body, mind, and character; often bad or destructive. The images argue that we have done little in society (besides reproduce) to earn our keep; that we have made only small contribution to culture, high or low, yet always push for more than we deserve. Sometimes cute or adorable, sometimes consoling, but only in that context, we are pleasant baubles to have around. In any other guise, we are a nuisance at best, a disaster at worst.

These and other stereotypical images of women are destructive to us. In their positive aspects, impossible to meet, in their negative, deprecatory and ugly, they flourish in the minds of women, who are forced to live them. Functioning in large part as social norms, they have great power to direct attitudes and behavior, among the group stereotyped as well as in the larger community. The tragedy of the female stereotype is that it impels women not only to appear substandard, but to become substandard; it moves to form us into the loathed monster. If the work of the stereotype be done, we are reduced to the weak, hapless creatures required by social lore, living in the mold, even experiencing ourselves according to the myth.

Limited experience, opportunity, and education, deemed appropriate for beings who must not become "too smart for our own good"; restrictive clothing and play, tailored for our more "alluring" and refined bodies;

disapproval for behavior (sports, for example, competition, and assertiveness) that might strengthen body or character; suitors who require subservience and fragility; adolescent girlfriends straining to become "desirable" women; parents prompting us to marriage or marriageability; these and countless other experiences and influences work together to make us believe the myth and copy the model. The model requires that we be pretty, gentle, and kind; we can become pretty, gentle, and kind. The model, however, also requires that we be silly, weak, and incompetent. Are we not required then to become silly, weak, and incompetent? Haven't we often tried? And as we come to fit the mold and exhibit the expected traits, we reinforce the stereotype, perpetuate the cycle, and give "truth" to the lie. And if the lie be true, then everything follows. Because women are incompetent and weak, they must be protected, set apart, and given a safe "place," guarded by their men. Since we are petty and evil, unable to get along even with each other, we must be controlled for the good of ourselves and society.

We deserve the contempt in which we are held.

Clearly, to live in the shadow of such attitudes is intolerable, even when they are covered over by chivalry or mystification, even when they are temporarily suspended for good behavior. Life and personhood defined within such constraints must be distorted, out of phase with even the barest elements of emotional and physical health, spiritual transcendence and joy. Furthermore, the misery occasioned by these ideals goes well beyond the psychological and spiritual elements of life. Because we are speaking here only about images, we have not yet raised the issue of more concrete oppression — poverty and physical abuse.

In the following chapter we will examine feminist responses to these images, feminist insights into the nature and effects of patriarchal stereotypes, the struggles women experience in freeing themselves, and the alternative, woman-identified images being forged in the struggle.

Selections

WHETHER WOMAN SHOULD HAVE BEEN MADE IN THE FIRST PRODUCTION OF THINGS?

ST. THOMAS AQUINAS

Thomas Aquinas (1227–1274), medieval philosopher and theologian, was named the official philosophic authority of the Catholic Church by Pope Leo XIII in 1879. His reasoning forms the basis of Catholic doctrine and pervades much of Protestant theology as well. As such, it has exerted tremendous influence on Western culture and hence on women's lives. Through the church, Aquinas's ideas continue in importance today, having their effect on arguments regarding contraception and abortion, women's place in the priesthood, women's role in the family, women's role in the economy, and so on.

In the following discussion, Aquinas asks whether one could say that because women are defective and sinful (more so than men) they ought not to have been created in the first innocent beginning of things by an all-perfect God. Certainly, women should have been created, he replies, for nature decrees that men must have "helpers," not in cultural works, but in reproduction. That is, women are necessary as biological assistants.

Aquinas was known for his reconciliation of Christian doctrine with the philosophy of Aristotle, increasingly important in the thirteenth century. The philosopher he refers to in his opening remarks is Aristotle, who theorized that "females are weaker and colder in nature, and we must look upon the female character as being a sort of natural deficiency" (*De Generatione Animalium*, IV, 6, 775a 15). Aristotle's analysis of woman as misbegotten male is one of a whole genre of theories, popular through the centuries, treating womanhood as a partial or defective instance of manhood.

FIRST ARTICLE

Whether Woman Should Have Been Made in the First Production of Things?

We proceed thus to the First Article: —

Objection 1. It would seem that woman should not have been made in the first production of things. For the Philosopher says that the *female is a misbegotten male.* But nothing misbegotten or defective should have been in the first production of things. Therefore woman should not have been made at that first production.

Obj. 2. Further, subjection and limitation were a result of sin, for to the woman was

"Whether Woman Should Have Been Made in the First Production of Things?" *Summa Theologicae*, Pars I, Q. 92 (The Production of Woman), Art. 1, in *Basic Writings of St. Thomas Aquinas*, ed. Anton C. Pegis (New York: Random House, 1945). Reprinted by permission of the estate of Anton C. Pegis.

it said after sin (*Gen.* iii. 16): *Thou shalt be under the man's power;* and Gregory says that, *Where there is no sin, there is no inequality.* But woman is naturally of less strength and dignity than man, *for the agent is always more honorable than the patient,* as Augustine says. Therefore woman should not have been made in the first production of things before sin.

Obj. 3. Further, occasions of sin should be cut off. But God foresaw that woman would be an occasion of sin to man. Therefore He should not have made woman.

On the contrary, It is written (*Gen.* ii. 18): *It is not good for man to be alone; let us make him a helper like to himself.*

I answer that, It was necessary for woman to be made, as the Scripture says, as *a helper* to man; not, indeed, as a helpmate in other works, as some say, since man can be more efficiently helped by another man in other works; but as a helper in the work of generation, but are generated by an agent observe the mode of generation carried out in various living things. Some living things do not possess in themselves the power of generation, but are generated by an agent of another species; and such are those plants and animals which are generated, without seed, from suitable matter through the active power of the heavenly bodies. Others possess the active and passive generative power together, as we see in plants which are generated from seed. For the noblest vital function in plants is generation, and so we observe that in these the active power of generation invariably accompanies the passive power. Among perfect animals, the active power of generation belongs to the male sex, and the passive power to the female. And as among animals there is a vital operation nobler than generation, to which their life is principally directed, so it happens that the male sex is not found in continual union with the female in perfect

animals, but only at the time of coition; so that we may consider that by coition the male and female are one, as in plants they are always united, even though in some cases one of them preponderates, and in some the other. But man is further ordered to a still nobler work of life, and that is intellectual operation. Therefore there was greater reason for the distinction of these two powers in man; so that the female should be produced separately from the male, and yet that they should be carnally united for generation. Therefore directly after the formation of woman, it was said: *And they shall be two in one flesh* (*Gen.* ii. 24).

Reply Obj. 1. As regards the individual nature, woman is defective and misbegotten, for the active power in the male seed tends to the production of a perfect likeness according to the masculine sex; while the production of woman comes from defect in the active power, or from some material indisposition, or even from some external influence, such as that of a south wind, which is moist, as the Philosopher observes. On the other hand, as regards universal human nature, woman is not misbegotten, but is included in nature's intention as directed to the work of generation. Now the universal intention of nature depends on God, Who is the universal Author of nature. Therefore, in producing nature, God formed not only the male but also the female.

Reply Obj. 2. Subjection is twofold. One is servile, by virtue of which a superior makes use of a subject for his own benefit; and this kind of subjection began after sin. There is another kind of subjection, which is called economic or civil, whereby the superior makes use of his subjects for their own benefit and good; and this kind of subjection existed even before sin. For the good of order would have been wanting in the human family if some were not governed by others wiser than themselves. So by such a kind of subjection woman is naturally subject to man, because in man the discernment of reason predominates. Nor is inequality among men excluded by the state of innocence, as we shall prove.

Reply Obj. 3. If God had deprived the world of all those things which proved an occasion of sin, the universe would have been imperfect. Nor was it fitting for the common good to be destroyed in order that individual evil might be avoided; especially as God is so powerful that He can direct any evil to a good end.

SCIENTIFIC ANALYSIS OF WOMAN

ANONYMOUS

In the nineteenth century, the German philosopher Arthur Schopenhauer wrote a well-known essay, "Of Women," in which he described women as not *the fair sex* but rather "the unesthetic sex," "that undersized, narrow-shouldered, broad-hipped, and short-legged race." He argued with seemingly objective aplomb that women were intellectually shortsighted and underequipped; petty, dishonest, manipulative, and lacking in deep sensibility; unable to get along with one another because of competition in the sexual arena, but past masters (mistresses?) at turning men to their advantage. Deplorable as these traits were, however, he suggested that they undoubtedly served the propagation of the race (woman's only proper sphere) by enabling women to seduce men into marriage. For that reason, woman's character was perhaps forgivable or justifiable, but she ought never be allowed freedom or power. Many treat Schopenhauer's essay as a joke, although other pieces very similar in substance have been written and taken seriously (the writings of Philip Wylie and Norman Mailer, for example). Yet such essays should be looked at carefully because they reflect and reveal the deeply misogynist undercurrents of our culture.

The following is a less erudite yet nonetheless potent statement of the same theme, the more chilling for its appearance in the contemporary popular idiom. It was given to me by my daughter's baby sitter, who told me that it was being passed around her high school with great hilarity.

If you are acquainted with chemistry, you may be interested in this scientific analysis of a familiar element, Woman.

Symbol — Wo

Discovered — First detected in pure form by Adam in Garden of Eden

Physical properties

1. Boils at anything
2. Freezes at anything

3. Melts when properly treated
4. Very bitter if not used well
5. Very unstable under pressure

Accepted weight — 118

Occurrence — Surplus quantity is found in metropolitan areas

Chemical properties

1. Possesses great affinity for gold, silver, platinum, and precious stones

2. Reacts violently if left alone
3. Has ability to absorb great quantities of food

Test — Turns green if placed beside a better-looking specimen

Uses

1. Highly ornamental

2. Useful as a catalyst in acceleration of low spirits
3. Useful as an equalizer in distribution of wealth
4. Probably the most effective income-reducing agent known to man

CAUTION — Highly explosive in inexperienced *hands.*

"I AM UNCLEAN . . ."

H. R. HAYS

The novelist and anthropologist H. R. Hays studied at Cornell and Columbia and has taught at the University of Minnesota, Fairleigh Dickinson, and Southampton. He is the author of several works in social anthropology: *From Ape to Angel, In the Beginning, Children of the Raven,* and *The Kingdom of Hawaii.*

  The Dangerous Sex, from which this selection is taken, is described by Frederic Wertham as "a long overdue and well-documented study of man's inhumanity to woman." Through an examination of the beliefs, customs, and mores of cultures from the primitive to the present, Hays chronicles the hostility and cruelty with which men have treated women, and seeks reasons in male fears and ignorance. The chapter reprinted here describes the highly prevalent treatment of woman as dirty, woman as cosmically dangerous. The biological processes of women have "big magic"; they are fraught with serious consequences and thus surrounded by "big scare." Interestingly, the theme of male fear of women, not a new or uncommon idea, is increasingly a factor in analyses of male-female relations.

When menstruating, a Surinam Negro woman lives in solitude. If anyone approaches her, she must cry out, "I am unclean."

  The notion that women's sexual processes are impure is worldwide and persistent; the magical fear of menstrual blood is particularly intense. In the first place, the fact that blood flows from the female genitals at regular intervals sets women off from the other sex and gives them the exceptional properties of mana in a world in which men set the norm. The taboos which surround the first menstruation are particularly severe. The phenomenon itself is frequently explained as a supernatural wound, the result of an attack by a bird, a snake or a lizard. The origin of the female genital as a result of castration or sadistic attack is also illustrated in myths concerning the creation of women. Since male fantasy is dominant in human institutions, a very early time is often referred to in which there were only men and no women. The Negritos of the Malay Peninsula

From H. R. Hays, *The Dangerous Sex* (New York: Putnam, 1964). Reprinted by permission.

maintain there was once an ancestral creator entity, the monitor lizard. Since his contemporaries were all men, the lizard caught one of them, cut off his genitals and made him into a woman who became the lizard's wife and the ancestor of the Negritos. When Christopher Columbus discovered the Indians inhabiting Haiti, whom he named Caribs, he left a friar among them as a missionary. Friar Pane recorded a story concerning the Indian ancestors who had no women yet felt they should have some. One day they observed certain creatures who were falling out of the trees or hiding in the branches. These alien beings had no sex organs whatsoever. The Carib ancestors bound them and tied woodpeckers to them in the proper place. The birds pecked out the desired sexual orifices. Not only do we have here the theme of women being created by castration appearing on opposite sides of the world but, significantly enough, the image of the vulva as a wound also occurs in the fantasies of male psychoanalytical patients.

New Guinea carvings show images of women with a crocodile attacking the vulva, a hornbill plunging its beak into the organ or a penislike snake emerging from it. On the one hand there is the idea of castration and on the other an image of the female genital being created by a sadistic attack by the penis, symbolized by lizard, bird beak, or snake. The mysterious and dangerous nature of the wound is uppermost in primitive tradition.

Blood in all of its manifestations is a source of mana. In the case of menstrual blood the ancient ambivalence is in evidence with the harmful aspect predominating. The dangers of contact and contagion are so great that women are nearly always secluded or forced to reside apart during their monthly periods. Special huts are built for them by the Bakairi of Brazil, the Shus-

wap of British Columbia, the Gauri of northern India, the Veddas of Ceylon, and the Algonkian of the North American forest. From this it can be seen that the custom covers the globe.

Then, too, a sort of fumigating sometimes takes place. Siberian Samoyed women step over fires of burning reindeer skin. They must also refrain from cooking food for their men. Among the Nootka of the Canadian northwest coast, at her first period a girl is given her private eating utensils and must eat alone for eight months. The Chippewa girl also eats alone, cannot cross a public road or talk to any man or boy. Eskimo girls at their first period are taboo for forty days. They must sit crouching in a corner, their faces to the wall, draw their hoods over their heads, let their hair hang over their faces and only leave the house when everyone else is asleep. Hermann Ploss describes a still more curious segregation practiced by the Australians of Queensland. The girl is taken to a shady place. Her mother draws a circle on the ground and digs a deep hole into which the girl must step. "The sandy soil is then filled in, leaving her buried up to the waist. A woven hedge of branches or twigs is set around her with an opening toward which she turns her face. Her mother kindles a fire at the opening, the girl remains in her nest of earth in a squatting posture with folded arms and hands resting downward on the sand heap that covers her lower limbs."

We are not told how long she must remain in the condition of the heroine of Beckett's play, *Happy Days,* but it is evident that the soil is supposed to purify or nullify her dangerous condition.

Among the Dogon of East Africa the menstrual taboo is so strong that a woman in this condition brings misfortune to everything she touches. Not only is she segregated in an isolated hut and provided with special eating utensils, but if she is seen passing through the village a general purification must take place. The Wogeo of South Australia believe that if a man has contact with a menstruating woman he will die from a wasting disease against which there is no remedy whatsoever.

The Hindus observe an endless number of prohibitions during the first three days of a woman's period. She must not weep, mount a horse, an ox or an elephant, be carried in a palanquin or drive in a vehicle.

In Hebrew tradition the menstruating woman is forbidden to work in a kitchen, sit at meals with other people, or drink from a glass used by others. Any contact with her husband is a sin and the penalty for intercourse during her period is death for both. Indeed the misfortunes which men suffer when they break the menstrual taboo vary but they are always severe. A Uganda Bantu woman by touching her husband's effects makes him sick; if she lays a hand on his weapons, he will be killed in the next fight. The natives of Malacca believe that coitus, or even contact, will cause the man to lose his virility.

The prohibitions which we have just been discussing occur in ancient or primitive cultures. Menstrual anxiety, however, is so deeply ingrained in the male psyche that it lingers in folk tradition. The peasants of eastern Europe believe that a woman must not bake bread, make pickles, churn butter or spin thread during her period or all will go wrong. Here, of course, is a survival of the idea that food is particularly susceptible to the deadly contagion. In Silesian folklore women during their periods are forbidden to plant seedlings or work in the garden. The Roman author Pliny tells us that contact of menstruous women with new wine or ripe fruit will sour both. The same author provides us with examples of ambivalence: "Hailstorms, whirlwinds and lightnings even

will be scared away by a woman uncovering her body while her courses are upon her. . . . Also if a woman strips herself naked while she is menstruating and walks around a field of wheat, the caterpillars, worms, beetles and other vermin will fall off the ears of corn [wheat]. Algonkian women walk around a cornfield for the same reason. Menstrual blood is also thought to cure leprosy and is actually by European peasants sometimes put into a man's coffee as a love charm. In Russian folklore it is said to cure warts and birthmarks. These instances are enough to show that the basic principle of ambivalent mana is involved. The overwhelming amount of evidence proves, however, that men do not envy the female ability to menstruate but fear it.

An example cited by Havelock Ellis shows that even in the late nineteenth century educated men were not free of this superstition. In 1891 a British doctor, William Goodell, wrote that he had to shake off the tradition that women must not be operated upon during their periods. "Our forefathers from time immemorial have thought and taught that the presence of a menstruating woman would pollute solemn religious rites, would sour milk, spoil the fermentation in wine vats, and much other mischief in a general way." Ellis also cites several instances of violinists who were convinced that the strings of their instruments continually broke while their wives were indisposed.

Even Hermann Ploss and Max Bartels in their gynecological and anthropological work *Woman,* first published in Germany in 1905, wrote: "But it seems very doubtful whether these superstitions and traditions will ever be eradicated. They are far too deeply and far too widely ramified in the mind and emotions of humanity."

It will be seen that all the basic predispositions to anxiety are involved. Women by their recurring supernatural wound are set apart as aliens from the male norm. Sensitivity to contact and contagion is aroused and the symbol of the whole complex is blood, the powerful magic liquid on which life depends.

But menstruation is not the only female process which is surrounded with precautions. Pregnancy and childbirth, although the focus of various ideas, again arouse anxiety connected with blood, impurity and contagion. In addition, the production of a live being from a woman's body undoubtedly endows her with the supernatural properties of mana. In most cases the woman must be segregated or else she must give birth alone in the forest as among the Negritos, some east coast African Negroes, the Kiwai Papuans and the Guaná of Paraguay. The Hottentots of South Africa, the Tahitians, the Todas of India and the Gilyaks of the island of Sakhalin are among those who build a special hut or tent.

The misfortunes brought about by pregnancy and childbirth parallel those of menstruation. Among the Indians of Costa Rica, a woman pregnant for the first time infects the whole neighborhood; she is blamed for any deaths which may occur and her husband is obliged to pay damages. Cape Town Bantu males believe that looking upon a lying-in woman will result in their being killed in battle. Some Brazilian Indians are sure that if the woman is not out of the house during childbirth weapons will lose their power. The Sulka of New Britain feel that in addition men will become cowardly and taro shoots will not sprout. A purification ceremony consists of chewing ginger, spitting it on twigs which are held in the smoke of a fire, and repeating certain charms. The twigs are then placed on the taro shoots, on weapons, and over doors and on roofs.

Those who aid the parturient woman are also sure to be infected by the contagion. Garcilaso de la Vega, the chronicler of the ancient Incas, wrote that no one must help a woman in childbirth, and any who did would be regarded as witches. Among the Hebrews the midwife was regarded as unclean. The whole concept of "lying in" — only recently dispelled by new medical theories requiring the new mother to be up and about as soon as possible — which was rationalized as necessary for the woman to regain her strength, originated in magical precautions, as is clearly shown by the extreme length of time during which primitive women were sequestered and by the ceremonies carried out to purify them. To cite a few examples: The time varied from forty days, among the Swahili of Africa, to two months among the Eskimo or two to three months in Tahiti. Significantly enough, the period was longer after the birth of a girl in India, among the Hebrews, among many New Guinea tribes, the Masai of West Africa, and the Cree Indians of North America.

An example of purification ceremonies is the bathing of Hebrew women in special bathhouses in which both menstruating and parturient women were cleansed. After her time of sequestration was over, the Hebrew woman was required to send a lamb and a dove to the priest as sacrifices. The Pueblo Indians treat the purification more lyrically. Five days after the child is born, its mother is ceremonially washed. She then walks in the retinue of a priest to view the sunrise, throwing up cornflowers and blowing them about in the air.

In accordance with the feeling that the exceptional is embued with mana, miscarriage, being more abnormal than ordinary birth, is regarded with particular apprehension. The African Bantu consider it a cause of drought. They also believe that if a woman succeeds in aborting herself and at once has sexual relations with a man his death will follow.

The samplings just given are selected from a wealth of evidence which demonstrates that the male attitude toward female sexual functions is basically apprehensive; women, in short, are dangerous. Taboos and fears of contagion, however, are not limited to the physical crises in their lives. When we investigate the ideas of contact still further, a host of activities requires avoidance of women in general.

Since nutrition is one of the basic needs of human beings, and food is brought into contact with the body, it is not surprising that food and eating are universally involved with magical precautions. Women being intrinsically dangerous, their relation to food is a psychological problem. We have already cited food and eating taboos in relation to menstruation. Among preliterates and in ancient civilizations it is the rule rather than the exception that women do not eat with their husbands. Although in later periods the idea that the dominant male must be served first also enters the picture, the germ of the custom is certainly the notion that female impurity will contaminate a man's food and do him harm. Throughout Africa men and women eat separately, and the same is true of many South American tribes. In Melanesia and Polynesia the same segregation is observed. The Todas, those hill people of India who have already been cited, also observe the taboo, as do the sophisticated Hindus. If the wife of one of the Hindus were to touch his food it would be rendered unfit for his use. The same precaution was widespread in North America. The early traveler and artist George Catlin said he never saw Indians and squaws eating together. Henry Rowe Schoolcraft, the first American anthropologist, when he was an Indian agent

among the Chippewa, married a half-Indian girl. Although his wife had been educated in England and helped him collect Algonkian folklore and her dark-skinned mother prevented a border incident by mediating between her people and the whites, the mother's conservatism was so intense that she could never be persuaded to eat with her son-in-law.

The two exclusive male activities of hunting and fighting are also very often associated with avoidance of women. Nothing is closer to man's maleness than his weapons and his hunting gear. In Tahiti, women are prohibited from touching weapons and fishing apparatus. In Queensland the natives throw away their fishing lines if women step over them, and elsewhere a woman is forbidden to step over objects, because in so doing the woman's sex passes over them and they are thus exposed to the seat of contagion. (When a Maori warrior wishes to absorb the phallic magic of a powerful chief, he crawls between his legs.) A Dakota Indian's weapons must not be touched by a woman and women of the Siberian hunting tribes must abide by the same taboo. If a woman touches a Zulu's assegai, he cannot use it again.

Cattle among the southern Bantu are an important form of male ego expression and in this case they are taboo to women. If women touch them the beasts will fall ill. Fighting cocks among the Malay are treated in the same way. This taboo, however, among the Bantu does not apply to girls who have not yet reached puberty or to old women who have passed the menopause, proving conclusively that it is the female sexual mana which is thought to do the damage.

The necessity of abstaining from intercourse with women before undertaking the chase and warfare has sometimes been explained as a fear of the debilitating effect of what is considered the weaker sex. Indeed it is often so rationalized by the primitives themselves. That this is a late addition is indicated by the fact that fasting often accompanies the ritual surrounding hunting and war and fasting can scarcely be construed as a method of conserving strength.

Sexual abstinence before war and hunting is practiced all over Polynesia and in many parts of Melanesia. The headhunters of Assam, in India, are particularly strict in observing this taboo. In one case the wife of a headman spoke to her husband, unaware that he was returning with a group of warriors who had taken trophy heads. When she learned what she had done she was so disturbed that she grew sick and died. In British Columbia and other areas of North America which were inhabited by the hunting tribes, the taboo against contact with women before hunting or fighting was carefully observed. The Huichol of Mexico did so, and explained that a deer would never enter the snare of a man who was sleeping with his wife. It would simply look at the trap, snort "pooh, pooh" and go away. Throughout Africa continence and avoidance were observed before war and hunting. Women were forbidden to approach the Zulu army except (as in the case of cattle) for old women past the menopause, because such women "have become men."

The hunting taboo can be exaggerated to the extent that the Bangalas of equatorial Africa remain continent while they are making nets to capture wild pigs and the Melanesian of the Torres Straits refrain from intercourse during the mating season of turtles (an important food), in a curious defiance of the principles of mimetic magic.

Most extreme of all is the taboo which functions on the principle that since the name is a part of the individual, its use will affect his well-being. The Bantu women of Nyasaland do not speak their husband's names or any words that may be synonymous. A Warramunga woman of Australia may not mention the ordinary name of a man, which she knows, and in addition he has a secret name which she does not even know. Similarly the Hindus, whom we have continually cited as taboo ridden, do not allow a woman to mention her husband's name. She must speak of him as the "man of the house" or "father of the household" and if she dreams of his name this will result in his untimely death.

The tiny Bushmen, who are one of the oldest peoples and who support life by the simplest of hunting and gathering techniques, exemplify nearly all of the avoidances we have been discussing. Men and women sit on different sides of their crude shelters of woven twigs or grasses — if a man occupies a woman's place he will become impotent. When a man sets out to shoot an eland or a giraffe, he must avoid intercourse or the poison on his arrows will lose its power. A Bushman woman gives birth secretly in the bush. If a man inadvertently steps over the spot he will lose his ability to hunt.

A Bushman myth emphasizes the alienation of the two sexes almost in terms of their being different tribes. In the early times men and women lived apart, the former hunting animals exclusively, the latter pursuing a gathering existence. Five of the men, who were out hunting, being careless creatures, let their fire go out. The women, who were careful and orderly, always kept their fire going. The men, having killed a springbok, became desperate for means to cook it, so one of their number set out to get fire, crossed the river, and met one of the women gathering seeds. When he asked her for some fire, she invited him to the feminine camp. While he was there she said, "You are very hungry. Just wait until I pound up these seeds and I will boil them and give you some." She made him some porridge. After he had eaten it, he said, "Well, it's nice food so I shall just stay with you." The men who were left waited and wondered. They still had the springbok and they still had no fire. The second man set out, only to be tempted by female cooking, and to take up residence in the camp of the women. The same thing happened to the third man. The two men left were very frightened. They suspected something terrible had happened to their comrades. They cast the divining bones but the omens were favorable. The fourth man set out timidly, only to end by joining his comrades. The last man became very frightened indeed and besides by now the springbok had rotted. He took his bow and arrows and ran away.

On the other side of the world, among the Pueblo and Zuñi Indians, myths which tell of the emergence of their forefathers from the ground also divide the sexes into two camps, although in this case the women are portrayed as less efficient than the men in their attempts to reach the upper world. In these traditional stories such matters as sex and marriage are completely ignored, the sexes are viewed as groups living apart, a theme which may be a reflection of the periodic segregation of women.

The earliest types of religion at any rate codify male anxiety by proclaiming that women shall remain inactive for a considerable portion of their lives. The same religious sanctions prohibit them from participating in many human activities, partly excluding them from the human condition. And all the evidence points to the fact that this situation began with the simplest types of group association, in all probability as far back as the Paleolithic.

Despite these barriers of alienation and fear, the sex drive after all does insure reproduction. The act of procreation, however, arouses still another type of ambivalence which affects the status of women and substantiates the view that the conditions of man's development as a social being prevent him from ever taking eros for granted.

THE FOULER SEX: WOMEN'S BODIES IN ADVERTISING

EMILY TOTH

Emily Toth, born in New York City in 1944, was educated in comparative literature at Johns Hopkins and Swarthmore. Her specialties include American and British literature of the nineteenth and twentieth centuries, popular culture, and minority literature. She has taught at several universities, has edited the journal *Regionalism and the Female Imagination,* and is the author of *The Curse: A Cultural History of Menstruation* (with Janice Delaney and Mary Jane Lupton, 1976) and *Female Wits* (1979).

The preceding discussion by H. R. Hays delineated in sharp relief the common cultural image of woman's body as the harborer of strong magic and dangerous mysteries against which men must be ever vigilant. The contemporary American version of that idea is expressed in the theme of woman as dirty: Woman's body au naturel is dirty, smelly, repugnant, a state against which woman must be ever vigilant. Hence she must engage endlessly in the effort to un-dirty it: washing, shaving, deodorizing, rescenting, and so on. Toth documents the expression and exploitation of this theme in advertising.

Probably no one has ever called the Three Weird Sisters of *Macbeth* feminists. Their coven is hierarchical, ruled over by Hecate — not collective. Not sisterly, they torment another woman, a sailor's wife (a "rump-fed ronyon"), as well as the man, Macbeth. Nor are the Three Weird Sisters even especially "feminine" in appearance, for Banquo comments upon their beards.

Nevertheless, one of their first chants applies to the contemporary female condition as aptly as it did to the moral and meteorological climate of Macbeth's Scotland:

Fair is foul, and foul is fair.

Today, American culture tells us that women are the fairer sex — but only if they mask their natural foulness, according to advertising in American women's magazines.[1]

Of course, ads in general function to create wants: a sleek new car; a sexy cigarette; another essential electrical appliance. The psychology employed in advertising is usually the same. Advertisers use the appeals of newness; of competition (be the first on your block; buy the product at "better" or "leading" stores); and of conformity ("most good citizens...", "more women..."). Although the products and the words used may change to be more contemporary, the emotions appealed to are generally the same ones. Both hopes and fears are involved.

In any case, magazine advertisements involving women's appearance create wants from hopes and fears which are intended to be ever-changing, as an ad in *Advertising Age* boasts:

A paper delivered at the Popular Culture Association Convention, Indianapolis, Indiana, April 13, 1973; reprinted by permission of the author.

Magazines turned legs into a rainbow. Magazines convinced a gal she needed a flutter of fur where plain little eyelashes used to wink.

Magazines have the power to make a girl forget her waist exists. And the very next year, make her buy a belt for every dress she owns...

Magazines help distressed damsels remake their wardrobes, faces, hair, body. And sometimes their whole way of being.

And the ladies love it. And beg for more.

When she gets involved with herself and fashion, in any magazine, she's a captive cover to cover.[2]

Women's magazines are one of the primary vehicles for this "captivity." Over fifty million women buy a women's magazine every month. That figure is practically three-quarters of the entire adult female population.[3]

Within women's magazines, more than half the ads are directed toward women's appearance, including fashions, exercise, cosmetics, underwear, and the like. Those ads directly involving women's bodies are characterized by a particular and peculiar negativity. Their emphasis tends to be on the avoidance of demons (witches?): encroaching fat; dangerous signs of aging; and (especially) loathsome odors.

The pictures set impossible standards for a youthful figure and regular features (both of which are limited, naturally, by heredity), while suggesting ways in which readers may attempt to measure up. The ways are invariably painful: dieting or mechanical methods, such as constricting undergarments.

Of course, one product leads to another: Ammen's Medicated Powder is recommended for "a woman's special irritation problems. When the confinement of bras, girdles, sanitary napkins leads to perspiration, your natural skin defenses can break down. Then constant rubbing and chafing can bring on minor irritations." (*Ladies' Home Journal*, June, 1967, p. 18).[4] Imperfections mean chafing and confinement, which mean medicated powder. In any case, garments are expected to be uncomfortable: one manufacturer advertises the superiority of its girdle because it has "No cutting when you bend. No riding when you sit . . . Works so naturally you'll forget it's on." (*Mademoiselle*, June, 1967, p. 32).

If a woman manages to bind her hips and waist into shape, she still has to make sure her breasts are up to standard. If they are small, she may want to wear The Fibber, for "If Nature didn't, Warner's will." (*Mademoiselle*, June 1968, p. 11). Or, for the more adventurous, there is Beauti-Breast, a "hydrodynamic contour cup" (*Cosmopolitan*, January, 1973, p. 71). The apparatus, which looks vaguely like a cup-shaped medieval torturing device for the breasts, should be used for fifteen minutes a day, "less time than it takes you to make up your face." The rewards are great, for M. S. of Baldwin Park writes:

Three children and six years of marriage took its toll from my bustline. After just one treatment, and only 1", my husband began to notice me again.

Hence it appears that if a woman can hide or otherwise manipulate her natural body, she may become a success. Like M. S., she may attract a man. In advertising involving women's bodies, unsuccessful women are pictured alone. A successful woman may be pictured with a man, who is invariably taller and usually darker than she. Most frequently, he is shown hovering behind the woman, who looks down demurely. He is her reward for being the fairest one of all.

Historically, disparagement of the female body is nothing new. The early Church Fathers, especially Tertullian, inveighed against women's fair beauty as a foul snare. Curls, especially, were a sign of lasciviousness. The author of *The Ayenbite of Inwit* (The Prick of Conscience, c. 1340) said that if a man had the eyes of a lynx, he would see that a fair body is no more than a white sack full of stinking dung, like a dunghill covered with snow.[5]

Although he criticized "fairing the foul with art's false borrow'd face" (Sonnet 127), Shakespeare seemed aware of bad breath as a problem:

And in some perfumes is there more delight
Than in the breath that from my mistress reeks.
(Sonnet 130)

Jonathan Swift criticized the stench of Mopsa's breath and of Hircina's armpits in *The Journal of a Modern Lady*, and seemed to praise Chloe with irony:

Such cleanliness from head to heel:
No humours gross, or frowzy steams,
No noisome whiffs, or sweaty streams,
Before, behind, above, below,
Could from her taintless body flow.[6]

Arthur Schopenhauer described women as "that undersized, narrow-shouldered, broad-hipped and short-legged race."[7] In William Faulkner's *Sound and the Fury*, Quentin Compson's father sees no beauty in women's bodily functions, for he defines the female as "Equilibrium of periodical filth between two moons balanced."[8]

Given these cultural views of themselves, it would be surprising if women did not absorb a dislike for their own bodily processes.

Women do learn to hate and fear their bodies: Germaine Greer writes of her menstruation as "revolting labours" and her fear that someone might *"smell* it." [9]

Advertising feeds on dislike, anxiety, fear, loathing, disgrace concerning women's bodies. This is especially true in ads involving menstruation, douching, and "feminine hygiene" sprays — the foci of this paper.

These ads are often evidence of what Jo Foxworth calls a national neurosis: "Deodorantus — Detergentitis — Anti-septiosis." [10] Menstruation, known in private life as The Curse, used to be elegantly unmentionable in ads: "Modess — Because." Now it is "that time of the month"; "those difficult days"; "those special days." The word *special,* in particular, is double-edged, suggesting not only "noteworthy," but also "problematic." Quest deodorant advertisers report that "Every woman must constantly face the special *feminine* problem of odor caused by body secretions and perspiration ... It's the special deodorant for a woman's special needs." (*Mademoiselle,* June, 1967, p. 158). *Special,* then, seems to denote difficulty rather than pride in being a woman.

Further, women are expected to feel they cannot talk directly about their periods. Unless they use Tampax, they may be forced into embarrassed excuses:

Tampax Tampons. So you won't have to make excuses. You're free to enjoy the magical water world. Anytime. No need to make excuses. Like "I have this bad cold." Or "I have this awful hangnail."

(*Mademoiselle,* June, 1971, p. 34)

Equally hush-hush is what to do with used menstrual paraphernalia. "Now — one more thing *not* to worry about ... that little discussed disposal problem. Now — neat, discreet, disposal bags come in each box of new Scott Confidets." (*Mademoiselle,* June, 1967, p. 50).[11]

Those ads which promote their products with a more positive tone tend to stress psychology over technology. For instance, the word *absorbent* appears far less frequently than the terms *secure, confident,* and *free.* Sometimes advertisers seem to suffer from a poverty of vocabulary:

The way you feel is free. Today and everyday, you feel free, confident, unhampered. Tampax tampons worn internally, make this possible. Keep you feeling cool and comfortably confident, in or out of the water ... for total freedom, total comfort ... Tampax.

(*McCall's,* June, 1967, p. 29)

Other "feminine hygiene" products, such as sprays and douches, also stress security and assurance on "nervous, unsure occasions," but almost uniformly refuse to show what the product is really for. Although one would not expect a picture of female genitals, one often does not even see a picture of a female. Instead, the ads show the packaged product. Cupid's Quiver (the first "gyna-cosmetic") appears in different, brightly-colored packages, according to the fragrance of the douching substance therein (*Ladies' Home Journal,* June, 1970, p. 132). A Massengill package appears with a "Freedom Now" button next to it (*Mademoiselle,* June, 1970, p. 86). When women *are* shown, rarely are they looking at anything in particular, except sometimes at themselves, in the mirror — for narcissism is encouraged by ads about women's bodies.

Women are *not* encouraged, however, to see or to think about any topics involving their natural odors. Norforms are advertised as superior to the "awkward and unsightly" douching apparatus, kept in its "hiding place." (*Mademoiselle,* June, 1968, p. 145). Norforms even offers its free information booklet "in a plain wrapper."

Women are supposed to be embarrassed at the mention of their natural smells. One of the first ads for Feminique trumpets: "Five years ago most women would have been too embarrassed to read this page," for it is about "a product that would have made your grandmother faint and your mother blush. All it should do to you is make you happy . . . Because now that 'The Pill' has freed you from worry, 'The Spray' will help make all that freedom worthwhile." (*Mademoiselle,* June, 1969, p. 31).

What will the spray do to make the freedom worthwhile? The ad doesn't say, but Jerry Della Femina (who brought out the commercials and named the spray after himself) told Judith Ramsey: "The sprays are a *psychological* product . . . Think of the women who are now going at sex with gusto and confidence. If there were a Nobel Peace Prize for more and better orgasms, I think I would qualify." [12]

The ads for non-menstrual vaginal products clearly do appeal to a certain kind of psychological need. Unlike napkins and tampons, sprays and douches are less clearly needed — blood, after all, is tangible, odors are not. Hence the need must be created — through negative-avoidance methods. Here euphemistic language comes into play.

One verbal device often used is *occupatio,* originally a medieval rhetorical figure. *Occupatio* is the mentioning of details under the guise of denying or omitting them: in effect, throwaway lines. For example, a Norforms ad suggests the drawbacks to douching: it is a nuisance, "unsightly," malodorous, and so forth. "Besides, your doctor may tell you not to douche every day." (*Mademoiselle,* June, 1968, p. 145). Under the guise of criticizing douching, the ad in fact implies that one must cleanse oneself internally every day — a need not established before.

Ads seek to serve, then, as definers for women's needs. The same advertisement defines "hygiene" as a smell problem, rather than a health problem: "As every married woman knows, embarrassing feminine odor that begins in the vaginal tract is a hygiene problem. You'd like to feel fresh, clean, and secure . . . but it's not always easy."

In addition to redefining words, vaginal spray ads (like menstrual ads) define — by their appeal — what they believe a woman to be. Although these "female problems" appear when one becomes a woman, manufacturers nearly always address themselves to "girls." Fittingly, then, their language is coy and stresses helplessness.

"The trickiest deodorant problem a girl has," according to Pristeen, *"isn't* under her pretty little arms." The *real* problem is "how to keep the most girl part of you" odor-free. (*Mademoiselle,* June, 1969, p. 45). Kotex tampons keep women "little-girl free" and "little-girl comfortable," for there is "nothing hard" about their insertion (*Mademoiselle,* June, 1967, p. 79). Not only are women thought to be little, vulnerable, and somewhat incompetent girls, but they are also addressed in cute rather than adult language: products try to take care of "bothersome," "troublesome," "worrisome" odors.

Sociolinguists have long noted that women use apologetic speech patterns more frequently than do men; that women interrupt themselves more often, and use more qualifying adjectives and interjections. Certainly this use of language is conditioned, and part of the conditioning may come from ads: *"Oh,* we didn't change it" (Massengill — *Mademoiselle,* June, 1968, p. 64); "Thank goodness!" and "What a relief!" (Norforms — *Mademoiselle,* June, 1970, p. 52). Jeneen exhorts women to get rid of "guess-how-much measuring" and avoid "mess and fuss." (*Ladies' Home Journal,* June, 1968, p. 32). Many ads have coy rhetorical questions in the copy, such as, "You like freedom, don't you?" (Massengill — *Mademoiselle,* June, 1970, p. 86) and "Wasn't that much easier than douching?" (Norforms — *Mademoiselle,* June, 1970, p. 52). Most ads have very short sentences.

Certainly, all advertising aims at a quick, clear message. But the language used in women's advertising would not be used in men's. Men are men, not boys; when black men are addressed as "boy," there is a similar disparagement as that involved in addressing adult women as "little girls." Men are expected to be self-confident and reliant, whereas American culture suggests that women are helpless, dependent, and somewhat scatter-brained.[13] Advertising both reports on and promotes this image.

The child-woman does, of course, get rewards. As in most other arenas of woman's life, she is pictured as happiest when she achieves male approval. "Be the woman your husband deserves" if you douche with Demure (*Ladies' Home Journal,* June, 1967, p. 120). You should "Be his. Be home. Be hard to forget. But be sure. Sure as Kotex napkins." (*Mademoiselle,* June, 1970, p. 99). Fresh "remembers you're a girl — somebody's girl." (*Mademoiselle,* June, 1971, p. 79). Both Feminique spray and Demure douche report that every husband wants his wife to be "feminine, in every sense of the word." (*Mademoiselle,* June, 1970).

The definition, then, of femininity and of womanhood means hiding what one smells like naturally in the "most girl part of you." Femininity is not the same as being female, moreover: femininity is a creation of artifice, not of nature. For "You don't sleep with teddy bears anymore . . . Your teddy bear loved you no matter what." [14] Your husband, however, is expected to be more discriminating. Pristeen "helps you feel completely, happily feminine," free from the odors "from every woman's natural body functions" (*Mademoiselle,* June, 1970, p. 43). Demure advertisements tell us that "The world's costliest perfumes are worthless — unless you're sure of your own natural fragrance." (*McCall's,* December, 1972, p. 133).

Ultimately it is unclear what is meant by either "femininity" or "natural," since using an artificial product like Demure, or like Koromex douche powder makes one "Totally feminine . . . It helps restore and maintain your normal physiological balance, naturally." (*Mademoiselle,* June, 1971, p. 38).

Just as definitions for words are not clear-cut, ads can also foster hostility and confusion between women, in that they promote conflicting messages. Both competition and conformity are invited — a paradoxical combination that perhaps makes sense only to one who can be foul and fair at the same time. The competition is often between generations of women. The Pristeen ad (see p. 5) reports that the modern woman is ahead of her grandmother who would faint, her mother who would blush; Modess announces that "Maybe you could sit down with your mother and teach her a few things." (*Mademoiselle,* September, 1969, p. 90). For douching, "Massengill tells it like your mother probably didn't." (*McCall's,* June, 1970, p. 20).

However, a woman can teach her mother only what she herself knows, so she must conform: "Could you be the last woman to be using just *one* deodorant? Don't be. Find out about FDS, the *other* deodorant" (*McCall's,* July, 1969, p. 53). Conformity is also stressed in the emphasis on quantity: "Millions of modern women" use Tampax (*Mademoiselle,* June, 1968, p. 70); "More women use Bidette every day" (*McCall's,* June, 1970, p. 135); "Massengill is used by more women" (*Mademoiselle,* June, 1968, p. 64).

Over a five-year period, from June 1967 through January 1973, advertising for intimate female products has changed, perhaps because of the "Sexual Revolution." Although Norforms and Demure ads have remained remarkably the same, the language in others has become much more explicit. Rather than vague euphemisms about not feeling "fresh" and "secure," many ads use an open language like that of Massengill douche: "After intercourse, it's a good vaginal cleanser . . . a good way to wash secretions or contraceptive creams or jellies out of your vagina." Yet the ad still concludes: "Clean is fresh." (*Glamour,* January, 1973, p. 25).

Another change is that ads for tampons now say "young girls" more frequently than "unmarried girls"; some even mention "virginity." Hence a young woman learning to use a tampon now would not have the difficulties encountered by Julie, the protagonist in Lois Gould's *Such Good Friends.* Julie's two friends teach her to use a tampon in the school lavatory, but Julie is confused about the instruction sheet.

> It says about unmarried girls, that's all — that it's safe for unmarried girls. They don't even *mention* the word hymen. Maybe it's designed not to go in if you're a virgin.[15]

Also, within the last few years, other new products besides vaginal sprays have been invented. Tassaway is a small, soft cup used to collect menstrual blood. Its ads are factual and appeal to the intelligence, using the terms "uterus" and "menses." According to Tassaway advertising, menstrual odor is caused by oxidation; Tassaway is more absorbent and more economical. (*McCall's,* October, 1970, R-10). Whereas other ads say there's "nothing hard" about insertion, Tassaway is more positive and less authoritative, quoting a satisfied customer: "Once you get the 'feel' of it you can't go wrong." Tassaway ads also say "women" rather than "little" or "girls"; the ads' sentence structures are longer and more complex. The Tassaway ad shows a respect for women's minds, and points to a direction in which ads for *necessary* products might go.

The medical necessity for vaginal sprays and douches has not, of course, been shown. They may, in fact, be disappearing cultural artifacts, for many health questions have been raised about them. Until recently, most contained hexachlorophene; they are also responsible for a great increase in the number of cases of vulvitis.[16] They may, however, have other uses which advertisers do not mention:

> Oven cleaner or vaginal deodorant sprayed direct in the eyes will blind an attacker.[17]

Further, the use of vaginal deodorants may have changed the nature of falling in love. According to Desmond Morris in *The Naked Ape,* falling in love is a kind of "olfactory imprinting"; in the sexual encounters of lower animals, the male sniffs the female more than she sniffs him. In humans, pubic hair and armpit-hair are the major scent-traps — and American women are urged to spray the one and shave the other. Odor-removal, then, can be viewed as a form of sexual control.[18]

The ads do, in any case, stress containment and control of a woman's natural body. One must "put on a happy face" despite those "special days" — in addition to painting, girdling, padding, and otherwise changing what has been divinely ordained.

The Three Weird Sisters in *Macbeth* are fortunate in that they are allowed to be themselves, beards and all. Further, *they* are the advertisers: they tell Macbeth what his future is to be. Perhaps there is a lesson in *Macbeth:* if women control the media, they will be able to define for themselves how they want their bodies to be; they will be able to say what is fair and what is foul.

Notes

1. I surveyed ads in *Mademoiselle, McCall's,* and *Ladies' Home Journal* over a five-year period, from June, 1967, through January, 1973. I also glanced at other women's magazines from time to time. With the three studied, I concentrated on the June issues, reasoning that stress on women's bodies would be greatest at the start of the summer. This time span is also significant in that feminine hygiene sprays were introduced within this time period.

2. Alice Embree, "Media Images I: Madison Avenue Brainwashing — The Facts," in *Sisterhood Is Powerful,* ed. Robin Morgan (New York: Vintage, 1970), p. 186.

3. Embree, p. 187.

4. Most of the ads cited ran for at least a year in all of the magazines studied. Some, like Demure douche solution, were virtually unchanged for several years. For each ad, I cite one place where it may be found, but there are many others.

5. Katherine M. Rogers, *The Troublesome Helpmate: A History of Misogyny* (Seattle: University of Washington, 1966), p. 69. *The Ayenbite of Inwit* is one of the few works suggesting improvement on the male anatomy: lynxes were thought to be able to see the insides as well as the outsides of objects. But the improvement in male anatomy would be for utility, not for beauty.

6. Cited in Rogers, 170–171.

7. Quoted in Una Stannard, "The Mask of Beauty," in *Woman in Sexist Society,* eds. Vivian Gornick and Barbara Moran (New York: Basic Books, 1971), p. 123.

8. William Faulkner, *The Sound and the Fury* (New York: Random House, 1946), p. 115.

9. Germaine Greer, *The Female Eunuch* (New York: McGraw-Hill, 1970), p. 41.

10. Jo Foxworth, "Madison Avenue Finds Foe in Crusade Against Germs," *Advertising Age* (October 6, 1969), p. 82.

11. Sasha, the protagonist in Alix Kates Shulman's *Memoirs of an Ex-Prom Queen* (New York: Knopf, 1972), brags that "At home and at school my Kotex disposal was down to an art." (67)

12. Judith Ramsey, "Those Vaginal Deodorants," *Ms.* (November, 1972), p. 32. Della Femina made a similar speech to Nora Ephron for *Esquire* ("Dealing with the, uh, Problem" — March, 1973). Della Femina told Ephron: "Somewhere out there, there is a girl who might be hung up about herself, and one day she goes out and buys Feminique and shoots up with it, and she comes home and that one night she feels more confident and she jumps her husband and for the first time in her life she has an orgasm. If I can feel I was responsible for one more orgasm in the world I feel I deserve the Nobel Peace Prize." (91)

13. There are male genital area sprays, such as Pub Below the Belt. But their ads are much rarer, and their sales are only 5% of those of vaginal sprays (Ephron, 186).

14. Demure ad, cited in Foxworth, 82.

15. Lois Gould, *Such Good Friends* (New York: Dell, 1970), p. 109.

16. The most significant lay report on the safety of vaginal products is "Should Genital Deodorants Be Used?" in *Consumer Reports* (January, 1972), pp. 39–41. It is summarized in Ramsey and Ephron, and in a pamphlet published by the St. Louis Organization for Women's Rights, entitled "Everything You Should Have Known about Female Hygiene Deodorants . . . and that the manufacturers were afraid you'd ask."

17. Robin Morgan, "News," in *Monster* (New York: Vintage, 1972), p. 67.

18. Desmond Morris, *The Naked Ape* (New York: Dell, 1967), pp. 64, 73.

SOPHY, OR WOMAN

JEAN-JACQUES ROUSSEAU

In histories of Western thought, Jean Jacques Rousseau (1712–1778) is generally grouped among the members of the French Enlightenment. He is noted as one of the foremost proponents of individual freedom and political rights. His most famous work, *The Social Contract* (1762), opens with the ringing phrase, "Man was born free, but is everywhere in bondage." That work and all his others proceed to investigate the sources of this bondage and to seek remedy.

Emile (1762) is Rousseau's theory of education, in which Emile and Sophy, prototype male and female, are followed from childhood into young adulthood as models of the properly educated. The emphasis in Emile's life is on freedom of intellectual and emotional expression, untrammeled though assisted development, rather than authoritarianism. But Sophy meets a different fate; women, who are created for the needs of men, "must be trained to bear the yoke from the first, so that they may not feel it, to master their own caprices and to submit themselves to the will of others."

From reading Rousseau we learn an important lesson: It is a measure of the extent and pervasiveness of sexism in our culture, and in the history of ideas, that Rousseau's happy acceptance of the enslavement of more than half of the human race does not interfere with his reputation as champion of human liberty, except among feminists.

But for her sex, a woman is a man; she has the same organs, the same needs, the same faculties. The machine is the same in its construction; its parts, its working, and its appearance are similar. Regard it as you will the difference is only in degree.

Yet where sex is concerned man and woman are unlike; each is the complement of the other; the difficulty in comparing them lies in our inability to decide, in either case, what is a matter of sex, and what is not. General differences present themselves to the comparative anatomist and even to the superficial observer; they seem not to be a matter of sex; yet they are really sex differences, though the connection eludes our observation. How far such differences may extend we cannot tell; all we know for certain is that where man and woman are alike we have to do with the characteristics of the species; where they are unlike, we have to do with the characteristics of sex. Considered from these two standpoints, we find so many instances of likeness and unlikeness that it is perhaps one of the greatest of marvels how nature has contrived to make two beings so like and yet so different.

These resemblances and differences must have an influence on the moral nature; this inference is obvious, and it is confirmed by experience; it shows the vanity of the disputes as to the superiority or the equality of the sexes; as if each sex, pursuing the path marked out for it by nature, were not more perfect in that very divergence than if it more closely resembled the other. A perfect man and a perfect woman should no more be alike in mind than in face, and perfection admits of neither less nor more.

In the union of the sexes each alike con-

From *Emile,* by Jean-Jacques Rousseau, translated by Barbara Foxley. An Everyman's Library Edition. Published in the United States by E. P. Dutton and in Canada by J. M. Dent, and reprinted with their permission.

tributes to the common end, but in different ways. From this diversity springs the first difference which may be observed between man and woman in their moral relations. The man should be strong and active; the woman should be weak and passive; the one must have both the power and the will; it is enough that the other should offer little resistance.

When this principle is admitted, it follows that woman is specially made for man's delight. If man in his turn ought to be pleasing in her eyes, the necessity is less urgent, his virtue is in his strength, he pleases because he is strong. I grant you this is not the law of love, but it is the law of nature, which is older than love itself.

If woman is made to please and to be in subjection to man, she ought to make herself pleasing in his eyes and not provoke him to anger; her strength is in her charms, by their means she should compel him to discover and use his strength. The surest way of arousing this strength is to make it necessary by resistance. Thus pride comes to the help of desire and each exults in the other's victory. This is the origin of attack and defence, of the boldness of one sex and the timidity of the other, and even of the shame and modesty with which nature has armed the weak for the conquest of the strong.

Who can possibly suppose that nature has prescribed the same advances to the one sex as to the other, or that the first to feel desire should be the first to show it? What strange depravity of judgment! The consequences of the act being so different for the two sexes, is it natural that they should enter upon it with equal boldness? How can any one fail to see that when the share of each is so unequal, if the one were not controlled by modesty as the other is controlled by nature, the result would be the destruction of both, and the human race

would perish through the very means ordained for its continuance?

Women so easily stir a man's senses and fan the ashes of a dying passion, that if philosophy ever succeeded in introducing this custom into any unlucky country, especially if it were a warm country where more women are born than men, the men, tyrannised over by the women, would at last become their victims, and would be dragged to their death without the least chance of escape.

Female animals are without this sense of shame, but what of that? Are their desires as boundless as those of women, which are curbed by this shame? The desires of the animals are the result of necessity, and when the need is satisfied, the desire ceases; they no longer make a feint of repulsing the male, they do it in earnest. Their seasons of complaisance are short and soon over. Impulse and restraint are alike the work of nature. But what would take the place of this negative instinct in women if you rob them of their modesty?

Emile

The Most High has deigned to do honour to mankind; he has endowed man with boundless passions, together with a law to guide them, so that man may be alike free and self-controlled; though swayed by these passions man is endowed with reason by which to control them. Woman is also endowed with boundless passions; God has given her modesty to restrain them. Moreover, he has given to both a present reward for the right use of their powers, in the delight which springs from that right use of them, *i.e.,* the taste for right conduct established as the law of our behaviour. To my mind this is far higher than the instinct of the beasts.

Whether the woman shares the man's

passion or not, whether she is willing or unwilling to satisfy it, she always repulses him and defends herself, though not always with the same vigour, and therefore not always with the same success. If the siege is to be successful, the besieged must permit or direct the attack. How skilfully can she stimulate the efforts of the aggressor. The freest and most delightful of activities does not permit of any real violence; reason and nature are alike against it; nature, in that she has given the weaker party strength enough to resist if she chooses; reason, in that actual violence is not only most brutal in itself, but it defeats its own ends, not only because the man thus declares war against his companion and thus gives her a right to defend her person and her liberty even at the cost of the enemy's life, but also because the woman alone is the judge of her condition, and a child would have no father if any man might usurp a father's rights.

Thus the different constitution of the two sexes leads us to a third conclusion, that the stronger party seems to be master, but is as a matter of fact dependent on the weaker, and that, not by any foolish custom of gallantry, nor yet by the magnanimity of the protector, but by an inexorable law of nature. For nature has endowed woman with a power of stimulating man's passions in excess of man's power of satisfying those passions, and has thus made him dependent on her goodwill, and compelled him in his turn to endeavour to please her, so that she may be willing to yield to his superior strength. Is it weakness which yields to force, or is it voluntary self-surrender? This uncertainty constitutes the chief charm of the man's victory, and the woman is usually cunning enough to leave him in doubt. In this respect the woman's mind exactly resembles her body; far from being ashamed of her weakness, she is proud of it; her soft muscles offer no resistance, she professes

that she cannot lift the lightest weight; she would be ashamed to be strong. And why? Not only to gain an appearance of refinement; she is too clever for that; she is providing herself beforehand with excuses, with the right to be weak if she chooses. . . .

The consequences of sex are wholly unlike for man and woman. The male is only a male now and again, the female is always a female, or at least all her youth; everything reminds her of her sex; the performance of her functions requires a special constitution. She needs care during pregnancy and freedom from work when her child is born; she must have a quiet, easy life while she nurses her children; their education calls for patience and gentleness, for a zeal and love which nothing can dismay; she forms a bond between father and child, she alone can win the father's love for his children and convince him that they are indeed his own. What loving care is required to preserve a united family! And there should be no question of virtue in all this, it must be a labour of love, without which the human race would be doomed to extinction.

The mutual duties of the two sexes are not, and cannot be, equally binding on both. Women do wrong to complain of the inequality of man-made laws; this inequality is not man's making, or at any rate it is not the result of mere prejudice, but of reason. She to whom nature has entrusted the care of the children must hold herself responsible for them to their father. No doubt every breach of faith is wrong, and every faithless husband, who robs his wife of the sole reward of the stern duties of her sex, is cruel and unjust; but the faithless wife is worse; she destroys the family and breaks the bonds of nature; when she gives her husband children who are not his own, she is false both to him and them, her crime is not infidelity but treason. To my mind, it is the source of dissension and of crime of every kind. Can any position be more wretched than that of the unhappy father who, when he clasps his child to his breast, is haunted by the suspicion that this is the child of another, the badge of his own dishonour, a thief who is robbing his own children of their inheritance. Under such circumstances the family is little more than a group of secret enemies, armed against each other by a guilty woman, who compels them to pretend to love one another.

Thus it is not enough that a wife should be faithful; her husband, along with his friends and neighbours, must believe in her fidelity; she must be modest, devoted, retiring; she should have the witness not only of a good conscience, but of a good reputation. In a word, if a father must love his children, he must be able to respect their mother. For these reasons it is not enough that the woman should be chaste, she must preserve her reputation and her good name. From these principles there arises not only a moral difference between the sexes, but also a fresh motive for duty and propriety, which prescribes to women in particular the most scrupulous attention to their conduct, their manners, their behaviour. Vague assertions as to the equality of the sexes and the similarity of their duties are only empty words; they are no answer to my argument.

It is a poor sort of logic to quote isolated exceptions against laws so firmly established. Women, you say, are not always bearing children. Granted; yet that is their proper business. Because there are a hundred or so of large towns in the world where women live licentiously and have few children, will you maintain that it is their business to have few children? And what would become of your towns if the remote country districts, with their simpler and purer women, did not make up for the barrenness of your fine ladies? There are plenty of country places where women with only four

or five children are reckoned unfruitful. In conclusion, although here and there a woman may have few children,* what difference does it make? Is it any the less a woman's business to be a mother? And do not the general laws of nature and morality make provision for this state of things?

Even if there were these long intervals, which you assume, between the periods of pregnancy, can a woman suddenly change her way of life without danger? Can she be a nursing mother to-day and a soldier to-morrow? Will she change her tastes and her feelings as a chameleon changes his colour? Will she pass at once from the privacy of household duties and indoor occupations to the buffeting of the winds, the toils, the labours, the perils of war? . . .

To cultivate the masculine virtues in women and to neglect their own is evidently to do them an injury. Women are too clear-sighted to be thus deceived; when they try to usurp our privileges they do not abandon their own; with this result: they are unable to make use of two incompatible things, so they fall below their own level as women, instead of rising to the level of men. If you are a sensible mother you will take my advice. Do not try to make your daughter a good man in defiance of nature. Make her a good woman, and be sure it will be better both for her and us.

Does this mean that she must be brought up in ignorance and kept to housework only? Is she to be man's handmaid or his helpmeet? Will he dispense with her greatest charm, her companionship? To keep her a slave will he prevent her knowing and feel-

---

* Without this the race would necessarily diminish; all things considered, for its preservation each woman ought to have about four children, for about half the children born die before they can become parents, and two must survive to replace the father and mother. See whether the towns will supply them?

ing? Will he make an automaton of her? No, indeed, that is not the teaching of nature, who has given women such a pleasant easy wit. On the contrary, nature means them to think, to will, to love, to cultivate their minds as well as their persons; she puts these weapons in their hands to make up for their lack of strength and to enable them to direct the strength of men. They should learn many things, but only such things as are suitable.

When I consider the special purpose of woman, when I observe her inclinations or reckon up her duties, everything combines to indicate the mode of education she requires. Men and women are made for each other, but their mutual dependence differs in degree; man is dependent on woman through his desires; woman is dependent on man through her desires and also through her needs; he could do without her better than she can do without him. She cannot fulfill her purpose in life without his aid, without his goodwill, without his respect; she is dependent on our feelings, on the price we put upon her virtue, and the opinion we have of her charms and her deserts. Nature herself has decreed that woman, both for herself and her children, should be at the mercy of man's judgment.

Worth alone will not suffice, a woman must be thought worthy; nor beauty, she must be admired; nor virtue, she must be respected. A woman's honour does not depend on her conduct alone, but on her reputation, and no woman who permits herself to be considered vile is really virtuous. A man has no one but himself to consider, and so long as he does right he may defy public opinion; but when a woman does right her task is only half finished, and what people think of her matters as much as what she really is. Hence her education must, in this respect, be different from man's education. "What will people think" is the grave of a

man's virtue and the throne of a woman's.

The children's health depends in the first place on the mother's, and the early education of man is also in a woman's hands; his morals, his passions, his tastes, his pleasures, his happiness itself, depend on her. A woman's education must therefore be planned in relation to man. To be pleasing in his sight, to win his respect and love, to train him in childhood, to tend him in manhood, to counsel and console, to make his life pleasant and happy, these are the duties of woman for all time, and this is what she should be taught while she is young. The further we depart from this principle, the further we shall be from our goal, and all our precepts will fail to secure her happiness or our own. . . .

Even the tiniest little girls love finery; they are not content to be pretty, they must be admired; their little airs and graces show that their heads are full of this idea, and as soon as they can understand they are controlled by "What will people think of you?" If you are foolish enough to try this way with little boys, it will not have the same effect; give them their freedom and their sports, and they care very little what people think; it is a work of time to bring them under the control of this law.

However acquired, this early education of little girls is an excellent thing in itself. As the birth of the body must precede the birth of the mind, so the training of the body must precede the cultivation of the mind. This is true of both sexes; but the aim of physical training for boys and girls is not the same; in the one case it is the development of strength, in the other of grace; not that these qualities should be peculiar to either sex, but that their relative values should be different. Women should be strong enough to do anything gracefully; men should be skilful enough to do anything easily.

The exaggeration of feminine delicacy leads to effeminacy in men. Women should not be strong like men but for them, so that their sons may be strong. Convents and boarding-schools, with their plain food and ample opportunities for amusements, races, and games in the open air and in the garden, are better in this respect than the home, where the little girl is fed on delicacies, continually encouraged or reproved, where she is kept sitting in a stuffy room, always under her mother's eye, afraid to stand or walk or speak or breathe, without a moment's freedom to play or jump or run or shout, or to be her natural, lively, little self; there is either harmful indulgence or misguided severity, and no trace of reason. In this fashion heart and body are alike destroyed. . . .

Boys and girls have many games in common, and this is as it should be; do they not play together when they are grown up? They have also special tastes of their own. Boys want movement and noise, drums, tops, toy-carts; girls prefer things which appeal to the eye, and can be used for dressing-up — mirrors, jewellery, finery, and specially dolls. The doll is the girl's special plaything; this shows her instinctive bent towards her life's work. The art of pleasing finds its physical basis in personal adornment, and this physical side of the art is the only one which the child can cultivate.

Here is a little girl busy all day with her doll; she is always changing its clothes, dressing and undressing it, trying new combinations of trimmings well or ill matched; her fingers are clumsy, her taste is crude, but there is no mistaking her bent; in this endless occupation time flies unheeded, the hours slip away unnoticed, even meals are forgotten. She is more eager for adornment than for food. "But she is dressing her doll, not herself," you will say. Just so; she sees her doll, she cannot see herself; she cannot

do anything for herself, she has neither the training, nor the talent, nor the strength; as yet she herself is nothing, she is engrossed in her doll and all her coquetry is devoted to it. This will not always be so; in due time she will be her own doll.

We have here a very early and clearly-marked bent; you have only to follow it and train it. What the little girl most clearly desires is to dress her doll, to make its bows, its tippets, its sashes, and its tuckers; she is dependent on other people's kindness in all this, and it would be much pleasanter to be able to do it herself. Here is a motive for her earliest lessons, they are not tasks prescribed, but favours bestowed. Little girls always dislike learning to read and write, but they are always ready to learn to sew. They think they are grown up, and in imagination they are using their knowledge for their own adornment. . . .

Show the sense of the tasks you set your little girls, but keep them busy. Idleness and insubordination are two very dangerous faults, and very hard to cure when once established. Girls should be attentive and industrious, but this is not enough by itself; they should early be accustomed to restraint. This misfortune, if such it be, is inherent in their sex, and they will never escape from it, unless to endure more cruel sufferings. All their life long, they will have to submit to the strictest and most enduring restraints, those of propriety. They must be trained to bear the yoke from the first, so that they may not feel it, to master their own caprices and to submit themselves to the will of others. If they were always eager to be at work, they should sometimes be compelled to do nothing. Their childish faults, unchecked and unheeded, may easily lead to dissipation, frivolity, and inconstancy. To guard against this, teach them above all things self-control. Under our senseless conditions, the life of a good woman is a perpetual struggle against self; it is only fair that woman should bear her share of the ills she has brought upon man.

Beware lest your girls become weary of their tasks and infatuated with their amusements; this often happens under our ordinary methods of education, where, as Fénelon says, all the tedium is on one side and all the pleasure on the other. If the rules already laid down are followed, the first of these dangers will be avoided, unless the child dislikes those about her. A little girl who is fond of her mother or her friend will work by her side all day without getting tired; the chatter alone will make up for any loss of liberty. But if her companion is distasteful to her, everything done under her direction will be distasteful too. Children who take no delight in their mother's company are not likely to turn out well; but to judge of their real feelings you must watch them and not trust to their words alone, for they are flatterers and deceitful and soon learn to conceal their thoughts. Neither should they be told that they ought to love their mother. Affection is not the result of duty, and in this respect constraint is out of place. Continual intercourse, constant care, habit itself, all these will lead a child to love her mother, if the mother does nothing to deserve the child's ill-will. The very control she exercises over the child, if well directed, will increase rather than diminish the affection, for women being made for dependence, girls feel themselves made to obey.

Just because they have, or ought to have, little freedom, they are apt to indulge themselves too fully with regard to such freedom as they have; they carry everything to extremes, and they devote themselves to their games with an enthusiasm even greater than that of boys. This is the second difficulty to which I referred. This enthusiasm must be kept in check, for it is the source of several vices commonly found among women, ca-

price and that extravagant admiration which leads a woman to regard a thing with rapture to-day and to be quite indifferent to it to-morrow. This fickleness of taste is as dangerous as exaggeration; and both spring from the same cause. Do not deprive them of mirth, laughter, noise, and romping games, but do not let them tire of one game and go off to another; do not leave them for a moment without restraint. Train them to break off their games and return to their other occupations without a murmur. Habit is all that is needed, as you have nature on your side.

This habitual restraint produces a docility which woman requires all her life long, for she will always be in subjection to a man, or to man's judgment, and she will never be free to set her own opinion above his. What is most wanted in a woman is gentleness; formed to obey a creature so imperfect as man, a creature often vicious and always faulty, she should early learn to submit to injustice and to suffer the wrongs inflicted on her by her husband without complaint; she must be gentle for her own sake, not his. Bitterness and obstinacy only multiply the sufferings of the wife and the misdeeds of the husband; the man feels that these are not the weapons to be used against him. Heaven did not make women attractive and persuasive that they might degenerate into bitterness, or meek that they should desire the mastery; their soft voice was not meant for hard words, nor their delicate features for the frowns of anger. When they lose their temper they forget themselves; often enough they have just cause of complaint; but when they scold they always put themselves in the wrong. We should each adopt the tone which befits our sex; a soft-hearted husband may make an overbearing wife, but a man, unless he is a perfect monster, will sooner or later yield to his wife's gentleness, and the victory will be hers.

Daughters must always be obedient, but mothers need not always be harsh. To make a girl docile you need not make her miserable; to make her modest you need not terrify her; on the contrary, I should not be sorry to see her allowed occasionally to exercise a little ingenuity, not to escape punishment for her disobedience, but to evade the necessity for obedience. Her dependence need not be made unpleasant, it is enough that she should realise that she is dependent. Cunning is a natural gift of woman, and so convinced am I that all our natural inclinations are right, that I would cultivate this among others, only guarding against its abuse. . . .

What is, is good, and no general law can be bad. This special skill with which the female sex is endowed is a fair equivalent for its lack of strength; without it woman would be man's slave, not his helpmeet. By her superiority in this respect she maintains her equality with man, and rules in obedience. She has everything against her, our faults and her own weakness and timidity; her beauty and her wiles are all that she has. Should she not cultivate both? Yet beauty is not universal; it may be destroyed by all sorts of accidents, it will disappear with years, and habit will destroy its influence. A woman's real resource is her wit; not that foolish wit which is so greatly admired in society, a wit which does nothing to make life happier; but that wit which is adapted to her condition, the art of taking advantage of our position and controlling us through our own strength. Words cannot tell how beneficial this is to man, what a charm it gives to the society of men and women, how it checks the petulant child and restrains the brutal husband; without it the home would be a scene of strife; with it, it is the abode of happiness. I know that this power is abused by the sly and the spiteful; but what is there that is not liable to abuse? Do not destroy the means of happiness because the wicked use them to our hurt. . . .

Women have ready tongues; they talk earlier, more easily, and more pleasantly than men. They are also said to talk more; this may be true, but I am prepared to reckon it to their credit; eyes and mouth are equally busy and for the same cause. A man says what he knows, a woman says what will please; the one needs knowledge, the other taste; utility should be the man's object; the woman speaks to give pleasure. There should be nothing in common but truth.

You should not check a girl's prattle like a boy's by the harsh question, "What is the use of that?" but by another question at least as difficult to answer, "What effect will that have?" At this early age when they know neither good nor evil, and are incapable of judging others, they should make this their rule and never say anything which is unpleasant to those about them; this rule is all the more difficult to apply because it must always be subordinated to our first rule, "Never tell a lie."

I can see many other difficulties, but they belong to a later stage. For the present it is enough for your little girls to speak the truth without grossness, and as they are naturally averse to what is gross, education easily teaches them to avoid it. In social intercourse I observe that a man's politeness is usually more helpful and a woman's more caressing. This distinction is natural, not artificial. A man seeks to serve, a woman seeks to please. Hence a woman's politeness is less insincere than ours, whatever we may think of her character; for she is only acting upon a fundamental instinct; but when a man professes to put my interests before his own, I detect the falsehood, however disguised. Hence it is easy for women to be polite, and easy to teach little girls politeness. The first lessons come by nature;

art only supplements them and determines the conventional form which politeness shall take. The courtesy of woman to woman is another matter; their manner is so constrained, their attentions so chilly, they find each other so wearisome, that they take little pains to conceal the fact, and seem sincere even in their falsehood, since they take so little pains to conceal it. Still young girls do sometimes become sincerely attached to one another. At their age good spirits take the place of a good disposition, and they are so pleased with themselves that they are pleased with every one else. Moreover, it is certain that they kiss each other more affectionately and caress each other more gracefully in the presence of men, for they are proud to be able to arouse their envy without danger to themselves by the sight of favours which they know will arouse that envy. . . .

If boys are incapable of forming any true idea of religion, much more is it beyond the grasp of girls; and for this reason I would speak of it all the sooner to little girls, for if we wait till they are ready for a serious discussion of these deep subjects we should be in danger of never speaking of religion at all. A woman's reason is practical, and therefore she soon arrives at a given conclusion, but she fails to discover it for herself. The social relation of the sexes is a wonderful thing. This relation produces a moral person of which woman is the eye and man the hand, but the two are so dependent on one another that the man teaches the woman what to see, while she teaches him what to do. If women could discover principles and if men had as good heads for detail, they would be mutually independent, they would live in perpetual strife, and there would be an end to all society. But in their mutual harmony each contributes to a common purpose; each follows the other's lead, each commands and each obeys.

As a woman's conduct is controlled by public opinion, so is her religion ruled by authority. The daughter should follow her mother's religion, the wife her husband's. Were that religion false, the docility which leads mother and daughter to submit to nature's laws would blot out the sin of error in the sight of God. Unable to judge for themselves they should accept the judgment of father and husband as that of the church.

While women unaided cannot deduce the rules of their faith, neither can they assign limits to that faith by the evidence of reason; they allow themselves to be driven hither and thither by all sorts of external influences, they are ever above or below the truth. Extreme in everything, they are either altogether reckless or altogether pious; you never find them able to combine virtue and piety. Their natural exaggeration is not wholly to blame; the ill-regulated control exercised over them by men is partly responsible. Loose morals bring religion into contempt; the terrors of remorse make it a tyrant; this is why women have always too much or too little religion.

As a woman's religion is controlled by authority it is more important to show her plainly what to believe than to explain the reasons for belief; for faith attached to ideas half-understood is the main source of fanaticism, and faith demanded on behalf of what is absurd leads to madness or unbelief. . . .

The reason which teaches a man his duties is not very complex; the reason which teaches a woman hers is even simpler. The obedience and fidelity which she owes to her husband, the tenderness and care due to her children, are such natural and self-evident consequences of her position that she cannot honestly refuse her consent to the inner voice which is her guide, nor fail to discern her duty in her natural inclination. . . .

People would be disgusted with a woman's whims if they were not skilfully managed, and when they are artistically distributed her servants are more than ever enslaved.

What is the secret of this art? Is it not the result of a delicate and continuous observation which shows her what is taking place in a man's heart, so that she is able to encourage or to check every hidden impulse? Can this art be acquired? No; it is born with women; it is common to them all, and men never show it to the same degree. It is one of the distinctive characters of the sex. Self-possession, penetration, delicate observation, this is a woman's science; the skill to make use of it is her chief accomplishment.

This is what is, and we have seen why it is so. It is said that women are false. They become false. They are really endowed with skill not duplicity; in the genuine inclinations of their sex they are not false even when they tell a lie. Why do you consult their words when it is not their mouths that speak? Consult their eyes, their colour, their breathing, their timid manner, their slight resistance, that is the language nature gave them for your answer. The lips always say "No," and rightly so; but the tone is not always the same, and that cannot lie. Has not a woman the same needs as a man, but without the same right to make them known? Her fate would be too cruel if she had no language in which to express her legitimate desires except the words which she dare not utter. Must her modesty condemn her to misery? Does she not require a means of indicating her inclinations without open expression? What skill is needed to hide from her lover what she would fain reveal! Is it not of vital importance that she should learn to touch his heart without showing that she cares for him? It is a pretty story that tale of Galatea with her apple and her clumsy flight. What more is needed? Will she tell the shepherd who pursues her among the willows that she only flees that he may follow? If she did, it would be a lie; for she would no longer attract him. The more modest a woman is, the more art she needs, even with her husband. Yes, I maintain that coquetry, kept within bounds, becomes modest and true, and out of it springs a law of right conduct. . . .

On these grounds I think we may decide in general terms what sort of education is suited to the female mind, and the objects to which we should turn its attention in early youth.

As I have already said, the duties of their sex are more easily recognised than performed. They must learn in the first place to love those duties by considering the advantages to be derived from them — that is the only way to make duty easy. Every age and condition has its own duties. We are quick to see our duty if we love it. Honour your position as a woman, and in whatever station of life to which it shall please heaven to call you, you will be well off. The essential thing is to be what nature has made you; women are only too ready to be what men would have them.

FEMININITY

SIGMUND FREUD

The Austrian psychologist Sigmund Freud (1856–1939) was one of the earliest theorists, and probably the most influential in the areas of clinical psychology and psychoanalysis. Although extraordinarily creative and insightful as groundbreaker in a new dimension, his work has been severely criticized for its ethnocentricity, its lack of objective verification (or perhaps even verifiability), and, more recently, its thorough sexism. Freud's theories on the nature of women's psychology include the following themes: (1) that for women, anatomy is destiny: more so than for men, women's lives and personalities are prescribed by their biological and reproductive nature; (2) that women are not only fundamentally different from men in character but inferior to them physically (in sexual capacity and equipment), emotionally (in stability and control), and ethically (in the sense of honesty and justice).

The essay reprinted here (written about 1933) is Freud's most famous treatise on femininity. It was at one time (until quite recently — into the forties or fifties) the official word on female psychology. Although Freud and this analysis have been challenged roundly from all quarters, its themes are still very influential and pervade much of contemporary clinical and popular thought.

LADIES AND GENTLEMEN, — All the while I am preparing to talk to you I am struggling with an internal difficulty. I feel uncertain, so to speak, of the extent of my licence. It is true that in the course of fifteen years of work psycho-analysis has changed and grown richer; but, in spite of that, an introduction to psycho-analysis might have been left without alteration or supplement. It is constantly in my mind that these lectures are without a *raison d'être.* For analysts I am saying too little and nothing at all that is new; but for you I am saying too much and saying things which you are not equipped to understand and which are not in your province. I have looked around for excuses and I have tried to justify each separate lecture

on different grounds. The first one, on the theory of dreams, was supposed to put you back again at one blow into the analytic atmosphere and to show you how durable our views have turned out to be. I was led on to the second one, which followed the paths from dreams to what is called occultism, by the opportunity of speaking my mind without constraint on a department of work in which prejudiced expectations are fighting to-day against passionate resistances, and I could hope that your judgement, educated to tolerance on the example of psycho-analysis, would not refuse to accompany me on the excursion. The third lecture, on the dissection of the personality, certainly made the hardest demands upon you with its unfamiliar subject-matter; but it was impossible for me to keep this first beginning of an ego-psychology back from you, and if we had possessed it fifteen years ago I should have had to mention it to you then. My last lecture, finally, which you were probably able to follow only by great exertions, brought forward necessary corrections — fresh attempts at solving the most important conundrums; and my introduction would have been leading you astray if I had been silent about them. As you see, when one starts making excuses it turns out in the end that it was all inevitable, all the work of destiny. I submit to it, and I beg you to do the same.

To-day's lecture, too, should have no place in an introduction; but it may serve to give you an example of a detailed piece of analytic work, and I can say two things to recommend it. It brings forward nothing but observed facts, almost without any speculative additions, and it deals with a subject which has a claim on your interest second almost to no other. Throughout history people have knocked their heads against the riddle of the nature of femininity —

Häupter in Hieroglyphenmützen,
Häupter in Turban und schwarzem Barett,
Perückenhäupter und tausend andre
Arme, schwitzende Menschenhäupter....*

Nor will *you* have escaped worrying over this problem — those of you who are men; to those of you who are women this will not apply — you are yourselves the problem. When you meet a human being, the first distinction you make is 'male or female?' and you are accustomed to make the distinction with unhesitating certainty. Anatomical science shares your certainty at one point and not much further. The male sexual product, the spermatozoon, and its vehicle are male; the ovum and the organism that harbours it are female. In both sexes organs have been formed which serve exclusively for the sexual functions; they were probably developed

from the same [innate] disposition into two different forms. Besides this, in both sexes the other organs, the bodily shapes and tissues, show the influence of the individual's sex, but this is inconstant and its amount variable; these are what are known as the secondary sexual characters. Science next tells you something that runs counter to your expectations and is probably calculated to confuse your feelings. It draws your attention to the fact that portions of the male sexual apparatus also appear in women's bodies, though in an atrophied state, and vice versa in the alternative case. It regards their occurrence as indications of *bisexuality,* as though an individual is not a man or a woman but always both — merely a certain amount more the one than the other. You will then be asked to make yourselves familiar with the idea that the proportion in which masculine and feminine are mixed in an individual is subject to quite considerable fluctuations. Since, however, apart from the very rarest cases, only one kind of sexual product — ova or semen — is nevertheless present in one person, you are bound to have doubts as to the decisive significance of those elements and must conclude that what constitutes masculinity or femininity is an unknown characteristic which anatomy cannot lay hold of.

Can psychology do so perhaps? We are accustomed to employ 'masculine' and 'feminine' as mental qualities as well, and have in the same way transferred the notion of bisexuality to mental life. Thus we speak of a person, whether male or female, as behaving in a masculine way in one connection and in a feminine way in another. But you will soon perceive that this is only giving way to anatomy or to convention. You cannot give the concepts of 'masculine' and 'feminine' *any* new connotation. The distinction is not a psychological one; when you

---

* Heads in hieroglyphic bonnets,
  Heads in turbans and black birettas,
  Heads in wigs and thousand other
  Wretched, sweating heads of humans. . . .
  (Heine, *Nordsee* [Second Cycle, VII, 'Fragen'].)

say 'masculine', you usually mean 'active', and when you say 'feminine', you usually mean 'passive'. Now it is true that a relation of the kind exists. The male sex-cell is actively mobile and searches out the female one, and the latter, the ovum, is immobile and waits passively. This behaviour of the elementary sexual organisms is indeed a model for the conduct of sexual individuals during intercourse. The male pursues the female for the purpose of sexual union, seizes hold of her and penetrates into her. But by this you have precisely reduced the characteristic of masculinity to the factor of aggressiveness so far as psychology is concerned. You may well doubt whether you have gained any real advantage from this when you reflect that in some classes of animals the females are the stronger and more aggressive and the male is active only in the single act of sexual union. This is so, for instance, with the spiders. Even the functions of rearing and caring for the young, which strike us as feminine *par excellence,* are not invariably attached to the female sex in animals. In quite high species we find that the sexes share the task of caring for the young between them or even that the male alone devotes himself to it. Even in the sphere of human sexual life you soon see how inadequate it is to make masculine behaviour coincide with activity and feminine with passivity. A mother is active in every sense towards her child; the act of lactation itself may equally be described as the mother suckling the baby or as her being sucked by it. The further you go from the narrow sexual sphere the more obvious will the 'error of superimposition' become. Women can display great activity in various directions, men are not able to live in company with their own kind unless they develop a large amount of passive adaptability. If you now tell me that these facts go to prove precisely that both men and women are bisexual in the psychological sense, I shall conclude that you have decided in your own minds to make 'active' coincide with 'masculine' and 'passive' with 'feminine'. But I advise you against it. It seems to me to serve no useful purpose and adds nothing to our knowledge.

One might consider characterizing femininity psychologically as giving preference to passive aims. This is not, of course, the same thing as passivity; to achieve a passive aim may call for a large amount of activity. It is perhaps the case that in a woman, on the basis of her share in the sexual function, a preference for passive behaviour and passive aims is carried over into her life to a greater or lesser extent, in proportion to the limits, restricted or far-reaching, within which her sexual life thus serves as a model. But we must beware in this of underestimating the influence of social customs, which similarly force women into passive situations. All this is still far from being cleared up. There is one particularly constant relation between femininity and instinctual life which we do not want to overlook. The suppression of women's aggressiveness which is prescribed for them constitutionally and imposed on them socially favours the development of powerful masochistic impulses, which succeed, as we know, in binding erotically the destructive trends which have been diverted inwards. Thus masochism, as people say, is truly feminine. But if, as happens so often, you meet with masochism in men, what is left to you but to say that these men exhibit very plain feminine traits?

And now you are already prepared to hear that psychology too is unable to solve the riddle of femininity. The explanation must no doubt come from elsewhere, and cannot come till we have learnt how in general the differentiation of living organisms into two sexes came about. We know nothing about it, yet the existence of two sexes is a most striking characteristic of organic life which distinguishes it sharply from inanimate nature. However, we find enough to study in those human individuals who, through the possession of female genitals, are characterized as manifestly or predominantly feminine. In conformity with its peculiar nature, psycho-analysis does not try to describe what a woman is — that would be a task it could scarcely perform — but sets about enquiring how she comes into being, how a woman develops out of a child with a bisexual disposition. In recent times we have begun to learn a little about this, thanks to the circumstance that several of our excellent women colleagues in analysis have begun to work at the question. The discussion of this has gained special attractiveness from the distinction between the sexes. For the ladies, whenever some comparison seemed to turn out unfavourable to their sex, were able to utter a suspicion that we, the male analysts, had been unable to overcome certain deeply-rooted prejudices against what was feminine, and that this was being paid for in the partiality of our researches. We, on the other hand, standing on the ground of bisexuality, had no difficulty in avoiding impoliteness. We had only to say: 'This doesn't apply to *you*. You're the exception; on this point you're more masculine than feminine.'

We approach the investigation of the sexual development of women with two expectations. The first is that here once more the constitution will not adapt itself to its function without a struggle. The second is that the decisive turning-points will already have been prepared for or completed before puberty. Both expectations are promptly confirmed. Furthermore, a comparison with what happens with boys tells us that the development of a little girl into a normal woman is more difficult and more complicated, since

it includes two extra tasks, to which there is nothing corresponding in the development of a man. Let us follow the parallel lines from their beginning. Undoubtedly the material is different to start with in boys and girls: it did not need psycho-analysis to establish that. The difference in the structure of the genitals is accompanied by other bodily differences which are too well known to call for mention. Differences emerge too in the instinctual disposition which give a glimpse of the later nature of women. A little girl is as a rule less aggressive, defiant and self-sufficient; she seems to have a greater need for being shown affection and on that account to be more dependent and pliant. It is probably only as a result of this pliancy that she can be taught more easily and quicker to control her excretions: urine and faeces are the first gifts that children make to those who look after them, and controlling them is the first concession to which the instinctual life of children can be induced. One gets an impression, too, that little girls are more intelligent and livelier than boys of the same age; they go out more to meet the external world and at the same time form stronger object-cathexes. I cannot say whether this lead in development has been confirmed by exact observations, but in any case there is no question that girls cannot be described as intellectually backward. These sexual differences are not, however, of great consequence: they can be outweighed by individual variations. For our immediate purposes they can be disregarded.

Both sexes seem to pass through the early phases of libidinal development in the same manner. It might have been expected that in girls there would already have been some lag in aggressiveness in the sadistic-anal phase, but such is not the case. Analysis of children's play has shown our women analysts that the aggressive impulses of little girls leave nothing to be desired in the way of abundance and violence. With their entry into the phallic phase the differences between the sexes are completely eclipsed by their agreements. We are now obliged to recognize that the little girl is a little man. In boys, as we know, this phase is marked by the fact that they have learnt how to derive pleasurable sensations from their small penis and connect its excited state with their ideas of sexual intercourse. Little girls do the same thing with their still smaller clitoris. It seems that with them all their masturbatory acts are carried out on this penis-equivalent, and that the truly feminine vagina is still undiscovered by both sexes. It is true that there are a few isolated reports of early vaginal sensations as well, but it could not be easy to distinguish these from sensations in the anus or vestibulum; in any case they cannot play a great part. We are entitled to keep to our view that in the phallic phase of girls the clitoris is the leading erotogenic zone. But it is not, of course, going to remain so. With the change to femininity the clitoris should wholly or in part hand over its sensitivity, and at the same time its importance, to the vagina. This would be one of the two tasks which a woman has to perform in the course of her development, whereas the more fortunate man has only to continue at the time of his sexual maturity the activity that he has previously carried out at the period of the early efflorescence of his sexuality.

We shall return to the part played by the clitoris; let us now turn to the second task with which a girl's development is burdened. A boy's mother is the first object of his love, and she remains so too during the formation of his Oedipus complex and, in essence, all through his life. For a girl too her first object must be her mother (and the figures of wet-nurses and foster-mothers that merge into her). The first object-cathexes occur in attachment to the satisfaction of the major

and simple vital needs, and the circumstances of the care of children are the same for both sexes. But in the Oedipus situation the girl's father has become her love-object, and we expect that in the normal course of development she will find her way from this paternal object to her final choice of an object. In the course of time, therefore, a girl has to change her erotogenic zone and her object — both of which a boy retains. The question then arises of how this happens: in particular, how does a girl pass from her mother to an attachment to her father? or, in other words, how does she pass from her masculine phase to the feminine one to which she is biologically destined?

It would be a solution of ideal simplicity if we could suppose that from a particular age onwards the elementary influence of the mutual attraction between the sexes makes itself felt and impels the small woman towards men, while the same law allows the boy to continue with his mother. We might suppose in addition that in this the children are following the pointer given them by the sexual preference of their parents. But we are not going to find things so easy; we scarcely know whether we are to believe seriously in the power of which poets talk so much and with such enthusiasm but which cannot be further dissected analytically. We have found an answer of quite another sort by means of laborious investigations, the material for which at least was easy to arrive at. For you must know that the number of women who remain till a late age tenderly dependent on a paternal object, or indeed on their real father, is very great. We have established some surprising facts about these women with an intense attachment of long duration to their father. We knew, of course, that there had been a preliminary stage of attachment to the mother, but we did not know that it could be so rich in content and so long-lasting, and could leave behind so many opportunities for fixations and dispositions. During this time the girl's father is only a troublesome rival; in some cases the attachment to her mother lasts beyond the fourth year of life. Almost everything that we find later in her relation to her father was already present in this earlier attachment and has been transferred subsequently on to her father. In short, we get an impression that we cannot understand women unless we appreciate this phase of their pre-Oedipus attachment to their mother.

We shall be glad, then, to know the nature of the girl's libidinal relations to her mother. The answer is that they are of very many different kinds. Since they persist through all three phases of infantile sexuality, they also take on the characteristics of the different phases and express themselves by oral, sadistic-anal and phallic wishes. These wishes represent active as well as passive impulses; if we relate them to the differentiation of the sexes which is to appear later — though we should avoid doing so as far as possible — we may call them masculine and feminine. Besides this, they are completely ambivalent, both affectionate and of a hostile and aggressive nature. The latter often only come to light after being changed into anxiety ideas. It is not always easy to point to a formulation of these early sexual wishes; what is most clearly expressed is a wish to get the mother with child and the corresponding wish to bear her a child — both belonging to the phallic period and sufficiently surprising, but established beyond doubt by analytic observation. The attractiveness of these investigations lies in the surprising detailed findings which they bring us. Thus, for instance, we discover the fear of being murdered or poisoned, which may later form the core of a paranoic illness, already present in this pre-Oedipus period, in relation to the mother. Or another case: you will recall an interesting episode in the history of analytic research which caused me many distressing hours. In the period in which the main interest was directed to discovering infantile sexual traumas, almost all my women patients told me that they had been seduced by their father. I was driven to recognize in the end that these reports were untrue and so came to understand that hysterical symptoms are derived from phantasies and not from real occurrences. It was only later that I was able to recognize in this phantasy of being seduced by the father the expression of the typical Oedipus complex in women. And now we find the phantasy of seduction once more in the pre-Oedipus prehistory of girls; but the seducer is regularly the mother. Here, however, the phantasy touches the ground of reality, for it was really the mother who by her activities over the child's bodily hygiene inevitably stimulated, and perhaps even roused for the first time, pleasurable sensations in her genitals.

I have no doubt you are ready to suspect that this portrayal of the abundance and strength of a little girl's sexual relations with her mother is very much overdrawn. After all, one has opportunities of seeing little girls and notices nothing of the sort. But the objection is not to the point. Enough can be seen in the children if one knows how to look. And besides, you should consider how little of its sexual wishes a child can bring to preconscious expression or communicate at all. Accordingly we are only within our rights if we study the residues and consequences of this emotional world in retrospect, in people in whom these processes of development had attained a specially clear and even excessive degree of expansion. Pathology has always done us the service of making discernible by isolation and exaggeration conditions which would remain concealed in a normal state. And since our investigations have been carried out on people who were by no means seriously abnormal, I think we should regard their outcome as deserving belief.

We will now turn our interest on to the single question of what it is that brings this powerful attachment of the girl to her mother to an end. This, as we know, is its usual fate: it is destined to make room for an attachment to her father. Here we come upon a fact which is a pointer to our further advance. This step in development does not involve only a simple change of object. The turning away from the mother is accompanied by hostility; the attachment to the mother ends in hate. A hate of that kind may become very striking and last all through life; it may be carefully overcompensated later on; as a rule one part of it is overcome while another part persists. Events of later years naturally influence this greatly. We will restrict ourselves, however, to studying it at the time at which the girl turns to her father and to enquiring into the motives for it. We are then given a long list of accusations and grievances against the mother which are supposed to justify the child's hostile feelings; they are of varying validity which we shall not fail to examine. A number of them are obvious rationalizations and the true sources of enmity remain to be found. I hope you will be interested if on this occasion I take you through all the details of a psychoanalytic investigation.

The reproach against the mother which goes back furthest is that she gave the child too little milk — which is construed against her as lack of love. Now there is some justification for this reproach in our families. Mothers often have insufficient nourishment to give their children and are content to suckle them for a few months, for half or three-quarters of a year. Among primitive peoples children are fed at their mother's breast for two or three years. The figure of the wet-nurse who suckles the child is as a rule merged into the mother; when this has not happened, the reproach is turned into another one — that the nurse, who fed the child so willingly, was sent away by the mother too early. But whatever the true state of affairs may have been, it is impossible that the child's reproach can be justified as often as it is met with. It seems, rather, that the child's avidity for its earliest nourishment is altogether insatiable, that it never gets over the pain of losing its mother's breast. I should not be surprised if the analysis of a primitive child, who could still suck at its mother's breast when it was already able to run about and talk, were to bring the same reproach to light. The fear of being poisoned is also probably connected with the withdrawal of the breast. Poison is nourishment that makes one ill. Perhaps children trace back their early illnesses too to this frustration. A fair amount of intellectual education is a prerequisite for believing in chance; primitive people and uneducated ones, and no doubt children as well, are able to assign a ground for everything that happens. Perhaps originally it was a reason on animistic lines. Even to-day in some strata of our population no one can die without having been killed by someone else — preferably by the doctor. And the regular reaction of a neurotic to the death of someone closely connected with him is to put the blame on himself for having caused the death.

The next accusation against the child's mother flares up when the next baby appears in the nursery. If possible the connection with oral frustration is preserved: the mother could not or would not give the child any more milk because she needed the nourishment for the new arrival. In cases in which the two children are so close in age that lactation is prejudiced by the second pregnancy, this reproach acquires a real basis, and it is a remarkable fact that a child, even with an age difference of only 11 months, is not too young to take notice of what is happening. But what the child grudges the unwanted intruder and rival is not only the suckling but all the other signs of maternal care. It feels that it has been dethroned, despoiled, prejudiced in its rights; it casts a jealous hatred upon the new baby and develops a grievance against the faithless mother which often finds expression in a disagreeable change in its behaviour. It becomes 'naughty', perhaps, irritable and disobedient and goes back on the advances it has made towards controlling its excretions. All of this has been very long familiar and is accepted as self-evident; but we rarely form a correct idea of the strength of these jealous impulses, of the tenacity with which they persist and of the magnitude of their influence on later development. Especially as this jealousy is constantly receiving fresh nourishment in the later years of childhood and the whole shock is repeated with the birth of each new brother or sister. Nor does it make much difference if the child happens to remain the mother's preferred favourite. A child's demands for love are immoderate, they make exclusive claims and tolerate no sharing.

An abundant source of a child's hostility to its mother is provided by its multifarious sexual wishes, which alter according to the phase of the libido and which cannot for the most part be satisfied. The strongest of these frustrations occur at the phallic period, if the mother forbids pleasurable activity with the genitals — often with severe threats and every sign of displeasure — activity to which, after all, she herself had introduced the child. One would think these were reasons enough to account for a girl's turning away from her mother. One would judge, if so, that the estrangement follows inevitably from the nature of children's sexuality, from the im-

moderate character of their demand for love and the impossibility of fulfilling their sexual wishes. It might be thought indeed that this first love-relation of the child's is doomed to dissolution for the very reason that it is the first, for these early object-cathexes are regularly ambivalent to a high degree. A powerful tendency to aggressiveness is always present beside a powerful love, and the more passionately a child loves its object the more sensitive does it become to disappointments and frustrations from that object; and in the end the love must succumb to the accumulated hostility. Or the idea that there is an original ambivalence such as this in erotic cathexes may be rejected, and it may be pointed out that it is the special nature of the mother-child relation that leads, with equal inevitability, to the destruction of the child's love; for even the mildest upbringing cannot avoid using compulsion and introducing restrictions, and any such intervention in the child's liberty must provoke as a reaction an inclination to rebelliousness and aggressiveness. A discussion of these possibilities might, I think, be most interesting; but an objection suddenly emerges which forces our interest in another direction. All these factors — the slights, the disappointments in love, the jealousy, the seduction followed by prohibition — are, after all, also in operation in the relation of a *boy* to his mother and are yet unable to alienate him from the maternal object. Unless we can find something that is specific for girls and is not present or not in the same way present in boys, we shall not have explained the termination of the attachment of girls to their mother.

I believe we have found this specific factor, and indeed where we expected to find it, even though in a surprising form. Where we expected to find it, I say, for it lies in the castration complex. After all, the anatomical distinction [between the sexes] must express itself in psychical consequences. It was, however, a surprise to learn from analyses that girls hold their mother responsible for their lack of a penis and do not forgive her for their being thus put at a disadvantage.

As you hear, then, we ascribe a castration complex to women as well. And for good reasons, though its content cannot be the same as with boys. In the latter the castration complex arises after they have learnt from the sight of the female genitals that the organ which they value so highly need not necessarily accompany the body. At this the boy recalls to mind the threats he brought on himself by his doings with that organ, he begins to give credence to them and falls under the influence of fear of castration, which will be the most powerful motive force in his subsequent development. The castration complex of girls is also started by the sight of the genitals of the other sex. They at once notice the difference and, it must be admitted, its significance too. They feel seriously wronged, often declare that they want to 'have something like it too', and fall a victim to 'envy for the penis', which will leave ineradicable traces on their development and the formation of their character and which will not be surmounted in even the most favourable cases without a severe expenditure of psychical energy. The girl's recognition of the fact of her being without a penis does not by any means imply that she submits to the fact easily. On the contrary, she continues to hold on for a long time to the wish to get something like it herself and she believes in that possibility for improbably long years; and analysis can show that, at a period when knowledge of reality has long since rejected the fulfillment of the wish as unattainable, it persists in the unconscious and retains a considerable cathexis of energy. The wish to get the longed-for penis eventually in spite of everything

may contribute to the motives that drive a mature woman to analysis, and what she may reasonably expect from analysis — a capacity, for instance, to carry on an intellectual profession — may often be recognized as a sublimated modification of this repressed wish.

One cannot very well doubt the importance of envy for the penis. You may take it as an instance of male injustice if I assert that envy and jealousy play an even greater part in the mental life of women than of men. It is not that I think these characteristics are absent in men or that I think they have no other roots in women than envy for the penis; but I am inclined to attribute their greater amount in women to this latter influence. Some analysts, however, have shown an inclination to depreciate the importance of this first instalment of penis-envy in the phallic phase. They are of opinion that what we find of this attitude in women is in the main a secondary structure which has come about on the occasion of later conflicts by regression to this early infantile impulse. This, however, is a general problem of depth psychology. In many pathological — or even unusual — instinctual attitudes (for instance, in all sexual perversions) the question arises of how much of their strength is to be attributed to early infantile fixations and how much to the influence of later experiences and developments. In such cases it is almost always a matter of complemental series such as we put forward in our discussion of the aetiology of the neuroses. Both factors play a part in varying amounts in the causation; a less on the one side is balanced by a more on the other. The infantile factor sets the pattern in all cases but does not always determine the issue, though it often does. Precisely in the case of penis-envy I should argue decidedly in favour of the preponderance of the infantile factor.

The discovery that she is castrated is a

turning-point in a girl's growth. Three possible lines of development start from it: one leads to sexual inhibition or to neurosis, the second to change of character in the sense of a masculinity complex, the third, finally, to normal femininity. We have learnt a fair amount, though not everything, about all three.

The essential content of the first is as follows: the little girl has hitherto lived in a masculine way, has been able to get pleasure by the excitation of her clitoris and has brought this activity into relation with her sexual wishes directed towards her mother, which are often active ones; now, owing to the influence of her penis-envy, she loses her enjoyment in her phallic sexuality. Her self-love is mortified by the comparison with the boy's far superior equipment and in consequence she renounces her masturbatory satisfaction from her clitoris, repudiates her love for her mother and at the same time not infrequently represses a good part of her sexual trends in general. No doubt her turning away from her mother does not occur all at once, for to begin with the girl regards her castration as an individual misfortune, and only gradually extends it to other females and finally to her mother as well. Her love was directed to her *phallic* mother; with the discovery that her mother is castrated it becomes possible to drop her as an object, so that the motives for hostility, which have long been accumulating, gain the upper hand. This means, therefore, that as a result of the discovery of women's lack of a penis they are debased in value for girls just as they are for boys and later perhaps for men.

You all know the immense aetiological importance attributed by our neurotic patients to their masturbation. They make it responsible for all their troubles and we have the greatest difficulty in persuading them that they are mistaken. In fact, how-

ever, we ought to admit to them that they are right, for masturbation is the executive agent of infantile sexuality, from the faulty development of which they are indeed suffering. But what neurotics mostly blame is the masturbation of the period of puberty; they have mostly forgotten that of early infancy, which is what is really in question. I wish I might have an opportunity some time of explaining to you at length how important all the factual details of early masturbation become for the individual's subsequent neurosis or character: whether or not it was discovered, how the parents struggled against it or permitted it, or whether he succeeded in suppressing it himself. All of this leaves permanent traces on his development. But I am on the whole glad that I need not do this. It would be a hard and tedious task and at the end of it you would put me in an embarrassing situation by quite certainly asking me to give you some practical advice as to how a parent or educator should deal with the masturbation of small children. From the development of girls, which is what my present lecture is concerned with, I can give you the example of a child herself trying to get free from masturbating. She does not always succeed in this. If envy for the penis has provoked a powerful impulse against clitoridal masturbation but this nevertheless refuses to give way, a violent struggle for liberation ensues in which the girl, as it were, herself takes over the role of her deposed mother and gives expression to her entire dissatisfaction with her inferior clitoris in her efforts against obtaining satisfaction from it. Many years later, when her masturbatory activity has long since been suppressed, an interest still persists which we must interpret as a defence against a temptation that is still dreaded. It manifests itself in the emergence of sympathy for those to whom similar difficulties are attributed, it plays a part as a motive in contracting a marriage and, indeed, it may determine the choice of a husband or lover. Disposing of early infantile masturbation is truly no easy or indifferent business.

Along with the abandonment of clitoridal masturbation a certain amount of activity is renounced. Passivity now has the upper hand, and the girl's turning to her father is accomplished principally with the help of passive instinctual impulses. You can see that a wave of development like this, which clears the phallic activity out of the way, smooths the ground for femininity. If too much is not lost in the course of it through repression, this femininity may turn out to be normal. The wish with which the girl turns to her father is no doubt originally the wish for the penis which her mother has refused her and which she now expects from her father. The feminine situation is only established, however, if the wish for a penis is replaced by one for a baby, if, that is, a baby takes the place of a penis in accordance with an ancient symbolic equivalence. It has not escaped us that the girl has wished for a baby earlier, in the undisturbed phallic phase: that, of course, was the meaning of her playing with dolls. But that play was not in fact an expression of her femininity; it served as an identification with her mother with the intention of substituting activity for passivity. *She* was playing the part of her mother and the doll was herself: now she could do with the baby everything that her mother used to do with her. Not until the emergence of the wish for a penis does the doll-baby become a baby from the girl's father, and thereafter the aim of the most powerful feminine wish. Her happiness is great if later on this wish for a baby finds fulfilment in reality, and quite especially so if the baby is a little boy who brings the longed-for penis with him. Often enough in her combined picture of 'a baby from her father' the emphasis is laid on the baby and her father

left unstressed. In this way the ancient masculine wish for the possession of a penis is still faintly visible through the femininity now achieved. But perhaps we ought rather to recognize this wish for a penis as being *par excellence* a feminine one.

With the transference of the wish for a penis-baby on to her father, the girl has entered the situation of the Oedipus complex. Her hostility to her mother, which did not need to be freshly created, is now greatly intensified, for she becomes the girl's rival, who receives from her father everything that she desires from him. For a long time the girl's Oedipus complex concealed her pre-Oedipus attachment to her mother from our view, though it is nevertheless so important and leaves such lasting fixations behind it. For girls the Oedipus situation is the outcome of a long and difficult development; it is a kind of preliminary solution, a position of rest which is not soon abandoned, especially as the beginning of the latency period is not far distant. And we are now struck by a difference between the two sexes, which is probably momentous, in regard to the relation of the Oedipus complex to the castration complex. In a boy the Oedipus complex, in which he desires his mother and would like to get rid of his father as being a rival, develops naturally from the phase of his phallic sexuality. The threat of castration compels him, however, to give up that attitude. Under the impression of the danger of losing his penis, the Oedipus complex is abandoned, repressed and, in the most normal cases, entirely destroyed, and a severe super-ego is set up as its heir. What happens with a girl is almost the opposite. The castration complex prepares for the Oedipus complex instead of destroying it; the girl is driven out of her attachment to her mother through the influence of her envy for the penis and she enters the Oedipus situation as though into a haven of refuge. In the absence of fear of castration the chief motive is lacking which leads boys to surmount the Oedipus complex. Girls remain in it for an indeterminate length of time; they demolish it late and, even so, incompletely. In these circumstances the formation of the super-ego must suffer; it cannot attain the strength and independence which give it its cultural significance, and feminists are not pleased when we point out to them the effects of this factor upon the average feminine character.

To go back a little. We mentioned as the second possible reaction to the discovery of female castration the development of a powerful masculinity complex. By this we mean that the girl refuses, as it were, to recognize the unwelcome fact and, defiantly rebellious, even exaggerates her previous masculinity, clings to her clitoridal activity and takes refuge in an identification with her phallic mother or her father. What can it be that decides in favour of this outcome? We can only suppose that it is a constitutional factor, a greater amount of activity, such as is ordinarily characteristic of a male. However that may be, the essence of this process is that at this point in development the wave of passivity is avoided which opens the way to the turn towards femininity. The extreme achievement of such a masculinity complex would appear to be the influencing of the choice of an object in the sense of manifest homosexuality. Analytic experience teaches us, to be sure, that female homosexuality is seldom or never a direct continuation of infantile masculinity. Even for a girl of this kind it seems necessary that she should take her father as an object for some time and enter the Oedipus situation. But afterwards, as a result of her inevitable disappointments from her father, she is driven to regress into her early masculinity complex. The significance of these disappointments must not be exaggerated;

a girl who is destined to become feminine is not spared them, though they do not have the same effect. The predominance of the constitutional factor seems indisputable; but the two phases in the development of female homosexuality are well mirrored in the practices of homosexuals, who play the parts of mother and baby with each other as often and as clearly as those of husband and wife.

What I have been telling you here may be described as the prehistory of women. It is a product of the very last few years and may have been of interest to you as an example of detailed analytic work. Since its subject is woman, I will venture on this occasion to mention by name a few of the women who have made valuable contributions to this investigation. Dr. Ruth Mack Brunswick [1928] was the first to describe a case of neurosis which went back to a fixation in the pre-Oedipus stage and had never reached the Oedipus situation at all. The case took the form of jealous paranoia and proved accessible to therapy. Dr. Jeanne Lampl-de Groot [1927] has established the incredible phallic activity of girls towards their mother by some assured observations, and Dr. Helene Deutsch [1932] has shown that the erotic actions of homosexual women reproduce the relations between mother and baby.

It is not my intention to pursue the further behaviour of femininity through puberty to the period of maturity. Our knowledge, moreover, would be insufficient for the purpose. But I will bring a few features together in what follows. Taking its prehistory as a starting-point, I will only emphasize here that the development of femininity remains exposed to disturbance by the residual phenomena of the early masculine period. Regressions to the fixations of the pre-Oedipus phases very frequently occur; in the course of some women's lives there is a repeated alternation between periods in which masculinity or femininity gains the upper hand. Some portion of what we men call 'the enigma of women' may perhaps be derived from this expression of bisexuality in women's lives. But another question seems to have become ripe for judgement in the course of these researches. We have called the motive force of sexual life 'the libido'. Sexual life is dominated by the polarity of masculine-feminine; thus the notion suggests itself of considering the relation of the libido to this antithesis. It would not be surprising if it were to turn out that each sexuality had its own special libido appropriated to it, so that one sort of libido would pursue the aims of a masculine sexual life and another sort those of a feminine one. But nothing of the kind is true. There is only one libido, which serves both the masculine and the feminine sexual functions. To it itself we cannot assign any sex; if, following the conventional equation of activity and masculinity, we are inclined to describe it as masculine, we must not forget that it also covers trends with a passive aim. Nevertheless the juxtaposition 'feminine libido' is without any justification. Furthermore, it is our impression that more constraint has been applied to the libido when it is pressed into the service of the feminine function, and that — to speak teleologically — Nature takes less careful account of its [that function's] demands than in the case of masculinity. And the reason for this may lie — thinking once again teleologically — in the fact that the accomplishment of the aim of biology has been entrusted to the aggressiveness of men and has been made to some extent independent of women's consent.

The sexual frigidity of women, the frequency of which appears to confirm this disregard, is a phenomenon that is still insufficiently understood. Sometimes it is psychogenic and in that case accessible to influence; but in other cases it suggests the hypothesis of its being constitutionally determined and even of there being a contributory anatomical factor.

I have promised to tell you of a few more psychical peculiarities of mature femininity, as we come across them in analytic observation. We do not lay claim to more than an average validity for these assertions; nor is it always easy to distinguish what should be ascribed to the influence of the sexual function and what to social breeding. Thus, we attribute a larger amount of narcissism to femininity, which also affects women's choice of object, so that to be loved is a stronger need for them than to love. The effect of penis-envy has a share, further, in the physical vanity of women, since they are bound to value their charms more highly as a late compensation for their original sexual inferiority. Shame, which is considered to be a feminine characteristic *par excellence* but is far more a matter of convention than might be supposed, has as its purpose, we believe, concealment of genital deficiency. We are not forgetting that at a later time shame takes on other functions. It seems that women have made few contributions to the discoveries and inventions in the history of civilization; there is, however, one technique which they may have invented — that of plaiting and weaving. If that is so, we should be tempted to guess the unconscious motive for the achievement. Nature herself would seem to have given the model which this achievement imitates by causing the growth at maturity of the pubic hair that conceals the genitals. The step that remained to be taken lay in making the threads adhere to one another, while on the body they stick into the skin and are only matted together. If you reject this idea as fantastic and regard my belief in the influence of lack of a penis on the configuration of femininity as an *idée fixe,* I am of course defenceless.

The determinants of women's choice of

an object are often made unrecognizable by social conditions. Where the choice is able to show itself freely, it is often made in accordance with the narcissistic ideal of the man whom the girl had wished to become. If a girl has remained in her attachment to her father — that is, in the Oedipus complex — her choice is made according to the paternal type. Since, when she turned from her mother to her father, the hostility of her ambivalent relation remained with her mother, a choice of this kind should guarantee a happy marriage. But very often the outcome is of a kind that presents a general threat to such a settlement of the conflict due to ambivalence. The hostility that has been left behind follows in the train of the positive attachment and spreads over on to the new object. The woman's husband, who to begin with inherited from her father, becomes after a time her mother's heir as well. So it may easily happen that the second half of a woman's life may be filled by the struggle against her husband, just as the shorter first half was filled by her rebellion against her mother. When this reaction has been lived through, a second marriage may easily turn out very much more satisfying. Another alteration in a woman's nature, for which lovers are unprepared, may occur in a marriage after the first child is born. Under the influence of a woman's becoming a mother herself, an identification with her own mother may be revived, against which she had striven up till the time of her marriage, and this may attract all the available libido to itself, so that the compulsion to repeat reproduces an unhappy marriage between her parents. The difference in a mother's reaction to the birth of a son or a daughter shows that the old factor of lack of a penis has even now not lost its strength. A mother is only brought unlimited satisfaction by her relation to a son; this is altogether the most perfect, the most free from ambivalence of

all human relationships. A mother can transfer to her son the ambition which she has been obliged to suppress in herself, and she can expect from him the satisfaction of all that has been left over in her of her masculinity complex. Even a marriage is not made secure until the wife has succeeded in making her husband her child as well and in acting as a mother to him.

A woman's identification with her mother allows us to distinguish two strata: the pre-Oedipus one which rests on her affectionate attachment to her mother and takes her as a model, and the later one from the Oedipus complex which seeks to get rid of her mother and take her place with her father. We are no doubt justified in saying that much of both of them is left over for the future and that neither of them is adequately surmounted in the course of development. But the phase of the affectionate pre-Oedipus attachment is the decisive one for a woman's future: during it preparations are made for the acquisition of the characteristics with which she will later fulfil her role in the sexual function and perform her invaluable social tasks. It is in this identification too that she acquires her attractiveness to a man, whose Oedipus attachment to his mother it kindles into passion. How often it happens, however, that it is only his son who obtains what he himself aspired to! One gets an impression that a man's love and a woman's are a phase apart psychologically.

The fact that women must be regarded as having little sense of justice is no doubt related to the predominance of envy in their mental life; for the demand for justice is a modification of envy and lays down the condition subject to which one can put envy aside. We also regard women as weaker in their social interests and as having less capacity for sublimating their instincts than men. The former is no doubt derived from the dissocial quality which unquestionably characterizes all sexual relations. Lovers find sufficiency in each other, and families too resist inclusion in more comprehensive associations. The aptitude for sublimation is subject to the greatest individual variations. On the other hand I cannot help mentioning an impression that we are constantly receiving during analytic practice. A man of about thirty strikes us as a youthful, somewhat unformed individual, whom we expect to make powerful use of the possibilities for development opened up to him by analysis. A woman of the same age, however, often frightens us by her psychical rigidity and unchangeability. Her libido has taken up final positions and seems incapable of exchanging them for others. There are no paths open to further development; it is as though the whole process had already run its course and remains thenceforward insusceptible to influence — as though, indeed, the difficult development to femininity had exhausted the possibilities of the person concerned. As therapists we lament this state of things, even if we succeed in putting an end to our patient's ailment by doing away with her neurotic conflict.

That is all I had to say to you about femininity. It is certainly incomplete and fragmentary and does not always sound friendly. But do not forget that I have only been describing women in so far as their nature is determined by their sexual function. It is true that that influence extends very far; but we do not overlook the fact that an individual woman may be a human being in other respects as well. If you want to know more about femininity, enquire from your own experiences of life, or turn to the poets, or wait until science can give you deeper and more coherent information.

WOMAN AS "OTHER"

SIMONE DE BEAUVOIR

Of great interest is the work of the French existentialist philosopher Simone de Beauvoir (born in Paris, 1908). *Le Deuxième Sexe* (*The Second Sex*) was published in France in 1949 and in the United States in 1953, a time and climate hospitable neither to feminist scholarship nor to activism. Coming at a time of transition for the women's movement, between the social-psychological debates of the twenties and thirties and the liberation movement of the sixties, the book was a work of great creativity and courage. Broad in range and at times complex in argument, it covers issues in philosophy, biology, psychology, sociology, anthropology, education, politics, history, and more. The unifying theme is summarized by H. M. Parshley in the Translator's Preface as follows:

> . . . Since patriarchal times women have in general been forced to occupy a secondary place in the world in relation to men, a position comparable in many respects with that of racial minorities in spite of the fact that women constitute numerically at least half of the human race, and further that this secondary standing is not imposed of necessity by natural "feminine" characteristics but rather by strong environmental forces of educational and social tradition under the purposeful control of men. This, the author maintains, has resulted in the general failure of women to take a place of human dignity as free and independent existents, associated with men on a plane of intellectual and professional equality, a condition that not only has limited their achievement in many fields but also has given rise to pervasive social

evils and has had a particularly vitiating effect on the sexual relations between men and women.

De Beauvoir's thesis is not new and was not new in 1949, but it had been ignored, and her treatment of it was unique. Today, she has been faulted for being nonpolitical in her orientation, not sufficiently concerned with remedy, and at times even sexist in her perspective. Although that may be true of the work in its present context, it was a criticism far less applicable in its day, and the book was widely read.

Existentialism is a philosophy that emphasizes direct experience, feeling, awareness, choice, commitment, and honesty. It strives for living "authentically," true to one's own values and insights, living fully, freely, taking responsibility for one's actions, sharpening one's understanding, and ultimately moving beyond the confines of the brute here and now as determined by the concrete social environment. In this, one is said to strive for *transcendence*. A major theme of *The Second Sex* is that women's peripheral existence denies them the chance for transcendence.

In the following selection, de Beauvoir analyzes the female condition of *otherness* or *alterity*. It is natural, she argues, for people, either individually or collectively, to understand their existence in terms of a fundamental duality: I (Self) and things not myself (Other). The mature adult juxtaposes her or his own needs and perceptions against those of others, understanding at the same time that the other person is doing so as well. To me, I am Self, you are Other; but to you, you are Self, I am Other. I realize and accept that this is so. De Beauvoir terms the equality of claims to self and otherness from different perspectives *reciprocity*. She points out, however, that the typical reciprocity of claims to selfness does not obtain between women and men. Men perceive themselves as Self and women as Other. That is as it should be. The problem de Beauvoir emphasizes is that women too perceive men as Self (as subject) and themselves as Other. Commonly, neither men nor women recognize the reciprocity of selfness for women.

. . . A man would never get the notion of writing a book on the peculiar situation of the human male.[1] But if I wish to define myself, I must first of all say: "I am a woman"; on this truth must be based all further discussion. A man never begins by presenting himself as an individual of a certain sex; it goes without saying that he is a man. The terms *masculine* and *feminine* are used symmetrically only as a matter of form, as on legal papers. In actuality the relation of the two sexes is not quite like that of two electrical poles, for man represents both the positive and the neutral, as is indicated by the common use of *man* to designate human beings in general; whereas woman represents only the negative, defined by limiting criteria, without reciprocity. In the midst of an abstract discussion it is vexing to hear a man say: "You think thus and so because you are a woman"; but I know that my only defense is to reply: "I think thus and so because it is true," thereby removing my subjective self from the argument. It would be out of the question to reply: "And you think the contrary because you are a man," for it is understood that the fact of being a man is no peculiarity. A man is in the right in being a man; it is the woman who is in the wrong. It amounts to this: just as for the ancients there was an absolute vertical with reference to which the oblique was defined, so there is an absolute human type, the masculine. Woman has ovaries, a uterus; these peculiarities imprison her in her subjectivity, circumscribe her within the limits of her own nature. It is often said that she thinks with her glands. Man superbly ignores the fact that his anatomy also includes glands, such as the testicles, and that they secrete hormones. He thinks of his body as a direct and normal connection with the world, which he believes he apprehends objectively, whereas he regards the body of woman as a hindrance, a prison, weighed down by everything peculiar to it. "The female is a female by virtue of a certain *lack* of qualities," said Aristotle; "we should regard the female nature as afflicted with a natural defectiveness." And St. Thomas for his part pronounced woman to be an "imperfect man," an "incidental" being. This is symbolized in Genesis where Eve is depicted as made from what Bossuet called "a supernumerary bone" of Adam.

Thus humanity is male and man defines woman not in herself but as relative to him; she is not regarded as an autonomous being. Michelet writes: "Woman, the relative being . . ." And Benda is most positive in his *Rapport d'Uriel*: "The body of man makes sense in itself quite apart from that of woman, whereas the latter seems wanting in significance by itself. . . . Man can think of himself without woman. She cannot think of herself without man." And she is simply what man decrees; thus she is called "the sex," by which is meant that she appears essentially to the male as a sexual being. For him she is sex — absolute sex, no less. She is defined and differentiated with reference to man and not he with reference to her; she is the incidental, the inessential as opposed to the essential. He is the Subject, he is the Absolute — she is the Other.[2]

The category of the *Other* is as primordial as consciousness itself. In the most primitive societies, in the most ancient mythologies, one finds the expression of a duality — that of the Self and the Other. This duality was not originally attached to the division of the sexes; it was not dependent upon any empirical facts. It is revealed in such works as that of Granet on Chinese thought and those of Dumézil on the East Indies and Rome. The feminine element was at first no more involved in such pairs as Varuna-Mitra, Uranus-Zeus, Sun-Moon, and Day-Night than it was in the contrasts between Good and Evil, lucky and unlucky auspices, right and left, God and Lucifer. Otherness is a fundamental category of human thought.

Thus it is that no group ever sets itself up as the One without at once setting up the Other over against itself. If three travelers chance to occupy the same compartment, that is enough to make vaguely hostile "others" out of all the rest of the passengers on the train. In small-town eyes all persons not belonging to the village are "strangers" and suspect; to the native of a country all who inhabit other countries are "foreigners"; Jews are "different" for the anti-Semite, Negroes are "inferior" for American racists, aborigines are "natives" for colonists, proletarians are the "lower class" for the privileged.

Lévi-Strauss, at the end of a profound work on the various forms of primitive societies, reaches the following conclusion: "Passage from the state of Nature to the state of Culture is marked by man's ability to view biological relations as a series of contrasts; duality, alternation, opposition, and symmetry, whether under definite or vague forms, constitute not so much phenomena to be explained as fundamental and immediately given data of social reality." [3] These phenomena would be incomprehensible if in fact human society were simply a *Mitsein* or fellowship based on solidarity and friendliness. Things become clear, on the contrary, if, following Hegel, we find in consciousness itself a fundamental hostility toward every other consciousness; the subject can be posed only in being opposed — he sets himself up as the essential, as opposed to the other, the inessential, the object.

But the other consciousness, the other ego, sets up a reciprocal claim. The native traveling abroad is shocked to find himself in turn regarded as a "stranger" by the natives of neighboring countries. As a matter of fact, wars, festivals, trading, treaties, and contests among tribes, nations, and classes tend to deprive the concept *Other* of its absolute sense and to make manifest its relativity; willy-nilly, individuals and groups are forced to realize the reciprocity of their relations. How is it, then, that this reciprocity has not been recognized between the sexes, that one of the contrasting terms is set up as the sole essential, denying any relativity in regard to its correlative and defining the latter as pure otherness? Why is it that women do not dispute male sovereignty? No subject will readily volunteer to become the object, the inessential; it is not the Other who, in defining himself as the Other, establishes the One. The Other is posed as such by the One in defining himself as the One. But if the Other is not to regain the status of being the One, he must be submissive enough to accept this alien point of view. Whence comes this submission in the case of woman?

There are, to be sure, other cases in which a certain category has been able to dominate another completely for a time. Very often this privilege depends upon inequality of numbers — the majority imposes its rule upon the minority or persecutes it. But women are not a minority, like the American Negroes or the Jews; there are as many women as men on earth. Again, the two groups concerned have often been originally independent; they may have been formerly unaware of each other's existence, or perhaps they recognized each other's autonomy. But a historical event has resulted in the subjugation of the weaker by the stronger. The scattering of the Jews, the introduction of slavery into America, the conquests of imperialism are examples in point. In these cases the oppressed retained at least the memory of former days; they possessed in common a past, a tradition, sometimes a religion or a culture.

The parallel drawn by Bebel between women and the proletariat is valid in that neither ever formed a minority or a separate collective unit of mankind. And instead of a single historical event it is in both cases a historical development that explains their status as a class and accounts for the membership of *particular individuals* in that class. But proletarians have not always existed, whereas there have always been women. They are women in virtue of their anatomy and physiology. Throughout history they have always been subordinated to men,[4] and hence their dependency is not the result of a historical event or a social change — it was not something that *occurred*. The reason why otherness in this case seems to be an absolute is in part that it lacks the contingent or incidental nature of historical facts. A condition brought about at a certain time can be abolished at some other time, as the Negroes of Haiti and others have proved; but it might seem that a natural condition is beyond the possibility of change. In truth, however, the nature of things is no more immutably given, once for all, than is historical reality. If woman seems to be the inessential which never becomes the essential, it is because she herself fails to bring about this change. Proletarians say "We"; Negroes also. Regarding themselves as subjects, they transform the bourgeois, the whites, into "others." But women do not say "We," except at some congress of feminists or similar formal demonstration; men say "women," and women use the same word in referring to themselves. They do not authentically assume a subjective attitude. The proletarians have accomplished the revolution in Russia, the Negroes in Haiti, the Indo-Chinese are battling for it in Indo-China; but the women's effort has never been anything more than a symbolic agitation. They have gained only what men have been willing to grant; they have taken nothing, they have only received.

The reason for this is that women lack concrete means for organizing themselves into a unit which can stand face to face with the correlative unit. They have no past, no history, no religion of their own; and they have no such solidarity of work and interest as that of the proletariat. They are not even promiscuously herded together in the way that creates community feeling among the American Negroes, the ghetto Jews, the workers of Saint-Denis, or the factory hands of Renault. They live dispersed among the males, attached through residence, housework, economic condition, and social standing to certain men — fathers or husbands — more firmly than they are to other women. If they belong to the bourgeoisie, they feel solidarity with men of that class, not with proletarian women; if they are white, their allegiance is to white men, not to Negro women. The proletariat can propose to massacre the ruling class, and a sufficiently fanatical Jew or Negro might dream of getting sole possession of the atomic bomb and making humanity wholly Jewish or black;

but woman cannot even dream of exterminating the males. The bond that unites her to her oppressors is not comparable to any other. The division of the sexes is a biological fact, not an event in human history. Male and female stand opposed within a primordial *Mitsein,* and woman has not broken it. The couple is a fundamental unity with its two halves riveted together, and the cleavage of society along the line of sex is impossible. Here is to be found the basic trait of woman: she is the Other in a totality of which the two components are necessary to one another.

One could suppose that this reciprocity might have facilitated the liberation of woman. When Hercules sat at the feet of Omphale and helped with her spinning, his desire for her held him captive; but why did she fail to gain a lasting power? To revenge herself on Jason, Medea killed their children; and this grim legend would seem to suggest that she might have obtained a formidable influence over him through his love for his offspring. In *Lysistrata* Aristophanes gaily depicts a band of women who joined forces to gain social ends through the sexual needs of their men; but this is only a play. In the legend of the Sabine women, the latter soon abandoned their plan of remaining sterile to punish their ravishers. In truth woman has not been socially emancipated through man's need — sexual desire and the desire for offspring — which makes the male dependent for satisfaction upon the female.

Master and slave, also, are united by a reciprocal need, in this case economic, which does not liberate the slave. In the relation of master to slave the master does not make a point of the need that he has for the other; he has in his grasp the power of satisfying this need through his own action; whereas the slave, in his dependent condition, his hope and fear, is quite conscious of the need he has for his master. Even if the need is at bottom equally urgent for both, it always works in favor of the oppressor and against the oppressed. That is why the liberation of the working class, for example, has been slow.

Now, woman has always been man's dependent, if not his slave; the two sexes have never shared the world in equality. And even today woman is heavily handicapped, though her situation is beginning to change. Almost nowhere is her legal status the same as man's,[5] and frequently it is much to her disadvantage. Even when her rights are legally recognized in the abstract, long-standing custom prevents their full expression in the mores. In the economic sphere men and women can almost be said to make up two castes; other things being equal, the former hold the better jobs, get higher wages, and have more opportunity for success than their new competitors. In industry and politics men have a great many more positions and they monopolize the most important posts. In addition to all this, they enjoy a traditional prestige that the education of children tends in every way to support, for the present enshrines the past — and in the past all history has been made by men. At the present time, when women are beginning to take part in the affairs of the world, it is still a world that belongs to men — they have no doubt of it at all and women have scarcely any. To decline to be the Other, to refuse to be a party to the deal — this would be for women to renounce all the advantages conferred upon them by their alliance with the superior caste. Man-the-sovereign will provide woman-the-liege with material protection and will undertake the moral justification of her existence; thus she can evade at once both economic risk and the metaphysical risk of a liberty in which ends and aims must be contrived without assistance.

Indeed, along with the ethical urge of each individual to affirm his subjective existence, there is also the temptation to forgo liberty and become a thing. This is an inauspicious road, for he who takes it — passive, lost, ruined — becomes henceforth the creature of another's will, frustrated in his transcendence and deprived of every value. But it is an easy road; on it one avoids the strain involved in undertaking an authentic existence. When man makes a woman the *Other,* he may, then, expect her to manifest deep-seated tendencies toward complicity. Thus, woman may fail to lay claim to the status of subject because she lacks definite resources, because she feels the necessary bond that ties her to man regardless of reciprocity, and because she is often very well pleased with her role as the *Other.*

But it will be asked at once: how did all this begin? It is easy to see that the duality of the sexes, like any duality, gives rise to conflict. And doubtless the winner will assume the status of absolute. But why should man have won from the start? It seems possible that women could have won the victory; or that the outcome of the conflict might never have been decided. How is it that this world has always belonged to the men and that things have begun to change only recently? Is this change a good thing? Will it bring about an equal sharing of the world between men and women?

These questions are not new, and they have often been answered. But the very fact that woman *is the Other* tends to cast suspicion upon all the justifications that men have ever been able to provide for it. These have all too evidently been dictated by men's interest. A little-known feminist of the seventeenth century, Poulain de la Barre, put it this way: "All that has been written about women by men should be suspect, for the men are at once judge and party to the lawsuit." Everywhere, at all times, the males have displayed their satisfaction in feeling that they are the lords of creation. "Blessed be God . . . that He did not make me a woman," say the Jews in their morning prayers, while their wives pray on a note of resignation: "Blessed be the Lord, who created me according to His will." The first among the blessings for which Plato thanked the gods was that he had been created free, not enslaved; the second, a man, not a woman. But the males could not enjoy this privilege fully unless they believed it to be founded on the absolute and the eternal; they sought to make the fact of their supremacy into a right. "Being men, those who have made and compiled the laws have favored their own sex, and jurists have elevated these laws into principles," to quote Poulain de la Barre once more.

Legislators, priests, philosophers, writers, and scientists have striven to show that the subordinate position of woman is willed in heaven and advantageous on earth. The religions invented by men reflect this wish for domination. In the legends of Eve and Pandora men have taken up arms against women. They have made use of philosophy and theology, as the quotations from Aristotle and St. Thomas have shown. Since ancient times satirists and moralists have delighted in showing up the weaknesses of women. We are familiar with the savage indictments hurled against women throughout French literature. Montherlant, for example, follows the tradition of Jean de Meung, though with less gusto. This hostility may at times be well founded, often it is gratuitous; but in truth it more or less successfully conceals a desire for self-justification. As Montaigne says, "It is easier to accuse one sex than to excuse the other." Sometimes what is going on is clear enough. For instance, the Roman law limiting the rights of woman

cited "the imbecility, the instability of the sex" just when the weakening of family ties seemed to threaten the interests of male heirs. And in the effort to keep the married woman under guardianship, appeal was made in the sixteenth century to the authority of St. Augustine, who declared that "woman is a creature neither decisive nor constant," at a time when the single woman was thought capable of managing her property. Montaigne understood clearly how arbitrary and unjust was woman's appointed lot: "Women are not in the wrong when they decline to accept the rules laid down for them, since the men make these rules without consulting them. No wonder intrigue and strife abound." But he did not go so far as to champion their cause.

It was only later, in the eighteenth century, that genuinely democratic men began to view the matter objectively. Diderot, among others, strove to show that woman is, like man, a human being. Later John Stuart Mill came fervently to her defense. But these philosophers displayed unusual impartiality. In the nineteenth century the feminist quarrel became again a quarrel of partisans. One of the consequences of the industrial revolution was the entrance of women into productive labor, and it was just here that the claims of the feminists emerged from the realm of theory and acquired an economic basis, while their opponents became the more aggressive. Although landed property lost power to some extent, the bourgeoisie clung to the old morality that found the guarantee of private property in the solidity of the family. Woman was ordered back into the home the more harshly as her emancipation became a real menace. Even within the working class the men endeavored to restrain woman's liberation, because they began to see the women as dangerous competitors — the more so because they were accustomed to work for lower wages.

In proving woman's inferiority, the anti-feminists then began to draw not only upon religion, philosophy, and theology, as before, but also upon science — biology, experimental psychology, etc. At most they were willing to grant "equality in difference" to the *other* sex. That profitable formula is most significant; it is precisely like the "equal but separate" formula of the Jim Crow laws aimed at the North American Negroes. As is well known, this so-called equalitarian segregation has resulted only in the most extreme discrimination. The similarity just noted is in no way due to chance, for whether it is a race, a caste, a class, or a sex that is reduced to a position of inferiority, the methods of justification are the same. "The eternal feminine" corresponds to "the black soul" and to "the Jewish character." True, the Jewish problem is on the whole very different from the other two — to the anti-Semite the Jew is not so much an inferior as he is an enemy for whom there is to be granted no place on earth, for whom annihilation is the fate desired. But there are deep similarities between the situation of woman and that of the Negro. Both are being emancipated today from a like paternalism, and the former master class wishes to "keep them in their place" — that is, the place chosen for them. In both cases the former masters lavish more or less sincere eulogies, either on the virtues of "the good Negro" with his dormant, childish, merry soul — the submissive Negro — or on the merits of the woman who is "truly feminine" — that is, frivolous, infantile, irresponsible — the submissive woman. In both cases the dominant class bases its argument on a state of affairs that it has itself created. As George Bernard Shaw puts it, in substance, "The American white relegates the black to

the rank of shoeshine boy; and he concludes from this that the black is good for nothing but shining shoes." This vicious circle is met with in all analogous circumstances; when an individual (or a group of individuals) is kept in a situation of inferiority, the fact is that he *is* inferior. But the significance of the verb *to be* must be rightly understood here; it is in bad faith to give it a static value when it really has the dynamic Hegelian sense of "to have become." Yes, women on the whole *are* today inferior to men; that is, their situation affords them fewer possibilities. The question is: should that state of affairs continue?

Many men hope that it will continue; not all have given up the battle. The conservative bourgeoisie still see in the emancipation of women a menace to their morality and their interests. Some men dread feminine competition. Recently a male student wrote in the *Hebdo-Latin:* "Every woman student who goes into medicine or law robs us of a job." He never questioned his rights in this world. And economic interests are not the only ones concerned. One of the benefits that oppression confers upon the oppressors is that the most humble among them is made to *feel* superior; thus, a "poor white" in the South can console himself with the thought that he is not a "dirty nigger" — and the more prosperous whites cleverly exploit this pride.

Similarly, the most mediocre of males feels himself a demigod as compared with women. It was much easier for M. de Montherlant to think himself a hero when he faced women (and women chosen for his purpose) than when he was obliged to act the man among men — something many women have done better than he, for that matter. And in September 1948, in one of his articles in the *Figaro littéraire,* Claude Mauriac — whose great originality is admired by all

— could [6] write regarding woman: "*We* listen on a tone [*sic!*] of polite indifference . . . to the most brilliant among them, well knowing that her wit reflects more or less luminously ideas that come from *us.*" Evidently the speaker referred to is not reflecting the ideas of Mauriac himself, for no one knows of his having any. It may be that she reflects ideas originating with men, but then, even among men there are those who have been known to appropriate ideas not their own; and one can well ask whether Claude Mauriac might not find more interesting a conversation reflecting Descartes, Marx, or Gide rather than himself. What is really remarkable is that by using the questionable *we* he identifies himself with St. Paul, Hegel, Lenin, and Nietzsche, and from the lofty eminence of their grandeur looks down disdainfully upon the bevy of women who make bold to converse with him on a footing of equality. In truth, I know of more than one woman who would refuse to suffer with patience Mauriac's "tone of polite indifference."

I have lingered on this example because the masculine attitude is here displayed with disarming ingenuousness. But men profit in many more subtle ways from the otherness, the alterity of woman. Here is miraculous balm for those afflicted with an inferiority complex, and indeed no one is more arrogant toward women, more aggressive or scornful, than the man who is anxious about his virility. Those who are not fear-ridden in the presence of their fellow men are much more disposed to recognize a fellow creature in woman; but even to these the myth of Women, the Other, is precious for many reasons.[7] They cannot be blamed for not cheerfully relinquishing all the benefits they derive from the myth, for they realize what they would lose in relinquishing woman as they fancy her to be, while they fail to realize what they have to gain from the woman of

tomorrow. Refusal to pose oneself as the Subject, unique and absolute, requires great self-denial. Furthermore, the vast majority of men make no such claim explicitly. They do not *postulate* woman as inferior, for today they are too thoroughly imbued with the ideal of democracy not to recognize all human beings as equals.

In the bossom of the family, woman seems in the eyes of childhood and youth to be clothed in the same social dignity as the adult males. Later on, the young man, desiring and loving, experiences the resistance, the independence of the woman desired and loved; in marriage, he respects woman as wife and mother, and in the concrete events of conjugal life she stands there before him as a free being. He can therefore feel that social subordination as between the sexes no longer exists and that on the whole, in spite of differences, woman is an equal. As, however, he observes some points of inferiority — the most important being unfitness for the professions — he attributes these to natural causes. When he is in a co-operative and benevolent relation with woman, his theme is the principle of abstract equality, and he does not base his attitude upon such inequality as may exist. But when he is in conflict with her, the situation is reversed: his theme will be the existing inequality, and he will even take it as justification for denying abstract equality.[8]

So it is that many men will affirm as if in good faith that women *are* the equals of man and that they have nothing to clamor for, while *at the same time* they will say that women can never be the equals of man and that their demands are in vain. It is, in point of fact, a difficult matter for man to realize the extreme importance of social discriminations which seem outwardly insignificant but which produce in woman moral and intellectual effects so profound that they appear to spring from her original nature.[9] The most sympathetic of men never fully comprehend woman's concrete situation. And there is no reason to put much trust in the men when they rush to the defense of privileges whose full extent they can hardly measure. We shall not, then, permit ourselves to be intimidated by the number and violence of the attacks launched against women, nor to be entrapped by the self-seeking eulogies bestowed on the "true woman," nor to profit by the enthusiasm for woman's destiny manifested by men who would not for the world have any part of it.

We should consider the arguments of the feminists with no less suspicion, however, for very often their controversial aim deprives them of all real value. If the "woman question" seems trivial, it is because masculine arrogance has made of it a "quarrel"; and when quarreling one no longer reasons well. People have tirelessly sought to prove that woman is superior, inferior, or equal to man. Some say that, having been created after Adam, she is evidently a secondary being; others say on the contrary that Adam was only a rough draft and that God succeeded in producing the human being in perfection when He created Eve. Woman's brain is smaller; yes, but it is relatively larger. Christ was made a man; yes, but perhaps for his greater humility. Each argument at once suggests its opposite, and both are often fallacious. If we are to gain understanding, we must get out of these ruts; we must discard the vague notions of superiority, inferiority, equality which have hitherto corrupted every discussion of the subject and start afresh.

Notes

1. The Kinsey Report [Alfred C. Kinsey and others: *Sexual Behavior in the Human Male*

(W. B. Saunders Co., 1948)] is no exception, for it is limited to describing the sexual characteristics of American men, which is quite a different matter.

2. E. Lévinas expresses this idea most explicitly in his essay *Temps et l'Autre*. "Is there not a case in which otherness, alterity [*altérité*], unquestionably marks the nature of a being, as its essence, an instance of otherness not consisting purely and simply in the opposition of two species of the same genus? I think that the feminine represents the contrary in its absolute sense, this contrariness being in no wise affected by any relation between it and its correlative and thus remaining absolutely other. Sex is not a certain specific difference ... no more is the sexual difference a mere contradiction. ... Nor does this difference lie in the duality of two complementary terms, for two complementary terms imply a pre-existing whole. ... Otherness reaches its full flowering in the feminine, a term of the same rank as consciousness but of opposite meaning."

I suppose that Lévinas does not forget that woman, too, is aware of her own consciousness, or ego. But it is striking that he deliberately takes a man's point of view, disregarding the reciprocity of subject and object. When he writes that woman is mystery, he implies that she is mystery for man. Thus his description, which is intended to be objective, is in fact an assertion of masculine privilege.

3. See C. Lévi-Strauss: *Les Structures élémentaires de la parenté*. My thanks are due to C. Lévi-Strauss for his kindness in furnishing me with the proofs of his work, which, among others, I have used liberally in Part II.

4. With rare exceptions, perhaps, like certain matriarchal rulers, queens, and the like. — Tr.

5. At the moment an "equal rights" amendment to the Constitution of the United States is before Congress. — Tr.

6. Or at least he thought he could.

7. A significant article on this theme by Michel Carrouges appeared in No. 292 of the *Cahiers du Sud*. He writes indignantly: "Would that there were no woman-myth at all but only a cohort of cooks, matrons, prostitutes, and bluestockings serving functions of pleasure or

usefulness!" That is to say, in his view woman has no existence in and for herself; he thinks only of her *function* in the male world. Her reason for existence lies in man. But then, in fact, her poetic "function" as a myth might be more valued than any other. The real problem is precisely to find out why woman should be defined with relation to man.

8. For example, a man will say that he considers his wife in no wise degraded because she has no gainful occupation. The profession of housewife is just as lofty, and so on. But when the first quarrel comes, he will exclaim: "Why, you couldn't make your living without me!"

9. The specific purpose of Book II of this study is to describe this process.

4

Counter Images: Feminist Response

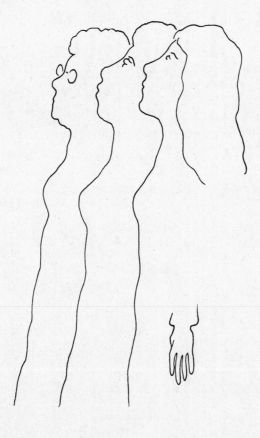

The Challengers

Subtract the effort to meet the stereotypic model, undo much of the indoctrination; add a streak of independence, self-affirmation and self-respect; toss in a growing knowledge of women's history and circumstance, pride in womanhood, and concern for other women; wrap all in a strong awareness of the entire process and condition—and you have some picture of the feminist woman, who today is challenging the old images and building new ones.

If patriarchy is hostile to women in general, even those who conform to masculist standards and regulations, one might imagine the attitudes it is likely to have toward the feminist woman, who rejects its regulations and constraints, refuses to accept the "place" constructed for her, and aspires instead to a space of her own regardless of its acceptability to the patriarchs. To the masculist a feminist woman is the very incarnation of a nightmare come true. According to myth, a woman unfettered by venerable convention, by the watchful eyes of fathers, brothers, and husbands, is dangerous. Now here are women not only unredeemed by their utility in service, but questioning convention, rebelling, refusing their appointed labors, lusting after male jobs, intruding on male territory, demanding preposterous freedoms, and worst of all, making headway!

To verify the hostility these women arouse, one need only turn to the usual indicators of social attitudes—TV stories, letters to the editor in newspapers and magazines, commentaries in books and magazines, political campaign rhetoric and election results, church sermons, in-group jokes, and many other sources. Notice how the feminist, the "libber," and her demands are presented. The libber, either ridiculed or despised, is first of all *unfeminine*. This term implies not only a lack of "charm" and expertise in certain "womanly" behaviors; it suggests as well a particular appearance—hard, often dirty, unkempt, badly dressed, not pretty—and a clear disadvantage in whatever it takes to attract men. The libber is perceived as in some way having trouble with sex and as having real problems relating to men because of bad experiences either in childhood (with her father) or later on (with husband, lover, or rapist). That is, the libber is maladjusted or just plain sick. From a representative cross section of hostile comment, one gathers that libbers want

- to become like men, to "sleep around," to reject their maternal prerogatives and special "power," to emasculate men, and to destroy civilization ... (George Gilder)[1]
- to indulge themselves, abrogate familial responsibility, and avoid sex ... (Midge Decter)[2]
- to reject their true "femininity," castrate men, have a penis of their own, and disrupt society ... (Sigmund Freud)[3]
- to surrender their womanliness, become "phallic women," and distort the innate balance of complementarity in life and nature ... (Karl Stern)[4]
- to destroy the universities, academic freedom, scholarship, etc.... (those against affirmative action)
- to give up all "the wonderful privileges" women in this country now enjoy ... (Phyllis Schlafly)

[1] George Gilder, *Sexual Suicide* (New York: Quadrangle, 1973), chap. 1.

[2] Midge Decter, *The New Chastity and Other Arguments Against Women's Liberation* (New York: Coward, McCann & Geoghegan, 1972).

[3] Especially in Sigmund Freud, "Femininity," lecture XXXIII, in *The Standard Edition of the Complete Psychological Works of Sigmund Freud*, trans. and ed. James Strachey et al. (London: Hogarth Press, 1964), vol. XXII.

[4] Karl Stern, *The Flight from Woman* (New York: Farrar, Straus & Giroux, 1965).

- to take jobs away from those who are "really oppressed." . . .
- to turn their children over to communist-inspired day care centers. . . .

Feminists, it is said, tend to get "shrill" or "strident," which means literally high-pitched, grating on the ear. These are terms one would expect masculists to use; they are (and are meant to be) deprecating. They not only refer to the higher pitch of the female voice, but they conjure up images of whining old crones and nagging shrews. They are a means of ridiculing and discounting feminist arguments: "Not only do I not accept the things you are saying, but I don't even take them seriously; I reduce them simply to the ugly noises of thwarted, aggressive women."

Yet I believe that, in a sense different from the intended one, the terms *shrill* and *strident* are accurate, for they reveal a deeper, perhaps unconscious truth. The arguments of the feminists *are* extremely grating — at least to traditional mind sets. In attacking the ancient categories and the lines between women and men, feminists are striking at values and feelings that run deep and have powerful emotional impact. If even the smallest changes in sex orientation (such as altering hair length) provoke marked reaction, certainly greater shifts will beget proportionately greater response. Feminists can and do expect to incur a great deal of anger and abuse, whether that is expressed as ridicule or as outright invective.

Women, feminist or nonfeminist, exist in a hostile environment. We live within a struggle. Feminists work within a struggle, philosophize, analyze, act, try, grow within a struggle. Our development, the way we grow, the things we learn, and the visions we create all bear that mark and must be understood in that context.

To one degree or another, feminists perceive themselves as revolutionaries. In Shula-mith Firestone's words: "If there were another word more all-embracing than revolution we would use it." [5] Yet we are revolutionaries on peculiar terrain, for we do not typically seek war, to exchange one hierarchy for another. We rarely hate our "enemies." In fact, we often hesitate to call anyone "enemy," not quite certain who or what that enemy might be. It is said that most of us live intimately in the homes of our oppressors, loving and caring for them. We are not decided on a firm, far-reaching revolutionary program, for it is too early in our analysis to settle on one set of strategies or goals. Yet with all, we *are* revolutionaries, for in altering the arrangements of work and relationships between women and men, in challenging the primacy of Martial/masculist values, we mean to change the very nature of life and society for all people.

There is a saying in the women's movement: the personal is the political. Such a phrase means several things: It means first that no gulf truly exists between the personal and social elements of our lives. It means that much of what we have taken in our lives to be personal matters — the problems of communication with our men, for example, or the failures in our sexual relationships — are actually not purely personal, but are also sociopolitical, a consequence of the power arrangements between women and men. "The personal is the political" means as well that the insights we gain into our private circumstances ultimately can have far-reaching political and social consequences.

Kate Millett defined politics as "power-structured relationships, arrangements whereby one group of persons is controlled by another." [6] If that is the case, then such ques-

[5] Shulamith Firestone, *The Dialectic of Sex* (New York: Bantam, 1971), p. 1.
[6] Kate Millett, *Sexual Politics* (New York: Doubleday, 1970), p. 23.

tions as "Why do I get up earlier than he does and prepare him breakfast before we both go off to our jobs?" are political questions, because they refer to the control of women's time and effort by men. That women are expected to wash, cook, clean, and serve and yet not be paid for their labors nor even recognized to be working, that women are placed by society in such a position and men are not is a political issue and no small matter, for it is but one symptom of the exploitation and domination of 51 percent of the population of the world by the remaining 49 percent. And if the exploitation of women by men is both model and manifestation of all forms of exploitation and oppression, as many feminists argue, then the understanding of male/female roles is of the profoundest importance, and the challengers' analyses of sexism, rather than petty and inconsequential as charged, are tremendously significant both for the 51 percent and for humanity in general.

The personal is the political, and feminists are fomenting a revolution out of consciousness-raising.

The Process: Coming to Understand

The process of learning and unlearning, of coming to recognize the nature and consequence of the images of women, and of reorienting oneself toward them is difficult, painstaking, and time consuming. Considering the length of time each of us has lived with the images and the extent of their power in our culture, it is not surprising that this is so.

Consciousness-Raising

Each of us has come to the task of becoming aware from her own set of circumstances and in her own way. Most women report a first moment, an event or happening in which they experienced "the explosion," the first rush of awareness or insight into sexism and its very personal connection with them. Triggered perhaps by a personal crisis — an unwanted pregnancy and its attendant social cruelties, or a divorce that left her burdened and impoverished, or perhaps by job discrimination, or a social humiliation, or even a feminist speech that freed the woman from some damaging beliefs — the explosion or insight once begun is almost always followed by a growing and developing awareness. Often the growth is conscious, sought after and cultivated. Sometimes it happens despite resistance, for the awareness, though freeing and exciting, is also painful and frightening.

This process of coming to understand sexism fully, at the highest level of awareness, is called consciousness-raising. It functions both to intensify awareness with regard to the implications of sexism and to stimulate the search for alternatives. Consciousness-raising takes a variety of forms, follows from various techniques (for example, self-examination, role reversal, shared discussion), and takes different paths with attendant effects and reactions.

The Insight: It's a Lie

How does the experience of consciousness proceed?

Suppose you spent your youth learning the trade of "femininity." Suppose Mama and Papa taught you to make yourself just right so that you could attract just the right man so that he could care for you and make you happy because women and men do those things, and it is right and proper and wonderful that it should be that way. Suppose you do just what is expected: You become feminine and sweet and sexy, and you find that man (or, rather, he finds you) and you marry and have three lovely children and he has a lovely job and you have a lovely house and...suppose suddenly it ends. Suppose you find yourself in your thirty-third year with three lovely children, no husband, meager support or none, no income, no skills, no joy. Suppose you see him with freedom, mobility, job skills, income, future. What do you say? Usually you say first, "What did I do wrong?" Perhaps in time you gain some insight and recognize that what went wrong were the assumptions and presuppositions, the whole set of beliefs. Then you say, "It was a lie."

Suppose it doesn't end. Suppose you have the lovely children, the lovely home, the lovely husband, and you aren't happy. You're depressed or restless or grouchy. You're always busy, but you're bored. What do you say? You say, "What's wrong with me? Why am I unsatisfied?" or perhaps you say, "It was a lie."

Suppose you did all the things you were advised to do in *Fascinating Womanhood*[7] — you were kind, thoughtful, playful, and selfless — but instead of "celestial love," you got misunderstanding, neglect, and hostility. What do you say?

Suppose it all went a different way. Suppose your youth was poor and hard. You learned to scrape and scrape. Now jobs are hard to find, and when they do come along they pay even less than a man's, and your men come and go, and you have some babies to support, but when employment projects open you hear, "Take care of the men — first things first." What do you say?

Or suppose the scenario is very different. You spent your youth learning and preparing and studying, and the future is bright because America is a land of opportunity. You know things are harder for a woman and you have to be twice as good, but you *are* twice as good. But suppose you can't find the kind of job you want: They just ask you how many words per minute you can type. Suppose they do give you that job (EEOC and Title IX, you know), but you find you're the only sales associate answering the phone or having a typewriter on your desk. What do you say?

When at last, for whatever reason and in whatever way, you recognize one lie, you get suspicious, and you begin to look at it all, and soon you see just how many lies there are. You think:

If women are stupid, incompetent, and petty as they say, but I am female and *not* those things, either I am not a woman, or it's a lie. And if it's a lie about me, it's a lie about other women, and if that's a lie then perhaps the rest is a lie. Perhaps it's a lie that women can't be trusted with important tasks; that for women beauty is more important than brains; that women are satisfied in the home of a he-male; that women don't need jobs or salary; that men should make the decisions; that women should *never* be "promiscuous"; that...

The questioning once begun has no limits. We discover lie upon lie, myth upon myth. The response? If it is not true that women are bad or incompetent, then all that subordination is just plain wrong. If the role won't work, we'll have to find us another way.

Where is it written that it must be the way it is?

What We Learn: The Images Tell Us

The heading of this section is presumptuous. What we learn when we begin to ask the questions is so vast that it could not be told in a thousand volumes. What I would like to

[7] Helen B. Andelin, *Fascinating Womanhood* (New York: Bantam, 1975).

describe here, however, are some of the insights feminists have had into themselves as women, into the effects of the myths and stereotypes, and into the possibilities without them.

The Splitting of the Androgyne: Complements

The term *androgyne* is composed of the two ancient Greek words *andros* and *gyne, man* and *woman*. In certain feminist theories[8] it refers to a person who is complete, who is characterized by combining the best qualities of what has traditionally been taken to be male and female. The androgyne, or the androgynous person, is strong and tender, rational and feeling, independent and receptive, and so on.

As we saw earlier, what obtains currently in the ideals of women and men is the exact opposite: Instead of androgyny there is complementarity. Women and men are expected to exhibit opposite and exclusive traits and behavior.

Patriarchal Ideals

Ideal Man	Ideal Woman
powerful, creative	nurturant, supportive
intelligent, rational	intuitive, emotional, cunning
independent, self-reliant	needful, dependent
strong	tender
courageous, daring	timid, fragile
responsible, resolute	capricious, childlike
temperate, cautious, sober	ebullient, exuberant
honest, forthright	tactful, evasive, artful
active, forceful	passive, receptive
honorable, principled, just	obedient, loyal, kind, merciful
self-affirming	self-abnegating
authoritative, decisive	compliant, submissive
successful, task oriented	contented, serene, being oriented
he does	she cares
he lives in the mind	she lives in the heart
he confronts the world	she withdraws from the world

It has been said by some of the sexists that men and women are complements to one another; that their complementarity is natural, desirable, and beautiful; that together these two, different but interlocking, provide for themselves, their families, and society all that is necessary and harmonious for human living. Actually, the theory of complementarity is based on a division of labor: men and women, each having their different natural capacities and abilities, have different (but equally important) tasks and spheres that are appropriate to their "natures."

Not only is this mystification, feminists argue, but one may make certain specific criticisms of the complementary arrangement.

• It may be rather pretty to envision two interlocking creatures walking hand in hand down life's highway, but in reality half a person and half a person equal two half persons, not one whole.

• As Plato pointed out in the third century B.C., human beings require balance and excellence in all of their qualities to function well. The ideal man of patriarchy may be eminently successful so far as society is concerned, but if he lacks the ability to feel and to experience fully the affective elements of living, he is gaining only half of what life has to offer, and he is apt to be a rather unpleasant person. The ideal patriarchal woman may be very fetching and capable of deep feeling, but she is also unable to care for herself in

---

[8] See Joyce Trebilcot, "Two Forms of Androgynism," in *Feminism and Philosophy,* ed. Mary Vetterling-Braggin, Frederick A. Elliston, and Jane English (Totowa, N.J.: Littlefield, Adams, 1977).

the material aspects of life, and hence she is at the mercy of people and events.

• It is unrealistic to believe that two people, entirely different in capacity and outlook, could successfully manage meaningful communication, mutual respect, and love. Rather than interlocking, these people are locked together in destructive though symbiotic partnership. The traditional complementary arrangement is logical and functional only in terms of social and economic efficiency, not in terms of human needs. Complementarity, a "division of labor," may be an effective way of accomplishing a variety of social tasks; and when marriage functioned as a social arrangement for satisfying certain community needs, complementarity might have been a productive perspective. But if marriage is to function as a *personal* arrangement, as a primary source of emotional support and profound human interchange, then complementarity is dysfunctional, and "interlocking" symbiosis is a psychological and spiritual disaster.

• Even if it were possible for two people to relate well in complementarity, women would still be at a marked disadvantage. In fact, we are.

In the first place, the thesis that in our society the two elements, male and female, are different but equal in value and importance is a lie. The system, patriarchal in origin and serving patriarchal ends, is built on the principle that men rule and women obey, that men take care of themselves and women take care of everyone but themselves. Even in the most benevolent of all worlds, that cannot be a very promising arrangement for women.

In the second place, though it is true that in a system of complementarity men and women are both in the position of using half and only half of their human capacities (and so losing half as well), the half that men keep is the half valued by society (which stands to

reason, given the control of the masculists), and the half that women keep is devalued. Though women are praised, there is always in that praise a patronizing undertone. The praise is awarded for traits that society deems substandard.

> Sigh no more, ladies
> Time is male
> and in his cups drinks to the fair.
> Bemused by gallantry, we hear
> our mediocrities over-praised,
> indolence read as abnegation,
> slattern thought styled intuition,
> every lapse forgiven, our crime
> only to cast too bold a shadow
> or smash the mould straight off.
> For that, solitary confinement,
> tear gas, attrition shelling.
> Few applicants for that honor.
> — Adrienne Rich[9]

Human Versus Female

In Chapter 2 we looked at the historical confusion of the concepts of *man* and *human*. In fact the patriarchal schema of complementary ideals is both cause and effect of that confusion. The configuration of traits and qualities reserved for men is coextensive with the configuration expected of excellent human beings: intelligence, independence, courage, honor, strength. Not so the configuration for a woman. Womanly perfection and human excellence in this schema are incompatible.

In effect, women are being asked to choose between their human selves and their sexual identities. Unlike men, who develop and im-

[9] Adrienne Rich, "Snapshots of a Daughter-in-Law," in *Snapshots of a Daughter-in-Law: Poems 1954–1962* (New York: Norton, 1956), p. 26.

prove their masculinity and humanity concurrently, women in patriarchy can only destroy their acceptability as females as they develop their human excellence, or else destroy their human potential as they become more "feminine."

A recent study translates this issue into the language of psychology.

A study by Inge Broverman and her colleagues suggests that many clinicians today view their female patients the way Freud viewed his. They gave 79 therapists (46 male and 33 female psychiatrists, psychologists and social workers) a sex-role-stereotype questionnaire. This test consists of 122 pairs of traits such as "very subjective . . . very objective" or "not at all aggressive . . . very aggressive."

The investigators asked the subjects to rate each set of traits on a scale from one to seven, in terms of where a healthy male should fall, a healthy female, or a healthy adult (sex unspecified). They found:

1. There was a high agreement among these clinicians on the attributes that characterize men, women and adults.
2. There were no major differences between the male and the female clinicians.
3. Clinicians have different standards of mental health for men and women. Their standards for a "healthy adult man" looked like those for a "healthy adult"; but healthy women differed from both by being: submissive, emotional, easily influenced, sensitive to being hurt, excitable, conceited about their appearance, dependent, not very adventurous, less competitive, unaggressive, unobjective — and besides, they dislike math and science. This "healthy woman" is not very likable, all in all! (In fact, other studies have shown that these traits, characteristic of normal women, are the least socially desirable.) For a woman to be "healthy," then, she must adjust to the behavioral norms for her sex even though these norms are not highly

valued by her society, her men — or her therapist.[10]

That is, behavior considered healthy for men was not considered healthy for women, and vice versa. Men and women were expected to display opposite characteristics. But the traits deemed *generally* healthy, desirable for *people* without regard to sex, were those expected of or prescribed for men. Women displaying those traits would be deemed "unfeminine." At the same time, women who were "feminine," who would be deemed healthy or adjusted as women, would by this schema have to be judged sick as people!

Feminists argue that complementarity is a disaster for both sexes, that the healthy person (of either sex) is the human being who excels in both configurations or perhaps rejects *any* configuration, who has the wherewithal to cope with the necessities and challenges of life as well as the sensibilities to do it in a way that is *for* life.

What's Wrong with "Femininity"?

In the preceding chapter we noted that the dichotomy in the female ideal required women to exemplify at once two incompatible characterizations, Mary and the Playmate, and we could see how destructive such a contradiction would be. But there are more things wrong with patriarchal female images, or "femininity," than only the contradictions wrought by dichotomy. For one thing, feminists argue, the pejorative stereotype of Woman the Inferior is simply false. For an-

10 Reported by Phyllis Chesler, "Men Drive Women Crazy," in *The Female Experience,* ed. Carol Tavris (Del Mar, Calif.: Communications Research Machines, 1973), p. 83.

other, neither of the supposedly nonpejorative images, Mary or Playmate, is a desirable model. In fact, they are demeaning and destructive.

The Myth of Female Inferiority

According to misogynist ideology, women are inferior in two ways: (1) women are morally inferior, evil, bad, sinful, dangerous, harmful, and dirty; (2) women are inferior in competence — physically, intellectually, and spiritually.

WOMEN ARE EVIL   That women are morally inferior to the point of being positively evil is a well-worn theme from antiquity to the present:

> Woman is a pitfall — a pitfall, a hole, a
> ditch.
> Woman is a sharp iron dagger that cuts a
> man's throat.
> — Mesopotamian poem[11]

> Man who trusts womankind trusts deceivers.
> — Hesiod [12]

> The beauty of woman is the greatest snare.
> — St. John Chrysostom[13]

> You are the devil's gateway . . . the first deserter of the divine law; you are she who persuaded him whom the devil was not valiant enough to attack. You destroyed so easily God's image, man. On account of your desert — that is, death — even the son of God had to die.
> — Tertullian[14]

> I have not left any calamity more detrimental to mankind than woman.
> — Islamic saying[15]

> Art thou not formed of foul slime? Art thou not full of uncleanness?
> — Rule for Anchoresses[16]

> God made Adam master over all creatures, to rule over all living things, but when Eve persuaded him that he was lord even over God she spoiled everything. . . . With tricks and cunning women deceive men.
> — Martin Luther[17]

> I cannot escape the notion . . . that for women the level of what is ethically normal is different from what it is in man.
> — Sigmund Freud [18]

So much for the pedestal. With these historical statements, I have not even scratched the surface. All you need do is look about you for further evidence of the belief in female malevolence. In fact, it would be a good exercise for you to do so.

Such allegations of evil can simply be dismissed. They are too nonsensical to refute. While patriarchal society prattles of women's destructiveness, feminists ask: Who creates and marches off to war? Who hunts living creatures for fun? Who fights for kicks? Who pillages the earth for profit? Who colonizes and exploits? What destruction have we wrought that is even nearly comparable to that?

WOMEN ARE INCOMPETENT   The charge that both requires and admits of refutation is that women are simply not as able as men, not as

11 Quoted in Vern L. and Bonnie Bullough, *The Subordinate Sex* (Baltimore: Penguin, 1974), p. 29. © 1974 by the Board of Trustees of the University of Illinois.
12 Ibid., p. 58.
13 Ibid., p. 98.
14 Ibid., p. 114.

15 Ibid., p. 145.
16 Ibid., p. 176.
17 Ibid., p. 198.
18 Quoted in Chesler, "Men Drive Women Crazy," p. 82.

competent in any task except those traditionally designated "women's work." It is said that women are less capable than men of doing any kind of work requiring a high degree of rationality, abstraction, and intelligence, because women are intellectually inferior and are characteristically not given to rationality and logic. It is said that, even in the best of circumstances, even unusually intelligent women are still not the equals of men in important and difficult work because they are temperamentally unsuited to seriousness of purpose, sustained effort, and strain. It is said that women are unable to withstand the pressure of competition either with people or with ideas and are therefore always destined to defeat. And finally, it is said that women who are not thus characteristically inferior are not "normal," are not attractive or natural or feminine, and are not even really women.

As evidence of women's inferiority, it is asserted that the great scientists, inventors, legislators, entrepreneurs, artists, humorists, authors, sportsmen, and warriors have always been men. Where are the female geniuses, the Beethovens, Shakespeares, and Platos? We are told that in business and industry, in the professions and professional schools, it is men who outnumber women, who outrank women, who achieve. Even today, argue the sexists, when women have all the opportunities of men, they still do not make it. Why? Because women have not the intelligence, the instincts, the grit, the motivation, the stamina, or the strength of men. In every way that counts, women are inferior.

This is the schema: Part I — It is unnatural and undesirable for women to do what men do; women must expend their energies serving, supporting, and pleasing; they must not be allowed to do what men do. Part II — Because women do not do the things men do, it is evident that they cannot do what men do and are therefore obviously inferior. The argument is circular, superficial, and fallacious, but it has tremendous power in society — at least as rationale — and it is believed by a majority, both female and male.

Feminists challenge the schema and refute the arguments. We contend that the socialization process and the structure of society, not "natural" capacities, account for the different levels of achievement and motivation in women and men. Although the literature is mixed and the research inconclusive, it appears safe to say that there is no evidence that men and women differ in intellectual capacity or IQ and a good deal of evidence to the contrary. Apparently males excel earlier in spatial perception and females in verbal perception, but even this difference may possibly be accounted for by social conditions, and it is certainly not sufficient to account for the wide divergence in interest, abilities, motivations, and achievements.

There is a great deal of evidence to suggest that "feminine" ideals, the images, models, and values described in Chapter 3, the constraints and circumstances imposed on women from childhood, are far more responsible for women's alleged and actual lack of motivation, grit, and aggressiveness than any inherent childlikeness or timidity. Differences in training, expectations, and experience produce ineffectualness and defeatism in women.

There is not now nor has there ever been equality of opportunity for women — in business, the professions, education, the arts, or any other socially prized and male-controlled venture. Even today the doors are only grudgingly open to women. Women are still ill paid for their work, segregated in function, last hired, first fired. Even if this were not so, the separate but not equal conditioning of females and the hostility and ignorance of the men already in positions of power make any claims to equality of opportunity a farce.

Women's dual roles and incompatible cultural requirements render success in a profession painfully expensive if not impossible.

The married woman who works outside the home usually carries two jobs — one paid (however humbly), one not paid. She is lawyer (teacher, doctor, pilot, secretary ...) and she is homemaker and mother. The price of such demands, both for her profession and for her personal health, should be obvious. The unmarried professional faces different costs: slurs on her womanhood, social disapprobation, at times loneliness. According to the image, ideal women are intuitive but not rational, lovely but not effectual. The successful professional, according to the myth, is the unsuccessful *femme*. To opt for a career, the story goes, is to relinquish one's happily-ever-after. Such visions, even unfounded, are disturbing. They do not do much for professional motivation, as Matina Horner discovered in her research into success avoidance in women.

In a study of women in and aspiring to management positions in industry, Margaret Hennig and Anne Jardim found that sex-role differences in attitudes, values, and outlook affect the course of professional careers for women and men.[19] They found that women and men have very different approaches to work itself and to careers, with formidable effects on their success potential. Hennig and Jardim posit that the socialization process is responsible for these differences, supporting and broadening the feminist thesis that something other than inferiority accounts for women's lack of professional success even where opportunity *appears* to exist.

To the questions "Why haven't women produced any geniuses? Why are there no female Shakespeares or Beethovens?" Virginia Woolf answered that we have not been allowed a "room of our own." We have been accorded bread, but not roses. We have not been allowed the spiritual atmosphere, the creative space men are heir to, the amenities that raise life above the mundane and encourage one to creativity.

The issues treated here all point to an important feminist argument: Many factors in the environment conspire to impede women's competence and accomplishments in many areas — hostile or deprecating attitudes of incumbent men, lack of support and assistance from all quarters, dual and/or incompatible professional and nonprofessional functions, pervasiveness of the male (alien, inhospitable) ambience, and socialization that erodes confidence and self-assertion. Rather than being inferior, women are hampered in developing competence in the most profound ways. To overcome the obstacles put in our way we must indeed be twice as good, but in more ways than we expected. It is not surprising that so many of us don't "succeed." It is extraordinary that any of us do.

And what we do accomplish often disappears! In the history books, achieving women are rarely given more than a few lines, and the experiences of ordinary women, unlike those of "the common man," are simply not considered. Our successes have often gone underground — they are attributed to men or are thought to be anonymous, because women were not permitted success. Female authors or artists often used male pen names or "protectors" or "co-authors" who co-authored them right out of their due. Ancient accomplishments are simply usurped by the patriarchy. Male historians and anthropologists "forget" to research the contributions of women to early civilization — the introduction of pottery, weaving, food preparation, and so on. Current anthologies of the arts do not bother to include women's works, because these are "substandard," "narrow," or "lacking in grandeur."

[19] Margaret Hennig and Anne Jardim, *The Managerial Woman* (New York: Doubleday/Anchor, 1977).

The Dark Side of the "Good" Woman

Refutation of the claim that women as a class are inferior does not exhaust the feminist offensive against patriarchal female images. The so-called positive images are a target as well, for even the ideals — Perfect Woman, Mary, or the Playmate — are destructive and counterproductive. Even in their praise, approval, and veneration, the ideals themselves actually disparage women and cause us to disparage ourselves and assist in the diminution of our lives.

Consider once again the major requirements of traditional femininity: beauty, self-effacement, fragility, and domesticity. History, poetry, literature, philosophy, and even science have eulogized the woman who embodies these qualities, but feminists have taken a closer look. Demystifying the image, translating myth into reality, through introspection and analysis, we have seen the dark side of the image.

BEAUTY AND ATTRACTIVENESS Attractiveness, at least in people, is by and large a cultural phenomenon; beauty is socially defined. In patriarchy men construct the ideal in their own interests, and women whose lives have no purpose outside of being chosen, whose identities and fortunes have been made subject to their appeal to men, have little choice but to struggle with the imperious requirements of "beauty," even though the ideal is impossible. For no human being can be perfect in hair, skin, teeth, shape, proportion, and scent, and furthermore be so "naturally" and endlessly. Constant comparison with the figures of screen and magazine that more nearly realize the ideal must leave us always defeated, always at a disadvantage, always self-deprecating.

Women are called narcissistic. We are chided for our obsession with clothing and fashion. We are ridiculed for our willingness to sit for hours under a hair drier and for slathering cream onto our skin at night. And yet what other choice is there *if we accept* the traditional role that bids us to use our appearance to attract and keep a mate? Can we reject that option if any life other than "being chosen" is deemed undesirable or even unacceptable, if "attractive" and "sexy" are society's primary terms of approbation for women?

SELF-EFFACEMENT The concept of submissiveness for women has changed since the Middle Ages. Few expect a woman to lower her head and whisper, "yes, sir." And yet the concept survives: No one likes an aggressive woman. We may quarrel, we may fight, but in the end, if we don't give in and lose often enough, we will lose our man. Assertiveness, the kind that goes beyond a little pluckiness, is still not considered acceptable in women; it is always translated into aggression.

And self-effacement? The husband who taunts in public is teasing. The wife who does the same is attacking her man's ego. She is not expected to say "yes, dear," but she is expected to yield the decisions, follow his job, entertain his friends. He drives when he chooses, he works late when he needs to. He storms out of the house when angry; she screams or she cries, but she stays put.

Women, it is said, are prone to depression. We get "neurotic," clingy, and nagging. What man who could not make his own decisions, place his needs high in priority, satisfy his desires and wishes, please himself, and follow his goals would not get depressed and "neurotic"? What man who was barred from creating his own pleasures and diversions wouldn't nag others for entertainment? The logical outcome of self-effacement is depression.

FRAGILITY Very close to self-effacement is fragility. Women are to be submissive because we are weaker, needful of protection and guidance. In gratitude and in our understanding of our best interests, we are to take direction from the stronger. Fragility — timidity, delicacy, needfulness — means vulnerability. It is, to be sure, very appealing to the male. But vulnerability of the sort required of women means dependence. To be fearful of strange situations, to be hesitant when decision is called for, to avoid risk, to learn *not* to defend oneself, to feign or even encourage physical weakness, to shrink from the world is to place oneself at the mercy of circumstance; it is to afford oneself dependence on others. Even if those on whom one depends are completely trustworthy, marvelously competent, and around forever, a person in such a situation must feel some lack of self-respect, a sense of inferiority and ineffectualness. For such people life is truncated, and the pleasures and rewards of independence, accomplishment, and power are unknown. Further, in a culture that clearly values competence, where human excellence is said to include independence and self-reliance, the endlessly vulnerable and dependent person is a figure of ridicule and contempt. We saw earlier that for women this was so.

DOMESTICITY *Kinder, Kirche, Küche,* "children, church, and cooking," was the slogan of ideal womanhood for Hitler's Germany, the Third Reich. Similarly, housekeeping and all of its attendant duties, care of children, including teaching, nursing, and other service occupations, and worship (*not* theology) are said to be the only legitimate occupations for women in patriarchy. What is more, the work is to be task oriented, not policy oriented; that is, we are to execute our jobs according to prescribed procedure, not to define those jobs, not to create their meaning and expression. Ours is to carry out that part

of any job that is repetitive, routine, uninteresting. Work that transcends the mundane belongs to men. Women may be cooks, not chefs; dressmakers, not designers; secretaries, not executives. We may busy ourselves with the pretties of curtains or vases, but we are not to presume to art.

The imminent, as the existentialists call it, the mundane, the here and now, the "what," is dull and petty unless it is lifted by the transcendent, the eternal, the why and the wherefore. Tasks and things do not have the scope or the breadth of ideas. Interest, scope, and depth belong to creativity. Interesting people are living, growing people; they are people themselves interested, excited, challenged and challenging, learning, and experiencing. *Kinder, Kirche, Küche,* however taxing of time and energy, cannot be creative unless so treated and perceived. In closing women to freedom of experience and movement, in disallowing as "unfeminine" an interest in the transcendent, in constricting our limits and our power, patriarchy confines us to the narrow and then condemns us for our "narrowness."

Patriarchal feminine ideals are monstrous. When successful, they destroy, and when we become the most perfect realizations of them, we are most damaged.

Responses: Feminist Reactions and Ideals

When feminist women look over the history of the tyranny of these beliefs and visions, when we note the destruction they have wrought and the exploitation they have legitimized, we are appalled and filled with emotion — anger, pain, grief, shock, determination.

We are called petty, prattling noisily about inconsequentials. Is the loss of potential, of self-respect and autonomy inconsequential?

Are economic deprivation and financial dependency inconsequential? Or the use and abuse of our bodies for the interests of others? Of infanticide, physical mutilation, footbinding, and other physical torture? Is 10,000 years of domination and exploitation of 51 percent of humanity inconsequential?

We are advised to be ladylike, to go slow, ask nicely, develop a sense of humor. Are we to swallow our pride once again and plead prettily for our liberation from those who have withheld it for 10,000 years and continue to withhold it? Are we to chuckle good-naturedly at centuries of restrictive clothing, at chastity belts and whalebone corsets, at enforced fatigue of body and mind, at slave labor and sexual servitude, at prostitution and rape? Are we to take these images in our stride, once more play the peacemakers and maintain the hated postures just a little longer while the masculists adjust to the idea of change?

No, say the feminists, we won't do it. If we are angry, it is because we have seen the attack. If we are noisy, it is because women are suffering. If we are strident, it is because the affirmation of women is grating on the ears of the masculists. "It is not that we are so radical," said Gloria Steinem, "but that there is something radically wrong with our world."

We have seen the visions of *woman the oppressed, woman the exploited, woman the outsider, woman the lost, woman the debased,* and we reject them all, opting instead for positive visions.

Feminists are building new visions. Throwing away the imperatives of "femininity" so badly conceived, canceling "ladylikeness," we are redefining what is desirable for us, what is commendable, what is possible. Our new heroines include *woman rediscovering herself,* in history and for today; *woman redeeming herself* in her own eyes; *woman rightfully angry,* rightfully fighting; and *woman the leader,* the pillar, who in the words of Wilma Scott Heide may "create the kind of world where the power of love exceeds the love of power." [20]

What we shall be, what we should and can be, is still an open question. Feminists are still very much involved in the matter of what we are not and should not be. We have been asked what we would wish to be, how life would be if we could have our way, and many have answered that it is hard to say. We have never known a time when we have not been subordinated and devalued; we have never known a time of freedom and self-determination. We are only beginning to learn our history and conceive our future — with few known models and precious little experience. In very large part the question of what we ought to be is the question philosophers have pursued for centuries: What is human excellence and virtue? Women are, after all, human beings, and our strivings and hopes are those of all humanity. How our ideals may be different from those of men or how our insights may alter the notion of human excellence is yet to be seen.

Certain things are so: We are being born, coming into life. We are struggling, and in the birth struggle there is joy. That has been expressed eloquently by Simone de Beauvoir, Germaine Greer, and Erica Jong.

The free woman is just being born; when she has won possession of herself perhaps Rimbaud's prophecy will be fulfilled: "There shall be poets! When woman's unmeasured bondage shall be broken, when she shall live for and through herself, man — hitherto detestable — having let her go, she, too, will be poet! Woman will find the unknown! Will her ideational worlds be different from ours?

[20] Wilma Scott Heide in the Introduction to *Hospitals, Paternalism, and the Role of the Nurse,* by JoAnn Ashley (New York: Teachers College Press, 1976), p. viii.

She will come upon strange, unfathomable, repellent, delightful things; we shall take them, we shall comprehend them." * It is not sure that her "ideational worlds" will be different from those of men, since it will be through attaining the same situation as theirs that she will find emancipation; to say in what degree she will remain different, in what degree these differences will retain their importance — this would be to hazard bold predictions indeed. What is certain is that hitherto woman's possibilities have been suppressed and lost to humanity, and that it is high time she be permitted to take her chances in her own interest and in the interest of all.

— Simone de Beauvoir[21]

The surest guide to the correctness of the path that women take is *joy in the struggle.* Revolution is the festival of the oppressed. For a long time there may be no perceptible reward for women other than their new sense of purpose and integrity. Joy does not mean riotous glee, but it does mean the purposive employment of energy in a self-chosen enterprise. It does mean pride and confidence. It does mean communication and cooperation with others based on delight in their company and your own. To be emancipated from helplessness and need and walk freely upon the earth that is your birthright. To refuse hobbles and deformity and take possession of your body and glory in its power, accepting its own laws of loveliness. To have something to desire, something to make, something to achieve, and at last something genuine to give. To be freed from guilt and shame and the tireless self-discipline of women. To stop pretending and dissembling, cajoling and manipulating, and begin to control and sympathize. To claim the masculine virtues of magnanimity and generosity and courage. It goes much further

than equal pay for equal work, for it ought to revolutionize the conditions of work completely. It does not understand the phrase "equality of opportunity," for it seems that the opportunities will have to be utterly changed and women's souls changed so that they desire opportunity instead of shrinking from it. The first significant discovery we shall make as we racket along our female road to freedom is that men are not free, and they will seek to make this an argument why nobody should be free. We can only reply that slaves enslave their masters, and by securing our own manumission we may show men the way that they could follow when they jumped off their own treadmill. Privileged women will pluck at your sleeve and seek to enlist you in the "fight" for reforms, but reforms are retrogressive. The old process must be broken, not made new. Bitter women will call you to rebellion, but you have too much to do. What *will* you do?

— Germaine Greer[22]

Narrowing life because of the fears,
narrowing it between the dust motes,
narrowing the pink baby
between the green-limbed monsters,
& the drooling idiots,
& the ghosts of Thalidomide infants,
narrowing hope,
always narrowing hope.

Mother sits on one shoulder hissing:
Life is dangerous.
Father sits on the other sighing:
Lucky you.
Grandmother, grandfather, big sister:
You'll die if you leave us,
you'll die if you ever leave us.

Sweetheart, baby sister,
you'll die anyway
& so will I.

---

* In a letter to Pierre Demeny, May 15, 1871.

[21] Simone de Beauvoir, *The Second Sex,* ed. and trans. H. M. Parshley (New York: Knopf, 1953), p. 715.

[22] Germaine Greer, *The Female Eunuch* (New York: McGraw-Hill, 1971), pp. 328–329. Copyright © 1970, 1971 by Germaine Greer. Reprinted by permission of the publishers, McGraw-Hill Book Company and Granada Publishing Limited.

Even if you walk the wide greensward,
even if you
& your beautiful big belly
embrace the world of men & trees,
even if you moan with pleasure,
& smoke the sweet grass
& feast on strawberries in bed,
you'll die anyway —
wide or narrow,
you're going to die.
As long as you're at it,
die wide.
Follow your belly to the green pasture.
Lie down in the sun's dapple.
Life is not as dangerous
as mother said.
It is more dangerous,
more wide.

— Erica Jong[23]

23 "For Claudia, Against Narrowness." From *Loveroot*
by Erica Jong. Copyright © 1968, 1969, 1973, 1974,
1975 by Erica Mann Jong. Reprinted by permission of
Holt, Rinehart and Winston, Publishers.

What might I, as typical of many feminists, include in an ideal? I would like to see

- women bearing all the marvelous traits of excellence chronicled by the great philosophers: strength, intelligence, temperance, independence, courage, principle, honor, and the rest
- women, beautiful and healthy in our bodies, comfortable with them, understanding them, proud of them
- women free of the fetters of possession and exploitation, free to define our own female beings, to direct the rites, events, and progress of our own lives and experience
- women caring for one another, proud of our womanhood, caring for any living thing in the way that is meaningful to us
- women contributing wholeheartedly and equally with men to civilization in whatever way we enjoy and believe to be right

Selections

WOMAN — WHICH INCLUDES MAN, OF COURSE: AN EXPERIENCE IN AWARENESS

THEODORA WELLS

Theodora Wells was born in 1926 and studied at the University of California at Berkeley and at the University of Southern California. She is a communication and management consultant, heading her own firm and conducting conferences and training in management development for women. Her *Breakthrough: Women into Management* was published in 1972. She is a member of the Women's Equity Action League (WEAL) and served on an advisory board of a feminist women's health collective. The following selection, particularly well known, is an "experience in awareness." It should be read and felt slowly and deeply.

There is much concern today about the future of man, which means, of course, both men and women — generic Man. For a woman to take exception to this use of the term "man" is often seen as defensive hairsplitting by an "emotional female."

The following experience is an invitation to awareness in which you are asked to feel into, and stay with, your feelings through each step, letting them absorb you. If you start intellectualizing, try to turn it down and let your feelings again surface to your awareness.

Consider reversing the generic term Man. Think of the future of Woman which, of course, includes both women and men. Feel into that, sense its meaning to you — as a woman — as a man.

Think of it always being that way, every day of your life. Feel the everpresence of woman and feel the nonpresence of man. Absorb what it tells you about the importance and value of being woman — of being man.

Recall that everything you have ever read all your life uses only female pronouns — she, her — meaning both girls and boys, both women and men. Recall that most of the voices on radio and most of the faces on TV are women's — when important events are covered — on commercials — and on the late talk shows. Recall that you have no male senator representing you in Washington.

Feel into the fact that women are the leaders, the power-centers, the prime-movers. Man, whose natural role is husband and father, fulfills himself through nurturing children and making the home a refuge for woman. This is only natural to balance the biological role of woman who devotes her entire body to the race during pregnancy.

Then feel further into the obvious biological explanation for woman as the ideal — her genital construction. By design, female genitals are compact and internal, protected by her body. Male genitals are so exposed that he must be protected from outside attack to assure the perpetuation of the race. His vulnerability clearly requires sheltering.

Thus, by nature, males are more passive than females, and have a desire in sexual relations to be symbolically engulfed by the protective body of the woman. Males psychologically yearn for this protection, fully realizing their masculinity at this time — feeling exposed and vulnerable at other times. The male is not fully adult until he has overcome his infantile tendency to penis orgasm and has achieved the mature surrender of the testicle orgasm. He then feels himself a "whole man" when engulfed by the woman.

If the male denies these feelings, he is unconsciously rejecting his masculinity. Therapy is thus indicated to help him adjust to his own nature. Of course, therapy is administered by a woman, who has the education and wisdom to facilitate openness leading to the male's growth and self-actualization.

To help him feel into his defensive emotionality, he is invited to get in touch with the "child" in him. He remembers his sister's jeering at his primitive genitals that "flop around foolishly." She can run, climb and ride horseback unencumbered. Obviously, since she is free to move, she is encouraged to develop her body and mind in preparation for her active responsibilities of adult womanhood. The male vulnerability needs female protection, so he is taught the less active, caring, virtues of homemaking.

Because of his clitoris-envy, he learns to strap up his genitals, and learns to feel ashamed and unclean because of his nocturnal emissions. Instead, he is encouraged to keep his body lean and dream of getting married, waiting for the time of his fulfillment — when "his woman" gives him a girl-child to carry on the family name. He knows that if it is a boy-child he has failed somehow — but they can try again.

In getting to your feelings on being a woman — on being a man — stay with the sensing you are now experiencing. As the words begin to surface, say what you feel from inside you.

THE HUMAN-NOT-QUITE-HUMAN

DOROTHY L. SAYERS

It is not well known that Dorothy Sayers (1893–1957), the writer of witty mystery novels and sometimes caustic essays on religion, politics, and popular behavior, was an extremely learned scholar and the author of works in theology and philosophy. *Unpopular Opinions*, a collection of her essays, includes two strong feminist pieces, "Are Women Human?" in which she argues against the separation of individuals into useless rigid categories (for example, male and female), and the essay reprinted in part below. Here Sayers elaborates on the confusion of malekind with mankind (in her language, *vir* and *homo*). She restates the common feminist theme: Women are generally perceived as females primarily, only incidentally human, whereas men are seen as human beings who happen to be male. In blistering terms she lays bare the hypocrisy and cruelty afforded women by men, particularly in more recent times.

The first thing that strikes the careless observer is that women are unlike men. They are "the opposite sex" — (though why "opposite" I do not know; what is the "neighbouring sex"?). But the fundamental thing is that women are more like men than anything else in the world. They are human beings. *Vir* is male and *Femina* is female: but *Homo* is male and female.

This is the equality claimed and the fact that is persistently evaded and denied. No matter what arguments are used, the discussion is vitiated from the start, because Man is always dealt with as both *Homo* and *Vir,* but Woman only as *Femina*.

I have seen it solemnly stated in a newspaper that the seats on the near side of a bus are always filled before those on the off side, because, "men find them more comfortable on account of the camber of the road, and women find they get a better view of the shop windows." As though the camber of the road did not affect male and female bodies equally. Men, you observe, are given a *Homo* reason; but Women, a *Femina* reason, because they are not fully human. . . .

Probably no man has ever troubled to imagine how strange his life would appear to himself if it were unrelentingly assessed in terms of his maleness; if everything he wore, said, or did had to be justified by reference to female approval; if he were compelled to regard himself, day in day out, not

as a member of society, but merely (*salvâ reverentiâ*) as a virile member of society. If the centre of his dress-consciousness were the cod-piece, his education directed to making him a spirited lover and meek paterfamilias; his interests held to be natural only in so far as they were sexual. If from school and lecture-room, Press and pulpit, he heard the persistent outpouring of a shrill and scolding voice, bidding him remember his biological function. If he were vexed by continual advice how to add a rough male touch to his typing, how to be learned without losing his masculine appeal, how to combine chemical research with seduction, how to play bridge without incurring the suspicion of impotence. If, instead of allowing with a smile that "women prefer cave-men," he felt the unrelenting pressure of a whole social structure forcing him to order all his goings in conformity with that pronouncement.

He would hear (and would he like hearing?) the female counterpart of Dr. Peck* informing him: "I am no supporter of the Horseback Hall doctrine of 'gun-tail, plough-tail and stud' as the only spheres for masculine action; but we do need a more definite conception of the nature and scope of man's life." In any book on sociology he would find, after the main portion dealing with human needs and rights, a supplementary chapter devoted to "The Position of the

From Dorothy L. Sayers, *Unpopular Opinions* (New York: Harcourt, Brace, 1947). Copyright 1947, renewed 1974 Dorothy L. Sayers.

* Dr. Peck had disclaimed adherence to the *Kinder, Kirche, Küche* school of thought.

Male in the Perfect State." His newspaper would assist him with a "Men's Corner," telling him how, by the expenditure of a good deal of money and a couple of hours a day, he could attract the girls and retain his wife's affection; and when he had succeeded in capturing a mate, his name would be taken from him, and society would present him with a special title to proclaim his achievement. People would write books called, "History of the Male," or "Males of the Bible," or "The Psychology of the Male," and he would be regaled daily with headlines, such as "Gentleman-Doctor's Discovery," "Male-Secretary Wins Calcutta Sweep," "Men-Artists at the Academy." If he gave an interview to a reporter, or performed any unusual exploit, he would find it recorded in such terms as these: "Professor Bract, although a distinguished botanist, is not in any way an unmanly man. He has, in fact, a wife and seven children. Tall and burly, the hands with which he handles his delicate specimens are as gnarled and powerful as those of a Canadian lumberjack, and when I swilled beer with him in his laboratory, he bawled his conclusions at me in a strong, gruff voice that implemented the promise of his swaggering moustache." Or: "There is nothing in the least feminine about the home surroundings of Mr. Focus, the famous children's photographer. His 'den' is panelled in teak and decorated with rude sculptures from Easter Island; over his austere iron bedstead hangs a fine reproduction of the Rape of the Sabines." Or: "I asked M. Sapristi, the renowned chef, whether kitchen-cult was not a rather unusual occupation for a man. 'Not a bit of it!' he replied, bluffly. 'It is the genius that counts, not the sex. As they say in *la belle Ecosse,* a man's a man for a' that' — and his gusty, manly guffaw blew three small patty pans from the dresser."

He would be edified by solemn discussions about "Should Men serve in Drapery Establishments?" and acrimonious ones about "Tea-Drinking Men"; by cross-shots of public affairs "from the masculine angle," and by irritable correspondence about men who expose their anatomy on beaches (so masculine of them), conceal it in dressing-gowns (too feminine of them), think about nothing but women, pretend an unnatural indifference to women, exploit their sex to get jobs, lower the tone of the office by their sexless appearance, and generally fail to please a public opinion which demands the incompatible. And at dinner-parties he would hear the wheedling, unctuous, predatory female voice demand: "And why should you trouble your handsome little head about politics?"

If, after a few centuries of this kind of treatment, the male was a little self-conscious, a little on the defensive, and a little bewildered about what was required of him, I should not blame him. If he traded a little upon his sex, I could forgive him. If he presented the world with a major social problem, I should scarcely be surprised. It would be more surprising if he retained any rag of sanity and self-respect.

"The rights of woman," says Dr. Peck, "considered in the economic sphere, seem to involve her in competition with men in the struggle for jobs." It does seem so indeed, and this is hardly to be wondered at; for the competition began to appear when the men took over the women's jobs by transferring them from the home to the factory. The mediæval woman had effective power and a measure of real (though not political) equality, for she had control of many industries — spinning, weaving, baking, brewing, distilling, perfumery, preserving, pickling — in which she worked with head as well as hands, in command of her own domestic staff. But now the control and direction — all the intelligent part — of those industries have gone to the men, and the women have been left, not with their "proper" *work* but with *employment* in those occupations. And at the same time, they are exhorted to be feminine and return to the home from which all intelligent occupation has been steadily removed.

. . . The period from which we are emerging was like no other: a period when empty head and idle hands were qualities for which a man prized his woman and despised her. When, by an odd, sadistic twist of morality, sexual intercourse was deemed to be a marital right to be religiously enforced upon a meek reluctance — as though the insatiable appetite of wives were not one of the oldest jokes in the world, older than mothers-in-law, and far more venerable than kippers. When to think about sex was considered indelicate in a woman, and to think about anything else unfeminine. When to "manage" a husband by lying and the exploitation of sex was held to be honesty and virtue. When the education that Thomas More gave his daughters was denounced as a devilish indulgence, and could only be wrung from the outraged holder of the purse-strings by tears and martyrdom and desperate revolt, in the teeth of the world's mockery and the reprobation of a scandalised Church. . . .

A BRIGHT WOMAN IS CAUGHT IN A DOUBLE BIND

MATINA HORNER

Psychologist Matina Horner was educated at Bryn Mawr and at the University of Michigan, where she took her doctorate and began her research into achievement motivation in women. In 1969 she joined the faculty of Harvard, continuing there her studies of success anxiety. In 1972, at the age of 32, she was named president of Radcliffe College, the youngest president since its founding. Matina Horner's now classic though controversial research into the "fear of success" syndrome in women presents evidence of certain complex attitudes toward work that tend to impede women's professional potential. Conflicts, fears, and confusion occasioned by the contradictions between traditional sex-role expectations and the requirements of a career can cause women to inhibit their own professional success.

Consider Phil, a bright young college sophomore. He has always done well in school, he is in the honors program, he has wanted to be a doctor as long as he can remember. We ask him to tell us a story based on one clue: *"After first-term finals, John finds himself at the top of his medical-school class.* Phil writes:

John is a conscientious young man who worked hard. He is pleased with himself. John has always wanted to go into medicine and is very dedicated ... John continues working hard and eventually graduates at the top of his class.

Now consider Monica, another honors student. She too has always done well and she too has visions of a flourishing career. We give her the same clue, but with "Anne" as the successful student — *after first-term finals, Anne finds herself at the top of her medical-school class.* Instead of identifying with Anne's triumph, Monica tells a bizarre tale:

Anne starts proclaiming her surprise and joy. Her fellow classmates are so disgusted with her behavior that they jump on her in a body and beat her. She is maimed for life.

Next we ask Monica and Phil to work on a series of achievement tests by themselves. Monica scores higher than Phil. Finally we get them together, competing against each other on the same kind of tests. Phil performs magnificently, but Monica dissolves into a bundle of nerves.

The glaring contrast between the two stories and the dramatic changes in performance in competitive situations illustrate important differences between men and women in reacting to achievement.

In 1953, David McClelland, John Atkinson and colleagues published the first major work on the "achievement motive." Through the use of the Thematic Apperception Test (TAT), they were able to isolate the psychological characteristic of a *need to achieve.* This seemed to be an internalized standard of excellence, motivating the individual to do

well in any achievement-oriented situation involving intelligence and leadership ability. Subsequent investigators studied innumerable facets of achievement motivation: how it is instilled in children, how it is expressed, how it relates to social class, even how it is connected to the rise and fall of civilizations. The result of all this research is an impressive and a theoretically consistent body of data about the achievement motive — in men.

Women, however, are conspicuously absent from almost all of the studies. In the few cases where the ladies were included, the results were contradictory or confusing. So women were eventually left out altogether. The predominantly male researchers apparently decided, as Freud had before them, that the only way to understand woman was to turn to the poets. Atkinson's 1958 book, *Motives in Fantasy, Action and Society,* is an 800-page compilation of all of the theories and facts on achievement motivation in men. Women got a footnote, reflecting the state of the science.

To help remedy this lopsided state of affairs, I undertook to explore the basis for sex differences in achievement motivation. But where to begin?

My first clue came from the one consistent finding on the women: they get higher test-anxiety scores than do the men. Eleanor Maccoby has suggested that the girl who is motivated to achieve is defying conventions of what girls "should" do. As a result, the intellectual woman pays a price in anxiety. Margaret Mead concurs, noting that intense intellectual striving can be viewed as "competitively aggressive behavior." And of course Freud thought that the whole essence of femininity lay in repressing aggressiveness (and hence intellectuality).

Thus consciously or unconsciously the girl equates intellectual achievement with loss of femininity. A bright woman is caught in a double bind. In testing and other achievement-oriented situations she worries not only about failure, but also about success. If she fails, she is not living up to her own standards of performance; if she succeeds she is not living up to societal expectations about the female role. Men in our society do not experience this kind of ambivalence, because they are not only permitted but actively encouraged to do well.

For women, then, the desire to achieve is often contaminated by what I call the *motive to avoid success.* I define it as the fear that success in competitive achievement situations will lead to negative consequences, such as unpopularity and loss of femininity. This motive, like the achievement motive itself, is a stable disposition within the person, acquired early in life along with other sex-role standards. When fear of success conflicts with a desire to be successful, the result is an inhibition of achievement motivation.

I began my study with several hypotheses about the motive to avoid success:

1. Of course, it would be far more characteristic of women than of men.

2. It would be more characteristic of women who are capable of success and who are career-oriented than of women not so motivated. Women who are not seeking success should not, after all, be threatened by it.

3. I anticipated that the anxiety over success would be greater in competitive situations (when one's intellectual performance is evaluated against someone else's) than in noncompetitive ones (when one works alone). The aggressive, masculine aspects of achievement striving are certainly more pronounced in competitive settings, particularly when the opponent is male. Women's

anxiety should therefore be greatest when they compete with men.

I administered the standard TAT achievement motivation measures to a sample of 90 girls and 88 boys, all undergraduates at the University of Michigan. In addition, I asked each to tell a story based on the clue described before: *After first-term finals, John (Anne) finds himself (herself) at the top of his (her) medical-school class.* The girls wrote about Anne, the boys about John.

Their stories were scored for "motive to avoid success" if they expressed any negative imagery that reflected concern about doing well. Generally, such imagery fell into three categories:

1. The most frequent Anne story reflected strong fears of social rejection as a result of success. The girls in this group showed anxiety about becoming unpopular, unmarriageable and lonely.

> Anne is an acne-faced bookworm. She runs to the bulletin board and finds she's at the top. As usual she smarts off. A chorus of groans is the rest of the class's reply.... She studies 12 hours a day, and lives at home to save money. "Well it certainly paid off. All the Friday and Saturday nights without dates, fun — I'll be the best woman doctor alive." And yet a twinge of sadness comes thru — she wonders what she really has ...

> Although Anne is happy with her success she fears what will happen to her social life. The male med. students don't seem to think very highly of a female who has beaten them in their field ... She will be a proud and successful but alas a very *lonely* doctor.

> Anne doesn't want to be number one in her class ... she feels she shouldn't rank so high because of social reasons. She drops down to ninth in the class and then marries the boy who graduates number one.

Anne is pretty darn proud of herself, but everyone hates and envies her.

2. Girls in the second category were less concerned with issues of social approval or disapproval; they were more worried about definitions of womanhood. Their stories expressed guilt and despair over success, and doubts about their femininity or normality.

Unfortunately Anne no longer feels so certain that she really wants to be a doctor. She is worried about herself and wonders if perhaps she isn't normal... Anne decides not to continue with her medical work but to take courses that have a deeper personal meaning for her.

Anne feels guilty ... She will finally have a nervous breakdown and quit medical school and marry a successful young doctor.

Anne is pleased. She had worked extraordinarily hard and her grades showed it. "It is not enough," Anne thinks. "I am not happy." She didn't even want to be a doctor. She is not sure what she wants. Anne says to hell with the whole business and goes into social work — not hardly as glamorous, prestigious or lucrative; but she is happy.

3. The third group of stories did not even try to confront the ambivalence about doing well. Girls in this category simply denied the possibility that any mere woman could be so successful. Some of them completely changed the content of the clue, or distorted it, or refused to believe it, or absolved Anne of responsibility for her success. These stories were remarkable for their psychological ingenuity:

Anne is a *code name* for a nonexistent person created by a group of med. students. They take turns writing exams for Anne.

Anne is really happy she's on top, though *Tom is higher than she* — though that's as it should be ... Anne doesn't mind Tom winning.

Anne is talking to her counselor. Counselor says she will make a fine *nurse*.

It was *luck* that Anne came out on top because she didn't want to go to medical school anyway.

Fifty-nine girls — over 65 per cent — told stories that fell into one or another of the above categories. But only eight boys, fewer than 10 per cent, showed evidence of the motive to avoid success. (These differences are significant at better than the .0005 level.) In fact, sometimes I think that most of the young men in the sample were incipient Horatio Algers. They expressed unequivocal delight at John's success (clearly John had worked hard for it), and projected a grand and glorious future for him. There was none of the hostility, bitterness and ambivalence that the girls felt for Anne. In short, the differences between male and female stories based on essentially the same clue were enormous.

Two of the stories are particularly revealing examples of this male-female contrast. The girls insisted that Anne give up her career for marriage:

Anne has a boyfriend, Carl, in the same class and they are quite serious ... She wants him to be scholastically higher than she is. Anne will deliberately lower her academic standing the next term, while she does all she subtly can to help Carl. His grades come up and Anne soon drops out of medical school. They marry and he goes on in school while she raises their family.

But of course the boys would ask John to do no such thing:

John has worked very hard and his long hours of study have paid off . . . He is thinking about his girl, Cheri, whom he will marry at the end of med. school. He realizes he can give her all the things she desires after he becomes established. He will go on in med. school and be successful in the long run.

Success inhibits social life for the girls; it enhances social life for the boys.

Earlier I suggested that the motive to avoid success is especially aroused in competitive situations. In the second part of this study I wanted to see whether the aggressive overtones of competition against men scared the girls away. Would competition raise their anxiety about success and thus lower their performance?

First I put all of the students together in a large competitive group, and gave them a series of achievement tests (verbal and arithmetic). I then assigned them randomly to one of three other experimental conditions. One-third worked on a similar set of tests, each in competition with a member of the same sex. One-third competed against a member of the opposite sex. The last third worked by themselves, a non-competitive condition.

Ability is an important factor in achievement motivation research. If you want to compare two persons on the strength of their *motivation* to succeed, how do you know that any differences in performance are not due to initial differences in *ability* to succeed? One way of avoiding this problem is to use each subject as his own control; that is, the performance of an individual working alone can be compared with his score in competition. Ability thus remains constant; any change in score must be due to motivational factors. This control over ability was, of course, possible only for the last third of my subjects: the 30 girls and 30 boys who had worked alone *and* in the large

group competition. I decided to look at their scores first.

Performance changed dramatically over the two situations. A large number of the men did far better when they were in competition than when they worked alone. For the women the reverse was true. Fewer than one-third of the women, but more than two-thirds of the men, got significantly higher scores in competition.

When we looked at just the girls in terms of the motive to avoid success, the comparisons were even more striking. As predicted, the students who felt ambivalent or anxious about doing well turned in their best scores when they worked by themselves. Seventy-seven per cent of the girls who feared success did better alone than in competition. Women who were low on the motive, however, behaved more like the men: 93 per cent of them got higher scores in competition. (Results significant at the .005.)

Female fear of success & performance

	Perform better working alone	Perform better in competition
High fear of success	13	4
Low fear of success	1	12

As a final test of motivational differences, I asked the students to indicate on a scale from 1 to 100 "How important was it for you to do well in this situation?" The high-fear-of-success girls said that it was much more important for them to do well when they worked alone than when they worked in either kind of competition. For the low-fear girls, such differences were not statistically significant. Their test scores were higher in competition, as we saw, and they thought that it was important to succeed no matter what the setting. And in all experimental conditions — working alone, or in competition against males or females — high-fear women consistently lagged behind their fearless comrades on the importance of doing well.

These findings suggest that most women will fully explore their intellectual potential only when they do not need to compete — and least of all when they are competing with men. This was most true of women with a strong anxiety about success. Unfortunately, these are often the same women who could be very successful if they were free from that anxiety. The girls in my sample who feared success also tended to have high intellectual ability and histories of academic success. (It is interesting to note that all but two of these girls were majoring in the humanities and in spite of very high grade points aspired to traditional female careers: housewife, mother, nurse, schoolteacher. Girls who did not fear success, however, were aspiring to graduate degrees and careers in such scientific areas as math, physics and chemistry.)

We can see from this small study that achievement motivation in women is much more complex than the same drive in men. Most men do not find many inhibiting forces in their path if they are able and motivated to succeed. As a result, they are not threatened by competition; in fact, surpassing an opponent is a source of pride and enhanced masculinity.

If a woman sets out to do well, however, she bumps into a number of obstacles. She learns that it really isn't ladylike to be too intellectual. She is warned that men will treat her with distrustful tolerance at best, and outright prejudice at worst, if she pursues a career. She learns the truth of Samuel Johnson's comment, "A man is in general better pleased when he has a good dinner upon his table, than when his wife talks Greek." So she doesn't learn Greek, and the motive to avoid success is born.

In recent years many legal and educational barriers to female achievement have been removed; but it is clear that a psychological barrier remains. The motive to avoid success has an all-too-important influence on the intellectual and professional lives of women in our society. But perhaps there is cause for optimism. Monica may have seen Anne maimed for life, but a few of the girls forecast a happier future for our medical student. Said one:

> Anne is quite a lady — not only is she tops academically, but she is liked and admired by her fellow students — quite a trick in a man-dominated field. She is brilliant — but she is also a woman. She will continue to be at or near the top. And . . . always a lady.

A ROOM OF ONE'S OWN

VIRGINIA WOOLF

Virginia Woolf (1882–1941), British author and co-founder (with her husband) of the Hogarth Press, grew up in literary circles and traveled with some of the most interesting British thinkers of her day. Her novels include *The Voyage Out* (1915), *Night and Day* (1919), *Monday or Tuesday* (1921), *Mrs. Dalloway* (1925), *To the Lighthouse* (1927), and *The Years* (1937). She wrote two famous feminist essays, *A Room of One's Own* (1929) and *Three Guineas* (1938). In 1941, fearful that she was going mad, she killed herself.

The following excerpt is from the first of two chapters in which, with vivid imagery, Woolf depicts the ambiance and style of the great British university ("Oxbridge") — its appearance, the rhythm of the day, the amenities within, the effect on the human spirit. Here the plain dinner served to the women of "Fernham College" is her metaphor for the historical poverty of women, the paucity of money, time, dignity, freedom, and peace that women are heir to. Angrily she develops the contrast between the "plain gravy soup" affordable by the women's colleges and the "partridges and wine" of the university's well-endowed male enclaves, between the commodious gentility of the "queer old gentlemen ... with tufts of fur upon their shoulders" and "all those women working year after year and finding it hard to get two thousand pounds together." She thinks of the women mothering "thirteen children," of the library to which women are not admitted, and of the insecurity women bear, and forces one to consider the effect of all this on the mind of the writer. Consider further, if you will, the effect of the entire configuration on the mind of any thinker, or potential artist or scientist or musician, and you have the beginnings of the answer to the question: Why are there no women geniuses?

Here was my soup. Dinner was being served in the great dining-hall. Far from being spring it was in fact an evening in October. Everybody was assembled in the big dining-room. Dinner was ready. Here was the soup. It was a plain gravy soup. There was nothing to stir the fancy in that. One could have seen through the transparent liquid any pattern that there might have been on the plate itself. But there was no pattern. The plate was plain. Next came beef with its attendant greens and potatoes — a homely trinity, suggesting the rumps of cattle in a muddy market, and sprouts curled and yellowed at the edge, and bargaining and cheapening, and women with string bags on Monday morning. There was no reason to complain of human nature's daily food, seeing that the supply was sufficient and coalminers doubtless were sitting down to less. Prunes and custard followed. And if any one complains that prunes, even when mitigated by custard, are an uncharitable vegetable (fruit they are not), stringy as a miser's heart and exuding a fluid such as might run in misers' veins who have denied themselves wine and warmth for eighty years and yet not given to the poor, he should reflect that there are people whose charity embraces even the prune. Biscuits and cheese came next, and here the water-jug was liberally passed round, for it is the nature of biscuits to be dry, and these were biscuits to the core. That was all. The meal was over. Everybody scraped their chairs back; the swing-doors swung violently to and fro; soon the hall was emptied of every sign of food and made ready no doubt for breakfast next morning. Down corridors and up staircases the youth of England went banging and singing. And was it for a guest, a stranger (for I had no more right here in Fernham than in Trinity or Somerville or Girton or Newnham or Christchurch), to say, "The dinner was not good," or to say (we were now, Mary Seton and I, in her sitting-room), "Could we not have dined up here alone?" for if I had said anything of the kind I should have been prying and searching into the secret economies of a house which to the stranger wears so fine a front of gaiety and courage. No, one could say nothing of the sort. Indeed, conversation for a moment flagged. The human frame being what it is, heart, body and brain all mixed together, and not contained in separate compartments as they will be no doubt in another million years, a good dinner is of great importance to good talk. One cannot think well, love well, sleep well, if one has not dined well. The lamp in the spine does not light on beef and prunes. We are all *probably* going to heaven, and Vandyck is, we *hope,* to meet us round the next corner — that is the dubious and qualifying state of mind that beef and prunes at the end of the day's work breed between them. Happily my friend, who taught science, had a cupboard where there was a squat bottle and little glasses — (but there should have been sole and partridge to begin with) — so that we were able to draw up to the fire and repair some of the damages of the day's living. In a minute or so we were slipping freely in and out among all those objects of curiosity and interest which form in the mind in the absence of a particular person, and are naturally to be discussed on coming together again — how somebody has married, another has not; one thinks this, another that; one has improved out of all knowledge, the other most amazingly gone to the bad — with all those speculations upon human nature and the character of the amazing world we live in which spring naturally from such beginnings. While these things were being said, however, I became shamefacedly aware of a current setting in of its own accord and carrying everything forward to an end of its own. One might be talking of Spain or Portugal, of book or racehorse, but the real interest of whatever was said was none of those things, but a scene of masons on a high roof some five centuries ago. Kings and nobles brought treasure in huge sacks

and poured it under the earth. This scene was for ever coming alive in my mind and placing itself by another of lean cows and a muddy market and withered greens and the stringy hearts of old men — these two pictures, disjointed and disconnected and nonsensical as they were, were for ever coming together and combating each other and had me entirely at their mercy. The best course, unless the whole talk was to be distorted, was to expose what was in my mind to the air, when with good luck it would fade and crumble like the head of the dead king when they opened the coffin at Windsor. Briefly, then, I told Miss Seton about the masons who had been all those years on the roof of the chapel, and about the kings and queens and nobles bearing sacks of gold and silver on their shoulders, which they shovelled into the earth; and then how the great financial magnates of our own time came and laid cheques and bonds, I suppose, where the others had laid ingots and rough lumps of gold. All that lies beneath the colleges down there, I said; but this college, where we are now sitting, what lies beneath its gallant red brick and the wild unkempt grasses of the garden? What force is behind that plain china off which we dined, and (here it popped out of my mouth before I could stop it) the beef, the custard and the prunes?

Well, said Mary Seton, about the year 1860 — Oh, but you know the story, she said, bored, I suppose, by the recital. And she told me — rooms were hired. Committees met. Envelopes were addressed. Circulars were drawn up. Meetings were held; letters were read out; so-and-so has promised so much; on the contrary, Mr. —— won't give a penny. The *Saturday Review* has been very rude. How can we raise a fund to pay for offices? Shall we hold a bazaar? Can't we find a pretty girl to sit in the front row? Let us look up what John Stuart Mill said on the subject. Can any one persuade the editor of the —— to print a letter? Can we get Lady —— to sign it? Lady —— is out of town. That was the way it was done, presumably, sixty years ago, and it was a prodigious effort, and a great deal of time was spent on it. And it was only after a long struggle and with the utmost difficulty that they got thirty thousand pounds together.* So obviously we cannot have wine and partridges and servants carrying tin dishes on their heads, she said. We cannot have sofas and separate rooms. "The amenities," she said, quoting from some book or other, "will have to wait." †

At the thought of all those women working year after year and finding it hard to get two thousand pounds together, and as much as they could do to get thirty thousand pounds, we burst out in scorn at the reprehensible poverty of our sex. What had our mothers been doing then that they had no wealth to leave us? Powdering their noses? Looking in at shop windows? Flaunting in the sun at Monte Carlo? There were some photographs on the mantelpiece. Mary's mother — if that was her picture — may have been a wastrel in her spare time (she had thirteen children by a minister of the church), but if so her gay and dissipated life had left too few traces of its pleasures on her face. She was a homely body; an old lady in a plaid shawl which was fastened by a large cameo; and she sat in a basket-chair,

encouraging a spaniel to look at the camera, with the amused, yet strained expression of one who is sure that the dog will move directly the bulb is pressed. Now if she had gone into business; had become a manufacturer of artificial silk or a magnate on the Stock Exchange; if she had left two or three hundred thousand pounds to Fernham, we could have been sitting at our ease tonight and the subject of our talk might have been archaeology, botany, anthropology, physics, the nature of the atom, mathematics, astronomy, relativity, geography. If only Mrs. Seton and her mother and her mother before her had learnt the great art of making money and had left their money, like their fathers and their grandfathers before them, to found fellowships and lectureships and prizes and scholarships appropriated to the use of their own sex, we might have dined very tolerably up here alone off a bird and a bottle of wine; we might have looked forward without undue confidence to a pleasant and honourable lifetime spent in the shelter of one of the liberally endowed professions. We might have been exploring or writing; mooning about the venerable places of the earth; sitting contemplative on the steps of the Parthenon, or going at ten to an office and coming home comfortably at half-past four to write a little poetry. Only, if Mrs. Seton and her like had gone into business at the age of fifteen, there would have been — that was the snag in the argument — no Mary. What, I asked, did Mary think of that? There between the curtains was the October night, calm and lovely, with a star or two caught in the yellowing trees. Was she ready to resign her share of it and her memories (for they had been a happy family, though a large one) of games and quarrels up in Scotland, which she is never tired of praising for the fineness of its air and the quality of its cakes, in order that Fernham might

* "We are told that we ought to ask for £30,000 at least. . . . It is not a large sum, considering that there is to be but one college of this sort for Great Britain, Ireland and the Colonies, and considering how easy it is to raise immense sums for boys' schools. But considering how few people really wish women to be educated, it is a good deal." — Lady Stephen, *Life of Miss Emily Davies*.

† Every penny which could be scraped together was set aside for building, and the amenities had to be postponed. — R. Strachey, *The Cause*.

have been endowed with fifty thousand pounds or so by a stroke of the pen? For, to endow a college would necessitate the suppression of families altogether. Making a fortune and bearing thirteen children — no human being could stand it. Consider the facts, we said. First there are nine months before the baby is born. Then the baby is born. Then there are three or four months spent in feeding the baby. After the baby is fed there are certainly five years spent in playing with the baby. You cannot, it seems, let children run about the streets. People who have seen them running wild in Russia say that the sight is not a pleasant one. People say, too, that human nature takes its shape in the years between one and five. If Mrs. Seton, I said, had been making money, what sort of memories would you have had of games and quarrels? What would you have known of Scotland, and its fine air and cakes and all the rest of it? But it is useless to ask these questions, because you would never have come into existence at all. Moreover, it is equally useless to ask what might have happened if Mrs. Seton and her mother and her mother before her had amassed great wealth and laid it under the foundations of college and library, because, in the first place, to earn money was impossible for them, and in the second, had it been possible, the law denied them the right to possess what money they earned. It is only for the last forty-eight years that Mrs. Seton has had a penny of her own. For all the centuries before that it would have been her husband's property — a thought which, perhaps, may have had its share in keeping Mrs. Seton and her mothers off the Stock Exchange. Every penny I earn, they may have said, will be taken from me and disposed of according to my husband's wisdom — perhaps to found a scholarship or to endow a fellowship in Balliol or Kings, so that

to earn money, even if I could earn money, is not a matter that interests me very greatly. I had better leave it to my husband.

At any rate, whether or not the blame rested on the old lady who was looking at the spaniel, there could be no doubt that for some reason or other our mothers had mismanaged their affairs very gravely. Not a penny could be spared for "amenities"; for partridges and wine, beadles and turf, books and cigars, libraries and leisure. To raise bare walls out of the bare earth was the utmost they could do.

So we talked standing at the window and looking, as so many thousands look every night, down on the domes and towers of the famous city beneath us. It was very beautiful, very mysterious in the autumn moonlight. The old stone looked very white and venerable. One thought of all the books that were assembled down there; of the pictures of old prelates and worthies hanging in the panelled rooms; of the painted windows that would be throwing strange globes and crescents on the pavement; of the tablets and memorials and inscriptions; of the fountains and the grass; of the quiet rooms looking across the quiet quadrangles. And (pardon me the thought) I thought, too, of the admirable smoke and drink and the deep armchairs and the pleasant carpets: of the urbanity, the geniality, the dignity which are the offspring of luxury and privacy and space. Certainly our mothers had not provided us with anything comparable to all this — our mothers who found it difficult to scrape together thirty thousand pounds, our mothers who bore thirteen children to ministers of religion at St. Andrews.

So I went back to my inn, and as I walked through the dark streets I pondered this and that, as one does at the end of the day's work. I pondered why it was that Mrs. Seton had no money to leave us; and what effect poverty has on the mind; and what effect wealth has on the mind; and I thought of the queer old gentlemen I had seen that morning with tufts of fur upon their shoulders; and I remembered how if one whistled one of them ran; and I thought of the organ booming in the chapel and of the shut doors of the library; and I thought how unpleasant it is to be locked out; and I thought how it is worse perhaps to be locked in; and, thinking of the safety and prosperity of the one sex and of the poverty and insecurity of the other and of the effect of tradition and of the lack of tradition upon the mind of a

writer, I thought at last that it was time to roll up the crumpled skin of the day, with its arguments and its impressions and its anger and its laughter, and cast it into the hedge. A thousand stars were flashing across the blue wastes of the sky. One seemed alone with an inscrutable society. All human beings were laid asleep — prone, horizontal, dumb. Nobody seemed stirring in the streets of Oxbridge. Even the door of the hotel sprang open at the touch of an invisible hand — not a boots was sitting up to light me to bed, it was so late.

I HAVE A MOTHERLAND

GENA COREA

Gena Corea, born in Hingham, Massachusetts, in 1946, was educated at the University of Massachusetts and in 1971 became an investigative reporter. She edited a feminist feature for the *Holyoke* (Mass.) *Transcript* until 1973 and then turned to free-lance writing. Her articles have appeared in the *New York Times, Ms.,* and *Glamour,* and she has written a weekly syndicated column, "Frankly Feminist," for the New Republic Feature Syndicate. Active in women's health care, she is a member of the National Women's Health Network and the author of *The Hidden Malpractice: How American Medicine Mistreats Women* (1977).

To all the distortions, the ultimate response is the search for truth and the affirmation of worth. Forceful and feeling, Corea's affirmation captures the emotions aroused in us when we recover the past and reconstitute our "place."

Sit down, wretch, and answer me: what have you done with my past?

Years ago you stood before me with a solemn face and told me I was an orphan. With the hand behind your back you pushed the heads of my parents — my proud, strong, angry ancestors — under time's river.

You hid the action of your right hand by

pointing with your left to my entire history, one sentence in a book: "In 1920, in a battle largely led by Susan B. Anthony, women won the right to vote."

But you never told me how strong Anthony was. How, year after year, she suffered scorn, ridicule and defeat and kept on working, not merely for suffrage, but for woman's full liberation.

You never described to me, white man, the courage of hundreds of nameless women who, though raised to be timid, taught to be frightened, nonetheless defied decorum and walked down strange streets, knocked on doors, stood up before hostile faces, and suffered jeers to collect signatures for suffrage petitions — petitions later joked about in Congress and then ignored.

Why didn't you tell me I had such magnificent foremothers?

Why, white man, in your history books, did you never tell me about spunky Abigail Adams asking her husband John to assign women the legal status of human being, rather than property, in the Constitution of the young United States?

And of her warning that, if forgotten, women were "determined to foment a rebellion"? Women were forgotten and women have been fomenting a rebellion but you hid from me the uprisings of my foremothers.

Why did you reverently describe to me the political and military strategies with which earlier Kissingers entertained themselves but keep from me the stories of how ordinary women lived their lives?

I know all about the glorious deaths of soldiers on the battlefield but nothing about the deaths of women in childbed.

Where is the Tomb of the Unknown Mother? Why did she die?

You told me about Carrie Nation, whom you pictured as a ludicrous, axe-wielding teetotaller, but not about Margaret Sanger, who brought to women the most important discovery since fire: contraception.

Why did you hide Anne Hutchinson, Lucy Stone, Sojourner Truth and Mary Walker from me? I could have been stronger if I'd known of them.

You tried to disinherit me. When I trembled before you like an orphan dependent on your good will, you said, "Oh, I'll take care of you, little one."

You kept me meek and grateful for your very small favors. You told me how benevolent you were to an orphan like me. How chivalrous you were, you said.

(Oh, why did you never tell me that way back in 1848, Sarah Grimke had called chivalry "practical contempt"?)

And in gratitude for your chivalry, your patronizing protection, I cooked your food, washed your clothes, cleaned your house, bore and raised your children.

You fraud! I'm your equal and you hid that from me.

When I envied you your freedom, your adventures, and dreamed of being, say, a lawyer, you frowned and told me that if I began to use my brain, I'd be sure to have labor pains and it wouldn't do for me, while trying a case in a court of law, to give birth to a child.

You put on black robes, held a thick book to your heart, rolled your eyes to heaven and solemnly announced that God wanted me to be just as I was.

How cruel of God, I whispered.

Blasphemer! you shouted in my ear. Heretic!

Let me read the thick book, I said.

No, you snapped, your brain's too small. You'll hurt it and go mad.

And all that time, all that time when I thought I was a strange mutation of a woman with strange longings to be whole, all that time, damn it, my ancesters had felt the same, thought the same, said the same.

And you, white man, hid their words, their struggles, their very existences from me. You left my ancestors out of history.

But now I know. I have a tribe, a people, a history, a past, an identity, a motherland, a tradition. I'm not an orphan. I'm not alone. And I'll tremble before you no more.

5

Origins and Explanations

Asking the Question

It is not long after one becomes sensitized to the nature of women's situation that one asks, Why? How did this situation come to be, and why is it so resistant to change? Although there is great diversity among peoples of the world, we can see that, for the most part, in society after society, across time and space, men dominate the upper levels of political, economic, and social power, and women are rarely or only partially included.[1] The work of men is generally valued more highly than that of women and is usually more highly compensated. Typically men are valued more in themselves as persons, a fact often expressed in social customs, rites, and laws. Men tend to outrank women in social status, and their privilege is frequently built on the services of women. The reverse is rarely the case.

What accounts for the fact that societies are so constructed that men dominate and disparage women? Has it always been so, or was there a time in the dim past when women were the equals of men or even, as some have suggested, the initiators and prime movers of civilization? If male dominance has indeed been universal in time, how is the superior position of men to be explained? Is it true, as patriarchy contends, that men are superior to women in ability, or did they win their place by the choice of the gods? If, on the other hand, male dominance has not always held sway, how did it come to be? Was there a primordial revolution of magnificent proportions, as is sometimes figured in ancient myths, or was there a gradual erosion of female power and autonomy, and what could have occasioned such erosion?

Many have argued that men and women are "different" in a variety of ways and it is these differences that account for women's position. Are women different in ways that matter to the direction in which civilization has evolved? Or did the way civilization has evolved create the differences? Are such behavioral differences biologically or culturally based? And what difference do the differences make, or *should* they make, for the way the culture is arranged — in the apportionment of political authority, economic benefits, and enjoyment of the amenities of life?

There are many ways to pose the question and just as many kinds of answers. Some are scientific or quasiscientific; others appear in mythic context, in political or even poetic language, directed as much toward response as toward understanding. Some speak in purely pragmatic terms, arguing efficiency or order, whereas others center on personal choices or cosmic decrees.

The question in various forms has been asked before, but now the women's movement has focused minds afresh on the issues it raises, and the analyses and investigations are becoming more urgent and often more sophisticated. In the religious communities, feminist theologians are challenging the traditional interpretations of language, dogma, and beliefs. In the sciences, feminists and nonfeminists alike are carrying on new and vigorous research into aspects of these issues barely touched or prejudicially treated before. Controversy and debate are sharp. New, more reliable information is being gathered, and new techniques are being generated to deal with this ancient question.

[1] In the social sciences today, particularly anthropology, energetic dialogue surrounds the issue of the universality or near universality of female subordination. Well known in this debate is the work of Alice Schlegel (see Alice Schlegel, ed., *Sexual Stratification: A Cross-Cultural View* [New York: Columbia University Press, 1977]) and of Michelle Rosaldo and Nancy Chodorow in the anthology *Women, Culture, and Society*, ed. Michelle Rosaldo and Louis Lamphere (Stanford: Stanford University Press, 1974).

New Data

Almost every field of intellectual endeavor is collecting new information on women's place, experience, and contributions in culture, past and present. Anthropologists have thrown new light on women's discoveries and inventions in early civilization — pottery, food preservation, tanning, and so on. Feminist historians have unearthed data on women never before recognized, events whose importance had been overlooked, activities never before understood. Psychologists and biologists are carefully re-examining studies of female/male differences, together with their relation to behavioral characteristics, in order to deal in a more objective way with traditional assumptions and theories. Linguists are discovering new connections between speech patterns and social effectiveness and power.

New Perspectives

The addition of feminist critique to intellectual dialogue is developing a new depth of sophistication in the nature of inquiry itself. Having challenged the reliability of traditional knowledge collected solely by men or within male structures, feminists are posing new questions that alter considerably the search for explanations. How viable and/or complete is much of the information we have on prehistory and primitive cultures, interpreted as it was through masculist bias? Can we depend on unsensitized males to have asked the pertinent questions about women; would women have confided freely in male researchers? Would the male researcher have evaluated properly the female data he collected? If the masculist psychologist has imposed his expectations on his research findings, won't they have been distorted, and

won't most of the theories of sex differences, for example, so integral to traditional theories of explanation, be unreliable? Might not there then have to be entirely new ways of piecing together the origins of patriarchy?[2]

The matter of terminology has been very sharply critiqued, as feminists have challenged the utility of many terms relevant to the issue. The term *domestic* is an interesting example. Literally the word means "pertaining to the home," and it is used in social science to describe tasks, artifacts, or behavior directly related to the home site or hearth, to the group's family or living arrangements. Anthropologists generally agree that almost universally women have carried on the "domestic" activities of society. However, there is evidence to show that almost any task assigned to women is likely to be deemed "domestic," but the same task assigned to men is likely to be categorized differently. For example, fashioning pottery for the tribe might be categorized as a "domestic" activity if done by women, but an "artistic" one if done by men. In other words, since the expectation is that women do the domestic work of the group, their tasks are automatically categorized as domestic; and, in a real round robin, women's work having been termed domestic, researchers feel safe to report that the domestic work of the tribe is always done by women!

Since one may ask today whether any knowledge that excludes female experience has utility, one may realistically challenge traditionally accepted theses such as the claim that women are oppressed because they have never united in their own self-interest. If

---

[2] For an interesting discussion of the relation of politics to scientific inquiry, see Donna Haraway, "Animal Sociology and a Natural Economy of the Body Politic, Part I: A Political Physiology of Dominance," *Signs,* 4, No. 1 (Autumn 1978), 21–36.

events such as the Roman women's opposition to the Oppian Laws; the movement of the Beguines in the Middle Ages; the later fights for temperance, birth control, and abortion rights are ignored and thus not integrated into the thesis, how reliable is it? Armchair theories in science will not do, nor will any other kind of sloppy thinking. The current surge of interest in the quest for explanations gives reason to be optimistic about discovery, but not without careful attention to the many complicated problems before us.

Our discussion must be preceded by certain cautions. First, no one as yet knows "the answer." There are vast gaps in data and analysis. Second, there may not be one answer, but many. Third, the several theories and suggestions presented here represent only a scattered example of those that exist, and even the challenges put to them do not constitute the full array of those that should be made. There is room in this book for only a beginning.

The Matter of Definition

No one as yet knows "the answer" to what? That is, exactly what is our question? Are we asking why women and men are "unequal"? Unequal in what? In political or personal power? What constitutes power? What kind of power do women not have? Unequal in opportunity? Opportunity for what? We have opportunity to gain income — we can marry it. From a value-free standpoint, why is that mode of opportunity less acceptable than any other? Are we unequal in status? Or are we just "different," that is, separate but "equal"? How does one measure status and compare it? How does one compare the power and status of one group of women in a culture (say, middle-class American white

women) with another (perhaps, wealthy black British women)?

If we ask why women are subordinate to men, what do we mean by "subordinate," and how do we indicate and include differences in subordination from culture to culture? How is subordination different from oppression, exploitation, discrimination, domination? What does the term *subordination* mean in the context of power? If it is true, as some have suggested, that though men hold formal power, wives frequently hold great informal power over men, then who is subordinate to whom, and in what way?

As you can see, there are many relevant terms and concepts, and each has its nuances and implications. One must be extraordinarily careful how they are used.

Any good investigator will point out that the first step in problem solving is a careful definition of the problem itself and of the terms employed. It is quite another matter to ask, "How did it come to be that men usurped female autonomy and prestige?" or "Why are men superior to women in power and accomplishments?" These questions, each in its own way, make certain assumptions and value judgments, express a particular perspective, and require a specific kind of research context. Neither defines the problem adequately because each is biased and circular: It assumes an answer before it begins to seek one.

In tracking down reliable explanations, one must guard against hidden assumptions and values, charged language ("usurped," "equality," "superior"), and bias-prone terminology ("domestic," "aggressive," "technological"). This in itself is a monumental task. How does one ask a question that is free of prior assumptions and value-laden concepts, yet is still meaningful? For example: "Under what conditions did the present cultural sexual arrangements come to be?" What arrangements? Which culture? What kind of origin — in time, in causative factors? Whereas the two formulations in the previous paragraph are too narrow and prejudicial, this one is too broad and omits the essence of the problem — which *is* valuational. Clearly, there must be a balance of attention to constructing formulations that are relatively objective and free of assumption, yet sufficiently concrete in perspective to be substantive.

Sexual Asymmetry and Concepts That Matter

Searching for a term that captures all of the issues that we have been raising, that is broad enough to admit of other kinds of circumstances, and that is relatively "objective," some feminists and social scientists have been using the term *sexual asymmetry,* which means simply a disproportion or dissimilarity based on sex. Broadly encompassing, flexible, and relatively nonprejudicial, the term functions in a number of different contexts — scientific, political, religious, and so on — and avoids many pitfalls. It is both meaningful and scientifically productive to ask, "What are the origins and causes of sexual asymmetry?" Yet in its scientific purity, the term *sexual asymmetry* also tends to be vague, and without the assistance of related concepts for fleshing it out (charged though they may be), discussion staying strictly within its limits might tend to become rather thin.

For purposes of our discussion, let us say that sexual asymmetry refers to a whole range of activities and situations where (1) policies regarding control over the wider community and the exercise of freedom to act or participate in affairs affecting all members of the group are determined solely or primarily on the grounds of sex, and (2) judgments of value or worth are made solely or primarily on the basis of sex. For example, in a culture where the legal right to vote for a leader of the entire group is limited to men *because they are men* (not bright men or strong men or educated men) and prohibited to women *because they are women* (not stupid women or poor women or malicious women), sexual asymmetry of the kind with which we are concerned exists. In a culture where men are deemed intrinsically more valuable than women, more worthy, better humans, more desirable *solely on the grounds of maleness,* sexual asymmetry exists.

Asymmetry takes many forms. In most cultures, we have said, the work of men is more highly prized than that of women, women are considered to be the inferiors of men (in a variety of ways), and people tend to disparage both the work and the persons of women. Such societies are misogynist. In our culture signs of misogyny range from the subtle to the blatant. Women are reputed to be stupid, petty, incompetent, or deceptive; are underpaid; and are excluded from many activities. Other cultures have featured infibulation, the chastity belt, purdah, and suttee.[3]

Although in some cultures women have considerable power within the family group or over other women, in every known society men make the policy that affects the group as a whole — men make policy for women (and for some other men), but women do not formally make policy for men. In such a case, women are *subordinate* to men, that is, women inhabit a lower order of rank and privilege. For example, men in our culture formally control all the institutions that determine the character and the rules of our experience — the legislature, the judiciary, the police, the law, the economy. Women control

---

3 *Infibulation:* the practice of sewing together the labia of the vagina to insure chastity; *purdah:* the practice in Islam of totally sequestering women; *suttee:* the practice in India, surviving now only in rural areas, of widows immolating themselves on the burning funeral pyres of their husbands.

the home, though *formally* only with the approval of the men they live with.

Oppression differs from subordination in that one person may be subordinate to another and yet not be oppressed, as when a child is subordinate to a benevolent parent or when a worker of lesser ability must yield to policy set by a more highly qualified person in a position of higher rank. To oppress means to bear down, to weigh upon, to burden. One is oppressed when one experiences life as a burden, when one is emotionally or spiritually crushed or tyrannized. A culture that demeaned a woman's self-image, destroyed her pride, misused her person for ends not her own, or appropriated the fruits of her labor without proper recompense (that is, exploited her labor) would be an oppressive culture. Many cultures oppress and exploit their women as our culture oppresses and exploits at least some of us, if not all (as many feminists argue). Through *discrimination* (different, disadvantageous treatment before the law), outright slavery, or social customs that serve to solidify male privilege, women are oppressed and exploited in most cultures.

When we ask, "What are the origins and causes of sexual asymmetry?" we are seeking an answer to the entire range of asymmetry from discrimination to misogyny.

Problems of Method

How do we go about finding meaningful and reliable answers to the questions we have asked? We are, after all, pursuing a situation that in myth is without beginnings and in social science traces back at least 10,000 years into prehistory, that traverses diverse cultures around the globe, and that may even have parallels in other species.

Scientifically, how do we deal with origins when the beginnings are lost? And where shall we count the beginnings? With re-

corded history? With early primitive peoples? With primates and hominoids? How helpful is information gleaned from current "primitive" groups when they diverge so even among themselves?

Under what circumstances and to what degree is the practice of drawing analogies between humans and other animals to count? Which animals? Shall we select those that meet one set of expectations, like the aggressive, asymmetrical gibbons, or shall we focus on the ever-faithful, one-time-mating gray lag goose, or perhaps the lion with its tough hunter female? Shall we confine ourselves to primates? And to what degree are any animal studies helpful when investigating a creature as uniquely malleable as the human being?

A great deal of important information is coming from new research into certain primate groups such as the chimpanzee, which are believed to be closely related to the kind of African ape that some four million years ago may have given rise to the hominids (the earliest members of the human family, such as *Australopithecus* and *Homo erectus*). Because fossil records (bones and teeth, for example, or organic tools) of this period are scarce, and because it is difficult to speculate reliably on behavior patterns of groups that are not observable, anthropologists use a combination of several kinds of evidence to generate hypotheses regarding the nature of early human social activities. For example, changes in the relative size of canine and molar teeth, within and across sexual categories, may tell us about diet (and therefore food-getting patterns) or about modes of defense, or even about degrees of sociability. Such speculations, supported or enlarged by the observation of existent populations of highly developed primates, offer possibilities for piecing together a picture of the evolution of early human organization.

There are social scientists, however, who

approach the problem differently. They contend that because *Homo sapiens* is a far more advanced and complex creature in terms of intelligence than the earliest hominids, and because reflective thinking is unique to that species, *Homo sapiens* is qualitatively different from its ancestors. Its behavior patterns and social organization therefore require a different kind and level of explanation. At this point one enters the sphere of psychological or mythic explanation, theological or secular.

Studying the art and artifacts of lost civilizations further along the evolutionary scale, some claim that there existed advanced cultures before our own which were matriarchal and matrilineal. Argued primarily from inferential information, such theories are very controversial. They raise the question: What counts as evidence? It is commonly understood that personal testimony (emic data) may be unreliable; there is the issue of subjectivity, of perspective, of lack of insight, even of deceit. Yet even purely objective, researcher-based analysis (etic) may suffer from ethnocentrism or oversimplification, and even with physical evidence there is the problem of interpretation. How then are such speculations or hypotheses to be verified?

A Series of Hypotheses

So far, all we have for "answers" to our problem is conjecture. There are hypotheses, no firm theories. The hypotheses, except for certain themes that appear to be common to all, range across a variety of perspectives, levels of explanation, and conclusions, some of them quite contradictory.

Biological Approaches

When one argues that asymmetry occurs because women and men have different capacities and behaviors based on their *innate, inherited physical differences* (such as hormonal patterns, brain size, or bone structure), then one argues from the biological perspective or level. This approach has included arguments that females and males differ *constitutionally* in such varied factors as intelligence, temperament, IQ, capacity to lead, physical endurance, propensity to "bond" with members of the same sex, sexuality, aggressiveness, even a sense of justice. It is contended that these biologically based differences account for *and justify* the social arrangements that constitute sexual asymmetry.

Such a point of view has the advantage of focusing on factors that are more easily observable, hence more amenable to investigation and verification than some others. And, as some of the discussion in the preceding chapter pointed out, research does indicate some real physical behavior-related differences between females and males. What remains, however, is to determine what these differences do or should mean. If it should be found, for example, that males are constitutionally more aggressive and hence more likely to compete and win than females[4] (there is some evidence to this effect) and thus more inclined to dominate or lead, one ought reasonably to ask whether this means that men *should* lead; or, since the world now suffers from an overabundance of aggressiveness, whether less aggressive persons (females?) should be socially encouraged to lead and males be discouraged.

To say that women are "naturally" this and men are "naturally" that (leaving aside

[4] Steven Goldberg, in *The Inevitability of Patriarchy* (New York: Morrow, 1974), argued precisely that: Males *are* constitutionally more aggressive, more likely to compete energetically and hence win. Socialization patterns merely recognize and support this reality. Patriarchy, therefore, is the inevitable arrangement because it is the most orderly, stable, and reflective of nature.

the question of the truth of the propositions) is an argument that has frequently been used by those who wish to maintain the status quo, not only in sexual arrangements but in many other forms as well. Yet one must remember that the terms *natural* and *desirable* are different. It is natural for animals to kill and maim (usually for food or protection, but sometimes for other reasons), but that does not make it desirable. It is natural for humans to die painfully of disease, but that does not make it desirable. The human species has never rested content with what is "natural." That is our splendor as well as our infamy. We have survived through adaptations that were not "natural." Cultures evolve because humans are malleable. We must not confuse the muddy scientific concept *natural* with the equally muddy ethical notion of desirability.

Sociological or Cultural Theories

The factor of malleability raises the familiar issue of the nature/nurture controversy. Which, it asks, is more responsible for human behavior, nature (physiological, inborn components) or nurture (the effects of society — socialization, enculturation, learning)? Although nature, our physical selves, constitutes the raw material of our beings and thus imposes its own limits on our development, investigators generally agree that nurture contributes the lion's share to our development.

In a famous cross-cultural study of three existing societies, Margaret Mead described extremely divergent gender-based behavior.[5] The Arapesh society approved behavior for both men and women that our culture would term *feminine* — unaggressive, maternal, and cooperative rather than competitive. Mundugumor men and women were exactly opposite in behavior, all of them expected to be extremely aggressive, violent, and nonmaternal. The Tchambuli culture, a mirror image of our own, prized dominant, impersonal, and managing women and emotionally dependent, less effective men. Mead concluded that such data threw great doubt on the biological basis of gender behavior and strongly supported the thesis that sex-linked behavioral characteristics and activities are the result of social conditions.

The emphasis on enculturation as the main source of sex-role behavior continues today, yet there has also been a move toward a reappraisal of biological and physiological factors on the part of both nonfeminists and feminists.[6]

Sociological theories like Mead's generally argue that female/male behavioral differences are more a matter of social than of biological degree: The traits we take to be feminine or masculine are prescribed by the mores of our culture and are learned or internalized through formal education, religion, media, and all the other institutions that define experience. Unlike biological explanations, which account for the temporal origins of asymmetry by saying simply, "It has always been that way, decreed by nature," sociological theories need additional elaboration to deal with origins. It is one thing to say that I as a woman have trait x because my society teaches it, and another to account for *why* my society teaches x. How and why did my society choose to teach x, and why does this society teach x while another teaches y?

[5] Margaret Mead, *Sex and Temperament in Three Primitive Societies* (New York: Morrow, 1935).

[6] See, for example, Edward O. Wilson, *Sociobiology: The New Synthesis* (Cambridge, Mass.: Harvard University Press, 1975) and Haraway, "Animal Sociology."

There are those, feminist and otherwise, who say that it is not necessary to ask why or how sexual norms originated. They argue that we need only evaluate them in the present context from the point of view of ethics (is it right, fair, or just to subordinate women?) or of social efficacy (does it benefit our society to maintain the present arrangement?). In common sense, there is much to be said for their argument. One does not have to ask when or how the first war began in order to believe that war is undesirable and must be ended. A medical researcher does not need to ask who had the first cancer in order to search for its cause. But origins and causes are logically related. If it is known how something comes to be, if it can be determined *what factors precede and precipitate an event,* in effect the cause has been found, and only in understanding causes of events can we hope to control them.

The problem, however, becomes complicated. Just as some people confuse natural with desirable, others sometimes confuse origin with justification. For example, George Gilder[7] argues that asymmetry originates in the males' exclusion from childbearing and in their drive to achieve parity through other modes of creativity. This, he argues, explains why men feel the need to exclude women from their modes of expression, why they become unpleasant if women refuse the place men have made for them, and *why women should not refuse that place.* Whatever one thinks of his first contention — that men dominate women to achieve parity — it can plainly be seen that, right or wrong, the thesis cannot stand logically as a justification, an ethical argument for asymmetry. Analogically, to say that *people commit murder because they are hostile, antisocial, and pressured* may explain why they do it, how their murderous impulses originate, but it does not support the thesis that *they should do it;* that is, it serves as no justification. Clearly, it is helpful to explore origins, but one must keep in mind exactly how it is helpful, what the exploration accomplishes, and what it leaves yet to be done.

By and large, sociological/cultural theories of origin are either *evolutionary* or *psychomythic.* Evolutionary theories argue that either individuals, entire cultures, or both have developed certain traits or norms as adaptations, as survival mechanisms in answer to the requirements of the environment.

INDIVIDUAL-EVOLUTIONARY THEORIES One famous example of the individual-evolutionary explanation is the "man-the-hunter" theory. Food, it begins, was the most important commodity of survival in primitive society, and meat, because scarce, the most prized. Because women in primitive circumstances were always with child one way or another, it was not practical for them to go on the hunt, which often took one miles and days away from the shelter and safety of the home site, and which required capabilities not easily performed with an attached child. For this reason, women stayed at home, raising children, foraging for vegetables and small game, and tending the hearth while men went hunting. Each sex developed (evolved) physical and behavioral traits appropriate to their tasks. This, some evolutionists say, explains not only work segregation based on sex, but also why men are prized above women (*they* brought the meat). It also reveals the origin of the different capabilities, traits, and personalities of females and males: Men are aggressive and bonding so they can hunt, whereas women are compliant and gentle because "the overall mood arising from such

[7] George Gilder, *Sexual Suicide* (New York: Quadrangle, 1973).

organic orientation, from so much waiting and letting grow and gentling and encouraging but never forcing, is a mood of compliance." [8]

For a time, the man-the-hunter theory was in great vogue with many people, feminists and nonfeminists alike. But now the entire configuration is coming into question. One may ask whether the male became aggressive because he had to hunt, or hunted because he was aggressive. (There were, after all, other sources of protein than that sought after in the hunt — even meat.) Which came first, man the hunter or man the warrior, and are the two related? Did women really evolve "compliance" because that temperament is necessary to raising children? Who says that it is necessary? Mead's Mundugumors certainly do not. Their women are aggressive, their children survive, and female aggressiveness does not lead to male unaggressiveness as some theories suggest. How does one account for male aggressiveness and rites of courage in cultures (for example, in Polynesia) where food (including protein) is plentiful and hunting is unnecessary? There are other evolutionary theories of this ilk — each with its own starting point.

Evolutionary theories that focus on the development of individual (male/female) differences are certainly more sophisticated than biological theories, but they leave much to be desired. Still paying scant attention to the power of socialization, they fail to take into account the changes in individual behavior that would be wrought by changing environments. Men no longer go off to hunt (however widely one chooses to define the term); brute strength, size, and aggressiveness are no longer adaptive traits for social survival, yet the value persists. Some other, wider factor

may be needed to explain the cultural definitions and expectations of woman and man.

CULTURAL-EVOLUTIONARY THEORIES A variation of the preceding kind of explanation, the cultural-evolutionary theories take the society rather than the individual as the basic unit to be explored. In this case it is the entire culture, as well as the individual, that evolves adaptive mechanisms; sexual mores, role definitions, and gender expectations are part of them. For example, if a society were located in an environment where conditions were particularly hard, with survival difficult and the death rate high, such a society would probably require a high birth rate to maintain an adequate population, and it might well develop values that encouraged women to conceive and bear many children, to view themselves primarily in their childbearing capacity, and so on. The cultural-evolutionary approach, then, seeks to understand sexual mores, attitudes, and behavior in terms of the environmental conditions that would give rise to them.

PSYCHO-MYTHIC THEORIES None of the theories thus far developed fully accounts for the whole range of sexual asymmetry. Too many puzzling questions are left unanswered. The kinds of explanations we have considered do not adequately explain the reasons for sex segregation, political subordination, or the divisions of labor based on sex. They do not even begin to explain the other, more virulent aspect of asymmetry — misogyny.

It is one thing to categorize people on the basis of a certain trait — old people do this, young people do that; large people do this, small people do that. But what gives sexism its essential characteristic, wherever it appears, is the element of valuation that is added to the categories. Not only are tasks separated by sex, but men's tasks are judged more valuable, women's less valuable. Not only is the

[8] Wolfgang Lederer, *The Fear of Women* (New York: Grune & Stratton, 1968), p. 87.

male's role to lead and the female's to follow, but leading is valued and following is not. Not only are men and women to exhibit complementary character traits, but male traits are praised and female traits are held in contempt. Nor is it only that men tend to do or be better things and hence are more deserving of praise. Rather, in reverse, the things that are praised are simply the things that men do; they are praised *because men do them*. For the most part, a task socially assigned to women is debased. Cross-cultural studies bear this out.

We hear much of the fact that 75 percent of all physicians in the USSR are women. However, it is rarely pointed out that in the Soviet Union the practice of medicine, except for some highly specialized fields, is considered merely a technical job and is not highly paid; for the most part, the higher-paid specialists and surgeons are men. Secretarial work had high status and was highly paid until it became a female occupation; so was teaching. Nursing, always female, has always suffered in power, prestige, and pay. The men who are now moving into the nursing field are being rewarded with preference in the highest paid, most select positions. Men are "encouraged" to enter nursing to "raise the level of the profession." Women are "permitted" to enter medicine or law because it is not just or legal to bar them; nothing is said about raising the level of the profession. Feminists have argued that women are always assigned to do the "shitwork" of society. More and more it becomes apparent that it is equally the other way around: Tasks are deemed unworthy if women do them.

The same analysis can be made of human behaviors. When men ask their wives more than once to do something, they are "reminding." Women who ask repeatedly are "nagging." When men are firm and resolute, they have backbone; women are stubborn or bitchy. When a man raises his voice in argu-

ment he is angry; a woman is hysterical. Menstruation in most societies is surrounded with taboos, disgust, and often horror. In this modern society that can utter any obscenity, can discuss freely any body function from nose blowing to orgasm, open admission of having one's period is still an occasion for shock and embarrassment. I dare say that would not be the case if menstruation were a male function. Erections are a source of pride to their owners. Much fuss is made over the length and breadth of a penis. What is the analogous situation for women? In patriarchy, it is as though the female carries with her an evil effusion and contaminates all that she touches.

Theories that explain only the *fact* of separation or categorization (men do this, women do that) and omit the *judgment* of devaluation (men and what they do are good; women and what they do are contemptible) or theories that disclaim the existence or importance of devaluation are missing the central point. The misogyny in sexual asymmetry is what renders it sexist and makes it oppressive. It is true that analyses of asymmetry are highly charged with value. One could argue that one man's misogyny is another man's reality — it is not misogyny to say that women are inferior; it is true! Many of us, however, know better, and the fact of misogyny, almost universal though varying in degree, must be explained.

The psycho-mythic explanations function on a level where this issue can be treated. A myth is a story that serves to explain and/or to express some important reality of life or nature. The creation story in the Bible, for example, represented the ancient Hebrew explanation of the origin of the world, of life, and of human suffering. Sometimes the stories are avowedly fictitious; others are regarded as true.

There are several theories of myths — that they represent certain human verities, common to all people (such as the confrontation with one's own mortality); that they are modes of expressing experiences or feelings inexpressible in ordinary language; or that they symbolize beliefs and needs in a person, too deep, too intense, or too socially bizarre to express directly. Their relation to psychological explanation, then, is clear.

A myth is generally taken to be an accurate representation of common, perhaps universal, human beliefs and attitudes. For this reason, myths are important for the analysis of sexual asymmetry. They are studied to reveal their hidden message about attitudes toward women, and feminists often explain certain arrangements regarding women as the social acting out of basic psycho-mythic beliefs or psychological needs. The Adam and Eve story, for example, is a powerfully revealing myth that has parallels in many cultures. Many societies, primitive and otherwise, have stories that credit the first human life and the power of birth to a male and then relegate the life-giving function to women, often as a discredited and burdensome task. Does this story reveal a universal male envy of female procreative powers? Does it perhaps hark back to a primitive matriarchy, if not a historical one then a symbolic one (as in the paradigmatic Mother)? And does this tale not neatly justify the subordination and oppression of women? Have not numerous churchmen contended that women's suppression justly results from the primordial betrayal in the Garden? Does this story not express a statement of women's evil, untrustworthiness, guile, naiveté, seduceability, and unworthiness before God? Does it not justify hatred and contempt?

If the story expresses and justifies misogyny, for most contemporary people — and other than in terms of the theory of womb envy — it does not explain it. Why must men control and condemn women? The psycho-mythic theories attempt to approach this central issue through various themes, such as a yearning for maternal safety (Elizabeth Janeway), the model of family aggression — man upon woman (Shulamith Firestone), or even penis envy (Sigmund Freud). Each theory seeks some universal theme, some common human reality to explain this universal behavior — misogynous sexual asymmetry.

The major strength of psycho-mythic theories is that they seek wide-ranging explanations, sufficiently inclusive to cover all the occurrences and variations of sexism. Also, they treat a psychological event — attitudes and beliefs — on a psychological level. The problem with psycho-mythic theories, however, is that they are almost impossible to verify — my myth against yours, my analysis against yours — and if used exclusively, they omit references to the very essential sociocultural elements, as Freud's theory did.

Conclusion

If there are no definitive theories of explanation, what is to be done? Search the following explanations carefully. Ponder the points they have in common, such as the centrality of childbearing or of hunting, and consider whether these themes are viable and/or sufficient. Notice the gaps in all the theories; use these as further points of departure.

Ultimately, reliable explanations will probably develop out of a combination of levels and perspectives. They will undoubtedly require a great deal more in the way of research, sophisticated analysis, and objective judgment than is now available.

Selections

ANTHROPOLOGICAL APPROACHES TO THE SUBORDINATION OF WOMEN

CHARLOTTE J. FRISBIE

Charlotte J. Frisbie was born in Hazleton, Pennsylvania, in 1940; studied music and ethnomusicology at Smith and Wesleyan; and took a doctorate in anthropology at the University of New Mexico. She now teaches at Southern Illinois University, Edwardsville. Specializing in cultural anthropology, ethnographic field techniques, and Native Americans, Frisbie has recently done a great deal of research on women in cross-cultural perspective. In the following selection she explains and summarizes the major issues and research in current anthropological studies of women.

Introduction

At the present time, the discipline of anthropology offers no single approach to discussions of the subordination of women. This is not because of a lack of interest in the topic, but because of the many problems related to evaluating the issue on the basis of available cross-cultural data. At present, although many anthropologists agree that women live in a man's world in many geographic areas, not all are convinced that this is a human universal, something shared by all people everywhere. Likewise, there is no agreement on any one particular explanation or interpretation of the phenomenon, where it is found; instead, there are several different approaches that are attracting further research energies and generating much discussion.

Before outlining some of the possible ap-

proaches to discussions of the subordination of women, it seems useful to review some of the inherent, relevant problems. Anthropological evaluations of women's statuses, roles, and actual lives in cross-cultural perspective depend not only on contemporary data gathered by doing fieldwork among the peoples in question, but also on ethnographies or descriptive reports of past work as well. It is often true that the latter sources lead researchers into a major problem, that of bias. Anthropology, like other disciplines, has benefited in numerous ways from the feminist movement; among them have been the development of an increased awareness of sexism within the discipline, and associated actions designed to reduce and hopefully, eliminate the problem. In cultural anthropology, that part of the discipline that deals with the lifeways of contemporary people, recent reviews of many available descriptive sources have resulted in one major conclusion — you are lucky if you can learn anything about women at all from reading these works! This is true for several reasons:

1. Since the beginning of the discipline, most fieldworkers and ethnographers have been male.
2. These people have done their fieldwork by talking to males, the public, visible people in cultures.
3. The perceptions of male informants have been accepted as representative of the entire culture, including the female part of the population.
4. Female anthropologists, for the most part, have been trained by males, and taught to carry on the above traditions.

Thus, with very few exceptions (for example, Mead 1928, 1935, 1949; Landes 1938; Kaberry 1939), earlier anthropological reports provide us with unidimensional descriptions of an androcentric nature. Women are either not mentioned at all, or treated as meaningless shadows and relegated to brief mention in footnotes or single text statements.

Lately, these characteristics have been among those identified as sexist, and energies have been expended to begin attacking such problems. This work, from the research perspective, involves fieldwork with women as well as men, critical analyses of the differences between the perceptions of women and men (be they informants or anthropologists) and heightened awareness of the pervasiveness of sexism within the discipline. Such efforts, by themselves, have led to a re-examination of the idea that women are subordinate to men throughout the world. Now, we wonder if this is really true, or if it is possible that this very picture reflects our own sexist, ethnocentric bias and the way in which much of our past work was done.

Although we are far from answering this question and others, a number of developments have already occurred. For example, students now are being trained to ask who did the fieldwork, with what part of the population, and from what perspective? Likewise, the last decade has yielded a number of worthwhile ethnographies that concern women in cultural contexts (for example, Fernea 1965, Goodale 1971, Strathern 1972, Wolf 1972, Chiñas 1973, and Murphy and Murphy 1974). Several collections have appeared, such as those edited by Pescatello (1973), Matthaisson (1974), Rosaldo and Lamphere (1974), Rohrlich-Leavitt (1975) and Reiter (1975), and texts have become available (for example, Martin and Voorhies 1975, Friedl 1975, Kessler 1976, and Hammond and Jablow 1976). Specific papers that deal with various theoretical aspects of sexist bias in anthropology are also available (for example, Ardener 1972; Schlegel 1975; Slocum 1975; Rohrlich-Leavitt, Sykes, and Weatherford 1975; and Sacks 1976).

Sexism is characteristic of physical as well as cultural anthropology. In this portion of the discipline, where the focus is on physical and cultural evolution and the relationship between humans and their nonhuman primate relatives, many questions are now being asked. To name just one, "Why have women been so consistently ignored in the story of human evolution, which has been taught for so long as the evolution of MAN, and what can be done about it?" This will receive further discussion below.

The Subordination of Women

Since not all anthropologists accept the subordination of women to men throughout evolutionary time and geographic space as a human universal, the question can be discussed from several different perspectives. This is possible, in part, anyway, because of available cross-cultural information about women's work. For a variety of reasons, this area of women's lives has received rather consistent research attention through time. Thus, we have a relatively good idea of the numerous ways in which women's work and men's work can be defined by humans around the world. An analysis of these data, or of the question of division of labor by sex (as it is properly termed) leads to the recognition of several universals. All humans use sex as one of the defining principles of labor; in other words, people everywhere have ideas about what constitutes women's work and men's work. While the particulars often vary — so that in one culture women weave, and in another men do, or in one, women build the shelters, and in another this is men's work — there are certain ideas that all humans share. Among these are the association of women with childbearing, childrearing and the related private or domestic sphere, and the association of men with warfare, control over significant resources, preferential access to authority and the related public, visible, political sphere. Furthermore, from what we now know, it appears that everywhere men's activities are the ones that are most highly valued, the ones that carry the greatest prestige. Given these universals, what can be said about the relative status of the sexes cross-culturally?

As might be expected, there are those who argue that women have been subordinate to males since time immemorial, and those who reject both the time immemorial and the universal implications of this statement. Let us turn now to each of these groups and examine the extreme positions before dealing with some alternative approaches.

Biological Determinists

Within anthropology there is a group which argues essentially that biology is destiny, and that because females are biologically designed to conceive, give birth and to support offspring through lactation, they are "naturally" designed for life in the restricted domestic or private sphere, rather than in the more widely ranging, public, political one. The arguments of this group, currently, are presented in two slightly different ways.

A group of people, including Ardrey (1966), Lorenz (1966), Morris (1968), Tiger (1969, 1970), and Tiger and Fox (1971), prefer to explain sex roles from a biological perspective. Essentially, this stance stresses nature rather than nurture, biology rather than culture, and innate rather than learned approaches to the question. The position focuses on the universals in human culture, rather than particular differences among groups. The argument states that culture, rather than being totally learned, is in part biologically based, and that this base explains the presence of human universals.

For biological determinists, sex roles and behavior are best explained by references to innate biological and psychological differences between the sexes. In brief, the view (which refers to savannah dwelling Hamadryas baboon information for supporting parallels) characteristically emphasizes the importance of size differences (sexual dimorphism); Man the Aggressor, Man the Hunter, Man the Dominant are important correlates. Males are viewed as physically larger, stronger, and hormonally more aggressive. Biologically, they are required to spend far less time than females in reproduction-related activities. In evolutionary terms, as our ancestors came down from the trees, they became vulnerable. According to biological determinists, males at this point learned to coordinate their behaviors for defense, and with time and increased male-male cooperation, the tendency for them to bond became genetic.

Females are characterized by more fatty tissues on the breasts and buttocks, pelvic areas constructed for childbirth and a wide variety of hormonal levels. Because of their biological adaptation for reproduction and their "natural" preoccupation with helpless infants, they are inhibited by inferior mobility, threat of miscarriage and hormonal changes that affect coordination and perception. Additionally, they lack genetic codes for bonding (except those related to male-female bonding for reproduction), and thus are not biologically suited for cooperative economic and political endeavors. Given this, females are most aptly described as "naturally" docile, nurturant followers who are "normally pregnant or nursing their infants."

Obviously, the biological determinist stance credits males with the development of human culture; with enough evolutionary time and the correlated increases in brain size and complexity, Man the Hunter and Tool Maker became Man the Thinker, the Language User, the Inventor, the City Dweller, and the Moon Rocket Builder. Females, biologically burdened by their reproductive capacities and helpless offspring, stayed in camp, dependent on Man the Hunter, Man the Dominant for their sustenance and survival. According to biological determinists, sex roles and behaviors were ever thus; they represent the product of millions of years of successful human adaptation. To tamper with them, or suggest that things should be different is, according to some, equivalent to heresy.

In the past few years, a newer, slightly more sophisticated version of biological determinism has been advanced, under the rubric of sociobiology (Trivers 1971, Alexander 1974, West Eberhard 1975, Wilson 1975, and Barash 1977). Defined as the study of the biological basis for social behavior, sociobiology implies the existence of a common thread that links together all social behaviors of all life forms, and calls for a new synthesis of disciplines involved in the study of behavior (be it that of termites, red-winged blackbirds, marmots, or humans). Unlike earlier biological determinists who see human behavior as an expression of innate, biologically based needs and drives, sociobiologists strive to relate social behavior to well-established evolutionary principles. Of these, the one receiving major emphasis at present is self-maximization of individual genotypes. In simple terms, this means that genes "call the shots," and that the lives of all living forms are organized around the tendency for genetic material to maximize itself over time through reproductive success, or enhanced genetic contributions to the next generation.

Although the above may appear quite unrelated to discussions of the subordination of women, it isn't. Sociobiologists argue that there are genes for particular social behaviors, and that these have spread by natural selection through evolutionary time. Among the behaviors frequently discussed as genetically based are the human capacities for aggression, cooperation, altruism, kin selection, and mating. Repeating the emphasis on the biological advantages of the initial human division of labor into Man the Hunter-Protector-Provider, and Woman the Reproducer-Child Rearer, Wilson and many others suggest that like aggression, the division of labor by sex is genetically based.

Obviously the sociobiological stance, which argues that genes prescribe the rules of life and determine much human behavior, can be used as a way of rationalizing the correctness, naturalness, and legitimacy of all kinds of social patterns and institutions, including male dominance over women. All you have to do is "prove" that men are genetically predisposed to be dominant, ritual-political leaders, and economic managers whereas women are genetically predisposed to cook, wash clothes and dishes, and care for children and homes. How far sociobiology will be pushed, at present, remains to be seen.

Environmentalists

In direct opposition to biological determinists are other contemporary anthropologists who align themselves with the nurture, culture, and learned side of the issue and argue that biology is not destiny (see, for example, Brown 1970, Chiñas 1973, Friedl 1975, Martin and Voorhies 1975, Reiter 1975, and Slocum 1975). In contrast to the group discussed earlier, this one, following Boasian tradition, stresses the uniqueness of culture, and focuses on human plasticity, variability, and differences rather than universals. Sex roles are viewed as functions of social and cultural conditioning rather than biological heredity.

Environmentalists, like their opponents, use ethnographic data and primatology studies to support their claims; in the former, the emphasis is on differences — examples of cultures where women have political roles, have control of significant resources, serve as warriors. In the latter, the preferred non-human primate is the chimpanzee, our closest living relative.

Much of the work already generated by environmentalists provides serious challenges to earlier anthropological models and theories that perpetuate sexism. For example, data now available from studies of foraging peoples (or those who depend on gathering, hunting, and fishing for survival), make it clear that among most foragers,

women provide the majority, and sometimes up to 80 percent, of the daily diet for the group. This they do through gathering wild vegetables, fruits, eggs, insects, and the like, and hunting small animals. The results of Man the Hunter's hunting are more valued, yes, but unpredictable. Given these data, environmentalists suggest that new models of cultural evolution that take into account the contributions of *both* women and men are long overdue. Lancaster (1975) and Tanner and Zihlman (1976) are among those attempting to correct the picture, while Leibowitz (1975) has called for a re-evaluation of the significance of sexual dimorphism (size difference) in evolutionary history.

Environmentalists are not arguing that their position is new, nor would they think of so doing since the study of human and behavioral flexibility and plasticity is what has characterized anthropology as a discipline since its inception. Witness the works of Margaret Mead (1935, 1949) for example, wherein clear cases were made for the importance of culture as the decisive factor in definitions of sex roles and personality types appropriate for both males and females. What environmentalists *are* saying is that the importance of social, environmental, and cultural factors needs to be restated at the present time, especially in view of the new biogenetic revival of the "anatomy is destiny" argument. From their perspective, male bias or androcentrism in anthropology is surmountable, as is male dominance, which is neither inevitable, natural, nor permanent in culture.

Other Approaches

Obviously, the biological and environmentalist positions described above represent two opposite approaches to a question that has been argued before and will continue to receive attention in the future. There is no easy answer to the question of how much of culture is genetically based, especially now that research on language acquisition supports the idea. It will only be possible to sort out all the related matters when we increase our now-limited comprehension of the science of heredity, the human brain, and other such phenomena. In the meantime, perhaps it is feasible to question both groups if only because of their exclusive, either-or approaches.

Although these two groups represent much of the anthropological work related to discussion of the subordination of women, there are some other approaches and developments that deserve at least brief mention.

NEW STRUCTURALISM   In recent years, a French anthropologist, Claude Lévi-Strauss (1963, 1969), has greatly affected much anthropological thinking. Basically interested in cognitive processes and committed to unraveling human universals, Lévi-Strauss has striven to reveal the mental structures that underlie human behavior. Using a variety of ethnographic data, he has suggested that these usually take the form of binary sets or oppositions. Included in these dichotomies are day-night, raw-cooked, life-death, young-old, sacred-profane, earth-sky, right-left, nature-culture, male-female, and the like. Humans, in time and space, share these mental structures, which exist at what can be termed the deep, structural level, rather than a surface one.

Several aspects of Lévi-Strauss's work are applicable to discussions of the subordination of women; among these are the equation of females and nature in opposition to males and culture, and his ideas on kinship. Viewing kinship as a primary force in all human lives and one that is central to cultural systems, Lévi-Strauss stresses its controlling aspects. As it turns out, though both sexes

are controlled, women bear the brunt of it all, just because they are the reproducers. Lévi-Strauss views marriage as the most basic form of gift exchange, and within it, women become gifts to be given and exchanged by men. Thus, from his perspective, the oppression of women stems from the social system, rather than from biological factors.

Lévi-Strauss's works are challenging, thought-provoking and difficult. To date, Ortner (1974) and Rubin (1975) have done creditable jobs in evaluating their implications for those interested in a cross-cultural view of women. It should be noted, however, that not all anthropologists are willing to accept the universality of binary mental structures, and some, such as Sacks (1976), find Lévi-Strauss's explanation of the oppression of women downright untenable, ethnographically.

REVIVAL OF MATRIARCHY THEORIES   One of the initial results of feminism in anthropology was a reawakening of interest in matriarchies. As originally proposed by nineteenth-century classical evolutionists, all humans progressed culturally through a series of stages, which began with promiscuity and ended with civilization. Confusing descent and political rule, and mistakenly equating the viable principle of matriliny (where descent is traced through females) with power and rule by women, some early anthropologists such as Bachofen (1861) suggested that there was a time when women were, in fact, in control. By the early twentieth century, however, the grandiose schemes of the nineteenth-century classical evolutionists had been rejected by most serious anthropologists, and that of matriarchies was among them. Recent re-examinations of the theories (Bamberger 1974, Webster 1975) have not suggested that reviving them has any anthropological value, although some writers such as Davis (1972), Morgan (1972), and Reed (1975) have chosen to do so.

MARXISM   Related to the interest in reviving the ideas of Bachofen and other classical evolutionists is that of re-examining the philosophies of Marx and Engels. These, especially as professionally interpreted by Leacock (1972), Sacks (1974), Rubin (1975), and Gough (1977), offer a picture of early human society that was based on sexual egalitarianism. Women and men were both engaged in equally significant work and communal ownership was the rule; women were neither oppressed nor exploited. However, with the domestication of animals and ensuing ideas of private ownership of property and production of surpluses, class societies emerged. With them, the nature and importance of the household changed, the nuclear family became economically isolated and women became subordinate and subservient to dominant men and dependent on them. This situation is typical of much of today's world because Europeans, through contact and colonialism, have spread not only capitalistic philosophies and political domination, but also all of their cultural attitudes and beliefs about the proper asymmetrical relationship between the sexes.

OTHER ALTERNATIVES   In addition to the approaches mentioned above, there are several other developments within contemporary anthropology that deserve brief mention because they are related to discussions of subordination of women. Perhaps it is most useful to view these as shifts in research methods which make it more possible to evaluate women's roles and statuses within specific cultures.

The first of these is known as *emic research*. Put simply, this approach stresses the native person's perspective, categories, and analysis of his or her own world. It asks and values the responses to questions such as how do women in *x* culture see themselves as individuals as well as in relation to their men, and how do the men see the women? Do they devalue themselves or each other? Do the women see themselves living in a man's world, oppressed and dominated by their men? Do the men see women as subordinate entities? This kind of research design contrasts with one that has been long established in anthropology, one that since the middle 1950s has been termed the *etic approach.* Here, the emphasized perspective is the external one, that of the outsider scientist, which is based on observation, comparative analysis, and evaluation. Although there is undoubtedly room and need for both perspectives, we have yet to balance our allegiances. Perhaps more ethnographic information, such as that provided by Chiñas (1973) for Isthmus Zapotec women and Briggs (1974) for Eskimo women, will encourage just that.

Another research technique that was especially useful when the discipline was initially identifying and attacking sexism is the distinction between the private-domestic-informal and the public-political-formal spheres or domains of life. In retrospect, this emphasis seems necessary, if only to awaken fieldworkers of both sexes to the fact that there are other things happening in culture besides what is visible and public, and by extension, male. Since women are found in the private sphere so often, a recognition of the importance of this opened up access to the other half of the population and encouraged the realization that male-female relations anywhere cannot be analyzed solely through male eyes and minds.

Studies and collections that have utilized this distinction (for example, Friedl 1967, Chiñas 1973, Matthiasson 1974 and Rosaldo 1974) have suggested that in some places in the world, women's and men's roles are "complementary but equal." The spheres and activities are different but they are seen as mutually interdependent, supportive, necessary, and of equal value by the people who experience them. With such data in hand, the idea that the subordination of women is a universal can be challenged as representing another figment of our imagination, another example of how our own values, attitudes, perceptions, and ethnocentrism have biased our analyses.

Summary

At the present time, no one approach characterizes anthropological perspectives on the subordination of women. This is true both in terms of the pervasiveness of subordination in time and space and the explanations for it where it can be documented. Although emphases on emic research and the private sphere have utility, some anthropologists are already challenging the notion that the private-public dichotomy is universal, suggesting that it is related specifically to class societies and not applicable to foragers.

At present, as Lamphere (1977) indicates, much of the anthropological work on the subordination of women focuses on an evaluation of women's roles among foragers, the one subsistence system wherein equality, as we envision and define it, seems possible. Some, relying heavily on emic data, argue that foraging males and females have "complementary but equal" relationships, whereas others (for example, Friedl 1975, Hammond and Jablow 1976, Lamphere 1977) challenge such interpretations, stating they ignore observable, etic realities.

Anthropologists recognize the serious need for continual research, thought, and discussion of the issues. Hopefully, in the near future, it will be possible to define such concepts as dominance, power, authority, equality, and subordinance so they are useful cross-culturally. Hopefully, it will be soon possible to build models that incorporate both emic and etic information without damaging either, and that take into account variables we already know are important, such as who controls resources and their allocation. At the moment, the questions are emerging faster than the answers, thereby stimulating the energies of current researchers. Undoubtedly, the issues will continue to challenge generations of forthcoming scholars.

References Cited

Alexander, R. D. 1974. "The Evolution of Social Behavior." *Annual Review of Ecology and Systematics* 5: 325–383.

Ardener, E. 1972. "Belief and the Problem of Women." In *The Interpretation of Rituals.* J. S. La Fontaine, ed. London: Tavistock Publications.

Ardrey, Robert. 1966. *The Territorial Imperative.* New York: Atheneum.

Bachofen, J. J. 1861. *Das Mutterecht.* Basle: Benno Schwabe and Company.

Bamberger, Joan. 1974. "The Myth of Matriarchy: Why Men Rule in Primitive Society." In *Women, Culture, and Society.* Michelle Rosaldo and Louise Lamphere, eds. Pp. 263–280. Stanford: Stanford University Press.

Barash, David. 1977. *Sociobiology and Behavior.* New York: Elsevier North-Holland, Inc.

Briggs, Jean. 1974. "Eskimo Women: Makers of Men." In *Many Sisters.* Carolyn J. Matthiasson, ed. Pp. 261–304. New York: Free Press.

Brown, Judith. 1970. "A Note on the Division of Labor by Sex." *American Anthropologist* 72: 1073–1078.

Chiñas, Beverly. 1973. *The Isthmus Zapotecs: Women's Roles in Cultural Context.* New York: Holt, Rinehart and Winston.

Davis, Elizabeth. 1971. *The First Sex.* New York: G. P. Putnam.

Fernea, E. W. 1965. *Guests of the Sheik*. Garden City, N.Y.: Doubleday/Anchor.

Friedl, Ernestine. 1967. "The Position of Women: Appearance and Reality." *Anthropological Quarterly 40*, 3: 97–108.

————. 1975. *Women and Men: An Anthropologist's View*. New York: Holt, Rinehart and Winston.

Goodale, Jane C. 1971. *Tiwi Wives: A Study of the Women of Melville Island, North Australia*. Seattle: University of Washington Press, American Ethnological Society, Monograph 51.

Gough, Kathleen. 1977. "An Anthropologist Looks at Engels." In *Women in a Man-Made World*. 2nd ed. Nona Glazer-Melbin and Helen Youngelson Waehrer, eds. Pp. 156–168. Chicago: Rand McNally. Orig. published 1972.

Hammond, Dorothy, and Alta Jablow. 1976. *Women in Cultures of the World*. Menlo Park, Calif.: Cummings Publishing Company.

Kaberry, Phyllis. 1939. *Aboriginal Woman: Sacred and Profane*. London: Routledge and Kegan Paul, Ltd.

Kessler, Evelyn. 1976. *Women: An Anthropological View*. New York: Holt, Rinehart and Winston.

Lamphere, Louise. 1977. "Review Essay: Anthropology." *SIGNS: Journal of Women Culture and Society 2*, 3: 612–627.

Lancaster, Jane. 1975. *Primate Behavior and the Emergence of Human Culture*. New York: Holt, Rinehart and Winston.

Landes, Ruth. 1938. *The Ojibwa Woman*. New York: Columbia University Press.

Leacock, Eleanor. 1972. "Introduction to Frederick Engels." In *The Origin of the Family, Private Property and the State*. E. B. Leacock, ed. New York: International Publishers.

Leibowitz, Lila. 1975. "Perspectives on the Evolution of Sex Differences." In *Toward an Anthropology of Women*. Rayna Reiter, ed. Pp. 20–35. New York: Monthly Review Press.

Lévi-Strauss, Claude. 1969. *The Elementary Structures of Kinship*. Boston: Beacon Press. Orig. French edition, 1949.

————. 1963. *Structural Anthropology*. New York: Basic Books, Inc.

Lorenz, Konrad. 1966. *On Aggression*. New York: Harcourt, Brace and World.

Martin, M. Kay, and Barbara Voorhies. 1975. *Female of the Species*. New York: Columbia University Press.

Matthiasson, Carolyn J., ed. 1974. *Many Sisters: Women in Cross-Cultural Perspective*. New York: Free Press.

Mead, Margaret. 1928. *Coming of Age in Samoa*. New York: Mentor Book Edition (1949).

————. 1935. *Sex and Temperament in Three Primitive Societies*. New York: Dell Publishing Company.

————. 1949. *Male and Female: A Study of the Sexes in a Changing World*. New York: Dell Publishing Company.

Morgan, Elaine. 1972. *Descent of Woman*. New York: Stein and Day.

Morris, Desmond. 1968. *The Naked Ape*. New York: McGraw-Hill.

Murphy, Yolanda, and Robert Murphy. 1974. *Women of the Forest*. New York: Columbia University Press.

Ortner, Sherry. 1974. "Is Female to Male as Nature Is to Culture?" In *Women, Culture, and Society*. Michelle Rosaldo and Louise Lamphere, eds. Pp. 67–88. Stanford: Stanford University Press.

Pescatello, Ann, ed. 1973. *Female and Male in Latin America*. Pittsburgh: University of Pittsburgh Press.

Reed, Evelyn. 1975. *Woman's Evolution: From Matriarchal Clan to Patriarchal Family*. New York: Pathfinder Press.

Reiter, Rayna, ed. 1975. *Toward an Anthropology of Women*. New York: Monthly Review Press.

Rohrlich-Leavitt, Ruby, ed. 1975. *Women Cross-Culturally: Change and Challenge*. The Hague: Mouton Press.

Rohrlich-Leavitt, Ruby, Barbara Sykes, and Elizabeth Weatherford. 1975. "Aboriginal Woman: Male and Female Anthropological Perspectives." In *Toward an Anthropology of Women*. Rayne Reiter, ed. Pp. 110–126. New York: Monthly Review Press.

Rosaldo, Michelle. 1974. "Woman, Culture, and Society: A Theoretical Overview." In *Woman, Culture, and Society*. Michelle Rosaldo and Louise Lamphere, eds. Pp. 17–42. Stanford: Stanford University Press.

Rosaldo, Michelle, and Louise Lamphere, eds.

1974. *Woman, Culture and Society.* Stanford: Stanford University Press.

Rubin, Gayle. 1975. "The Traffic in Women: Notes on the 'Political Economy' of Sex." In *Toward an Anthropology of Women.* Rayna Reiter, ed. Pp. 157–210. New York: Monthly Review Press.

Sacks, Karen. 1974. "Engels Revisited: Women, the Organization of Production and Private Property." In *Woman, Culture, and Society.* Michelle Rosaldo and Louise Lamphere, eds. Pp. 207–222. Stanford: Stanford University Press.

———. 1976. "State Bias and Women's Status." *American Anthropologist 78,* 3: 565–569.

Schlegel, Alice. 1974. "Women Anthropologists Look at Women." *Reviews in Anthropology 1,* 6: 553–560.

Slocum, Sally. 1975. "Woman the Gatherer: Male Bias in Anthropology." In *Toward an Anthropology of Women.* Rayna Reiter, ed. Pp. 36–50. New York: Monthly Review Press.

Strathern, Marilyn. 1972. *Women in Between.* New York: Seminar Press.

Tanner, Nancy, and Adrienne Zihlman. 1976. "Women in Evolution Part 1: Innovation and Selection in Human Origins." *SIGNS 1,* 3, 1: 585–608.

Tiger, Lionel. 1969. *Men in Groups.* New York: Random House.

———. 1970. "Male Dominance? Yes, Alas. A Sexist Plot? No." *New York Times Magazine.* October 25.

Tiger, Lionel, and Robin Fox. 1971. *The Imperial Animal.* New York: Holt, Rinehart and Winston.

Trivers, R. L. 1971. "The Evolution of Reciprocal Altruism." *Quarterly Review of Biology* 46: 35–37.

Webster, Paula. 1975. "Matriarchy: A Vision of Power." In *Toward an Anthropology of Women.* Rayna Reiter, ed. Pp. 141–156. New York: Monthly Review Press.

West Eberhard, M. J. 1975. "The Evolution of Social Behavior by Kin Selection." *Quarterly Review of Biology,* 50: 1–33.

Wilson, Edward O. 1975. *Sociobiology, The New Synthesis.* Cambridge, Mass.: Harvard University Press.

Wolf, M. 1976. *Women and the Family in Rural Taiwan.* Stanford: Stanford University Press.

MALE DOMINANCE? YES, ALAS.
A SEXIST PLOT? NO.

LIONEL TIGER

Anthropologist Lionel Tiger was born in Montreal, Canada, in 1937; studied at McGill and the University of London; and has been the recipient of several research grants. He has taught at the University of British Columbia and at Rutgers. Among feminists he is best known for his work *Men in Groups* (1969) in which he developed the thesis that men's hunting activity created in them the ability to "bond," to form close, lasting, mutually protective and productive associations, an ability that women did not have and would never develop except in reproductive activities. (Ultimately, men may bond with one another to do society's work; women bond only with their children and mate and thus become excluded from communal affairs.)

In this essay, Tiger represents the school of thought that argues for the biological-evolutionary basis of sex-role behavior and social-sexual systems. Men and women are physiologically, biologically different because they have evolved that way in answer to environmental survival factors. These differences account for male/female behavioral differences and for current male dominance.

The feminists' angry rebuke to us males could not be more correct and more justified. Women everywhere earn less money than men, possess less power over their communities than men, have more difficulty becoming eminent than men, and do so far less often; as a group they have lower status than men and less public prestige. Surely no one, myself included, would want to argue that such a situation is good or even tolerable: this must be the moral given or baseline from which all discussion of the feminist movement proceeds. However, if you want to change a system you have got to understand it.

The feminist critique is rooted in the assumption that there are no important differences between the sexes (except reproductive) which are not culturally determined and that, in fact, any differences which do exist result mainly from a universal conspiracy among males to keep females different — and inferior.

"Groups who rule by birthright are fast disappearing," says Kate Millett in her "Sexual Politics," "yet there remains one ancient and universal scheme for the domination of one birth group by another — the scheme that prevails in the area of sex." She claims that new research "suggests that the possibilities of innate temperamental differences seem more remote than ever. . . . In doing so it gives fairly concrete positive evidence of the overwhelmingly *cultural* character of gender, i.e., personality structure in terms of sexual category."

Not only do men keep women subordinate, goes the argument, they also make an elaborate pretense of placing them on a pretty pedestal — by means of literature and social science designed to make women feel

they are most feminine, most productive and most natural when they raise men's children, cook men's food, share men's beds, and believe in the ideology that what's good for men and boys is best for women and girls.

As well as being of general intellectual interest, the feminists' attack on males is also one of the strongest indictments of science and the scientific method that it is possible to make. On generous scientific grounds, it seems clear to me that the evidence which feminists such as Kate Millett and Ti-Grace Atkinson use to support their case is, on balance, irresponsible in its selection and so narrowly and unfairly interpreted that it will finally do damage to the prospects of women's actual liberation.

Briefly, there is considerable evidence that differences between males and females do not result simply from male conspiracy, that they are directly related to our evolution as an animal, that they occur in such a wide variety of situations and cultures that the feminist explanation is inadequate in itself to help us understand them, and that there are biological bases for sexual differences which have nothing to do with oppressing females but rather with ensuring the safety of communities and the healthy growth of children. Furthermore, these differences reach back not only to the early states of our history as a civilization, but further back to our formative time as a species; accordingly, sexual differences in physique, hormone secretions, energy and endurance, and possibly even in ways of relating to other people, may be linked to our genetic heritage in direct and influential ways. To say that these differences have existed for a long time and have some biological basis is not — as some people too hastily conclude — to say that human beings are condemned to live in ancient arrangements with no hope of real change. But without understanding what they are and how they came about in the first place, the women and men who want to change our sexual patterns will fail.

First, we have to look at the unpleasant facts. In all communities, the central political decisions are overwhelmingly taken by males and the "public forum" is dominated by males. In a few progressive countries women may be actively involved in legislatures — for example, in Finland and Norway — but by and large the pattern is that even where females have had the vote for many years and where there is open encouragement of female political activity, the number of women participating in managing governments is tiny. The rule is, the higher up the hierarchy you look, the less likely it is you'll find a woman official. The same pattern applies in labor unions, businesses, recreational groups and religious hierarchies. All over the world armies and other fighting groups are all-male. In a few places where women are trained to fight, it remains unusual for them to join men in the front lines (except where defense of home territory is involved, as is sometimes the case for the Vietnamese, for example, and for Israelis living in some border kibbutzim). The task of forming a raiding and fighting party and leaving the home bases to attack elsewhere is universally and unexceptionally male. So is controlling other persons by force, as in police work and similar enterprises.

Other things being equal, women's work is of lower status than men's, and when women begin to move in on an occupation, it loses standing in comparison with others. Though in this country individual women have considerable power to dispose of family income and wealth, typically their investment decisions are guided by males; the products they buy and the manner in which they are stimulated to do so are managed by men. Even proponents of the kibbutz system in Israel — still the most radical, long-term effort at constructing the ideal society which we can observe — concede that insofar as relations between men and women are concerned, the result of over two generations of extremely shrewd and wholehearted effort is far from acceptable to sexual egalitarians. And in this country, those who have set up communes to avoid the effects of private property, patriarchy, restrictive sexual and familial life, and technocracy have discovered that simply because there is more heavy physical labor on the commune, the distinction between men's work and women's work is far sharper than in the larger society from which they hope to escape.

The political misfortune in this is clear. However, the scientific question remains: why is this the case? I've already noted the feminist answer: patriarchy exists because it has existed for so long and so universally. Despite enormous variation in standard of living, religious belief, economies, ecologies, political history, ideology and kinship systems of different societies, the same pattern broadly prevails *because* males have always dominated females in an effective and widespread scheme. But coming from feminists, this is a curious explanation, because it implies that all men everywhere are sufficiently clever and persistent to subdue permanently all women everywhere. If this is so, the conclusion follows mercilessly that men *should* govern. And if women so universally accept this state of affairs, then perhaps they are actually incapable of political action. That is nonsense, and unflattering to women, and unduly optimistic about male political acumen.

In all this general discussion, one of the

most useful laws of science has been over-looked, the so-called Law of Parsimony (or Occam's Razor). This dictates that you can-not explain a behavioral phenomenon by a higher, more complex process if a lower or simpler one will do. To take a simple case: The other day in the paperback section of Brentano's in Greenwich Village, a beautiful woman was looking at books. She wore no bra and her blouse was aggressively unbut-toned; all the supposedly cerebral men around couldn't take their horn-rimmed eyes off her. Now it is possible that the reason we stared was that we had been brain-washed by sexist books like Mailer's and Henry Miller's and our male chauvinist egos were aroused by the challenge of conquest. But the law of parsimony demands we con-sider that since sexual attraction is a basic signaling system which all animals have, this woman was signaling something which the men around her were dutifully responding to. Obviously, there were some higher proc-esses involved, too, but the simple erotic one was probably primary in this case.

If male dominance extends over the whole species — and has existed for so long — we seem constrained by the law of parsimony to look first into the biological information and theory at our disposal for an explana-tion. This includes comparative information about the other primates who exhibit many of the behavior patterns which feminists claim are unique impositions on human fe-males by human males. It also requires us to see what effect our evolution in the past has on our behavior in the present, which feminists — along with many of the social scientists they criticize — by and large are unwilling to do.

Their reasoning derives from the Pav-lovian biology of the nineteen-twenties and thirties, which taught that habit and condi-tioning could account for almost all men's behavior — and inherited characteristics for very little. Like the Lysenkoists in Russia and the positivists in this country, the fem-inists believe that changing the environments of the human animal will soon change the animal itself. For this, there is no evidence. Moreover, the argument ignores the theory that remains one of the strongest in science today — Darwin's explanation of the evolu-tion of the species through natural selection and inheritance.

Modern biology in part represents an ex-tremely important synthesis of sociology and genetics: we are able to understand the complicated social behavior of animals and can also work out how this behavior can be transmitted in the genetic codes. By now, many people are familiar with the work of the animal ethologists such as Konrad Lo-renz, George Schaller and Jane Goodall. Through their experiments and field studies, and those of their colleagues, we have come to appreciate that higher animals other than man also live in relatively elaborate social systems, with traditions, much learning, and considerable variation among different groups of the same species. And yet there remains a central pattern of behavior which is common to a species and appears to be passed down genetically from generation to generation. Three decades ago, how this was transmitted would have been difficult to say. But now we know that the intricate DNA genetic code makes it possible for the indi-vidual to inherit not only simple physical characteristics, such as size, shape and chemical makeup, but also a whole set of propensities for particular social behavior which goes with a given physiology. And we can deduce from systematic observations of behavior that these propensities can be in-hibited or released in the encounter with other members of the species, and modified over generations by the process of natural selection. This is most important, because it is a decisive advance from the notion of "instinct," which was defined as a relatively automatic matter of feeling hunger, blinking, and kicking softly at the doctor who hits one's knee with a small hammer.

Now we see that the question of what can be inherited is much more complex than we once thought, that all animals are "programed" not only to grow, come to sexual maturity, reproduce, become old and die, but also to interact with each other in rather predictable ways. Of course, there is considerable variation in how animals behave, just as there is in how they look, how quickly they run or swim, how much food they eat, and how large they grow. Just as with humans, there is considerable diversity but also a great amount of consistency and predictability.

We now want to know what the human biological inheritance is, or put another way, what is "in the wiring" of the average male and female, and how it got there. Almost certainly the most dismal difference between males and females is that men create large fighting groups, then with care, enthusiasm, and miserable effectiveness proceed to maim and kill each other. Feminists associate this grim pattern with *machismo* — the need for men to assert themselves in rough-and-tumble ways and to commit mayhem in the name of masculinity. Why men show *macho* and not women, the feminists do not wholly clarify, but the fact that women don't and men do is strikingly plain enough. Yet, among the possible reasons, there is a simple and clear biological factor the feminists overlook — the effect of the sex hormones on behavior.

In a report to a UNESCO conference on aggression I attended in Paris last May, David Hamburg of the department of psy-

chiatry at Stanford described the role of testosterone in stimulating aggressive behavior. In experiments on primates, when both males and females are given extra testosterone, they show much more aggressive hyper-male activity. Humans have similar reactions under artificial manipulation of hormone levels. Among boys and girls before puberty, boys show more testosterone than girls. But at adolescence, the changes are startling: Testosterone in boys increases at least tenfold, and possibly as much as 30 times. On the other hand, girls' testosterone levels only double, from a lower base to begin with. These levels remain stable throughout the life cycle.

In one sense this seems unimportant, because the absolute amounts of these hormone substances are so tiny. And yet hormones are like poisons — a tiny amount can have a gross effect. Hence we see adolescent males — not only among humans but in some other primate species, too — flooded at puberty with a natural chemical which apparently stimulates marked aggressive behavior. When females are given extra amounts, their behavior — independent of socialization, advertising, the male conspiracy — becomes more male-like, more aggressive, more assertive. I choose the example of aggression to discuss "the wiring" and its effect on what we do because no one is likely to claim any longer that the male capacity for violent corporate aggression is a sign of superiority or courage in the world we live in.

Other differences, too, are not unusual in the world of little boys and girls. Parents and teachers are familiar with the marked difference in the rate of maturity between girls and boys: the girls generally outpace the boys for at least the first 14 years of life in school performance, physical control, ability to withstand disease and accident, emotional control, and capacity to engage in detailed work. The pattern persists into sexual maturity; the earlier social competence of women is widely recognized when women marry men some years older than they. Among humans the contrast in rates of maturation are nowhere as marked as in some of the primates — for example, those whose females may mature at $3^1/_2$ years of age and males at 7. As John Tanner of London University has shown in his book, "Human Growth," girls at adolescence are about 18 months ahead of boys, just as they have been physically more mature than boys at all ages from birth. These differences are tangible, measurable and cross-cultural; they must reflect in some degree the genetic heritage which underlies such predictable regularities — though it must be emphasized that we are speaking of propensities that overlap and not absolute differences.

Now what could be the advantage to the human species of this extensive difference of male-female production of testosterone —given its implication for behavior? In a real if extremely simplified sense, evolution is conditioning over time. In other words, just as dogs can be rewarded for salivating at the sound of a bell, so members of a species do things which become rewarded genetically by the greater ability of the performers of the effective actions to survive and to reproduce. So what our information about sex hormones may mean is that there was an advantage to the evolving human species in selecting males with high testosterone levels and females with much lower levels. Our new information about human evolution from archeological research gives us a reason for this difference: hunting.

From all the available evidence, hunting was the critical human adaptation as long ago as 2 million, or 14, or even 20 million years ago. We have been farming for 13,000 years at most, and until about 5,000 years ago the majority of us were hunter-gatherers. We have been industrialized for barely 200 years. For 99 per cent of our history our survival depended on what bio-anthropologist William Laughlin of the University of Connecticut calls "the master pattern of the human species."

During this vast time span, the hunting-based behavioral adaptations which distinguish us from the other primates were selected in the same way we evolved our huge higher brains, our striding walk, our upright posture, and the apparatus for speech. And one of the most important of our evolutions underlies precisely the feminists' complaint: males hunted and females did not, and my suggestion is that, in addition to other indices such as size, running and throwing ability, and endurance, the differences between male and female hormone patterns reflect this reality.

It's worth reviewing this briefly. Among the other primates, an individual who is old enough gathers virtually all the food he or she will eat. Almost no primates eat meat, and there is no division of labor as far as getting food is concerned. Among humans, however, a division of work on the basis of sex is universal. A strong explanation for this is that our hunting past stimulated a behavioral specialization — males hunted, females gathered — which is clearly still very much part of us, though often in only symbolic and contorted forms. The ancient pattern seems to persist: men and women unite to reproduce young, but they separate to produce food and artifacts. Highly volatile adolescent males are subjected to rigorous and frequently painful initiations and training in the active manly arts; females — more equable, less accident-prone, less gripped by symbolic fantasies of heroic triumph —

rarely undergo initiations as violent and abusive as those males suffer. That is, it appears that females are much less truculent, much less in need of control, much less committed to extensive self-assertion. The possibility must be faced that this general characteristic of the species reflects the physiological one — that female bodies are less driven by those internal secretions which mark the rambunctious and often dangerous males.

If millions of years of evolution have a lot to do with the temperament of the individual male, it may also help explain the deep emotional ties that bind men together in groups. In a book that I published last year, "Men in Groups," I suggested that there is a biological program that results in a "bonding" between males which is as important for politics as the program of male-female bonding is for reproduction. The results of this male bonding propensity could be seen easily and everywhere: in sports, rock groups (who ever said males weren't emotional?), the American Legion, the men's houses of Indians, the secret societies of both Yale seniors and Australian aborigines, and — most unhappily of all — the bizarre and fantasy-ridden male enterprises called armies.

So not only were there traditional and casual barriers to female participation in the powerful groups of human communities but more elusive and fundamental ones as well. It might take far more radical steps than we feared to approach the sexual equality we say we want.

I have said that males hunted and females gathered. This is not to imply that what females did was less valuable for survival. In his detailed studies of the Kalahari Bushmen, my colleague Richard Lee of Rutgers has shown that in this group, at least, the food women gather is 80 per cent of the diet. What the Kalahari males bring back from the hunt is useful, but not essential. How representative the Bushmen are of all hunters, and particularly of our ancestors, is another question, but Lee's general suggestion presumably applies in many hunting-gathering communities. Nonetheless, all societies make some distinction between men's work and women's work. As Cynthia Epstein of Queens College has pointed out in her excellent study, "Woman's Place" (the most sensitive and probing modern analysis of the sociology of female employment), these distinctions are not necessarily sensible or logical. Still and all, we are an animal as committed to sexual segregation for certain purposes — particularly those having to do with hunting, danger, war, and passionate corporate drama — as we are to sexual conjunction for others — in particular for conceiving and rearing children, and sharing food.

Once again, we get perspective of this matter from studying other primates. While among the other primates there is no sexual division of labor for food-getting, there is still considerable difference between what males and females do. In fact, from primatological work only now becoming available, an unexpected and fascinating body of information is emerging about encounters among primate females, their hierarchies, how they structure relationships over generations and how they learn their social roles. From the work of researchers at the Japanese Monkey Center, from Vernon Reynolds and his wife, Frankie, of Bristol University, from Jane Lancaster of Rutgers, Suzanne Ripley of the Smithsonian Institution and Phyllis Jay Dolhinow of the University of California, we are beginning to learn that there are indeed elaborate patterns of female bonding and that these are based to a large extent on kinship relationships rather than the political ones that frequently bind males. Furthermore, these kinship-like structures appear to be essential for comfortable and viable community life, and they provide security for the young in a web of affiliations which persist over their lifetimes. Hence, the core social bonds at the intimate level are mediated through the females, while at the public or political level, the central relationships remain very much a male monopoly. It is extremely unlikely for a female to assume political leadership of a group when a suitable adult male is available, even though the females may be far more experienced than a young leader-male, and though females seem perfectly capable of leading groups in interim periods when no suitable male is present.

One possible, if elusive, clue to the different social roles of male and female is suggested by research into the frequency of their smiles by Daniel G. Freedman of the Committee for the Study of Human Development at the University of Chicago. The underlying proposition is that smiling is an affiliative gesture of deference, a permissive, accommodating expression rather than a commanding or threatening one. Certainly among other primates, the smile is associated with fear, and humans too talk of the "nervous smile." Freedman and his associates found that among human infants two days old, females smiled spontaneously at a significantly higher rate than males. This was *eyes-closed smiling* — in the absence of a social relationship — and suggests the affinity for this particular motor pattern which girls have.

In another study — using the ingenious method of looking at photos of students in high school and college yearbooks since 1900 — the same sexual difference was maintained. While everyone smiled less during periods of economic depression (they also had fewer babies), still the significant sexual difference persisted. And in his field studies of primates, Irven DeVore of Harvard University has found that females smile more often than males as a result of fear.

Intriguingly enough, some of the techniques of political organization which feminists are exploring suggest significant differences from conventional male procedures. For one thing, the principle of competitive, individual leadership is rejected in favor of an attempt at cooperative, group action. In their "consciousness-raising" sessions, the exchange and discussion of personal intimacies serves as a basis for eventual political activity; these groups gather in a circle, formalities are minimal and sisterhood is emphasized. In a sense, the feminist approach to politics is genuinely radical; if it works, it could well be an important contribution not only to the lives of women but to the political conduct of men and the body politic in general.

So far I have argued that the feminist critique takes for granted what important scientific evidence does not permit us to take for granted: that only explicit cultural control — in fact, conspiracy — lies behind the very great differences in certain male and female social behaviors. Feminists such as Kate Millett suggest that once upon a time there was a matriarchy that became corrupted by patriarchal force, which to this day oppresses women. However, the archeological facts available suggest that there is an unbroken line from the male-dominated primate systems I have described here through the hunting stage of our evolution — from which we have not changed genetically — to the most sophisticated and complicated, male-dominated technocratic societies.

Because they ignore biological factors (like many other reformers), the feminists run the risk of basing their legitimate demand for legal and economic equality on a vulnerable foundation. Their denial of significant physiological differences can also deter real occupational and educational success by women — a possibility that is suggested by a variety of studies of the menstrual cycle. The relationship of the cycle to social performance is by no means simple, nor is the evidence conclusive. But studies such as those done over a period of some 15 years by Katherina Dalton of University College, University of London, must be considered: One of her estimates is that roughly 40 per cent of women suffer from a variety of distressing symptoms during the final week or so of the menstrual cycle (other researchers see a higher figure). Dalton's investigation of admission to mental hospitals revealed that 46 per cent of the female admissions occurred during the seven or eight days preceding and during menstruation; at this time, too, 53 per cent of attempted suicides by females occurred.

In another of her studies, 45 per cent of industrial employes who reported sick did so during this period; 49 per cent of crimes committed by women prisoners happened at this time and so did 45 per cent of the punishments meted out to schoolgirls. Dalton also discovered that schoolgirls who were prefects and monitors doled out significantly greater numbers of punishments to others during the menstrual period, and she raises the question of whether or not this is also true of women magistrates, teachers and other figures in authority.

She presents evidence that students writing examinations during the premenstruum earn roughly 14 to 15 per cent poorer grades than they do at other times of the month. If what happens in England also happens here (there could well be cultural and psychological differences between the reactions of the two female populations), then an American girl writing her Graduate Record Examinations over a two-day period or a week-long set of finals during the premenstruum begins with a disadvantage which almost certainly condemns her to no higher than a second-class grade. A whole career in the educational system can be unfairly jeopardized because of this phenomenon. In another sphere, a study by the British Road Research Laboratory suggests that about 60 per cent of all traffic accidents of females occur during about 25 per cent of the days of the month — apparently before and during menstruation. Since women are generally safer drivers than men, certainly in the younger age groups, this may not be a considerable hazard to the public. But for individual women driving cars or writing examinations, these findings may be relevant — and important.

So the paradox is that when they deny there are meaningful differences between males and females because of such a predictable phenomenon as menstruation, feminists may help make it more difficult for women to compete openly and equally for scholarships, jobs, entry to graduate schools, and the variety of other prerequisites of wealth and status. This emphatically does not mean women shouldn't have responsible or competitive jobs; it may mean that in a community committed to genuine equal opportunity examinations and schedules of work — for example, the flying time of women pilots — could be adjusted to the realities of female experience and not, as now, wholly to the male-oriented work week and pattern. (Interestingly, Valentina Tereshkova-Nikolayeva, the first woman astronaut, affirms that women can be as capable astronauts as men, but that allowance should be made for the effect of the cycle on physiology.) The human species is faced with two overwhelming problems — war and overpopulation. The first results from the social bonding of males, and is not our concern here. The second results from the sexual bonding of males and females. Men and women make love and have children not simply because the patriarchal conspiracy offers women no other major form of satisfaction, but because an old pattern rooted in the genetic codes and reflected in our life cycles — particularly in the flurries of adolescence — draw men and women to each other and to the infants their conjunction yields.

There is no conspiracy in becoming adolescent and sprouting breasts and becoming interested in boys in a new way. Madison Avenue did not invent the fact that female bodies and the movement and sound of women are stimulating to men. Anyone who has pushed a baby carriage down the street will know how many passers-by peek at a young infant and how quickly the presence of a baby will help strangers talk. Throughout the primates, females with newborn infants enjoy high status and babies are enormously attractive to all members of the community. Can it be that human females, who have more of a stake in maternity than males, are responding to the crisis of population and devaluation of this role in the stringent, probing, feminist way? In other words, is the rhetoric about sexual politics really political, or is it, ironically, another expression of sexual difference? More poignantly still, may it perhaps reflect also the currently drastic excess of females over males of marriageable age — because of the disruptions of the Second World War and the baby boom which followed — and hence the probability that a huge number of mature women remain "sexually unemployed" insofar as they will probably be unable to arrange reproductive lives in the limited ways our sexual rigidities allow?

Child-rearing remains the most labor-intensive task left to members of mechanized societies, and it can't be speeded up. Day-care centers for children can obviously be a sensible feature of a civilized society. But it is another thing for Kate Millett to recommend that child care be entrusted to "trained persons of both sexes" — an idea which is not promising in view of the experiences of orphanages and foster homes. As John Bowlby has argued in his book on child-rearing and deprivation, "Attachment," children need inputs of behavior as much as they require food, and there is considerable evidence that those who do not have a mother or mother-figure on which to focus their affections and security in early childhood suffer irreparable difficulty later on.

Now, it is not clear that fathers cannot do as well. Millions of children are currently being raised by fathers without wives, and it is true that adult males obviously have, as Margaret Mead has suggested, a strong interest in infants. On the other hand, the long and intimate relationship a pregnant woman has with her gestating child must prime her to respond to the child differently from even the most doting father. Even if this has not been demonstrated conclusively, it remains a possibility, just as it is possible that breast-feeding mothers — still the majority at the present time — have, in comparison to fathers, some different if not more substantial commitment to their children because of the hormonal and other physiological processes involved. And if nothing else, the fact that the whole human species has overwhelmingly elected to have children raised at least in the first years by women suggests conformity to nature rather than to male conspiracy.

There is good psychological and primatological evidence that it is necessary for young children to separate themselves increasingly from their parents as they mature. But unless the day-care program of the women's liberationists takes carefully into account what mothers know too well — the routinely incessant and innocent demands of young children for both care and encounter — then too many women who have spent too many days with this understanding will reject the more appealing aspects of the movement. A rejection of the intimacies of family life such as they are, and an implication that females interested sexually in males as husbands and progenitors are somehow inferior and don't know their own minds, can also serve only to frighten off potential supporters.

The theorists who proclaim the withering away of the state of sexual differences may well be proved as wrong as those Marxists who assumed that the State would wither away once it had changed the social arrangements of the people. The problem the feminists face is not just to change a culture and an economy, but to change a primate who is very old genetically and who seems stubbornly committed to relatively little variation in basic sexual structures. This is not to say that some change cannot and will not be achieved, if for no other reason than that the population crush may affect this animal as it has some others — by drastically altering his behavior patterns (though we may as yet be far from the densities which will seriously inhibit breeding).

In an article on the relationship between women's rights and socialism (New Left Review, November-December, 1966), the English sociologist Juliet Mitchell called the feminist struggle "The Longest Revolution." If there is to be a revolution, it will be of infinitely greater duration than Mitchell anticipated. Our biological heritage is the product of millions of years of successful adaptation and it recurs in each generation with only tiny alterations. It is simply prudent that those concerned with changing sex roles understand the possible biological importance of what they want to do, and take careful measure of what these phenomena mean. If they do not, the primary victims of their misanalysis, unfortunately, will be — as usual — women and their daughters.

WOMAN THE GATHERER: MALE BIAS IN ANTHROPOLOGY

SALLY SLOCUM

Sally Slocum, born in Indiana in 1939 and educated at the University of California and the University of Colorado, is an anthropologist with a wide array of skills and experience. A stained-glass craftswoman, a professional dancer, and a participant in archeological surveys, she has taught courses in physical anthropology, paleontology, and ethnology, among other subjects, and has made major contributions to research and teaching in Women's Studies.

Crystallizing, then rejecting the male bias in anthropology that allowed theories like Man-the-Hunter to develop uncritically, Slocum here proffers a different perspective: Central to human community and social organization is the sharing of food that for many reasons must precede organized hunting. Such sharing must have originated in the mother-infant relationship and then enlarged into wider bonding. This concept might prove a far more fruitful explanatory factor than the notions of hunting, weaponry, and male bonding.

The perspective of women is, in many ways, equally foreign to an anthropology that has been developed and pursued primarily by males. There is a strong male bias in the questions asked, and the interpretations given. This bias has hindered the full development of our discipline as "the study of the human animal" (I don't want to call it "the study of man" for reasons that will become evident). I am going to demonstrate the Western male bias by reexamining the matter of evolution of Homo sapiens from our nonhuman primate ancestors. In particular, the concept of "Man the Hunter" as developed by Sherwood Washburn and C. Lancaster (1968) and others is my focus. This critique is offered in hopes of transcending the male bias that limits our knowledge by limiting the questions we ask.

Though male bias could be shown in other areas, hominid evolution is particularly convenient for my purpose because it involves speculations and inferences from a rather small amount of data. In such a case, hidden assumptions and premises that lie behind the speculations and inferences are more easily demonstrated. Male bias exists not only in the ways in which the scanty data are interpreted, but in the very language used. All too often the word "man" is used in such an ambiguous fashion that it is impossible to decide whether it refers to males or to the human species in general, including both males and females. In fact, one frequently is led to suspect that in the minds of many anthropologists, "man," supposedly meaning the human species, is actually exactly synonymous with "males."

This ambiguous use of language is par-

ticularly evident in the writing that surrounds the concept of Man the Hunter. Washburn and Lancaster make it clear that it is specifically males who hunt, that hunting is much more than simply an economic activity, and that most of the characteristics which we think of as specifically human can be causally related to hunting. They tell us that hunting is a whole pattern of activity and way of life: "The biology, psychology, and customs that separate us from the apes — all these we owe to the hunters of time past" (1968:303). If this line of reasoning is followed to its logical conclusion, one must agree with Jane Kephart when she says:

> Since only males hunt, and the psychology of the species was set by hunting, we are forced to conclude that females are scarcely human, that is, do not have built-in the basic psychology of the species: to kill and hunt and ultimately to kill others of the same species. The argument implies built-in aggression in human males, as well as the assumed passivity of human females and their exclusion from the mainstream of human development. (1970:5)

To support their argument that hunting is important to human males, Washburn and Lancaster point to the fact that many modern males still hunt, though it is no longer economically necessary. I could point out that many modern males play golf, play the violin, or tend gardens: these, as well as hunting, are things their culture teaches them. Using a "survival" as evidence to demonstrate an important fact of cultural evolution can be accorded no more validity when proposed by a modern anthropologist than when proposed by Tylor.

Regardless of its status as a survival, hunting, by implication as well as direct statement, is pictured as a male activity to the exclusion of females. This activity, on which we are told depends the psychology, biology, and customs of our species, is strictly male. A theory that leaves out half

From Sally Slocum, "Woman the Gatherer: Male Bias in Anthropology," in *Toward an Anthropology of Women*, ed. Rayna Reiter (New York: Monthly Review Press, 1975). Copyright © 1975 by Rayna R. Reiter. Reprinted by permission of Monthly Review Press.

the human species is unbalanced. The theory of Man the Hunter is not only unbalanced; it leads to the conclusion that the basic human adaptation was the desire of males to hunt and kill. This not only gives too much importance to aggression, which is after all only one factor of human life, but it derives culture from killing. I am going to suggest a less biased reading of the evidence, which gives a more valid and logical picture of human evolution, and at the same time a more hopeful one. First I will note the evidence, discuss the more traditional reading of it, and then offer an alternative reconstruction.

The data we have to work from are a combination of fossil and archeological materials, knowledge of living nonhuman primates, and knowledge of living humans. Since we assume that the protohominid ancestors of Homo sapiens developed in a continuous fashion from a base of characteristics similar to those of living nonhuman primates, the most important facts seem to be the ways in which humans differ from nonhuman primates, and the ways in which we are similar. The differences are as follows: longer gestation period; more difficult birth; neoteny, in that human infants are less well developed at birth; long period of infant dependency; absence of body hair; year-round sexual receptivity of females, resulting in the possibility of bearing a second infant while the first is still at the breast or still dependent; erect bipedalism; possession of a large and complex brain that makes possible the creation of elaborate symbolic systems, languages, and cultures, and also results in most behavior being under cortical control; food sharing; and finally, living in families. (For the purposes of this paper I define families as follows: a situation where each individual has defined responsibilities and obligations to a specific set of others of both sexes and various ages. I use this definition because, among humans, the family is a *social* unit, regardless of any biological or genetic relationship which may or may not exist among its members.)

In addition to the many well-known close physiological resemblances, we share with nonhuman primates the following characteristics: living in social groups; close mother-infant bonds; affectional relationships; a large capacity for learning and a related paucity of innate behaviors; ability to take part in dominance hierarchies; a rather complex nonsymbolic communication system which can handle with considerable subtlety such information as the mood and emotional state of the individual, and the attitude and status of each individual toward the other members of the social group.

The fossil and archeological evidence consists of various bones labeled Ramapithecus, Australopithecus, Homo habilis, Homo erectus, etc.; and artifacts such as stone tools representing various cultural traditions, evidence of use of fire, etc. From this evidence we can make reasonable inferences about diet, posture and locomotion, and changes in the brain as shown by increased cranial capacity, ability to make tools, and other evidences of cultural creation. Since we assume that complexity of material culture requires language, we infer the beginnings of language somewhere between Australopithecus and Homo erectus.

Given this data, the speculative reconstruction begins. As I was taught anthropology, the story goes something like this. Obscure selection pressures pushed the protohominid in the direction of erect bipedalism — perhaps the advantages of freeing the hands for food carrying or for tool use. Freeing the hands allowed more manipulation of the environment in the direction of tools for gathering and hunting food. Through a hand-eye-brain feedback process, coordination, efficiency, and skill were increased. The new behavior was adaptive, and selection pressure pushed the protohominid further along the same lines of development. Diet changed as the increase in skill allowed the addition of more animal protein. Larger brains were selected for, making possible transmission of information concerning tool making, and organizing cooperative hunting. It is assumed that as increased brain size was selected for, so also was neoteny — immaturity of infants at birth with a corresponding increase in their period of dependency, allowing more time for learning at the same time as this learning became necessary through the further reduction of instinctual behaviors and their replacement by symbolically invented ones.

Here is where one may discover a large logical gap. From the difficult-to-explain beginning trends toward neoteny and increased brain size, the story jumps to Man the Hunter. The statement is made that the females were more burdened with dependent infants and could not follow the rigorous hunt. Therefore they stayed at a "home base," gathering what food they could, while the males developed cooperative hunting techniques, increased their communicative and organizational skills through hunting, and brought the meat back to the dependent females and young. Incest prohibitions, marriage, and the family (so the story goes) grew out of the need to eliminate competition between males for females. A pattern developed of a male hunter becoming the main support of "his" dependent females and young (in other words, the development of the nuclear family for no apparent reason). Thus the peculiarly human social and emotional bonds can be traced to the hunter bringing back the food to share. Hunting, according to Washburn and Lancaster, in-

volved "cooperation among males, planning, knowledge of many species and large areas, and technical skill" (1968:296). They even profess to discover the beginnings of art in the weapons of the hunter. They point out that the symmetrical Acheulian biface tools are the earliest beautiful man-made objects. Though we don't know what these tools were used for, they argue somewhat tautologically that the symmetry indicates they may have been swung, because symmetry only makes a difference when irregularities might lead to deviations in the line of flight. "It may well be that it was the attempt to produce efficient high-speed weapons that first produced beautiful, symmetrical objects" (1968: 298).

So, while the males were out hunting, developing all their skills, learning to cooperate, inventing language, inventing art, creating tools and weapons, the poor dependent females were sitting back at the home base having one child after another (many of them dying in the process), and waiting for the males to bring home the bacon. While this reconstruction is certainly ingenious, it gives one the decided impression that only half the species — the male half — did any evolving. In addition to containing a number of logical gaps, the argument becomes somewhat doubtful in the light of modern knowledge of genetics and primate behavior.

The skills usually spoken of as being necessary to, or developed through, hunting are things like coordination, endurance, good vision, and the ability to plan, communicate, and cooperate. I have heard of no evidence to indicate that these skills are either carried on the Y chromosome, or are triggered into existence by the influence of the Y chromosome. In fact, on just about any test we can design (psychological, aptitude, intelligence, etc.) males and females score just about the same. The variation is on an individual, not a sex, basis.

Every human individual gets half its genes from a male and half from a female; genes sort randomly. It is possible for a female to end up with all her genes from male ancestors, and for a male to end up with all his genes from female ancestors. The logic of the hunting argument would have us believe that all the selection pressure was on the males, leaving the females simply as drags on the species. The rapid increase in brain size and complexity was thus due entirely to half the species; the main function of the female half was to suffer and die in the attempt to give birth to their large-brained male infants. An unbiased reading of the evidence indicates there was selection pressure on both sexes, and that hunting was not in fact the basic adaptation of the species from which flowed all the traits we think of as specifically human. Hunting does not deserve the primary place it has been given in the reconstruction of human evolution, as I will demonstrate by offering the following alternate version.

Picture the primate band: each individual gathers its own food, and the major enduring relationship is the mother-infant bond. It is in similar circumstances that we imagine the evolving protohominids. We don't know what started them in the direction of neoteny and increased brain size, but once begun the trends would prove adaptive. To explain the shift from the primate individual gathering to human food sharing, we cannot simply jump to hunting. Hunting cannot explain its own origin. It is much more logical to assume that as the period of infant dependency began to lengthen, *the mothers would begin to increase the scope of their gathering to provide food for their still-dependent infants.* The already strong primate mother-infant bond would begin to extend over a longer time period, increasing the depth and scope of social relationships, and giving rise to the first sharing of food.

It is an example of male bias to picture these females with young as totally or even mainly dependent on males for food. Among modern hunter-gatherers, even in the marginal environments where most live, the females can usually gather enough to support themselves and their families. In these groups gathering provides the major portion of the diet, and there is no reason to assume that this was not also the case in the Pliocene or early Pleistocene. In the modern groups women and children both gather and hunt small animals, though they usually do not go on the longer hunts. So, we can assume a group of evolving protohominids, gathering and perhaps beginning to hunt small animals, with the mothers gathering quite efficiently both for themselves and for their offspring.

It is equally biased, and quite unreasonable, to assume an early or rapid development of a pattern in which one male was responsible for "his" female(s) and young. In most primate groups when a female comes into estrus she initiates coitus or signals her readiness by presenting. The idea that a male would have much voice in "choosing" a female, or maintain any sort of individual, long-term control over her or her offspring, is surely a modern invention which could have had no place in early hominid life. (Sexual control over females through rape or the threat of rape seems to be a modern human invention. Primate females are not raped because they are willing throughout estrus, and primate males appear not to attempt coitus at other times, regardless of physiological ability.) In fact, there seems to me no reason for suggesting the development of male-female adult pair-bonding until much later. Long-term monogamy is a fairly rare pattern even among modern humans — I think it is a peculiarly Western male bias to suppose its existence in proto-human society. An argument has been made (by Morris, 1967, and others) that traces the development of male-female pair-bonding to the shift of sexual characteristics to the front of the body, the importance of the face in communication, and the development of face-to-face coitus. This argument is insufficient in the first place because of the assumption that face-to-face coitus is the "normal," "natural," or even the most common position among humans (historical evidence casts grave doubt on this assumption). It is much more probable that the coitus position was invented *after* pair-bonding had developed for other reasons.

Rather than adult male-female sexual pairs, a temporary consort-type relationship is much more logical in hominid evolution. It is even a more accurate description of the modern human pattern: the most dominant males (chief, headman, brave warrior, good hunter, etc.), mate with the most dominant females (in estrus, young and beautiful, fertile, rich, etc.), for varying periods of time. Changing sexual partners is frequent and common. We have no way of knowing when females began to be fertile year-round, but this change is not a necessary condition for the development of families. We need not bring in any notion of paternity, or the development of male-female pairs, or any sort of marriage in order to account for either families or food sharing.

The lengthening period of infant dependency would have strengthened and deepened the mother-infant bond; the earliest families would have consisted of *females and their children*. In such groups, over time, the sibling bond would have increased in importance also. The most universal, and presumably oldest, form of incest prohibition is between mother and son. There are indications of such avoidance even among modern monkeys. It could develop logically

from the mother-children family: as the period of infant dependency lengthened, and the age of sexual maturity advanced, a mother might no longer be capable of childbearing when her son reached maturity. Another factor which may have operated is the situation found in many primates today where only the most dominant males have access to fertile females. Thus a young son, even after reaching sexual maturity, would still have to spend time working his way up the male hierarchy before gaining access to females. The length of time it would take him increases the possibility that his mother would no longer be fertile.

Food sharing and the family developed from the mother-infant bond. The techniques of hunting large animals were probably much later developments, after the mother-children family pattern was established. When hunting did begin, and the adult males brought back food to share, the most likely recipients would be first their mothers, and second their siblings. In other words, a hunter would share food *not* with a wife or sexual partner, but with those who had shared food with him: his mother and siblings.

It is frequently suggested or implied that the first tools were, in fact, the weapons of the hunters. Modern humans have become so accustomed to the thought of tools and weapons that it is easy for us to imagine the first manlike creature who picked up a stone or club. However, since we don't really know what the early stone tools such as hand-axes were used for, it is equally probable that they were not weapons at all, but rather *aids in gathering*. We know that gathering was important long before much animal protein was added to the diet, and continued to be important. Bones, sticks, and hand-axes could be used for digging up tubers or roots, or to pulverize tough vegetable matter for easier eating. If, however, instead of thinking in terms of tools and weapons, we think in terms of *cultural inventions,* a new aspect is presented. I suggest that two of the *earliest and most important* cultural inventions were containers to hold the products of gathering, and some sort of sling or net to carry babies. The latter in particular must have been extremely important with the loss of body hair and the increasing immaturity of neonates, who could not cling and had less and less to cling to. Plenty of material was available — vines, hides, human hair. If the infant could be securely fastened to the mother's body, she could go about her tasks much more efficiently. Once a technique for carrying babies was developed, it could be extended to the idea of carrying food, and eventually to other sorts of cultural inventions — choppers and grinders for food preparation, and even weapons. Among modern hunter-gatherers, regardless of the poverty of their material culture, food carriers and baby carriers are always important items in their equipment.

A major point in the Man the Hunter argument is that cooperative hunting among males demanded more skill in social organization and communication, and thus provided selection pressure for increased brain size. I suggest that longer periods of infant dependency, more difficult births, and longer gestation periods also demanded more skills in social organization and communication — creating selective pressure for increased brain size without looking to hunting as an explanation. The need to organize for feeding after weaning, learning to handle the more complex social-emotional bonds that were developing, the new skills and cultural inventions surrounding more extensive gathering — all would demand larger brains. Too much attention has been given to the skills required by hunting, and too little to the skills required for gathering and the raising of dependent young. The techniques required for efficient gathering include location and identification of plant varieties, seasonal and geographical knowledge, containers for carrying the food, and tools for its preparation. Among modern hunting-gathering groups this knowledge is an extremely complex, well-developed, and important part of their cultural equipment. Caring for a curious, energetic, but still dependent human infant is difficult and demanding. Not only must the infant be watched, it must be taught the customs, dangers, and knowledge of its group. For the early hominids, as their cultural equipment and symbolic communication increased, the job of training the young would demand more skill. Selection pressure for better brains came from many directions.

Much has been made of the argument that cooperation among males demanded by hunting acted as a force to reduce competition for females. I suggest that competition for females has been greatly exaggerated. It could easily have been handled in the usual way for primates — according to male status relationships already worked out — and need not be pictured as particularly violent or extreme. The seeds of male cooperation already exist in primates when they act to protect the band from predators. Such dangers may well have increased with a shift to savannah living, and the longer dependency of infants. If biological roots are sought to explain the greater aggressiveness of males, it would be more fruitful to look toward their function as protectors, rather than any supposedly basic hunting adaptation. The only division of labor that regularly exists in primate groups is the females caring for infants and the males protecting the group from predators. The possibilities for both cooperation and aggression in males lies in this protective function.

The emphasis on hunting as a prime moving factor in hominid evolution distorts the data. It is simply too big a jump to go from the primate individual gathering pattern to a hominid cooperative hunting-sharing pattern without some intervening changes. Cooperative hunting of big game animals could only have developed *after* the trends toward neoteny and increased brain size had begun. Big-game hunting becomes a more logical development when it is viewed as growing out of a complex of changes which included sharing the products of gathering among mothers and children, deepening social bonds over time, increase in brain size, and the beginnings of cultural invention for purposes such as baby carrying, food carrying, and food preparation. Such hunting not only needed the prior development of some skills in social organization and communication; it probably also had to await the development of the "home base." It is difficult to imagine that most or all of the adult primate males in a group would go off on a hunting expedition, leaving the females and young exposed to the danger of predators, without some way of communicating to arrange for their defense, or at least a way of saying, "Don't worry, we'll be back in two days." Until that degree of communicative skill developed, we must assume either that the whole band traveled *and hunted* together, or that the males simply did not go off on large cooperative hunts.

The development of cooperative hunting requires, as a prior condition, an increase in brain size. Once such a trend is established, hunting skills would take part in a feedback process of selection for better brains just as would other cultural inventions and developments such as gathering skills. By itself, hunting fails to explain any part of human evolution and fails to explain itself.

Anthropology has always rested on the assumption that the mark of our species is our ability to *symbol*, to bring into existence forms of behavior and interaction, and material tools with which to adjust and control the environment. To explain human nature as evolving from the desire of males to hunt and kill is to negate most of anthropology. Our species survived and adapted through the invention of *culture*, of which hunting is simply a part. It is often stated that hunting *must* be viewed as the "natural" species' adaptation because it lasted as long as it did, nine-tenths of all human history. However:

> Man the Hunter lasted as long as "he" did from no natural propensity toward hunting any more than toward computer programming or violin playing or nuclear warfare, but because that was what the historical circumstances allowed. We ignore the first premise of our science if we fail to admit that "man" is no more natural a hunter than "he" is naturally a golfer, for after symboling became possible our species left forever the ecological niche of the necessity of any one adaptation, and made all adaptations possible for ourselves. (Kephart, 1970:23)

That the concept of Man the Hunter influenced anthropology for as long as it did is a reflection of male bias in the discipline. This bias can be seen in the tendency to equate "man," "human," and "male"; to look at culture almost entirely from a male point of view; to search for examples of the behavior of males and assume that this is sufficient for explanation, ignoring almost totally the female half of the species; and to filter this male bias through the "ideal" modern Western pattern of one male supporting a dependent wife and minor children.

The basis of any discipline is not the answers it gets, but the questions it asks. As an exercise in the anthropology of knowledge, this paper stems from asking a simple question: what were the females doing while the males were out hunting? It was only possible for me to ask this question after I had become politically conscious of myself as a woman. Such is the prestige of males in our society that a woman, in anthropology or any other profession, can only gain respect or be attended to if she deals with questions deemed important by men. Though there have been women anthropologists for years, it is rare to be able to discern any difference between their work and that of male anthropologists. Learning to be an anthropologist has involved learning to think from a male perspective, so it should not be surprising that women have asked the same kinds of questions as men. But political consciousness, whether among women, blacks, American Indians, or any other group, leads to reexamination and reevaluation of taken-for-granted assumptions. It is a difficult process, challenging the conventional wisdom, and this paper is simply a beginning. The male bias in anthropology that I have illustrated here is just as real as the white bias, the middle-class bias, and the academic bias that exist in the discipline. It is our task, as anthropologists, to create a "study of the human species" in spite of, or perhaps because of, or maybe even by means of, our individual biases and unique perspectives.

THE ORIGIN OF THE FAMILY

FRIEDRICH ENGELS

Friedrich Engels was born in Bermen, Germany, in 1820 and died in England in 1895. Together with Karl Marx he developed much of the social and economic theory that is known today as Marxist communism. Among works that he wrote or co-authored are *The Condition of the Working Class in England* (1844), *The German Ideology* (1845), and *The Communist Manifesto* (1848).

The essay excerpted here, *The Origin of the Family, Private Property, and the State,* written in 1884, is an integration of the theoretical concepts of Marxism, particularly the materialistic conception of history, and the work of the anthropologist Lewis Morgan in *Ancient Society* (1877). Essentially, Engels traces the development of society from a time of primitive egalitarianism, when there were no classes and no families as we know them, to a time when private property, its acquisition and maintenance, makes rigid family structures a possibility and a necessity.

In pretechnological times, Engels believed, men and women lived together in large integrated communities (called tribes or clans), all working together for subsistence and survival. Women were charged with the care of the household and were well respected and politically equal to the men, who provided food and engaged in the "productive" work. However, as technology developed and it became possible to produce more than could be immediately used by the group, surplus emerged and with it private property, productive goods controlled by individual men. The accumulation of goods that could be publicly exchanged for others yielded power; and since women's work could not be amassed, and women served only their now-segregated families, women became wards of men, losing their status and power in an exchange economy and becoming wholly subordinated. As the importance of private property developed, the matter of inheritance altered the significance of children, and women's reproductive labor was appropriated by men as their productive labor had been. Hence (as many feminists today also theorize) the imperatives of virginity, chastity, and monogamy developed for women as the patterns of inheritance persuaded men to insure their paternity. Ultimately, it is argued, with the passing of private property and class, monogamy will disappear, marriage and sex will be based on love and choice, and women's original freedom and value will be restored.

Reconstructing thus the past history of the family, Morgan, in agreement with most of his colleagues, arrives at a primitive stage when unrestricted sexual freedom prevailed within the tribe, every woman belonging equally to every man and every man to every woman. Since the 18th century there had been talk of such a primitive state, but only in general phrases. Bachofen — and this is one of his great merits — was the first to take the existence of such a state seriously and to search for its traces in historical and religious survivals. Today we know that the traces he found do not lead back to a social stage of promiscuous sexual intercourse, but to a much later form — namely, group marriage. The primitive social stage of promiscuity, if it ever existed, belongs to such a remote epoch that we can hardly expect to prove its existence *directly* by discovering its social fossils among backward savages. Bachofen's merit consists in having brought this question to the forefront for examination.*. . .

According to Morgan, from this primitive state of promiscuous intercourse there developed, probably very early:

1. The Consanguine Family, the First Stage of the Family

Here the marriage groups are separated according to generations: all the grandfathers and grandmothers within the limits of the family are all husbands and wives of one another; so are also their children, the fathers and mothers; the latter's children will form a third circle of common husbands and wives; and their children, the great-grand-children of the first group, will form a fourth. In this form of marriage, therefore, only ancestors and progeny, and parents and children, are excluded from the rights and duties (as we should say) of marriage with one another. . . .

2. The Punaluan Family

If the first advance in organization consisted in the exclusion of parents and children from sexual intercourse with one another, the second was the exclusion of sister and brother. On account of the greater nearness in age, this second advance was infinitely more important, but also more difficult, than the first. It was effected gradually, beginning proba-

From Friedrich Engels, *The Origin of the Family, Private Property, and the State,* ed. Eleanor Burke Leacock (New York: International Publishers, 1972). Reprinted by permission of International Publishers Co., Inc. Copyright © 1972.

* Bachofen proves how little he understood his own discovery, or rather his guess, by using the term ''hetaerism'' to describe this primitive state. For the Greeks, when they introduced the word, hetaerism meant intercourse of men, unmarried or living in monogamy, with unmarried women; it always presupposes a definite form of marriage outside which this intercourse takes place and includes at least the possibility of prostitution. The word was never used in any other sense, and it is in this sense that I use it with Morgan.

bly with the exclusion from sexual intercourse of one's own brothers and sisters (children of the same mother) first in isolated cases and then by degrees as a general rule (even in this century exceptions were found in Hawaii), and ending with the prohibition of marriage even between collateral brothers and sisters, or, as we should say, between first, second, and third cousins. . . .

3. The Pairing Family

A certain amount of pairing, for a longer or shorter period, already occurred in group marriage or even earlier; the man had a chief wife among his wives (one can hardly yet speak of a favorite wife), and for her he was the most important among her husbands. This fact has contributed considerably to the confusion of the missionaries, who have regarded group marriage sometimes as promiscuous community of wives, sometimes as unbridled adultery. But these customary pairings were bound to grow more stable as the gens developed and the classes of "brothers" and "sisters" between whom marriage was impossible became more numerous. The impulse given by the gens to the prevention of marriage between blood relatives extended still further. Thus among the Iroquois and most of the other Indians at the lower stage of barbarism, we find that marriage is prohibited between *all* relatives enumerated in their system — which includes several hundred degrees of kinship. The increasing complication of these prohibitions made group marriages more and more impossible; they were displaced by the *pairing family*. In this stage, one man lives with one woman, but the relationship is such that polygamy and occasional infidelity re-

main the right of the men, even though for economic reasons polygamy is rare, while from the woman the strictest fidelity is generally demanded throughout the time she lives with the man and adultery on her part is cruelly punished. The marriage tie can, however, be easily dissolved by either partner; after separation, the children still belong as before to the mother alone.

In this ever extending exclusion of blood relatives from the bond of marriage, natural selection continues its work. In Morgan's words:

> The influence of the new practice, which brought unrelated persons into the marriage relation, tended to create a more vigorous stock physically and mentally. . . . When two advancing tribes, with strong mental and physical characters, are brought together and blended into one people by the accidents of barbarous life, the new skull and brain would widen and lengthen to the sum of the capabilities of both [1963:468].

Tribes with gentile constitution were thus bound to gain supremacy over more backward tribes, or else to carry them along by their example.

Thus the history of the family in primitive times consists in the progressive narrowing of the circle, originally embracing the whole tribe, within which the two sexes have a common conjugal relation. The continuous exclusion, first of nearer, then of more and more remote relatives, and at last even of relatives by marriage, ends by making any kind of group marriage practically impossible. Finally, their remains only the single, still loosely linked pair, the molecule with whose dissolution marriage itself ceases. This in itself shows what a small part individual sex love, in the modern sense of the word, played in the rise of monogamy. Yet stronger proof is afforded by the practice of all peoples at this stage of development. Whereas in the earlier forms of the family, men never lacked women but, on the contrary, had too many rather than too few, women had now become scarce and highly sought after. Hence it is with the pairing marriage that there begins the capture and purchase of women — widespread *symptoms,* but no more than symptoms, of the much deeper change that had occurred. These symptoms, mere methods of procuring wives, the pedantic Scot McLennan has transmogrified into special classes of families under the names of "marriage by capture" and "marriage by purchase." In general, whether among the American Indians or other peoples (at the same stage), the conclusion of a marriage is the affair not of the two parties concerned, who are often not consulted at all, but of their mothers. Two persons entirely unknown to each other are often thus affianced; they learn that the bargain has been struck when the time for marrying approaches. Before the wedding the bridegroom gives presents to the bride's gentile relatives (to those on the mother's side, therefore, not to the father and his relations) which are regarded as gift payments in return for the girl. The marriage is still terminable at the desire of either partner, but among many tribes, the Iroquois for example, public opinion has gradually developed against such separations. When differences arise between husband and wife, the gens relatives of both partners act as mediators, and only if these efforts prove fruitless does a separation take place, the wife then keeping the children and each partner being free to marry again.

The pairing family, itself too weak and unstable to make an independent household necessary or even desirable, in no wise destroys the communistic household inherited from earlier times. Communistic housekeeping, however, means the supremacy of women in the house; just as the exclusive recognition of the female parent, owing to the impossibility of recognizing the male parent with certainty, means that the women — the mothers — are held in high respect. One of the most absurd notions taken over from 18th century enlightenment is that in the beginning of society woman was the slave of man. Among all savages and all barbarians of the lower and middle stages, and to a certain extent of the upper stage also, the position of women is not only free, but honorable. As to what it still is in the pairing marriage, let us hear the evidence of Ashur Wright, for many years missionary among the Iroquois Senecas:

As to their family system, when occupying the old long houses [communistic households comprising several families], it is probable that some one clan [gens] predominated, the women taking in husbands, however, from the other clans [gentes]. . . . Usually, the female portion ruled the house. . . . The stores were in common; but woe to the luckless husband or lover who was too shiftless to do his share of the providing. No matter how many children, or whatever goods he might have in the house, he might at any time be ordered to pick up his blanket and budge; and after such orders it would not be healthful for him to attempt to disobey. The house would be too hot for him; and . . . he must retreat to his own clan [gens]; or, as was often done, go and start a new matrimonial alliance in some other. The women were the great power among the clans [gentes], as everywhere else. They did not hesitate, when occasion required, "to knock off the horns," as it was technically called, from the head of a chief, and send him back to the ranks of the warriors [Morgan, 1963: 464 *fn*].

The communistic household, in which most or all of the women belong to one and the same gens, while the men come from various gentes, is the material foundation of that supremacy of the women which was general in primitive times, and which it is Bachofen's third great merit to have discovered. The reports of travelers and missionaries, I may add, to the effect that women among savages and barbarians are overburdened with work in no way contradict what has been said. The division of labor between the two sexes is determined by quite other causes than by the position of woman in society. Among peoples where the women have to work far harder than we think suitable, there is often much more real respect for women than among our Europeans. The lady of civilization, surrounded by false homage and estranged from all real work, has an infinitely lower social position than the hard-working woman of barbarism, who was regarded among her people as a real lady (lady, *frowa, Frau* — mistress) and who was also a lady in character. . . .

Bachofen is also perfectly right when he consistently maintains that the transition from what he calls "hetaerism" or *"Sumpfzeugung"* to monogamy was brought about primarily through the women. The more the traditional sexual relations lost the naive primitive character of forest life, owing to the development of economic conditions with consequent undermining of the old communism and growing density of population, the more oppressive and humiliating must the women have felt them to be, and the greater their longing for the right of chastity, of temporary or permanent marriage with one man only, as a way of release. This advance could not in any case have originated with the men if only because it has never occurred to them, even to this day, to renounce the pleasures of actual group marriage. Only when the women had brought about the transition to pairing marriage were the men able to introduce strict monogamy — though indeed only for women. . . .

Once it had passed into the private possession of families and there rapidly begun to augment, this wealth dealt a severe blow to the society founded on pairing marriage and the matriarchal gens. Pairing marriage had brought a new element into the family. By the side of the natural mother of the child it placed its natural and attested father with a better warrant of paternity, probably, than that of many a "father" today. According to the division of labor within the family at that time, it was the man's part to obtain food and the instruments of labor necessary for the purpose. He therefore also owned the instruments of labor, and in the event of husband and wife separating, he took them with him, just as she retained her household goods. Therefore, according to the social custom of the time, the man was also the owner of the new source of subsistence, the cattle, and later of the new instruments of labor, the slaves. But according to the custom of the same society, his children could not inherit from him. For as regards inheritance, the position was as follows:

At first, according to mother right — so long, therefore, as descent was reckoned only in the female line — and according to the original custom of inheritance within the gens, the gentile relatives inherited from a deceased fellow member of their gens. His property had to remain within the gens. His effects being insignificant, they probably always passed in practice to his nearest gentile relations — that is, to his blood relations on the mother's side. The children of the dead man, however, did not belong to his gens, but to that of their mother; it was from her that they inherited, at first conjointly with her other blood-relations, later perhaps with rights of priority; they could not inherit from their father because they did not belong to his gens within which his property had to remain. When the owner of the herds died, therefore, his herds would go first to his brothers and sisters and to his sister's children, or to the issue of his mother's sisters. But his own children were disinherited.

Thus on the one hand, in proportion as wealth increased it made the man's position in the family more important than the woman's, and on the other hand created an impulse to exploit this strengthened position in order to overthrow, in favor of his children, the traditional order of inheritance. This, however, was impossible so long as descent was reckoned according to mother right. Mother right, therefore, had to be overthrown, and overthrown it was. This was by no means so difficult as it looks to us today. For this revolution — one of the most decisive ever experienced by humanity — could take place without disturbing a single one of the living members of a gens. All could remain as they were. A simple decree sufficed that in the future the offspring of the male members should remain within the gens, but that of the female should be excluded by being transferred to the gens of their father. The reckoning of descent in the female line and the matriarchal law of inheritance were thereby overthrown, and the male line of descent and the paternal law of inheritance were substituted for them. As to how and when this revolution took place among civilized peoples, we have no knowledge. It falls entirely within prehistoric times. But that it *did* take place is more than sufficiently proved by the abundant traces of mother right which have been collected, particularly by Bachofen. . . .

The overthrow of mother right was the *world historical defeat of the female sex.*

The man took command in the home also; the woman was degraded and reduced to servitude; she became the slave of his lust and a mere instrument for the production of children. This degraded position of the woman, especially conspicuous among the Greeks of the heroic and still more of the classical age, has gradually been palliated and glossed over, and sometimes clothed in a milder form; in no sense has it been abolished.

The establishment of the exclusive supremacy of the man shows its effects first in the patriarchal family, which now emerges as an intermediate form. Its essential characteristic is not polygyny, of which more later, but "the organization of a number of persons, bond and free, into a family under paternal power for the purpose of holding lands and for the care of flocks and herds. . . . (In the Semitic form) the chiefs, at least, lived in polygamy. . . . Those held to servitude and those employed as servants lived in the marriage relation" [Morgan, 1963: 474].

Its essential features are the incorporation of unfree persons and paternal power; hence the perfect type of this form of family is the Roman. The original meaning of the word "family" (*familia*) is not that compound of sentimentality and domestic strife which forms the ideal of the present-day philistine; among the Romans it did not at first even refer to the married pair and their children but only to the slaves. *Famulus* means domestic slave, and *familia* is the total number of slaves belonging to one man. As late as the time of Gaius, the *familia, id est patrimonium* (family, that is, the patrimony, the inheritance) was bequeathed by will. The term was invented by the Romans to denote a new social organism whose head ruled over wife and children and a number of slaves, and was invested under Roman paternal power with rights of life and death over them all.

> This term, therefore, is no older than the iron-clad family system of the Latin tribes, which came in after field agriculture and after legalized servitude, as well as after the separation of the Greeks and Latins [Morgan, 1963: 478].

Marx adds:

> The modern family contains in germ not only slavery (*servitus*) but also serfdom, since from the beginning it is related to agricultural services. It contains *in miniature* all the contradictions which later extend throughout society and its state.

Such a form of family shows the transition of the pairing family to monogamy. In order to make certain of the wife's fidelity and therefore of the paternity of the children, she is delivered over unconditionally into the power of the husband; if he kills her, he is only exercising his rights.

With the patriarchal family, we enter the field of written history. . . .

4. The Monogamous Family

It develops out of the pairing family, as previously shown, in the transitional period between the upper and middle stages of barbarism; its decisive victory is one of the signs that civilization is beginning. It is based on the supremacy of the man, the express purpose being to produce children of undisputed paternity; such paternity is demanded because these children are later to come into their father's property as his natural heirs. It is distinguished from pairing marriage by the much greater strength of the marriage tie, which can no longer be dissolved at either partner's wish. As a rule, it is now only the man who can dissolve it and

put away his wife. The right of conjugal infidelity also remains secured to him, at any rate by custom (the *Code Napoléon* explicitly accords it to the husband as long as he does not bring his concubine into the house), and as social life develops he exercises his right more and more; should the wife recall the old form of sexual life and attempt to revive it, she is punished more severely than ever. . . .

Sex love in the relationship with a woman becomes and can only become the real rule among the oppressed classes, which means today among the proletariat — whether this relation is officially sanctioned or not. But here all the foundations of typical monogamy are cleared away. Here there is no property, for the preservation and inheritance of which monogamy and male supremacy were established; hence there is no incentive to make this male supremacy effective. What is more, there are no means of making it so. Bourgeois law, which protects this supremacy, exists only for the possessing class and their dealings with the proletarians. The law costs money and, on account of the worker's poverty, it has no validity for his relation to his wife. Here quite other personal and social conditions decide. And now that large-scale industry has taken the wife out of the home onto the labor market and into the factory, and made her often the breadwinner of the family, no basis for any kind of male supremacy is left in the proletarian household, except, perhaps, for something of the brutality toward women that has spread since the introduction of monogamy. The proletarian family is therefore no longer monogamous in the strict sense, even where there is passionate love and firmest loyalty on both sides and maybe all the blessings of religious and civil authority. Here, therefore, the eternal attendants of monogamy, hetaerism and adultery, play only an almost vanishing part. The wife has in fact regained the right to dissolve the marriage, and if two people cannot get on with one another, they prefer to separate. In short, proletarian marriage is monogamous in the etymological sense of the word, but not at all in its historical sense. . . .

As regards the legal equality of husband and wife in marriage, the position is no better. The legal inequality of the two partners bequeathed to us from earlier social conditions is not the cause but the effect of the economic oppression of the woman. In the old communistic household, which comprised many couples and their children, the task entrusted to the women of managing the household was as much a public, a socially necessary industry as the procuring of food by the men. With the patriarchal family and still more with the single monogamous family, a change came. Household management lost its public character. It no longer concerned society. It became a *private service;* the wife became the head servant, excluded from all participation in social production. Not until the coming of modern large-scale industry was the road to social production opened to her again — and then only to the proletarian wife. But it was opened in such a manner that, if she carries out her duties in the private service of her family, she remains excluded from public production and unable to earn; and if she wants to take part in public production and earn independently, she cannot carry out family duties. And the wife's position in the factory is the position of women in all branches of business, right up to medicine and the law. The modern individual family is founded on the open or concealed domestic slavery of the wife, and modern society is a mass composed of these individual families as its molecules.

In the great majority of cases today, at least in the possessing classes, the husband is obliged to earn a living and support his family, and that in itself gives him a position of supremacy without any need for special legal titles and privileges. Within the family he is the bourgeois, and the wife represents the proletariat. In the industrial world, the specific character of the economic oppression burdening the proletariat is visible in all its sharpness only when all special legal privileges of the capitalist class have been abolished and complete legal equality of both classes established. The democratic republic does not do away with the opposition of the two classes; on the contrary, it provides the clear field on which the fight can be fought out. And in the same way, the peculiar character of the supremacy of the husband over the wife in the modern family, the necessity of creating real social equality between them and the way to do it, will only be seen in the clear light of day when both possess legally complete equality of rights. Then it will be plain that the first condition for the liberation of the wife is to bring the whole female sex back into public industry, and that this in turn demands that the characteristic of the monogamous family as the economic unit of society be abolished.

We thus have three principal forms of marriage which correspond broadly to the three principal stages of human development: for the period of savagery, group marriage; for barbarism, pairing marriage; for civilization, monogamy supplemented by adultery and prostitution. Between pairing marriage and monogamy intervenes a period in the upper stage of barbarism when men have female slaves at their command and polygamy is practiced.

As our whole presentation has shown, the progress which manifests itself in these successive forms is connected with the peculiarity that women, but not men, are increasingly deprived of the sexual freedom of group marriage. In fact, for men group marriage actually still exists even to this day. What for the woman is a crime entailing grave legal and social consequences is considered honorable in a man or, at the worse, a slight moral blemish which he cheerfully bears. But the more the hetaerism of the past is changed in our time by capitalist commodity production and brought into conformity with it, the more, that is to say, it is transformed into undisguised prostitution, the more demoralizing are its effects. And it demoralizes men far more than women. Among women, prostitution degrades only the unfortunate ones who become its victims, and even these by no means to the extent commonly believed. But it degrades the character of the whole male world. A long engagement particularly is in nine cases out of ten a regular preparatory school for conjugal infidelity.

We are now approaching a social revolution in which the economic foundations of monogamy as they have existed hitherto will disappear just as surely as those of its complement — prostitution. Monogamy arose from the concentration of considerable wealth in the hands of a single individual — a man — and from the need to bequeath this wealth to the children of that man and of no other. For this purpose, the monogamy of the woman was required, not that of the man, so this monogamy of the woman did not in any way interfere with open or concealed polygamy on the part of the man. But by transforming by far the greater portion, at any rate, of permanent, heritable wealth — the means of production — into social property, the coming social revolution will reduce to a minimum all this anxiety about bequeathing and inheriting. Having arisen from economic causes, will monogamy then disappear when these causes disappear?

One might answer, not without reason: far from disappearing, it will on the contrary begin to be realized completely. For with the transformation of the means of production into social property there will disappear also wage labor, the proletariat, and therefore the necessity for a certain — statistically calculable — number of women to surrender themselves for money. Prostitution disappears; monogamy, instead of collapsing, at last becomes a reality — also for men.

In any case, therefore, the position of men will be very much altered. But the position of women, of *all* women, also undergoes significant change. With the transfer of the means of production into common ownership, the single family ceases to be the economic unit of society. Private housekeeping is transformed into a social industry. The care and education of the children becomes a public affair; society looks after all children alike, whether they are legitimate or not. This removes all the anxiety about the "consequences," which today is the most essential social — moral as well as economic — factor that prevents a girl from giving herself completely to the man she loves. Will not that suffice to bring about the gradual growth of unconstrained sexual intercourse and with it a more tolerant public opinion in regard to a maiden's honor and a woman's shame? And finally, have we not seen that in the modern world monogamy and prostitution are indeed contradictions, but inseparable contradictions, poles of the same state of society? Can prostitution disappear without dragging monogamy with it into the abyss? . . .

Full freedom of marriage can therefore only be generally established when the abolition of capitalist production and of the property relations created by it has removed all the accompanying economic considerations which still exert such a powerful influence on the choice of a marriage partner. For then there is no other motive left except mutual inclination.

And as sexual love is by its nature exclusive — although at present this exclusiveness is fully realized only in the woman — the marriage based on sexual love is by its nature individual marriage. We have seen how right Bachofen was in regarding the advance from group marriage to individual marriage as primarily due to the women. Only the step from pairing marriage to monogamy can be put down to the credit of the men, and historically the essence of this was to make the position of the women worse and the infidelities of the men easier. If now the economic considerations also disappear which made women put up with the habitual infidelity of their husbands — concern for their own means of existence and still more for their children's future — then, according to all previous experience, the equality of woman thereby achieved will tend infinitely more to make men really monogamous than to make women polyandrous.

But what will quite certainly disappear from monogamy are all the features stamped upon it through its origin in property relations; these are, in the first place, supremacy of the man and secondly, the indissolubility of marriage. The supremacy of the man in marriage is the simple consequence of his economic supremacy, and with the abolition of the latter will disappear of itself. The indissolubility of marriage is partly a consequence of the economic situation in which monogamy arose, partly tradition from the period when the connection between this economic situation and monogamy was not yet fully understood and was carried to ex-

tremes under a religious form. Today it is already broken through at a thousand points. If only the marriage based on love is moral, then also only the marriage is moral in which love continues. But the intense emotion of individual sex love varies very much in duration from one individual to another, especially among men, and if affection definitely comes to an end or is supplanted by a new passionate love, separation is a benefit for both partners as well as for society — only people will then be spared having to wade through the useless mire of a divorce case.

What we can now conjecture about the way in which sexual relations will be ordered after the impending overthrow of capitalist production is mainly of a negative character, limited for the most part to what will disappear. But what will there be new? That will be answered when a new generation has grown up: a generation of men who never in their lives have known what it is to buy a woman's surrender with money or any other social instrument of power; a generation of women who have never known what it is to give themselves to a man from any other considerations than real love or to refuse to give themselves to their lover from fear of the economic consequences. When these people are in the world, they will care precious little what anybody today thinks they ought to do; they will make their own practice and their corresponding public opinion about the practice of each individual — and that will be the end of it.

THE MASS PSYCHOLOGY OF RAPE

SUSAN BROWNMILLER

Susan Brownmiller was born in Brooklyn, New York, in 1935; was educated at Cornell University; served as a reporter for NBC-TV and as a newswriter for ABC-TV; has worked as a free-lance writer; and is the author of *Shirley Chisholm* (1970) and the controversial and well-known *Against Our Will* (1975). Her treatment of the concept of rape is historical, anthropological, and political. Her thesis here is psychological and mythical (in the positive sense) as well as sociological. Forcible rape, in its violence and cruelty, is a conscious act of intimidation. Women's fear and vulnerability force them to seek protection. Perhaps man's domination of women has its source in his exclusive ability to fend off other attackers.

1. The Mass Psychology of Rape: An Introduction

... Man's structural capacity to rape and woman's corresponding structural vulnerability are as basic to the physiology of both our sexes as the primal act of sex itself. Had it not been for this accident of biology, an accommodation requiring the locking together of two separate parts, penis and vagina, there would be neither copulation nor rape as we know it. Anatomically one might want to improve on the design of nature, but such speculation appears to my mind as unrealistic. The human sex act accomplishes its historic purpose of generation of the species and it also affords some intimacy and pleasure. I have no basic quarrel with the procedure. But, nevertheless, we cannot work around the fact that in terms of human anatomy the possibility of forcible intercourse incontrovertibly exists. This single factor may have been sufficient to have caused the creation of a male ideology of rape. When men discovered that they could

rape, they proceeded to do it. Later, much later, under certain circumstances they even came to consider rape a crime.

In the violent landscape inhabited by primitive woman and man, some woman somewhere had a prescient vision of her right to her own physical integrity, and in my mind's eye I can picture her fighting like hell to preserve it. After a thunderbolt of recognition that this particular incarnation of hairy, two-legged hominid was not the Homo sapiens with whom she would like to freely join parts, it might have been she, and not some man, who picked up the first stone and hurled it. How surprised he must have been, and what an unexpected battle must have taken place. Fleet of foot and spirited, she would have kicked, bitten, pushed and run, *but she could not retaliate in kind.*

The dim perception that had entered prehistoric woman's consciousness must have had an equal but opposite reaction in the mind of her male assailant. For if the first rape was an unexpected battle founded on the first woman's refusal, the second rape was indubitably planned. Indeed, one of the earliest forms of male bonding must have been the gang rape of one woman by a band of marauding men. This accomplished, rape became not only a male prerogative, but man's basic weapon of force against woman, the principal agent of his will and her fear. His forcible entry into her body, despite her physical protestations and struggle, became the vehicle of his victorious conquest over her being, the ultimate test of his superior strength, the triumph of his manhood.

Man's discovery that his genitalia could serve as a weapon to generate fear must rank as one of the most important discoveries of prehistoric times, along with the use of fire and the first crude stone axe. From prehistoric times to the present, I believe, rape has played a critical function. It is nothing more or less than a conscious process of intimidation by which *all men* keep *all women* in a state of fear.

2. In the Beginning Was the Law

From the humblest beginnings of the social order based on a primitive system of retaliatory force — the *lex talionis:* an eye for an eye — woman was unequal before the law. By anatomical fiat — the inescapable construction of their genital organs — the human male was a natural predator and the human female served as his natural prey. Not only might the female be subjected at will to a thoroughly detestable physical conquest from which there could be no retaliation in kind — a rape for a rape — but the consequences of such a brutal struggle might be death or injury, not to mention impregnation and the birth of a dependent child.

One possibility, and one possibility alone, was available to woman. Those of her own sex whom she might call to her aid were more often than not smaller and weaker than her male attackers. More critical, they lacked the basic physical wherewithal for punitive vengeance; at best they could maintain only a limited defensive action. But among those creatures who were her predators, some

might serve as her chosen protectors. Perhaps it was thus that the risky bargain was struck. Female fear of an open season of rape, and not a natural inclination toward monogamy, motherhood or love, was probably the single causative factor in the original subjugation of woman by man, the most important key to her historic dependence, her domestication by protective mating.

Once the male took title to a specific female body, and surely for him this was a great sexual convenience as well as a testament to his warring stature, he had to assume the burden of fighting off all other potential attackers, or scare them off by the retaliatory threat of raping *their* women. But the price of woman's protection *by some men* against an abuse *by others* was steep. Disappointed and disillusioned by the inherent female incapacity to protect, she became estranged in a very real sense from other females, a problem that haunts the social organization of women to this very day. And those who did assume the historic burden of her protection — later formalized as husband, father, brother, clan — extracted more than a pound of flesh. They reduced her status to that of chattel. The historic price of woman's protection by man against man was the imposition of chastity and monogamy. A crime committed against her body became a crime against the male estate.

The earliest form of permanent, protective conjugal relationship, the accommodation called mating that we now know as marriage, appears to have been institutionalized by the male's forcible abduction and rape of the female. No quaint formality, bride capture, as it came to be known, was a very real struggle: a male took title to a female, staked a claim to her body, as it were, by an act of violence. Forcible seizure was a perfectly acceptable way — to men — of acquiring women, and it existed in England as late as the fifteenth century. Eleanor of Aquitaine, according to a biographer, lived her early life in terror of being "rapt" by a vassal who might through appropriation of her body gain title to her considerable property. Bride capture exists to this day in the rain forests of the Philippines, where the Tasadays were recently discovered to be plying their Stone Age civilization. Remnants of the philosophy of forcible abduction and marriage still influence the social mores of rural Sicily and parts of Africa. A proverb of the exogamous Bantu-speaking Gusiis of southwest Kenya goes "Those whom we marry are those whom we fight."

It seems eminently sensible to hypothe-size that man's violent capture and rape of the female led first to the establishment of a rudimentary mate-protectorate and then sometime later to the full-blown male solid-ification of power, the patriarchy. As the first permanent acquisition of man, his first piece of real property, woman was, in fact, the original building block, the cornerstone, of the "house of the father." Man's forcible ex-tension of his boundaries to his mate and later to their offspring was the beginning of his concept of ownership. Concepts of hier-archy, slavery and private property flowed from, and could only be predicated upon, the initial subjugation of woman. . . .

GENESIS

The myth that the origin of male authority rested in some great cataclysmic female sin is not peculiar to the Judeo-Christian tradition or to the Western world. Again and again it appears in societies primitive and highly advanced: Woman is evil and dangerous and to make things right the gods decree that man should maintain order through control.

Chapter 2

Thus the heavens and the earth were finished, and all the host of them. [2]And on the seventh day God ended his work which he had made; and he rested on the seventh day from all his work which he had made. [3]And God blessed the seventh day, and sanctified it: because that in it he had rested from all his work which God created and made.

[4]These *are* the generations of the heavens and of the earth when they were created, in the day that the Lord God made the earth and the heavens.

[5]And no plant of the field was yet on the earth, and no herb of the field had yet grown: for the Lord God had not caused it to rain upon the earth, and *there was* not a man to till the ground. [6]But there went up a mist from the earth, and watered the whole face of the ground. [7]And the Lord God formed man *of* the dust of the ground, and breathed into his nostrils the breath of life; and man became a living soul.

[8]And the Lord God planted a garden east-ward in Eden; and there he put the man whom he had formed. [9]And out of the ground made the Lord God to grow every tree that is pleasant to the sight, and good for food; the tree of life also in the midst of the gar-den, and the tree of knowledge of good and evil. [10]And a river went out of Eden to water the garden; and from thence it was parted, and became into four heads. [11]The name of

the first *is* Pishon: that *is* it which compasseth the whole land of Havilah, where *there is* gold; [12]And the gold of that land *is* good: there *is* bdellium and the onyx stone. [13]And the name of the second river *is* Gihon: the same *is* it that compasseth the whole land of Ethiopia. [14]And the name of the third river *is* Hiddekel: that *is* it which goeth toward the east of Assyria. And the fourth river is Euphrates.

[15]And the Lord God took the man, and put him into the garden of Eden to till it and to keep it. [16]And the Lord God commanded the man saying, Of every tree of the garden thou mayest freely eat: [17]But of the tree of the knowledge of good and evil, thou shalt not eat of it; for in the day that thou eatest thereof thou shalt surely die.

[18]And the Lord God said, *it is* not good that the man should be alone; I will make him a help meet for him. [19]And out of the ground the Lord formed every beast of the field, and every fowl of the air; and brought *them* unto Adam to see what he would call them: and whatsoever Adam called every living creature, that *was* the name thereof. [20]And Adam gave names to all cattle, and to the fowl of the air, and to every beast of the field; but for Adam there was not found a help meet for him. [21]And the Lord God caused a deep sleep to fall upon Adam, and he slept: and he took one of his ribs, and closed up the flesh instead thereof; [22]And the rib, which the Lord God had taken from man, made he a woman, and brought her unto the man. [23]And Adam said, This *is* now bone of my bones, and flesh of my flesh: she shall be called Woman, because she was taken out of Man. [24]Therefore shall a man leave his father and his mother, and shall cleave unto his wife: and they shall be one flesh.

[25]And they were both naked, the man and his wife, and were not ashamed.

Chapter 3

Now the serpent was more subtle than any beast of the field which the Lord God had made. And he said unto the woman, Yea, hath God said, Ye shall not eat of every tree of the garden? [2]And the woman said unto the serpent, We may eat of the fruit of the trees of the garden: [3]But of the fruit of the tree which *is* in the midst of the garden, God hath said, Ye shall not eat of it, neither shall ye touch it, lest ye die. [4]And the serpent said unto the woman, Ye shall not surely die: [5]For God doth know that in the day ye eat thereof, then your eyes shall be opened, and ye shall be as gods, knowing good and evil. [6]And when the woman saw that the tree *was* good for food, and that it *was* pleasant to the eyes, and a tree to be desired to make *one* wise, she took of the fruit thereof, and did eat, and gave also unto her husband with her; and he did eat. [7]And the eyes of them both were opened, and they knew that they *were* naked; and they sewed fig leaves together, and made themselves aprons. [8]And they heard the voice of the Lord God walking in the garden in the cool of the day: and Adam and his wife hid themselves from the presence of the Lord God amongst the trees of the garden. [9]And the Lord God called unto Adam, and said unto him, Where *art* thou? [10]And he said, I heard thy voice in the garden, and I was afraid, because I *was* naked; and I hid myself. [11]And he said, Who told thee that thou *wast* naked? Hast thou eaten of the tree, whereof I commanded thee that thou shouldest not eat? [12]And the man said, The woman whom thou gavest *to be* with me, she gave me of the tree, and I did eat. [13]And the Lord God said unto the woman, What *is* this *that* thou hast done? And the woman said, The serpent beguiled me, and I did eat. [14]And the Lord God said unto the serpent,

Because thou hast done this, thou _art_ cursed above all cattle, and above every beast of the field; upon thy belly shalt thou go, and dust shalt thou eat all the days of thy life: [15]And I will put enmity between thee and the woman, and between thy seed and her seed; he shall bruise thy head, and thou shalt bruise his heel. [16]Unto the woman he said, I will greatly multiply thy sorrow and thy conception; in sorrow thou shalt bring forth children; and thy desire _shall be_ to thy husband, and he shall rule over thee. [17]And unto Adam he said, Because thou hast hearkened unto the voice of thy wife, and hast eaten of the tree, of which I commanded thee, saying, Thou shalt not eat of it; cursed _is_ the ground for thy sake; in sorrow shalt thou eat _of_ it all the days of thy life; [18]Thorns also and thistles shall it bring forth to thee, and thou shalt eat the herb of the field; [19]In the sweat of thy face shalt thou eat bread, till thou return unto the ground; for out of it wast thou taken; for dust thou _art,_ and unto dust shalt thou return.

[20]And Adam called his wife's name Eve; because she was the mother of all living.

[21]Unto Adam also and to his wife did the Lord God make coats of skins, and clothed them.

[22]And the Lord God said, Behold, the man is become as one of us, to know good and evil: and now, lest he put forth his hand, and take also of the tree of life, and eat, and live for ever: [23]Therefore the Lord God sent him forth from the garden of Eden, to till the ground from whence he was taken. [24]So he drove out the man; and he placed at the east of the garden of Eden the Cherubim, and a flaming sword which turned every way, to keep the way of the tree of life.

MAN'S WORLD, WOMAN'S PLACE

ELIZABETH JANEWAY

Novelist and social critic Elizabeth Janeway, born in Brooklyn in 1913, was educated at Barnard and has been awarded honorary degrees from several institutions. She is the author of ten novels, including _Daisy Kenyon_ (1945), _The Vikings_ (1951), and _Leaving Home_ (1953). Her feminist works, _Man's World, Woman's Place_ (1971) and _Between Myth and Morning: Women Awakening_ (1974), have won her recognition in the women's movement. In the following discussion Janeway penetrates the psycho-mythic source of sex-role patterns. She argues that the cliches and themes of gender we hear oft repeated in our culture — that "woman's place is in the home," that "women must stand behind their men," and so on — are really the expression of a deeply rooted human need and image: the paradigmatic Golden Age of beginnings, when for each of us all was as it should be, a Virtuous Lady tended us, and peace reigned.

Chapter 3

In earlier centuries most women in America worked, and they worked throughout the whole of their adult lives. In fact, whether a farm family was affluent or impoverished frequently hinged on the competence of the wife.... Exceptions were the small minority of families in middle- and upper-income classes who lived in urban centers. The major change in the pattern of women's lives occurred after the Civil War when accelerating industrialization and urbanization ushered in a rapid increase in the urban middle classes.... This isolation of women from work was a significant phenomenon in American life for only about eighty years — from the Civil War to World War II.

Eli Ginzberg
Life Styles of Educated Women[1]

Logic and reason deal with the relationship between facts. They tend, therefore, to speak in the indicative mood — as does Professor Ginzberg when he notes the long history of working women and the economic value of their labor. Myth, however, will not be argued down by facts. It may seem to be making straightforward statements, but actually these conceal another mood, the imperative. Myth exists in a state of tension. It is not really describing a situation, but trying by means of this description *to bring about* what it declares to exist. One might think that the hopeful, optative mood was more appropriate to wish fulfillment, but myth is more demanding than that. It doesn't merely wish, it wills; and when it speaks, it commands action.

Contrast a mythical statement with a factual one like Ginzberg's, and the difference in semantic value is clear. Here is Merle Miller, also talking about women at work: "They are almost always insecure and neurotic; they are out of place in the business world and ill at ease at home.... Eventually they nearly always fail at either their careers or their marriages, frequently at both.... I am convinced that if at quitting time tomorrow all the married women in this country over thirty who have jobs were to resign, the republic would not only survive, it would be considerably better off." [2]

True, Miller was writing some years ago; but there is nothing in his words to indicate that he intended to confine their application to a particular time or place (this universality, as we shall see, is characteristic of myth). It is easy enough, moreover, to find equivalent assertions put forward today. Here are a few garnered from the stalwart and articulate Americans who reply to the questions put by The Inquiring Fotographer of the New York *Daily News*: "A woman's success in business has to be due to a man's help, either her husband or a male boss at work. She can't succeed in a big way without male help or encouragement." "Women are jealous of the success men have." "How many wives are successful outside the home? At what?" "Women have little practical common sense and even less native ability. They should remain what most of them are, housewives and mothers." [3] What Miller and the man in the street are giving us is clearly not a description of a situation, but a wish that something would happen. The wish gives rise to a demand, that women should go home.

But the trouble with mythic demands, as I suggested in the last chapter, is that either they don't work because the action they desire isn't appropriate to the end they seek, or the action doesn't take place at all. Women have not gone home, and they show less and less of a will to do so, even those who carry no banner of militancy. If the militants force a door open, there are women behind them waiting to surge forward into the gap, whether the jobs they are offered are as bank executives or telephone repairmen.

The myth, however, pays no attention and continues to repeat its command: Women, go home to the place where you belong.

Why should this be? If we decide to question the myth rationally and ask *why* women should go home, we often get a perfectly rational and relevant answer: Women belong at home for the sake of the family, and particularly of the children. Within empirical limits, this is true. Children do indeed need to be brought up, and brought up in intimate, familiar surroundings. They need love, stability, consistent and unequivocal care and lasting relationships with people who are profoundly enough interested in them to look after them with warmth, gaiety and patience. They need sound human patterns on which to model themselves and guidance, as they grow, for the many possible experiences and ways of living which await them. Psychologists of every stamp agree that emotionally disturbed adults grow out of emotionally deprived children, emotionally swamped children, or children caught in circumstances which subject them to strain they can't cope with. . . .

Given this situation, isn't it sensible and logical to say that women belong at home? Of course it is, if the proposition is put sensibly, with regard to facts and not to the universals of myth. If we do this, we will set down a statement more or less like the following: "In American society as it is organized at present, the place for many married women during certain years of their lives is in the home, unless they are able to provide satisfactory substitute care. The time it is wise for them to spend at home can be figured as a function of the number and the ages of the children for whom they have accepted responsibility." Many men and women have no difficulty at all in altering the mythic statement to conform with this limited proposition, or in living with its requirements once they have done so.

It is when the proposition becomes a universal command that we move into the realm of mythology. The imperative mood is even more central to myth than is its emotional content. New formulations of natural law, after all, may also produce emotional reactions, as Galileo and Darwin both discovered; but neither they nor their followers felt any need to *order* the laity to obey the laws of gravity or of evolution. Their laws were provable and testable in the real world. But mythic "laws" are based on longings, not on objective facts. The statements they make aren't provable. Instead, they can be analyzed to yield an order or a preaching. In psychological terms, they are not rational, but rationalizations, ways of saying, "I want this and so it must be right." In order to externalize and legitimize their wants, myth-makers insist that this is indeed a law, binding on all.

To deal with this problem, we need to change our question so as to isolate the mythic element in the proposition we are considering. Let us ask, as we go around in circles, why women belong at home if they are not married, or married but not raising children, or alone for hours every day with children in school and husbands at business; if home is no longer an economic center, and the time and energy required for cleaning and cooking has been drastically reduced by modern inventions?

The myth is quite ready to reply on its own terms. Here is a recent formulation of an old, old answer. It comes from a popular book by an intelligent and talented woman, and it is especially useful for our investigation because it makes no pretense of depending on logic or facts. "By and large . . . the world runs better when men and women keep in their own spheres. I do not say women are better off, but society in general is. And that is, after all, the mysterious honor and obligation of women — to keep this planet in orbit. We are the self-immolators, the sacrificers, the givers, not the eaters-up of life. To say to us arbitrarily, as some psychologists and propagandists do, that it is our *duty* to be busy elsewhere than at home is pretentious nonsense. Few jobs are worth disrupting family life for unless the family profits by it rather than the housewife herself." [4]

This quotation from Phyllis McGinley's book, *Sixpence in Her Shoe,* raises a number of interesting points. . . .

This approach to woman's place and woman's role transfers the whole question to a realm where emotion holds sway and factual data become irrelevant. Who, for instance, are these "psychologists and propagandists [who say] that it is our *duty* to be busy elsewhere than at home"? In a considerable body of reading on the subject I have not run into any. Even the militants (and Miss McGinley's book appeared in 1964, before the Women's Liberation Front was dreamed of) don't go around ringing other women's doorbells and telling them to get out of the house and go to work. They want to go to work themselves, to earn equal wages with men when they get there and be granted equal opportunities to compete for jobs at all levels. Why should this be felt as so menacing? It can only be on the grounds that this desire of theirs challenges the *universality* of myth. Otherwise, why should Miss McGinley, an excellent professional writer and a talented poet herself, *care* what they do?

But of course she is telling us why, and this is the most interesting implication of her words by far, for it ties our contemporary tag, Woman's place is in the home, into a far older and greater structure of mythology. Women belong at home, says Miss McGinley, because "the world runs better when men and women keep in their own spheres." The general good of society requires that each sex keep its place and play its proper role, or else . . . Or else what? Miss McGinley is joking when she declares that this keeps the planet in orbit, but the metaphor does imply that some kind of world order would be overthrown.

Now the preservation of the order of the world is the formally stated function and consciously held purpose of myth, and of the ritual behavior it demands, in all the societies where it is accepted as a living force. "Myth," wrote Malinowski, "fulfills in primitive culture an indispensable function: it expresses, enhances and codifies belief; it safeguards and enforces morality; it vouches for the efficiency of ritual and contains practical rules for the guidance of man . . . it is not an intellectual explanation or an artistic imagery, but a pragmatic charter of primitive faith and moral wisdom . . . a statement of a primeval, greater and more relevant reality, by which the present life, fates and activities of mankind are determined." [5] One does not challenge such beliefs without shaking the order which they impose and inviting the return of the primordial chaos out of which the world was made and from which it is preserved only by proper belief and behavior. This is why the myth must insist on its universality.

All of this Miss McGinley is hinting at: the reason for staying in one's own sphere is the preservation of the order of the universe. But she certainly knows, as well as anyone, that not all women are keeping to their sphere. The statistics of the Labor Department, let alone the slogans of the Women's Movement, make that clear. If women are indeed able to shift the orbit of the planet by their actions, *then they have already shifted it;* or, to return her metaphor to its place, they have appreciably changed the structure of society; and since society is better off if they don't (in this view), it must have been a change for the worse.

This takes us a step further forward. Not only is Miss McGinley writing in a context of myth, we can now make out which myth it is that her formulation accords with. As it happens, it is one of the rare myths which psychoanalysis has dealt with fruitfully and interpreted persuasively as being closely connected with woman's place in the family and her role as the nurturer of children. This is the myth of the Golden Age, the myth that tells us that society has indeed fallen from a happier state. . . .

"This golden age out of the far-distant past is early infancy," wrote Bruno Bettelheim, summing up the judgment of psychoanalysis. "It was an age when nothing was asked of us and all that we wanted was given. This is the kernel of historic and psychological truth in our dreams of a paradise lost." [6] And certainly, in the first weeks of our lives, each of us rested, a tiny ferocious ogre of greed, in the supporting arms of unquestioning love. Our timeless, overwhelming needs and desires were satisfied miraculously with no words spoken, for we had no words to speak. We were hungry and we were fed, we were thirsty and were given drink. When we roared with rage we were comforted by a ministering woman, whose place was nearby and whose role was our care. This Golden Age of beginnings is a universal, personal myth drawn from experience we all share.

The importance of these glinting, gilded memories varies with the individual. But within their ambience the statement, Woman's place is in the home, expresses a wish to go back to that Age of Gold when every desire was anticipated, to a land where fruit fell from the trees and roast duck flew through the air, a fairytale paradise which our earliest memories assure us once existed. Normally these memories form a kind of subsoil for later pleasures: they have taught us how to enjoy experience and

reach satisfaction. As we grow toward a mature control of our lives we grow away from them. But "normally" is a tricky word. Suppose that other people, or external circumstances, deny our right to control our lives? One way or another, there are many dwellers in this world who have never been, and can never be, satisfied *enough;* and there are times and situations which are so exacting that they "normally" increase the proportion of those who can't find satisfaction of their needs in the real world. None of us is ever satisfied on all counts, but there are degrees of want, and periods and situations when satisfaction seems impossible.

When this happens, myth wells up out of dream and memory, and if times are bad enough, memories of happiness once enjoyed refuse to stay put in the past. The glimmer of a lost paradise nourishes longing for a paradise regained. When what is real and actual becomes too hurtful and limiting to bear, the tatters of past contentment are rewoven into Utopian hopes and millennial strivings. If we were happy once, the logic of emotion asks, why can't we be happy again? And the Golden Age rises out of the past and flames across the future as an apocalyptic vision. Promises are on every tongue. "The World's great age begins anew." "We shall overcome." "Harvest time is here, so God himself has hired me for his harvest. I have sharpened my scythe, for my thoughts are most strongly fixed on the truth, and my lips, hands, skin, hair, soul, body, life curse the unbelievers." [7] . . .

Now that we have set our proposition, Woman's place is in the home, in its mythic context of the lost Golden Age of early infancy, let us ask again what it means. In this relationship, we can see, it is a demand for the renewal of past happiness, which might be stated badly this way: "I want a woman of my own, whom I can command, and who will respond willingly, to comfort me in my lack and loneliness and frustration as my mother did long ago." With such a plea we can surely sympathize. This is the internal, remembered reality which corresponds with the external social reality, the emotion imprinted by the fact that children need mothering and get it most often and most easily from their mothers. Out of the need, however, grows the demanding mythic imperative, for our statement goes on to assert that a man does not just need a woman, he has a right to her and that right is a part of the order of the world. When she left her sphere she violated "the mysterious honor and obligation of women," the planet shook in its orbit, and the Age of Gold came to an end.

Phyllis McGinley's formulation of woman's obligation to her traditional role has brought us this far. Let us now look at another illustration of the emotional syntax of myth. In the summer of 1967 a study group of college students and young professionals was invited to stay for two weeks in the Bedford-Stuyvesant area of Brooklyn, visit local welfare and anti-poverty programs, and talk to a wide range of city officials and community workers. This Cornerstone Project, as it was known, had been set up the year before less as a frontal attack on the problems of the ghetto than as an effort to give young white middle-class men and women a feeling for what life there is like.

If myth rises out of deprivation and longing, out of the inability to control one's own life, if it clings to remembered happiness and dreams of its renewal in a new order of things, then we must surely expect the ghetto to breed such hopes. And indeed we find just such a mythic imagining reported by *The New York Times* in a story about a seminar held for the members of the Cornerstone Project. What is more interesting is the way in which it echoes Miss McGinley's

words about woman's place and role. After all, in suburbia there are homes for women to be in and the pattern of life demands that they be kept up, that the children be clean and neatly dressed, ferried to dancing school and Cub Scouts, that meals be hot, cookies baked, husbands welcomed home and friends entertained. The real world, in other words, provides a plausible color to the idea that women belong at home.

For black women, the world is a different place. More black mothers work than do whites by a considerable margin, and some of those who are at home are there because they stand to lose their welfare money if they take a job. They are more often heads of families, and since Daniel Moynihan's well-known study appeared, the lack of a father figure in black families has become a sociologist's cliché. Any statement out of the ghetto, then, declaring that women are properly subordinate to men must be a statement made out of need, not reality, a statement of myth, not fact. Yet one was made.

"On a recent evening," runs the *Times* report on the Cornerstone Project, "the guest was Reginald Ecklestein, director of the narcotics program for Youth in Action, the local anti-poverty agency. 'The only way an addict can be cured,' began the bearded young Negro, 'is through a woman.

" 'In my program I tell young girls they must be patient,' he went on. 'The black man in Bedford-Stuyvesant is hostile and even barbaric. Women have to understand that. Women were put here to be hurt.' " (It is unclear whether by "here" he meant the world or Bedford-Stuyvesant; but in that labyrinthine ghetto, perhaps it hardly matters. The world beyond is very far away.)

"A girl in the audience slowly raised her hand. 'How do the girls help the boys?' she asked. 'Do they talk to them, draw them out, give them sex?'

" 'They have to listen,' Mr. Ecklestein replied. 'If she doesn't listen, he has to turn to something else, like drugs. The only way a man can be a man, is if a woman is a woman. A woman shouldn't compete with a man, she should make him aware of what his capabilities are.' " [8]

"Women are put here to be hurt," says Mr. Ecklestein to the earnest young audience which has traveled into the hell of the ghetto to learn and understand somewhat as Dante visited the Inferno. Miss McGinley agrees: "We [women] are the self-immolators, the sacrificers, the givers." The questioning girl in the audience who thinks of sex as a gift from a woman to a man speaks in the same key; of this, more later.

"A woman shouldn't compete with a man," says Mr. Ecklestein, out of the dark and bitter slums. "If she doesn't listen, he has to turn to something else, like drugs." And back from suburbia comes the response, "The world runs better when men and women keep to their own spheres. I do not say women are better off, but society in general is."

What is it our speakers are telling us as their responses chime and agree? On the face of it, they are demanding that women subordinate themselves and their natural talents to men; not just some women to some men in certain circumstances, but all women to all men always. Nor can they offer logical reasons for this, but instead invoke such misty concepts as the natural order of things, in which men are capable and women put here to be hurt. Here once again, played back more than a hundred years after the first feminists joined together to resist it, is the old myth of feminine weakness, of woman's incapacity and lack of value compared to the male. To the rational mind it is infuriating to hear it all again, with just as little basis as ever, just as little common

sense; as if the natural order of things didn't produce capable women and silly men as frequently, repetitiously and monotonously as it breeds competent men and foolish women.

But let us remember that we are not talking about reasoned proposals, we are investigating myth. If we listen once more to these voices, perhaps we shall hear behind the demand for feminine subordination the statement of something quite different. "The mysterious honor and obligation of woman is to keep this planet in orbit." "The only way a man can be a man is if a woman is a woman." Is this really a description of weakness? Or does the myth mask another, older, more frightening and more fertile — the myth of female power?

Chapter 4

If a person continues to see only giants, it means he is still looking at the world through the eyes of a child. I have a feeling that man's fear of woman comes from having first seen her as the mother, creator of men.

Anais Nin
Diary, 1931–1934 [1]

"The only way a man can be a man is if a woman is a woman." We are still in the land of myth, but we are no longer talking about woman's weakness, limitations and incapacity. Instead we are being told that a man cannot fulfill his own nature and reach his full potential in life without a woman intervening to help. True, the form of this intervention is expected to be her withdrawal: "A woman shouldn't compete with a man, she should make him aware of what his capabilities are." But the fact that the action required of her is to stand back and let men act for her doesn't make the help she gives any less necessary or primary. She is being asked to withdraw by her own decision, of her own free will, to submit voluntarily. We can tell that it is important for her to *choose* submission, not just to submit willy-nilly, because she is offered something in return.

What she is offered is the knowledge that by her submission she does what the man cannot do alone: she bestows on him his full status. Her submission makes him a man. She and she alone has the power to create his mature strength, to show him his new, adult, face, to grant rebirth where once she gave birth. His dignity depends on her. Or so this contemporary iteration of an ancient belief declares.

This is the myth of female power and it is very old indeed, so old that we cannot trace its origin. The depths of pre-history allow much room for surmise, and perhaps Joseph Campbell goes rather far when he suggests (in his lengthy study of mythology, *The Masks of God*) that "In the very earliest ages of human history the magical force and wonder of the female was no less a marvel than the universe itself; and this gave to woman a prodigious power, which it has been one of the chief concerns of the masculine part of the population to break, control, and employ for its own ends." Campbell cites as evidence the "many primitive hunting races [who] have the legend of a still more primitive age than their own, in which women were the sole possessors of the magic art." [2] Certainly where shamanism, the religion of the archaic hunters across the northern hemisphere, survived into recorded time, women are often found as sorceresses and shamanesses and in some areas special powers are reserved to them.

Was the Golden Age, then, the Age of Matriarchy? My own feeling is that both concepts belong equally to the realm of myth; but whether or not a system of matriarchy ever actually existed, there is no doubt that women were seen, in the dim past, as su-

preme guardians and givers of fertility. Everywhere in ancient cave painting, engraving and sculpture we find evidence which confirms the profound significance that early man attributed to woman as sexual being. The very earliest art we know, which has been dated to the twenty- to thirty-thousand-year-old Aurignacian period of the Stone Age, includes the famous figurines of abundantly pregnant women, like the often reproduced "Venus of Willendorf." In these forms, small enough to fit in the hand but sometimes reflected in life-size wall engravings, an almost featureless head bends over swollen breasts and belly, and huge buttocks dwindle to narrow legs. More than a pregnant woman, this is the essence of pregnancy itself. Campbell believes that these "earliest examples of the 'graven image' . . . were the first objects of worship of the species Homo sapiens." [3]

These Venus-figures have been found over a huge range of territory, from western Europe past the Urals into Siberia, and everywhere they maintain a remarkable degree of similarity. Whatever they represent, it is an emotion that was central to a way of life which endured for millenniums. "Undoubtedly," writes Paolo Graziosi, the well-known Italian student of Paleolithic art, "the people of this ancient phase of the Upper Paleolithic were interested in the reproduction of the female form and emphasized the features specifically connected with sexuality and procreation; in every part of Europe and even outside it, this interest is . . . always displayed with the almost identical aesthetic canons, leading us to believe that so widespread a phenomenon must have had its roots in a deep reason, in a potent impulse, such as the diffusion of certain magical or religious beliefs." [4]

At the time when Stone Age artists were carving these representations of their beliefs, the power of the female to create life must have seemed awesome indeed for, let us remember, there can as yet have been no understanding of the part the father played. Anthropologists in recent times have found numerous primitive peoples who were un-aware that the male seed was as necessary to procreation as the female ovum and womb. The myth of female magical power certainly had its origin in a period when the mother was the only parent, when her im-pregnation was as easily attributed to the wind, or the dew, or an ancestral spirit, as to the man she lived with. Kinship systems which reckon descent through the female line and assign power over children to their mother's brother instead of to the father also recall such an era even though the physical role of the father is now understood in the societies where they exist.

Indeed, the myth of female power may be fossilized in many other beliefs and rituals found among primitive people around the world. Initiation ceremonies, in which medi-cine men or secret societies or the elders of the tribe confer adult status on boys, have been interpreted as efforts by men to act out the rite of birth which nature denies them. The initiation ceremony can be seen as a statement that though women give birth to children in the ordinary course of events, men, by enacting the sacred rites of pas-sage, turn these unfinished creatures into *men,* and that the latter act is as necessary as the former; without it, the children would never arrive at full adulthood. In token of this rebirth, the initiates often take new names and are always granted new dignities and privileges. The ceremonial social act thus becomes as significant as the process of natural birth and growth. It represents the acknowledgment by society of this growth, through the authority of the men in charge.

Now we find a young social worker facing the problem of how boys can grow to ma-turity today and be acknowledged by society as men. In our society no established ritual exists. Maturity, it has been assumed, comes automatically with age. Even in the Jewish community where the bar mitzvah ceremony is still honored and performed, this pleasant festival has no real effect on the life of the boy who goes through it. His schooling does not end, nor do his parents allow him one jot more of adult privilege than he enjoyed before. Western belief has held for centuries that the individual can be left to himself to grow into a place in a free, expanding world where power is easily available and adult status need not be conferred because it is there for the taking.

This era is over, Reginald Ecklestein is saying: "The black man in Bedford-Stuyve-sant is hostile and barbaric. Women have to understand that [and] make him aware of what his capabilities are." Because society can no longer assure the transformation of barbaric children into responsible adults, women must be called in. Once more, meta-phorically but unmistakably, we are witness-ing an invocation of the ancient, magical force of the female who gives birth. Let her now put forth her power to aid in the rebirth of boys as men. The world of the ghetto, and not the world of the ghetto alone, has be-come so fragmented and disorganized that there are no longer social institutions or spiritual leaders who can effect the change of boy to man, irresponsibility to authority, dreaming to action. Where reality offers no hope, the world of myth is called in.

So the myth of female weakness which preaches subordination of woman to man can, it seems, mask its contrary, the myth of female power. This is a step forward in our exploration, but not of course a final resolution, for the myth of female power is as much a projection of need and a focus for fears as is its twin. We may find in this connection, however, an answer to an old puzzle: why have women so often and so persistently acquiesced in declaring themselves subordinate to men? Why have so many, as the suffragists indignantly phrased it, "hugged their chains"? Why have women preached to women that their role calls for abnegation, withdrawal from a direct confrontation with the world of action, and submission to the male — father, brother, husband, son, lover — who will mediate between them and events? These injunctions go far beyond the ordinary agreement that the world is divided between men and women, each with a different sort of job to do, but each job respected. They order women to give up not only activity, but dignity as well.

The immediate, pragmatic answer is that many women prefer to be subordinate because they have been brought up to be. We can't dismiss the obvious fact that habit, timidity and conditioning keep many people in uncomfortable places, whatever their sex. Laziness and greed are powerful persuaders too, for why should one want to change one's position if one is looked after and cosseted where one is? Rightly or wrongly, many women are persuaded that submission, frivolity and charm will get them more out of life than any other strategy. Some of them are right. Moreover, the traditional feminine role (which we will analyze in detail later) pushes women toward this pattern of behavior and also idealizes it: women are praised for being "feminine," which is another example of mythic illogic. Why should anyone be praised for being what she is supposed to be by nature? . . .

So let us persist in our belief that there must be some better explanation for women's acquiescence in the myth of female weakness than the response that that's the way they are made. Surely one reason can be found in the myth of female power which lies behind the myth of weakness. As Anais Nin intuitively guessed, in the quotation at the head of this chapter, the source of the myth of female power lies just where the myth of the Golden Age takes its rise: in the mother-child relationship. But now this relationship is being seen the other way around.

What we are looking at is the effective memory of the mother's power over the child which is *in reality* as complete as the child *imagines* its power over the mother to be. The grown child remembers the mother as slave, as loving nurturer who tends and watches and serves. But the mother is also the master. Having created the child as a living entity (and except for one not-unique act by the father she has created it. I am speaking of psychological, not scientific, truth), she now has the power to create it as a social being, a member of the community; and without her this creation will not take place, whatever ritual initiation the men like to indulge themselves in acting out. The child will not grow into an adult without her care, and the kind of adult it grows into will depend on her. Of course she is circumscribed by custom, responsible to her husband and his family for the baby; but the process of nurturing is hers and its rewards are hers. Every day she undertakes anew to love and to care for the child she has borne. It is this continued repeated choosing that authenticates her relationship with the child and sets up the psychological structure which is realized as the experience of motherhood.

Meanwhile, the child is in her power, is her toy. She can mold it and shape its habits, play with it, tease it, teach it and frustrate it, push it toward the fulfillment of her own desires and mock her husband's hopes, if she wishes to. *He* may assert his power over her and over the children, but she knows what she knows: that for a time *her* power is always greater. She can deceive him more easily than her children can deceive her, and she can manipulate them, frighten them and change them to a greater degree than she can be forced to change herself. This is real power; and to some women the fact that it is secret, where female weakness is apparent, makes it all the more attractive.

Indeed, the less control which a woman exercises over other areas of her life, the greater will be the satisfaction she derives from managing the lives of her children. . . .

So when women cling to their traditional role, it is not primarily because they find masochistic pleasure in being dominated (though no doubt some do) but because this role offers them power too: private power in return for public submission. This is the regular, orthodox bargain by which men run the world and allow women to rule in their own place. Some times it is a better bargain than at others. When women's activities are publicly acknowledged to have social and economic value, when within their place they can control the work to be done and order its processes, when they do not feel themselves isolated and cut off from man's world by a barrier of incomprehension, then the bargain will be accepted unquestioningly by a great majority of women. Enough authority within their traditional place balances an external subordination that is not too wounding.

Let us not stop here, however, with a summing-up because there is more to be learned from this arrangement if we follow Erikson's advice and look at it from another angle. The balance of private power and public submission which women accept touches only the factual aspect of their position. It assumes that power and weakness are separate and opposite things, contraries that contradict and offset each other. But they are not, not in the realm of myth which grows out of the interior world of feeling.

In that inner world, opposites are two sides of the same coin, as Freud found in his dream analysis. Positive and negative show the same picture. Power and weak-

ness flow into each other. They are not divided, but are aspects of the same inner emotional tension. In mythic identification of power and weakness, women immolate themselves as a sign of strength. They are the givers; but how can one give if one does not possess riches and substance? . . .

Notes

Chapter 3

1. Ginzberg, Eli, *Life Styles of Educated Women.* New York: Columbia University Press, 1966. Page 7.
2. Miller, Merle, "Marriage à la Mode," in *Women Today,* Bragdon, Elizabeth, ed. Indianapolis: The Bobbs Merrill Company, 1953.
3. Quotes from The Inquiring Fotographer (sic), *The New York Daily News,* November 12, 1969, and December 28, 1969.
4. McGinley, Phyllis, *Sixpence in Her Shoe.* New York: The Macmillan Company, 1964. Page 47.
5. Malinowski, Bronislaw, *Myth in Primitive Psychology,* 1926, quoted in Eliade, Mircea, *Myth and Reality.* New York: Harper & Row, 1963. Page 20.
6. Bettelheim, Bruno, *The Empty Fortress.* New York: The Free Press, 1967. Page 14.
7. Cohn, Norman, *The Pursuit of the Millennium.* London: Secker and Warburg, 1957. Page 255. The quotation is from Thomas Müntzer, the German Anabaptist and millenary preacher, 1489–1525.
8. The report on the Cornerstone Project meeting appeared in *The New York Times,* July 30, 1967.

Chapter 4

1. Nin, Anais, *Diary, 1931–1934.* New York: The Swallow Press, Harcourt, Brace and World, Inc., 1966. Page 53.
2. Campbell, Joseph, *The Masks of God: Primitive Mythology.* New York: The Viking Press, 1959. Page 315.
3. *Ibid.,* page 325.
4. Graziosi, Paolo, *Paleolithic Art.* New York: McGraw-Hill, 1960. Page 60.

II

Sexism Realized:

Women's Lives in Patriarchy

"We have been foreigners not only to the fortresses of political power but also to those citadels in which thought processes have been spun out. . . . Women are beginning to recognize that the value system that has been thrust upon us by the various cultural institutions of patriarchy has amounted to a kind of gang rape of minds as well as of bodies."

— MARY DALY, *Beyond God the Father*

So far we have been examining the consciousness of patriarchy, the abstract concepts, myths, beliefs, and values that underlie the sexual caste system. We now turn to the material expression of that consciousness and the effects it has on the lives of women. Permeating the experience of women in the most concrete ways, sexism is built into almost everything that women do or that is done to us, lodged in the most personal facets of our lives, and the most public. In the following chapters we will explore in some detail the outward realization of sexist consciousness, the patterns and structures, institutionalized and informal, that give female lives their particular color and shape.

Chapter 6 focuses on the part of women's lives ordinarily called the private sphere — personal relationships, marriage and unmarriage, love, romance, and sex. We shall look at women's lifestyles, the way we live, and at our life space, the way we psychologically perceive it.

Chapter 7 directs attention to the institutional sphere, to work and economics, to women's legal status, and to the quality and character of women's participation in public policy making, all of which are intricately interrelated.

Finally, Chapter 8 treats the psychoperceptual undergirding of the entire system, the intellectual modes through which patriarchy formulates, maintains, and solidifies sexist consciousness.

6

Women's Private Space: Asymmetry Becomes the Double Standard

The Lady in the Space

Earlier we looked at the external images and models constructed for women in patriarchy, and we examined woman's designated "place," but we have not yet ascertained the impact of these constructions for the woman within. How do these forces shape women's internal space, our private lives, the way we live on the most intimate level with ourselves and with others?

We women are simply people, human beings, with the needs, dreams, and desires people are wont to experience. How we relate to others on a one-to-one basis; how we relate to ourselves, our bodies, and our feelings; and how we relate to the physical space around us are the concrete realities that make up private lives on a daily basis. But there are aspects of our lives as *women,* particularly women in a sexist world, that profoundly alter and color those concrete human realities. It is in the tension between the two, our experience as people and our experience as women, in the conflicts that arise between their divergent states and expectations, that we live our realities and inhabit our private space. Let us turn, then, to a close examination of the constructions of our private, personal space and their effects on the quality of our lives.

A Story

Once upon a time there was a very beautiful little girl named Cinderella (Snow White, Sleeping Beauty, Rapunzel...). Her nature was as lovely as her face. Gentle, kind, accepting, modest, obedient, and sweet, she never complained or became peevish, though she suffered greatly at the hands of circumstance and cruel people. Because she was good-natured and uncomplaining, because she asked for little and gave a great deal, her beauty shone, and a handsome prince came along, fell in love with her, and took her away to his castle, where the pair lived happily ever after. At that point, the story always ends.

This is a story that in its many tellings is very dear to the hearts of most little girls, who hear it practically in the crib, read and repeat it endlessly, play-act and live it vicariously, and dream of its realization in their own lives. It tells us a great deal about the way women are expected to be and the way we come to see our existence.

The story teaches us, in the most effective way, that we are born to be chosen, admired, and sought after, that to succeed in being chosen follows upon certain attributes: physical beauty, "good nature" (willingness to take unwarranted abuse), modesty, self-effacement, piety, vulnerability, suffering, and good luck. We learn that even if we do not have these attributes or, for that matter, dislike them, we had better appear to have them. For the essence of the story is the fact of *being chosen* rather than choosing, of being noticed for our "feminine qualities," of gaining success from endurance and patience rather than initiative, which belongs to the man. The story goes beyond the façade of his asking and her assenting, straight to the unvarnished truth: It is the Prince who picks what he wants; our chief responsibility is to make ourselves as worthy of his interest as we can. Our only appropriate direct action lies in the orchestrating of an effect. The story teaches us, in an extension of the principle of passivity, that it is not through our own efforts that we are to be happy (or safe or comfortable), but through the intervention of a powerful protector who alone can bestow on us status and security. He alone has the power to make us happy, for clearly we are (or ought to be) unable to do that for ourselves.

It is the element in these tales of relinquishing initiative and the power to make ourselves happy or safe that is so potent a factor in the molding of the approved feminine character. We come to believe not only that we are too weak and small to take care of ourselves, that we are and must be dependent, but that it is wrong to be any other way. Self-assertive women like Cinderella's stepmother and sisters are portrayed with disapprobation and come to bad ends. It is fixed in our minds that women who take for themselves, by themselves, are selfish and wicked, whereas admirable females earn for themselves through renunciation what they do not take directly.

The attitude born of all this is a sense that only through the intercession of another can we *be made* happy, that we are to receive the positive goods in life only from another in return for beauty of face and nature and for services rendered. Most of us do not learn until much later that in giving up the right as well as the responsibility of framing our own fortunes, we place ourselves at the mercy of circumstance and of anyone who may wish to exercise the power we have abrogated. We do not learn until later, after the pain it brings, that we have bartered our souls for the illusion of protection.

The Matter of Marriage

Enter Mr. Right (alias the Prince or the One). He will "come along," we will "fall in love," we will know instinctively that we belong together — forever. We will marry, have children, and live happily ever after. The End.

That fantasy, for women who marry and women who do not, exercises incredible power on the living of our lives.

The Myth

Some years ago, in a course I was teaching in introductory philosophy, I used to ask the students to begin the term's work with an essay entitled, "What I Want Out of Life." Those were the years before I had acquired what now is known as a feminist consciousness, and the results surprised me. With great regularity, the papers of the men in the class differed from the women's. The men's papers generally followed a familiar theme: I want to finish school, get a good job, have a good income, a nice place to live, friends, fun things to do. Many said they wanted to be happy; a few remembered to hope for health. The women too said they wanted to be happy. They wanted to finish school, work for a while, fall in love, get married. Finis. Did the men, I asked, mean to get married? Oh sure, they said. That was understood. It came along the way. For the women, it *was* the way. It was as though the women looked into the future only so far as the "magic event." Then the Cinderella tale took over: "happily ever after."

It is most telling, I think, that the favorite female fairy tales end with the wedding, and all else is subsumed under the heading of "ever-after." It is as though these tales teach that our whole existence is to be wrapped up in the quest for a mate; that once we acquire the mate all else is decided; that after the wedding, definition of what follows is irrelevant because it is indistinguishable from any other ever-after; that what follows really has little importance, because we have already done the all-important; that life with the Prince in his castle is the only happily-ever-after that is possible for us, there being no viable alternatives; that all the other aspects of our lives, public as well as private, are determined in large measure by the overwhelming pervasiveness of the wifely estate.

As children listening to stories and as young women creating our own, how closely did we really look at ever-after land? We had vague images of doll houses kept clean and chic by pretty homemakers fastidiously dressed and coifed as in the pages of women's magazines. Many of us saw ourselves happily dusting, cherishing contented babies, and expressing our creativity through all the daily acts of family concern. We knew we would be loved and appreciated, sharing a husband's life, supporting him as he encouraged us, fulfilling ourselves in the haven of his world.

Promise and Disillusionment

The pervasive American mystique of marriage promises to women a roster of assurances.

* You will have someone to make you happy.
* You will be loved and cherished till death.
* You will be cared for and protected from all the dangers of the world.
* You will have sexual intimacy and satisfaction.
* You will have someone to understand and support you.
* You will have companionship and safety from loneliness.
* You will have a father for your children.
* You will be socially secure as part of a couple.
* You will have a place in this world, a meaning, and you will love it.
* You will gain status and prestige as someone's chosen wife. You will not be an "old maid."
* You will be financially secure.
* You will be happy.

That's the promise.

Feminists cast a suspicious glance at the promise. "Demystifying" marriage, we have drawn up a roster of our own: the untruths

and half-truths, the traps and games, the dissimulations and dangers of the traditional marriage mystique. It is not that feminism is in principle incompatible with marriage. (Although some feminists believe that it is, others do not, and many feminists marry.) Rather, it is that traditional marriage arrangements and presuppositions are often destructive to women in the most concrete way, and feminists, discovering these realities, seek to warn and redress.

The Case Against Traditional Marriage

Following Emile Durkheim, Jessie Bernard, a feminist sociologist, commented that "marriage is not the same for women as for men; it is not nearly as good." [1] Bernard concluded from extensive research that although men ridicule married life and display contempt for it, they benefit considerably from marriage whereas women lose a great deal. In several studies it was found that married men have greater psychic health than single men, that they suffer depression and anxiety less frequently than their single counterparts, that they advance faster professionally and socially and have better incomes than single men. Furthermore, the remarriage rate for divorced men and widowers is very high; they remarry more often and sooner than either women or never-married men. [2] Apparently they know what is good for them.

Married women, on the other hand, experience greater depression, anxiety, and fear than single women, are more apt to show severe neurotic symptoms, and have lower

---

[1] "The Paradox of the Happy Marriage," in *Women in Sexist Society,* ed. Vivian Gornick and Barbara Moran (New York: Basic Books, 1971), p. 147.

[2] Ibid. See also Jessie Bernard, *The Future of Marriage* (New York: Bantam, 1972).

self-esteem than single women or married men. What is interesting as well, as Tavris and Offir report, homemakers are even more apt to display these problems than working wives, and when single men in any category (never-married, divorced, or widowed) are compared with single women, the men are more likely to suffer from psychological difficulties.[3]

After all the ball-and-chain jokes, all the tavern mythology about carefree bachelors and manipulative women, and all the masculist assertions that marriage is a terrific deal for women and a disaster for men, are not these findings a revelation? Yet, if one demystifies, they really should come as no surprise. In so many ways, in emotional exchange, in economics, in work, in independence, in freedom and mobility, in autonomy and authenticity, traditional marriage truly offers to women and men a double standard, and women's part of that standard is the less advantaged.

CONJUGAL OBLIGATION   In patriarchy, a man and a woman marry, each taking on certain responsibilities. He agrees to love, honor, cherish, and provide her with the physical necessities of life. She agrees to love and to obey (a term now out of vogue in modern marriage ceremonies, although the power relationship in which it originates is not); and she takes on a whole composite of responsibilities, diverse, unspecified, generally lumped under the heading of wife/housewife. On the surface it might appear an even exchange, but it is not. Actually, it is a rather extraordinary exchange, and an enigmatic one, for it is at base quite different from what it appears to be or is reputed to be. Overladen with social mythology and expectation, it is rarely seen

for what it is, and the parties concerned often interpret and perceive it very differently.

In the patriarchal barroom myth, marriage for men is a trap. A man in the excellent condition of bachelorhood, free and unencumbered, encounters a lady, wily and manipulative, who tricks him into "falling in love." He becomes so besotted with her that he loses his good sense and marries her. The door slams shut; he will find out only later that he has been entrapped and is now the captive of a "ball and chain" who, for the rest of his life, will nag him, keep tabs on him, spend his money, and bring him difficulties. The lady, on the other hand, has a "good deal"; having snared her meal ticket, she can spend her time in relative comfort and leisure, talking on the telephone, coffee-klatsching, or playing bridge after completing the few odd jobs around the house. "And they say women are the dumb ones!" Actually, of course, both women and men know the myth to be false, but it is unclear to both just how false. In some form and to some degree, the myth is believed (or else Jessie Bernard's findings would not surprise us), and in its tension with reality it exerts considerable pressure on the attitudes and behaviors of husbands and wives.

Let us take a different and demystifying look at traditional marriage. In patriarchy, a man and a woman marry; they strike a bargain, make an exchange (not fully understood at the time of marriage), and each takes on certain responsibilities and privileges. The bare bones of the agreement require that the husband is to provide the physical necessities of life through his income — shelter, food, clothing, and so on — and that in return for these the wife is to provide care of the home and family. But what do these respective duties, obligations, and privileges actually entail for each?

The patriarchal husband's responsibilities are quite explicit: He must work or in some

[3] Carol Tavris and Carole Offir, *The Longest War* (New York: Harcourt Brace Jovanovich, 1977), p. 222.

fashion secure financial maintenance of the home and family. He must act as "head of household," making policy decisions for the family and bearing responsibility for them. He is to protect his wife and children from danger, whatever that might be in their circumstances, and guide and mold their behavior and character. Although the law does not specify the quantity or the quality of the provisions a man must secure for his family, the culture does, for according to the imperatives of Mars a man proves his worthiness through success in the marketplace (the modern hunt). Society, and often his wife or children, may judge a man ill if he does not provide according to the standard of living decreed by the media. There is then an intense pressure on husbands to provide always bigger and better, and the pressure may be burdensome and unremitting.

A different aspect to the prescription to "provide" is often overlooked in discussions about masculine responsibility, and I have rarely heard it voiced. "Provision" means work. It means one must have a job, of whatever nature, and must remain regularly at a job in order to obtain all one needs. Husbands frequently point out that they work very hard "to get you what you need" and therefore should be loved, respected, served, and accorded the right to make family decisions. What they do not say is that they would work in any event, married or unmarried, for one needs to eat, dress, and have shelter, married or not. They do not say that they work for more than only income, that even in routine or laborious jobs there is a satisfaction in earning, and that life without work outside the house would drive them mad — a point certainly supported by Studs Terkel's *Working*.[4] They do not say that there is a tremendous satisfaction in looking about one's family

home and noting that whatever is there, whatever its condition, it has been provided by one's efforts, and that because of those efforts, one is autonomous and worthy. We need not denigrate the value and importance of giving or the pressure of provision. We need only consider that there is in that labor a very positive and meaningful reward that must not be overlooked in evaluating its claims to compensation. The experience of autonomy and self-worth that follows on providing is the reason many women give for returning to work outside the home or even for leaving "comfortable" marriages.

The husband's duty to protect is enigmatic in the twentieth century. Certainly the simple job of protection from physical danger is impossible in such a complex society. That work is now largely passed to public institutions, and the remainder of the responsibility is shared equally by husband and wife. In terms of children's safety, the lion's share of that work is accomplished by the mother, who typically takes almost total charge of her offspring. Even when she is not with them, it is she who worries and protects through vigilance with regard to a ride to school, an adequate baby sitter, a competent physician, appropriate companions, and countless other matters. It is she too who "guides"; fathers could hardly be expected to provide much guidance to children in the average twelve minutes a day they spend with them![5]

Head of household, then, becomes an interesting concept. If it does not mean protection, guidance, and modeling, what it means in essence is power, control over household and family in return for breadwinning, which is neither all sacrifice nor peculiar to marriage. And the head of household has certain real privileges that he enjoys both as husband and as male: considerably more freedom, au-

---

[4] Studs Terkel, *Working* (New York: Pantheon, 1974).

[5] Tavris and Offir, *The Longest War*, p. 232.

tonomy, and service. The service, by and large, is provided by his wife.

One of the most extraordinary features of being a wife in patriarchy is the unification of certain aspects of the role — the married woman *is* a housewife; she doesn't *do* housewifing. She is not simply a mate, a coworker and partner in the business of life; she is a certain identity, one that carries with it a particular (mixed) status, a "place," and some identifiable and rather unchanging tasks. Upon marriage, the patriarchal wife yields her own individual identity (a fact attested to by her change of name), subsumes it under her husband's, and commits her life — her time, interests, and energies — to the needs of the family group, husband and offspring. She becomes, in essence, a servant and general laborer,[6] a position, furthermore, from which she may never return while the marriage endures. For regardless of whatever else a wife may be involved in — work outside the home, community affairs, pursuit of a creative career — patriarchy defines as her first priorities her duties as wife/housewife. Should she choose not to keep house, she is no less the housewife; she is simply a housewife not doing her job.

A husband barters some of his income and freedom for the kind of services and satisfactions a wife provides. What does a wife barter? For the financial security (now not a clear return for the more than 44 percent of all married women who work outside the home[7]), for the status of being married, for love and companionship, women take on their general, almost limitless labors of service to their home and family. Whereas a husband takes on a "job" involving specifiable hours, tasks, and rewards, a wife takes on a lifestyle. Her tasks are not wholly specified, but comprise the satisfaction of almost every kind of physical and emotional need voiced by her husband and children, as well as those services that may be required for smooth maintenance of family life. Her labor is limited neither by time nor by personal need. She is expected to perform at whatever hour needs arise — breakfast at whatever time the family must rise, dinner when they return home. Were this job to be advertised outside the home, it might carry the warning that the job makes tremendous demands on one's personal time, including split shifts and a great deal of overtime.

Unlike her husband, whose skills and education define the kind of work he will do, the housewife is assigned work that is elemental and undifferentiated by skill. For the college educated and the illiterate, the common denominator is housework — sweeping floors, washing clothes, scouring ovens, cleaning toilets, washing dishes, dumping garbage — and she who performs such menial tasks earns for herself the status incumbent upon them: low. She is "just a housewife." The tasks themselves are no joy. However glorified in the poetry of *Woman's Day* magazine, however falsified in media commercials, housework in the real world is boring, ugly, tiresome, repetitive, unsatisfying, and carried on in isolation. Factory or office work may be dull and tiresome, but there are people around; one can see and be seen, talk and interact, change scenes. One of the worst aspects of housewifing is the awful sense of being locked up with sameness, day after day after day.

Labor to maintain the house itself is not the only responsibility of the housewife. In addition to the care of the home, she is also expected to manage care of the inhabitants of the home, and this really remarkable assign-

---

[6] If such an analysis seems overly harsh, I recommend to your attention such extremely popular and well-purchased books as Marabel Morgan's *Total Woman* (Old Tappan, N.J.: Revell, 1973) and Helen Andelin's *Fascinating Womanhood* (New York: Bantam, 1975).

[7] *1975 Handbook on Women Workers*, U.S. Dept. of Labor, Women's Bureau.

ment makes the contemporary wife's role what it is. Housewives have nearly complete responsibility for the care of their children, not only to feed, clothe, and teach them, but to monitor the quality of their school experience, organize their religious, social, and health needs, provide for child care when parents are not at home, and so on. More to the point, the mother is held responsible for the emotional needs of her children, and it is left very unclear at which point needs become demands. Given current child-centered sensitivities to the warnings of doctors Freud and Spock, many mothers are extremely hesitant to deny children any demand on time, privacy, or strength without suffering considerable guilt and concern. In essence, the demands of parenting, physical and emotional, are stringent, and most mothers have to function for the most part as single parents.

Care of inhabitants does not end with children, for a wife is expected to care for her husband in very much the same way she cares for offspring. She is to feed him, cook his favorite dishes, buy and maintain his clothes, arrange his home to suit him, pack his suitcase when he goes on a trip, arrange entertainment for him on Saturday night, entertain his business friends, arrange doctor's appointments for him (even against his will), listen to him, support and "understand" him. In some circles a wife is responsible even for the spiritual health of her husband. Priests in some parishes advise that it is sinful for a wife to deny her husband sex lest he be led into temptation outside the home, and Jews believe it to be a wife's duty to provide for her husband a living environment in which he may successfully seek blessings from God.

Whereas a husband's contributions to family maintenance are "public" or communal, the wife's work is frequently personal or private, and it is this aspect of her labor, in addition to the rest, that renders it a form of service (in the sense of a servant). The husband may mow a lawn, repair a door, or dump garbage, tasks pertaining to the household collectively, but he would not be expected to mend his wife's slacks or gauge and replenish her toiletries. In the traditional household, wives render to their husbands a plethora of personal services; the reverse is rarely true.

Wives do not receive a salary for their work, although their husbands share their incomes with them, sometimes generously. There is a great deal of difference between receiving an established and agreed on sum of money in return for one's labor and receiving money as a "gift," that is, at the giver's own choosing. Although wife labor is extensive and time-consuming, often taxing, and absolutely necessary for the household, and although husbands could not advance professionally nor be half so productive without it, wives are not perceived as earning; hence they are in the position of dependents. The money they are given by their husbands is perceived by all, institutions and individuals, as a grant. Therefore, they must endure the disadvantages and indignities of pensioners. Dependent wives are cautioned as to how they are to spend their *husband's* money; they are to express gratitude for sums earmarked for their own personal use (such as clothing), and they must wait until their husbands decide it is time to replace the washer. To put aside a savings of their own out of "granted" money is perceived as deceptive and is rarely done, and wives sometimes find themselves trapped in intolerable marriages by finances.

The cruelest jab in the housewife's situation (and one not often recognized) is the derogation of her labor to the status of nonwork. Because our society (unlike some others) affords no economic recognition of housework (such as social security or compensation), because the work is accomplished at home in the service of the family rather than in the public marketplace, because "women's work" is always devalued and demeaned, the housewife is perceived and treated as a nonworker, nonproductive, with the accompanying stigmas and trials. "Does your wife work?" one might ask. "No, she's at home." "Do you work?" one woman asks another. "No, I'm just a housewife." Even women, housewives themselves, must be reminded that, paid or not, recognized or not, *homemaking is a job.*

The effects of the classification of homemaking as nonwork are far-reaching and powerful. It has already been shown that the housewife is reduced to a state of financial dependence, which in turn diminishes her power in the family, her own self-image, and her standing in society. The problems, however, go much farther.

By allowing herself to be completely dependent on the income of her husband, by accruing no formally recognized history of labor (such as social security benefits or a pension) that would be compensable in later years, and by collecting no savings of her own, a wife makes her future financial security subject to the continuance of her marriage or her husband's good will. By removing herself from the labor force, by not developing or enhancing marketable skills, she further erodes the possibility of financial independence in or out of marriage.

Consider a woman who, after twenty years as a housewife, finds herself in an intolerable marriage situation. With dependent children, no savings, no job, no work history, and no marketable skills, what is she to do? She may remain trapped and unhappy, or she may leave. Divorced, she suffers then not only loss of companionship and social status; she must also expect a terribly diminished standard of living, severe strains of economic survival with little experience to withstand them, and no career or professional interests to sustain

her. Furthermore, alimony and child support are largely inadequate or nonexistent.[8]

Just as the traditional homemaker often finds herself in a traditional bind, the wife who opts for an alternative to dependence by working outside the home may also find herself severely hampered by the nonwork status of homemaking. As of 1976, more than 40 percent of all married women were working for salary outside the home. Over thirteen million had children under 18, over five million had children under 6, and the number is steadily rising.[9] Such women share the responsibilities of economic maintenance with their husbands. Do they commonly receive a proportional increase in status, power, privilege, and autonomy? Do they in return receive from their husbands an equal share of their efforts for homemaking? In this country as in nearly every other in the world, the answer is generally no.

Under any circumstances, husbands rarely take equal responsibility for the maintenance of the household. In the case of the wife working only at home, the logic goes this way: If homemaking is nonwork, it is not a job with visible, recognized, and acknowledged demands. The homemaker has no right, therefore, to expect her husband to share in household tasks, for she is "not working" and he is! How can she legitimately expect him to add her responsibilities to his burden? The same logic holds even when the wife is publicly employed. Such a wife actually carries two jobs, a salaried one and a nonsalaried one, but since homemaking is not recognized as "work," her two-job

[8] See Lenore Weitzman, "Legal Equality in Marriage," in *Woman in a Man-Made World*, ed. Nona Glazer and Helen Y. Waehrer (Chicago: Rand McNally, 1977).

[9] *Fact Sheets on Institutional Sexism*, March 1976 (New York: Council on Interracial Books for Children, Inc., 1976), p. 2.

status is not recognized. She merely has certain wifely or womanly "responsibilities" at home, and the husband's contributions are usually treated as a gift or favor rather than a rightful responsibility (he "helps").

We are familiar with the media images of the (double)-working wife: She must "organize her time" very carefully in order to meet all her responsibilities and not "neglect" her family. Smiling all the while, taking Geritol to maintain her health and her sex appeal, she hurries home from work to get supper on; she spends the evenings and weekends cleaning, washing, using Downy (to get noticed); and she finds time to use Aviance perfume and carry on all that follows.

Two jobs, however, are more than taxing. Parenting, cleaning, cooking, shopping, and working for salary take their toll: Physically, psychologically, and creatively, one runs down. It is a truism in the business and professional world that one cannot produce at peak performance if one is cut in too many ways. For this reason, most institutions have formal prohibitions against moonlighting. Yet moonlighting is a way of life for most married working women. Worse, it is never even clear which job is *the* job and which is moonlighting.

Many wives are becoming sensitive to their circumstances. They have begun to recognize that a cultural construction and not a cosmic imperative burdens them with homemaking, and they have begun to expect sharing with their mates. Many husbands have come to recognize the unfairness of it all, and they are moving (however grudgingly, however painfully) toward carrying some of the load.

THE EMOTIONAL ECONOMY If the fairy-tale image of marriage promises women anything at all, it promises abundant satisfaction of emotional needs. When the prince arrives he is supposed to bring with him love everlasting, constant attention, affection, devotion,

understanding, companionship, appreciation, and, most of all, the desire and wherewithal to make his princess happy. To be sure, a great deal of this fantasy is wrong-headed and ill-conceived. No one can make another happy, however much he or she might want to, and no one can provide another with complete solace and total understanding. Nor can or should anyone shower another with constant attention and concern. Yet still, people can and do care for one another, need one another, and share feelings, and sociologists tend to agree that marriage as an institution survives today primarily because it is seen as providing the major source and vehicle for these kinds of interactions.

Love, as we know, is a complicated term and an enigmatic concept. Love is different things to different people in varied circumstances, and it is often experienced and expressed in very individual ways. It is not so enduring, dependable, and consistent as it has been reputed to be, nor can it conquer all or justify every kind of action. Yet it would be wrong to lapse into cynicism and to denigrate the experience. However difficult it is to understand or define, however changeable, and however distorted by myth, love as a concept persists in the human vocabulary. There is ample evidence that human beings cannot thrive without the kind of succor provided by what is generally called love, and that life can be arid and unwholesome without some measure of love's joy.

Certainly, the intense kind of personal contact that either is or begets love may be gleaned from a variety of relationships, several in kind and in number. But our culture rarely affords us an environment in which such relationships can grow, and we are discouraged rather than encouraged to participate in the kind of encounter crucial to love. Marriage, however, formal or otherwise, is just such an environment, and it does include an expectation that the partners will have at least this — a sharing of communication, concern, and mutual support, an exchange of sensitivity, compassion, and nurture. Such sharing and mutuality can be termed the emotional economy of the relationship.

For various reasons, all lodged in patriarchy, it is in this exchange that women often experience their greatest disappointment in traditional marriage. The emotional economy, like the work economy, is out of balance, and once more the wife typically occupies the disadvantaged position. In the traditional patriarchal marriage, although women usually express a greater interest in love and emotional exchange, and although women are thought to need and want more open expressions of affection, wives are apt to receive considerably less personal affection than their husbands. Despite or because of the high priority women often place on the love relationship, wives are more apt to love than be loved, support rather than be supported, nurture rather than be nurtured, even though they appear to seek the exchanges more than men do. The sexist role and character definitions of Venus and Mars decree that women should become more overtly and intricately bound up with the behaviors and feelings of interpersonal contact. Ultimately, women become very good at loving, but for the patriarchal male it is a clumsy business at best.

There is a good deal of controversy in the women's movement over whether women do or do not have any special ability for love and feeling. The contention that we have such a unique ability has been used by sexists to exclude us from any activity *not* based on serving, any activity *not* based on feeling. But such a division is more patriarchal than rational; the idea that one who is capable of emotion and sensitivity is incapable of discipline and rational judgment is absurd. We need not fear to consider that women's experience and world may have developed in us a particular ability to live and act more lovingly, more considerately. It bespeaks no *undesirable* softness (again, the Martial belief that "softness" is contemptible), no lack of intellect or strength.

It appears to me that women are very much concerned with the human and the loving, and that most of us do exercise an immense ability to understand, nurture, and support, a fact of which we may be duly proud. There is a problem, however, with our concern for concern, for in patriarchy our commitment and ability to love can become distorted. Since love and service are prescribed as women's only allowable activities, they are forced out of perspective and out of proportion. In male-identified women, loving can become disproportionate: first, in that loving and serving others is not kept in balance with loving and caring for oneself; and second, in that the activities and interests of love are not balanced by other kinds of interests and activities, and indeed often crowd out other sources of pleasure, satisfaction, and meaning. Such a situation is destructive, creating an overdependence on the exchanges of love (or some distorted facsimile) and an inability to draw on other resources.

Romance and love are important to men, but so are a lot of other things. Woman's prescribed role as subordinate housekeeper and her prescribed passive, dependent, and emotional character are at the heart of the saying that love is central for women, but peripheral for men; that for women, love is abstract, emotional, and spiritual, whereas for men it is concrete, physical, and sexual. In relation to love, women and men move in two different realities, and that is the rub.

How does traditional marriage turn the differences in male and female loving into the asymmetry of its emotional economy? Wives and husbands, that is to say, women and men who happen to be married, both need love and nurture, although their expression of that need and the way they relate to it may differ. But given traditional female/male role definition, husbands are far more likely than wives to have that need well satisfied. Women, trained as we are for caring and service, often treat fulfilling another's needs not only as an obligation, a task, or responsibility, but as a desirable activity, something we wish to do. We are in a sense "aggressive" about taking the initiative in caring; ferreting out, anticipating, or pursuing the emotional needs of those we love. We want to "help." Just as we might to a child, we often say to a mate (although not necessarily in these words), "Let me take care of you, let me 'mother' you."

But who is mothering Mother? Trained to see unrestricted tenderness as effeminate, uncomfortable with feeling in general and need in particular, the traditional male is not usually adept at that aspect of the caring and emotional exchange termed *psychological nurturance*. For men in patriarchy, love is to be expressed not directly, emotionally, on a one-to-one basis, but indirectly through providing, through modeling, and through caring for the material possessions of the family. Such indirect provision can be a form of expressing love, but in the husband/wife division of labor, it is a form of caring in which the wife once again makes equal, if not greater, contributions. Husbands work, but wives work too, only their work is not defined or recognized or compensated. Furthermore, in terms of service and love, a wife's work is considerably more direct, personal, and expressive. She not only prepares food, but prepares his favorite food; not only cleans clothes, but maintains his personal items in an intimate and personal way.

It is often said that men express their most intimate feelings through their sexual lovemaking, and this may be true. One cannot now presume to know how often or in what degree it is true. Yet in journals, conferences, workshops, and consciousness-raising groups, women of all ages have revealed that they very often sense a lack of emotional contact with their mates in sex. It appears that although women and men are both capable of separating love and sex, women are considerably less apt to do so, particularly with their mates.

Yet if there were no qualifications, if it were true that a man typically expresses his love equally, though differently, through provision and through sex, it would not alleviate the matter of his wife's not receiving adequate emotional support and nurturance. The need for intimate contact in the realm of feeling and understanding is profound and important; few can do well without it. The fact is that wives do get less of this kind of contact, less attention, less direct concern. There is great imbalance in the emotional economy of the patriarchal couple.

After-Marriage: Divorce and Widowhood

Few consider as they "walk down the aisle" that marriages end, either in divorce or in death. Since in our culture one is never free of a once-married state, but instead is always perceived as a "formerly married person," when a marriage ends there follows a period of after-marriage, a time with its own particular character and issues, a time that ends either in remarriage or in death. It is a time experienced more by women than by men, since women are more frequently widowed than men, more men than women remarry after the death of a spouse or divorce, and men remarry sooner. It is a time experienced very differently by women and by men, since social attitudes and judgments toward the unmarried, social rules and options (such as dating behavior or age expectations), and economic environments are frequently determined by sex.

The character and quality of one's life and experience in after-marriage are largely determined by the arrangements and life decisions made by the partners earlier. Quite naturally, the seeds sown in marriage continue to be harvested at its end. As we might expect, the woman of a traditional marriage, a woman who has built her life around and patterned her behaviors after the prescribed patriarchal model, truncated and distorted as it is, is apt to find her condition after marriage similarly truncated and distorted. Traditional imperatives fix a woman's whole identity within her marriage and make her dependent on it in a very profound way; the more traditional the arrangements of the relationship, the more profound the dependence. Passivity, economic and psychological dependence on one's mate, withdrawal from confrontation with public life, and discouragement from developing resources outside of marriage do not bode well for life outside marriage, that is, after-marriage. To live life alone well and happily requires personal strength, preparation, and experience, none of which are encouraged in women in patriarchal marriage. Hence the wife as ex-wife or widow is likely to suffer tremendously at her marriage's end and for some time thereafter, even if she grows considerably, for she has lost valuable time.

Although the experiences of divorce and widowhood have some fundamental and important differences, in patriarchy they have much in common. A widow and a divorcée are both once-were wives, having had similar roles and identity prescriptions in their former lives. They both are perceived and treated as half-beings, anomalies in a universe of couples. They are generally unprepared both economically and psychologically for life alone; and they frequently have the same burdens — children to raise alone, hostility or tolerant contempt from outsiders, increased responsibilities with decreased resources.

The Feminine Role in Marriage: A Setup

Typically in our culture a woman marries young, directly out of high school, during college or right after. Before or without settling career questions, before becoming independent or self-sufficient, she moves out of her parents' home, or away from her roommates, into the home she shares with her husband. Directly she settles into the wife's role and lifestyle, forming her adult character, norms, and expectations and determining her future through decisions made within the economic and social structures of her marriage.

THE ECONOMIC SETUP A typical patriarchal wife works at home, parenting and housekeeping, during a large portion of her life. That is her primary occupation, her expenditure of energy. In her work at home she accrues neither savings of her own, nor salary, nor social security benefits, nor workmen's compensation, nor pension. She develops no special marketable skills, no experience, no work history, no seniority. On the open market she's worth little or nothing; in fact, the longer she has maintained her home posture, the less she is worth outside.

A traditional wife may work outside the home, especially if her income is absolutely necessary for the family's subsistence. The wife's salary is generally treated as an augmentation of the husband's. Since in the patriarchal context neither mate perceives the wife's job as primary, little attention is likely to be paid to the quality of the job situation, its potential for growth or advancement, its benefits and status in the work world. Even professionally trained women may settle for irregular positions or status. And because patriarchy prescribes that the husband's job is more important than the wife's, wives must quit work to follow transferred husbands; they must be the ones who stay home from work to care for sick babies or mate; they must accommodate their work behavior to the needs of their families. Such expectations and behaviors do not make for professionalism or the rewards that follow upon it. In essence, during marriage a husband builds a career, a future, marketable skills, experience, and seniority. But a wife who invests her time, energy, and service in promoting her husband's financial future, mistakenly believing it to be her own, is impoverishing her own earning potential and independent economic security.

A majority of wives are procurement officers for their households. They shop, not only for groceries, but often for furniture, household goods, and private and personal needs. For this reason, they often pay bills, keep the checkbook and the records, and do the banking. Yet despite claims to the contrary, dependent wives do not "control" the money in the family or the nation, except as delegated. They execute policy, they do not form it. Patriarchal wives may make such momentous decisions as which toilet paper to buy or where to purchase their vegetables (hence their manipulation by advertising media), but they must wait for their husbands to outline the larger budget — how much money to spend on food or clothes or mortgage, when to replace an appliance. The intricacies of insurance, long-range planning and budgeting, and investments are generally left to the male in the traditional household.

Furthermore, although the wife may sign the check or the credit card, she usually does so under her husband's name. Until recently wives could not have their own charge accounts, and the homemaker without salary still cannot. The result — the wife accrues no credit of her own; it all goes to Mr. and Mrs. X (or, more succinctly, to Mr. X). At the end of marriage, these financial chickens will very likely come home to roost.

THE SOCIAL SETUP One of the really delightful aspects of marriage, when it goes well, is the friendly companionship, the opportunity to talk, to do things with one another, to interact with others in a kind of community, to have company and sharing in work and play. And yet this very positive facet of the relationship is a two-edged sword; unbalanced by the functioning existence of two separate realms of being for each partner, "togetherness" can be a trap. In patriarchy, it is usually the wife who lacks the separate realm of being.

A traditional wife's lifestyle, made up of the concrete details of her day, is built around her husband. She sleeps with him, rises with him, takes breakfast and dinner with him. She plans her day around him, work and play. Rarely does a traditional wife socialize in mixed company without her husband. Outside of occasional all-female events, socializing occurs in couples: one invites the Smiths and the Joneses for dinner or goes out for an evening with the Browns, two by two. It would be unusual for the typical wife to go to a party by herself, unescorted at least by another couple. She is not likely to travel any distance alone, or to vacation or play or dine out or go to a theater by herself — or even with another woman except in rare instances. A traditional married friend of mine laughingly reported that she and her husband were "joined at the hip." In traditional marriage, coupledom reigns.

A "togetherness" marriage does not encourage women to develop companion or buddy relationships with other women or even with men, and it inhibits the growth of a life outside of marriage. Isolated in her home during the day, with the children and/

or her husband in the evening, with couples on the weekend, the traditional wife develops a social existence, together with a perspective on interaction, that is based almost entirely within marriage and the world of couples.

A patriarchal wife's social status and identity too are grounded squarely within her marriage. She is John's wife — John the mechanic, John whose last name (and therefore hers) is Smith, John whose social status (and therefore hers) is X. Her friends are friends of the marriage, attached to the couple collectively, rarely to either of them individually. These things are more true of a woman in marriage than of a man. It is she who takes on his name and the social standing of his work, she who must live where his work is, she who entertains his business friends or working buddies. It is she, moreover, at home with reduced opportunity for people contact, with little interest in her own work or future, who builds her life space around the world of her husband, whatever its character and potential.

Feminists often quip, "In marriage two become one, and he's the one!" In the traditional household, for the homemaking wife, this is very nearly so. Imagine the extent of the trauma to one so completely absorbed in a marriage, if that union should end.

Dénouement: The Experience of After-Marriage

Typically, the patriarchal wife has put all her eggs into one basket; she has built her life around her marriage. How does she find herself at that marriage's end?

THE DIVORCÉE The longer and more traditionally a woman has lived as a patriarchal wife, the more her whole being has been adapted to one kind of existence, and the harder will be her transition into and experience of a new life. A great proportion of divorces occur well into marriages, after ten, twenty, even thirty years.

The divorced patriarchal wife is apt to find herself financially strapped. She has probably been left with the house (after all, there are three children who must be sheltered), but maintenance of that home is likely to pose problems. Mortgage payments are usually too high for what salary she may get (between 60 and 80 percent of former wives do not receive child support or alimony), and she is usually unable through inexperience to deal with repairs herself. Maintenance people must be hired, usually at exorbitant rates. Perhaps she has been awarded the family car. How long will it be before it too begins to fail, and how able will she be to replace it and maintain payments?

A job is in order. What is she trained for or ready for? Who wants her after ten or twenty-nine years outside the job market? What salary is she likely to earn? If she worked during her marriage at an "auxiliary" job, how likely is it to supply the entire needs of her family now if it was only auxiliary earlier? If her children are young, she must bear the burden of full-time work and full-time single parenting in the intensely difficult emotional environment of after-marriage. If she is one of the minority of women who receive some financial contributions from their ex-husbands, she must bear the burden of continued dependence, fretful interactions with him, and all the problems that emanate from that circumstance.

Responsibility lies heavily on her life. Her children's psychological, financial, and material needs must be met. She must return to work, an alien experience, maintain the semblance of a stable home, and at the same time deal with her own sense of loss and anxiety. There is too little time, too little money, too little peace.

Loneliness closes in. Inexperienced at cultivating friendships, at seeking out and encouraging camaraderie, resistant to the different modes of interaction in single life, she finds at the same time that her old friends are dropping away. They are couples; she, a single, is no longer part of their world, the world she had with her husband. To the community of couples, the single woman is a pariah; more so the divorcée because of the image she carries of wantonness, danger, threat. Seeking new relationships, she often finds something different from what is sought. When a woman leaves her marriage, she takes on a new image and a new status in male/female encounters. It is assumed that she is "on the prowl," and she often finds herself treated as a sexual mark. A new "meaningful relationship"? The later the divorce, the less likely, and the more limited her range of options.

Resentful, lonely, frightened, the divorced patriarchal wife has a good deal of building to do. It can be done, and frequently is done, but the prescriptions of patriarchy — "femininity," wifely subordination, and social discrimination — make the challenge a difficult one.

THE WIDOW Much that is true of the divorcée is true of the widow. Also financially strapped,[10] thrust into loneliness and new responsibilities, the widow discovers she has lost more than a husband. She has lost status and identity as well. No longer a part of a couple, she too becomes a pariah in her singleness, intensified as it is by the stigma of death that she is perceived to carry. Friends who were so kind "at the end" drift away, embarrassed by her grief, uncomfortable with her new condition as not quite whole.

---

[10] Carol J. Barrett, "Women in Widowhood," *Signs*, 2, No. 4 (Summer 1978), 856.

Living with Oneself

There are two alternatives: married or ————. What's the other term? Unmarried? Single? Each of these terms has the ring of "wrongness." *Unmarried* is clearly the negative of married, which is the norm, the "natural" and acceptable and positive state in our society. *Single* implies that there must be a double. The wrongness intimated by the terms is the wrongness assigned to the state, and I cannot find a term in our language for the unmarried state in women (*bachelor* is male) that does not carry with it a linguistic stigma.

It would be better, feminists believe, to focus elsewhere when considering alternatives. The crucial question (although our culture would disagree) is not whether we are married or unmarried or after-married, but whether we are whole or not whole, whether we are living fully and well or not. If we can be successful at living *with* ourselves, then the matter of whether or not we live *by* ourselves becomes secondary (though not unimportant). The ability and capacity to function well and happily with oneself and for oneself, encouraged to some extent in men, is discouraged in women in patriarchy. Self-sufficient, viable women do not make good servants. They make happier people, however, and, should they choose, better companions.

Living well, achieving peace and what happiness is afforded on this most peculiar planet, requires many hard-won qualities: personal strength, courage, discipline, balance, perspective, endurance, humor, compassion, and intelligence. It requires a sense of self-worth, a sense of the integrity and inviolability of one's own being, a sense of pride. It requires self-awareness and understanding. It requires preparation, training, and experience, the wherewithal to use one's power in advantageous ways in whatever circumstances one finds oneself. It requires a commitment made to the self to live well, to choose life for its own sake. When a person comes to see that there is good in the experiencing of good, that there is joy in doing what is personally meaningful, then one is prepared to live with oneself, alone or in company. When one keeps in mind that ultimately we walk quite by ourselves in this life, that for many reasons other people and other circumstances come and go, that we must always depend first on ourselves to meet our needs, emotional or material, then one does not relinquish one's power or safety into another's keeping.

A woman, as well as a man, must foster and maintain her own personal integrity and viability, whatever her circumstances or relationships, however much she may love another or commit herself. In that case, she does not as a female take upon herself any greater risks than are already presented to women quite naturally by life and society, but rather diminishes them, and she greatly increases the likelihood of happiness. A woman so described, independent, capable, viable, may not be the darling of patriarchy. She may find herself out of step with many and rejected by some. But she is far more a person, more fully able to relate to those who would accept her, more likely to contribute to her whole community. Besides, the alternative is destructive.

Our Bodies: Negotiable Chattel

With few exceptions the history of thought and philosophy has rarely given important space to the manner in which one relates to one's own body in the formation of the self-image. Possibly because of masculist fear of sensuality and feelings,[11] or because men as a class have so long had control over their own bodies, "intellectuals" (until very recently) have given the subject short shrift. Nonetheless, our bodies are the material representations of ourselves, both to others and to ourselves. On many levels, from the superficial (such as the way we dress) to the very profound (such as the way we encounter and treat own own decay), the treatment and attitudes we perceive directed toward our bodies often determine the way we see the other aspects of ourselves. The relationship between our physical selves and our psycho-social selves is very close.

If we look about, we can see many examples of the psycho-social importance of control over one's body and its needs. One of the first and most compelling forms of control exercised over new army recruits, one that molds them into obedience and dependence, is the control the authorities take over their physical selves, through appearance (in dress and hair), through management of body functions (eating, sleeping, elimination), and through providing for body needs (from medical treatment to cigarettes). It has been reported that one of the major factors in the breakdown of resistance in victims of Nazi concentration camps was the removal of their clothing and their subjection to other physical humiliations. To a lesser extent, the same thing is true in prisons. Studies in the psychology of nursing and hospital care point out that a patient's loss of control over the care of her or his own body, apart from the illness itself, often leads to a diminution of the sense of health and well-being, and therefore patients are to be encouraged to meet their own physical needs as much as possible. Nowhere, of course, can we see more clearly the close relationship between body control and confident, independent maturity than in the development of children. With each new step toward meeting physical needs and wants, with each step away from control

11 See Sheila Ruth, "Methodocracy, Misogyny, and Bad Faith: Sexism in the Philosophical Establishment," *Metaphilosophy*, January 1979.

through physical discipline, the child grows in independence and viability.

Because in patriarchy, in our world, it is the class of men as a whole, not women, who wield power over the circumstances and exigencies of women's physical selves, women can be reduced to the status of dependent children. Through the institutionalization of masculine authority — in medicine, education, politics, communication, and law enforcement — and through brute power, men have obtained for themselves the use, maintenance, even "protection" of women's bodies. Until conditions change, women are in the childlike position of seeking out the *pater* for the satisfaction of physical needs and for the determination of the disposition of our bodies.

Appearance

Let us begin with something that might seem superficial (but is not): our appearance. We saw in Chapter 4 that women are taught very early that the way we come into this world is not the way we ought to remain. Unlike men, who are expected to groom and reorder themselves in small ways, we are pressed to conform in very profound ways to the current ideal of physical attractiveness. Who sets the standards of female beauty? Certainly not women, although properly conditioned and prodded we avidly pursue the entire business for approval of the patriarchs. It is men who design fashions, who control the media, the advertising, the magazines, the films, the cosmetic firms, the department stores, and who ultimately manipulate us into believing we set the trends.

To adorn and paint one's body out of a *self-defined* love of play and color may be self-expressive and healthy. To reject one's natural self and subject it instead to the requirements of an *alien* mold created by a separate reigning group for their interests, to

yield one's physical representation for another's approval and protection, is destructive, because it is so terribly close to yielding one's intricately related psychological and spiritual self.

"I am, physically and nonphysically, who I am" is authentic. "I am and will become what the whim of the ruling patriarchs wish me to be" is near nonexistence.

Health

When children are troubled with physical ailments, they must seek out their guardians for help. So must women. There being relatively few women in health practice (a situation deftly arranged by patriarchy), when we are ill or face physical changes and "passages," *by law* and by custom we must turn to those formally charged with our care: men. Consider how absurd and humiliating men would think it if they had to ask women for assistance whenever they had a urinary disorder, a dysfunction of the penis, or a sexual or reproductive problem! In any sane world pregnancy and childbirth would be women's province. Yet in our world it is men, through the American Medical Association and the American Hospital Association, who determine almost entirely how these experiences are to proceed, where and how we are to give birth, what procedures will be followed, who may accompany us, who may assist. Women, at home or in clinics, may not legally contribute even informally in these affairs unless they are licensed by male-controlled agencies of various kinds.

Research into female medical needs, into surgical techniques and drug therapy for a variety of female experiences from menopause to depression, is carried on almost exclusively by males with the aid and support of the giant (male-dominated) research and grant agencies. Under policy and practice written by men, male physicians develop, prescribe, and test contraceptives for women and may withhold them if they choose, not without a certain degree of misogyny, as Ellen Frankfort and Barbara Seaman have pointed out.[12]

Through entrance into medical schools, licensing, lobby, and legislation, patriarchy limits the participation and authority of women in health care, hence over our own care. Historically the AMA and AHA have fought any growth of power and prestige in the nursing associations. Now men are being encouraged to join the nursing profession to "raise the level of the profession," and, in passing, to capture the more highly skilled and highly paid positions of authority in hospital nursing programs and in the American Nursing Association.

Control over our reproductive and medical needs is exacerbated by masculist/masculine control over the law. Women have little power in the making of policy because, as you will see in the following chapter, we are systematically excluded from anything like full participation in government — legislative, executive, or judicial on any level. Legal policy regarding reproduction, contraception, abortion, and illegitimacy is written, interpreted, and executed essentially by men.

The matter of abortion is extremely complex both ethically and legally, and the arguments for and against are numerous and complicated. The following three points are crucial: First, in determining the matter of abortion laws and statutes, supreme court decisions, and constitutional amendments, great care must be taken to distinguish legal rights and responsibilities from what one perceives to be moral obligations. There are many acts

one might wish performed or not performed, on moral or ethical grounds, that cannot or should not be compelled or prohibited by law. Second, attention should be paid to the matter of consistency. People not actively or even ideologically opposed to killing in war or by capital punishment are clamoring for laws against the killing of a not-yet-conscious fetus. People little concerned with the quality of the ensuing life of either mother or child are determined to maintain the biological life. Although it is fallacious to attack an argument on the basis of who proposes it, the question of motivation may always be pertinent. Motivation is at the psychological heart of discrimination — as when one discriminates between two kinds of "killing": one (war) allowable, the other (abortion) not — and therefore is at the heart of oppression. Third, it is valuable to place the entire issue in historical context. There are strong analogies to the movement in the 1930s to legalize the prescription, use, and sale of contraceptives. Those in favor argued, as today, on the grounds of constitutionality, personal freedom, the quality of life for all, and the benefits of population control to society. Then, as now, their opponents accused them of immorality, murder (of future generations), opposition to God's will, and the destruction of the family and the social order. Consider the lessons to be learned from this.

Sexuality

The matter of women's sexuality is a large and many-faceted topic, rarely treated seriously in intellectual exchange. Yet in the analysis of our life space, our sexuality is an extremely important issue. It is ironic, as well as indicative of the role we are to play in patriarchal society, that the aspect of our nature that is considered definitive of us by the male hegemony is also the aspect of our-

---

[12] Ellen Frankfort, *Vaginal Politics* (New York: Quadrangle, 1972); Barbara Seaman, *Free and Female* (New York: Coward, McCann & Geoghegan, 1972).

selves from which we are commanded to be the most alienated.

In Chapter 3 we saw that, except for our role as Mother (procreator or nurturer), our only function in patriarchy is to serve as sexual Playmate. In the patriarchal environment we are submerged in that guise. Our clothing is designed, our movements are trained, and our behavior is coached to be seductive. And yet, though sex and appearing sexy is so much a prescribed part of the curriculum, for women the enjoyment of sex or sensuality, the use of sex to women's own ends, has been prohibited.

The women's movement has argued that in patriarchy women are all reduced to the status of "sex objects." That does not mean merely that we are sometimes the object of sexual interest or desire (which we might all on some occasion wish to be), but that we are formally perceived and treated as objects for sex, sex-things. Unlike a human being, a thing is not perceived to have feelings, needs, and rights, because a thing is not perceived as a subjectivity, a conscious perceptual center. In patriarchy, women in their sexual roles are ideally to function not as self-affirming, self-fulfilling human beings, but as beautiful dolls to be looked at, touched, felt, experienced for arousal, used for titillation (for sexual release or the sale of merchandise), to be enjoyed, consumed, and ultimately used up and traded in for a newer model thing. We may respond or even enjoy, but not for our own pleasure (only bad women are selfish) but for the greater pleasure of the user. Our sexual role in patriarchy is to be acted upon, not to act ourselves, except insofar as this served the users' interest or needs.

Full sexuality and sensuality is utterly conscious and healthily self-centered as well as other-centered. As long as we accept the patriarchal image of women as copulating machines, as long as we allow ourselves to be washed, perfumed, painted, and dressed

like the ultimate sex object in *Story of O*,[13] playing a part, totally selfless, there will be alienation in sex and alienation from our bodies. In patriarchy, women are objectified, passive, and self-abnegating, but authentic functioning sexuality is subjective, forceful, and self-affirming.

Perhaps there is much to be learned from lesbian love and sex. As women loving women because they are women, lesbians point out that they are in a special position with regard to liberating female sexuality. Free of the social politics of dominance and submission, free of the usual gender-based roles and prescriptions, more positive and self-affirming, more acutely aware of the needs of their partners because, in a sense, they are their partners, lesbian women contend that they are more able to discover and express authentic female sexuality than their heterosexual counterparts. Certainly the experiences of many lesbian couples have valuable implications for any nonexploitative relationships.

Protection

In the system of chivalry, men protect women against men. This is not unlike the protection relationship which the Mafia established with small businesses in the early part of this century. Indeed, chivalry is an age-old protection racket which depends for its existence on rape.[14]

Ordinarily, nations and cultures grant their membership the right of self-protection. Self-defense is deemed both natural and appropriate. In patriarchy, however, so far as women are concerned, that is not true. No written

[13] Pauline Reage, *Story of O*, trans. Sabine d'Estrée (New York: Grove Press, 1965).

[14] Susan Griffin, "Rape: The All-American Crime," *Ramparts*, 10 (September 1971), 30.

law prohibits us from defending our persons against attack; that would be unthinkable! Instead we are kept from defending ourselves by two main devices: (1) The kinds of attack directed specifically against women (such as rape or many forms of prostitution), are simply defined away as not an attack or not a crime. The burden is shifted to the victim to prove not only that certain acts take place but that they are indeed criminal. (2) The entire set of behavioral rules and presuppositions imposed on women through the requirements of "femininity" render us passive, weak, and unable to defend ourselves, nor are we allowed by law to compensate physically, with weapons or similar protective devices, for our lesser strength and size. In patriarchy, men as a class are charged with the protection of women. This is ironic, since for the most part it is men as a class from whom we must be protected. It is men who rape, batter, exploit, and prostitute women for their own interests.

Nor is the issue easily explained away by the proposition that the part of the group that attacks is different from that part that defends. The same man who rapes may also be a husband or lover, though not necessarily of the raped woman. The same man who batters and beats a woman frequently is her own husband or lover. When one accepts friendship or companionship from a man, a date, a ride, a dinner, one cannot be sure what payment may be exacted, even forcefully, in return.

Those who, like slaves or prisoners, are not permitted or are not able to defend themselves against any kind of attack by any thing or person are deprived of a basic prerequisite to freedom, integrity, confidence, viability, and independence. It matters little whether the prohibition to self-defense is imposed by law or by lore. Total dependence on others for protection, particularly when those others are the very persons from whom one must be protected, is not workable.

It may be said that women are not protected simply by men, but by law, the courts, judges, and the police. Feminists point out that the percentage of women in legislatures, courts, and police forces is small; the number who have any power in those areas is smaller yet, and they are hampered by a legacy of masculist decision making.

Women beaten and battered by their husbands are only now beginning to receive even meager attention. Women raped and abused — by strangers, lovers, or relatives — have little recourse and receive little restitution. Women are forced by a patriarchal economy and society to barter their bodies for goods and survival, and they are harassed and imprisoned. The use of brute force by men against women, in an environment in which we may not defend ourselves, is an act of political terror meant to keep us in the "place" devised for us.

Conclusion

This discussion has barely begun to uncover the many facets and layers of women's more private experiences in patriarchy. There is much more to examine, much more to tell, but that will have to happen in another place. The story up to now has necessarily been harsh and polemical. As feminists point out, recognition of some of the harsh realities is the first spur to change. Change will meet resistance, and resistance begets resistance.

There are, however, positive elements to keep firmly in mind. Having been excluded from the inner power circle of patriarchy, women have also not been absorbed by it. Women have a unique position in society in that we have a more rounded, more balanced apprehension of it. Having lived and grown and studied in patriarchy, we know it intimately. Having lived on its periphery, often in contest with it, we understand it more critically. We are therefore in a much stronger position to change and heal it than those more nearly at its center. We have extraordinary social contributions to make.

We have, too, special options in our personal lives. Many have contended that the character of our experience and the more satisfying life that flows from it are born of challenge. I believe that, and so do many other feminists.

It is extremely difficult to break from the familiar, which is comfortable even in its inadequacy. It is difficult to alter behaviors, relationships, and values that hold at least some good and some attraction for us in order to move toward something that we can only dimly see at times, but something that we know must be better. May Sarton has said, "It is only when we can believe that we are creating the soul that life has any meaning, but when we can believe it — and I do and always have — then there is nothing we do that is without meaning and nothing that we suffer that does not hold the seed of creation in it." [15] Because the oppression of women has been in large part an oppression of our souls (our character, our integrity, and our spirit), feminist activism is as much as anything else an attempt to reclaim our souls, to rebuild them. This is the source of the buoyant excitement so many feminists carry, even side by side with the pain of recognition. It is the source of our pride in the achievements and successes we win. Rewards are only as great as the risks one has to take to gain them.

[15] May Sarton, *Journal of a Solitude* (New York: Norton, 1973), p. 67.

Selections

LOVE

SHULAMITH FIRESTONE

Shulamith Firestone was one of the founders of the women's liberation movement. She participated in the creation of Redstockings and the New York Radical Feminists. Her *Dialectic of Sex,* now a classic in the movement, appeared in 1970, as did *Notes,* a radical feminist journal that she co-edited.

"Love," argues Firestone, "perhaps even more than childbearing, is the pivot of women's oppression today." Women's need for love is known, almost to the point of cliché, but men's dependence on it is rarely articulated and understood, for men are wont to deny it. Although they use and (parasitically) live off the energy of women's love, Firestone contends, they do not return it in kind. Ultimately love comes to mean very different things to women and to men and has divergent effects on their respective experiences and lives.

A book on radical feminism that did not deal with love would be a political failure. For love, perhaps even more than childbearing, is the pivot of women's oppression today. I realize this has frightening implications: Do we want to get rid of love?

The panic felt at any threat to love is a good clue to its political significance. Another sign that love is central to any analysis of women or sex psychology is its omission from culture itself, its relegation to "personal life." (And whoever heard of logic in the bedroom?) Yes, it is portrayed in novels, even metaphysics, but in them it is described, or better, recreated, not analyzed.

Love has never been *understood,* though it may have been fully *experienced,* and that experience communicated.

There is reason for this absence of analysis: *Women and Love are underpinnings. Examine them and you threaten the very structure of culture.*

The tired question "What were women doing while men created masterpieces?" deserves more than the obvious reply: Women were barred from culture, exploited in their role of mother. Or its reverse: Women had no need for paintings since they created children. Love is tied to culture in much deeper ways than that. Men were thinking, writing, and creating, because women were pouring their energy into those men; women are not creating culture because they are preoccupied with love.

That women live for love and men for work is a truism. Freud was the first to attempt to ground this dichotomy in the individual psyche: the male child, sexually rejected by the first person in his attention, his mother, "sublimates" his "libido" — his reservoir of sexual (life) energies — into long term projects, in the hope of gaining love in a more generalized form; thus he displaces his need for love into a need for recognition. This process does not occur as much in the female: most women never stop seeking direct warmth and approval.

There is also much truth in the clichés that "behind every man there is a woman," and that "women are the power behind [read: voltage in] the throne." (Male) culture was built on the love of women, and at their expense. Women provided the substance of those male masterpieces; and for millennia they have done the work, and suffered the costs, of one-way emotional relationships the benefits of which went to men and to the work of men. So if women are a parasitical class living off, and at the margins of, the male economy, the reverse too is true: (*Male*) *culture was* (*and is*) *parasitical, feeding on the emotional strength of women without reciprocity.*

Moreover, we tend to forget that this culture is not universal, but rather sectarian, presenting only half the spectrum. The very structure of culture itself, as we shall see, is saturated with the sexual polarity, as well as being in every degree run by, for, and in the interests of male society. But while the male half is termed all of culture, men have not forgotten there is a female "emotional" half: They live it on the sly. As the result of their battle to reject the female in themselves (the Oedipus Complex as we have explained it) they are unable to take love seriously as a cultural matter; but they can't do without it altogether. Love is the underbelly of (male) culture just as love is the weak spot of every man, bent on proving his virility in that large male world of "travel and adventure." Women have always known how men need love, and how they deny this need. Perhaps this explains the peculiar contempt women so universally feel for men ("men are so dumb"), for they can see their men are posturing in the outside world. . . .

But abstractions about love are only one more symptom of its diseased state. (As one female patient of Reik so astutely put it, "Men take love either too seriously or not seriously enough.") Let's look at it more concretely, as we now experience it in its corrupted form. Once again we shall quote from the Reikian Confessional. . . .

WOMEN:

Later on he called me a sweet girl. . . . I didn't answer . . . what could I say? . . . but I knew I was not a sweet girl at all and that he sees me as someone I'm not.

No man can love a girl the way a girl loves a man.

I can go a long time without sex, but not without love.

It's like H$_2$O instead of water.

I sometimes think that all men are sex-crazy and sex-starved. All they can think about when they are with a girl is going to bed with her.

Have I nothing to offer this man but this body?

I took off my dress and my bra and stretched myself out on his bed and waited. For an instant I thought of myself as an animal of sacrifice on the altar.

I don't understand the feelings of men. My husband has me. Why does he need other women? What have they got that I haven't got?

Believe me, if all wives whose husbands had affairs left them, we would only have divorced women in this country.

After my husband had quite a few affairs, I flirted with the fantasy of taking a lover. Why not? What's sauce for the gander is sauce for the goose. . . . But I was stupid as a goose: I didn't have it in me to have an extramarital affair.

I asked several people whether men also sometimes cry themselves to sleep. I don't believe it.

MEN (for further illustration, see *Screw*):

It's not true that only the external appearance of a woman matters. The underwear is also important.

It's not difficult to make it with a girl. What's difficult is to make an end of it.

The girl asked me whether I cared for her mind. I was tempted to answer I cared more for her behind.

"Are you going already?" she said when she opened her eyes. It was a bedroom cliché whether I left after an hour or after two days.

Perhaps it's necessary to fool the woman and to pretend you love her. But why should I fool myself?

When she is sick, she turns me off. But when I'm sick she feels sorry for me and is more affectionate than usual.

It is not enough for my wife that I have to hear her talking all the time — blah, blah, blah. She also expects me to hear what she is saying.

Simone de Beauvoir said it: "The word love has by no means the same sense for both sexes, and this is one cause of the serious misunderstandings which divide them." Above I have illustrated some of the traditional differences between men and women in love that come up so frequently in parlor discussions of the "double standard," where it is generally agreed: That women are monogamous, better at loving, possessive, "clinging," more interested in (highly involved) "relationships" than in sex per se, and they confuse affection with sexual desire. That men are interested in nothing but a screw (Wham, bam, thank you M'am!), or else romanticize the woman ridiculously; that once sure of her, they become notorious philanderers, never satisfied; that they mistake sex for emotion. All this bears out what we have discussed — the difference in the psychosexual organizations of the two sexes, determined by the first relationship to the mother.

I draw three conclusions based on these differences:

1. That men can't love. (Male hormones?? Women traditionally expect and accept an emotional invalidism in men that they would find intolerable in a woman.)
2. That women's "clinging" behavior is necessitated by their objective social situation.
3. That this situation has not changed significantly from what it ever was.

Men can't love. We have seen why it is that men have difficulty loving and that while men may love, they usually "fall in love" — with their own projected image. Most often they are pounding down a woman's door one day, and thoroughly disillusioned with her the next; but it is rare for women to leave men, and then it is usually for more than ample reason.

It is dangerous to feel sorry for one's oppressor — women are especially prone to this failing — but I am tempted to do it in this case. Being unable to love is hell. This is the way it proceeds: as soon as the man feels any pressure from the other partner to commit himself, he panics and may react in one of several ways:

1. He may rush out and screw ten other women to prove that the first woman has no hold over him. If she accepts this, he may continue to see her on this basis. The other

women verify his (false) freedom; periodic arguments about them keep his panic at bay. But the women are a paper tiger, for nothing very deep could be happening with them anyway: he is balancing them against each other so that none of them can get much of him. Many smart women, recognizing this to be only a safety valve on their man's anxiety, give him "a long leash." For the real issue under all the fights about other women is that the man is unable to commit himself.

2. He may consistently exhibit unpredictable behavior, standing her up frequently, being indefinite about the next date, telling her that "my work comes first," or offering a variety of other excuses. That is, though he senses her anxiety, he refuses to reassure her in any way, or even to recognize her anxiety as legitimate. For he *needs* her anxiety as a steady reminder that he is still free, that the door is not entirely closed.

3. When he *is* forced into (an uneasy) commitment, he makes her pay for it: by ogling other women in her presence, by comparing her unfavorably to past girlfriends or movie stars, by snide reminders in front of friends that she is his "ball and chain," by calling her a "nag," a "bitch," "a shrew," or by suggesting that if he were only a bachelor he would be a lot better off. His ambivalence about women's "inferiority" comes out: by being committed to one, he has somehow made the hated female identification, which he now must repeatedly deny if he is to maintain his self-respect in the (male) community. This steady derogation is not entirely put on: for in fact every other girl suddenly does look a lot better, he can't help feeling he has missed something — and, naturally, his woman is to blame. For he has never given up the search for the ideal; she has forced him to resign from it. Probably he will go to his grave feeling cheated, never realizing that there isn't much

difference between one woman and the other, that it is the loving that *creates* the difference.

There are many variations of straining at the bit. Many men go from one casual thing to another, getting out every time it begins to get hot. And yet to live without love in the end proves intolerable to men just as it does to women. The question that remains for every normal male is, then, *how do I get someone to love me without her demanding an equal commitment in return?*

.   .   .

Women's "clinging" behavior is required by the objective social situation. The female *response* to such a situation of male hysteria at any prospect of mutual commitment was the development of subtle methods of manipulation, to force as much commitment as *could* be forced from men. Over the centuries strategies have been devised, tested, and passed on from mother to daughter in secret tête-à-têtes, passed around at "kaffeeklatsches" ("I never understand what it is women spend so much time talking about!"), or, in recent times, via the telephone. These are not trivial gossip sessions at all (as women prefer men to believe), but desperate strategies for survival. More real brilliance goes into one one-hour coed telephone dialogue about men than into that same coed's four years of college study, or for that matter, than into most male political maneuvers. It is no wonder, then, that even the few women without "family obligations" always arrive exhausted at the starting line of any serious endeavor. It takes one's major energy for the best portion of one's creative years to "make a good catch," and a good part of the rest of one's life to "hold" that catch. ("To be in love can be a full-time job for a woman, like that of a profession for a man.") Women who choose to drop out of this race are choosing a life without love, something that, as we have seen, most *men* don't have the courage to do.

But unfortunately The Manhunt is characterized by an emotional urgency beyond this simple desire for return commitment. It is compounded by the very class reality that produced the male inability to love in the first place. In a male-run society that defines women as an inferior and parasitical class, a woman who does not achieve male approval in some form is doomed. To legitimate her existence, a woman must be *more* than woman, she must continually search for an out from her inferior definition;* and men are the only ones in a position to bestow on her this state of grace. But because the woman is rarely allowed to realize herself through activity in the larger (male) society — and when she is, she is seldom granted the recognition she deserves — it becomes easier to try for the recognition of one man than of many; and in fact this is exactly the choice most women make. Thus once more the phenomenon of love, good in itself, is corrupted by its class context: women must have love not only for healthy reasons but actually to validate their existence.

In addition, the continued *economic* dependence of women makes a situation of healthy love between equals impossible. Women today still live under a system of patronage: With few exceptions, they have the choice, not between either freedom or marriage, but between being either public or private property. Women who merge with a member of the ruling class can at least hope that some of his privilege will, so to speak, rub off. But women without men are in the same situation as orphans: they are a helpless sub-class lacking the protection of the powerful. This is the antithesis of freedom when they are still (negatively) defined by a class situation: for now they are in a situation of *magnified* vulnerability. To participate in one's subjection by choosing one's master often gives the illusion of free choice; but in reality a woman is never free to choose love without external motivations. For her at the present time, the two things, love and status, must remain inextricably intertwined. . . .

* Thus the peculiar situation that women never object to the insulting of women as a class, *as long as* they individually are excepted. The worst insult for a woman is that she is "just like a woman," i.e., no better; the highest compliment that she has the brains, talent, or strength of a man. In fact, like every member of an oppressed class, she herself participates in the insulting of others like herself, hoping thereby to make it obvious that *she* as an individual is above their behavior. Thus women as a class are set against each other ["Divide and Conquer"], the "other woman" believing that the wife is a "bitch" who "doesn't understand him," and the wife believing that the other woman is an "opportunist" who is "taking advantage" of him — while the culprit himself sneaks away free.

THE PROBLEM THAT HAS NO NAME

BETTY FRIEDAN

Betty Friedan, born in Peoria, Illinois, in 1921 and educated at Smith College and the University of California at Berkeley, has been active in the current wave of the women's movement almost from its beginning. Some have credited her book, *The Feminine Mystique,* with precipitating the feminist dialogue among the general public. She founded NOW, the National Organization for Women, in 1966; organized the Women's Strike for Equality (1970); and co-convened the National Women's Political Caucus (1971). Having taught at several universities, Friedan is now a member of several national boards and associations.

In this selection from the first chapter of *The Feminine Mystique* Friedan describes the inchoate sense of something wrong lodged in the minds and feelings of countless American housewives, a sense that puts the lie to the "feminine mystique," the cultural image of wifely and domestic bliss. Friedan's work has power not only because it so accurately delineates the nature of the mystique, but because it captures as well the flaws in the image, the fall from grace of happily-ever-after-land.

The problem lay buried, unspoken, for many years in the minds of American women. It was a strange stirring, a sense of dissatisfaction, a yearning that women suffered in the middle of the twentieth century in the United States. Each suburban wife struggled with it alone. As she made the beds, shopped for groceries, matched slipcover material, ate peanut butter sandwiches with her children, chauffeured Cub Scouts and Brownies, lay beside her husband at night — she was afraid to ask even of herself the silent question — "Is this all?"

For over fifteen years there was no word of this yearning in the millions of words written about women, for women, in all the columns, books and articles by experts telling women their role was to seek fulfillment as wives and mothers. Over and over women heard in voices of tradition and of Freudian sophistication that they could desire no greater destiny than to glory in their own femininity. Experts told them how to catch a man and keep him, how to breastfeed children and handle their toilet training, how to cope with sibling rivalry and adolescent rebellion; how to buy a dishwasher, bake bread, cook gourmet snails, and build a swimming pool with their own hands; how to dress, look, and act more feminine and make marriage more exciting; how to keep their husbands from dying young and their

sons from growing into delinquents. They were taught to pity the neurotic, unfeminine, unhappy women who wanted to be poets or physicists or presidents. They learned that truly feminine women do not want careers, higher education, political rights — the independence and the opportunities that the old-fashioned feminists fought for. Some women, in their forties and fifties, still remembered painfully giving up those dreams, but most of the younger women no longer even thought about them. A thousand expert voices applauded their femininity, their adjustment, their new maturity. All they had to do was devote their lives from earliest girlhood to finding a husband and bearing children. . . .

The suburban housewife — she was the dream image of the young American women and the envy, it was said, of women all over the world. The American housewife — freed by science and labor-saving appliances from the drudgery, the dangers of childbirth and the illnesses of her grandmother. She was healthy, beautiful, educated, concerned only about her husband, her children, her home. She had found true feminine fulfillment. As a housewife and mother, she was respected as a full and equal partner to man in his world. She was free to choose automobiles, clothes, appliances, supermarkets; she had everything that women ever dreamed of.

In the fifteen years after World War II, this mystique of feminine fulfillment became the cherished and self-perpetuating core of contemporary American culture. Millions of women lived their lives in the image of those pretty pictures of the American suburban housewife, kissing their husbands goodbye in front of the picture window, depositing their stationwagonsful of children at school, and smiling as they ran the new electric waxer over the spotless kitchen floor. They baked their own bread, sewed their own and their children's clothes, kept their new washing machines and dryers running all day. They changed the sheets on the beds twice a week instead of once, took the rug-hooking class in adult education, and pitied their poor frustrated mothers, who had dreamed of having a career. Their only dream was to be perfect wives and mothers; their highest ambition to have five children and a beautiful house, their only fight to get and keep their husbands. They had no thought for the unfeminine problems of the world outside the home; they wanted the men to make the major decisions. They gloried in their role as women, and wrote proudly on the census blank: "Occupation: housewife." ...

If a woman had a problem in the 1950's and 1960's, she knew that something must be wrong with her marriage, or with herself. Other women were satisfied with their lives, she thought. What kind of a woman was she if she did not feel this mysterious fulfillment waxing the kitchen floor? She was so ashamed to admit her dissatisfaction that she never knew how many other women shared it. If she tried to tell her husband, he didn't understand what she was talking about. She did not really understand it herself. For over fifteen years women in America found it harder to talk about this problem than about sex. Even the psychoanalysts had no name for it. When a woman went to a psychiatrist for help, as many women did, she would say, "I'm so ashamed," or "I must be hopelessly neurotic." "I don't know what's wrong with women today," a suburban psychiatrist said uneasily. "I only know

something is wrong because most of my patients happen to be women. And their problem isn't sexual." Most women with this problem did not go to see a psychoanalyst, however. "There's nothing wrong really," they kept telling themselves. "There isn't any problem."

But on an April morning in 1959, I heard a mother of four, having coffee with four other mothers in a suburban development fifteen miles from New York, say in a tone of quiet desperation, "the problem." And the others knew, without words, that she was not talking about a problem with her husband, or her children, or her home. Suddenly they realized they all shared the same problem, the problem that has no name. They began, hesitantly, to talk about it. Later, after they had picked up their children at nursery school and taken them home to nap, two of the women cried, in sheer relief, just to know they were not alone.

Gradually I came to realize that the problem that has no name was shared by countless women in America. As a magazine writer I often interviewed women about problems with their children, or their marriages, or their houses, or their communities. But after a while I began to recognize the telltale signs of this other problem. I saw the same signs in suburban ranch houses and split-levels on Long Island and in New Jersey and Westchester County; in colonial houses in a small Massachusetts town; on patios in Memphis; in suburban and city apartments; in living rooms in the Midwest. Sometimes I sensed the problem, not as a reporter, but as a suburban housewife, for during this time I was also bringing up my own three children in Rockland County, New York. I heard echoes of the problem in college dormitories and semi-private maternity wards, at PTA meetings and luncheons of the League of Women Voters, at suburban cocktail parties, in station wagons waiting for trains, and in snatches of conversation overheard at Schrafft's. The groping words I heard from other women, on quiet afternoons when children were at school or on quiet evenings when husbands worked late, I think I understood first as a woman long before I understood their larger social and psychological implications.

Just what was this problem that has no name? What were the words women used when they tried to express it? Sometimes a woman would say "I feel empty somehow ... incomplete." Or she would say, "I feel as if I don't exist." Sometimes she blotted out the feeling with a tranquilizer. Sometimes she thought the problem was with her husband, or her children, or that what she really needed was to redecorate her house, or move to a better neighborhood, or have an affair, or another baby. Sometimes, she went to a doctor with symptoms she could hardly describe: "A tired feeling ... I get so angry with the children it scares me ... I feel like crying without any reason." (A Cleveland doctor called it "the housewife's syndrome.") A number of women told me about great bleeding blisters that break out on their hands and arms. "I call it the housewife's blight," said a family doctor in Pennsylvania. "I see it so often lately in these young women with four, five and six children who bury themselves in their dishpans. But it isn't caused by detergent and it isn't cured by cortisone." ...

.   .   .

In 1960, the problem that has no name burst like a boil through the image of the happy American housewife. In the television commercials the pretty housewives still beamed over their foaming dishpans and *Time*'s cover story on "The Suburban Wife, an American Phenomenon" protested: "Having too good a time ... to believe that they

should be unhappy." But the actual unhappiness of the American housewife was suddenly being reported — from the *New York Times* and *Newsweek* to *Good Housekeeping* and CBS Television ("The Trapped Housewife"), although almost everybody who talked about it found some superficial reason to dismiss it. It was attributed to incompetent appliance repairmen (*New York Times*), or the distances children must be chauffeured in the suburbs (*Time*), or too much PTA (*Redbook*). Some said it was the old problem — education: more and more women had education, which naturally made them unhappy in their role as housewives. "The road from Freud to Frigidaire, from Sophocles to Spock, has turned out to be a bumpy one," reported the *New York Times* (June 28, 1960). "Many young women — certainly not all — whose education plunged them into a world of ideas feel stifled in their homes. They find their routine lives out of joint with their training. Like shut-ins, they feel left out. In the last year, the problem of the educated housewife has provided the meat of dozens of speeches made by troubled presidents of women's colleges who maintain, in the face of complaints, that sixteen years of academic training is realistic preparation for wifehood and motherhood."

There was much sympathy for the educated housewife. ("Like a two-headed schizophrenic ... once she wrote a paper on the Graveyard poets; now she writes notes to the milkman. Once she determined the boiling point of sulphuric acid; now she determines her boiling point with the overdue repairman. ... The housewife often is reduced to screams and tears. ... No one, it seems, is appreciative, least of all herself, of the kind of person she becomes in the process of turning from poetess into shrew.")

Home economists suggested more realistic preparation for housewives, such as high-school workshops in home appliances. College educators suggested more discussion groups on home management and the family, to prepare women for the adjustment to domestic life. A spate of articles appeared in the mass magazines offering "Fifty-eight Ways to Make Your Marriage More Exciting." No month went by without a new book by a psychiatrist or sexologist offering technical advice on finding greater fulfillment through sex.

A male humorist joked in *Harper's Bazaar* (July, 1960) that the problem could be solved by taking away woman's right to vote. ("In the pre-19th Amendment era, the American woman was placid, sheltered and sure of her role in American society. She left all the political decisions to her husband and he, in turn, left all the family decisions to her. Today a woman has to make both the family *and* the political decisions, and it's too much for her.")

A number of educators suggested seriously that women no longer be admitted to the four-year colleges and universities: in the growing college crisis, the education which girls could not use as housewives was more urgently needed than ever by boys to do the work of the atomic age.

The problem was also dismissed with drastic solutions no one could take seriously. (A woman writer proposed in *Harper's* that women be drafted for compulsory service as nurses' aides and baby-sitters.) And it was smoothed over with the age-old panaceas: "love is their answer," "the only answer is inner help," "the secret of completeness — children," "a private means of intellectual fulfillment," "to cure this toothache of the spirit — the simple formula of handing one's self and one's will over to God." *

* See the Seventy-fifth Anniversary Issue of *Good Housekeeping*, May, 1960, "The Gift of Self," a symposium by Margaret Mead, Jessamyn West, *et al.*

The problem was dismissed by telling the housewife she doesn't realize how lucky she is — her own boss, no time clock, no junior executive gunning for her job. What if she isn't happy — does she think men are happy in this world? Does she really, secretly, still want to be a man? Doesn't she know yet how lucky she is to be a woman? . . .

Even so, most men, and some women, still did not know that this problem was real. But those who had faced it honestly knew that all the superficial remedies, the sympathetic advice, the scolding words and the cheering words were somehow drowning the problem in unreality. A bitter laugh was beginning to be heard from American women. They were admired, envied, pitied, theorized over until they were sick of it, offered drastic solutions or silly choices that no one could take seriously. They got all kinds of advice from the growing armies of marriage and child-guidance counselors, psychotherapists, and armchair psychologists, on how to adjust to their role as housewives. No other road to fulfillment was offered to American women in the middle of the twentieth century. Most adjusted to their role and suffered or ignored the problem that has no name. It can be less painful for a woman, not to hear the strange, dissatisfied voice stirring within her.

It is no longer possible to ignore that voice, to dismiss the desperation of so many American women. This is not what being a woman means, no matter what the experts say. For human suffering there is a reason; perhaps the reason has not been found because the right questions have not been asked, or pressed far enough. I do not accept the answer that there is no problem because American women have luxuries that women in other times and lands never dreamed of; part of the strange newness of the problem is that it cannot be understood in terms of the age-old material problems of man: poverty, sickness, hunger, cold. The women who suffer this problem have a hunger that food cannot fill. . . .

Can the problem that has no name be somehow related to the domestic routine of the housewife? When a woman tries to put the problem into words, she often merely describes the daily life she leads. What is there in this recital of comfortable domestic detail that could possibly cause such a feeling of desperation? Is she trapped simply by the enormous demands of her role as modern housewife: wife, mistress, mother, nurse, consumer, cook, chauffeur; expert on interior decoration, child care, appliance repair, furniture refinishing, nutrition, and education? Her day is fragmented as she rushes from dishwasher to washing machine to telephone to dryer to station wagon to supermarket, and delivers Johnny to the Little League field, takes Janey to dancing class, gets the lawnmower fixed and meets the 6:45. She can never spend more than 15 minutes on any one thing; she has no time to read books, only magazines; even if she had time, she has lost the power to concentrate. At the end of the day, she is so terribly tired that sometimes her husband has to take over and put the children to bed.

Thus terrible tiredness took so many women to doctors in the 1950's that one decided to investigate it. He found, surprisingly, that his patients suffering from "housewife's fatigue" slept more than an adult needed to sleep — as much as ten hours a day — and that the actual energy they expended on housework did not tax their capacity. The real problem must be something else, he decided — perhaps boredom. Some doctors told their women patients they must get out of the house for a day, treat themselves to a movie in town. Others prescribed tranquilizers. Many suburban housewives were taking tranquilizers like cough drops. "You wake up in the morning, and you feel as if there's no point in going on another day like this. So you take a tranquilizer because it makes you not care so much that it's pointless."

It is easy to see the concrete details that trap the suburban housewife, the continual demands on her time. But the chains that bind her in her trap are chains in her own mind and spirit. They are chains made up of mistaken ideas and misinterpreted facts, of incomplete truths and unreal choices. They are not easily seen and not easily shaken off.

How can any woman see the whole truth within the bounds of her own life? How can she believe that voice inside herself, when it denies the conventional, accepted truths by which she has been living? And yet the women I have talked to, who are finally listening to that inner voice, seem in some incredible way to be groping through to a truth that has defied the experts.

WIVING

MIDGE DECTER

Midge Decter was born in St. Paul, Minnesota, and attended the University of Minnesota and then the Jewish Theological Seminary. She has served on the staff of *Midstream* and *Commentary* magazines and as an editor of *Harper's Magazine* and at Basic Books. She is the author of *The Liberated Woman and Other Americans* (1971); *Liberal Parents, Radical*

Children (1975); and *The New Chastity and Other Arguments Against Women's Liberation* (1972), from which the following excerpt is taken.

Decter's discussion is useful to us here because (1) it states in the most positive and sophisticated terms the traditional philosophy of "complementary" marriage, and (2) it characterizes very well both what antifeminists perceive to be the stance of the women's liberation movement as well as their response to it. In Decter's view, feminists are simply spoiled petulant little girls, demanding gratification without return, seeking to avoid the responsibilities of maturity in sexual relations and in social obligation.

The Rock and the Waves

However determinedly the movement has evaded the issue by concentrating on the manipulations of men and society, the plain unvarnished fact is that every woman wants to marry. She may want in addition to be a doctor or a lawyer, to spend her days in travel or her nights being swept across a ballroom floor; she may dream of participating in great projects or quest for great power, long to be a celebrity or a recluse enjoying the ease of large stretches of solitude. But, except should some pathology, some unnatural fear or lust for punishment, erect a barrier between self and desire, she will want as a basic pinning for her life to be married. Women's Liberation in grudging acknowledgment of this fact says that women wish for marriage only because from the cradle on they are trained, if not simply blackmailed, to do so. The truth is, however — certainly, anyway, in the contemporary world — that marriage is an institution maintained and protected by women, for the sake of and at the behest of women, and in accordance with their deepest wishes. Men have, to be sure, for the most part willingly and in some measure perhaps even eagerly, supported them in this. For marriage is not

without its very great benefit to men. Nevertheless, the true balance of the situation is that marriage is something asked by women and agreed to by men.

A woman wants to be married for the simplest and most self-evident of reasons. She requires both in her nature and by virtue of what are her immediate practical needs (if indeed the two can even be separated) the assurance that a single man has undertaken to love, cherish, and support her. As a sexual being, her true freedom and self-realization lie in a sustained and ever more easy, ever more emotionally intimate commitment to one man — a commitment in which she may know herself to be desirable and to be acceptable for who and what she simply, individually is. As a social being, her true sense of value lies in activity that flows essentially from her connection to a stable personal order. And as a spiritual being, her true fulfillment lies in the exercise of her special capacity for sustaining and refining and enriching the materials of everyday existence. Some degree of freedom and self-realization, of feeling valuable and fulfilled, she must achieve by herself; and some of it depends entirely on her ability to forge for her life the conditions in which the necessary outside intervention can propitiously entertain and be brought to bear. For this she needs a husband — one man — who will agree to keep her safe while she brings forth her gifts and who by accepting these gifts will not only provide the measure of their value, and so of hers, but will help her to her own sense of having contributed fully to the human estate. . . .

Contracting the Terms

Why, then — whatever truly may be its dangers and difficulties, and they are of course considerable — should Women's Liberation seek to characterize marriage as the very model of the exploitation of women by men? Why should this institution, entered into by each individual couple for the sake of bringing a much-needed fixity and security to its female member, now be pronounced the means whereby her personhood is most utterly violated — her needs set at nothing and her wishes disregarded? Marriage in the vast majority of cases devolves upon women the obligations of housewifery, which the movement abominates for its routinization of a certain measure of selflessness. It also devolves upon them the obligations of adult heterosexuality, which the movement abominates for its imposition of the need for complicity in the all too frail and mortal existence of the Other. But beyond even these there is something the movement would deny on women's behalf: and that is the idea that for a woman to take upon herself the sharing of a single destiny with a man in any way conduces to her own welfare.

Being married is a condition described in the literature and public utterance of Women's Liberation only in terms of the services, emotional as well as practical, that it calls upon a woman to perform. The all-sympathetic and all-forbearing wife described by Judy Syfers ("My God, who *wouldn't* want a wife?") is a woman whose marriage is entirely the expression of her husband's convenience. She responds fully to his sexual advances and at the same time makes no erotic demands of her own. She undergoes the risk of Pill or messy trouble of diaphragm in order to keep *him* safely unencumbered of too many children. And she observes the sexual morality of the double standard in order that he may be free "to relate to people as fully as possible," at the same time enjoying an "intellectual life" uncluttered with jealousies. That such a wife has probably never existed (or husband either), that such an unbelievably callow perception of anything, let alone marriage, passes comfortably into the general polemic of the movement's free-swinging sexual politics, is only secondary. Miss Syfers is after all playing with us, using the weight of satiric exaggeration to make her point. That point, however, turns out to be different from the one she seems to have imagined she was making. For the author's mode works not merely to underline the bitter injustice of this wife's existence but to describe it exclusively in terms outside her own power to exercise any control. Nothing has been said about how she managed to get into such a predicament: presumably just by agreeing to marry. Miss Syfers's advertisement of wifely virtue is based upon some assumed male fantasy of perfection. Now, viewing marriage through the medium of male fantasy — a common occurrence in the movement's discussion of the subject — would seem to serve the purpose of illustrating how and why men have been so keenly intent upon marrying through the ages. Actually, though, it is an implicit confession that women are the ones who marry freely and of their own volition: were they married under duress, simply because society had in a number of ways trapped them into it, they could afford to be a great deal less concerned with the problem of what might be truly pleasing to their husbands. The wife who complains that in order to make her man happy she must meet a series of unfair demands is a wife who has in the first place promised both herself and her husband to be "good" — and finds it difficult to do so. "Why do you ask so much of me?" is the self-protective challenge thrown out by someone who has initially offered, by word or deed, to do as asked. For the movement to throw out this challenge — and throw it out, moreover, in relation to a level of wifely promise that would make most men wonder whether they had not blundered into Eden before the Fall — not only confirms that marriage has at least for some time been women's institution but that it has been one for which they feel themselves to have incurred some unhappy burden of debt.

One of the results of the movement's efforts at "consciousness raising," for instance, has been the drawing up by individual couples of a new and privately tailored marriage contract. Essentially these contracts, though they may differ in detail, all involve the effort to reorganize the family duties so as to relieve the woman of any specialized wifely ones. No particular realm — i.e., housework, nurture of the young, hospitality — is to be left to her sole attendance, and in this way she is to become truly her husband's equal. One such document merits special attention. Drawn up, or anyway first made public, in 1970, it has with good cause come to be seen as a primary working model for Liberationist marriage. This is the agreement devised by Mrs. Alix Cates Shulman. It includes a detailed breakdown and allocation of all jobs connected with looking after the children and the house:

> Cooking: Breakfasts during the week are divided equally; husband does all weekend breakfasts (including shopping for them and dishes). Wife does all dinners except Sunday nights.... Whoever invites guests does shopping, cooking and dishes....

> Cleaning: Husband does dishes Tuesday, Thursday, and Sunday. Wife does Monday, Wednesday, and Saturday. Friday is split according to who has done extra work during the week....

> Laundry:... Wife does home laundry. Husband does dry-cleaning delivery and pick-up. Wife strips beds, husband remakes them.[1]

In the Shulman household, no chore has a sexual connotation, and none is performed without its exact corresponding compensation in leisure time. Apart from what such a document reveals about the sense of life and work and human relations shared by those who privately undertake to live in accordance with it, there is considerable public significance in its endeavors to give a precise name to the network of mutual marital obligations. For in the statement of principles with which the agreement begins, there is a brief but telling reference to the question of who supports this menage whose other operations have been so minutely parceled out. And here it is made clear that the husband's financial contribution is under no circumstances to be entered on the credit side of his sheet in the family ledger:

> We reject the notion that the work which brings in more money is more valuable. The ability to earn more money is a privilege which must not be compounded by enabling the larger earner to buy out of his/her duties and put the burden on the partner who earns less or on another person hired from the outside.[2]

In other words, the husband's bearing the major burden of wage-earning is entirely irrelevant to an assessment of what he owes or what is owed to him. It is his *privilege* to make the money with which to provide a home for his wife and children. If anything, this privilege obligates him even more to household performance (note that he may not even hire a servant to "buy out" of his duties).

All this is quite in keeping with the movement's more general announcement that the system, once crudely regarded as a division of labor between the sexes, whereby men support their wives and expect in exchange a certain attention to their needs, is in reality nothing more than a plot to keep women from playing their rightful role in the world. The traditionally male side of this bargain may count for a great deal in the husband's own life: if he succeeds, he is puffed with feelings of pride, and if he fails, he suffers a severe blow in the region of his masculinity. But to the marriage itself, in the view of the movement, to the private bookkeeping of relations between husband and wife, to the safety and protection of the home, the well-being of children, his strivings in the world count virtually for nil. His career is not a contribution to but an area of liberation from his true responsibilities to marriage.

It might seem curious that at the very time when women, among them an ever growing proportion of wives and mothers, have come to take a noticeable place in the professions and in the labor force generally, wage-earning should be declared an insignificant contribution to the household welfare. One might think that women who produce income themselves would be all the more prepared to regard economic activity as an entitlement to extra consideration at home. The truth is, however, that precisely to the extent that women are discovering for themselves how very difficult — how fraught with stress and anxiety — is the activity of making one's way in the world of work, Women's Liberation has sought to devalue the currency through which participation in

that world might be traded off for domestic indulgence. Nor, given the movement's genuine underlying attitudes toward men and toward the question of women's relation to men, is there anything strange about this. Women's connection with work and the making of money, at least among the middle classes who constitute the movement's basic constituency, is that of volunteers. Married women work because it pleases them — in a variety of ways and for a variety of reasons — to do so. They are free to earn less money if doing so provides them with an opportunity to do something more interesting or satisfying to them. They are free to leave a job whose conditions are not to their liking. They are free, that is, to continue to behave like dependents. But such a relation to work prevents their being economically "equal" to their husbands — and this, regardless of how much money either of them makes. Thus women cannot relieve themselves of their debt to assume the major responsibility for supervising the running of the household unless they can declare their husbands to be volunteers as well. From this follows the idea that wage-earning is a privilege, something undertaken by men because it pleases them also, and, in short, entitling them to nothing.

But the debt for economic support is not the only, and perhaps not even the major, marital debt that Women's Liberation affirms in the very passion of its denial. Women, including the financially independent among them, have clearly required marriage for the several other forms of male support it brings them. There is the sexual commitment of one man, which the movement has termed a male conspiracy to stunt and so control women's natural erotic insatiability. There is the commitment to father and protect their children, which, as we shall see, the movement has termed a male conspiracy to exploit women's reproductive capacities for the uses of society. And probably above all, there is the commitment — difficult to define but easy to discern in the expression of women's desires — to confirm and abet and support them in their pursuit of private happiness. This Women's Liberation has termed a male strategy for tricking women into playing their necessary part in the men's pursuit of happiness. In the words of Shulamith Firestone:

> She is lifted out of the class [of merely being like all other women] because she is now an appendage of a member of the master class; and he cannot associate with her unless he raises her status. But she has not been freed, she has been promoted to "housenigger," she has been elevated only to be used in a different way.[3]

A husband's kindnesses and attentions to his wife, along with his concern that she be well housed and well fed and sexually gratified, are, that is to say, only the plans from which he means to construct a towering edifice to his own vanity. The Liberationist does not, like an ordinary nagging wife, demand more of such attentions but wishes rather to assert that they are so inadequate as to mean nothing to her. They are not, indeed, attentions to *her* at all but just a deceptive means for eroding her individual freedom. A house nigger after all is someone whose slavery has been made only a tiny bit more palatable but who is supposed to be obligated by this to be all the more slavish.

This mode of standing the marital transaction exactly on its head, of repaying, as it were, kindness with the imputation of evil motive, is no everyday form of complaint. In fact, it resembles nothing so much as the tantrum of a young child who, unable to

claim that he has received no parental indulgence, screams all the louder that such indulgence was meant in the first place to dismiss him and that thus his need is even greater than before.

What is Women's Liberation really saying about marriage? The most outspokenly radical arms of the movement, of course — like WITCH, the Redstockings, the Feminists, who include among them not only women politically committed to a complete withdrawal from men and the smashing of "their" society but also a considerable number of outright proselytizers to lesbianism — advocate the abolition of marriage altogether. Woman will live in communes, or ultimately, when society has been altered so as to include no further possibility for male-style struggle and strife, they will settle at peace among those others who have now in all but the most trivial of biological details been rendered indistinguishable from themselves. The more "moderate" Liberationists, no doubt among them women who still mean to marry or have already done so, would, short of destroying it, effect a certain reformation of the institution's basic arrangements. There is to be a new form of marriage, in which either, as decreed by such documents as Mrs. Shulman's marriage contract, the wife may regard the fulfillment of any demands but her own as a privilege — marital obligation residing exclusively in a husband's fulfillment of her desires — or in which there is neither husband nor wife but two entirely autonomous androgynes who in order not to be lonely share the same premises.

Margaret Mead, the most reliable bellwether for changes in man-woman relationships over the past thirty years, now suggests that the family of the future won't even be based on sex or a sexual relationship. Many people will get the emotional reassurance now provided by marriage from individuals of the same or opposite sex who are simpatico rather than sexually compelling.[4]

In other words, whether marriage is actually abolished or sustained, whether women are to live in communes, as lesbians, or in fully formal heterosexual coupledom, there will be no more husbands. Margaret Mead has been a bellwether, as Caroline Bird says, not for changes in man-woman relationships but for changes in the way it has been acceptably enlightened to speak about them. And the household she speaks of here is a household described in feminine terms; it is a household come into existence for emotional reassurance and based on *simpático* — neither a new rationale nor a new basis for women, but new only in its expression of a sense of marriage that makes not the least allowance for the special participation of men. The significance of its sexlessness is not that it predicts a time when men will no longer have their lusty will of women, not even their wives, but that it makes possible an image of married life from which has been expunged any idea of the alien masculine which was once so thoughtlessly accepted by women as the inevitable quid for the quo of marriage.

A world without husbands is a world without daily reminder of the obligation incurred by being married. This is an obligation that inheres in no particular details, for the details of marital exchange vary from culture to culture and yet some basic principle of marriage remains. In denouncing this, that, or the other feature of bourgeois family life, the movement does not seek to deal with, or alter, the transient implications of marriage but the universal ones. Its very falsifications — such as, for instance, that the modern middle-class wife is a timid and cowering victim of her husband's proclivities toward physical and verbal violence — bespeak its disregard of the social facts. In proclaiming that marriage is a male system created for the purpose of subjugating women, Women's Liberation seeks not to describe the experience of living women but only to express their own longing for the renunciation of their debt. For the eternal obligation of marriage, be women huntresses or debutantes, queens, breadwinners, or housekeepers, is the obligation to incorporate somewhere within one's life the settlement with a principle different from one's own. A wife need no longer keep her house, have children or, having them, tend to them, live within the means provided by her husband or in a place or in a style exclusively determined by him. Were she now to succeed in altering his role in marriage to be indistinguishable from hers, she could demand marriage — the necessary confirmation of her womanly nature — without feeling herself bound to make that one last, ultimate, and inescapable return. As with work and sex, being a wife in the way that Women's Liberation has demanded the right for her to be would help to keep her as unformed, as able to act without genuine consequence, as the little girl she imagines she once was and longs to continue to be.

Notes

1. Alix Cates Shulman, "The Shulmans' Marriage Agreement," *Ms.* (December 20, 1971), p. 72.
2. *Ibid.*, p. 72.
3. Shulamith Firestone, *The Dialectic of Sex* (New York, Bantam Books, 1971), p. 142.
4. Caroline Bird, *Born Female: The High Cost of Keeping Women Down* (New York, Pocket Books, 1969), p. xiii.

A DEFENSE OF ABORTION

JUDITH JARVIS THOMSON

Judith Jarvis Thomson, a philosopher with special interest in values and ethics, was educated at Barnard College, Cambridge University, and Columbia University. Her research has appeared in *Mind, Journal of Philosophy, Philosophical Quarterly,* and other journals. A member of many learned societies, she is currently teaching at the Massachusetts Institute of Technology.

The matter of abortion has legal, political, economic, social, and moral implications, all of which have been debated and discussed at one time or another. The moral-ethical issues, however, seem most crucial to the others and to ultimate decisions. Here Thomson treats the ethical questions: Does an unborn fetus have a "right to life" even against the rights of its mother, whose body and person must be at its disposal? What is meant by a "right to life," and on what terms can it be justified? What is the obligation of any one human being, in any circumstance, to the preservation of other life, and how does this relate to mother and child? These and other issues Thomson unfolds and attempts to confront. The experiential factors per se are not treated: for example, the social context in which pregnancies occur, wanted and unwanted, legitimate and illegitimate; the personal trauma of decision; or the host of ambivalences surrounding the emotional consequences of adoption for the biological parents. All of these are of course crucial and should be assessed. They are, however, rarely at issue in judicial decision making; Thomson's themes are.

*Most opposition to abortion relies on the premise that the fetus is a human being, a person, from the moment of conception. The premise is argued for, but, as I think, not well. Take, for example, the most common argument. We are asked to notice that the development of a human being from conception through birth into childhood is continuous; then it is said that to draw a line, to choose a point in this development and say "before this point the thing is not a person, after this point it is a person" is to make an arbitrary choice, a choice for which in the nature of things no good reason can be given. It is concluded that the fetus is, or anyway that we had better say it is, a person from the moment of conception. But this conclusion does not follow. Similar things might be said about the development of an acorn into an oak tree, and it does not follow that acorns are oak trees, or that we had better say they are. Arguments of this form are sometimes called "slippery slope arguments" — the phrase is perhaps self-explanatory — and it is dismaying that opponents of abortion rely on them so heavily and uncritically.

I am inclined to agree, however, that the prospects for "drawing a line" in the development of the fetus look dim. I am inclined to think also that we shall probably have to agree that the fetus has already become a human person well before birth. Indeed, it comes as a surprise when one first learns how early in its life it begins to acquire human characteristics. By the tenth week, for example, it already has a face, arms and legs, fingers and toes; it has internal organs, and brain activity is detectable.[1] On the

Judith Jarvis Thomson, "A Defense of Abortion," *Philosophy & Public Affairs* 1, no. 1 (Fall 1971). Copyright © 1971 by Princeton University Press. Reprinted by permission.

* I am very much indebted to James Thomson for discussion, criticism, and many helpful suggestions.

other hand, I think that the premise is false, that the fetus is not a person from the moment of conception. A newly fertilized ovum, a newly implanted clump of cells, is no more a person than an acorn is an oak tree. But I shall not discuss any of this. For it seems to me to be of great interest to ask what happens if, for the sake of argument, we allow the premise. How, precisely, are we supposed to get from there to the conclusion that abortion is morally impermissible? Opponents of abortion commonly spend most of their time establishing that the fetus is a person, and hardly any time explaining the step from there to the impermissibility of abortion. Perhaps they think the step too simple and obvious to require much comment. Or perhaps instead they are simply being economical in argument. Many of those who defend abortion rely on the premise that the fetus is not a person, but only a bit of tissue that will become a person at birth; and why pay out more arguments than you have to? Whatever the explanation, I suggest that the step they take is neither easy nor obvious, that it calls for closer examination than it is commonly given, and that when we do give it this closer examination we shall feel inclined to reject it.

I propose, then, that we grant that the fetus is a person from the moment of conception. How does the argument go from here? Something like this, I take it. Every person has a right to life. So the fetus has a right to life. No doubt the mother has a right to decide what shall happen in and to her body; everyone would grant that. But surely a person's right to life is stronger and more stringent than the mother's right to decide what happens in and to her body, and so outweighs it. So the fetus may not be killed; an abortion may not be performed.

It sounds plausible. But now let me ask you to imagine this. You wake up in the morning and find yourself back to back in bed with an unconscious violinist. A famous unconscious violinist. He has been found to have a fatal kidney ailment, and the Society of Music Lovers has canvassed all the available medical records and found that you alone have the right blood type to help. They have therefore kidnapped you, and last night the violinist's circulatory system was plugged into yours, so that your kidneys can be used to extract poisons from his blood as well as your own. The director of the hospital now tells you, "Look, we're sorry the Society of Music Lovers did this to you — we would never have permitted it if we had known. But still, they did it, and the violinist now is plugged into you. To unplug you would be to kill him. But never mind, it's only for nine months. By then he will have recovered from his ailment, and can safely be unplugged from you." Is it morally incumbent on you to accede to this situation? No doubt it would be very nice of you if you did, a great kindness. But do you *have* to accede to it? What if it were not nine months, but nine years? Or longer still? What if the director of the hospital says, "Tough luck, I agree, but you've now got to stay in bed, with the violinist plugged into you, for the rest of your life. Because remember this. All persons have a right to life, and violinists are persons. Granted you have a right to decide what happens in and to your body, but a person's right to life outweighs your right to decide what happens in and to your body. So you cannot ever be unplugged from him." I imagine you would regard this as outrageous, which suggests that something really is wrong with that plausible-sounding argument I mentioned a moment ago.

In this case, of course, you were kidnapped; you didn't volunteer for the operation that plugged the violinist into your kidneys. Can those who oppose abortion on the ground I mentioned make an exception for a pregnancy due to rape? Certainly. They can say that persons have a right to life only if they didn't come into existence because of rape; or they can say that all persons have a right to life, but that some have less of a right to life than others, in particular, that those who came into existence because of rape have less. But these statements have a rather unpleasant sound. Surely the question of whether you have a right to life at all, or how much of it you have, shouldn't turn on the question of whether or not you are the product of a rape. And in fact the people who oppose abortion on the ground I mentioned do not make this distinction, and hence do not make an exception in case of rape.

Nor do they make an exception for a case in which the mother has to spend the nine months of her pregnancy in bed. They would agree that would be a great pity, and hard on the mother; but all the same, all persons have a right to life, the fetus is a person, and so on. I suspect, in fact, that they would not make an exception for a case in which, miraculously enough, the pregnancy went on for nine years, or even the rest of the mother's life.

Some won't even make an exception for a case in which continuation of the pregnancy is likely to shorten the mother's life; they regard abortion as impermissible even to save the mother's life. Such cases are nowadays very rare, and many opponents of abortion do not accept this extreme view. All the same, it is a good place to begin: a number of points of interest come out in respect to it.

1. Let us call the view that abortion is impermissible even to save the mother's life "the extreme view." I want to suggest first that it does not issue from the argument I mentioned earlier without the addition of some fairly powerful premises. Suppose a woman has become pregnant, and now learns that she has a cardiac condition such

that she will die if she carries the baby to term. What may be done for her? The fetus, being a person, has a right to life, but as the mother is a person too, so has she a right to life. Presumably they have an equal right to life. How is it supposed to come out that an abortion may not be performed? If mother and child have an equal right to life, shouldn't we perhaps flip a coin? Or should we add to the mother's right to life her right to decide what happens in and to her body, which everybody seems to be ready to grant — the sum of her rights now outweighing the fetus' right to life?

The most familiar argument here is the following. We are told that performing the abortion would be directly killing[2] the child, whereas doing nothing would not be killing the mother, but only letting her die. Moreover, in killing the child, one would be killing an innocent person, for the child has committed no crime, and is not aiming at his mother's death. And then there are a variety of ways in which this might be continued. (1) But as directly killing an innocent person is always and absolutely impermissible, an abortion may not be performed. Or, (2) as directly killing an innocent person is murder, and murder is always and absolutely impermissible, an abortion may not be performed.[3] Or, (3) as one's duty to refrain from directly killing an innocent person is more stringent than one's duty to keep a person from dying, an abortion may not be performed. Or, (4) if one's only options are directly killing an innocent person or letting a person die, one must prefer letting the person die, and thus an abortion may not be performed.[4]

Some people seem to have thought that these are not further premises which must be added if the conclusion is to be reached, but that they follow from the very fact that an innocent person has a right to life.[5] But this seems to me to be a mistake, and perhaps the simplest way to show this is to bring out that while we must certainly grant that innocent persons have a right to life, the theses in (1) through (4) are all false. Take (2), for example. If directly killing an innocent person is murder, and thus is impermissible, then the mother's directly killing the innocent person inside her is murder, and thus is impermissible. But it cannot seriously be thought to be murder if the mother performs an abortion on herself to save her life. It cannot seriously be said that she *must* refrain, that she *must* sit passively by and wait for her death. Let us look again at the case of you and the violinist. There you are, in bed with the violinist, and the director of the hospital says to you, "It's all most distressing, and I deeply sympathize, but you see this is putting an additional strain on your kidneys, and you'll be dead within the month. But you *have* to stay where you are all the same. Because unplugging you would be directly killing an innocent violinist, and that's murder, and that's impermissible." If anything in the world is true, it is that you do not commit murder, you do not do what is impermissible, if you reach around to your back and unplug yourself from that violinist to save your life.

The main focus of attention in writings on abortion has been on what a third party may or may not do in answer to a request from a woman for an abortion. This is in a way understandable. Things being as they are, there isn't much a woman can safely do to abort herself. So the question asked is what a third party may do, and what the mother may do, if it is mentioned at all, is deduced, almost as an afterthought, from what it is concluded that third parties may do. But it seems to me that to treat the matter in this way is to refuse to grant to the mother that very status of person which is so firmly insisted on for the fetus. For we cannot simply read off what a person may do from what a third party may do. Suppose you find yourself trapped in a tiny house with a growing child. I mean a very tiny house, and a rapidly growing child — you are already up against the wall of the house and in a few minutes you'll be crushed to death. The child on the other hand won't be crushed to death; if nothing is done to stop him from growing he'll be hurt, but in the end he'll simply burst open the house and walk out a free man. Now I could well understand it if a bystander were to say, "There's nothing we can do for you. We cannot choose between your life and his, we cannot be the ones to decide who is to live, we cannot intervene." But it cannot be concluded that you too can do nothing, that you cannot attack it to save your life. However innocent the child may be, you do not have to wait passively while it crushes you to death. Perhaps a pregnant woman is vaguely felt to have the status of house, to which we don't allow the right of self-defense. But if the woman houses the child, it should be remembered that she is a person who houses it.

I should perhaps stop to say explicitly that I am not claiming that people have a right to do anything whatever to save their lives. I think, rather, that there are drastic limits to the right of self-defense. If someone threatens you with death unless you torture someone else to death, I think you have not the right, even to save your life, to do so. But the case under consideration here is very different. In our case there are only two people involved, one whose life is threatened, and one who threatens it. Both are innocent: the one who is threatened is not threatened because of any fault, the one who threatens does not threaten because of any fault. For this reason we may feel that we bystanders cannot intervene. But the person threatened can.

In sum, a woman surely can defend her life against the threat to it posed by the unborn child, even if doing so involves its death. And this shows not merely that the theses in (1) through (4) are false; it shows also that the extreme view of abortion is false, and so we need not canvass any other possible ways of arriving at it from the argument I mentioned at the outset.

2. The extreme view could of course be weakened to say that while abortion is permissible to save the mother's life, it may not be performed by a third party, but only by the mother herself. But this cannot be right either. For what we have to keep in mind is that the mother and the unborn child are not like two tenants in a small house which has, by an unfortunate mistake, been rented to both: the mother *owns* the house. The fact that she does adds to the offensiveness of deducing that the mother can do nothing from the supposition that third parties can do nothing. But it does more than this: it casts a bright light on the supposition that third parties can do nothing. Certainly it lets us see that a third party who says "I cannot choose between you" is fooling himself if he thinks this is impartiality. If Jones has found and fastened on a certain coat, which he needs to keep him from freezing, but which Smith also needs to keep him from freezing, then it is not impartiality that says "I cannot choose between you" when Smith owns the coat. Women have said again and again "This body is *my* body!" and they have reason to feel angry, reason to feel that it has been like shouting into the wind. Smith, after all, is hardly likely to bless us if we say to him, "Of course it's your coat, anybody would grant that it is. But no one may choose between you and Jones who is to have it."

We should really ask what it is that says "no one may choose" in the face of the fact that the body that houses the child is the mother's body. It may be simply a failure to appreciate this fact. But it may be something more interesting, namely the sense that one has a right to refuse to lay hands on people, even where it would be just and fair to do so, even where justice seems to require that somebody do so. Thus justice might call for somebody to get Smith's coat back from Jones, and yet you have a right to refuse to be the one to lay hands on Jones, a right to refuse to do physical violence to him. This, I think, must be granted. But then what should be said is not "no one may choose," but only "*I* cannot choose," and indeed not even this, but "*I* will not *act*," leaving it open that somebody else can or should, and in particular that anyone in a position of authority, with the job of securing people's rights, both can and should. So this is no difficulty. I have not been arguing that any given third party must accede to the mother's request that he perform an abortion to save her life, but only that he may.

I suppose that in some views of human life the mother's body is only on loan to her, the loan not being one which gives her any prior claim to it. One who held this view might well think it impartiality to say "I cannot choose." But I shall simply ignore this possibility. My own view is that if a human being has any just, prior claim to anything at all, he has a just, prior claim to his own body. And perhaps this needn't be argued for here anyway, since, as I mentioned, the arguments against abortion we are looking at do grant that the woman has a right to decide what happens in and to her body.

But although they do grant it, I have tried to show that they do not take seriously what is done in granting it. I suggest the same thing will reappear even more clearly when we turn away from cases in which the mother's life is at stake, and attend, as I propose we now do, to the vastly more common cases in which a woman wants an abortion for some less weighty reason than preserving her own life.

3. Where the mother's life is not at stake,

the argument I mentioned at the outset seems to have a much stronger pull. "Everyone has a right to life, so the unborn person has a right to life." And isn't the child's right to life weightier than anything other than the mother's own right to life, which she might put forward as ground for an abortion?

This argument treats the right to life as if it were unproblematic. It is not, and this seems to me to be precisely the source of the mistake.

For we should now, at long last, ask what it comes to, to have a right to life. In some views having a right to life includes having a right to be given at least the bare minimum one needs for continued life. But suppose that what in fact *is* the bare minimum a man needs for continued life is something he has no right at all to be given? If I am sick unto death, and the only thing that will save my life is the touch of Henry Fonda's cool hand on my fevered brow, then all the same, I have no right to be given the touch of Henry Fonda's cool hand on my fevered brow. It would be frightfully nice of him to fly in from the West Coast to provide it. It would be less nice, though no doubt well meant, if my friends flew out to the West Coast and carried Henry Fonda back with them. But I have no right at all against anybody that he should do this for me. Or again, to return to the story I told earlier, the fact that for continued life that violinist needs the continued use of your kidneys does not establish that he has a right to be given the continued use of your kidneys. He certainly has no right against you that *you* should give him continued use of your kidneys. For nobody has any right to use your kidneys unless you give him such a right; and nobody has the right against you that you shall give him this right — if you do allow him to go on using your kidneys, this is a kindness on your part, and not something he can

claim from you as his due. Nor has he any right against anybody else that *they* should give him continued use of your kidneys. Certainly he had no right against the Society of Music Lovers that they should plug him into you in the first place. And if you now start to unplug yourself, having learned that you will otherwise have to spend nine years in bed with him, there is nobody in the world who must try to prevent you, in order to see to it that he is given something he has a right to be given.

Some people are rather stricter about the right to life. In their view, it does not include the right to be given anything, but amounts to, and only to, the right not to be killed by anybody. But here a related difficulty arises. If everybody is to refrain from killing that violinist, then everybody must refrain from doing a great many different sorts of things. Everybody must refrain from slitting his throat, everybody must refrain from shooting him — and everybody must refrain from unplugging you from him. But does he have a right against everybody that they shall refrain from unplugging you from him? To refrain from doing this is to allow him to continue to use your kidneys. It could be argued that he has a right against us that *we* should allow him to continue to use your kidneys. That is, while he had no right against us that we should give him the use of your kidneys, it might be argued that he anyway has a right against us that we shall not now intervene and deprive him of the use of your kidneys. I shall come back to third-party interventions later. But certainly the violinist has no right against you that *you* shall allow him to continue to use your kidneys. As I said, if you do allow him to use them, it is a kindness on your part, and not something you owe him.

The difficulty I point to here is not peculiar to the right to life. It reappears in connection with all the other natural rights; and it is something which an adequate account of rights must deal with. For present purposes it is enough just to draw attention to it. But I would stress that I am not arguing that people do not have a right to life — quite to the contrary, it seems to me that the primary control we must place on the acceptability of an account of rights is that it should turn out in that account to be a truth that all persons have a right to life. I am arguing only that having a right to life does not guarantee having either a right to be given the use of or a right to be allowed continued use of another person's body — even if one needs it for life itself. So the right to life will not serve the opponents of abortion in the very simple and clear way in which they seem to have thought it would.

4. There is another way to bring out the difficulty. In the most ordinary sort of case, to deprive someone of what he has a right to is to treat him unjustly. Suppose a boy and his small brother are jointly given a box of chocolates for Christmas. If the older boy takes the box and refuses to give his brother any of the chocolates, he is unjust to him, for the brother has been given a right to half of them. But suppose that, having learned that otherwise it means nine years in bed with that violinist, you unplug yourself from him. You surely are not being unjust to him, for you gave him no right to use your kidneys, and no one else can have given him any such right. But we have to notice that in unplugging yourself, you are killing him; and violinists, like everybody else, have a right to life, and thus in the view we were considering just now, the right not to be killed. So here you do what he supposedly has a right you shall not do, but you do not act unjustly to him in doing it.

The emendation which may be made at this point is this: the right to life consists not in the right not to be killed, but rather in the right not to be killed unjustly. This runs a risk of circularity, but never mind: it would enable us to square the fact that the violinist has a right to life with the fact that you do not act unjustly toward him in unplugging yourself, thereby killing him. For if you do not kill him unjustly, you do not violate his right to life, and so it is no wonder you do him no injustice.

But if this emendation is accepted, the gap in the argument against abortion stares us plainly in the face: it is by no means enough to show that the fetus is a person, and to remind us that all persons have a right to life — we need to be shown also that killing the fetus violates its right to life, i.e., that abortion is unjust killing. And is it?

I suppose we may take it as a datum that in a case of pregnancy due to rape the mother has not given the unborn person a right to the use of her body for food and shelter. Indeed, in what pregnancy could it be supposed that the mother has given the unborn person such a right? It is not as if there were unborn persons drifting about the world, to whom a woman who wants a child says "I invite you in."

But it might be argued that there are other ways one can have acquired a right to the use of another person's body than by having been invited to use it by that person. Suppose a woman voluntarily indulges in intercourse, knowing of the chance it will issue in pregnancy, and then she does become pregnant; is she not in part responsible for the presence, in fact the very existence, of the unborn person inside her? No doubt she did not invite it in. But doesn't her partial responsibility for its being there itself give it a right to the use of her body? [6] If so, then her aborting it would be more like the boy's taking away the chocolates, and less like your unplugging yourself from the violinist — doing so would be depriving it of what it does have a right to, and thus would be doing it an injustice.

And then, too, it might be asked whether or not she can kill it even to save her own life: If she voluntarily called it into existence, how can she now kill it, even in self-defense?

The first thing to be said about this is that it is something new. Opponents of abortion have been so concerned to make out the independence of the fetus, in order to establish that it has a right to life, just as its mother does, that they have tended to overlook the possible support they might gain from making out that the fetus is *dependent* on the mother, in order to establish that she has a special kind of responsibility for it, a responsibility that gives it rights against her which are not possessed by any independent person — such as an ailing violinist who is a stranger to her.

On the other hand, this argument would give the unborn person a right to its mother's body only if her pregnancy resulted from a voluntary act, undertaken in full knowledge of the chance a pregnancy might result from it. It would leave out entirely the unborn person whose existence is due to rape. Pending the availability of some further argument, then, we would be left with the conclusion that unborn persons whose existence is due to rape have no right to the use of their mothers' bodies, and thus that aborting them is not depriving them of anything they have a right to and hence is not unjust killing.

And we should also notice that it is not at all plain that this argument really does go even as far as it purports to. For there are cases and cases, and the details make a difference. If the room is stuffy, and I therefore open a window to air it, and a burglar climbs in, it would be absurd to say, "Ah, now he can stay, she's given him a right to the use of her house — for she is partially responsible for his presence there, having voluntarily done what enabled him to get in, in full knowledge that there are such things as

burglars, and that burglars burgle." It would be still more absurd to say this if I had had bars installed outside my windows, precisely to prevent burglars from getting in, and a burglar got in only because of a defect in the bars. It remains equally absurd if we imagine it is not a burglar who climbs in, but an innocent person who blunders or falls in. Again, suppose it were like this: people-seeds drift about in the air like pollen, and if you open your windows, one may drift in and take root in your carpets or upholstery. You don't want children, so you fix up your windows with fine mesh screens, the very best you can buy. As can happen, however, and on very, very rare occasions does happen, one of the screens is defective; and a seed drifts in and takes root. Does the person-plant who now develops have a right to the use of your house? Surely not — despite the fact that you voluntarily opened your windows, you knowingly kept carpets and upholstered furniture, and you knew that screens were sometimes defective. Someone may argue that you are responsible for its rooting, that it does have a right to your house, because after all you *could* have lived out your life with bare floors and furniture, or with sealed windows and doors. But this won't do — for by the same token anyone can avoid a pregnancy due to rape by having a hysterectomy, or anyway by never leaving home without a (reliable!) army.

It seems to me that the argument we are looking at can establish at most that there are *some* cases in which the unborn person has a right to the use of its mother's body, and therefore *some* cases in which abortion is unjust killing. There is room for much discussion and argument as to precisely which, if any. But I think we should sidestep this issue and leave it open, for at any rate the argument certainly does not establish that all abortion is unjust killing.

5. There is room for yet another argument

here, however. We surely must all grant that there may be cases in which it would be morally indecent to detach a person from your body at the cost of his life. Suppose you learn that what the violinist needs is not nine years of your life, but only one hour: all you need do to save his life is to spend one hour in that bed with him. Suppose also that letting him use your kidneys for that one hour would not affect your health in the slightest. Admittedly you were kidnapped. Admittedly you did not give anyone permission to plug him into you. Nevertheless it seems to me plain you *ought* to allow him to use your kidneys for that hour — it would be indecent to refuse.

Again, suppose pregnancy lasted only an hour, and constituted no threat to life or health. And suppose that a woman becomes pregnant as a result of rape. Admittedly she did not voluntarily do anything to bring about the existence of a child. Admittedly she did nothing at all which would give the unborn person a right to the use of her body. All the same it might well be said, as in the newly emended violinist story, that she *ought* to allow it to remain for that hour — that it would be indecent in her to refuse.

Now some people are inclined to use the term "right" in such a way that it follows from the fact that you ought to allow a person to use your body for the hour he needs, that he has a right to use your body for the hour he needs, even though he has not been given that right by any person or act. They may say that it follows also that if you refuse, you act unjustly toward him. This use of the term is perhaps so common that it cannot be called wrong; nevertheless it seems to me to be an unfortunate loosening of what we would do better to keep a tight rein on. Suppose that box of chocolates I mentioned earlier had not been given to both boys jointly, but was given only to the older boy. There he sits, stolidly eating

his way through the box, his small brother watching enviously. Here we are likely to say "You ought not to be so mean. You ought to give your brother some of those chocolates." My own view is that it just does not follow from the truth of this that the brother has any right to any of the chocolates. If the boy refuses to give his brother any, he is greedy, stingy, callous — but not unjust. I suppose that the people I have in mind will say it does follow that the brother has a right to some of the chocolates, and thus that the boy does act unjustly if he refuses to give his brother any. But the effect of saying this is to obscure what we should keep distinct, namely the difference between the boy's refusal in this case and the boy's refusal in the earlier case, in which the box was given to both boys jointly, and in which the small brother thus had what was from any point of view clear title to half.

A further objection to so using the term "right" that from the fact that A ought to do a thing for B, it follows that B has a right against A that A do it for him, is that it is going to make the question of whether or not a man has a right to a thing turn on how easy it is to provide him with it; and this seems not merely unfortunate, but morally unacceptable. Take the case of Henry Fonda again. I said earlier that I had no right to the touch of his cool hand on my fevered brow, even though I needed it to save my life. I said it would be frightfully nice of him to fly in from the West Coast to provide me with it, but that I had no right against him that he should do so. But suppose he isn't on the West Coast. Suppose he has only to walk across the room, place a hand briefly on my brow — and lo, my life is saved. Then surely he ought to do it, it would be indecent to refuse. Is it to be said "Ah, well, it follows that in this case she has a right to the touch of his hand on her brow, and so it would be an injustice in him to refuse"? So that I have a right to it when it is easy for him to provide it, though no right when it's hard? It's rather a shocking idea that anyone's rights should fade away and disappear as it gets harder and harder to accord them to him.

So my own view is that even though you ought to let the violinist use your kidneys for the one hour he needs, we should not conclude that he has a right to do so — we should say that if you refuse, you are, like the boy who owns all the chocolates and will give none away, self-centered and callous, indecent in fact, but not unjust. And similarly, that even supposing a case in which a woman pregnant due to rape ought to allow the unborn person to use her body for the hour he needs, we should not conclude that he has a right to do so; we should conclude that she is self-centered, callous, indecent, but not unjust, if she refuses. The complaints are no less grave; they are just different. However, there is no need to insist on this point. If anyone does wish to deduce "he has a right" from "you ought," then all the same he must surely grant that there are cases in which it is not morally required of you that you allow that violinist to use your kidneys, and in which he does not have a right to use them, and in which you do not do him an injustice if you refuse. And so also for mother and unborn child. Except in such cases as the unborn person has a right to demand it — and we were leaving open the possibility that there may be such cases — nobody is morally *required* to make large sacrifices, of health, of all other interests and concerns, of all other duties and commitments, for nine years, or even for nine months, in order to keep another person alive.

6. We have in fact to distinguish between two kinds of Samaritan: the Good Samaritan and what we might call the Minimally Decent Samaritan. The story of the Good Samaritan, you will remember, goes like this:

A certain man went down from Jerusalem to Jericho, and fell among thieves, which stripped him of his raiment, and wounded him, and departed, leaving him half dead.

And by chance there came down a certain priest that way; and when he saw him, he passed by on the other side.

And likewise a Levite, when he was at the place, came and looked on him, and passed by on the other side.

But a certain Samaritan, as he journeyed, came where he was; and when he saw him he had compassion on him.

And went to him, and bound up his wounds, pouring in oil and wine, and set him on his own beast, and brought him to an inn, and took care of him.

And on the morrow, when he departed, he took out two pence, and gave them to the host, and said unto him, "Take care of him; and whatsoever thou spendest more, when I come again, I will repay thee."

Luke 10:30–35

The Good Samaritan went out of his way, at some cost to himself, to help one in need of it. We are not told what the options were, that is, whether or not the priest and the Levite could have helped by doing less than the Good Samaritan did, but assuming they could have, then the fact they did nothing at all shows they were not even Minimally Decent Samaritans, not because they were not Samaritans, but because they were not even minimally decent.

These things are a matter of degree, of course, but there is a difference, and it comes out perhaps most clearly in the story of Kitty Genovese, who, as you will remember, was murdered while thirty-eight people watched or listened, and did nothing at all to help her. A Good Samaritan would have rushed out to give direct assistance against the murderer. Or perhaps we had better allow that it would have been a Splendid Samaritan who did this, on the ground that it would have involved a risk of death for himself. But the thirty-eight not only did not do this, they did not even trouble to pick up a phone to call the police. Minimally Decent Samaritanism would call for doing at least that, and their not having done it was monstrous.

After telling the story of the Good Samaritan, Jesus said "Go, and do thou likewise." Perhaps he meant that we are morally required to act as the Good Samaritan did. Perhaps he was urging people to do more than is morally required of them. At all events it seems plain that it was not morally required of any of the thirty-eight that he rush out to give direct assistance at the risk of his own life, and that it is not morally required of anyone that he give long stretches of his life — nine years or nine months — to sustaining the life of a person who has no special right (we were leaving open the possibility of this) to demand it.

Indeed, with one rather striking class of exceptions, no one in any country in the world is *legally* required to do anywhere near as much as this for anyone else. The class of exceptions is obvious. My main concern here is not the state of the law in respect to abortion, but it is worth drawing attention to the fact that in no state in this country is any man compelled by law to be even a Minimally Decent Samaritan to any person; there is no law under which charges could be brought against the thirty-eight who stood by while Kitty Genovese died. By contrast, in most states in this country women are compelled by law to be not merely Minimally Decent Samaritans, but Good Samaritans to unborn persons inside them. This doesn't by itself settle anything one way or the other, because it may well be argued that there should be laws in this country — as there are in many European countries — compelling at least Minimally Decent Samaritanism.[7] But it does show that there is a gross injustice in the existing state of the law. And it shows also that the groups currently working against liberalization of abortion laws, in fact working toward having it declared unconstitutional for a state to permit abortion, had better start working for the adoption of Good Samaritan laws generally, or earn the charge that they are acting in bad faith.

I should think, myself, that Minimally Decent Samaritan laws would be one thing, Good Samaritan laws quite another, and in fact highly improper. But we are not here concerned with the law. What we should ask is not whether anybody should be compelled by law to be a Good Samaritan, but whether we must accede to a situation in which somebody is being compelled — by nature, perhaps — to be a Good Samaritan. We have, in other words, to look now at third-party interventions. I have been arguing that no person is morally required to make large sacrifices to sustain the life of another who has no right to demand them, and this even where the sacrifices do not include life itself; we are not morally required to be Good Samaritans or anyway Very Good Samaritans to one another. But what if a man cannot extricate himself from such a situation? What if he appeals to us to extricate him? It seems to me plain that there are cases in which we can, cases in which a Good Samaritan would extricate him. There you are, you were kidnapped, and nine years in bed with that violinist lie ahead of you. You have your own life to lead. You are sorry, but you simply cannot see giving up so much of your life to the sustaining of his. You cannot extricate yourself, and ask us to do so. I should have thought that — in light of his having no right to the use of your body — it was obvious that we do not have to accede to your being forced to give up so much. We can do what you ask. There is no injustice to the violinist in our doing so.

7. Following the lead of the opponents of

abortion, I have throughout been speaking of the fetus merely as a person, and what I have been asking is whether or not the argument we began with, which proceeds only from the fetus' being a person, really does establish its conclusion. I have argued that it does not.

But of course there are arguments and arguments, and it may be said that I have simply fastened on the wrong one. It may be said that what is important is not merely the fact that the fetus is a person, but that it is a person for whom the woman has a special kind of responsibility issuing from the fact that she is its mother. And it might be argued that all my analogies are therefore irrelevant — for you do not have that special kind of responsibility for that violinist, Henry Fonda does not have that special kind of responsibility for me. And our attention might be drawn to the fact that men and women both *are* compelled by law to provide support for their children.

I have in effect dealt (briefly) with this argument in section 4 above; but a (still briefer) recapitulation now may be in order. Surely we do not have any such "special responsibility" for a person unless we have assumed it, explicitly or implicitly. If a set of parents do not try to prevent pregnancy, do not obtain an abortion, and then at the time of birth of the child do not put it out for adoption, but rather take it home with them, then they have assumed responsibility for it, they have given it rights, and they cannot *now* withdraw support from it at the cost of its life because they now find it difficult to go on providing for it. But if they have taken all reasonable precautions against having a child, they do not simply by virtue of their biological relationship to the child who comes into existence have a special responsibility for it. They may wish to assume responsibility for it, or they may not wish to. And I am suggesting that if assuming

responsibility for it would require large sacrifices, then they may refuse. A Good Samaritan would not refuse — or anyway, a Splendid Samaritan, if the sacrifices that had to be made were enormous. But then so would a Good Samaritan assume responsibility for that violinist; so would Henry Fonda, if he is a Good Samaritan, fly in from the West Coast and assume responsibility for me.

8. My argument will be found unsatisfactory on two counts by many of those who want to regard abortion as morally permissible. First, while I do argue that abortion is not impermissible, I do not argue that it is always permissible. There may well be cases in which carrying the child to term requires only Minimally Decent Samaritanism of the mother, and this is a standard we must not fall below. I am inclined to think it a merit of my account precisely that it does *not* give a general yes or a general no. It allows for and supports our sense that, for example, a sick and desperately frightened fourteen-year-old schoolgirl, pregnant due to rape, may *of course* choose abortion, and that any law which rules this out is an insane law. And it also allows for and supports our sense that in other cases resort to abortion is even positively indecent. It would be indecent in the woman to request an abortion, and indecent in a doctor to perform it, if she is in her seventh month, and wants the abortion just to avoid the nuisance of postponing a trip abroad. The very fact that the arguments I have been drawing attention to treat all cases of abortion, or even all cases of abortion in which the mother's life is not at stake, as morally on a par ought to have made them suspect at the outset.

Secondly, while I am arguing for the permissibility of abortion in some cases, I am not arguing for the right to secure the death of the unborn child. It is easy to confuse these two things in that up to a certain point in the life of the fetus it is not able to survive outside the mother's body; hence removing it from her body guarantees its death. But they are importantly different. I have argued that you are not morally required to spend nine months in bed, sustaining the life of that violinist; but to say this is by no means to say that if, when you unplug yourself, there is a miracle and he survives, you then have a right to turn round and slit his throat. You may detach yourself even if this costs him his life; you have no right to be guaranteed his death, by some other means, if unplugging yourself does not kill him. There are some people who will feel dissatisfied by this feature of my argument. A woman may be utterly devastated by the thought of a child, a bit of herself, put out for adoption and never seen or heard of again. She may therefore want not merely that the child be detached from her, but more, that it die. Some opponents of abortion are inclined to regard this as beneath contempt — thereby showing insensitivity to what is surely a powerful source of despair. All the same, I agree that the desire for the child's death is not one which anybody may gratify, should it turn out to be possible to detach the child alive.

At this place, however, it should be remembered that we have only been pretending throughout that the fetus is a human being from the moment of conception. A very early abortion is surely not the killing of a person, and so is not dealt with by anything I have said here.

Notes

1. Daniel Callahan, _Abortion: Law, Choice and Morality_ (New York, 1970), p. 373. This book gives a fascinating survey of the available information on abortion. The Jewish tradition is surveyed in David M. Feldman, _Birth Control in Jewish Law_ (New York, 1968), Part 5, the Catholic tradition in John T. Noonan, Jr., "An Almost Absolute Value in History," in _The Morality of Abortion,_ ed. John T. Noonan, Jr. (Cambridge, Mass., 1970).

2. The term "direct" in the arguments I refer to is a technical one. Roughly, what is meant by "direct killing" is either killing as an end in itself, or killing as a means to some end, for example, the end of saving someone else's life. See note 5, below, for an example of its use.

3. Cf. _Encyclical Letter of Pope Pius XI on Christian Marriage,_ St. Paul Editions (Boston, n.d.), p. 32: "however much we may pity the mother whose health and even life is gravely imperiled in the performance of the duty allotted to her by nature, nevertheless what could ever be a sufficient reason for excusing in any way the direct murder of the innocent? This is precisely what we are dealing with here." Noonan (_The Morality of Abortion,_ p. 43) reads this as follows: "What cause can ever avail to excuse in any way the direct killing of the innocent? For it is a question of that."

4. The thesis in (4) is in an interesting way weaker than those in (1), (2), and (3): they rule out abortion even in cases in which both mother _and_ child will die if the abortion is not performed. By contrast, one who held the view expressed in (4) could consistently say that one needn't prefer letting two persons die to killing one.

5. Cf. the following passage from Pius XII, _Address to the Italian Catholic Society of Midwives:_ "The baby in the maternal breast has the right to life immediately from God. — Hence there is no man, no human authority, no science, no medical, eugenic, social, economic or moral 'indication' which can establish or grant a valid juridical ground for a direct deliberate disposition of an innocent human life, that is a disposition which looks to its destruction either as an end or as a means to another end perhaps in itself not illicit. — The baby, still not born, is a man in the same degree and for the same reason as the mother" (quoted in Noonan, _The Morality of Abortion,_ p. 45).

6. The need for a discussion of this argument was brought home to me by members of the Society for Ethical and Legal Philosophy, to whom this paper was originally presented.
7. For a discussion of the difficulties involved,

and a survey of the European experience with such laws, see *The Good Samaritan and the Law,* ed. James M. Ratcliffe (New York, 1966).

RAPE: THE ALL-AMERICAN CRIME

SUSAN GRIFFIN

Susan Griffin has taught Women's Studies at the University of California at Berkeley and at San Francisco State University. Thirty-six years old and living in Berkeley with her ten-year-old daughter, she has recently earned her living by full-time writing. Her play *Voices* has been produced widely here and in Europe; for a local television performance it won an Emmy. She recently completed a prose-poetry work, *Woman and Nature: The Roaring Inside Her* (1978). One of the founders of the Feminist Writer's Guild, she considers her writing a political activity.

Griffin's analytical commentary on rape is one of the most powerful yet rationally perceptive on the subject to come out of the women's movement. She analyzes the effect of rape not only on the primary victim but on all women, all of whom are victims of rape as a political act of terror against the female sex.

I

I have never been free of the fear of rape. From a very early age I, like most women, have thought of rape as part of my natural environment — something to be feared and prayed against like fire or lightning. I never asked why men raped; I simply thought it one of the many mysteries of human nature.

I was, however, curious enough about the violent side of humanity to read every crime magazine I was able to ferret away from my grandfather. Each issue featured at least one "sex crime," with pictures of a victim, usually in a pearl necklace, and of the ditch or the orchard where her body was found. I was never certain why the victims were

always women, nor what the motives of the murderer were, but I did guess that the world was not a safe place for women. I observed that my grandmother was meticulous about locks, and quick to draw the shades before anyone removed so much as a shoe. I sensed that danger lurked outside.

At the age of eight, my suspicions were confirmed. My grandmother took me to the back of the house where the men wouldn't hear, and told me that strange men wanted to do harm to little girls. I learned not to walk on dark streets, not to talk to strangers, or get into strange cars, to lock doors, and to be modest. She never explained why a man would want to harm a little girl, and I never asked.

If I thought for a while that my grandmother's fears were imaginary, the illusion was brief. That year, on the way home from school, a schoolmate a few years older than

I tried to rape me. Later, in an obscure aisle of the local library (while I was reading *Freddy the Pig*) I turned to discover a man exposing himself. Then, the friendly man around the corner was arrested for child molesting.

My initiation to sexuality was typical. Every woman has similar stories to tell — the first man who attacked her may have been a neighbor, a family friend, an uncle, her doctor, or perhaps her own father. And women who grow up in New York City always have tales about the subway.

But though rape and the fear of rape are a daily part of every woman's consciousness, the subject is so rarely discussed by that unofficial staff of male intellectuals (who write the books which study seemingly every other form of male activity) that one begins to suspect a conspiracy of silence. And indeed, the obscurity of rape in print exists in marked contrast to the frequency of rape in reality, for *forcible rape is the most frequently committed violent crime in America today.* The Federal Bureau of Investigation classes three crimes as violent: murder, aggravated assault and forcible rape. In 1968, 31,060 rapes were *reported.* According to the FBI and independent criminologists, however, to approach accuracy this figure must be multiplied by at least a factor of ten to compensate for the fact that most rapes are not reported; when these compensatory mathematics are used, there are more rapes committed than aggravated assaults and homicides.

When I asked Berkeley, California's Police Inspector in charge of rape investigation if he knew why men rape women, he replied that he had not spoken with "these people and delved into what really makes them tick, because that really isn't my job. . . ." However, when I asked him how a woman might prevent being raped, he was not so reticent, "I wouldn't advise any female to go walking around alone at night . . . and she should lock her car at all times." The Inspector illustrated his warning with a grisly story about a man who lay in wait for women in the back seats of their cars, while they were shopping in a local supermarket. This man eventually murdered one of his rape victims. "Always lock your car," the Inspector repeated, and then added, without a hint of irony, "Of course, you don't have to be paranoid about this type of thing."

The Inspector wondered why I wanted to write about rape. Like most men he did not understand the urgency of the topic, for, after all, men are not raped. But like most women I had spent considerable time speculating on the true nature of the rapist. When I was very young, my image of the "sexual offender" was a nightmarish amalgamation of the bogey man and Captain Hook: he wore a black cape, and he cackled. As I matured, so did my image of the rapist. Born into the psychoanalytic age, I tried to "understand" the rapist. Rape, I came to believe, was only one of many unfortunate evils produced by sexual repression. Reasoning by tautology, I concluded that any man who would rape a woman must be out of his mind.

Yet, though the theory that rapists are insane is a popular one, this belief has no basis in fact. According to Professor Menachem Amir's study of 646 rape cases in Philadelphia, *Patterns in Forcible Rape,* men who rape are not abnormal. Amir writes, "Studies indicate that sex offenders do not constitute a unique or psychopathological type; nor are they as a group invariably more disturbed than the control groups to which they are compared." Alan Taylor, a parole officer who has worked with rapists in the prison facilities at San Luis Obispo, California, stated the question in plainer language, "Those men were the most normal men there. They had a lot of hang-ups, but they were the same hang-ups as men walking out on the street."

Another canon in the apologetics of rape is that, if it were not for learned social controls, all men would rape. Rape is held to be natural behavior, and not to rape must be learned. But in truth rape is not universal to the human species. Moreover, studies of rape in our culture reveal that, far from being impulsive behavior, most rape is planned. Professor Amir's study reveals that in cases of group rape (the "gangbang" of masculine slang) 90 percent of the rapes were planned; in pair rapes, 83 percent of the rapes were planned; and in single rapes, 58 percent were planned. These figures should significantly discredit the image of the rapist as a man who is suddenly overcome by sexual needs society does not allow him to fulfill.

Far from the social control of rape being learned, comparisons with other cultures lead one to suspect that, in our society, it is rape itself that is learned. (The fact that rape is against the law should not be considered proof that rape is not in fact encouraged as part of our culture.)

This culture's concept of rape as an illegal, but still understandable, form of behavior is not a universal one. In her study *Sex and Temperament,* Margaret Mead describes a society that does not share our views. The Arapesh do not ". . . have any conception of the male nature that might make rape understandable to them." Indeed our interpretation of rape is a product of our conception of the nature of male sexuality. A common retort to the question, why don't women rape men, is the myth that men have greater sexual needs, that their sexuality is more urgent than women's. And it is the nature of human beings to want to live up to what is expected of them.

And this same culture which expects aggression from the male expects passivity

from the female. Conveniently, the companion myth about the nature of female sexuality is that all women secretly want to be raped. Lurking beneath her modest female exterior is a subconscious desire to be ravished. The following description of a stag movie, written by Brenda Starr in Los Angeles' underground paper, *Everywoman,* typifies this male fantasy. The movie "showed a woman in her underclothes reading on her bed. She is interrupted by a rapist with a knife. He immediately wins her over with his charm and they get busy sucking and fucking." An advertisement in the *Berkeley Barb* reads, "Now as all women know from their daydreams, rape has a lot of advantages. Best of all it's so simple. No preparation necessary, no planning ahead of time, no wondering if you should or shouldn't; just whang! bang!" Thanks to Masters and Johnson even the scientific canon recognizes that for the female, "whang! bang!" can scarcely be described as pleasurable.

Still, the male psyche persists in believing that, protestations and struggles to the contrary, deep inside her mysterious feminine soul, the female victim has wished for her own fate. A young woman who was raped by the husband of a friend said that days after the incident the man returned to her home, pounded on the door and screamed to her, "Jane, Jane. You loved it. You know you loved it."

The theory that women like being raped extends itself by deduction into the proposition that most or much of rape is provoked by the victim. But this too is only myth. Though provocation, considered a mitigating factor in a court of law, may consist of only "a gesture," according to the Federal Commission on Crimes of Violence, only 4 percent of reported rapes involved any precipitative behavior by the woman.

The notion that rape is enjoyed by the

victim is also convenient for the man who, though he would not commit forcible rape, enjoys the idea of its existence, as if rape confirms that enormous sexual potency which he secretly knows to be his own. It is for the pleasure of the armchair rapist that detailed accounts of violent rapes exist in the media. Indeed, many men appear to take sexual pleasure from nearly all forms of violence. Whatever the motivation, male sexuality and violence in our culture seem to be inseparable. James Bond alternately whips out his revolver and his cock, and though there is no known connection between the skills of gun-fighting and love-making, pacifism seems suspiciously effeminate.

In a recent fictional treatment of the Manson case, Frank Conroy writes of his vicarious titillation when describing the murders to his wife:

> "Every single person there was killed." She didn't move.
>
> "It sounds like there was torture," I said. As the words left my mouth I knew there was no need to say them to frighten her into believing that she needed me for protection.

The pleasure he feels as his wife's protector is inextricably mixed with pleasure in the violence itself. Conroy writes, "I was excited by the killings, as one is excited by catastrophe on a grand scale, as one is alert to pre-echoes of unknown changes, hints of unrevealed secrets, rumblings of chaos. . . ."

The attraction of the male in our culture to violence and death is a tradition Manson and his admirers are carrying on with tireless avidity (even presuming Manson's innocence, he dreams of the purification of fire and destruction). It was Malraux in his *Anti-Memoirs* who said that, for the male, facing death was *the* illuminating experience analogous to childbirth for the female. Certainly our culture does glorify war and shroud the agonies of the gun-fighter in veils of mystery.

And in the spectrum of male behavior, rape, the perfect combination of sex and violence, is the penultimate act. Erotic pleasure cannot be separated from culture, and in our culture male eroticism is wedded to power. Not only should a man be taller and stronger than a female in the perfect love-match, but he must also demonstrate his superior strength in gestures of dominance which are perceived as amorous. Though the law attempts to make a clear division between rape and sexual intercourse, in fact the courts find it difficult to distinguish between a case where the decision to copulate was mutual and one where a man forced himself upon his partner.

The scenario is even further complicated by the expectation that, not only does a woman mean "yes" when she says "no," but that a really decent woman ought to begin by saying "no," and then be led down the primrose path to acquiescence. Ovid, the author of Western Civilization's most celebrated sex-manual, makes this expectation perfectly clear:

> . . . and when I beg you to say "yes," say "no." Then let me lie outside your bolted door. . . . So Love grows strong. . . .

That the basic elements of rape are involved in all heterosexual relationships may explain why men often identify with the offender in this crime. But to regard the rapist as the victim, a man driven by his inherent sexual needs to take what will not be given him, reveals a basic ignorance of sexual politics. For in our culture heterosexual love finds an erotic expression through male dominance and female submission. A man who derives pleasure from raping a woman clearly must enjoy force and dominance as much or more than the simple pleasures of the flesh. Coitus cannot be experienced in isolation. The weather, the state of the nation, the level of sugar in the blood — all will affect a man's ability to achieve orgasm. If a man can achieve sexual pleasure after terrorizing and humiliating the object of his passion, and in fact while inflicting pain upon her, one must assume he derives pleasure directly from terrorizing, humiliating and harming a woman. According to Amir's study of forcible rape, on a statistical average the man who has been convicted of rape was found to have a normal sexual personality, tending to be different from the normal, well-adjusted male only in having a greater tendency to express violence and rage.

And if the professional rapist is to be separated from the average dominant heterosexual, it may be mainly a quantitative difference. For the existence of rape as an index to masculinity is not entirely metaphorical. Though this measure of masculinity seems to be more publicly exhibited among "bad boys" or aging bikers who practice sexual initiation through group rape, in fact, "good boys" engage in the same rites to prove their manhood. In Stockton, a small town in California which epitomizes silent-majority America, a bachelor party was given last summer for a young man about to be married. A woman was hired to dance "topless" for the amusement of the guests. At the high point of the evening the bridegroom-to-be dragged the woman into a bedroom. No move was made by any of his companions to stop what was clearly going to be an attempted rape. Far from it. As the woman described, "I tried to keep him away — told him of my Herpes Genitalis, et cetera, but he couldn't face the guys if he didn't screw me." After the bridegroom had finished raping the woman and returned with

her to the party, far from chastizing him, his friends heckled the woman and covered her with wine.

It was fortunate for the dancer that the bridegroom's friends did not follow him into the bedroom for, though one might suppose that in group rape, since the victim is outnumbered, less force would be inflicted on her, in fact, Amir's studies indicate, "the most excessive degrees of violence occurred in group rape." Far from discouraging violence, the presence of other men may in fact encourage sadism, and even cause the behavior. In an unpublished study of group rape by Gilbert Geis and Duncan Chappell, the authors refer to a study by W. H. Blanchard which relates, "The leader of the male group . . . apparently precipitated and maintained the activity, despite misgivings, because of a need to fulfill the role that the other two men had assigned to him. 'I was scared when it began to happen,' he says. 'I wanted to leave but I didn't want to say it to the other guys — you know — that I was scared.' "

Thus it becomes clear that not only does our culture teach men the rudiments of rape, but society, or more specifically other men, encourage the practice of it.

II

Every man I meet wants to protect me. Can't figure out what from.
Mae West

If a male society rewards aggressive, domineering sexual behavior, it contains within itself a sexual schizophrenia. For the masculine man is also expected to prove his mettle as a protector of women. To the naive eye, this dichotomy implies that men fall into one of two categories: those who rape and those who protect. In fact, life does not prove so simple. In a study euphemistically entitled "Sex Aggression by College Men," it was discovered that men who believe in a double standard of morality for men and women, who in fact believe most fervently in the ultimate value of virginity, are more liable to commit "this aggressive variety of sexual exploitation."

(At this point in our narrative it should come as no surprise that Sir Thomas Malory, creator of that classic tale of chivalry, *The Knights of the Round Table,* was himself arrested and found guilty for repeated incidents of rape.)

In the system of chivalry, men protect women against men. This is not unlike the protection relationship which the mafia established with small businesses in the early part of this century. Indeed, chivalry is an age-old protection racket which depends for its existence on rape.

According to the male mythology which defines and perpetuates rape, it is an animal instinct inherent in the male. The story goes that sometime in our pre-historical past, the male, more hirsute and burly than today's counterparts, roamed about an uncivilized landscape until he found a desirable female. (Oddly enough, this female is *not* pictured as more muscular than the modern woman.) Her mate does not bother with courtship. He simply grabs her by the hair and drags her to the closest cave. Presumably, one of the major advantages of modern civilization for the female has been the civilizing of the male. We call it chivalry.

But women do not get chivalry for free. According to the logic of sexual politics, we too have to civilize our behavior. (Enter chastity. Enter virginity. Enter monogamy.) For the female, civilized behavior means chastity before marriage and faithfulness within it. Chivalrous behavior in the male is supposed to protect that chastity from involuntary defilement. The fly in the ointment of this otherwise peaceful system is the fallen woman. She does not behave. And therefore she does not deserve protection. Or, to use another argument, a major tenet of the same value system: what has once been defiled cannot again be violated. One begins to suspect that it is the behavior of the fallen woman, and not that of the male, that civilization aims to control.

The assumption that a woman who does not respect the double standard deserves whatever she gets (or at the very least "asks for it") operates in the courts today. While in some states a man's previous rape convictions are not considered admissible evidence, the sexual reputation of the rape victim is considered a crucial element of the facts upon which the court must decide innocence or guilt.

The court's respect for the double standard manifested itself particularly clearly in the case of the People v. Jerry Plotkin. Mr. Plotkin, a 36-year-old jeweler, was tried for rape last spring in a San Francisco Superior Court. According to the woman who brought the charges, Plotkin, along with three other men, forced her at gunpoint to enter a car one night in October 1970. She was taken to Mr. Plotkin's fashionable apartment where he and the three other men first raped her and then, in the delicate language of the *S.F. Chronicle,* "subjected her to perverted sex acts." She was, she said, set free in the morning with the warning that she would be killed if she spoke to anyone about the event. She did report the incident to the police who then searched Plotkin's apartment and discovered a long list of names of women. Her name was on the list and had been crossed out.

In addition to the woman's account of her abduction and rape, the prosecution submitted four of Plotkin's address books containing the names of hundreds of women. Plotkin claimed he did not know all of the women since some of the names had been given to him by friends and he had not yet called on them. Several women, however, did testify in court that Plotkin had, to cite the *Chronicle,* "lured them up to his apartment under one pretext or another, and forced his sexual attentions on them."

Plotkin's defense rested on two premises. First, through his own testimony Plotkin established a reputation for himself as a sexual libertine who frequently picked up girls in bars and took them to his house where sexual relations often took place. He was the Playboy. He claimed that the accusation of rape, therefore, was false — this incident had simply been one of many casual sexual relationships, the victim one of many playmates. The second premise of the defense was that his accuser was also a sexual libertine. However, the picture created of the young woman (fully 13 years younger than Plotkin) was not akin to the light-hearted, gay-bachelor image projected by the defendant. On the contrary, the day after the defense cross-examined the woman, the *Chronicle* printed a story headlined, "Grueling Day For Rape Case Victim." (A leaflet passed out by women in front of the courtroom was more succinct, "rape was committed by four men in a private apartment in October; on Thursday, it was done by a judge and a lawyer in a public courtroom.")

Through skillful questioning fraught with innuendo, Plotkin's defense attorney James Martin MacInnis portrayed the young woman as a licentious opportunist and unfit mother. MacInnis began by asking the young woman (then employed as a secretary) whether or not it was true that she was "familiar with liquor" and had worked as a "cocktail waitress." The young woman replied (the *Chronicle* wrote "admitted") that she had worked once or twice as a cocktail waitress. The attorney then asked if she had worked as a

secretary in the financial district but had "left that employment after it was discovered that you had sexual intercourse on a couch in the office." The woman replied, "That is a lie. I left because I didn't like working in a one-girl office. It was too lonely." Then the defense asked if, while working as an attendant at a health club, "you were accused of having a sexual affair with a man?" Again the woman denied the story, "I was never accused of that."

Plotkin's attorney then sought to establish that his client's accuser was living with a married man. She responded that the man was separated from his wife. Finally he told the court that she had "spent the night" with another man who lived in the same building.

At this point in the testimony the woman asked Plotkin's defense attorney, "Am I on trial? . . . It is embarrassing and personal to admit these things to all these people. . . . I did not commit a crime. I am a human being." The lawyer, true to the chivalry of his class, apologized and immediately resumed questioning her, turning his attention to her children. (She is divorced, and the children at the time of the trial were in a foster home.) "Isn't it true that your two children have a sex game in which one gets on top of another and they — " "That is a lie!" the young woman interrupted him. She ended her testimony by explaining "They are wonderful children. They are not perverted."

The jury, divided in favor of acquittal ten to two, asked the court stenographer to read the woman's testimony back to them. After this reading, the Superior Court acquitted the defendant of both the charges of rape and kidnapping.

According to the double standard a woman who has had sexual intercourse out of wedlock cannot be raped. Rape is not only a crime of aggression against the body; it is a transgression against chastity as defined by men. When a woman is forced into a sexual relationship, she has, according to the male ethos, been violated. But she is also defiled if she does not behave according to the double standard, by maintaining her chastity, or confining her sexual activities to a monogamous relationship.

One should not assume, however, that a woman can avoid the possibility of rape simply by behaving. Though myth would have it that mainly "bad girls" are raped, this theory has no basis in fact. Available statistics would lead one to believe that a safer course is promiscuity. In a study of rape done in the District of Columbia, it was found that 82 percent of the rape victims had a "good reputation." Even the Police Inspector's advice to stay off the streets is rather useless, for almost half of reported rapes occur in the home of the victim and are committed by a man she has never before seen. Like indiscriminate terrorism, rape can happen to any woman, and few women are ever without this knowledge.

But the courts and the police, both dominated by white males, continue to suspect the rape victim, *sui generis,* of provoking or asking for her own assault. According to Amir's study, the police tend to believe that a woman without a good reputation cannot be raped. The rape victim is usually submitted to countless questions about her own sexual mores and behavior by the police investigator. This preoccupation is partially justified by the legal requirements for prosecution in a rape case. The rape victim must have been penetrated, and she must have made it clear to her assailant that she did not want penetration (unless of course she is unconscious). A refusal to accompany a man to some isolated place to allow him to touch her does not in the eyes of the court, constitute rape. She must have said "no" at the crucial genital moment. And the rape victim, to qualify as such, must also have put up a physical struggle — unless she can prove that to do so would have been to endanger her life.

But the zealous interest the police frequently exhibit in the physical details of a rape case is only partially explained by the requirements of the court. A woman who was raped in Berkeley was asked to tell the story of her rape four different times "right out in the street," while her assailant was escaping. She was then required to submit to a pelvic examination to prove that penetration had taken place. Later, she was taken to the police station where she was asked the same questions again: "Were you forced?" "Did he penetrate?" "Are you sure your life was in danger and you had no other choice?" This woman had been pulled off the street by a man who held a 10-inch knife at her throat and forcibly raped her. She was raped at midnight and was not able to return to her home until five in the morning. Police contacted her twice again in the next week, once by telephone at two in the morning and once at four in the morning. In her words, "The rape was probably the least traumatic incident of the whole evening. If I'm ever raped again, . . . I wouldn't report it to the police because of all the degradation. . . ."

If white women are subjected to unnecessary and often hostile questioning after having been raped, third world women are often not believed at all. According to the white male ethos (which is not only sexist but racist), third world women are defined from birth as "impure." Thus the white male is provided with a pool of women who are fair game for sexual imperialism. Third world women frequently do not report rape and for good reason. When blues singer Billie Holliday was 10 years old, she was taken off to a local house by a neighbor and raped. Her mother brought the police to rescue her, and she was taken to the local police station crying and bleeding:

> When we got there, instead of treating me and Mom like somebody who called the cops for help, they treated me like I'd killed somebody. . . . I guess they had me figured for having enticed this old goat into the whorehouse. . . . All I know for sure is they threw me into a cell . . . a fat white matron . . . saw I was still bleeding, she felt sorry for me and gave me a couple glasses of milk. But nobody else did anything for me except give me filthy looks and snicker to themselves.
>
> After a couple of days in a cell they dragged me into a court. Mr. Dick got sentenced to five years. They sentenced me to a Catholic institution.

Clearly the white man's chivalry is aimed only to protect the chastity of "his" women.

As a final irony, that same system of sexual values from which chivalry is derived has also provided womankind with an unwritten code of behavior, called femininity, which makes a feminine woman the perfect victim of sexual aggression. If being chaste does not ward off the possibility of assault, being feminine certainly increases the chances that it will succeed. To be submissive is to defer to masculine strength; is to lack muscular development or any interest in defending oneself; is to let doors be opened, to have one's arm held when crossing the street. To be feminine is to wear shoes which make it difficult to run; skirts which inhibit one's stride; underclothes which inhibit the circulation. Is it not an intriguing observation that those very clothes which are thought to be flattering to the female and attractive to the male are those which make it impossible for a woman to defend herself against aggression?

Each girl as she grows into womanhood is taught fear. Fear is the form in which the female internalizes both chivalry and the double standard. Since, biologically speaking, women in fact have the same if not greater potential for sexual expression as do men, the woman who is taught that she must behave differently from a man must also learn to distrust her own carnality. She must deny her own feelings and learn not to act from them. She fears herself. This is the essence of passivity, and of course, a woman's passivity is not simply sexual but functions to cripple her from self-expression in every area of her life.

Passivity itself prevents a woman from ever considering her own potential for self-defense and forces her to look to men for protection. The woman is taught fear, but this time fear of the other; and yet her only relief from this fear is to seek out the other. Moreover, the passive woman is taught to regard herself as impotent, unable to act, unable even to perceive, in no way self-sufficient, and, finally, as the object and not the subject of human behavior. It is in this sense that a woman is deprived of the status of a human being. She is not free to be.

III

Since Ibsen's Nora slammed the door on her patriarchical husband, woman's attempt to be free has been more or less fashionable. In this 19th century portrait of a woman leaving her marriage, Nora tells her husband, "Our home has been nothing but a playroom. I have been your doll-wife just as at home I was papa's doll-child." And, at least on the stage, "The Doll's House" crumbled, leaving audiences with hope for the fate of the modern woman. And today, as in the past, womankind has not lacked examples of liberated women to emulate: Emma Goldman, Greta Garbo and Isadora Duncan all denounced marriage and the double standard, and believed their right to freedom included sexual independence; but still their example has not affected the lives of millions of women who continue to marry, divorce and remarry, living out their lives dependent on the status and economic power of men. Patriarchy still holds the average woman prisoner not because she lacks the courage of an Isadora Duncan, but because the material conditions of her life prevent her from being anything but an object.

In the *Elementary Structures of Kinship,* Claude Levi-Strauss gives to marriage this universal description, "It is always a system of exchange that we find at the origin of the rules of marriage." In this system of exchange, a woman is the "most precious possession." Levi-Strauss continues that the custom of including women as booty in the marketplace is still so general that "a whole volume would not be sufficient to enumerate instances of it." Levi-Strauss makes it clear that he does not exclude Western Civilization from his definition of "universal" and cites examples from modern wedding ceremonies. (The marriage ceremony is still one in which the husband and wife become one, and "that one is the husband.")

The legal proscription against rape reflects this possessory view of women. An article in the 1952–53 *Yale Law Journal* describes the legal rationale behind laws against rape: "In our society sexual taboos, often enacted into law, buttress a system of monogamy based upon the law of 'free bargaining' of the potential spouses. Within this process the woman's power to withhold or grant sexual access is an important bargaining weapon." Presumably then, laws against rape are intended to protect the right of a woman, not for physical self-determination, but for physical "bargaining." The article

goes on to explain explicitly why the preservation of the bodies of women is important to men:

> The consent standard in our society does more than protect a significant item of social currency for women; it fosters, and is in turn bolstered by, a masculine pride in the exclusive possession of a sexual object. The consent of a woman to sexual intercourse awards the man a privilege of bodily access, a personal "prize" whose value is enhanced by sole ownership. An additional reason for the man's condemnation of rape may be found in the threat to his status from a decrease in the "value" of his sexual possession which would result from forcible violation.

The passage concludes by making clear whose interest the law is designed to protect. "The man responds to this undercutting of his status as *possessor* of the girl with hostility toward the rapist; no other restitution device is available. The law of rape provides an orderly outlet for his vengeance." Presumably the female victim in any case will have been sufficiently socialized so as not to consciously feel any strong need for vengeance. If she does feel this need, society does not speak to it.

The laws against rape exist to protect rights of the male as possessor of the female body, and not the right of the female over her own body. Even without this enlightening passage from the *Yale Law Review,* the laws themselves are clear: In no state can a man be accused of raping his wife. How can any man steal what already belongs to him? It is in the sense of rape as theft of another man's property that Kate Millett writes, "Traditionally rape has been viewed as an offense one male commits against another — a matter of abusing his woman." In raping another man's woman, a man may aggrandize his own manhood and concurrently reduce that of another man. Thus a man's honor is not subject directly to rape, but only indirectly, through "his" woman.

If the basic social unit is the family, in which the woman is a possession of her husband, the superstructure of society is a male hierarchy, in which men dominate other men (or patriarchal families dominate other patriarchal families). And it is no small irony that, while the very social fabric of our male-dominated culture denies women equal access to political, economic and legal power, the literature, myth and humor of our culture depicts women not only as the power behind the throne, but the real source of the oppression of men. The religious version of this fairy tale blames Eve for both carnality and eating of the tree of knowledge, at the same time making her gullible to the obvious devices of a serpent. Adam, of course, is merely the trusting victim of love. Certainly this is a biased story. But no more biased than the one television audiences receive today from the latest slick comedians. Through a media which is owned by men, censored by a State dominated by men, all the evils of this social system which make a man's life unpleasant are blamed upon "the wife." The theory is: were it not for the female who waits and plots to "trap" the male into marriage, modern man would be able to achieve Olympian freedom. She is made the scapegoat for a system which is in fact run by men.

Nowhere is this more clear than in the white racist use of the concept of white womanhood. The white male's open rape of black women, coupled with his overweening concern for the chastity and protection of his wife and daughters, represents an extreme of sexist and racist hypocrisy. While on the one hand she was held up as the standard for purity and virtue, on the other the Southern white woman was never asked if she wanted to be on a pedestal, and in

fact any deviance from the male-defined standards for white womanhood was treated severely. (It is a powerful commentary on American racism that the historical role of Blacks as slaves, and thus possessions without power, has robbed black women of legal and economic protection through marriage. Thus black women in Southern society and in the ghettoes of the North have long been easy game for white rapists.) The fear that black men would rape white women was, and is, classic paranoia. Quoting from Ann Breen's unpublished study of racism and sexism in the South *"The New South: White Man's Country,"* Frederick Douglass legitimately points out that, had the black man wished to rape white women, he had ample opportunity to do so during the civil war when white women, the wives, sisters, daughters and mothers of the rebels, were left in the care of Blacks. But yet not a single act of rape was committed during this time. The Ku Klux Klan, who tarred and feathered black men and lynched them in the honor of the purity of white womanhood, also applied tar and feathers to a Southern white woman accused of bigamy, which leads one to suspect that Southern white men were not so much outraged at the violation of the woman as a person, in the few instances where rape was actually committed by black men, but at the violation of his property rights." In the situation where a black man was found to be having sexual relations with a white woman, the white woman could exercise skin-privilege, and claim that she had been raped, in which case the black man was lynched. But if she did not claim rape, she herself was subject to lynching.

In constructing the myth of white womanhood so as to justify the lynching and oppression of black men and women, the white male has created a convenient symbol of his own power which has resulted in black hostility toward the white "bitch," accompanied by an unreasonable fear on the part of many white women of the black rapist. Moreover, it is not surprising that after being told for two centuries that he wants to rape white women, occasionally a black man does actually commit that act. But it is crucial to note that the frequency of this practice is outrageously exaggerated in the white mythos. Ninety percent of reported rape is intra- not inter-racial.

In *Soul on Ice,* Eldridge Cleaver has described the mixing of a rage against white power with the internalized sexism of a black man raping a white woman. "Somehow I arrived at the conclusion that, as a matter of principle, it was of paramount importance for me to have an antagonistic, ruthless attitude toward white women. . . . Rape was an insurrectionary act. It delighted me that I was defying and trampling upon the white man's law, upon his system of values and that I was defiling his women — and this point, I believe, was the most satisfying to me because I was very resentful over the historical fact of how the white man has used the black woman." Thus a black man uses white women to take out his rage against white men. But in fact, whenever a rape of a white woman by a black man does take place, it is again the white man who benefits. First, the act itself terrorizes the white woman and makes her more dependent on the white male for protection. Then, if the woman prosecutes her attacker, the white man is afforded legal opportunity to exercise overt racism. Of course, the knowledge of the rape helps to perpetuate two myths which are beneficial to white male rule — the bestiality of the black man and the desirability of white women. Finally, the white man surely benefits because he himself is not the object of attack — he has been allowed to stay in power.

Indeed, the existence of rape in any form is beneficial to the ruling class of white males. For rape is a kind of terrorism which severely limits the freedom of women and makes women dependent on men. Moreover, in the act of rape, the rage that one man may harbor toward another higher in the male hierarchy can be deflected toward a female scapegoat. For every man there is always someone lower on the social scale on whom he can take out his aggressions. And this is any woman alive.

This oppressive attitude towards women finds its institutionalization in the traditional family. For it is assumed that a man "wears the pants" in his family — he exercises the option of rule whenever he so chooses. Not that he makes all the decisions — clearly women make most of the important day-to-day decisions in a family. But when a conflict of interest arises, it is the man's interest which will prevail. His word, in itself, is more powerful. He lords it over his wife in the same way his boss lords it over him, so that the very process of exercising his power becomes as important an act as obtaining whatever it is his power can get for him. This notion of power is key to the male ego in this culture, for the two acceptable measures of masculinity are a man's power over women and his power over other men. A man may boast to his friends that "I have 20 men working for me." It is also aggrandizement of his ego if he has the financial power to clothe his wife in furs and jewels. And, if a man lacks the wherewithal to acquire such power, he can always express his rage through equally masculine activities — rape and theft. Since male society defines the female as a possession, it is not surprising that the felony most often committed together with rape is theft. As the following classic tale of rape points out, the elements of theft, violence and forced sexual relations merge into an indistinguishable whole.

The woman who told this story was acquainted with the man who tried to rape her. When the man learned that she was going to be staying alone for the weekend, he began early in the day a polite campaign to get her to go out with him. When she continued to refuse his request, his chivalrous mask dropped away:

I had locked all the doors because I was afraid, and I don't know how he got in; it was probably through the screen door. When I woke up, he was shaking my leg. His eyes were red, and I knew he had been drinking or smoking. I thought I would try to talk my way out of it. He started by saying that he wanted to sleep with me, and then he got angrier and angrier, until he started to say, "I want pussy," "I want pussy." Then, I got scared and tried to push him away. That's when he started to force himself on me. It was awful. It was the most humiliating, terrible feeling. He was forcing my legs apart and ripping my clothes off. And it was painful. I did fight him — he was slightly drunk and I was able to keep him away. I had taken judo a few years back, but I was afraid to throw a chop for fear that he'd kill me. I could see he was getting more and more violent. I was thinking wildly of some way to get out of this alive, and then I said to him, "Do you want money. I'll give you money." We had money but I was also thinking that if I got to the back room I could telephone the police — as if the police would have even helped. It was a stupid thing to think of because obviously he would follow me. And he did. When he saw me pick up the phone, he tried to tie the cord around my neck. I screamed at him that I did have the money in another room, that I was going to call the police because I was scared, but that I would never tell anybody what happened. It would be an absolute secret. He said, okay, and I went to get the money. But when he got it, all of a sudden he got this crazy look in his eye and he said to me, "Now I'm going to kill you." Then I started saying my prayers. I knew there was nothing I could do. He started

to hit me — I still wasn't sure if he wanted to rape me at this point — or just to kill me. He was hurting me, but hadn't yet gotten me into a strangle-hold because he was still drunk and off balance. Somehow we pushed into the kitchen where I kept looking at this big knife. But I didn't pick it up. Somehow, no matter how much I hated him at that moment, I still couldn't imagine putting the knife in his flesh, and then I was afraid he would grab it and stick it into me. Then he was hitting me again and somehow we pushed through the back door of the kitchen and onto the porch steps. We fell down the steps and that's when he started to strangle me. He was on top of me. He just went on and on until finally I lost consciousness. I did scream, though my screams sounded like whispers to me. But what happened was that a cab driver happened by and frightened him away. The cab driver revived me — I was out only a minute at the most. And then I ran across the street and I grabbed the woman who was our neighbor and screamed at her, "Am I alive? Am I still alive?"

·   ·   ·

Rape is an act of aggression in which the victim is denied her self-determination. It is an act of violence which, if not actually followed by beatings or murder, nevertheless always carries with it the threat of death. And finally, rape is a form of mass terrorism, for the victims of rape are chosen indiscriminately, but the propagandists for male supremacy broadcast that it is women who cause rape by being unchaste or in the wrong place at the wrong time — in essence, by behaving as though they were free.

The threat of rape is used to deny women employment. (In California, the Berkeley Public Library, until pushed by the Federal Employment Practices Commission, refused to hire female shelvers because of perverted men in the stacks.) The fear of rape keeps women off the streets at night. Keeps women at home. Keeps women passive and modest for fear that they be thought provocative.

It is part of human dignity to be able to defend oneself, and women are learning. Some women have learned karate; some to shoot guns. And yet we will not be free until the threat of rape and the atmosphere of violence is ended, and to end that the nature of male behavior must change.

But rape is not an isolated act that can be rooted out from patriarchy without ending patriarchy itself. The same men and power structure who victimize women are engaged in the act of raping Vietnam, raping Black people and the very earth we live upon. Rape is a classic act of domination where, in the words of Kate Millett, "the emotions of hatred, contempt, and the desire to break or violate personality," takes place. This breaking of the personality characterizes modern life itself. No simple reforms can eliminate rape. As the symbolic expression of the white male hierarchy, rape is the quintessential act of our civilization, one which, Valerie Solanis warns, is in danger of "humping itself to death."

7

Discrimination:
Institutionalized Asymmetry

Sexism is not fully realized only in women's personal lives. As a major part of the consciousness of our culture, it is expressed as well through all the public institutions, formalized in law and custom. Women's demeaned and subordinated image is reflected in our position in the major public sectors of society. Marginal in importance and participation, in the economy women are poor; in politics and government, powerless; before the law, discriminated against and deprived of citizens' rights. In each instance the reality of the situation is denied, distorted, or justified by the same body of myth, lore, and mystification that governs women's personal lives. Let us look at the facts of the position that women actually do occupy in the economy, in politics, and before the law. Keep in mind that these social structures are interrelated and reinforcing. An intricate web of circumstances determines women's standing in each area, and that in turn determines the nuances of our personal lives.

Women in the Economy

The Myth: Lucky Ladies

Everyone has heard tales of pampered wives who play bridge and drink coffee while harried husbands labor to win the dollars so carelessly dropped at the supermarket or dress shop. The wives earn no money of their own, but *since they spend it, they control it;* everyone in America "knows" that. There are tales of gay divorcées reveling in windfalls snatched from vanquished ex-husbands, merry widows collecting fat sums from hard-earned insurance policies and social security, lazy but comfortable welfare mothers ripping off the state and living on steak. Such types compose a partial list of the privileged, well-off women reputed to represent the majority of the female population.

The Reality: Women Are Poor

Compared with men, in every category women are by and large disadvantaged. Within and across job classifications women have lower salaries, generally have less disposable income, are more likely to fall below nationally set poverty standards, and in several ways have far less recourse to remedy.

SOME FACTS REGARDING WOMEN'S EARNINGS AND INCOME   At present, on the average and across all occupations, full-time women workers earn about 59 percent of the salaries of men. In 1977, women's median income was $8,618, men's was $14,626.[1]

Generally women are employed and segregated in the lowest paid occupations and jobs. About 80 percent of the female labor force in 1978 worked in clerical, sales, service, and factory jobs.[2] In 1976, women constituted 87.7 percent of all cashiers, 98.5 percent of all secretaries, 85.2 percent of all food-counter workers, but 12.8 percent of all physicians, 1.8 percent of all engineers, and 9.2 percent of all lawyers. Between 90 and 91 percent of all bank tellers and bookkeepers are women, but only 24.7 percent of all bank officials are women.[3]

Even within occupations, women earn less than men. For example, in sales, men's median weekly salary in 1976 was $244, whereas women earned $111, only 45 percent of the figure for men. (As Gloria Steinem pointed out, in department stores men sell stoves and refrigerators; women sell men's underwear. Why? Surely not because of appropriate experience.) Even in clerical work, women's

[1] "An Overview of Women in the Workforce" (Washington, D.C.: National Commission on Working Women, Center for Women and Work), 1978.

[2] Ibid.

[3] *U.S. Working Women: A Databook* (Washington, D.C.: Dept. of Labor, Bureau of Labor Statistics, 1977), p. 9.

Figure 7.1 Fully employed women continue to earn less than fully employed men of either white or minority (includes all races other than white) races.

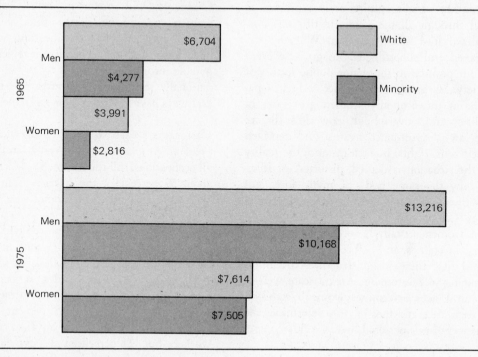

Source: Prepared by the Women's Bureau, Employment Standards Administration, U.S. Department of Labor, from data published by the Bureau of the Census, U.S. Department of Commerce, and presented in *The Spirit of Houston,* The First National Women's Conference, National Commission on the Observance of International Women's Year, U.S. Department of State, Washington, D.C., 1978.

median weekly earning in 1976, $147, was only 64 percent of men's $228.[4]

According to data from the 1970 *Census of Population,* the per capita income of male heads of households was twice that of female heads of households. Single men had one and one-half times the per capita income of single women.[5]

Only 14 percent of divorced or separated women are awarded alimony by the courts. Of those, only 46 percent collect regularly. Of the 44 percent of divorced mothers awarded child support, 45 percent collect regularly.[6]

Since women earn less over a lifetime, their social security and retirement benefits are smaller. Employed women whose husbands paid into the social security system receive only their husband's benefits, not both theirs and his. This situation is worsened because women often retire with benefits at

[4] Ibid.

[5] Susan A. Macmanus and Nikki R. Van Hightower, "The Impacts of Local Government Tax Structures on Women: Inefficiencies and Inequalities," *Social Science Journal,* 14, No. 2 (April 1977), 105.

[6] Market Opinion Research, Detroit, Michigan. Study done for International Women's Year Commission, Department of State, 1975.

62 rather than 65, receiving, therefore, even lower rates and having even smaller monthly benefits.

SOME FACTS REGARDING POVERTY In March 1978, 14.4 percent of American families were headed by women. Their yearly income in 1977 was barely half that of their male counterparts: $7,765 compared with $14,538 for male-headed families.[7]

In 1978, families headed by women constituted 48 percent of all poor families, and the proportion is growing.

Of households headed by women, 33 percent lived in poverty in 1977 compared with 5.6 percent of households headed by men.[8]

Sixty percent of all widows live in poverty. Three million elderly women live in poverty,[9] a larger number and proportion than men. In 1978 half the American women over 65 years of age had incomes below $3,000 per year. The average female retiree received less than $81 per month.[10]

SOME FACTS REGARDING CONTROL OF MONEY In 1972, men held 90 percent of all jobs paying $10,000 and over.[11]

Of stock owned by individuals in 1972, 24 percent was owned by men compared with 18 percent owned by women, and the difference is likely to be greater since frequently stock actually owned by men is held for tax

purposes in the name of wives or other women in the men's personal lives.[12]

In 1977, only six women held stock exchange seats.[13]

In forty-two of the fifty states, those without community property laws, a husband has complete control over his earnings and the standard of living he provides his family.[14] A wife spends a husband's earnings only by his consent. No actual legal control or decision making resides with the wife.

Upon a husband's death, a nonworking wife inherits the home or possessions acquired with her husband, and she is liable to pay inheritance tax on them. She is not legally perceived to own them outright since she is not perceived as having contributed financially to their acquisition.

SOME FACTS REGARDING WOMEN'S CONTRIBUTION TO THE ECONOMY Women work because they need to. Of the female labor force in 1976, 24 percent were single; 19 percent were widowed, divorced, or separated; and 23 percent had husbands earning less than $10,000.[15]

In 1976, 21.6 million married (husband present) women worked. They contributed 26.3 percent of the family income. In families earning less than $10,000 per year, however, they contributed 59.5 percent of the income, and 44.7 percent in families earning less than $15,000.[16]

DISCRIMINATION EVERYWHERE Women workers are channeled into occupations that are seen as "appropriate" for women, continuations of the roles females are expected to

7 "An Overview of Women in the Workforce."

8 See the article by Elyce J. Rotella at the end of this chapter, page 329ff.

9 "Women and Money: Beyond the Cookie Jar," *Equal Rights Monitor*, May–June 1977, p. 7.

10 "Hard Facts About Retirement for Women," *Changing Times*, June 1978, p. 13.

11 Shirley Bernard, "Women's Economic Status: Some Clichés and Some Facts" *Women: A Feminist Perspective* ed. Jo Freeman (Palo Alto, Calif.: Mayfield, 1975), p. 240.

12 Ibid., p. 241.

13 "Women and Money," p. 7.

14 Ibid., p. 6.

15 Data from Women's Bureau, Employment Standards Administration; see Fig. 7.2.

16 *U.S. Working Women*, p. 38.

Figure 7.2 Most women work because of economic need (women in the labor force, by marital status, March 1976).

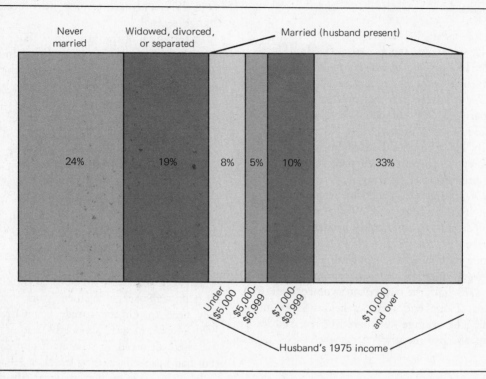

Source: Prepared by the Women's Bureau, Employment Standards Administration, from data published by the Bureau of Labor Statistics, U.S. Department of Labor, and presented in *The Spirit of Houston,* The First National Women's Conference, National Commission on the Observance of International Women's Year, U.S. Department of State, Washington, D.C., 1978.

fulfill: for example, serving and facilitating (secretaries, waitresses, nurses, "gal Fridays"), child care (teachers on the elementary level, pediatricians), sex and decoration (receptionists, airline hostesses, entertainers). Occupations historically reserved for women are notoriously underpaid regardless of the level of expertise needed to perform them, and they are generally controlled by male administrators who make it impossible, one way or the other, for women to set their own market and hence their own demands.

When women try to break out of these occupational ghettos they face other problems.

Various practices, official or otherwise, challenge entry into male-dominated areas — apprenticeship programs in trade unions, employment traps (for example, odd hours, machines too heavy for females), discriminatory hiring, and so on. Women who do manage entry are generally channeled to the low-earning end of the spectrum. Sales, for example, was shown earlier to favor men financially; high-line items may be reserved for men by seniority rules, for example, which disadvantage women who more frequently are temporary, part-time, or returning workers.

Unemployment rates are much higher for

women than for men, probably even higher than they appear to be, for the number of women who have not yet worked but want to cannot be properly evaluated. Federal retraining and work assistance programs have been extremely discriminatory, aiming at the male worker and offering little to the female.

Aid to Families with Dependent Children (AFDC), too, encourages and even insures female poverty. AFDC benefits are barely sufficient for subsistence, yet the mother with no husband, few skills, and children to care for is in a bind. Although job "retraining" may be supported, "education" is not. Often, the kind of jobs an AFDC mother may train for cannot give her sufficient income to secure both adequate child care and subsistence, yet the education that would make work outside the home truly profitable remains generally out of her reach. If she works to earn income additional to AFDC in order to make her life more tolerable, she stands to lose her public aid, leaving her few alternatives. With aid for abortion and contraception denied her, the plight of the welfare mother worsens.

Why?

What are the ideological factors that underlie the economic position of women? It is not too difficult to guess. Shirley Bernard expresses them in terms of "dominance."

> In a society where money means power, most of the money must come to the dominant group if it is to maintain the status quo. In our society white males are dominant; [as shown by Census Bureau figures for 1970], they earn substantially more than nonwhites and females. Among full-time workers, nonwhite males, who share "maleness" with the dominant group, earn about 70 percent as much as white males. White females, who share "whiteness" with the dominant group, earn about 58 percent as much as white

males. Nonwhite females, who share no characteristic of the dominant group, earn about 50 percent as much as white males.[17]

The notion of dominance is a shorthand that can be unpacked to reveal the entire range of beliefs and attitudes inherent in the patriarchal mind set. Once again, the nature of women's role and the gender ideal are the factors underlying women's disadvantaged position.

THE ROLE: WOMAN'S WORK In earlier chapters we saw that historically women have been perceived as created to be helpmeets to men, whereas men have been and are perceived as the central actors in society. In addition to performing the animalic functions of procreation and nursing, it is women's central responsibility to serve as underlaborers to men, to manage for them the necessary minutiae that muddy the waters of real creativity. For this function women are ideally suited, being less intelligent and less rational than men, hence both less capable of true accomplishment and more tolerant of detail and routine.

ON THE JOB Until very recently, and then only because of advances pressed by the women's movement, the "branch offices" of the public economic sector have been very much a study in patriarchal dominance. In offices, factories, hospitals, schools, and elsewhere, men "did the job," and women "helped." He managed while she answered his phone, sharpened his pencils, typed his letters, and perked his coffee. He cured the sick while she followed his orders, applied his prescriptions, and perked his coffee. He flew the airplane while she checked the tickets, served the customers, and perked his coffee. The rare woman who got to run the show

17 Bernard, "Women's Economic Status," p. 239.

was a peculiarity and a bewilderment, causing problems for her own self-image as well as for her male colleagues and subordinates.

Salaries reflected the relative positions, for line workers earn more than their assistants. Moreover, women *by virtue of being women,* regardless of position occupied, regardless of degree of education and ability required to do their job, earned less, whether in women's occupations or in others. Thus, nurses, schoolteachers, professional secretaries, and other traditionally female workers have been notoriously underpaid relative to their education, skill, and experience. Women in managerial or authoritative positions could not look forward to the rank, salary, or privilege of men of the same status.

A myth of contemporary culture is that these conditions no longer exist. However, little has actually changed. In fact, in some ways women have lost ground. The average salary of full-time women workers relative to men has actually dropped in the last several years, and there are proportionally fewer women in professional high-salaried positions than a generation earlier. Part of this may be accounted for by the greater numbers of women entering the public work force, but considering the legal and cultural drives toward parity in opportunity and compensation, the situation is disheartening.

Even where external structure and appearance seem to change, often the underlying reality is not different. An executive secretary with ten years' experience may be "promoted" to district sales manager (entry-level position for managerial class) with men several years her junior, but she may be the only one of her group with a typewriter on her desk. A female high school teacher may now receive salary equal to that of her male counterpart for her teaching, but if her extra duties at home or her sex role preclude her from requesting playground duties or coaching, she may thereby be denied the extra income that

raises the job above the average. "Maid" and "Janitor" may be redefined as "Maintenance Worker-2" and receive equal pay, but if only men make it to "Maintenance Worker-3" (supervisor) the equal opportunity is only a sham.

It is important to recognize the force and weight of the ideological and psychological dynamics straining to maintain the status quo, straining to thwart structural changes. The female sex-role and gender ideal is a major, if not the major, determinant of women's position in the work place. Michael Korda, a publishing house executive, contends that in the work place men perceive women workers, whether colleagues or subordinates, as extensions of their wives or other women in their personal lives. That is, they see women as females first and workers second, and this perception conditions men's attitudes and behavior toward women on the job.[18]

The anthropologist George Gilder offers a further, even more psychologically profound insight into men's resistance to women's economic equality.[19] In primitive times, Gilder theorizes, men proved and maintained their masculine identity through the hunt by facing hardship and death. Today, although industrialism has obviated the hunt per se, men still need to exhibit and reinforce their sense of masculinity. Their work, therefore, whatever it is, has been substituted for their old arena, making it a kind of symbolic hunt. It is thus crucial for men to maintain their job's aura of manliness, its rituals and traditions, and most of all its separation from women and all things female. As women encroach upon a field of endeavor, we throw doubt on its manliness, destroying its ability to function as a symbolic hunt, sending men

[18] Michael Korda, *Male Chauvinism! How It Works* (New York: Random House, 1972).
[19] George Gilder, *Sexual Suicide* (New York: Quadrangle, 1973).

scurrying to more distant bastions of masculinity. In essence, in Gilder's view, the plain fact of the work place is that for psycho-sexual reasons men simply do not want women there: Other arguments are mere rationales. Whatever one thinks of the man-the-hunter theory, the truth probably lies in this deeper region: Men do not want female equality at work. Gilder concludes that women should stay out, leave men their bastions and their sources of identity. Feminists, of course, go another way. Martyrdom or sacrifice on the altar of masculinity is a price too high either for women or for the totality of humankind. Women not only *need* to work; as citizens, women have a right to work, just as men do, even if it were for "frivolous" reasons such as sport, or happiness, or fulfillment, or the "proving of one's identity." Men will have to find other ways to prove their masculinity or other means of satisfaction. Women, however, must change as well.

GENDER: SUBLIMINAL EFFECTS It is true that very often a woman's relationship to a job or career is different from a man's. Part of that difference comes as a result of external conditions — the double burden of home and child care, barriers to opportunity, misogynist attitudes and behaviors. But other factors in those different relations to work reside within ourselves as women, our own attitudes and behavior, the often hidden or subliminal effects of our feminine socialization and our gender conditioning.

As detailed earlier, we are raised to see ourselves as being second to men, husbands, and employer/workers, our interests and actions subordinate to their needs and wishes. As wives, our husbands' jobs, desires, and values are to supersede our own. According to traditional rules, we work or fulfill ourselves only after we accomplish our "primary duties." Even the modern, liberated woman is subject to the tremendous force of that

other commitment. Not wanting to choose between work and family, subject to a social structure that decrees her responsible for the home, a woman in the work place is indeed doubly burdened. Like it or not, aware of it or not, married or not, the weight of that burden imposed on us is real, and it does interfere with our work. Even under the best conditions, no wife clears for us the bothersome details of living or guarantees us unhampered mobility.

Very few of us were raised to see ourselves primarily as workers of one kind or another in the public marketplace. Even for women who work full-time all their lives, there is the inbred image of women as temporary or marginal workers, as supplementary rather than central earners. We have often been more apt, then, to accept inadequate incomes, reduced benefits, or poor conditions. To meet home demands we may settle for part-time shifts, poor hours, or local jobs, all of which can be terribly exploitative.

The problem goes even deeper, for in addition to these reduced expectations of work, most of us are conditioned to carry reduced expectations of ourselves. Modeling after our mothers as young girls, serving our brothers and fathers, we learned to serve in general. Comfortable with the familiar behavior of subordination, we tend not to be sufficiently uncomfortable with the same requirements at work. Passively we absorb inappropriate use of our energy and time in a way that men would not tolerate. Accustomed to placing our attachments to men above many things, we might be more loyal to an exploitative employer than to a union of sister employees.

But even when we learn these things and consciously try to transcend the inherited values of femininity, we are still subject to the "outposts in the head." We must not only unlearn the destructive patterns we have been given, but we must somehow make up for the experiences we did not have, those reserved for males only, experiences such as the competition of team sports or the support system of the male in-group.

Women Before the Law: Some Relevant Principles

There are some essential features of law that we should keep in mind to help us understand women's relationship to the legal system: Laws are the rules of the game. When we speak of the law in our society we mean a collection of rules and procedures codified, formalized, made explicit; we mean the conceptual framework within which such "rules" are written, a set of values, attitudes, and general principles toward people, community, and government; we mean a kind of overriding loyalty to the concept of law as such, to living by the rules we set for ourselves; and we mean the whole system of legislation, courts, procedures, and people that actualizes the abstract concepts.

Since laws that contradict or clash with social mores are most likely to be disregarded or disobeyed, a law, to carry weight and command obedience in its own right (without undue force), must express or coincide with the ideas and perceptions of a majority of the people governed. Therefore, law can be understood to represent the formal expression of nonformal or sociocultural ideals and commitments — norms, mores, values — the unwritten rules of the game for any people.

Laws are written by people who hold power. In our society, law is enacted by legislatures made up of individuals said to be representative of a majority of voters. It is from this representativeness that legislators in large part are supposed to derive their power, and it is from their ability to express the will of the public that they maintain it. To a degree, the legislators do express the public will; and to a degree, they do not. What is true, however, is that the laws we live by are written and enacted by those people who, one way or the other, maintain their place in the legislatures by being able to satisfy their constituents that they are expressing the common will. That is why and how laws so clearly reflect the character of current mores, and specifically the mores of those who have and exercise power.

Our legal system relies heavily on precedent, continuity, and conservatism to give it stability and to ensure orderliness, credibility, and respect. Judicial decisions made today are largely based on decisions made earlier and on an interpretation of what is perceived to be the original intent of the framers of any law. Change in the body of law is meant to come slowly and cautiously. To a large degree, the past directs the present and the future, and the system tends very strongly to maintain the status quo.

Law, Women, and Men

When we relate these principles of law to women's position in society, the source of certain aspects of our situation becomes abundantly clear. The law, in conceptualization, policy, practice, execution, and application, is almost entirely masculine.

In overwhelming proportions the people in power who have written the laws, interpreted, argued, used, and enforced them, have been men. Legislators, judges, teachers and philosophers of law, court officials, lawyers, and police have been and are now predominantly male. Women, having been barred one way or another from the areas of power and decision making, are represented in absurdly small numbers in every aspect of politics and law. The representation of feminists, women consciously committed to women's rights and needs, is even smaller. Until as recently as 1920, the entire constituency that legislators and public officials had to satisfy was male. Before suffrage, women had no formal power at all. Today, without unity of common goals, without significant spheres of public influence, women's clout is little better.

It is a small wonder, therefore, that the law should reflect a male perspective. Given that the creators of our legal system and the constituency for whom it was created were and are the sons of patriarchy, consciously and unconsciously heir to all the perceptions, attitudes, and values it entails, our legal system is very sexist. It clearly accepts the traditional images and values of male and female, awards to men privilege and advantage in every sphere of life, public and private, and sanctions and reinforces the subordination of women to men. Judicial decisions on every level and in every area of concern — domestic relations, civil rights, labor and employment, crime, and others — reflect the common social themes regarding "femininity" and the sexes: that men and women, being "naturally" different in capacities, needs, and function, should occupy different spheres of activity;[20] that because women are weak and dependent, we should be "protected," both from the ugliness of life and the dangers of our own inferiority; that because women are both morally and intellectually less competent than men, less rational and trustworthy, we should be under greater constraint.

What this means to us as women is that the legal system, which is allegedly designed to protect and assist citizens in the activities of their lives, often thwarts us instead. It means that when we go to the courts for redress of crimes or injustice, we go as little girls to a father, as supplicants, and we go to a system that sees us and the world in a way

that is very much to our detriment. Male lawyers must argue for us (often missing issues central to our experience). Male judges must apply masculist laws to our female circumstances (interpreting them from their privileged male position). Male police must believe us and accept the credibility of beings said to have no credibility. These circumstances make the legal system a very different place for women than it is for men. The statistics bearing on rape, wife battering, child support, or prison sentences for women, to name just a few conspicuous areas of unevenhanded justice, bear this out. We know, furthermore, that since the law tends to conservatism and the status quo, we cannot expect change easily or soon, especially without some very powerful catalysts.

Points and Instances: A Short History

Law is based on precedent, and the past directs the future. Regarding the law, what kind of past do women have?

From earliest times in Western culture, as one might expect in patriarchy, the position of women has been marginal and shaky. Jo Freeman, like Kate Millett, argues that our identification and relationship to men can be understood in terms of caste.[21] Unlike a class, from which one may emerge, a caste is a rigid category of stratification based on characteristics one has no hand in determining — birth, color, or sex, for example. Women's caste, from which one cannot emerge, entails certain functions, activities, and behaviors. It imposes on us a whole separate set of expectations with attendant rewards and punishments. Maintaining this caste (this "place")

[20] Barbara A. Brown, Thomas I. Emerson, Gail Falk, and Ann E. Freedman, "The Equal Rights Amendment: A Constitutional Basis for Equal Rights for Women," *Yale Law Journal*, 80 (1971), 876.

[21] Jo Freeman, "The Legal Basis of the Sexual Caste System," *Valparaiso University Law Review*, 5, No. 2 (1971), pp. 203ff.

has been a major occupation of the legal system.

FROM THE BEGINNINGS Freeman[22] describes as follows the origin of women's legal status in classical and common law:

> The sexual caste system is the longest, most firmly entrenched caste system known to Western civilization. Only one other caste has as long a tradition of separate law — that of children. Here an interesting irony emerges. Children have never been entitled to the rights of adults. This has been tolerated in part because their status as dependents is temporary. But for women, the status of childhood has been permanent. There is a long standing legal tradition reaching back to early Roman law which defines women as perpetual children. This tradition, known as the "Perpetual Tutelage of Women," has not been systematically recognized, but the definition of women as minors who never grow up, who must always be under the guidance of a male, has been carried down in modified form to the present day. Many vestiges of it can still be seen in the legal system and its judicial opinions.
>
> Roman law was an improvement over Greek society. In that cradle of democracy only men could be citizens in the *polis*. In fact, most women were slaves, and most slaves were women. In ancient Rome both the status of women and slaves improved slightly as they incorporated into the family under the rule of *patria potestas* or power of the father. This term designated not so much a familial relationship as a property relationship. All the land was owned by families, not individuals, and was under the control of the oldest male. Women and slaves could not assume proprietorship and in fact frequently were considered to be forms of property. The woman had to give any income she might receive to the head of the household and had no rights to her own children, to divorce or to any life outside the family. The relationship of women to man was designated by the concept of *manus* [that is, hand] under which the woman stood. Women had no rights under law — not even legal recognition. In any civil or criminal case she had to be represented by the *pater* who accepted legal judgment on himself and in turn judged her according to his whims. Unlike slaves, women could not be emancipated [that is, removed from under the hand] but could only go from under one hand to another. This was the nature of the marital relationship. At marriage a woman was "born again" into the household of the bridegroom's family and became the "daughter of her husband."
>
> Although later practice of Roman law was much less severe than the ancient rules, some of the more stringent aspects were incorporated into Canon Law and from there passed to the English Common Law. Interpretation and spread of the law varied throughout Europe, but it was through the English Common Law that such legal conceptions of women were made a part of American legal tradition.
>
> Even here history played tricks on women. Throughout the sixteenth and seventeenth centuries tremendous liberalizations were taking place in the common law attitude toward women. This was particularly true in the American colonies where rapidly accelerating commercial expansion often made it profitable to ignore old social rules. Many women owned their own businesses or were able to act as attorney in their husband's place when necessary. According to one authority:
>
> > The new legal rights which married women acquired to a greater or lesser degree throughout the colonies evolved out of the revised concept of the institution of marriage which resulted from the Protestant Revolution and out of the different economic and social conditions of colonial America. [R. Morris, *Studies in*

the History of American Law (1959), p. 126]

When Blackstone wrote his soon-to-be-famous *Commentaries on the Laws of England,* however, he chose to ignore these new trends in favor of codifying the old common law rules. Published in 1765, his work was used in Britain as a textbook, but in the United States it became a legal Bible. Concise and readable, it was frequently the only treatise to be found in law libraries in the United States until the middle of the nineteenth century, and novice attorneys rarely delved past its pages when seeking the roots of legal tradition.

It is in the Common Law that the caste distinctions between the sexes can most clearly be seen. Their roles are defined as separate and reciprocal. This is particularly clear in the marital law, and, indeed, this law was so explicit and that regarding single women so nonexistent that one would gather that the Common Law could not imagine the existence of women in the unmarried or never-married state. Single women were presumed to have the same rights in private law as single men. But when a woman married, these rights were lost, suspended under the feudal doctrine of "coverture." As Blackstone described: "By marriage, the husband and wife are one person in law; that is, the very being or legal existence of the woman is suspended during the marriage, or at least is incorporated and consolidated into that of the husband, under whose wing, protection, and cover, she performs everything."

As a result of this doctrine a married woman incurred many substantive and procedural disabilities. These were alleviated in part for women with property by the development of the "equitable trust" in the chancery courts — a device which had previously been associated with the protection of infants and idiots. But the early American legal system frequently lacked chancery courts; they usually had limited equity jurisdiction, and such relief was never a real possibility for women of limited financial means or education.

Blackstone had given short shrift to equity law, and the multitude of American attorneys that read the law from his pages applied the doctrine of coverture rather than that of equity. Thus when Edward Mansfield wrote the first major analysis of *The Legal Rights, Liabilities and Duties of Women* in 1845, he still found it necessary to pay homage to Blackstone:

> It appears that the husband's control over the person of his wife is so complete that he may claim her society altogether; that he may reclaim her if she goes away or is detained by others; that he may use constraint upon her liberty to prevent her going away, or to prevent improper conduct; that he may maintain suits for injuries to her person; that she cannot sue alone; and that she cannot execute a deed or valid conveyance without the concurrence of her husband. In most respects she loses the power of personal independence, and altogether that of separate action in legal matters.

WHERE DO WE GO FROM HERE? ERA? Historically, ours was a system of justice that, for good or ill, maintained separate systems of justice for women and men. The effect has been a legacy of discrimination and inequality that heavily influences juridical behavior today and supports sexism in the society at large.

Our legal structure will continue to support and command an inferior status for women so long as it permits any differentiation in legal treatment on the basis of sex. This is so for three distinct but related reasons. First, discrimination is a necessary concomitant of any sex-based law because a large number of women do not fit the female stereotype upon which such laws are predicated. Second, all aspects of separate treatment for women are inevitably interrelated; discrimination in one area creates discriminatory patterns in another. Thus a woman who has been denied equal access to education will be disadvantaged in employment even though she receives equal treatment there. Third, whatever the motivation for different treatment, the result is to create a dual system of rights and responsibilities in which the rights of each group are governed by a different set of values. History and experience have taught us that in such a dual system one group is always dominant and the other subordinate. As long as woman's place is defined as separate, a male-dominated society will define her place as inferior.[23]

Attempts at change have been spotty and largely ineffectual. The protections of the Fifth and Fourteenth amendments to the Constitution have not been consistently applied to women's cases; piecemeal legislative changes have been sparse and slow; judicial review has been "casual," [24] peremptory, or sexist itself.

Most feminists and many legislators and judicial experts maintain that what is necessary is one consistent, coherent principle of equal rights for women and men, a principle of law that would serve as mandate and policy for the public sector and for the courts. The embodiment of that principle is, of course, the Equal Rights Amendment:

Section 1: Equality of rights under the law shall not be denied or abridged by the United States or by any state on account of sex.

Section 2: The Congress shall have the power to enforce, by appropriate legislation, the provisions of this article.

Section 3. This amendment shall take effect two years after the date of ratification.

Put quite simply, the question is whether women are finally to be counted as full human beings before the law and in society.

Opponents to the amendment have argued on grounds both hysterical and spurious: (1) ERA would legitimate abortion (false), homosexual marriage (false), and extraordinary federal control over personal matters (false); (2) ERA would deny the sanctity of the family (false), a woman's right not to have outside employment (false), and "privacy" (false); (3) ERA will require equal numbers of women and men in the army and in combat (false), coed bathrooms (false), women to share barracks with men in the service (false), children to be placed in state-run child-care facilities (false).[25]

Most of these issues are created precisely to frighten both women and men into rejecting ERA. Should that fail, one argues that ERA is simply not necessary: The Fourteenth Amendment is sufficient to remedy instances of discrimination. Proponents of ERA point out, however, that review under the Fourteenth Amendment has been inconsistent and inefficient, and that ERA, in making sex an absolutely prohibited classification for law, would go a much longer way toward guaranteeing women equality of economic, educational, and political opportunity.

With all the public controversy, it is sometimes surprising to discover that the great majority of voters are for ERA. By 1978 the amendment had been passed by thirty-five states (see Figure 7.3), and even in many states that have not ratified, polls consistently show a majority of popular approval. It

[23] Brown et al., "The Equal Rights Amendment." Reprinted by permission of The Yale Law Journal Company, Fred B. Rothman & Company, and the authors from the *Yale Law Journal,* Vol. 80, pp. 873–74.

[24] Brown et al., "The Equal Rights Amendment," p. 876.

[25] See "Ladies! Have You Heard?" published by Missouri Men to Stop ERA, 2501 Leonard, St. Charles, Missouri.

Figure 7.3 Most of the U.S. is ready for the ERA. States shown in the shaded areas have already ratified the Equal Rights Amendment. If only three of the remaining states (shown unshaded here) join the majority by June 30, 1982, ERA will become the 27th amendment to the Constitution. States yet to ratify are Alabama, Arizona, Arkansas, Florida, Georgia, Illinois, Louisiana, Mississippi, Missouri, Nevada, North Carolina, Oklahoma, South Carolina, Utah, and Virginia.

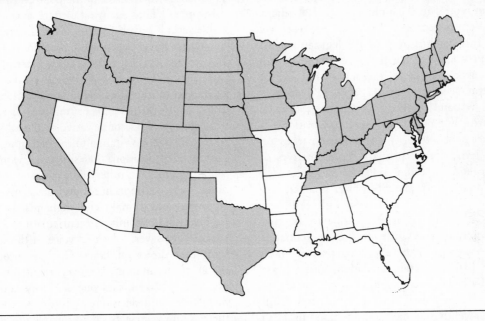

Source: *The Spirit of Houston,* The First National Women's Conference, National Commission on the Observance of International Women's Year, U.S. Department of State, Washington, D.C., 1978.

would appear that the minority opposed to ERA are entrenched in the power structure, are better supported financially, and are better organized.

The Equal Rights Amendment will be a valuable tool, to be sure, but we must keep in mind that ERA, like suffrage, cannot guarantee equality. It can function only as a tool, provided it is used properly. To gain equality, women must move to full participation in every sector of American life. Most particularly, women must develop influence and strength in government and politics, for there lies the heart of public power, the formal source of law, policy, and enforcement.

Women, Government, and Politics

To govern is to exercise authority, to wield power, to manage and guide the affairs of state and the citizenry. In this arena decisions and rules are made that affect every aspect of our lives, public and private, from how and where we may work to whether or not we may terminate a pregnancy. Yet here again, whether in the creation of law and public policy, in its interpretation, or in its execution, female citizens are absurdly underrepresented.

On the federal level, there have never been

more than nineteen women in the House of Representatives nor more than two in the Senate at one time.[26] No woman has ever been president or seriously considered for that office. No woman has ever occupied a top-level cabinet position or held major authority in central international or national affairs.

Women represent less than 8 percent of the membership of the state legislatures. As of 1976, only one female judge sat on the federal appellate level, and only 3 out of 333 federal district court judges were women.[27] No woman has ever sat on the Supreme Court. Women rarely serve in positions of power and authority in political parties on any level, nor as primary representatives of large and important pressure groups.

So far as formal public power is concerned, at present women have very little. Yet perhaps it would be more accurate to say that we *exercise* very little, for our potential is quite strong. After all, we represent more than half the total population, and we are legally entitled to vote, hold office, participate in and manipulate the political process. Until very recently, we have simply failed to do so to any extent.

There are a variety of reasons for women's minimal participation in the political process. Of course, a long history of enforced formal suppression, including disfranchisement and legal discrimination, has left a legacy of prejudicial attitudes and policies. Informal suppression, the effects of female roles and gender stereotypes, functions as effectively. The negative image of the authoritative women, the burdens of childrearing and homemaking, and the absence of social support for functioning outside of the assigned

"place" have all coalesced to keep women from organizing and unifying to challenge discrimination, exploitation, and sexism in the political arena and in the wider society.

Most important, until recently women did not identify themselves in the political process as women. That is, we failed to recognize ourselves as a distinct, meaningful category or class, as a legitimate pressure group, formed around and appropriately pressing for our own self-defined needs and goals. We have seen ourselves as Republicans or Democrats, as working class or middle class, as black or white, as conservative or liberal, and so on, but we have failed to make a most important identification, that simply of women, who, regardless of other connections and loyalties, have common needs and problems and have the right to make civil demands.

The result of inferior participation is an absence of power, a lack of voice in the decisions that direct our lives. Without proportional representation in government, one is not a free citizen, and one can only endure the whims and decisions of those in power; there is no recourse. Such a principle is clearly expressed in the early formulative documents of the American system, and it is obviously reflected in women's position in society. Men hold power and generally make decisions that they believe to be suitable. Women's perspective can be reflected in law only to the degree that women have public power and a political vote. We must not see ourselves as dependents or supplicants. The U.S. government is based on the principle that all citizens have a right to make their needs and wishes known, and to press for them in orderly fashion so that social balance may be achieved through the interplay of these pressures and social justice ultimately gained. We as women must affirm ourselves as full citizens, with the full complement of social responsibility and hence the full measure of social rights.

[26] Marianne Githens and Jewel L. Prestage, eds., *A Portait of Marginality* (New York: McKay, 1977), pp. 3–4.

[27] Ibid.

Selections

WOMEN'S ROLES IN ECONOMIC LIFE

ELYCE J. ROTELLA

Elyce J. Rotella was born in Johnstown, Pennsylvania, in 1946. She was educated in economic history at the University of Pennsylvania, where her doctoral research analyzed the rise in women's labor force participation in the United States at the turn of the century. Her other research includes work on the economics of fertility and the factor of mathematics training in women's earnings. While at the University of Pennsylvania she was active in the founding of the Women's Studies program. More recently she has served on the faculties of Women's Studies and Economics at San Diego State University. She is currently working on mathematics anxiety in women.

In this article Rotella describes and explains the concepts necessary to understand women's position in the American economy and details some of the data on women's present condition and status.

Any economy, no matter how it is organized, must decide how the resources of the society will be used to produce the goods and services that the members of the society will consume. A large portion of the productive resources of any society consists of the labor power of people. Therefore, the amounts and kinds of work that people do is of fundamental interest to anyone trying to understand an economy, and for that reason economists and other social scientists have long been interested in the ways that tasks are divided among the members of society. There are many reasons for the division of labor among individuals: The most obvious are differences in interest, ability and acquired skills. If all people were equally able to obtain all kinds of training, we would expect that persons would choose tasks simply

according to their interests and abilities. However, we know that in reality people's choices are limited in a number of ways. For example, some people are expected to follow in their parents' footsteps; some very able people do not go to college or receive other kinds of training because their families are poor; and some people's choices are limited by the expectations society has of the proper roles for them to play.

Both women's and men's choices are limited by sex roles. In all societies sex is an important determinant of the division of tasks. Most people believe that the sexual division of labor that prevails in their own society is natural and is determined by the biological differences between the sexes. However, there is actually considerable variation among societies in the tasks that are assigned to females and males. For example, farming is thought to be men's work in Western European societies, but in much of Africa farming was done by women until very recently. The one set of tasks that virtually all societies have assigned to women is child-rearing, although there are cultures in which it is customary for men to be quite involved in the care of children.

In this paper we will focus on the economic roles that women play in twentieth-century American society. Although much of what will be said can also be applied to many women in the rest of the world, it should be kept in mind that there are significant differences between cultures in the sexual division of labor. In addition the sexual division of labor has changed considerably over time, so that there are some tasks women routinely perform today that it would have been unthinkable for them to perform in the past.

The Economic System

Everyone in the economic system plays two basic roles — producer and consumer. People fulfill their producer role by using the resources that they control to make goods and provide services. For most people their most important productive resource is labor power, and they sell their labor to businesses or agencies that organize the production of goods and services that are sold in the market. In exchange for their labor people receive income in the form of wage earnings, which then makes it possible for them to fulfill their other basic economic role, that of consumer. In an advanced market economy, such as the modern U.S. economy, a very large proportion of goods and services are produced and sold in markets. This differs from the situation in subsistence economies in which most people consume the

things they produce themselves; in such economies few goods are traded in markets.

Consumers use their earnings to purchase the goods and services they need and want. Clearly, those people who receive the highest earnings in exchange for their labor are able to enjoy the consumption of the largest amounts of goods and services. In addition to spending the earnings that they receive in exchange for their own resources, some people are able to consume more market goods and services because they can use the earned income of others. For example, children are able to consume market goods because of their parents' earnings, and full-time housewives consume on the basis of their husbands' earnings.

In this paper we mainly will be examining women's roles as producers in the American economy, but we must keep in mind the close connection that exists among production, earnings, and consumption.

The Division of Women's Labor Between the Home and the Market

Women may use all of their labor power to work in their homes producing goods and services for themselves and their families. In this case they do not receive a money wage directly in exchange for their labor. In order to consume market goods and services they must be able to use the income earned by someone else, usually other family members. Such women are full-time homemakers, and they are fulfilling the economic role that our culture has, in the past century especially, considered to be the preferred and "natural" role for married women.

Many other women work for pay, that is, they exchange their labor services for a money wage in the market. Women who work for pay or who are looking for a paying job are said to be members of the labor force. The proportion of all women who are members of the labor force is called the *female labor force participation rate.*

Column one (1) in Table 1 shows how the female labor force participation rate has changed over this century. We can see that in 1900 only 20 percent of all women were at work for pay and that by 1978 over half of all women were in the labor force. This rise in the proportion of all women who work for pay is one of the most dramatic changes that has taken place in the U.S. economy in this century. It is very important to note that the pattern of increase in female labor force participation has not been the same in all time periods. The increase was quite slow up until 1940. The very rapid increase from 1940 to 1945 was due to the movement of women into the labor force during the Second World War when many men were fighting and there was a severe labor shortage. It was not until 1960 that female labor force participation reached the level that had prevailed in 1945. Since 1960 the growth of women's labor force participation has been extremely rapid.

Column two (2) in Table 1 shows how women's share of the total labor force has changed. In 1900 only 18 of every 100 paid workers were women. In 1978 women made up over 41 percent of the American labor force, and this number is still rising. Clearly then, paid employment is more important in the lives of American women today than it was in the past, and women are more important in the labor force.

This dramatic increase in women's participation in the labor force has caused economists to investigate the factors that affect women's decisions about how to structure their work lives. Marital status and family responsibilities have been found to have an important effect. Table 2 shows participation rates by marital status for selected years

Table 1 Women's labor force participation rate and women's share of the labor force

Year	(1) Women's labor force participation rate [a]	(2) Women's share of the labor force [b]
1900	20.0	18.1
1920	22.7	20.4
1930	23.6	21.9
1940	28.9	25.4
1945	38.1	36.1
1950	33.9	29.6
1955	35.7	31.6
1960	37.7	33.4
1965	39.2	35.2
1970	43.3	38.1
1974	45.6	39.4
1975	46.3	39.9
1976	47.3	40.5
1977	48.5	40.8
1978 (Sept)	50.6	41.4

[a] Women's Labor Force Participation Rate = $\dfrac{\text{women in the labor force}}{\text{women in the population}}$

[b] Women's Share of the Labor Force = $\dfrac{\text{women in the labor force}}{\text{total labor force}}$

since 1950; and for married women, it shows the effect of the presence of children in the home. Participation by single women was considerably higher than that of other groups at all dates. Although work force participation by women in all marital status groups has increased, the most notable increases were those of married women (husband present), who almost doubled their participation rate in just twenty-seven years. Since the overwhelming majority of American women marry (only 7 percent of women aged 30 to 34 in 1977 had never been married), it is these women whose actions domi-

Table 2 Women's labor force participation by marital status and presence of children

	1950	1960	1970	1977 (March)
Single (never married)	50.5	44.1	53.0	58.9
Widowed, divorced, husband absent	37.8	40.0	39.1	41.8
Married (husband present)	23.8	30.5	40.8	46.6
Married (husband present)				
With children 6 to 17 only	28.3	39.0	49.2	55.6
With children under 6	11.9	18.6	30.3	39.3
With children 3 to 5 (none under 3)	NA	25.1	37.0	46.4
With children under 3	NA	15.3	25.8	34.3

nate the female work force and who have been responsible for the bulk of the female labor force growth since the Second World War. Some of this increase in participation has also been due to the rise in the proportion of women who are not currently married because of the increase in the divorce rate and because of the recent trend toward later marriage for women.

Since married women are usually expected to bear the primary responsibility for housework and child care, it is not surprising that marriage and children reduce the likelihood that women will work for pay. When such women do work in the market, they generally assume the "double burden" of having two jobs. Recent surveys show that husbands' help with housework does not increase substantially when their wives are employed. It is interesting (and perhaps surprising) to see that, even in the face of this "double burden," labor force participation by married women with children is rising very rapidly. Indeed, the greatest increases are occurring among women with young children. In 1950 only 11.9 percent of married women with children under 6 were in the labor force; in 1977 this figure was 39.3 percent, an increase of over 230 percent. In 1976, 38 percent of all children under age 6

had employed mothers, up from 28 percent in 1970.

This remarkable increase in labor force participation by women who have the greatest demands on their time in the home has taken place even though there has been no substantial increase in the availability of institutionalized child care. In 1975 only 1.7 percent of all children aged 3 to 13 who had a mother in the labor force were in day care centers. Most children of employed mothers were cared for in their own home by a parent or other relative.

Certainly then, the last quarter-century has witnessed drastic changes in the ways that women organize their work lives. The graphs in Figure 1 picture the variation in women's labor force participation with age. Prior to 1950 the pattern was one in which the bulk of women in the labor force were young and unmarried. Until quite recently most women who worked for pay left the labor force when they married and did not return unless they were required to seek employment because of economic misfortune such as widowhood. The curves for both 1900 and 1940 drop off sharply after age 25. Beginning with 1950 we see the phenomenon that has come to be called re-entry, a return to the labor force by women over 35

Figure 1 Female participation in the labor force, by age, 1900–1978.

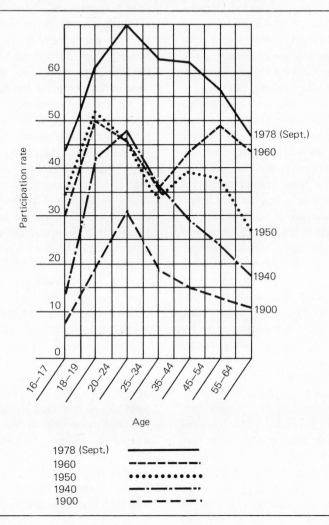

whose children are grown or in school. This pattern is even more pronounced in the curve for 1960 where the highest participation rates belong to women aged 45 to 54. The most recent curve shows higher participation for women in all age groups, and the dip between the peaks has nearly disappeared as participation rates of women aged 25 to 34 (many of them mothers) have risen.

We can gain some understanding of the rise in women's labor force participation by focusing on the process through which people make decisions about how to use their time. For everyone time is a scarce resource, and we must all decide how to allocate our time among the various things that we would like to do. Everyone must spend some time every day in sleep and in essential body maintenance functions. Beyond this we can decide to use our time for work or for leisure. All people (except workaholics) enjoy leisure and hope to have some leisure time each day. The time that we choose to work can be spent either working for pay or working in situations in which we are not paid for our labor. If we work for pay, we receive earnings, which allow us to enjoy consumption of goods and services that are bought in the market. If we work not-for-pay, we produce goods and services that we ourselves or someone else consumes. Most work not-for-pay takes place in the home (dishwashing, gardening, child care, and so on), but a substantial amount of volunteer work is also performed in other settings. Everyone, of course, performs some work not-for-pay in the home so everyone must decide how to allocate their work time between work for pay and work not-for-pay. However, since women are expected to be the major producers of goods and services in the home, the decision of dividing time between work at home and work for pay in the market is particularly important for them.

Throughout this century the wages that women can earn in the labor force have increased, and this increase is one factor that has been shown to be very important for explaining women's decisions about work for pay versus work not-for-pay. When the wage that a woman can earn by being in the labor force increases, the cost to her and her family of having her stay out of the labor force and work at home to produce goods and services for the family to consume will also increase. For example, if a woman could earn $400 per week by working as an engineer, she and her family would have to give up $400 per week if she stays at home to be a full-time homemaker. Clearly then, the incentive for a woman to go into the labor force will increase when her market wage increases, and women with high po-

tential wages will be less likely to be full-time homemakers. This is part of the reason that women who have high levels of education are much more likely to be in the labor force. Educated women have higher potential earnings, and they are probably more able to find pleasant and fulfilling jobs.

As women increase their time in market work and reduce their time in home work they substitute products they buy in the market for some of the goods and services they might have produced at home. This means that earning women and their families are more likely to eat in restaurants, to send out clothes to laundries, and to use institutional child care and baby sitters. It is not, however, possible to substitute purchased products for all home production. Therefore, studies have found that women who have the "double burden" of being homemakers and wage earners work more total hours per week than any other group in society.

The rise over time in women's wages and in women's labor force participation has a number of implications for the institutions of marriage and the family. We might expect to see marriage transformed as women become more able to provide for their own economic well-being. In the traditional marriage common in Western cultures the division of labor has been between the breadwinner-husband and the homemaker-wife. The husband specialized in market work for pay, and the wife specialized in home work not-for-pay. In this arrangement the wife was dependent on her husband's earnings in order to be able to consume market goods and services, and a woman who was concerned with her economic well-being had to be careful to choose a husband with good earning potential. As more women work in the market, this dependency should lessen. There are a number of possible results. Women may choose to marry later, and some may choose not to marry at all. Women with unhappy marriages may be more likely to divorce if they can earn their own income. All women who wish to marry may be freer to choose husbands on the basis of affection and attraction rather than on the basis of men's potential as income providers.

This analysis also has implications for the decisions that people make about how many children to have. As women's potential market wage rises, the cost of their time spent in household duties rises. Therefore the cost to families of having children to care for goes up if the mother is to stay at home to provide child care instead of working for pay. This leads to the incentive to have smaller families and is undoubtedly part of the reason for declining fertility among American women. It is possible that this negative effect on fertility could be reduced in the future if there are more low-cost day care centers available or if fathers take a greater part in the duties of child-rearing.

The major reasons that women work for pay are related to financial needs of themselves and their families. In 1977, 45 percent of all employed women were unmarried. Most of these women were dependent on themselves alone for financial support. In addition, many of these women were heads of families and used their earnings to support children. Many employed women are married to men who earn low wages, and these women's earnings often make the difference between the family living below or above the poverty level. In March 1978 among all husband-wife families, only 28 percent had the husband as the only earner in the family. On average, wives' earnings accounted for 26 percent of family income in 1976. However, in husband-wife families with full-time employed wives and incomes under $10,000, wives contributed nearly 60 percent of total family income.

In the past there has been a strong in-verse relationship between husband's earnings and wife's labor force participation. Women with high-earning husbands were much less likely to work for pay than were women who were married to men with lower earnings. Since 1960 this association has been weakening as more highly educated women (who are usually married to high-earning men) enter the labor force. At present there is no consistent relationship between husband's earnings and wife's likelihood of employment. From this we can conclude that married women are more responsive to the positive effects of their own wages, which tend to pull them into the work force, than they are to the negative effects of their husbands' earnings, which in the past have tended to keep them at home.

Black women have always had higher levels of labor force participation than have white women, though the differential has narrowed considerably since the Second World War. Undoubtedly, this is due in part to the greater financial need in black families because black workers have lower earnings and higher unemployment rates than do white workers.

Women's Earnings

We have seen that women's earnings are an important factor affecting the decision of how women will allocate their time between work at home and work for pay in the market. Women's earnings have increased over time, which has tended to pull women into the labor force, but men's earnings have also increased, and the gap between women's and men's earnings has actually widened over the past twenty years. In this section we want to look at what determines women's market earnings and at some of the causes of the differential between men's and women's earnings.

Some of the difference between the annual earnings of women and men is due to the fact that more women work part-time and part-year. In 1977, 71 percent of employed women worked at full-time jobs compared with 89 percent of men who worked full-time. Only 41.4 percent of employed women worked full-time, full-year in 1975. However, when we compare the earnings of women and men full-time, full-year workers, we still find a substantial earnings gap. In 1977 women who worked full-time and full-year had a median income of $8,600. This was 59 percent of the $14,600 median income of men. In 1956 the similar ratio was 63 percent. Therefore, over the same period of time that women have been increasing their labor force participation, their earnings position relative to men's has deteriorated.

The earnings gap may be caused by two situations: (1) women may be doing the same work as men but receiving lower wages, or (2) women may be doing different work from men, with women's jobs receiving lower pay. In truth, both of these situations exist, but the second one, the different occupational distribution of men and women, is the chief cause of the earnings gap.

In general, economists think that the wages that workers receive are related to the value of the goods and services they produce. It is not surprising that highly productive workers in skilled jobs receive higher earnings than do less productive workers. We do not have accurate direct data on workers' productivity, but we do have expectations about the kinds of qualities that cause workers to be more productive. Education, job training, and experience on the job should lead to higher productivity and therefore to higher earnings. The gap between women's and men's earnings could reflect a gap between women's

and men's productivities. Researchers have tried to see if this is true by comparing the earnings of women and men who have had the same education and training. What they have found is that some of the difference in earnings can be explained by differences in education and experience, but a much larger portion remains unexplained. Even when we compare the earnings of women and men in the same broad occupational categories we find that the gap persists.

Discrimination against women in the labor market is the other cause of the earnings gap. Discrimination can take a number of different forms. When women are paid less than equally productive men, they are being discriminated against. When women are excluded from some jobs or training so that they are forced to work in jobs in which their productivity is not as high as it might be, their earnings are lowered due to discrimination. Sometimes employers assume that all women have the same characteristics and make employment decisions about individual women based on the expected average attributes of women as a group. For example, employers may believe that all women will have high labor market turnover because some women drop out of the labor force in order to fulfill household responsibilities. In such cases, the women who are judged by the expected group characteristics rather than by their own individual characteristics are said to be victims of statistical discrimination.

In most studies, discrimination has been found to be the largest cause of the earnings gap. However, the major form that discrimination takes is not "unequal pay for equal work," though there are many cases of women receiving lower pay for doing substantially the same work as men. The biggest cause of the earnings gap and the major form of discrimination against women is that women and men are, by and large, employed in different occupations; and the pay in women's occupations is lower than the pay in men's occupations.

The Sex Distribution of Occupations

In Table 3 we can see how women and men workers are distributed among the major occupational categories of the U.S. labor force. There are very striking differences in the distributions. Almost 14 percent of males were employed as managers and administrators whereas only 5.9 percent of women were so employed. Nearly 35 percent of all female workers were in clerical jobs compared to only 6.3 percent of men. Nearly 21 percent of men, but only 1.6 percent of women, were craft workers. Much higher proportions of women than men were employed as private household workers and as other service workers. In the professional and technical fields where the figures for females and males are similar, the degree of aggregation in the data hides the large differences that actually exist because the overwhelming proportion of female professionals are teachers, nurses, librarians, and social workers whereas male professionals are in a much broader mix of fields.

When we look at occupational breakdowns of the U.S. labor force that are more detailed than the breakdown in Table 3, we see an even greater disparity between women's and men's jobs. In fact, women's employment is concentrated in a very small number of occupational categories. The U.S. Bureau of Labor Statistics divides the work force into about 250 occupations. In 1977 nearly 38 percent of all women workers were employed in just 10 occupations — secretary, retail trade salesworker, bookkeeper,

Table 3 Occupational distribution of females and males, 1977

Occupational group	Percent of labor force in group	
	Females	Males
Professional and technical	15.9	14.6
Managers and administrators	5.9	13.9
Clerical	34.7	6.3
Salesworkers	6.8	6.0
Craftsworkers	1.6	20.9
Operatives	11.8	17.6
Nonfarm laborers	1.2	7.6
Private household workers	3.1	0.7
Other service workers	17.9	8.7
Farm workers	1.3	4.2

private household worker, elementary school teacher, waitress, typist, cashier, sewer and stitcher, and registered nurse. Men's employment showed a much smaller degree of occupational concentration.

Not only are women workers concentrated in a very small number of jobs, but many of the jobs that women hold are held almost exclusively by women. That is, the occupational structure is highly segregated by sex, with most women being employed in jobs in which the overwhelming majority of workers are women. Because of the attention given to women in nontraditional jobs we might think that there has been considerable change in recent years in the degree of concentration of women's employment and in the degree of sex segregation of occupations. Most studies, however, show that this is not the case and that the relatively few token women in men's jobs have not yet caused a major change in the sex distribution of employment. In fact, there has been very little change over this entire century. Most women today are working in the same kinds of jobs that women held in 1920: teaching, clerical work, unskilled and semi-skilled manufacturing jobs, and service work. There has, however, been a notable increase in the numbers of women physicians, lawyers, and bank managers since 1970. And although the number of women skilled craft workers is still extremely small, the rate of increase since 1970 has been quite rapid.

The extreme degree of concentration and segregation that we observe in the occupational structure has implications for women's earnings and for the male-female earnings gap. If women's ability to enter occupations is limited so that they are able to take fewer kinds of jobs than men, then women's wages will be lowered because so many more women are available to work for a limited number of opportunities. If more women enter the labor force and most of them try to get jobs in women's occupations, then there will be extreme competition for these jobs and women's wages will fall. The result will be that the earnings gap between women and men will widen. If discrimination increases competition for "women's jobs" and therefore reduces competition for "men's jobs," then women's wages will be artificially low and men's wages will be artificially high. This analysis implies that the gap between women's and men's earnings will not narrow substantially until there is a lessening of sex stereotyping of occupations.

Sex stereotyping of occupations acts to limit women's opportunities in two ways: (1) employers will discriminate against women who want to work in "men's jobs" because they are uncomfortable with the idea of women doing these jobs or because they

think that women cannot perform them, and (2) women will tend to limit their aspirations and training to traditional "women's jobs" because they believe that these are their only options. In order for the degree of occupational segregation to change it will be necessary to change employers' attitudes and actions toward women in nontraditional fields. It will also be necessary to raise women's aspirations so that they train and apply for jobs in nontraditional fields.

There are some indications that the sex structure of occupations may change substantially in the future. Since the 1950s women have been increasing their levels of education much faster than have men. Although there are still many more college-educated men than college-educated women, the gap is narrowing very fast. In 1950, only 31 bachelor's degrees were earned by women for every 100 that were awarded to men. By 1977, the ratio was 84 women to 100 men; and in 1977, for the first time, more women than men were attending colleges in the United States. Even more important than college attendance per se are the changes in women's occupational aspirations and in the kinds of training that women are choosing. These changes have taken place in a very short time. From 1971 to 1976, women's share of college degrees awarded in a number of nontraditional fields increased dramatically: in business and management, from 9 percent to 20 percent; in engineering, from 1 percent to 3 percent; and in computer science from 14 percent to 20 percent. All of these majors provide training for jobs that have higher earnings than do traditional women's jobs. Changes are also taking place at levels of education above the bachelor's degree, with rapid increases in the numbers of women receiving master's and doctoral degrees, and especially dramatic changes in the numbers of women enrolled in professional schools. In the five years from 1971 to 1976, women's share of those receiving law degrees went from 7 percent to 19 percent and in medicine from 9 percent to 16 percent. Women have been expanding their employment in skilled craft jobs at a rapid pace, though they made up less than 5 percent of craft workers in 1976. In 1973, only 1 percent of all registered apprentices were women, which suggests that women have been getting training for craft jobs through other means than traditional apprenticeship programs. However, since 1973 a number of programs have been started to help women to get into apprenticeship programs and have met with notable success. If these trends continue, we would expect to see an unprecedented change in the sex distribution of occupations in the future. However, it will be necessary for antidiscrimination laws to be carefully enforced to assure that these newly trained women do not encounter discrimination when they enter the job market.

Unemployment and Poverty

Women's disadvantaged position in the economy shows up in a number of problems that affect women more harshly than they affect men. Women are more likely to suffer from unemployment than are men. In September 1978 the female unemployment rate was 7.6 percent whereas the male rate was 4.4 percent, and the gap between female and male unemployment rates has tended to widen since 1960. For black women the unemployment rate was much higher (13.0 percent). There is evidence to suggest that the female unemployment rate is actually higher than this because women are more likely to be discouraged workers, which means

that they are likely to have dropped out of the labor force because they believe that there are no jobs available.

The various economic disadvantages that women face in economic life combine to produce a much greater incidence of poverty among the female population. Women who head families are particularly likely to be poor. In March 1977, 13.6 percent of all families in the United States were female-headed. (This means that there was no male present in these families.) Thirty-three percent of the female-headed families were living below poverty level compared with only 5.6 percent of male-headed families who were poor. Nearly all (92 percent) of these female-headed poor families had children under the age of 18. The problem is particularly severe for black women and Spanish-speaking women who face additional problems in the economy. In 1977, when less than 6 percent of all male-headed families were below the poverty line, 25 percent of all white female-headed families, 52 percent of all black female-headed families, and 53 percent of all Spanish-speaking female-headed families were living below the poverty level.

Older women are more likely to be poor than are people in any other group in the economy. In March 1977, 10 percent of all people in the United States over the age of 16 were living in poverty; but 18 percent of all women aged 65 and over were poor. (The comparable figure for older men was 11 percent.) The large majority of these women are widows living on savings, pensions, and social security. Because American women live, on the average, about eight years longer than American men, there are many more older women than there are older men. For these women the economic problems of being female are compounded by the economic problems of being old.

Summary

This century has witnessed very dramatic increases in participation by women in the American labor force. The bulk of this increase has taken place since the Second World War and has been largely due to increased participation by married women. Up until 1965 the greatest increases in participation were attributable to middle-aged women returning to the labor force after their families were grown, but in the very recent past the most notable increases have come from young mothers and from young unmarried women. Studies of women's labor force participation have found that increases in women's wages are very important for explaining the greater propensity of women to work for pay. As women's educational level, and therefore their potential market wage, has risen, the implied price of home-produced goods and services has also risen, thus increasing the incentive to work for pay instead of working full-time in the home.

The growth in women's labor force participation has been associated with increases in women's wages; but since men's wages have risen even faster over time, the gap between women's and men's earnings has widened. The gap between women's and men's earnings may be a reflection of productivity differences between women and men or it may be due to discrimination against women. Studies have found that although there are individual differences between women and men in education, training, and job experience, the major portion of the earnings gap is due to discrimination as reflected in the differing occupational distributions of women and men workers. Women's employment tends to be concentrated in a relatively small number of low-paid jobs. Since the growth in women's labor force participation has not been accompanied by any very substantial decrease in the amount of sex segregation in the occupational structure, most of the new women workers have sought jobs in traditional women's fields. This development has increased competition for those jobs and exerted downward pressure on women's wages relative to men's wages. Certainly any substantial decrease in the size of the female-male earnings gap will require less sex segregation in the occupational structure.

Since 1970 there has been some movement of women into nontraditional professional, managerial, and craft jobs. Though the number of women employed in nontraditional fields is still very small, these employment changes may indicate that in the future the occupational structure will look very different from what it has been in the past. In addition, changes in the kinds of education and training being pursued by women suggest that more women are planning to enter nontraditional fields.

And, although there are indications that there may be substantial changes in economic opportunities for women in the occupational structure, the picture for women who are close to the bottom of the economic ladder does not show any such hopeful light. The unemployment rate of women is higher than the unemployment rate of men, and the gap has been increasing. The number of female-headed families is increasing rapidly as the divorce rate and the nonmarital birth rate increases. These families have a very high chance of falling into poverty and are unlikely to improve their position without considerable help in the form of subsidized child care and job training.

It is difficult to predict how women's economic roles will change in the future. There are indications that we may see substantial changes in some occupational areas, but the earnings gap between women and men is not narrowing and women make up an extremely large proportion of the poor. Most employed women bear the "double burden" of working in the labor force while they maintain primary responsibility for work in the home. Many feminist commentators have argued that the division of labor in the market will not change very substantially until the division of labor in the home changes.

SOCIAL SECURITY: WHO'S SECURE?

TISH SOMMERS

Tish Sommers, born in Cambria, California, in 1914, describes herself as a "free-lance agitator" on the agist front. Educated in psychology at the University of California at Berkeley and at UCLA, and in Hispanic studies at the University of Wisconsin, she has participated in and coordinated community action and civil rights organizations since 1943. She has served on the national board of NOW (1971–1972), helped to coordinate its Task Force on Older Women, and founded the Alliance for Displaced Homemakers. Her book *The Not-So-Helpless Female* was published in 1973, and her articles have appeared in various magazines, among them *Aging, Ms., Prime Time,* and *Civil Rights Digest.* In 1976 she was appointed to the California Commission on Aging by Governor Brown.

In the following selection Sommers articulates some of the nature and sources of the institutionally reinforced poverty of older women and suggests some reforms. It is important to note that the legislation she refers to by Martha Keys and Donald Fraser, an earnings split credit plan, is gaining some momentum. (See Hon. Donald Fraser, *Congressional Record,* Vol. 124, No. 61, 5/1/78, and Hon. Martha Keys, *Congressional Record,* Vol. 124, No. 160, 10/5/78.)

A Feminist Critique of Social Security

Since the purpose of Social Security, interpreted broadly, is to provide security in old age or disablement, how well does it serve women? Like any program, it must be judged by its results. Or in equal opportunity parlance, what is the impact of this, our key retirement plan, on the economic welfare of a *majority* of our citizens? I emphasize majority, because women comprise 59 percent of persons over 65 and almost two-thirds of those over 75.

Reprinted from *Equal Rights Monitor,* 2, No. 9 (August 1976), by permission of the Institute for Studies in Equality.

According to Martha Griffiths (former Democratic representative from Michigan), "Fourteen percent of aged women, compared to one percent of aged men, have no income. Among persons age 65 or over who have income, the median annual income of men is over $3,750 (little enough) while that of women is $1,900. Forty-two percent of women, versus 19 percent of men, received less than $120 a month in Social Security in 1972."

Benefit levels are much higher for retired male workers than female. Men are more than three times as likely as women to be entitled to the maximum. And women are three times more likely than men to be entitled to the minimum. Of the 4.3 million, or 22 percent of the elderly who live in poverty, over two-thirds are women, mostly widows.

Why are we so poor? Let's analyze the reasons:

SEX DISCRIMINATION IN EMPLOYMENT BEGETS SEX DISCRIMINATION IN RETIREMENT The exclusion from "man-paying" jobs continues to haunt us into our old age. In 1971, the median annual earnings for women were $2,986, just 40 percent of the men's median earnings of $7,388, and it is on earnings that the benefit formula is based. Since women typically earn low wages, they also receive low benefits as retirees or disabled workers. So, after a lifetime of hard work at low-paying, often exploitive jobs, a woman retires at 65 to receive the minimum payment.

WOMEN ARE PUNISHED FOR MOTHERHOOD The long periods women are out of the job market for child rearing show up later in reduced benefits. If staying home and taking care of children is so important to the fabric of American society that we are denied child-care centers for that reason, wouldn't you think that we would be entitled to retirement benefits like other workers for doing that job?

On the contrary, the *benefit formula* averages out earnings, so that every year out of child raising is counted as a zero, thus reducing the average earnings. Though the five lowest years are not included, given the child-care situation in this country and the presumed responsibility of women for young children, this method of computing benefits has a decidedly negative impact for mothers.

According to an SSA document (Mallan, 1974), if women had the same work lives as men (that is, if they didn't take time out for motherhood), only 11 percent, as opposed to 24 percent, would receive minimum benefits, and twice as many would receive the maximum. Motherhood and apple pie may be

sacred in America; neither provides security in later life.

IF YOU CAN'T SUPPORT YOURSELF, YOU'LL HAVE TO TAKE LESS FOR LIFE This is better known as actuarial reduction. If you are entitled to benefits, you may elect to take them at 62. BUT the monthly payment will be reduced by actuarial tables to the equivalent on a lifetime basis of what you would receive if you waited until 65. In 1970, half the women workers and only a third of the men claimed benefits at age 62. Seventy percent of women did not hold out until they were 65.

Why would they do that? For many there was no choice; older women, especially those without a job, have a terrible time finding one. In times like these, the only jobs available to them are really exploitive — physically and emotionally draining jobs of baby sitting, live-in domestic work, homemaker and chore services for the elderly — all at low pay scales — or part-time work, such as in department stores, which take advantage of older women to avoid paying fringe benefits.

Employment figures for women show a sharp drop when we reach our fifties, though you would expect them to rise because the children are grown. In 1972, the labor force participation rate for women aged 45–54 was 53.9 percent. At ages 55 to 64 it dropped to 42.1 percent. Yet, these are crucial years for collecting those Social Security quarter credits. Since 1972, as we all know, jobs have not been easy to come by. What do you do when you find yourself unable to find a job that pays enough to live on, or one that you can physically cope with? In many cases, such women opt for early retirement and lifelong poverty.

PAY TWICE — COLLECT ONCE All wage earners pay into Social Security at the same rate, regardless of the family situation. But benefits go to individuals and their dependents. When more than one person works in the family, retirement income may be no greater than if only the presumed breadwinner paid into the system. The employed wife receives no benefit for *her* payroll tax contribution.

The inequity is a real one. For example, a retired couple in which only the husband had worked, averaging $9,000 a year, would receive $531.80 a month — his benefit plus an additional 50 percent for his dependent wife. Another couple averaging the same income of $9,000 (his $6,000, hers $3,000), would receive a smaller benefit; their monthly benefits would be only $444.50.

NO CREDIT FOR LABOR IN THE HOME According to a recent study, more than 28 million non-salaried wives and mothers perform about $340 billion worth of services each year, as housekeeper, decorator, cleaning woman, bookkeeper, cook, dietitian, nurse, gardener, chauffeur, shopper, seamstress and psychologist.

That list, of course, is far from complete. If a homemaker drew a paycheck, her annual earnings would be well over $12,000. If she weren't a wife, how many men could afford her? Yet her services, extolled to the skies annually on Mother's Day, don't even rate a Social Security card. The largest body of workers, still uncovered by what purports to be a universal retirement system, are homemakers.

But she is covered, says the SSA. That's why dependency benefits were added in 1939. Let's examine that.

PITFALLS OF HOMEMAKER DEPENDENCY In the first place, a homemaker has no coverage for disability. So what happens if she has an accident? If someone has to be hired to replace her services, there is exactly the same impact on family income as though a wage earner lost a salary. And income replace-ment is the presumed function of disability insurance.

There are other pitfalls. If benefits follow the breadwinner, what happens when a dependent homemaker is divorced, which is happening in epidemic proportion these days? We can now receive benefits if we were married 20 years. But if a homemaker is divorced by her husband after 19 years, she loses all rights to Social Security as his dependent, even though her labor at home made possible her husband's labor at work. One more year and she would have squeezed under the wire. If marriage as a partnership is recognized at 20 years, it could only be one-twentieth less so after 19 years.

I was married 23 years, but I happened to be older than my husband (it's not that rare, just hidden). I will not be eligible until *he* reaches 65, and suppose he elects to postpone retirement? I would have to wait still longer. And it is not just retirement income I lose. What about Medicare?

THE WIDOW'S GAP When the youngest child reaches 18, the widow's benefits cease until she reaches 60, or is *totally* disabled. Yet the homemaker-widow at 50 faces severe job handicaps because of her age, sex and lack of "recent job experience." She is ineligible for Aid for Families with Dependent Children (AFDC) or medical benefits and, in some states, even general assistance. Her plight is exploited by those seeking cheap labor.

The Weisenfeld case touched on this question. According to that decision, the law was written on the premise that a mother should have a choice of staying home while there were young children; once they are grown, it is presumed that savings or the grown children will support her.

The decision demands a new look at the realities of modern life. What savings? How many grown children support their mothers?

What do they do, these widows who fall

in the gap? Some of them write to me. "I was 54 years old this past Christmas Day," says a woman widowed since 1971. "My husband earned the family income and I remained home to raise three sons and take care of my husband's parents and my mother. As of right now, I receive survivor's Social Security but next year my son turns 18. How do I eat and what if I get sick?"

THE DISPLACED HOMEMAKER . . . A NEW CATEGORY OF DISADVANTAGED PERSONS There are today 2.2 million women who have fulfilled a role lauded by society and now find themselves "displaced" in their middle years . . . widowed, divorced or separated. Too old to find jobs and too young for Social Security, they are victims of changing family roles, "liberalized" divorce laws and the fact that, when men remarry, they often choose younger brides.

Unlike other workers, displaced homemakers have no cushion to soften their sudden loss of support — no unemployment insurance, no emergency job programs, no union benefits. Their situation harks back to the pre-thirties sink-or-swim conditions.

At what age do women become eligible for senior citizens' programs, Medicare and Social Security? Usually at that magic figure, 65, that Bismarck picked as the age *men* could retire from the work force. However, homemakers often face mandatory retirement much earlier, complete with the trauma of feeling useless and "over the hill." Suicides peak for women in the middle years, while they go up sharply for men after 65.

In other words, the displaced homemaker is a discarded segment of our population, outside all the social protection from sudden hardships won through collective effort — unemployment insurance, workers' compensation, even AFDC and Supplemental Security Income (SSI).

THE REGRESSIVE NATURE OF THE PAYROLL TAX FALLS HEAVIEST ON THE LOWEST PAID, MOST OF WHOM ARE WOMEN This is part of the price we pay for limiting Social Security to payroll deductions. The tax has increased 800 percent during the last 20 years — more than 10 times the rise in the cost of living. Though masked by insurance terminology, this "contribution" is the biggest tax bite that most working persons pay. Those earning salaries over $32,000 pay less than two percent of their income on Social Security taxes; those earning under $10,000 pay almost six percent.

Sexism Institutionalized

Now add up all these points, and what do you have? A classic syndrome of institutionalized sexism. Social Security, as it now stands, is highly discriminatory against women — not in an abstract, "equal under the law," sense but in the far more real test of how well it keeps the wolf from the door. There, it serves us very poorly.

The underlying culprit is what Justice Brennan termed an "archaic" presumption: Man the breadwinner, woman the homemaker-dependent. Benefits calculated on earning rates, motherhood penalized by averaging earnings, no benefits for homemakers, dependents' benefits tied to the breadwinner, actuarial deductions, regressive tax rates — all these and more.

In the long run, it condemns a very large number of us to abject poverty. In no time of life is the payoff of woman's traditional role more clearly revealed than in old age. No wonder we feminists are beginning to reach a whole new segment of the population who never before understood what the "womanlibbers" were talking about!

Where Do we Go from Here?

Having made this scathing attack on Social Security, I will now beat a hasty retreat. For heaven's sakes, let's not get rid of Social Security until we have something better! Because that's *all* we have.

Our Social Security blanket is a patchwork quilt. The squares are all out of kilter. If there was once a consistent design, so many new swatches have been added that now the pattern is lopsided. If one inequity is patched, another is created. However, we have a hard winter coming up, so let's keep on mending until a new blanket is woven.

Suggested Changes

Here are some suggested patches (in shocking pink): On point one — the impact of low wages on retirement income — any legislation to increase the minimum payment would be of help, since the minimum is what so many of us receive. Since old women are at the bottom of the heap, major attention should be placed at raising the system from the bottom.

Punishment of women for motherhood, point two, could be lessened by providing credits for this socially important service to the nation. At the very least, child-rearing years — however many there are — could be excluded while averaging out benefit levels. This could, of course apply to men as well as to women.

Actuarial reductions are addressed in legislation such as Rosenthal's (D., N.Y.) sweeping reform bill, HR 5149. Perhaps more specific measures might be introduced, such as elimination of the actuarial reduction for those who receive minimum benefits, those who have been out of the job market for a prescribed period or persons with partial disability. In other words, if you *can't* work, you must have a liveable income.

On the fourth point — pay twice, collect once — several bills have been introduced into the 94th Congress which would combine earnings of spouses. HR 775 (Murphy, D., N.Y.) for example, would provide payment of benefits to married couples based on combined earnings records where higher, if both live in the same household. Payment would be computed by combining average monthly wages as if those were the wage of an individual and multiplying by 75 percent.

Abzug's (D., N.Y.) HR 4357 would also permit the payment of benefits to a married couple on its combined earnings record.

Credits for Home Labor

Credits for labor in the home was an idea pioneered by former representative Martha Griffiths. One piece of legislation in the current Congress is the Jordan (D., Tex.) and Burke (D., Calif.) bill HR 3009, which provides benefits for homemakers based on a self-employment concept. Three options for computing the amount to be paid are offered. While such a law would serve to establish the principle of homemaking as labor like any other, it would offer protection only to a limited number of families who could afford to pay double taxes without double income.

A far-reaching bill introduced by Fraser (D., Minn.) views marriage as a partnership, with credits going to both partners on an optional basis, similar to a joint income tax return.

Numerous bills have been introduced to compensate for the pitfalls of homemaker dependency. The arbitrary 20-year rule for divorced women to qualify for wife's or widow's benefits would be reduced to five in an Abzug bill, HR 159. Another pitfall, that of seniors living together to prevent benefit losses, has been a favorite television topic this season, and a number of legislators have responded. Among bills which would provide that remarriage would not cut benefits are Heckler's (R., Mass.) HR 3006, Young's (R., Fla.) HR 5284 and Koch's (D., N.Y.) 580.

Simultaneous benefits would be permitted under Holtzman's (D., N.Y.) HR 3242, providing the individuals may receive simultaneously old age or disability *and* widow's benefits.

The widow's gap is tackled in HR 5149, which would (among other things) provide payment of widow's or widower's benefits at age 50 regardless of disability and without actuarial reduction.

The Displaced Homemakers

For those who don't currently fit within the Social Security system — the displaced homemakers — we have been working for special legislation, spearheaded by the Alliance for Displaced Homemakers and the NOW Task Force on Older Women. Yvonne Burke's (D., Calif.) HR 10272 tackles the problem, and a Senate version has been introduced by John Tunney (D., Calif.). These bills would provide multipurpose service programs and training to help such persons move from dependency to self-sufficiency, laying the basis for bringing displaced homemakers under unemployment compensation programs.

To insure that such programs would not be ill-prepared, a demonstration center was set up in California, involving displaced homemakers in its preparations. A key facet of the California program is job creation, based on the principle that a homemaker's job skills and life experiences can be recycled into socially useful jobs which she can help develop.

The movement is spreading into other states. The remarkable response to "displaced homemaker" legislation, both on the state and national levels, indicates that we have struck a nerve.

The New Security Blanket

As we patch up the old Social Security system, we should all be hard at work devising something better; the issue of income maintenance, particularly in old age, needs a whole new look.

While social change has been moving at a gallop, social policy has followed at a crawl. Forty years after the introduction of Social Security is high time to review that "archaic assumption" that man is the breadwinner, and woman is the homemaker.

Prognosticator Jeane Dixon foresees the streets filled again as in the sixties, this time not with young people but with elders. If she's right, and I hope she is, older women will be in the front ranks. With our Post Menopausal Zest (or PMZ, as Margaret Mead calls it), we will become a force to be reckoned with.

Once our own self-concept becomes strong and positive and we move into action, we can confront ageism with the same vigor that young women attack sexism, giving us extraordinary new energy — energy that will turn traditional ballot box support into potent political clout.

WHO SHALL CARE FOR OUR CHILDREN?

ROSALYN F. BAXANDALL

Rosalyn F. Baxandall teaches labor studies and women's history at the State University of New York, College at Old Westbury. She was one of the earliest contemporary feminists active in creating day care centers and in working for their financial support by local government. She co-edited *America's Working Women: A Documentary History, 1600 to the Present* and is currently writing a book on romantic love.

Changed conditions in society are required before women can attain economic parity. Women cannot aspire to, or be expected to attain, professional or financial success without an equal reduction of other responsibilities. On the one hand, the private sector might be expected to respond to the changing requirements of changing women as it always has, by providing services or goods to fill needs, supply for demand. One could foresee, for example, companies providing reasonably priced and available housekeeping services, cooks, baby sitters, and so on. On the other hand, the public sector should be expected to provide for the needs of citizens as it always has: through a variety of public agencies. The matter of child care is crucial. More than any other responsibility, the care of the young has drained women's time and energy beyond the point of necessity or sense. Adequate, dependable child care facilities have been a perennial feminist goal. Baxandall's paper explores this issue. As you read, consider two things: the place of child care in the economic condition of women, and the issue of child care as a political, social, and legal matter.

The Need

More mothers are working outside the home now than ever before. In the 1940's only 9 percent of all mothers with children under eighteen worked for wages. In 1977, 51 percent of mothers with minor children worked, including 41 percent with children under six and 35 percent with children under three. The labor-participation rate of mothers has increased two times faster than the participation rate of all women, and the labor-participation rate has increased even more rapidly for mothers of pre-school-age children than it has for mothers of school-age children. More mothers (65 percent) work when the husband has absented himself from the family household than when the husband is present (48 percent).[21]

Day-care facilities have not increased commensurately with the increase in employment of mothers. Licensed public and voluntary day-care centers now care for only one-sixth the number of children cared for at the end of World War II.[22] The gap between availability and need has widened over a period of thirty years. Only in the last few years has the trend been reversed, and that only to a slight degree.[23]

What are the child-care arrangements for these children of working mothers? Of those aged 3 to 13, 83 percent were cared for in their own homes, 70 percent by their parents or other relatives and 9.4 percent by a nonrelative. Nearly 10 percent looked after themselves, undoubtedly an underestimate, as most women would hesitate to admit that

From "Who Shall Care for Our Children? The History and Development of Day Care in the United States," by Rosalyn F. Baxandall, in *Women: A Feminist Perspective*, 2nd ed., ed. Jo Freeman (Palo Alto, Calif.: Mayfield Publishing Co., 1979). Reprinted by permission of Rosalyn Fraad Baxandall.

they have no other alternative. Only 1.7 percent of the children were in group care.[24]

How many parents would use day care if it were available? The figures are of course impossible to provide. An indication of need is that in New York City in 1970 there were 8,000 children on the waiting list for day-care centers operated by the Department of Social Services. No official waiting lists exist or are available from Central Head Start, but many Head Start centers in 1970 recorded waiting lists as long as the lists of those currently enrolled.[25] Many women are known to be unable to take jobs because there is no day care for their children. The Labor Department made a study of underemployment and unemployment in ten high-poverty areas. They found that one out of every five residents who was not in the labor force but who desired a regular job, gave as the principal reason for not looking for work an inability to arrange child care.[26]

Families who can afford to pay for day care do not have enough nursery facilities either. For one thing, the suburban areas where many of them live have health and zoning laws precluding establishment of nursery schools in many residential areas.[27] At private nurseries in 1970, competition for admission was record-high, with applications outnumbering vacancies by as much as 150 to one.[28]

Attitudes Toward Day Care

Since there seems clearly to be a desperate need for day care, why is the need unmet? Part of the reason is that day care has been stigmatized by its welfare origins. It is thought of as something needed by the problem family. The *Ladies' Home Journal* carried a series on day care from June through November of 1967. One conclusion of this series was that "the concept of day care has not been more widely accepted because it was being presented as something solely for the poor and not for every mother." [29] Day care is often equated with maternal deprivation and emotional problems. Mr. Charles Tobin, secretary of the New York State Welfare Conference, said, "The child who needs day care has a family problem which makes it impossible for his parents to fulfill their parental responsibilities without supplementary help." [30]

Psychiatrists and social workers with their stress on the early mother-child relationship have certainly contributed to the negative attitude toward day care. No one has ever bothered to explore the importance of the *paternal relationship,* or other alternatives to the maternal nexus. As Barbara Wooten, a British sociologist, wrote: "But so long as the study of the role of the father continues to be so much neglected as compared with that of the mother, no opinion on the subject [the emphasis on the young child's need for its mother] can be regarded as more than purely speculative.[31] In the Soviet Union, where group child care from infancy onward is provided for all children as a right, Bronfenbrenner found that not only were the children better socialized, but there was greater companionship between parents and children, and Soviet parents spent even more time with their children than did American parents.[32]

Studies show that there are no detrimental effects on the child if the mother makes an effort to spend an hour or two a day with the child when she is home. Another study illustrates that if a mother enjoys her job, a child benefits from the mother's working. There seems no reason, then, to equate day care with maternal deprivation.[33]

A general prejudice against women's working has also prevented the development of adequate child care facilities outside the home in the United States. A 1960's study that originated in the Child Welfare League found that the average opinionmaker in the community, including the educator and the social worker, does not believe women should work. If they do work, they are working for frivolous reasons and therefore might better take care of their own children.[34] Another kind of negative attitude toward working women is exemplified by Samuel Nocella, International Vice President of the Amalgamated Clothing Workers, who says: "We have looked upon the presence of women in industry a little cynically because years ago we felt that the only way we could solve the problem of unemployment was for women to stay home so that men could have jobs."[35]

The attitude toward women's employment has often been tied in with the general mythology, or conventional wisdom, regarding a nurturing role for women. Part of this myth holds that only the biological mother can effectively "mother," and that a child will obviously therefore be harmed by the mother's absence in a work situation. The welfare mother has been the brunt, then, of contradictory attitudes: on the one hand she is urged to get off the tax rolls and into the job market; on the other hand she is mindful of the approval to be had from staying home to care for her children. Studies show that there is, on the whole, no higher rate of delinquency among the children of working mothers, nor is there evidence that either the husband-wife or the child-parent relationship is impaired.[36] Maternal employment has not been shown to have other harmful consequences for children either.[37] In general, the impact of a mother's employment on her child or children varies with the adequacy of the substitute arrangement, or the mother-child relationship prior to the separation for work, and with the mother's motivation to work and the gratification she receives from her employment.[38] In fact, "group care . . . has positive features. Often

those in charge of children's groups are better trained, more patient, and objective in dealing with children than the mothers. A child can be allowed greater freedom to run, climb, and throw in a nursery school than in a home full of breakable objects."[39] "There has been some speculation that greater variety of stimulation provided by several close mother figures may be intellectually stimulating and promote flexibility."[40] Day care in various experiments and full-scale programs in the Soviet Union, East Germany, Czechoslovakia, Hungary, Israel, Greece, and France seems to have benefited children.[41]

Since day care has never been studied from a feminist perspective, there have been few studies on the importance of day care *for the mother*. However, anyone who has been a mother knows that mothers need some kind of break from routine, some breathing spell, and some time for recreation, socializing, and creative pursuits — impossible on any meaningful scale without day care of some kind. In fact, most mothers are better mothers when they have some satisfying independent life of their own.[42] Mothers should not be forced to place their children in day-care centers, but the option should always be present.

Part of the reason why professionals in the child-care field oppose women's working and group care for children of working mothers is that these professionals equate maternal separation, even for a few hours a day, with maternal deprivation. They seem to think that maternal separation for any reason and in any manner has to have traumatic, deleterious effects on young children.[43] This misunderstanding comes out of the Bowlby, Spitz, Roudinesco, and Goldfarb studies showing that children who lived in impersonal institutions and were totally bereft, not only of maternal care but also of adequate maternal substitution, developed irreversible psychopathic or autistic characteristics. But these studies have little bearing on the situation of the child of a working mother generally considered; and they probably have little relevance even to questions of maternal deprivation. Barbara Wooten has questioned the scientific validity of these maternal-deprivation studies, inasmuch as they tended to use only disturbed children in institutions as a sample, never following the subjects into later experiences, whereas their clinical observations and statistics altered with time.[44] Regrettably, these studies are still respected in professional psychological and educational circles. It is true generally that scientific evaluations of the effects of day care on mothers and children are colored by cultural norms. And in a society where one must be considered abnormal in order to qualify for the day-care center, how is the evaluation of such services to be contemplated along guidelines that might with accuracy be termed scientific?

Perspectives and Problems

Day care can be viewed as a benefit in kind, as opposed to a cash benefit. Benefits in kind are preferred when a quality service is too expensive to be purchased in an individual basis.[45] In 1970 it was estimated that decent day care cost $1,600 per year per child.[46] Together with large sums of money, complex administrative and technological and educational skills are required if the demand for adequate day care is to be met. Individual families cannot be expected to meet these expensive complex demands themselves. Even if they could, there is a view of society whereby the wellbeing of children is too important a priority to be left to individual family discretion; childhood and education are societal rather than individual functions, since they ensure the con-

tinuity and survival of the society as a whole.

Day care, then, should be seen as a universal entitlement, like public education, rather than as it is now perceived, as a means-tested provision on the order of welfare. Means tests are not efficient as a way of concentrating help on those in need.[47] Means tests usually degrade and stigmatize and therefore only reinforce the conditions they are intended to alleviate and widen the inequity gap they purport to diminish.[48] In a society such as ours, which sets great emphasis on monetary reward and success, an admission of poverty and failure can prove so detrimental that it outweighs the reward it brings.[49] Many liberal-minded people believe that those who could pay for day care should do so on a sliding scale. However, because of the lingering welfare associations of day care, I feel the only way to make day care available without stigma must be to treat it as an unconditionally free public utility.

One of the problems with benefits in kind, however, is that they are often employed as mechanisms for social control.[50] Day care has in the past been used in this way. At present, day care is made available only on condition that women on welfare become enrolled in special Work Incentive Programs (WIN) and Concentrated Employment Programs (CEPS). Another proposal that would have combined day care with work was the Nixon Administration's Family Assistance Plan (FAP).

In FAP plans, the welfare recipients would be provided vouchers enabling them to purchase day care from government or private profit-making centers. This would constitute a windfall for private, franchised centers that would exist for profit rather than owing to any special evinced vocation for child care. Such centers would naturally seek to cut corners to increase their profits. The existing ones generally are overcrowded, with inadequate equipment and untrained part-time personnel. They are geared not toward child development but rather toward the readiest means to give parents the impression that their children are happy. They also seek to inveigle the parents into purchasing the products made by the day-care franchisers.[51]

The only way to prevent this balance-sheet-dominated kind of day care is to be insistent about having genuine parental control. With this, certain criteria and health and education standards should be maintained in day care. Unlike the present Code enforcement, such standards and criteria should not militate against experimentation and innovation. Different communities should be able to develop varying centers to meet their needs. For example: in an area where many parents are employed at night, the day-care center should be open 24 hours a day. In contrast, where parents seek care for half-days only, this too should be made possible, and with due budgetary benefit.

Day care has begun to be a factor in labor-market planning. Recently the AVCO Corporation of Dorchester, Massachusetts, Bell Telephone, Whirlpool, and the Rochester Clothing Company have commenced to use day care as a fringe benefit to attract and attach women workers to relative poorly paid jobs.[52] This is a genuine benefit and may take the place of another $100 or more a month in salary. Moreover, insofar as it succeeds in reducing turnover, it may be taken up by other industries. However, since many of the women in most need of the program would find it difficult to get another job, clearly the plan can also be used to control workers. Women are also less apt to engage in action that threatens the firm: organizing strikes, picketing, etc., when the threat is not only loss of a job, but loss of day care.

Day care should be financed by the federal government. This should be done from general tax revenue, rather than from any wage-related tax. Wage-related taxes are often employed to reinforce a psychological relationship between participation in the labor force and receipt of a benefit.[53] And taxes applied from the general tax revenues are on the whole considered to be of universal benefit. It is true the cost of universal day care stands to be enormous — perhaps as much as 6 to 10 billion dollars annually. The issue, however, is not in fact one of economic feasibility. In the world's wealthiest country the issue is rather one of priorities and readiness. Day-care services might best be administered under a special Early Childhood Agency rather than distributed among the existing (bureaucratic, outmoded, but entrenched) education or welfare systems. It would probably prove simpler to innovate, and to go directly to the task with a new agency structured for it. Early childhood education is a special field, with educational, health, nutritional, developmental, and behavioral components.

Another question often raised when universal day care is proposed is that of work incentive. Will the widespread availability of day care encourage women to engage in economically productive labor? And if so, with what consequences? Already we have explored the social and psychological consequences, and found no necessarily detrimental results, but rather the possibility of beneficial results both for the mother and for the child. As to economic consequences, these might include an even stronger influx of women into the labor market, adding to the unemployment problem. Yet with a growing unemployment among men to match the institutionalized unemployment (housewifery) among women, there might be more incentive for a rethinking of the entire question of the duration and constitution of the work week. Part-time work for all might prove to be a partial solution to unemployment and to family needs alike, especially if men are encouraged to share in housekeeping. Also, it might be argued that day care could in the short run reduce the public assistance rolls, as it would leave welfare mothers free to work. It is estimated that in New York City alone, 250,000 women on welfare would be employable if day-care centers and job training were provided.[54]

At present, the absence of day care operates as a work disincentive. The cost of babysitters and nurseries, transportation, work clothing, and lunches often makes it financially unfeasible for women to work, especially those with low pay. Work-related expenses plus taxes are estimated to take 50 percent of a mother's paycheck.[55]

In the past a combination of voluntary and publicly sponsored day care has been controlled by boards of directors, the welfare apparatus, or the tendencies of the labor market, and shaped to respond to the welfare and therapeutic needs of special families and the labor-productive sector. Yet day care is a unique and invaluable service. It is not interchangeable with other institutions for the structuring of human resources. Obstacles to universal day care seem to consist of its origin in welfare arrangements; negative attitudes on the subject of working women; the psychiatric social-work emphasis on the mother's role in early childhood; the tradition of a single dominant maternal role; the confusion between separation and deprivation; the association of day care with communism;[56] and a general emphasis in our modern psychological and educational theory on individual as opposed to group or contextual development and achievement.[57]

It is time for Americans to face the present realities — the breakdown of the nuclear family, the transformation of women's roles, the new awareness of human (child and parental) needs. It is accordingly time to reorient day-care policy to correspond to this changed reality. This in turn must call forth federally funded, community-controlled, universal day care, under a distinct administration for early childhood purposes.

Notes

21. U.S. Department of Labor News Release 77–792, Table 3.
22. Florence Ruderman, *Child Care and Working Mothers: A Study of Arrangements Made for Daytime Care of Children*, Child Welfare League of America, 1968, p. 10.
23. Mary Keyserling, "Working Mothers and Their Children: The Urgent Need for Day-Care Services," in *Report of a Consultation on Working Women and Day-Care Needs* (Washington, D.C.: United States Department of Labor, June 1, 1967), see footnote 20, p. 3.
24. Seth Low and Pearl Spindler, *Child-Care Arrangements of Working Mothers in the United States*, Children's Bureau and Women's Bureau, 1968, pp. 15–16 (based on a study done in 1965).
25. *Children Are Waiting* (Washington, D.C.: Human Resources Administration, Task Force on Early Childhood Development, July 1970), p. 8.
26. Keyserling, pp. 5–6.
27. *Ibid.*, p. 6.
28. Martin Tolchin, "Nursery Schools Arouse Rivalry," *New York Times*, Feb. 17, 1964.
29. Keyserling, p. 8.
30. *Guides to State Welfare Agencies for the Development of Day-Care Services,* (Washington, D.C.: United States Dept. of Health, Education, and Welfare, Children's Bureau, Welfare Administration, 1963).
31. Barbara Wooton, *Social Science and Social Pathology* (New York: Macmillan, 1959), p. 144.
32. Urie Bronfenbrenner, *Two Worlds of Childhood: U.S. and U.S.S.R.* (New York: Russell Sage Foundation, 1970).

33. F. Ivan Nye and Lois Wladis Hoffman, eds., *The Employed Mother in America* (Chicago: Rand McNally, 1963).

34. Joseph Reid, "Legislation for Day Care," in *Report,* p. 35.

35. "Innovative Approaches — a Panel," *Ibid.,* p. 55.

36. Rose A. John, "Child Development and the Part-Time Mother," *Children* (Nov.–Dec. 1959), 213–18; and Leon Yarrow, "Conceptualizing the Early Environment," in Laura L. Dittman, ed., *Early Child Care: The New Perspectives* (New York: Atherton, 1968), pp. 15–27.

37. Bettye Caldwell and Julius Richmond, "Programmed Day Care for the Very Young Child — A Preliminary Report," *Child Welfare,* 44 (Mar. 1965), 134–42; and Stig Sjolin, "Care of Well Children in Day-Care Centers," *Care of Children in Day Care Centers* (Geneva: World Health Organization, 1964), p. 22.

38. Milton Willner, "Day Care, a Reassessment," *Child Welfare,* 44 (Mar. 1967), 126–27.

39. Eleanor Maccoby, "Children and Working Mothers," *Children,* 5–6 (1958–59), 86.

40. Yarrow, pp. 22–23.

41. Dale Meers and Allen Marans, "Group Care of Infants in Other Countries," in Dittman, pp. 234–82.

42. Willner, p. 129.

43. Julius Richmond, "Twenty Percent of the Nation," *Spotlight on Day Care: Proceedings of the National Conference on Day-Care Services, May 13–15, 1965* (Washington, D.C.: United States Department of Health, Education, and Welfare), p. 45.

44. Wooton, pp. 146, 151, 153.

45. Gerald Holden, "A Consideration of Benefits in Kind for Children," *Children's Allowances and the Economic Welfare of Children* (New York: Citizens' Committee for Children, 1968), pp. 150–52.

46. *New York Times,* Nov. 30, 1970, p. 51.

47. David Bull, "Action for Welfare Rights," in *The Fifth Social Service: Nine Fabian Essays* (London: Fabian Society, May 1970; pamphlet), p. 148.

48. Peter Townsend, Introduction, "Does Selectivity Mean a Nation Divided," *Social Services for All: Eleven Fabian Essays* (London: Fabian Society, Sept. 1968), pp. 1–6.

49. Brian Abel Smith, Conclusion, "The Need for Social Planning," *Ibid.,* p. 114.

50. Holden, p. 151; and Alva Myrdal, *Nation and Family* (Cambridge, Mass.: M.I.T. Press, 1941), p. 150.

51. Joseph Featherstone, "The Day-Care Problem: Kentucky Fried Chicken," *The New Republic,* Sept. 12, 1970, pp. 12–16; and Ann Cook and Herbert Mack, "Business Education, the Discovery Center Hustle," *Social Policy* (Sept.–Oct. 1970), pp. 3–11; *New York Times,* Dec. 27, 1969. For example, if Creative Playthings (a toy corporation) runs a day-care center, they will try to convince the parents of the children that certain Creative Playthings toys are needed for the children's educational development.

52. *New York Times,* Jan. 21, 1970, pp. 59 and 65, and Oct. 29, 1970.

53. Shlakman, p. 28.

54. *New York Times,* Dec. 15 and 29, 1970.

55. Nadine Brozan, "To Many Working Mothers, a Job is Almost a Losing Proposition," *New York Times,* Jan. 5, 1971, p. 30.

56. Anna Mayer, *Day Care as a Social Instrument, a Policy Paper,* Columbia University School of Social Work, Jan. 1965, p. 129, quoting Raymond J. Gallagher, Secretary of the National Conference of Catholic Charities, in testimony on Public Welfare Amendments of 1962, Bill No. 10032, *Congressional Record,* 87th Congress, 2d Sess., pp. 578–80.

57. Rochelle Paul Wortis, "Child-Rearing and Women's Liberation," paper delivered at Women's Weekend, Ruskin College, Oxford University, February 28, 1970; pamphlet, p. 1.

WOMEN AND THE LAW

SHIRLEY RAISSI BYSIEWICZ

Shirley Raissi Bysiewicz, currently professor of law and law librarian at the University of Connecticut School of Law, has been actively involved in the women's legal situation for several years. As a member of the Connecticut Bar Association she has served on the Civil Rights Committee and the Committee on the Status of Women, and in 1978 won awards for her contributions to the bar and to the status of women. She is a member of the National Association of Women Lawyers, the Women's Equity Action League (WEAL), and the Task Force of the Governor's Commission on the Status of Women. She has written several articles and book reviews and is co-author of *Effective Legal Research* (1979).

In this selection Bysiewicz describes women's current legal status: women's position before the law, in terms of discrimination and its remedies; and women's position in the law, as members of the profession.

Introduction

Legal equality for women does not fully exist. In the eighteenth and nineteenth centuries, the legal status of women in the United States was comparable to that of blacks under slavery. Neither blacks nor married women had the legal capacity to hold property or to serve as guardians of their own children. Neither blacks nor women could hold office, serve on juries, or bring suit in their own names. The legal status of both women and blacks improved, albeit at different speeds. The Married Women's Property Acts, first enacted in Mississippi in 1839 and later adopted by all American jurisdictions, opened the door to a measure of economic independence for married women. According to Leo Kanowitz, in his book *Women and the Law: An Unfinished Revolution,* the Married Women's Property Acts, though varying from state to state, did redress the contract and property relations between husband and wife, and removed the procedural disabilities of married women. Basically, the Property Acts granted married women the right to make contracts, to sue and be sued without joining their husbands, to manage and control the property

they brought with them to their marriage, to engage in employment without their husbands' permission, and to retain the earnings derived from such employment.

The improved status of women may be attributed to recent federal legislation, to the adoption of similar legislation by the states, as well as to several landmark decisions by the United States Supreme Court striking down state laws and practices that violated the Equal Protection Clause of the Fourteenth Amendment. The court decisions and legislative enactments have altered women's status in employment, education, control of their own bodies, marriage, divorce, financial status, and the criminal law. The Equal Protection guarantee was not applied by the United States Supreme Court to sex discrimination until 1971 in the *Reed* v. *Reed* case, when the court invalidated an Idaho statute which stated that as between persons equally entitled to administer a decedent's estate, "males must be preferred to females." The painstaking process of constitutional litigation that resulted in recent changes in the law, has only accomplished part of the job. Many state statutes (i.e., Louisiana law does not allow a married woman to manage her own earnings) that tolerate gender-based discrimination are likely to remain in force unless the proposed Equal Rights Amendment to the Constitution is ratified.

Employment Discrimination

Prior to the passage of major federal legislation, sex-based employment discrimination prevented women from earning salaries comparable to men when they performed the same jobs. More important, in many instances, women were closed out of positions held by men. The Equal Pay Act, passed by Congress in 1963, forbids companies from paying women less than men for substantially the same work. However, according to a U.S. Department of Labor publication, women workers in 1960 were primarily engaged in housekeeping, nursing, and secretarial work and women engaging in these occupations were largely unaffected by the Equal Pay Act as few men were employed in these fields. Jobs found to be equal under the law so as to require employers to raise the wages of women workers included factory assembly-line employees; janitors and maids in colleges; sales-clerks in department stores, regardless of the kind of merchandise sold; orderlies and nurse's aides. Other jobs where women gained back wages as provided by the law included bank tellers, laboratory technicians, and machine operators.

The most important law prohibiting sex discrimination in employment is Title VII of the 1964 Civil Rights Act. This law has the greatest potential for effecting change in employment practices. It is the broadest law of all, covering almost all forms of race, color, religion, national origin, and sex discrimination. The inclusion in the Civil Rights Act of the prohibition against sex discrimination was serendipitous. The provision was added by opponents of the bill as a result of efforts to block passage of the basic legislation "rather than solicitude for women's employment rights."

Title VII has been a fertile source of litigation defining women's rights under the Act. One of the first United States Supreme Court cases interpreting the statute was *Phillips* v. *Martin Marietta Corp.* Ida Phillips, mother of three preschool-age children, was denied employment by the Marietta Corporation even though the company would hire the fathers of preschoolers. The Supreme Court overturned the decisions of the lower courts and found the practice of having "one hiring policy for women and another for men — each having preschool age children" discriminatory, therefore illegal under Title VII.

In addition to the Equal Pay Act, Executive Order 11246, signed by President Johnson, and Executive Order 11375, amending the earlier order, were powerful directives aimed at eliminating employment discrimination in the federal government. Executive orders have the force and effect of legislative enactments on agencies of the federal government. Executive Order 11246 forbids any employer who has a contract with the federal government to discriminate against minority workers. Executive Order 11375 amended the earlier order by prohibiting discrimination on the basis of sex. As a result of the executive order, every agency or department within the executive branch must obtain a promise from all contractors with whom it deals that the company will not discriminate against its employees.[1] Executive Order 11478, issued by President Nixon, further modified the earlier Johnson order by forbidding the federal government, as an employer, to discriminate on the basis of sex.

Most states have passed statutes similar to Title VII of the Equal Pay Act forbidding employment discrimination on the basis of sex. There are state public works laws modeled on Executive Order 11246, as amended, and public employee laws modeled on Executive Order 11478. A national commitment to equality by way of passage of the ERA would ensure better compliance to existing statutes and executive orders that forbid gender-based discrimination.

Educational Discrimination

Although women constitute approximately half the working population, education still prepares them to be housewives. Oberlin College made history 140 years ago by admitting women and blacks, thereby allowing women to receive a college education for the first time in the United States, yet sexism persisted. Women students were required to wash the male students' clothes, clean their rooms, and serve them at the table. Then, as now, "[s]ex segregation in the labor force and traditional sex-role allocations at home . . . are reinforced by educational arrangements from preschool to graduate schools."

Until 1972, when Congress passed the Education Amendment Act, no federal law specifically prohibited sex discrimination in education even though such discrimination had been prohibited in employment for almost a decade by Title VII of the Civil Rights Act of 1964. Title IX of the Education Amendments Act of 1972 forbids sex discrimination by any school, preschool through graduate, that receives federal funds. Title IX defines sex discrimination very broadly:

No person in the United States shall, on the basis of sex, be excluded from participation in, be denied the benefits of, or be subject to discrimination under any education program or activity receiving Federal financial assistance.

The Act, however, does not reach religious schools if a particular religion's tenets require sex discrimination. Title IX also exempts military schools, which are defined as schools training individuals for the U.S. military services or for the merchant marine.

In addition to the general exceptions for religious institutions and military schools, Title IX does not affect admissions to private elementary and secondary schools, or to private undergraduate institutions that do not receive federal funds. Also exempt from the admissions discrimination ban are undergraduate programs of public institutions that have admitted only one sex since their founding; traditionally one-sex institutions in the process of becoming co-educational have seven years to complete this transition before facing the threat of the loss of federal funds. Furthermore, the sanction provided would be limited to the particular program in which noncompliance exists.

The Department of Health, Education, and Welfare has the primary responsibility for administering Title IX. Under Title IX the legal sanction, if sex-based discrimination is proven, is the loss of federal funds. It is in this respect that Title IX differs from the protections afforded by the Equal Protection Clause of the Fourteenth Amendment. As of 1978, HEW is understaffed to handle the institutional reviews for a finding of discrimination. The severity of the penalty of withdrawal of federal monies has made its use virtually nonexistent. In order to bring suit for an alleged Constitutional violation there must be a showing of state action — discrimination carried out by state or local government. This does mean that women may sue any public school and any state college without further changes in the law. But since the effect of the Fourteenth Amendment on sex discrimination is not uniformly defined by the courts, there is no guarantee that any particular lawsuit will be successful. As of

1977 there are no court decisions interpreting Title IX.

Title IX applies not only to schools, but also to organizations and agencies receiving federal aid for education. It covers both students and employees and, more specifically, prohibits discrimination based on sex in the following areas: admissions, student aid, student housing, access to courses, sport participation, club membership, and employment. Feminists are using Title IX and the Equal Protection Clause imaginatively, but these legal weapons do not yet reach all forms of educational discrimination. Title IX does not provide language for a private right to sue. As of 1978, lawsuits are pending by private parties to determine the status of individuals suing educational institutions receiving federal funds on the basis of sex-based discrimination. Because the case-by-case judicial approach is not well suited to bring about equality in the field of education, the enactment of ERA would pave the way for equality.

Although some states have provisions outlawing discrimination, it is difficult to ascertain their effectiveness. Some administered by state civil rights agencies provide for a complaint procedure and full enforcement powers; others merely forbid some forms of discrimination but provide no enforcement mechanism.

Effective July 1, 1979 a reorganization plan places enforcement of Executive Order 11246 to the Office of Federal Contract Compliance Programs; enforcement of equal employment opportunity will be shifted to the EEOC; enforcement of the Equal Pay Act will also be shifted to the EEOC.

Women in the Law Profession

Nineteenth-century women aspiring to the practice of law fared poorly. The notorious case of *Bradwell* v. *The State* citation illustrates their difficulties. Myra Bradwell, a married Illinois resident, applied to the state bar and was denied admission. Although she was otherwise qualified as to education and moral character, the court held that she was unsuited to the practice of law as a result of the legal disability that prevented a married woman from entering into contracts thereby barring the creation of the contractual relationship between attorney and client which the court deemed necessary to the practice of law. With only one justice dissenting, the United States Supreme Court affirmed the state court decision. The Court reasoned that the privileges and immunities clause of Article IV, Section 2 of the Federal Constitution was inapplicable to Ms. Bradwell's claim. She was a citizen of Illinois, and because admission to the bar of a state is not one of the privileges and immunities of United States citizenship, the Fourteenth Amendment did not secure the asserted right. The Due Process and Equal Protection Clauses of the Fourteenth Amendment were not considered by the Court. It is hardly surprising that single women fared no better. In the *Motion to Admit Miss Lavinia Goodell to the Bar of this Court,* the Wisconsin Supreme Court denied the motion, reasoning that women are best suited to bear and nurture children. What the court wrote is typical of the attitude toward women shared by those who made and practiced law:

> The peculiar qualities of womanhood, its gentle graces, its quick sensibility, its tender susceptibility, its purity, its delicacy, its emotional impulses, its subordination of hard reason to sympathetic feeling, are surely not qualifications for forensic strife. Nature has tempered woman as little for the juridical conflicts of the courtroom, as for the physical conflicts of the battlefield. . . . It would be revolting to all female sense of the innocence and sanctity

357

Table 1 Women in legal education. *Statistics**

School year	Total men & women enrolled	Women enrolled	% of women enrolled to total
1963	49,552	1,883	3.8%
1964	54,265	2,183	4.0%
1965	59,744	2,537	4.2%
1966	62,556	2,678	4.2%
1967	64,406	2,906	4.5%
1968	62,779	3,704	5.8%
1969	68,386	4,715	6.8%
1970	82,499	7,031	8.5%
1971	94,468	8,914	9.4%
1972	101,707	12,173	11.8%
1973	106,102	16,760	15.7%
1974	110,713	21,788	19.6%
1975	116,991	26,737	22.8%
1976	117,451	29,982	25.5%
1977	118,557	32,538	27.4%

* Statistics taken from "Legal Education and Bar Admissions Statistics, 1963–1977," in *Law Schools & Bar Admission Requirements*, (Chicago: ABA, 1978), p. 54.

of their sex, shocking to man's reverence for womanhood and faith in woman, on which hinge all the better affections and humanities of life, that woman should be permitted to mix professionally in all the nastiness of the world which finds its way into courts of justice; all the unclean issues, all the collateral questions of sodomy, incest, rape, seduction, fornication, adultery, pregnancy, bastardy, legitimacy, prostitution, lascivious cohabitation, abortion, infanticide, obscene publications, libel and slander of sex, impotence, divorce . . . Reverence for all womanhood would suffer in the public spectacle of woman so instructed and so engaged.

Certainly women's status in the profession of law has improved since Ms. Goodell sought admission to the bar. Statistical surveys attest to the inroads made by women into the legal profession (see Table 1).

The spectacular rise in women's enrollment in law schools in the 1970s (see ABA figures) is a significant indicator of the impact of the women's movement on the career aspirations of female students, and there is a growing number of women "preparing for a profession that, perhaps more than any other in the United States, has been sex-typed as male." A survey conducted by social scientists based on interview and questionnaire responses by women and men in the fields of law, medicine and architecture, notes:

Sex discrimination as perceived by male and female professionals is common in law, medicine and architecture but is a significantly accentuated characteristic of law. While lawyers may have a special skill in discerning these attitudes, sex discriminatory action seems characteristic of the profession and appears to be accepted by a number of its professionals.[2]

Despite the persistence of these attitudes, enrollment of women in law schools has increased dramatically, and may be dated to the late 1960s as the idea of equal opportunity for men and women began to take hold.

In 1970, the Association of American Law Schools became one of the first national academic associations to prohibit sex discrimination in admissions, employment, and placement at member schools. The association's ban on sex discrimination was inspired by a 1970 survey on the status of women in law schools. A follow-up survey in 1972 revealed a distinct improvement, although the placement field figures indicated that there is still a distance to go before women have true equality in the profession. Figures compiled by the National Association for Law Placement revealed that in 1976 women were finally approaching the percentages achieved by men in finding employment after law school.

National Association for Law
Placement, Class of 1976

Eighty-nine of 123 participating law schools provided information concerning employment of women graduates. Of the total of 24,667 graduates from the reporting schools, 3,717 were women. The status of 18,393 of the total number of graduates was known, including 2,880 women. Of these, 16,939 or 92 percent of the total were employed, compared with 2,610 or 91 percent of the women. The employed women were distributed among employment categories as follows:

- 41.3 percent of the women were in private practice, compared with 52.4 percent of the total
- 22.4 percent of the women worked in government jobs compared with 17.5 percent of the total
- 8.8 percent of the women worked in corporations, compared with 10 percent of the total
- 12 percent of the women had judicial clerkships, compared with 9.1 percent of the total
- 9.4 percent of the women worked in public interest/indigent services, compared with 5 percent of the total
- 4.6 percent of the women worked in academic positions compared with 3.4 percent of the total
- 6 percent of the women worked in the military compared with 1.7 percent of the total
- .9 percent were engaged in a miscellaneous category, including prepaid schemes, matching the .9 percent of the total.

Abortion, Contraception, and Sterilization

The issue of abortion has received a great deal of attention in the courts and remains one of the most controversial issues of the decade. Beginning in the late 1960s, state laws prohibiting abortion were challenged as unconstitutional in that they restricted a woman's right to control her body, and thereby interfered with her right to privacy. In 1973, the United States Supreme Court confronted the issue in the historic opinions of *Roe* v. *Wade* and *Doe* v. *Bolton.* The Court ruled that abortion laws were unconstitutional invasions of a woman's privacy, which included "a woman's decision whether or not to terminate her pregnancy." In *Roe* v. *Wade,* the Court held that states could not prohibit abortions during the first trimester of pregnancy, the rationale being that during this period the woman's interest in controlling her own body outweighed the state's interest in preserving her health and the life of the fetus. After the first trimester the state's competing interest took precedence. Implementation of the Court's decisions as well as unresolved issues remain, and the boundaries of these decisions will expand and contract in the light of subsequent cases.

Presently, there are no legally enforceable restrictions on a woman's right to birth control. In *Griswold* v. *Connecticut,* the Supreme Court struck down a Connecticut law prohibiting the use of birth control, as the law interfered with a married couple's right to privacy. This decision was expanded to include unmarried persons in a 1972 decision, *Eisenstadt* v. *Baird,* where the Court invalidated a Massachusetts law that forbade distribution of contraceptives to the unmarried as an unconstitutional denial of equal protection for single people.

There are not state or federal laws prohibiting voluntary sterilization, although some doctors may refuse to operate on a woman below a certain age or a woman who does not have a certain number of children. Restrictive hospital regulations may also present difficulties to women seeking sterilization. Such regulations may be struck down, however, by legal challenges to hospitals receiving public funds in the light of the Supreme Court's decisions in *Roe* v. *Wade, Doe* v. *Bolton* and *Eisenstadt* v. *Baird.* These decisions make it clear that the state may not have such an all-encompassing anti–birth control policy as to interfere with a woman's right to control her own body. Indeed, the courts are increasingly recognizing the assertion made by the Boston Women's Health Collective in *Our Bodies, Our Selves:*

> All of us ought to have the right to make our own decisions about having children: if we will have children, when we will have children, and how many children we will have.[3]

Marriage and Divorce

Marriage

Historically, the position of the married woman marked her as her husband's chattel. Blackstone, in his commentaries on the *Law of England* described the legal status of the married woman:

> By marriage the husband and wife are one person in law: that is, the very being or legal existence of the woman is suspended during marriage, or at least is incorporated into that of her husband; under whose wing, protection and cover, she performs everything and is therefore called by French law a *feme-covert* ... under the protection and influence of her husband, her baron or lord; and her condition during her marriage is called her coverture.[4]

Elements of coverture still persist in women's legal position. First, women forfeited control of their property and the right to sue or be sued when they married. Today the married woman does not surrender her entire "legal personality" to her husband as she did in Blackstone's day. It was not until 1960, however, in *United States* v. *Dege,* that the Supreme Court recognized that a married couple was *two* human beings. In that case, a husband and wife were charged with conspiring to commit an offense in violation of a federal statute. The lower court had dismissed the indictment reasoning that since a wife was assumed to be one with her husband, the pair could not be capable of conspiring with themselves. The Supreme Court, reversing the lower court, held that a husband and wife are not legally incapable of violating a criminal conspiracy statute.

Second, a woman customarily changes her surname for that of her husband upon marriage. Kanowitz has written that the name change for women is "firmly rooted in Anglo-American social custom"; and research has shown that this is not sanctioned by statutory law.

Third, marriage has traditionally deprived a woman, but not a man, of the privilege accorded all other responsible adults, that of choosing her own legal domicile. In most states, when a woman marries, her husband's domicile automatically supersedes her own. If her husband's legal domicile is different from her premarital domicile, a married woman must, for example, re-register to vote, be subjected to unfavorable income tax consequences, lose the right to attend a university in her home state as a resident student, and she may be deprived of the privilege of running for office in her home state if her husband's legal domicile is outside the state. Again, the rationale has been that since the husband earned the money for the support of the family, he had the right to decide where the family should reside.

There is no federal law governing marriage and divorce. Traditionally jurisdiction over domestic relations belongs to the individual states. As a consequence, laws governing marriage and divorce vary from state to state. The Uniform Marriage and Divorce Act suggests statutory guidelines, but state legislatures are under no compulsion to adopt the act. It is only where state policy clearly violates constitutional guarantees that the federal courts will decide family law matters.

Divorce

The old belief that someone had to be at fault in order for a divorce to be granted still permeates the divorce process. Although a number of states are adopting no-fault grounds for divorce, the issue of fault is *still* considered in the determination of child custody, support, and division of property. Thus, the adversarial process dominates the dissolution of marriages. The most recent effort of divorce reformers is to achieve a policy shift from divorces based on the fault of one partner, to dissolution based on the nonjudgmental recognition that the marriage has ended as a viable institution.

The issue of what form the statutory basis for marriage dissolution should take is not primarily a problem of sex-based discrimination. There are, nevertheless, a few grounds for divorce available to one sex but not to the other. For example, in his review of the statutes, Kanowitz[5] found that whereas many states permit a wife to divorce her husband for nonsupport, only a few states permit a husband to base his action on the same ground.

An increasing number of marriages end in divorce, and the issue of alimony is of concern to the states whose welfare systems could be impossibly overburdened by divorced women, most of whom have dependent children. Alimony, created under English law, was administered by the ecclesiastical courts and was granted in cases of legal separation, but not in cases of dissolution. When divorce jurisdiction was transferred from the ecclesiastical courts to the civil courts, and separation became a ground for divorce, alimony was extended to provide support for a former wife following divorce.

The Uniform Marriage and Divorce Act creates a system of marital property for the purpose of division on divorce or legal separation. The Reporters' Comment makes clear that the authors of the act intended a relationship between the Disposition of Property Section (8307) and the Maintenance Section (8308), which addresses the alimony problem:

> The dual intention . . . is to encourage the court to provide for the financial needs of the spouses by property disposition rather than by an award of maintenance. Only if the available property is insufficient for the purpose and if the spouse who seeks maintenance is unable to secure employment appropriate to his skills and interests or is occupied with child care may an award of maintenance be ordered.

Finances

Credit

The Federal Equal Credit Opportunity Act now requires that creditors such as banks, department stores, and finance companies treat a woman in the same manner as they would a man. Both federal and state laws have attempted to overcome the notion that women are poor credit risks. In general, it is a violation of the federal law to discriminate on the basis of sex in the granting, continuation, or revocation of credit. Another recent federal law, the Fair Credit Reporting Act, requires that whenever credit is denied on the basis of a consumer credit agency report, the creditor must reveal the name and address of the agency that reported the poor rating. Furthermore, married women have the right to a separate account from their husbands', and where married couples have joint accounts, the law requires that the creditor maintain a credit rating for both husband and wife.

Taxation of Income

Although present tax law does not specifically single out working women for disadvantageous treatment, the financial imposition it places on the family where both spouses are employed is substantial. In 1948 Congress enacted the joint income tax return provision for married couples (the Internal Revenue Code of 1954, §6013). Until the Tax Reform Act of 1969, it was generally and correctly understood that in the majority of cases, the tax law favored the marital union by allowing a saving in federal income tax. This tended to place a heavy comparative tax penalty on the unmarried while affording a substantial tax advantage to the one-earner family. But the Tax Reform Act of 1969, in attempting to ameliorate the unfairly heavy burden the income tax statutes imposed on the unmarried, failed to recognize the adverse financial impact of the laws on the two-earner family, and the effect of the tax laws is to discourage married women from working.

Estates and Trusts

The modernization of the law of interstate succession progressed slowly in England.

Historically, although everyone had testamentary capacity, a married woman could not make an effective will because her husband acquired ownership of her property. Although English law was based on concepts and practices unsuited to American conditions, state legislatures adopted the substance of English statutes, and courts often deferred to English precedent in construing them. In the landmark case of *Reed* v. *Reed,* the Supreme Court invalidated an Idaho statute that preferred males to females as administrators of estates. This case had broad implications for the legal status of women not only in estate law, but also because it marked the first time the Supreme Court invalidated a statute on grounds of sex discrimination.

Concerning inheritance by a wife, most trusts today are set up to "protect women themselves." The prevalent view seems to be that a woman should be relieved of the responsibilities and duties of management of the estate. A trust is created so the wife will not dissipate the inheritance through unwise investment or through improvident expenditure.

Criminal Law

The laws defining the crimes of which women and girls are convicted are biased against the female offender. Recently, courts have invalidated statutes providing unequal sentences for men and women on the ground that they violated the Equal Protection guarantee of the Fourteenth Amendment. Yet a double standard continues to exist in a variety of ways. For example, prostitutes are prosecuted more vigorously and more often than are the customers who patronize them. Although the law is not written so as to afford protection to the customer, the enforcement of prostitution laws achieves this result. Until recently many girls were sent to reform schools because they engaged in sexual activity whereas boys who did so were regarded as healthy and normal. In Utah, the defense of "passion killing" is allowed to the wronged husband but not to the wronged wife.

Historically married women have suffered various legal inequities because of their marital status. Battered wives are another example of silent victims. However, a November 1977 Michigan case may initiate a more compassionate judicial system for the battered woman. In that Michigan trial, Mrs. Francine Hughes was charged with the first-degree murder of her husband. Her unprecedented defense, that years of repeated beatings drove her to set fire to the house in which James Hughes died, won her an acquittal.

Conditions in penal institutions for women continue to be inferior to those for men, especially in rehabilitative programs, staff, and equipment.

Equal Rights Amendment

Forty-nine years after it was first proposed, Congress passed the Equal Rights Amendment to the Constitution. In order for ERA to become part of the Constitution, however, it must be ratified by thirty-eight state legislatures by June 27, 1982. As of November 1978, thirty-five states had ratified. The proposed amendment provides that

> equality of rights under the law shall not be denied or abridged by the United States or by any state on account of sex.

Like the Equal Protection Clause of the Fourteenth Amendment, ERA prohibits discrimination by federal, state, and local governments, but is limited by the concept of "state action." Thus, only where the govern-

ment is somehow implicated may sex discrimination be prohibited. Hence, where there is no state action women will need other laws to protect them against discrimination. The Federal Equal Credit Opportunity Act, for example, protects women against the discrimination practiced by banks and other lending institutions. Without this act, women would not be protected since the requisite state action in a bank's activities is not found sufficient reason to invoke the protection of ERA or the Equal Protection Clause of the Fourteenth Amendment.

ERA would require that the United States Constitution be applied without favor to every individual no matter what sex the person may be. Thus, ERA would give men as well as women the right not to be discriminated against on the basis of sex. It would reach a broad range of widely used sex discriminatory practices and would securely and permanently outlaw certain practices harmful to women. It would prohibit denial of social security and other government benefits to the families of employed women, when these benefits are paid to the families of employed men. Also, it would eliminate all sex-based legal presumptions with regard to the ownership or control of marital property, such as the presumption that all household goods are owned by the husband.

Pending ratification of ERA by the requisite thirty-eight states, some women are protected by the equal rights provisions in their state constitutions. According to a publication of the U.S. Department of Labor, a total of sixteen states have equal rights amendments to their state constitutions.

Urging passage of ERA, Davidson and others have written in a personal note to their text that

> . . . the amendment would eliminate the historical impediment to unqualified judicial recognition of equal rights and responsibilities for

men and women as constitutional principle; it would end legislative inertia that keeps discriminatory laws on the books ... and it would serve as a clear statement of the nation's moral and legal commitment to a system in which women and men stand as full and equal individuals before the law.[6]

Notes

1. The contractor must also pledge to take affirmative action to ensure nondiscriminatory treatment, such as employment, promotion, demotion, recruitment, layoffs, training, and apprenticeship programs.
2. Bradley Soule and Kay Standley, "Lawyers' Perceptions of Sex Discrimination in Their Profession," *American Bar Association Journal,* 59 (1973), 1144.
3. Boston Women's Health Course Collective, *Our Bodies, Our Selves* (Boston, New England Free Press, 1971), p. 4.
4. Blackstone, William, *Commentaries on the Law,* Gavit, ed. (1941), p. 189.
5. Leo Kanowitz, *Women and the Law: The Unfinished Revolution* (Albuquerque, N.M.: University of New Mexico Press, 1969), p. 40.
6. Kenneth M. Davidson, Ruth Bader Ginsburg, and Herman Hill Kay, *Sex-Based Discrimination: Text, Cases and Materials* (St. Paul, Minn.: West Publishing Co., 1974), p. 116.

Bibliography

American Bar Association. *Law Schools and Bar Admission Requirements: A Review of Legal Education in the United States — Fall, 1976.* Chicago: American Bar Association, 1977.

Blackstone, William. *Commentaries on the Law,* Gavit, ed. Washington, D.C.: Washington Law Book Company, 1941.

Boston Women's Health Course Collective. *Our Bodies, Our Selves.* Boston: New England Free Press, 1971.

Bysiewicz, Shirley Raissi. "1972 AALS Questionnaire on Women in Legal Education." *Journal of Legal Education,* 25 (1973), p. 503.

Davidson, Kenneth M., Ruth Bader Ginsburg and Herman Hill Kay, *Sex-Based Discrimination: Text, Cases and Materials.* St. Paul, Minn.: West Publishing Co., 1974; Supplement, 1975.

Kanowitz, Leo. *Women and the Law: The Unfinished Revolution.* Albuquerque, N.M.: University of New Mexico Press, 1969.

Mears, Judith. *Women and the Law: A Handbook for Connecticut.* Hartford: Connecticut Civil Liberties Union, 1977.

National Association for Law Placement. *Class of 1976 Employment Report.* Sacramento, Calif.: National Association for Law Placement, 1977.

Ross, Susan C. *The Rights of Women: The Basic ACLU Guide to Women's Rights.* New York: Avon, 1973.

Soule, Bradley, and Kay Standley, "Lawyers' Perceptions of Sex Discrimination in Their Profession," *American Bar Association Journal,* 59, (1973), 1144.

U.S. Women's Bureau. *Handbook on Women Workers.* Washington, D.C.: U.S. Department of Labor, 1969.

U.S. Women's Bureau. *State Equal Rights Amendments.* Washington, D.C.: U.S. Department of Labor, 1976.

LET'S HAVE E.R.A. AS A SIGNAL

RUTH BADER GINSBURG

Ruth Bader Ginsburg, born in Brooklyn in 1933 and educated at Cornell University and Harvard and Columbia law schools, is a distinguished attorney and a professor of law at Columbia. She has written a number of articles, monographs, and books on sex-based discrimination. Since 1971 she has frequently participated in litigation before the Supreme

Court, and she has served actively on the boards of such organizations as the American Civil Liberties Union, the American Foreign Law Association, the Women's Law Fund, the Women's Equity Action League, and the Women's Action Alliance. Ginsburg has written often on the Equal Rights Amendment. Here she explains why, in the light of women's legal history and experience, this amendment is crucial to equal treatment and opportunity before the law.

Last year we celebrated the two hundredth anniversary of the Declaration of Independence, but for most American women it's more important to look at four questions that relate to the present decade of the 1970s. First, how have jurists treated official line drawing by gender before the present decade? Second, how has the judicial response altered in the current decade? Third, what is the purpose and function of the equal rights amendment to the federal Constitution? And finally, how may the presence (or absence) of the equal rights amendment affect Supreme Court precedent?

The State of the Art to 1971

"Anything goes" seems to be a fair summary of the Supreme Court's decisions until 1971. The Court consistently had affirmed governmental authority to classify by gender, as a trilogy of cases illustrates — *Muller* v. *Oregon,* 208 U.S. 412 (1908); *Goesaert* v. *Cleary,* 335 U.S. 464 (1948); and *Hoyt* v. *Florida,* 368 U.S. 57 (1961).

In 1905, in the now long-discredited *Lochner* v. *New York,* 198 U.S. 45, the Court rebuffed a state's attempt to enact protective labor legislation for all workers, men and women alike. But in 1908 in *Muller* the Court upheld a ten-hour day for women only. The decision reflects themes first sounded in nineteenth century decisions —

Reprinted with permission from the *American Bar Association Journal,* 63 (January 1977), 70–73.

first, that women's place in a world controlled by men is divinely ordained (a thought Justice Bradley expressed in his concurring opinion in *Bradwell* v. *Illinois,* 16 Wall. 130 (1873)); and second, that while men can fend for themselves, women must "rest upon and look to [men] for protection." Somewhat inconsistently, the Court added in *Muller* that women require the aid of the law "to protect her from the greed as well as the passion of man."

Next in the trilogy, *Goesaert* illustrates the danger lurking behind "protective" labels. This decision upheld a Michigan statute that allowed women to work as waitresses in taverns but barred them from the more lucrative job of bartender. The law protects women, said the state, while male bartenders plus their union joined in a chivalrous chorus.

One of the plaintiffs was a female bar owner whose daughter, a coplaintiff, assisted in operating the business. The state had protected away mother's and daughter's right to compete with male bar owners. If the Goesaerts would not pay a man to do a job the two women were fully capable of doing themselves, they would have to close up shop. The Supreme Court opinion in *Goesaert* declares and proceeds from this premise: "Michigan could, beyond question, forbid all women from working behind a bar."

Increasingly, as this century has worn on, women who needed jobs to support themselves and in many cases their families became skeptical of this kind of "protection" from the law. From their vantage point, restrictive labor laws operate less to protect women than to protect men's jobs from women's competition.

In the last in the series, *Hoyt,* a unanimous Supreme Court held it permissible to limit women's jury service to those who volunteered. This system yielded the result that lay participation in the administration of justice was virtually all male.

By the late 1960s a revived and burgeoning feminist movement spotlighted the altered life patterns of women. Two factors contributed in particular to this changed atmosphere — the virtual disappearance of food and goods cultivated or produced at home and the access to more effective means of birth control. The Equal Pay Act of 1963 (29 U.S.C. § 206(d)) and Title VII of the Civil Rights Act of 1964 (42 U.S.C. § 2000 (e) *et seq.*) began to focus national attention on the adversely discriminatory treatment that women encountered in the labor market.

The Judicial Response after 1971

The United States Court of Appeals for the District of Columbia Circuit in 1974 summarized the post-1971 developments this way: Supreme Court precedent with respect to gender-based discrimination is "still evolving," "rapidly changing, and variously interpreted" (509 F. 2d 508, 510). In the same year in an article in the *New York University Law Review* Prof. John Johnston, Jr., commented that the courts are "not certain what constitutes sex discrimination, how virulent this form of discrimination is or how it should be analyzed in terms of due process and equal protection." My own appraisal, expressed in an article in *The Supreme Court Review, 1975,* is that the Supreme

Court had taken a few remarkable steps in a new direction, but it had shied away from doctrinal development and had left open avenues of retreat.

The first break from the "anything goes" pattern was *Reed* v. *Reed,* 404 U.S. 71, in which the Supreme Court declared unconstitutional an Idaho law providing that as between persons "equally entitled" to administer a decedent's estate, "males must be preferred to females." A year and a half later, in *Frontiero* v. *Richardson,* 411 U.S. 677 (1973), married women in the uniformed services were held entitled to the same fringe benefits as married men. Under the law that the Supreme Court declared unconstitutional, married men automatically received a housing allowance and medical care for their wives, while married women received these benefits only if they supplied all their own support and more than half of their husband's.

In 1974 the Supreme Court retrenched, first in *Kahn* v. *Shevin,* 416 U.S. 351, a decision upholding exclusion of widowers from the Florida statute that grants widows a real property tax exemption. This exemption saved the real-property-owning widow the grand sum of fifteen dollars annually. A benign favor for (widowed) women? The Supreme Court said the fifteen dollar saving compensated women for past economic disadvantage. Florida gave three classes this little tax break: the blind, the totally and permanently disabled, and widows.

Later in 1974 the Court returned a decision impossible to rationalize as a favor to women. In *Geduldig* v. *Aiello,* 417 U.S. 484, the court upheld a California statute that excluded women disabled by pregnancy from a workers' income protection disability insurance plan. On the other hand, the Supreme Court has held that school teachers may not be dismissed or placed on involuntary leave arbitrarily at a fixed stage in pregnancy (414 U.S. 632 (1974)) and that pregnant women ready and willing to work may not be denied unemployment compensation (423 U.S. 44 (1975)).

Absence of a consistent, comprehensible approach to this issue was further indicated last month. In *General Electric Company* v. *Gilbert,* 45 U.S.L.W. 4031 (December 7, 1976), the Court confronted an employer's plan providing nonoccupational sickness and accident benefits to all employees, save only those with disabilities arising from pregnancy. Construing Title VII of the Civil Rights Act of 1964, the Court declared this exclusion entailed no gender-based discrimination at all!

With no pregnant problems on its calendar, 1975 brought the Supreme Court back to the 1971–73 track. In *Taylor* v. *Louisiana,* 419 U.S. 522, the Court overturned its 1961 *Hoyt* women's jury service decision and declared unconstitutional a Louisiana provision that restricted jury service by women to volunteers. In *Stanton* v. *Stanton,* 421 U.S. 7, the Court declared unconstitutional a Utah law that required parents to support a son until he is twenty-one but a daughter only until she is eighteen. And in *Weinberger* v. *Wiesenfeld,* 420 U.S. 636, the Court struck down one of a series of Social Security sex lines. It held a widowed father to be entitled to the same benefits to care for his child that a widowed mother receives.

Is *Wiesenfeld* a men's rights case? Only derivatively. The discrimination started with Paula Wiesenfeld, a wage-earning woman. When she died, her social insurance provided less protection for her family than the social insurance of a wage-earning man. Paula Wiesenfeld paid social security taxes without any discount. But the payout to her survivors, husband Stephen and son Jason Paul, was subject to a drastic discount.

Do We Need the E.R.A.?

The key to the Supreme Court's performance in the 1970s is not so much the specific results of decided cases but how those results were reached. The justices so far have avoided articulating general principles and have shown a tendency to deal with each case as an isolated instance in a narrow frame. No opinion attracting five votes acknowledges a clear perception of what computer runs or federal and state statutes so plainly reveal — that the particular statutes presented to the Supreme Court are part of a pervasive design, a design reflecting distinctly nonneutral notions about "the way women (or men) are."

Why does the Court shy away from doctrinal development? For an altogether understandable reason. Justice Powell explained the problem in his *Frontiero* concurring opinion. The Court must act with particular circumspection, he said, in the dim zone between constitutional interpretation (a proper judicial task) and constitutional amendment (a job for federal and state legislatures).

But the equal protection guarantee exists for all persons, and the Supreme Court has indeed acknowledged that women are "persons" within the meaning of the Fourteenth Amendment. Why, then, the reluctance to interpret the equal protection principle dynamically in this area? Because it is historic fact that neither the founding fathers nor the Reconstruction Congress had women's emancipation on the agenda. When the Thirteenth, Fourteenth, and Fifteenth amendments were added to the Constitution, women were denied the vote, the most basic right of adult citizens. If they were married, in many states they could not contract, hold property, or litigate on their own behalf. Courts are sensitive to that history.

Race discrimination decisions may be anchored with some security to the design of those who drafted the Constitution. Indeed, in the 1872 *Slaughter-House Cases,* 16 Wall. 36, the Court said that the Fourteenth Amendment's equal protection clause is so clearly a provision for the black race that the Court doubted whether any other form of official discrimination would ever be held to come within its purview.

Recognition of women as "persons" occurred in the Supreme Court's 1874 *Minor* v. *Happersett,* 21 Wall. 162, opinion, a decision rejecting a woman's claim to the franchise. Beyond doubt women are "persons" and may be "citizens" within the meaning of the Fourteenth Amendment, the Court said. So are children, it went on to explain, and no one would suggest children have a constitutional right to the franchise.

The adoption of the equal rights amendment would relieve the Court's uneasiness in the gray zone between interpretation and amendment of the Constitution. It would remove the historical impediment — the absence of any intention by eighteenth and nineteenth century Constitution makers to deal with gender-based discrimination. It would add to our fundamental instrument of government a principle under which the judiciary may develop the coherent opinion pattern lacking up to now. It also should end the legislative inertia that retards social change by keeping obsolete discriminatory laws on the books. And, as Justice Stevens observed in his confirmation hearings, the amendment would have symbolic importance. It would serve as a forthright statement of our moral and legal commitment to a system in which neither sons nor daughters are pigeonholed by government because of their sex. Rather, so far as laws and officialdom are concerned, males and females will be free to grow, develop, and aspire in accordance with their individual talents, preferences, and capacities.

What Are the Consequences?

What are the consequences of the High Court's unwillingness to articulate a principle of general application governing legislative line drawing by gender?

A look at the Court's docket for this current term indicates the situation. First, Oklahoma's 3.2 beer law is before the Court (No. 75–628). This is a "protective" statute with an unusual twist in that it permits girls to buy 3.2 beer or work in a beer parlor at the age of eighteen, while boys must wait until they are twenty-one. The plaintiff, Carolyn Whitener, is an entrepreneur who sells 3.2 beer, and her coplaintiff is an apparently thirsty young man. It is an embarrassment that a law of this kind is retained by a legislature and must occupy the attention of the highest court in the nation.

Second, there is another Social Security Act challenge (No. 75–699). W, a wage earner, dies. H, her spouse, is not himself covered under social security. H seeks survivors' benefits under W's account. The law says H is not entitled unless W outearned H three to one. For a spouse to qualify under a female wage earner's account, the female must provide all her own support, plus half of his — in other words, three fourths of the total family support.

If the situation were the other way around — if a male were the covered worker, a female the survivor — the survivor would qualify for benefits without regard to H's and W's respective contributions to family income. Women are put on a par with men for social security contribution purposes, but the payout under a woman's account is less than the payout under a man's.

That very same gender differential was declared unconstitutional in *Frontiero* v. *Richardson,* the 1973 military fringe benefits case. And *Weinberger* v. *Wiesenfeld,* the 1975 social security case, overturned a differential that the solicitor general described as "closely analogous." Yet despite a unanimous decision in *Wiesenfeld* and a near unanimous (eight-to-one) judgment in *Frontiero,* the Court did not deem it appropriate to affirm summarily. And the solicitor general argues, with some justification, that each precedent in the 1970s was written for one case and one day alone.

With the E.R.A. on the books, we may expect Congress and state legislatures to undertake in earnest, systematically and pervasively, the law revision so long deferred. History should teach that the entire job is not likely to be done until the E.R.A. supplies the signal. In the event of legislative default, the courts will be guided by a constitutional text clearly and cleanly in point.

Without the E.R.A., the judiciary will continue to be plagued with a succession of cases challenging laws and official practices that belong on history's scrap heap. The Supreme Court will confront again and again the need for principled decisions to guide

the lower courts and the difficulty of anchoring those decisions to the text of eighteenth and nineteenth century draftsmen.

The American Bar Association endorsed the equal rights amendment in August of 1974. The resolution aroused scant opposition. No one spoke against it in the House of Delegates; only a dozen or so "nay" votes were audible. The resolution included a commitment to work for ratification by the number of states required to write the amendment into the Constitution.

That commitment is hardly fulfilled. It is my hope that the Association, as a reasoned voice for the profession, will move swiftly this year to carry out its 1974 undertaking and its pledge to play an active role in educating the public. For the American Bar Association, perhaps more than any other professional organization, has the capacity and resources to dispel misunderstanding on this issue and to explain why the E.R.A. is the way for a society that believes in the essential human dignity and interdependence of each man and each woman.

WOMEN IN THE POLITICAL PROCESS

SUSAN GLUCK MEZEY

Susan Gluck Mezey was educated at Brooklyn College and Syracuse University. She has taught in departments of political science and government in eight institutions, including Thammasat University in Bangkok, the University of Hawaii, Wesleyan University in Connecticut, and currently teaches at De Paul University in Chicago. Her special research interests include minority group politics and American politics; she has researched women's political status since 1974.

Beginning with the history of women's political activity in this country, Mezey here recounts why women have only recently become aware of a potential for political power and why it is so difficult to overcome the barriers to a realization of that potential. She describes the issues and data of women's present status, the facts and myths that impinge on women's political actions both as voters and as officeholders.

Issues concerning the status of women in society cannot be treated as the dilemmas only of individual women, but must also be seen as the issues and concerns of a group in society that is organizing around political goals and seeking to redress grievances through the political process. Many women are no longer content to accept inferiority in a society that preaches equality and justice for all, and they have discovered a need to seek political solutions and to develop strategies that will effect changes within the political system. They are attempting to make the woman's predicament a focus of concern for the political system and to allow their own kind to represent them within its institutions of power. The women's movement, which grew out of the realization that discrimination on the basis of sex must be fought on a group level, is primarily concerned with the development of political power and with the extension of this power into influence in public policy making.

Historical Perspective

The Matter of Partisanship

Women have only recently become aware of their potential for political power. The suffrage movement had not prepared them to assume the burden of political activity. In fact, women were discouraged from seeking political office, from engaging in partisan political activity, and even from becoming part of the informed voting public. Much of this discouragement proceeded from a view of women as second-class citizens with second-class minds and the firm belief that women must remain within their sphere of household activities; however, the responsibility must also rest with those in the leadership of the suffrage struggle who did not anticipate or desire political activity beyond enfranchisement.

Throughout many of the events surrounding the struggle to win the vote, leaders of the women's suffrage movement were at odds with each other over what strategy should be followed to achieve victory and, more important, over what women should do with the vote once suffrage was achieved.[1] Many of the leaders saw the victory of enfranchisement as the ultimate goal of women in the United States. Others, such as Susan B. Anthony, saw the vote simply as a tool necessary to achieve a better status for women in the country and equality with men in all areas of endeavor. There was, nevertheless, agreement over the importance of achieving the vote as a first step, or in the case of some, as a final step, in the fight for equality. However, the effects of the schism became apparent in the events that followed enfranchisement.

Among those women who saw themselves participating in politics at all (and the numbers were very low in the early twenties), many saw themselves as providing a moral force for the political scene. Women were to be the reformers, the "good government" people who did not want to achieve power for themselves, but instead wanted to ensure that the political game was played in a moral and upright manner.

The divergent attitudes of the newly enfranchised suffragettes on the issue of partisanship could have been predicted from the pre-1920 struggle between the National American Women Suffrage Association (NAWSA) and the Congressional Union for Woman Suffrage (CU), later known as the Woman's Party.

The guiding principles of the NAWSA included opposition to partisan politics, a distrust of all politicians, and a disdain for those who soiled themselves by playing the political game of power and influence. Its idea was to urge those in power to give women the vote through moral persuasion and righteousness. The CU, to the contrary, felt it was necessary to use the power of numbers in the individual states where women were permitted to vote to *force* politicians to vote for national women's suffrage. Alice Paul, leader of the CU, urged women to combine their strength into a voting bloc and make the parties compete for the women's vote by rewarding their friends and punishing their enemies in both parties. The CU was thereby accused of "partisanship" by the NAWSA, obviously a transgression of vast importance in the suffrage struggle. However, in reality the CU was less concerned with other issues of the day as long as prosuffrage politicians of either party were rewarded and antisuffrage members of either party were punished. In essence the vital difference between the tactics of the two groups was that the conservative NAWSA was *asking* for enfranchisement whereas the CU was *demanding* it.

It is difficult to determine which strategy was more effective since the conservative policy had been in force since the late 1800s, and one can say that the eventual victory in 1919 was perhaps an inevitable result of the long struggle. The CU did not begin to exert its influence until about 1915–1916, and by then suffrage was almost a foregone conclusion. This history sets the stage for the character of the women's movement after 1920.

Participation After Enfranchisement

"We just scattered" was the judgment of one of the veterans of the battle for suffrage when asked to explain why women didn't use their proven organizational ability and energy to take part in partisan politics after the ratification of the Nineteenth Amendment.[2] The ladies were urged by such women as Mrs. Barclay Hazard, an original opponent of suffrage, to place themselves "in an absolutely independent position, freed from all party affiliations, untrammeled by political obligations."[3] Women hastened to take this advice and formed clubs such as the League of Women Voters as well as women's auxiliaries of the political parties, which kept them unsullied and innocent, untouched by partisan conflict and corruption; it also kept them away from avenues of potential power and influence.

The ineffectual impact of women on the political scene was deprecated by H. L. Mencken in his *In Defense of Women,* published two years after the franchise was won. He stated: "Years ago I predicted that these suffragettes, tired out by victory, would turn out to be idiots. They are now hard at work proving it. Half of them devote themselves to advocating reforms, chiefly of a sexual nature, so utterly preposterous that even male politicians and newspaper editors laugh at them; the other half succumb absurdly to the blandishments of the old-time male politicians, and so enroll themselves in the great political parties. . . . Thereafter she is nothing but an obscure cog in an ancient and creaking machine."[4]

A somewhat kinder, yet equally disparaging view was presented by William O'Neill in 1969 in his book *Everyone was Brave.*

> . . . when the vote was gained, it made little difference to the feminine condition. A few women were elected to office, political campaigning became more refined, and the sex lives of candidates were more vigorously policed. The ballot did not materially help women to advance their most urgent causes; even worse, it did not help women to better themselves or improve their status. The struggle for women's rights ended during the 1920's, leaving men in clear possession of the commanding places in American life.[5]

Contemporary Issues

Political Participation

"A firmly entrenched truth in the literature on political socialization and voting behavior is the claim that substantial and significant differences exist between men and women in terms of their attitudes and behaviors toward politics." [6] The most frequently cited differences between male and female political behavior are that women vote less than men do, that women are not as interested in politics as men are, that women are more affected than men by subjective factors such as good looks or pleasing personalities, that women are more candidate-oriented than issue-oriented, and finally, that women are less equipped to understand the real issues in society and are less mature in their political interest, political efficacy (the feeling that one can do something to influence a political decision), political knowledge, and political participation. [7]

It is accurate that women have generally voted less than men; surveys have also indicated that women are less interested in and less informed than men about politics. Women were also found to be less confident of their ability to influence the political system. [8] Although these results were based on survey data, they were taken from interviews conducted in the 1950s and 1960s — well before the rise of the women's rights movement. Since then, data from the Survey Research Center at the University of Michigan show that women have been closing the gap in many political activities: from voting in presidential elections to wearing political buttons or stickers. Differences remain primarily in the areas of influencing others to vote and interest in politics; here men still lead women. [9]

One of the problems associated with examining sex differences in political behavior is the tendency to lump all women together and to ignore individual differences within the female sex. Analysis of female voting behavior indicates that age, education, employment, race, and region all affect the rate at which women vote. Generally speaking, younger, better-educated, white, employed, non-Southern, nonrural women are likelier to vote than their counterparts. The future of female political participation is hopeful since "recent research results indicate that sex differences in voting turnout have decreased due to education, increased employment of women outside the home, and changing cultural and social patterns." [10]

Differences that have been found within the sex rather than between sexes suggest that female voting behavior is multidimensional; factors other than sex per se have an impact on women's tendencies to vote and influence political decisions. A study of mothers with young children showed that the presence of preschool-aged children and infants greatly affected the efficacy level of women who would have had high political efficacy. [11] Occupation, education, and social class also affect political efficacy. [12] Recent evidence indicates that sex-role ideology, or the way a person thinks the sexes should behave, is a better predictor of political behavior than gender or sex. [13]

The claim that women are more influenced by good looks and charming personalities is often heard around election time. Presumably, a candidate who looks attractive will readily gather votes from women. A glance at the voting records of women in the 1960 and 1964 elections reveals that a greater percentage of women voted for Nixon than for Kennedy, and more women opted for Johnson over Goldwater. Although personal attractiveness is always a subjective judgment, these election results should do a great deal to combat the myth of women succumbing to a handsome face.[14]

Sex differences in issue preferences, although generally slight, have been found in issues pertaining to force and violence and societal problems such as drug usage, gun control, and racial integration.[15] Charges of women's inability to deal with "real" political issues often stem from such differences between the sexes: Women are considered politically naive because they don't conform to the male model of political reality.

Two nationally based surveys conducted in the early 1970s do indeed show that women are less favorably disposed toward war and violent intervention, more receptive to gun control than men are, and less inclined to favor capital punishment. Women were less likely to favor increased defense spending and much less likely to agree on the imposition of the death penalty. A great majority of women stated that they believed in a system of strict gun control whereas men were much more divided on the subject. More women than men felt that regular users of soft drugs such as marijuana should be given medical and psychological treatment rather than stiff prison terms. Women similarly disagreed with the imposition of severe prison sentences for users of hard drugs like heroin, whereas men were more likely to opt for imprisonment over rehabilitation. Women were also more compassionate toward the plight of blacks in America and were more inclined to say that racial tension is a serious problem.

Evidence that women have different issue orientations from men is often used to show that women lack political "savvy"; the woman is portrayed as an immature citizen. It is time that women's political views were accepted as simply different from men's without the negative judgments that usually follow. One could, for example, argue that women have achieved a higher level of maturity because they have eschewed the aggressive, destructive solutions of war that men tend to favor. Perhaps, one could also argue that women are to be commended for their far-seeing acceptance of the inevitability of change in society with regard to racial integration and drug use.

The evidence on voting behavior and political participation indicates that women's voting patterns are changing as they become more educated and continue to seek employment outside the home. The broadening effects of education and employment suggest that extrinsic factors have been largely responsible for women's lower feelings of efficacy and political performance. The structural conditions that give rise to these factors require alteration if women are to compete as equals in the political world. There is also evidence suggesting that sex-role socialization (learning sex-appropriate behavior) may also be responsible for differential political participation between men and women. Whether the differential may be traced to external situational factors that keep women from expressing themselves politically or to sex-role conditioning that teaches women not to become complete and competent political participants, it seems clear that changes in women's lifestyles are necessary prerequisites to changes in women's political performances.[16]

Political Activism

Although the record shows that women have always taken part in political campaigns, it is only recently that they are beginning to achieve positions of importance as campaign workers and managers. Much of the literature relating to women as campaign workers and political activists points to women's status and role in society as the major problem for politically inclined women; party women do not get rewarded for activism the same way that men do. Since a man's political activity is often seen as an extension of his occupational or breadwinner role, he is often praised for enhancing his status and position and behaving with civic virtue. A woman's party activity is often seen as conflicting with her proper role as caretaker of the home, and she is more often pilloried than praised for engaging in partisan electoral activity.[17] The fact that women themselves have internalized this attitude was made apparent in a study of female delegates to the 1972 Democratic and Republican National Conventions. These women portrayed themselves in traditional female roles and were anxious to avoid either the appearance or the reality of striving, ambition, or personal achievement.[18] Furthermore, women in the electorate echo this view; over half the respondents in the 1972 Virginia Slims Poll agreed that "to be really active in politics, women have to neglect their husbands and children." Almost half also agreed "it is almost impossible to be a good wife and mother and hold public office too."[19]

An earlier study of delegates to national nominating conventions showed that female participants were usually subordinate to male participants in terms of social backgrounds and political careers. The men were better educated, in better occupational categories, and in higher economic strata.[20] Their political experiences were quite distinctive: Male delegates were more likely to hold elective or appointive office, they had more experience managing campaigns and writing campaign speeches, and they had sought and won office more frequently than the female delegates. Even though women were serving as party delegates and in positions of nominal equality with their male counterparts, they actually occupied secondary roles largely because of social role differentiation. The study concludes that "any change in the direction of feminine equality among political elites will occur only through a more profound social revolution which alters basic sex roles in that direction. Only when women come to the point of sharing equally in other occupations and roles prized and dominated by males may we expect to see this equity."[21]

Even when women achieve positions of importance in the party hierarchy, they never become quite as important as their male colleagues. A study of California party leaders showed that women spent as much, if not more, time on party activity than men in the organization, but they had not gathered the rewards of public office or powerful party positions.[22] The study also revealed that women party leaders held fewer of the prestigious national or state offices than men and were more likely to be in local offices such as school boards or local councils. The authors pointed out that these local offices are usually less well paid and always less powerful than the statewide offices.

These studies of political activists indicate that women often work as hard as men in organizational activities in the political process but continue to occupy secondary roles within the party bureaucracy. Clearly one of the reasons women remain severely under-represented in political positions of power is that they are failing to break out of the role of second-class citizens in society in general and politics in particular. Many women politicians, however, having broken down the barriers of their own negative self-image and societal disapproval, point to the party bureaucracy and leadership as the real source of discrimination against women. Frieda Gehlen's analysis of women in Congress, and Jeane Kirkpatrick's study of women in state legislatures indicate that the party leadership is the major roadblock for aspiring women. In her book on American women in public life, Peggy Lamson states: "If blame is to be attached to any group of men it must not be to those who pull the voting machine lever inside the polling booth but to those who pull the strings inside the political parties." [23] In sum, the consensus from women in a position to know is that political women are often deterred from active participation and achievement of positions of power because there are men in party hierarchies who act as gatekeepers. This view is further reinforced by two studies which conclude that sex itself is not a very significant factor at the voting booth. The effects of sex are largely felt before women get their names on the ballot.

In a study of women in local elections, the authors concluded: "Our data suggest that the main problems are associated with becoming candidates rather than gaining election after female candidates are on the ballot." [24] Women won almost half the races in which they were entered. "These findings clearly demonstrate that female candidates for council office are not victimized by insurmountable prejudice at the polls." [25] The same conclusions were drawn by the authors of a study on male and female candidates in congressional elections.[26] When controlling for the effects of party and incumbency in several elections from 1972 to 1974, the authors noted that sex played only a minimal role, if any, in electoral outcomes. The main problems for women lie in the recruitment and nomination processes. Women representatives are so few in number because they are not nominated to fill these positions. Once nominated, sex is not a major detriment to their electoral success.

These studies of the effects of sex on electoral outcomes provide further enlightenment on the problems that women in politics encounter. Although voters may vote for women without many qualms, very often they do not get the opportunity to do so. Much of the blame for this situation must be attached to party leaders who are reluctant to promote women's candidacies; blame must also be attached to women themselves who do not seek out electoral contests in which they can compete. Underlying the prejudices of the party hierarchies and the hesitancies of female politicos is a pervasive pattern of sexism in society, which has succeeded in keeping women in subordinate positions in society and has not encouraged them to transcend the domestic role to which society has relegated them.

Political Office-Holding

Learning how the pattern of sexism operates against female politicians can best be accomplished by examining the women in political office and noting the difficulties and problems they face. The most obvious fact about women in political office is that so few exist. Women constitute about 10 percent of elected positions on municipal councils, less than 10 percent in state houses and state senates, and less than 5 percent in the United States Congress. Scholars have noted that "women tend to be better represented in offices which carry less prestige and power." [27]

Although the presence of women in public office is not as unusual as it once was, women still lag far behind men in holding positions of political power. Those who have examined this disparity have pointed to social and cultural constraints that make it difficult for women to commit themselves to public life; these constraints are said to stem from their role as primary caretakers of the home and children.[28] A result of this role is that women enter public life at more advanced ages than their male colleagues. This age difference has been found at all levels of political office — from local public officials to members of the United States Congress. Whether the women serve in local political institutions, the state legislature, or the United States House of Representatives, there is typically more delay for women than for men in making the decision to become officeholders; such delay is usually caused by women's responsibilities as wives and mothers.[29] It is apparent that the vast majority of women do not begin political careers until their childrearing years are over.

A study of women and men in the state of Hawaii found that the median age of initial entry into politics of women officeholders was more than five years greater than the median age of entry for male officeholders.[30] Similarly, the median age of the women's children was five years greater than that of the men. Men also had more children than women at the time they were initially elected to office. This study suggests that women are more affected by their home responsibilities than men are since their status and the status of their families have to be more inclined toward freeing the woman for her outside activity. Such freedom is usually found among older women with older children. Clearly, if women are going to achieve some greater measure of political equality, they must be relieved of their primary responsibility for child care. The negative effects of women's late entry into politics are seen in the problems of sustaining a political career, the difficulty of establishing a power base and lack of seniority within representative institutions.[31]

Another basic problem that women face — even after the childrearing age is over — is the need for support from their spouses for their involvement in an outside profession or occupation. Although more and more women in the United States are now working at full-time jobs, the percentage of housewives among political office-holding women is still very high. It is important to look at the homefront to determine whether women face greater problems at home once they make the decision to enter public life. It is difficult to anticipate the answer to this question since evidence exists to support both sides. The stereotyped image of the career woman suggests that she neglects the home and hearth and all its inhabitants and therefore engenders resentment and hostility from within. At least two studies of political women, however, suggest the opposite — that political women carve out professional careers with the consent and cooperation of their mates and families.

A group of state legislators were quite emphatic about their need for supportive husbands: "All the married legislators agree that a cooperative husband is the first requirement for successfully juggling family and career." [32] Another study of women state legislators specifically found that women legislators received more support and encouragement from their husbands than male legislators received from their wives. The study concluded that women are probably less likely to run for legislative office at all unless their spouses are positive and supportive.[33]

The evidence therefore indicates that marriage places a greater restraint on women politicians than on men politicians; women have a greater need for support. Although the husbands of the state legislators in both studies appear to be tolerant and understanding, if women politicians must be assured of their spouse's support before entering politics, women are likely to feel more inhibited about pursuing political careers. Women forced to choose between politics and their families would be hard pressed in most cases to commit themselves to political careers, thus greatly limiting the pool of available female political actors.

Marriage, children, and obligations as homemakers contribute to erecting barriers to women contemplating political lives. Solutions to the problems faced by aspiring female politicians must be enacted on a societal level if women are to be able to participate equally with men. Some solutions that suggest themselves are greater availability of child-care facilities, better preparation of women for careers that lead to politics, such as business or law, and a more equitable division of labor within the household. These are long-term solutions that must be implemented if the political process is to be equally accessible to men and women.

Conclusion

This discussion of women in the political process has ranged over the entire area of political participation — from voting and influencing the government to public office-holding. Throughout it has been apparent that women have not been sufficiently represented as decision makers in the political system; there has also been some cause for optimism since changes in female participation rates have been occurring, and increasing numbers of women have been making their voices felt — within and without political institutions.

Factors that bear primary responsibility for the inferior role of women in the political process have been traced to the division of labor within society, which relegates women to subordinate roles in nonpolitical areas as well as within the political world. Women's social roles have been translated into political roles; equality must be won in the social realm before equality can be won in the political realm. The victory of enfranchisement must finally be completed with the victory of equality; only then will the political process fully reflect and engender an equal role for women in society.

Notes

1. See Virginia Sapiro, "You Can Lead a Lady to Vote, But What Will She Do with It? The Problem of a Woman's Bloc Vote," in _New Research on Women and Sex Roles,_ ed. Dorothy McGuigan (Michigan: Center for Continuing Education of Women, 1974); Martin Gruberg, _Women in American Politics_ (Oshkosh, Wis.: Academia Press, 1968); Marion K. Sanders, _The Lady and the Vote_ (Boston: Houghton Mifflin Co., 1956); and Aileen S. Kraditor, _The Ideas of the Woman Suffrage Movement 1890–1920_ (New York: Doubleday, 1971) for further information on woman's suffrage and the events immediately following the victory of enfranchisement.
2. Sanders, _The Lady,_ p. 141.
3. Sanders, _The Lady,_ p. 143.
4. Cited in Mary Costello, "Women Voters," in _Editorial Research Reports on the Women's Movement_ (Washington, D.C.: The Congressional Quarterly, 1973), pp. 119–120.
5. Costello, "Women Voters," p. 120.
6. Sandra Sue Volgy and Thomas Volgy, "Women and Politics: Political Correlates of Sex-Role Acceptance," _Social Science Quarterly,_ 55 (March 1975), 967. See also Kent Tedin, David Brady, and Arnold Vedlitz, "Sex Differences in Political Attitudes and Behavior: The Case for Situational Factors," _Journal of Politics,_ 39 (May 1977), 448–456.
7. See Angus Campbell, et al., _The American Voter_ (New York: John Wiley, 1960); Robert E. Lane, _Political Life_ (Glencoe, Ill.: The Free

Press, 1959); Gabriel Almond and Sidney Verba, *The Civic Culture* (Boston: Little, Brown, 1965); and Dean Jaros, *Socialization to Politics* (New York: Praeger Publishers, 1974) for discussion of these differences between the sexes. See also Jane S. Jaquette, "Introduction: Women in American Politics," in *Women in Politics,* ed. Jane S. Jaquette (New York: John Wiley, 1974); and Marjorie Lansing, "The American Woman Voter and Activist," in *Women in Politics,* ed. Jane S. Jaquette (New York: John Wiley, 1974) for their evaluation and discussion of this literature.

8. Tedin et al., "Sex Differences." Note: "the literature on both socialization and public opinion/political participation indicates that men are often more politically expressive on these variables than are women." See Tedin et al., "Sex Differences," p. 453. This study also lends support to this finding.

9. See Susan Hansen, Linda Franz, and Margaret Netemeyer-Mays, "Women's Political Participation and Policy Preferences," *Social Science Quarterly,* 56 (March 1976), 576–590; and John Soule and Wilma McGrath, "A Comparative Study of Male-Female Political Attitudes at Citizen and Elite Levels," in *Portrait of Marginality,* ed. Marianne Githens and Jewel Prestage (New York: David McKay, 1977), pp. 178–195.

10. Hansen, et al., "Women's Political Participation," p. 578.

11. Naomi Lynn and Cornelia Butler Flora, "Motherhood and Political Participation: A Changing Sense of Self," *Journal of Military and Political Sociology,* I (March 1973), 91–103.

12. Cornelia Butler Flora, "Working-Class Women's Political Participation," in *Portrait of Marginality,* ed. Marianne Githens and Jewel Prestage (New York: David McKay, 1977), pp. 75–95.

13. See Volgy and Volgy, "Women and Politics"; and Marjorie Randon Hershey, "The Politics of Androgyny?" *American Politics Quarterly,* 5 (July 1977), 261–287.

14. Lansing, "The American Woman," p. 15, presents figures for presidential voting from 1956 to 1972. The figures show that women essentially voted the way that men voted and not overwhelmingly for the "more attractive" candidate.

15. See *The 1970 and 1972 Virginia Slims American Women's Public Opinion Poll* (studies conducted by Louis Harris).

16. Tedin et al. "Sex Differences"; and Anthony Orum, Roberta Cohen, Sherri Grasmuck, and Amy Orum, "Sex Socialization and Politics," *American Sociological Review,* 39 (April 1974), 197–209 discuss the effects of situational factors.

17. See Naomi Lynn, "Women in American Politics: An Overview," in *Women: A Feminist Perspective,* ed. Jo Freeman (Palo Alto, Calif.: Mayfield Company, 1975), pp. 364–385; and Jeane Kirkpatrick, *The New Presidential Elite* (New York: Russell Sage Foundation, 1976).

18. Naomi Lynn and Cornelia Butler Flora, "Societal Punishment and Aspects of Female Political Participation: 1972 National Convention Delegates," in *Portrait of Marginality,* ed. Marianne Githens and Jewel Prestage, pp. 139–149.

19. *Virginia Slims Poll,* p. 30.

20. M. Kent Jenning and Norman Thomas, "Men and Women in Party Elites: Social Roles and Political Resources," *Midwest Journal of Political Science,* 12 (November 1968), 469–492.

21. Ibid., p. 492.

22. Edmund Costantini and Kenneth Craik, "Women as Politicians: The Social Background, Personality and Political Careers of Female Party Leaders," *Journal of Social Issues,* 28 (1972), 217–236.

23. In her discussion of women's role in the party hierarchy, Kirkpatrick quotes Peggy Lamson to support her view. See Kirkpatrick, *The New Presidential Elite,* pp. 459–462.

24. Albert Karnig and B. Oliver Walter, "Elections of Women to City Councils," *Social Science Quarterly,* 56 (March 1976), 608.

25. Ibid.

26. R. Darcy and Sarah Slavin Schramm, "When Women Run Against Men," *The Public Opinion Quarterly,* 41 (Spring 1977), 1–12.

27. Karnig and Walter, "Elections," p. 608. See

also Wilma Rule Krauss, "Political Implications of Gender Roles," *American Political Science Review,* 68 (December 1974), 1711. Irene Diamond notes that women are more apt to be in political positions where competition is low and less apt to be in public offices where competition is high. See Irene Diamond, *Sex Roles in the State House* (New Haven: Yale University Press, 1977).

28. See Jeane Kirkpatrick, *Political Woman* (New York: Basic Books, 1974); Costantini and Craik, "Women as Politicians"; Jennings and Thomas, "Men and Women"; Marcia Manning Lee, "Why So Few Women Hold Public Office: Democracy and Sexual Roles," *Political Science Quarterly,* 91 (Summer 1976), 297–314; and Lynn and Flora, "Societal Punishment and Aspects of Female Political Participation."

29. Kirkpatrick, *Political Woman*; Lee, "Why So Few"; Emmy Werner, "Women in Congress: 1918–1964," *Western Political Quarterly,* 19 (March 1966), 16–30; and Lynn and Flora, "Societal Punishment and Aspects of Female Political Participation."

30. Susan Gluck Mezey, "Does Sex Make a Difference? A Case Study of Women in Politics," *Western Political Quarterly* (March 1979). Some of the following discussion is taken from that article.

31. See Werner, "Women in Congress," Paula Dubeck, "Women and Access to Political Office: A Comparison of Female and Male State Legislators," *Sociological Quarterly,* 17 (Winter 1976), 42–52; Frieda Gehlen, "Women Members of Congress: A Distinctive Role," in *Portrait of Marginality,* ed. Marianne Githens and Jewel Prestage, pp. 304–319.

32. Kirkpatrick, *Political Woman,* p. 231.

33. Emily Stoper, "Wife and Politician: Role Strain Among Women in Public Office," in *Portrait of Marginality,* ed. Marianne Githens and Jewel Prestage, pp. 320–337.

8

Distortions in Perspective and Understanding: Asymmetry in Abstraction

Mind Control as an Instrument of Patriarchy

Despite the incredible injustice done to women, few people (women or men) take the whole business seriously or consider it cause for much guilt or concern. In fact, many find the fuss a little ridiculous if not meaningless. People point out that most women as well as men are in the nonfeminist or antifeminist camp. Don't they too laugh at the jokes? Don't they back legislators and legislation against so-called women's rights? And even if all this nonsense has anything to it, women are their own worst enemies, now aren't they?

It is true that women have acted side by side with men in the control of women by patriarchy. If one but thinks a minute of the tremendous feat involved in the subjugation of one half of the world's population by the other half, one sees that it would have to be so. Women are and always have been more than half the human population, and there could have been great power in that numerical superiority had it been tapped. Women can be creative, resourceful, and courageous and could have stood in their own behalf. Yet for centuries women have typically supported the patriarchal status quo, have "backed their men," and have demanded that their daughters and granddaughters do so as well, binding their feet and their minds and instructing them in the duties of good women. How are we to account for that? Could there be something to the charge that women are their own worst enemies or that there is simply nothing to bother about? Or does the answer lie elsewhere?

Students of politics and government often talk of the impossibility of world domination by a monolithic power on the grounds of size and space. It would be unlikely, they argue, that any power could draw a communication

or policing network so encompassing, an executive agency so vast that it could maintain control. And yet, although patriarchal societies are not themselves a monolith, patriarchy per se is, and for centuries it has maintained a grip of control over women and over the substructures that guide the political, economic, and cultural arrangements governing our lives. How does it do this?

It is not a new or surprising idea that the most potent form of control is one that reigns not over the body but over the mind. Science fiction and cold war drama are full of concern for brainwashing, conditioning, and mind control. To place into the belief system of an individual the idea that the restraints governing her or him are inevitable, right, proper, and desirable is to place a perpetual sentry at the door to a free existence. There is no need for external guards. The job is done and the control is intact so long as the belief remains.

Some time ago in a conference of the Society for Women in Philosophy, as the members were discussing the nature of domination and control, one woman suggested that the most stable and effective form of slavery was one in which the oppressed group were socialized to love their slavery. A second woman countered that an even more perfect form of slavery was one in which the slaves were *unaware* of their condition, unaware that they were controlled, believing that they freely chose their life and situation. The control of women by patriarchy is effected in just such a way, by mastery of beliefs and attitudes through the management of all the institutions and agencies of thought formation and dissemination.

For the most part, without counterbalancing ideas and perspectives, most women (and men) are unaware that their behavior, opportunities, and life possibilities are controlled by masculism and masculists, and that women did not freely come to choose "femininity" and its trappings.[1]

Women and men really live and move in two different conceptual universes. We see the world, values, and ourselves differently because in the most pointed ways patriarchy has arranged for the agencies of thought (for example, education, art, and the media) to foster and maintain two separate and asymmetrical conceptual environments in which to learn, grow, and act; two separate and asymmetrical images of reality to absorb. Not only are women and men trained to divergent perspectives on the world, we come to have very dissimilar postures to life and to the inner reality. We come to answer differently the questions, Who am I? What am I? What shall I be?

If patriarchy is to prevail, it must instill and ensure its consciousness in the minds of its subjects, particularly women, since the rebellion of women would mean its demise. Let us sharpen our awareness of the many ways by which patriarchal culture exerts control over the direction of our understanding. Let us look at some of the more powerful agencies of idea formation, their modes and their products.

Education

One learns patriarchal consciousness in many ways, from formal teaching environments and from informal or subliminal messages. Schools, from the primary grades through college do not teach only the three Rs and the officially recognized "knowledge" in books and curricula. Self-consciously or not, they also teach values, attitudes, expectations, and world views. In functioning both as trainer for participation in the wider society and as a reflection of that society, the schools transmit to their students the rather traditional views on sexual identity, and very early they convey, create, and reinforce in females and males the segregated conceptual systems of the sexes.

The Environment

Consider the administrative hierarchy of the typical primary school and high school. Quite like the arrangement of women and men in most institutions (male doctor to female assistants, male manager to clerks or secretaries, male pilot to his hostesses, male always in charge), the school presents to the students the traditional picture of masculine power. On the front lines, in the classrooms and in the outer offices behind typewriters, one finds women — accessible, concrete, "live" personnel. In the inner office, apart from the common folk, distant and powerful, resides the principal, in 95 percent of the cases in the United States, a male. Further removed and even more powerful are the school boards and the superintendents, of whom approximately 97 percent are male.

Female teachers often function with regard to the principal in the same way that female parents at home function with regard to male parents. They present and maintain policy set by the authority figure, but when children are very difficult, they are sent to that ultimate power for more "meaningful" discipline. When on occasion the principal visits the classroom, students are aware that something special is happening. The effect on both female and male children is potent and enduring. The arrangement says something very different to boys and girls about what they may become, what they can expect out

---

[1] For a thorough survey of the factors involved in the socialization process, see Lenore J. Weitzman, "Sex-Role Socialization," in *Women: A Feminist Perspective,* 2nd ed., ed. Jo Freeman (Palo Alto, Calif.: Mayfield Publishing Co., 1979).

of people in life, what they can do and accomplish. The consciousness of the two sexes forms rather differently amid such cues and statements.

The cues gain credence and color as they are played out in the same environment among the children themselves. Children are separated and reminded that they are different: *Boys on this side of the room, girls over there.* Their sense of competition is deepened: *Let's have a contest, boys against the girls.* Their place on the power-strength continuum is fixed: *I want three boys to carry the projector for me.* Little girls are taught to "behave like ladies": *Keep your legs down. Don't be rowdy.* Boys are told to be nice young *men,* or to help little Suzy. In my daughter's kindergarten room, toys were arranged against two walls — dolls, cradle, ironing board, brooms, and cupboards on one side; trucks, blocks, and a horse on the other. Circumstances do not change in high school. Boys gravitate to science and technology, girls to literature. Boys begin to excel and girls to channel their interest away from study and toward pleasing the boys. Shop classes for boys and home economics for girls reinforce the expected directions. In my high school, girls were required to take shop, but we spent the semester making jewelry while the boys made wooden cabinets.

Segregated gym classes with separate curricula train differently not only the body but the mind. Boys' team sports, competitive, aggressive and demanding, teach the participants teamwork, the value of practice and readiness, the effectiveness of perseverance and determination, the willingness to face risk for gain. Girls interested in sports, even hockey or track, are often mocked. The super femmes lead cheers. They win their kudos standing on the sidelines in abbreviated frocks, tossing their legs about, and shouting, "Come on, men!"

Consider for a moment the effects of those two divergent vantage points, the self-perceptions, the abilities, and the lessons gleaned from them. Think about those two so different sets of perceptions — *I, player* and *I, cheerleader; I, center* and *I, periphery* — and how they will function twenty years later.

The Curriculum

The school system, through its structures and patterns of education, says different things to female and male students because it evolves out of a sexist society. So do the people within them. Teachers, principals, authors, and scientists who grow and work in a sexist environment develop sexist world views, beliefs, and perspectives. What they say and teach is therefore also sexist. Books, films, magazines, pamphlets, and papers are usually sexist and masculist, are taught by teachers who rarely notice or question that perspective, and are therefore presented as truth. Sexist theories presented as truth in books have the weight of all history behind them. Even more than propositions about women and men that are consciously and pointedly spoken, the unspoken intimation or subliminal statement has power because it is not even available for comment or critique.

From nursery school through college, then, the learning experience, both formal and supportive, is different for females and males. Traditional behaviors for each sex are taught, rewarded, and required, usually unconsciously. Different images of what women and men are and should be are communicated by the institutions and validated by the history of "truth" as it is maintained in the books.

Females are presented with the same vision of themselves that we meet in the culture at large. From books, teachers, counselors, extracurricular activities, and aptitude tests, we learn to be passive, quiet, nurturing, surreptitiously bossy, incompetent ladies, wives, and mothers, and all the rest of the baggage we call the content of sexism. Given the power of the school experience, and given its early, continuous, and pervasive entry into our lives, it is hardly surprising that we should imbibe its formulations, believe them and internalize them.

Education is, therefore, one of the major contributors to the fixing of a "feminine" (that is, masculist) consciousness in women, the consciousness that allows patriarchy to prevail in our own private worlds because it appears "right." If the schools, the teachers, and the books say it is right, who are we to say it is wrong?

Change

Since the impetus of the women's movement and Title IX, sensitivity is increasing at the college level, in high schools, even in Parent–Teachers Associations and school boards. For teachers now in training, courses on sexism in education are frequently available. Book publishers, newly sensitized to the issue by groups such as the National Organization for Women (NOW) and the Women's Equity Action League (WEAL) are setting new guidelines for language and expression. Schools are integrating the gym classes and the playing teams. Universities and professional schools are under pressure to add women to their faculty and staff, not only for their own benefit, but as role models for the next generation of contributors.

In any society the educational process, formal or otherwise, is a primary effector of enculturation, a major arm of social control and stability. We must expect it, on the one hand, to reflect the beliefs and structures of the wider culture and thus to be basically conservative. On the other hand, in our times education presents itself as well in another

image — as the purveyor of knowledge and truth, as a foil to stasis and hardening of the intellectual arteries, as the proponent of constructive growth and change. That is an impressive image, believed by many, that carries with it an impressive responsibility: the duty to ensure that, however difficult the task, new insights and understanding will be absorbed and integrated into the existing body of knowledge and passed on to the next generation. In that duty lies the hopeful optimism of Women's Studies and contemporary feminists. It is the reason for treating the educational system as a primary target for vigilance and activity.

The Media

A medium, in the sense referred to here, is a mode or agency of public thought communication. In our culture the important media include newspapers, radio and television, magazines, advertising, books, and films. They are the primary means of projecting and carrying ideas among the various segments of the population. Media not only carry information, they are also very powerful in framing attitudes and forming opinions. In a word, media teach, and they teach not only with what they say, but with how they say it.

Television, Magazines, News Reporting

One of the most pervasive elements of media in our lives, especially for children, is television. More than any other modern invention, television has affected the content and nature of our thought, because it so thoroughly and so early pervades our conscious waking time, for some people as much as four or five hours a day. During those hours, we see programs and advertising replete with the traditional stereotypes and images, the age-old misogynistic attitudes. On the sitcoms and weekly dramas are the long-suffering wives, the manipulative young beauties, the wronged lovers, the mindless females pursuing husbands, lovers, or other fantasies. In cowboy land women are dance hall queens (prostitutes) or damsels in distress. In crime drama they are the victims of bizarre crimes of murder and rape, or perhaps the neglected wives of policemen or bad guys. Sometimes women manage to get on the police force, but they usually can be counted on to mess things up or become victimized in some way and to require saving by the male heroes. There are exceptions now, thanks to the movement, but they are rare. The occasional single women, even the self-sufficient ones, tend to appear in light comedy. Seldom seen are staunch women, realistically presented, wrestling with the simple human problems and issues that we are all heir to.

Advertising, more insidious even than programming because it is more covert in its statements, offers the same fare. Here are women still groaning over ring-around-the-collar (their husbands' dirt, mind you), twittering to one another over the joys of some fabric softener, and decaffeinating their husbands. Now and again we are presented with a professional woman, but she is generally wife or mother madly juggling her time with the aid of Product X so as not to neglect her family. On the other hand, there are the straight sexual ads: this perfume, hair color, soap, or toothpaste will give you the sex appeal you now lack; if you buy it, you will finally capture your elusive prince. Worse yet are the ads that use female bodies as a shill to the male buyer: semiclad ladies smiling seductively, draped across automobiles or cooing over shaving cream.

Where are the real women, the millions of working women, the divorced and widowed women, the professional women, the intelligent competent women? Where are the items truly important to us, truly meaningful: dramas about women trying to break into professions; working to stay intact; struggling to hold down jobs, care for children, and maintain peace of mind all at the same time? Where are the products truly useful to us, those that really might save work rather than create it?

Magazines and newspapers are no better. Most women's magazines are typically owned and published by men. It is they who select the articles and the advertising. It is they who decide *and tell us* what women want to see or think about. Consider the "women's pages" in most newspapers. They contain recipes, wedding and engagement announcements, fashions, and the like. Some women are interested in those things, and some are not. Some women are interested in them a little or once in a while, and some are interested in them a great deal. Some men are interested in those items. But when the editor dubs that section "Women's Pages" he is saying to the readers that this is what women are and should be interested in and, correlatively, that the rest of the paper is not for women. Readers, then, both male and female, draw the conclusion, consciously or not, that "real" women are indeed fixed on that part of the universe. Men get a distorted view of women, women a distorted view of themselves. One could hardly imagine calling the sports section the "Men's Pages." What would that make the rest of the paper?

The problem of what is "real" and what is not is rather complex in terms of social presentation. The media not only reflect cultural images but they create, teach, and reify them as well. Girls and young women, in being constantly bombarded with certain images of beauty, are being taught that those images *are* beauty, that they should and must have it. Women who see themselves portrayed only as happy housekeepers and feckless ladies are being taught that women really are such things and are anomalous in any other guise. The woman who sees those images and does not fit them rarely says to herself, "Those images aren't real." Because she comes to those images with the working assumption that the media offer true representations of reality, she believes the images. For her, the images are real; it is she who is not. She must either accept herself as anomaly (with all the attendant conflict) or change to conform. Until alternative visions are given realistic treatment by the mass media, until they are given social reification and approval by that treatment, they remain subversive, alien, or abnormal. Media treatment of the alternative visions, however, has not been kind or even natural. How many newscasters have we seen chuckle as they reported this or that quaint meeting of the libbers? How many times have we seen newsworthy items about women relegated to the last five minutes of the broadcast (the always-leave-them-laughing spot)?

The language, of course, is central. The repeated, politically directed use of certain language, particularly words in juxtaposition, can either hide the real meaning of a concept or distort it radically. Consider the term *beauty pageant*. The name alone proclaims that the contestants are beautiful, that they represent beauty per se. But standards of beauty are not absolute. My nineteenth-century European grandmother, for example, worried endlessly that my size 9 frame was far too skinny ever to lure a husband; would she find the contestants of the pageant beautiful? And I wonder, after coming to terms with the artifice and plasticity of contemporary feminine make-up and mannerisms, after spending time with and learning to admire very different kinds of women, whether most women would indeed find the pageant contestants beautiful. Can the term itself be wrong? The power of language is such that

it can distort reality, forming it to its own image. That is why the language and images employed by the media have been so much a focal point of the movement.

Art and Films

In a university in which I taught, a young instructor was made to remove his painting from a student-faculty art exhibit because his subject was a nude male with full portrayal of genitals. Several nudes (female nudes are always referred to simply as "nudes") remained aloft without comment, their breasts and pubes in plain view.

An avant-garde festival of erotic film at another university advertised itself with a poster picturing the face of the devil superimposed on the nude lower torso of a woman. Complaints to the administration by female faculty and students did not bring it down.

Pop music, rock particularly, has become very misogynistic and savagely aggressive. Many all-male rock groups wear their sexuality as costume and chant diatribes against "silicone sisters" and delectable poison. Album covers have appeared depicting chained women, half-clad or sexually expressive, their chests to the floor, their heads beneath the shoe of some arrogant male, the leader of the group. The girls in the audience, "liberated" and "modern," scream for more, pay for the concerts, and buy the albums. The number of female rock groups or females in the groups is minuscule.

The point of these representative instances is that the perspective is male. Nude women are respectable because men find them "beautiful," like to look at them, and are accustomed to employing them. Nude males are not respectable because the blatant presentation of the unadorned male body removes the aura of godliness, distance, and power from their persons and reduces them to the common, as women have been reduced.[2] It is fashionable today for men to belittle women and their bodies, and modern chic decrees that women who object are just not "with it." Women who deplore pornography because of its contemptuous treatment of women are simply dismissed as prudes and poor sports.

The male hegemony of consciousness sets the rules and standards. This is art, this is not. This is presentable, this is not. The depiction of naked women, invitingly arranged, is presentable art; the same depiction of men is irresponsible (and probably perceived as antimale). Literature relating to war, manhood, and mayhem is grandeur and art; that relating to childbirth, to families, or to women's experiences is petty craft of marginal interest.

The same circumstances obtain in the movies, that great shaper of American attitudes. In her study of the treatment of women in the movies, Molly Haskell explains that as the film industry has grown more and more to resemble an "art," with production of a film in the hands of one great "artist" (such as Bergman or Antonioni), the films increasingly reflect that (male) artist's point of view, and women's images have plunged in importance, centrality, and worth. Crediting the early strong images of women to decentralized control of the industry and to charismatic, strong-willed women (such as Bette Davis or Joan Crawford), Haskell describes the devolution of the female image to the nonsubstantive sex symbols and ultimate rape victims that we know today.[3]

Art in the hands of men only is masculist and misogynistic, but it touts itself as the highest form of human expression and truth. Who dares to challenge Art? Which of us, particularly women, can successfully pit ourselves against the soothsayers of the artistic elite? In their power wrought of the insecurities of the rest of us, they decree, "This is transcending truth; this is the esthetic perspective," and like the people in Hans Christian Andersen's story, we bow to the naked emperor in his imaginary clothes. Once again, the weight of the ages stands against women's consciousness.

Social Science

Science, both in its effects and as a concept, is an extremely important factor in the lives of twentieth-century people. Side by side with its data, procedures, and theories stands the scientific world view, a whole way of looking at truth and reality and of relating to life.

Some social analysts have suggested that in contemporary times science functions much as a god or as a substitute for God, providing a basis for truth and knowledge, an agent to be trusted and depended on for salvation, even a ground of value. Placing very high conceptual priorities on the judgments and evaluations of science and scientists is part of our cultural ethos. A large segment of the intelligentsia and the moderately educated public maintains the belief that Science *is* Truth, the only dependable, sane truth for up-to-date, rational, right-minded people. The corollary to the Science-is-Truth theme is the notion that we should all live our lives in accordance with the truths and findings of Science. Although the idea is rarely articulated in quite this way, a close appraisal of the new intellectual scene reveals the "modern" imperative: Live your life in such a way that Science would be proud of you. As medievals yearned to please God and stand in

[2] For a discussion of the psychological and political implications of dress, see Helene E. Robert, "The Exquisite Slave: The Role of Clothes in the Making of the Victorian Woman," *Signs,* 2, No. 3 (1977), 554–569.

[3] Molly Haskell, *From Reverence to Rape: The Treatment of Women in the Movies* (New York: Holt, Rinehart & Winston, 1973).

a state of grace, moderns yearn for a state of "health."

Because today's people want so badly to be judged "healthy," social science, that part of the investigative spectrum that focuses specifically on human behavior, has become very much like a faith. On at least two levels, as a technical/academic enterprise and as a "philosophy" of life for popular culture, social science — and especially psychology — serves as a kind of religion. It forms eternal verities about human nature and goals, decrees standards of perfection (health) toward which one is advised to strive, separates the "good" people (healthy, normal, "okay") from the bad (unhealthy, abnormal, "not okay"), determines social priorities both for individuals and for the state, and carries sufficient esteem in the community to socialize the population according to a certain vision of behavior.

Clearly the impact of the theories of social science on the conduct of our lives is tremendous. For women that is something of a disaster, for both the technical enterprise of the social sciences and the contemporary pop ethic which has evolved from it are rabidly sexist.

The Formal Enterprise

For a variety of reasons — the newness of the study, the complexity of its subject matter, and the absence of clearly articulated concepts and procedures — social science, at least for now and possibly forever, requires a far greater degree of interpretive latitude than its natural-science counterparts. That is a polite way of saying that social science is still quite subjective and therefore resistant to the traditional forms of verification. Because of this, theories of the social sciences generally bear the mark of the people who develop them, and they tend to be "culture bound," reflective of their time and place.

The culture and the greatest part of the personnel of the social sciences have always been predominantly male. For the most part it was men who developed the methods of research and the procedures for verification, who originated the earliest axioms and perspectives from which current developments have evolved, and who ultimately fixed the application of those perspectives, carrying theory out of the laboratory into the streets. With few exceptions, the women who gained some recognition for their work were adherents and popularizers of the existent male-identified systems rather than creators of their own models. In fact, their female support lent those antifemale systems greater weight, not only in academe but in the minds of the people who received them. Theories from the pens of men immersed in the Victorian world view brought all the familiar misogynistic stereotypes into greater respectability, enshrined as science, or truth. At last it was not only taught by experience but was also explained by science that women are petty, self-centered, and unprincipled. Sigmund Freud, for example, had shown how such traits followed from penis envy and the castration complex.

Although some of the most blatant expressions of misogyny have changed (the expression, not the beliefs), the situation is little better today. Sexism in the social sciences is absolutely crucial to the formation and character of women's consciousness in contemporary society. The precepts of science and social science have become the theoretical underpinnings of the public-serving institutions of our culture — education, social service, or medicine — and through them misogynistic doctrines masquerading as scientific truth are being infused formally into our entire conceptual environment. Every teacher, social worker, nurse, and doctor has received the rudiments of elementary psychology, and has been properly oriented to the importance of social "adjustment," strong male models, and clear sexual identity distinction. It is a rare child who escapes Erikson or Piaget, a rare ob-gyn patient who eludes Freud. Women are getting extra doses of distortion, officially sanctioned and therefore extremely powerful and convincing.

The other branch of the formal enterprise, the so-called helping professions, is similarly suffused with sexist ideology and perspective. As Phyllis Chesler has pointed out in her *Women and Madness,* the helping professions may turn out to be more hindrance than help for the woman staggering under the collective weight of patriarchy's consciousness-makers.

The Psych-Hype Ethic[4]

If the formal segment of social science is sexist and destructive, even more so is its popularized offspring, the contemporary culture's philosophy of life, what I call the *psych-hype ethic*. Since science itself has ascended so high in the contemporary consciousness, it is not surprising that the popular scene, both the material environment and its conceptual framework, should be permeated by scientific or neoscientific perspectives.

The scientific "naturalistic" image of humankind, around which is built a whole genre of life philosophies, depicts a creature, temporarily existent on a minor planet, "just" an animal like any other, subject only to its biological needs and impulses, bumping with difficulty against all the other such creatures. All of this, of course, is in one sense very true. What transforms this picture from a basic description of the human condition into a fertile setting for the psych-hype ethic is a

gross insensitivity to the complexities of such an image, a lack of sophistication in the business of trying to develop value systems out of factual data, and a kind of immature manipulativeness on the part of its proponents.

The premise of the psych-hype begins: "Hey, man, we're here only for a short time; tomorrow we may all go up in smoke. So let's not get hung up on the small stuff, and let's get it on. That morality junk we grew up with is just a bunch of stuff to keep us in line; dump it because it messes you over. What matters is feeling good and being happy."

The psych-hype deepens: "You gotta love yourself, man, take care of your needs. Trust your gut feelings, and put yourself first. Do what you want so long as you live and let live and don't get on anybody else's case. Stay free. Don't let anybody tie you into something rigid, because you gotta stay loose, and when something isn't good for you [that is, gets difficult — like a job, or a theory, or a relationship] you gotta split. Love everyone. Risk your innermost self and trust people. Don't be demanding. Be tolerant. Different strokes for different folks."

Such a vision is extremely seductive at first glance, especially to the young, who are seeking alternatives to the destructive and non-viable elements in our culture. Ostensibly it throws off the shackling inconsistencies and counterhumane tendencies of former theologies and moralities; it calls for freedom, love, and trust; it integrates behavioral values with current knowledge and environment; and it liberates what it terms the *feminine* in culture, the affective, feeling, emotional, and spiritual side of experience.

On the surface it looks good. Actually, as it functions among people, it carries another message and practices another style, for it is a perfect rationale for exploitative behavior. Psych-hype groupies tend to be extremely destructive. Demystify the theme to the bare

4 The following discussion is taken in part from Sheila Ruth, "A Feminist World-View," *Women's Studies International Quarterly,* June 1978.

bones of what is really being said and you have this: "Do what you want without too much serious thought; do what feels easy. Love everyone, but keep your distance. 'Risk' your innermost feelings [that is, reveal your fears], but exchange nothing deeply important with anyone. Don't get obligated; don't make demands or get committed to any thing, any place, or any person. Stay loose [that is, relaxed, nonfeeling, reserved]. On the other hand, 'feel,' free your 'feminine,' and let everyone else 'feel,' so long as it remains convenient, unscary, undemanding. Get 'spiritual'; trot off to Arika, TM, or the Andes for a short course in Nirvana, but persevere at nothing. Put your own needs and interests first even when that is not appropriate, for obligation or responsibility is only conformist sham."

Commentators on the lifestyle have variously called the ethic narcissistic (which it is), childish (which it is), inconsistent and counterproductive (which it is). I call it masculist, Mars all over. Leave aside the fact that its father is the body of theory and value created by (masculist) social science; its direction is decidedly male. Who needs to liberate the feminine, the affective, the spiritual? Women have so much of that we are accused of being emotional and irrational. Who has difficulty resolving the need to trust and risk with the fear of incurring emotional pain? Whose trip is it typically to keep one's distance, stay uncommitted and "safe," and yet be intensely loved? The inconsistencies and conflicts are basically male conflicts, and although we might have all sympathy with men's desire to work them out, we should consider the impact this world view has on today's women.

Although the ethic's lifestyle poses as an alternative to outdated, antihuman attitudes, in fact, so far as the concrete effects on women are concerned, it has turned out to be just a continuation of the same old thing.

So far as the "new," laid-back, okay, coun-

terculture young man is concerned, women are still subject to the classic servant/saint–witch/bitch dichotomy. Listen critically to Bob Dylan extolling the praises of his erstwhile lady, running gentle on his mind because she lets him, among other things, leave his sleeping bag rolled up behind her couch while he's off exploring railroad tracks. Bless him, he *will* return. One wonders whether he'd so lovingly care for *her* things while *she* went off a-wandering. The old tender services of woman to man — waiting, serving, preserving, letting him have his way — are re-created intact in this and countless other pop songs, reminding women of their place just as surely as did the preachers of old.

Enter Jack Nicholson in *Five Easy Pieces*, poor alienated psych-hype hero par excellence, searching for himself unsuccessfully, while he uses and abuses the women he encounters. The images of women in the film are classic: cheap waitresses, dykish lesbians, uptight spinsters, stupid or neurotic females with nothing to contribute, nothing to receive. Hip women in the audience are expected to contemplate the "intense, universal, ramifications" of this "important film," to empathize with said hero, and applaud his rebellion. Women are not supposed to question the treatment or fate of his female victims. Some might argue that the villain is the man, not the ethic. Others might answer: Test the tree by the fruit it produces.

From *Easy Rider* to savagely misogynistic rock groups, from Transactional Analysis or encounter weekends to a burst of angry young art, we are subjected to the same old stereotypes, insidiously hidden within the folds of a "new" consciousness, powerfully compelling for appearing so young, rebellious, and radical.

Questioning or challenging this ethic, furthermore, leads as certainly to the judgment of "bad" woman as did challenging the old ethic, only in the new consciousness, the term *bad* is expressed in different language: hung up, uptight, heavy, or "not okay." "The old lady" is a good old broad, so long as she does her bit [serves], doesn't get heavy [assertive], and stays cool. The woman who chooses not to sleep with a particular man at a particular time can be comfortably put down as hung up, while her more serviceable sisters earn the praise of being game chicks. The woman who is not content to make coffee instead of policy is a drag. She who hesitates to play the game wholeheartedly and at once is obviously afraid to "risk," is not ready for "community," needs to "let go."

The new anti-game ethic is full of games, but they are not played equally by all; the pressures are not applied to each in equal strength. Given our readiness as women to risk, love, give, and trust, it is not surprising that we are often the losers, that we fail to perceive the misogyny and the game, and that we let ourselves be convinced of our responsibility to "lay back," both personally and politically. If women are beginning to realize and resist the sexism in traditional social scientific perspectives, very few are prepared for the onslaught of the subliminal woman-hating in what is supposed to be a philosophy for the new generation.

Religion

Religion as it is practiced through or by the social institutions of a people is as much a reflection and expression of that culture's ideals, attitudes, and needs as it is their creator. The Judeo-Christian tradition of the West is, of course, no exception. As Western culture is patriarchal, so is its religion, and so is its god.

Although Christians (and sometimes Jews) argue that God is without sex, neither female nor male, that contention is contradicted by a host of beliefs indicating the maleness of

their God. Currently some fathers of the various churches have opposed the ordination of women on the grounds that it would be sacrilegious because the maleness of Christ proves that men were meant for the priestly office. (One could argue to separate God and Jesus, but I do not think that holds functionally, in the minds of the faithful.) In medieval times the Church explained that women rather than men were likely to be witches because, among other things, men had been saved from that most awful danger by the fact that Christ was male. Today the use of feminine pronouns, *she* or *her,* to refer to the deity brings a very hostile response. Certainly the Catholic imagery of the Church standing analogously to Christ as a wife stands to a husband supports once more the identification of God as male.

So in our culture God is traditionally conceived to be male. What can be made of that? A great deal can be made of that. The relationships among the concrete, material conditions of a culture, including its social organization, and its myths, mores, and ideals are intricate and close. The maleness of the Western god, his character and behavior, is as much a source of the content of our culture's masculist perspectives as it is an indicator. If men are to be gods, their god must be male. Likewise, if God in His heaven is male, then on earth men can be the only true gods. The entire conceptual system of Martial thought is elevated and deified by its incarnation in the person of the "One True God," ultimate male, just as the sociopolitical structures of patriarchy are reinforced by their justification through theology. The relationship between masculist theology and patriarchal society is the reason why it is both possible and necessary to insist on the masculinity of the priesthood or the authority of the hierarchy. It is the source of the masculine cast to biblical imagery and to male privilege in church doctrine.

Once again, consider the Genesis story of Adam and Eve, a story whose theme appears in numerous patriarchal mythologies. It can be understood through feminist analysis to function both as an expression of male psychological conflict resolved through myth and as a masculist construct justifying male domination of women. Early in the creation Adam appears, formed *in the likeness and image* of God (a concept, though unclear, frequently employed to support the ascendancy of maleness). Pure and happy, Adam spends his hours exercising his divinely given dominion over the earth until God decides that he needs a helpmeet. As Adam sleeps, Eve is taken by God from Adam's rib, from his body, formed into a Woman (so called because she was "taken out of man") and presented to him. Shortly thereafter, Eve is beguiled by a serpent into disobedience, and taking Adam along with her into disfavor with God, she causes the expulsion from the Garden of Eden, the downfall of all humankind, and death. The serpent is henceforth sentenced to the dust, Eve herself to her husband's yoke, and Adam, because he "hearkened to the voice of [his] wife," is condemned to labor, sweat, and sorrow.

Many meanings have been placed on the story. Freud made much of the phallic symbolism of the serpent, building around it a sexual interpretation of the tale. Others have focused on the matter of human growth through separation from parental protection and subsequent trial by life. As feminists, however, we can see other, more pragmatic applications.

We can see the masculist myth of Adam, the man, created "in the image of God" (in appearance? in power?), the first progenitor, the first earthly parent. So what if women and not men are able to conceive and bear young? Man did it *first* and produced woman, who produces young only secondarily. And man did it best — cleanly and neatly while he slept, without the fuss and mess of human conception, labor, and childbirth. We can see Eve, the woman, second in creation, an afterthought, a helpmeet, first approached by the snake, easily seduced, equally seducing, placed for sinfulness and stupidity under the yoke of her husband, condemned to painful childbirth and suffering. In a single stroke, the awesome female power of procreation is discounted (as punishment for sin); supreme parenting is comfortably settled upon the male (God and Adam, a theme reiterated and developed in the doctrine of the Virgin Birth); the man is firmly fixed in a position of dominance over women (his wife and, one assumes, other females); and the exploitation and subjection of woman is justified — she sinned, she was stupid and led humanity into disgrace and misery, she was condemned to the yoke by God. Men go out and work (albeit in sweat), and women bring forth children. Men rule and leave off hearkening to their wives, whereas woman's desire is to her husband. All is conveniently explained and justified.

As one might expect, the impact of the masculist character of theology and religion is vast, not only on women's lives and perspectives but on the entire culture.

Patriarchal Religion and Women

If the religion into which we are given and by which we are expected to live is masculist and misogynist, in that context what would it mean to be a "religious" woman?

Although we may rarely focus on them, we are all aware of certain realities of Western religious tradition.

• The God of this tradition (Judaism or Christianity) is male. So are its priests, its potentates and hierarchies, its power centers. So are its philosophers, apologists, and policymakers. So are its favorite sons. Encyclicals of the Pope to this day are addressed: Honored Brothers and Dear Sons ...

• The latest Savior and messiah of the tradition, Jesus, was himself male. So were the apostles and his disciples. There never was any question of his faithful female followers becoming disciples; it was outside the realm of consideration.

• In the tradition, women are conspicuously absent from power, from participation in theory or policy, from full human status. (Aquinas, remember, pointed out that women's souls were not fully developed, and a Jewish male begins his morning prayers with thanksgiving for not having been born a woman.)

• In both Judaism and Christianity the ideal woman is a fecund animal who tends to her young, to her husband's home and service, who "humbly" accepts the dominion of her husband and the male hegemony. Docile, quiet, passive, obedient, and meek, she neither questions nor challenges.

• The Christian ideal, Mary, perfect in submission ("Thy will be done") and sexual purity, took no active part in the drama of Christ. Receptacle only of God's seed, she nurtured her young male god; she herself neither directed nor taught, nor hazarded an instrusion into the march of events. She is the female model.

• According to the tradition, woman's progenitor was Eve, mother of evil, precipitator of The Fall. She resides in each of us.

• According to the early fathers, women's bodies are evil, seductive, damning, dirty. Women are carnal; men are spiritual. Women are body; men are mind. Women are sex, and sex is evil. Women are pleasure and passion, and that too is condemned.

Consider the impact on your self-image of being "in the likeness of God," like Jesus, the Pope, and the "Brothers of the Church," and contrast it with never finding yourself expressed in the sacred pronoun. Utter: God, He ...; God, Him. Say: God, She.... Imagine the experience of seeing oneself reflected in the sacred images of power, Christ walking on clouds, God forming Adam with His powerful arm. Imagine, instead, modeling after the suffering Mary or shamefully hiding one's inner Eve, one's sexuality. Think of looking high into the pulpit, seeing the Man proclaiming the Word of Him, knowing that that is ever out of the grasp of oneself or any of one's kind, because of one's lesser excellence and status. Ask again: If one's religion is sexist, masculist, and misogynist, what does it mean to be a religious woman?

No wonder victimization is a sacred principle of womanhood, sacrifice a magic contribution, self-effacement a high.

> Patriarchal religion adds to the problem by intensifying the process through which women internalize the consciousness of the oppressor. The males' judgment having been metamorphosed into God's judgment, it becomes the religious duty of women to accept the burden of guilt, seeing the self with male chauvinist eyes. What is more, the process does not stop with religion's demanding that women internalize such images. It happens that those conditioned to see themselves as "bad" or "sick" in a real sense become such. Women who are conditioned to live out the abject role assigned to the female sex actually appear to "deserve" the contempt heaped upon "the second sex." [5]

God, Mars, and Culture

To speak of a patriarchal religion and its effect on culture is to consider the cultural impact of the deification of masculist per-

[5] Mary Daly, *Beyond God the Father* (Boston: Beacon Press, 1973) p. 49.

spective, for as pointed out earlier, the forms of institutional religious worship are a reflection of cultural ideals, expressed in a different language. What makes the religious expression of those ideals so important and powerful is its claim to absolute cosmic validity and its subsequent persuasive force over society.

What we find when we turn analysis sensitive to masculist conceptualizations upon the patriarchal Western tradition is precisely what we would expect to find: a Martial god, an authoritarian ethic, and a warrior personality/consciousness.

In patriarchy, God rules. He creates out of nothing. Superior and external to the rest, He orders, fixes, requires, commands, and does unto. He gets angry at disobedience, "loves" on condition, rewards and punishes according to the meeting of His standards, and trains His followers through a series of trials and challenges. Jesus was supposed to have been the "completion" of the person of God — gentle, merciful, and forgiving; but outside of His ultimate sacrifice and readiness to accept us (provided that ...), one may not experience His sweetness in execess of His power, not practically. Put all together, the Trinity as the One generally functions in the Church more as the Power than as the Lamb.

That claims of the gentleness or lovingness of God are unconvincing among the laity is underscored smartly by the popular centrality of Mary as the image of mercy and kindness. In Catholicism, it is the female who captures the heart and serves the needs of the people. The Queen of Heaven, to whom most of the finest churches are dedicated, is the Mother, free from the angry, frightening qualities of Mars/God — forgiving where He is stern, understanding where He is legalistic, accessible where He is distant. It is no accident that Mary is absent from Protestantism, which has been both more ascetic than Catholicism and more unrelenting in its emphasis on sin and punishment.

God is good, we are told, although there are no standards outside of His own will against which we may judge Him. He is good (right) because He is God, that is, He is The Chief. Everybody else is expected to be good too, that is, obedient to the will of the Chief, not merely through coercion but through choice — ultimate obedience. If one is not good, God punishes. If one suffers sufficiently, one might be redeemed (forgiven), but that too is solely up to God. The pattern of the God–Person relationship is clearly disciplinarian and authoritarian.

Other relationships in which God resides are equally authoritarian although in a different context. The relationships are generally expressed as dualistic oppositions in which God has ascendancy: God against nature, Spirit against body, life against death, God vis-à-vis humanity. The relations are ones of strain, either of striving or of contention.

And of course the ethos of strain and contention permeates the lives of the people who are both its subject and its instigators. One strives constantly to "be good," to conform, to measure up to an image that is not in harmony with what it is to be human because it is derived from only one aspect and one segment of humanity: maleness. One strives and strains, but usually fails, and follows with guilt and penitence and atonement and forgiveness and striving and failing again.

The tone is antihumanistic. You sinned, it bellows. You are bad. Your body is bad; sex is bad; pleasure is bad. You should be ashamed. Try harder, ever harder. Salvation is possible only through vicarious identification with the Sacrificial Lamb. Even the treatment of love is formally rather heavy, generally ascetic, weighted with obligation and prohibitions, not particularly self-affirming. Certainly the qualities of mirth and gaiety have not been extant or even a consideration until very recently, and then only under pressure of the new ethic. Levity, in fact, has usually been treated with suspicion and disdain if not outright suppression.

The character of this perspective permeates our culture conceptually and spiritually, expressing itself in our thoughts, institutions, attitudes, and expectations. It is difficult to be self-affirming, constructively self-confident, healthily self-loving in the face of an image of humanity that is "sinful and debased." It is difficult to put into positive ethical perspective the needs and directions of one's natural self in a context that is condemnatory and almost hysterically antinature. It is nearly impossible for self-affirming people to comprehend the healthy possibility of worship, to know what or how or whether to worship when official worship is composed of self-abnegation.

The worship of Mars, the religion of masculism, means for culture an obeisance to all the warrior values we saw in Chapter 2. That is very harmful for a people because it gives them a distorted value base on which to build their society.

Feminist Alternatives

There are other ways to treat religion than as the submission of one's will and understanding to the prescriptions and doctrines of a powerful authority. There are those who view worship as a total emotional, rational, and physical experience of the elements of life, so beautiful, meaningful, and profound that they transcend temporary matters and deserve our most concentrated attention and respect. Perhaps such an experience may be possible through a very sensitive portrayal of the Western tradition, through Judaism or Christianity, but certainly not through the secularized, garden variety, patriarchal projections to which we are accustomed.

Many feminists question whether there can be a reformed, nonsexist portrayal of the Judeo-Christian religions, whether the historical identification of God as male can be reversed, whether its hierarchical, authoritarian character can be purged without obliterating its nature altogether.[6] Feminists ask whether women can or should relate to a religion that worships male gods and ideals in male language, demeans women's full humanity, and prohibits the full exercise of women's potentials. Can or should we participate in religious institutions that have been historically misogynistic and that even now form policy for our lives while blocking our power to contribute to those formulations? Is reform possible or even worthwhile?

Feminists both within and outside of the traditional religious institutions raise some rather intriguing questions about "God-talk" and by doing so perhaps point the way to some revitalization of religious experience. Just as conjecture, we might muse, would a feminist theology, projecting a female conceptualization of deity, a female god, or a series of female and male gods have been less authoritarian, less demanding and constraining than the ones we know? Would the deity Herself, free of masculist ideals, have been visualized as a more tolerant, accepting being, and would such a religion have been more affirming? Is there need for a deity at all, or could we, as Mary Daly proposes, think of God not as a person at all, as a noun, but rather as a verb, the Holy Verb *to be*.

Some feminists entirely reject any interest in religion or forms of worship, arguing that religion channels one's energy into the wrong directions, that women's situation requires strong political action, not wasteful dreaming. One can certainly sympathize with such a

---

6 See particularly the works of Mary Daly: *Beyond God the Father* (1973) and *Gyn/Ecology* (1978).

view, given the history of religion for women and given traditional definitions. On the other hand, I perceive feminism to be at base a spiritual movement. Feminists seek increased opportunity for participation and gain, not as ends in themselves, not simply for the power they entail, but for the growth in the quality of life they represent, and that is a spiritual matter. In such a context, "religion," worship, or reverence may prove fruitful, and it should not be dismissed without careful scrutiny simply because of its past association and its usurpation by patriarchy.

Conclusion

As we critically examine the agencies of thought formation in our culture, we see a network of interlocking and mutually supporting institutions and ideas that form our conceptual environment and thus direct and control the consciousness of society.

Ideas that appear repeatedly in varying formulations throughout the network become very powerful forces of socialization and indoctrination because they are continually reinforced by their pervasiveness and by their constant reiteration in successive languages and contexts. Their repetitiveness alone affords them a cumulative effect on awareness that renders them nearly unquestionable if not undeniable. We have seen, in case after case, that our culture's agencies of thought maintain and promote *as truth* the traditional misogynistic themes and images of women's inferiority, guilt, and "place." The wonder is not that women absorb and believe them, not that we are prone to participate in our own oppression, but that any of us ever break through at all!

And yet we do break through, we do come to recognize the falsehoods and the injustices, and we do seek and strive to live by more accurate, more constructive perspectives. That in a nutshell is what feminism is. However heterogeneous some of the theories, perspectives, methods, or goals, feminism is constant in its recognition of the falseness and perversity of distorted masculist images of womanhood; it is constant in its affirmation of the worth of women in every sense. The following chapter is a small glimpse at the career of that affirmation.

Selections

SEXUAL STEREOTYPES START EARLY

FLORENCE HOWE

Florence Howe, professor of humanities at the State University of New York, College at Old Westbury, has been active in feminism and ethnic liberation for many years and was one of the pioneers of Women's Studies. She served actively for women's rights through the Modern Language Association; edited a series of pamphlets on Women's Studies through the Feminist Press, which she founded; and published a variety of directories in Women's Studies including *Who's Who and Where in Women's Studies*. She is co-author, with Paul Lauter, of *The Conspiracy of the Young* (1970) and editor of *Women and the Power to Change* (1975).

The following excerpt from Howe's commentary on women's education vividly and concretely portrays the process, probably very familiar to most of you, of indirect teaching of sex stereotypes. Remember, as you read, the messages about women and men that you received in school. Note the ways in which the college environment fosters and validates those messages.

Children learn about sex roles very early in their lives, probably before they are eighteen months old, certainly long before they enter school. They learn these roles through relatively simple patterns that most of us take for granted. We throw boy-babies up in the air and roughhouse with them. We coo over girl-babies and handle them delicately. We choose sex-related colors and toys for our children from their earliest days. We encourage the energy and physical activity of our sons, just as we expect girls to be quieter

and more docile. We love both our sons and daughters with equal fervor, we protest, and yet we are disappointed when there is no male child to carry on the family name. . . .

How much blame should be placed on public education? A substantial portion, although it is true that schools reflect the society they serve. Indeed, schools function to reinforce the sexual stereotypes that children have been taught by their parents, friends, and the mass culture we live in. It is also perfectly understandable that sexual stereotypes demeaning to women are also perpetuated by women — mothers in the first place, and teachers in the second — as well as by men — fathers, the few male teachers in elementary schools, high school teachers, and many male administrators and educators at the top of the school's hierarchy. . . .

Sexual stereotypes are assumed differences, social conventions or norms, learned behavior, attitudes, and expectations. Most stereotypes are well-known to all of us, for they are simple — not to say simple-minded. Men are smart, women are dumb but beautiful, etc. A recent annotated catalogue of children's books (distributed by the National Council of Teachers of English to thousands of teachers and used for ordering books with federal funds) lists titles under the headings "Especially for Girls" and "Especially for Boys." Verbs and adjectives are remarkably predictable through the listings. Boys "decipher and discover," "earn and train," or "foil" someone; girls "struggle," "overcome difficulties," "feel lost," "help solve," or "help [someone] out." One boy's story has "strange power," another moves "from truancy to triumph." A girl, on the other hand, "learns to face the real world" or makes a "difficult adjustment." Late or early, in catalogues or on shelves, the boys of children's books are active and capable, the girls passive and in trouble. All studies of children's literature — and there have been many besides my own — support this conclusion.

Ask yourself whether you would be surprised to find the following social contexts in a fifth-grade arithmetic textbook:

1. girls playing marbles; boys sewing;
2. girls earning money, building things, and going places; boys buying ribbons for a sewing project;
3. girls working at physical activities; boys babysitting and, you guessed it, sewing.

Of course you would be surprised — so would I. What I have done here is to reverse the sexes as found in a fifth-grade arithmetic text. I was not surprised, since several years ago an intrepid freshman offered to report on third-grade arithmetic texts for me and found similar types of sexual roles prescribed: Boys were generally making things or earning money; girls were cooking or spending money on such things as sewing equipment. . . .

Children learn sexual stereotypes at an early age, and, by the time they get to fifth grade, it may be terribly difficult, perhaps hardly possible by traditional means, to change their attitudes about sex roles — whether they are male or female. For more than a decade, Paul Torrance, a psychologist particularly interested in creativity, has been conducting interesting and useful experiments with young children. Using a Products Improvement Test, for example, Torrance asked first-grade boys and girls to "make toys more fun to play with." Many six-year-old boys refused to try the nurse's kit, "protesting," Torrance reports, "I'm a boy! I don't play with things like that." Several creative boys turned the nurse's kit into a doctor's kit and were then "quite free to think of improvements." By the third grade, however, "boys excelled girls even on the nurse's kit, probably because," Torrance explains, "girls have been conditioned by this time to accept toys as they are and not to manipulate or change them."

Later experiments with third, fourth, and fifth-graders using science toys further verify what Torrance calls "the inhibiting effects of sex-role conditioning." "Girls were quite reluctant," he reports, "to work with these science toys and frequently protested: 'I'm a girl; I'm not supposed to know anything about things like that!' " Boys, even in these early grades, were about twice as good as girls at explaining ideas about toys. In 1959, Torrance reported his findings to parents and teachers in one school and asked for their cooperation in attempting to change the attitudes of the girls. In 1960, when he retested them, using similar science toys, the girls participated willingly and even with apparent enjoyment. And they performed as well as the boys. But in one significant respect nothing had changed: The boys' contributions were more highly valued — both by other boys and by girls — than the girls' contributions, regardless of the fact that, in terms of sex, boys and girls had scored equally. "Apparently," Torrance writes, "the school climate has helped to make it more acceptable for girls to play around with science things, but boys' ideas about science things are still supposed to be better than those of girls."

Torrance's experiments tell us both how useful and how limited education may be for women in a culture in which assumptions about their inferiority run deep in their own consciousness as well as in the consciousness of men. While it is encouraging to note that a year's effort had changed behavior patterns significantly, it is also clear that attitudes of nine-, ten-, and eleven-year-olds are not so easily modifiable, at least not through the means Torrance used.

Torrance's experiments also make clear that, whatever most of us have hitherto assumed, boys and girls are *not* treated alike in elementary school. If we consider those non-curricular aspects of the school environment that the late anthropologist Jules Henry labeled the "noise" of schools, chief among them is the general attitude of teachers, whatever their sex, that girls are likely to "love" reading and to "hate" mathematics and science. As we know from the Rosenthal study of teacher expectations, *Pygmalion in the Classroom,* such expectations significantly determine student behavior and attitudes. Girls are not expected to think logically or to understand scientific principles; they accept that estimate internally and give up on mathematics and science relatively early. And what encouragement awaits the interested few in high school? For ex-

ample, in six high school science texts published since 1966 and used in the Baltimore city public schools — all of the books rich in illustrations — I found photographs of one female lab assistant, one woman doctor, one woman scientist, and Rachel Carson. It is no wonder that the percentage of women doctors and engineers in the United States has remained constant at 6 per cent and 1 per cent respectively for the past fifty years.

Though there is no evidence that their early physical needs are different from or less than boys', girls are offered fewer activities even in kindergarten. They may sit and watch while boys, at the request of the female teacher, change the seating arrangement in the room. Of course, it's not simply a matter of physical exercise or ability: Boys are learning how to behave as males, and girls are learning to be "ladies" who enjoy being "waited on." If there are student-organized activities to be arranged, boys are typically in charge, with girls assisting, perhaps in the stereotyped role of secretary. Boys are allowed and expected to be noisy and aggressive, even on occasion to express anger; girls must learn "to control themselves" and behave like "young ladies." On the other hand, boys are expected not to cry, though there are perfectly good reasons why children of both sexes ought to be allowed that avenue of expression. Surprisingly early, boys and girls are separated for physical education and hygiene, and all the reports now being published indicate preferential treatment for boys and nearly total neglect of girls.

In junior high schools, sexual stereotyping becomes, if anything, more overt. Curricular sex-typing continues and is extended to such "shop" subjects as cooking and sewing, on the one hand, and metal- and woodworking, printing, ceramics, on the other. In vocational high schools, the stereotyping becomes outright channeling, and here the legal battles have begun for equality of opportunity. Recently, the testimony of junior high and high school girls in New York has become available in a pamphlet prepared by the New York City chapter of NOW (*Report on Sex Bias in the Public Schools,* available from Anne Grant West, 453 Seventh St., Brooklyn, N.Y. 11215). Here are a few items:

Well, within my physics class last year, our teacher asked if there was anybody interested in being a lab assistant, in the physics lab, and when I raised my hand, he told all the girls to put their hands down because he was only interested in working with boys.

There is an Honor Guard . . . students who, instead of participating in gym for the term, are monitors in the hall, and I asked my gym teacher if I could be on the Honor Guard Squad. She said it was only open to boys. I then went to the head of the Honor Guard . . . who said that he thought girls were much too nasty to be Honor Guards. He thought they would be too mean in working on the job, and I left it at that.

We asked for basketball. They said there wasn't enough equipment. The boys prefer to have it first. Then we will have what is left over. We haven't really gotten anywhere.

Finally, I quote more extensively from one case:

MOTHER: I asked Miss Jonas if my daughter could take metalworking or mechanics, and she said there is no freedom of choice. That is what she said.
THE COURT: That is it?
ANSWER: I also asked her whose decision this was, that there was no freedom of choice. And she told me it was the decision of the board of education. I didn't ask her anything else because she clearly showed me that it was

against the school policy for girls to be in the class. She said it was a board of education decision.
QUESTION: Did she use that phrase, "no freedom of choice"?
ANSWER: Exactly that phrase — no freedom of choice. That is what made me so angry that I wanted to start this whole thing.

.   .   .

THE COURT: Now, after this lawsuit was filed, they then permitted you to take the course; is that correct?
DAUGHTER: No, we had to fight about it for quite a while.
QUESTION: But eventually they did let you in the second semester?
ANSWER: They only let me in there.
Q: You are the only girl?
A: Yes.
Q: How did you do in the course?
A: I got a medal for it from all the boys there.
Q: Will you show the court?
A: Yes (indicating).
Q: And what does the medal say?
A: Metal 1970 Van Wyck.
Q: And why did they give you that medal?
A: Because I was the best one out of all the boys.
THE COURT: I do not want any giggling or noises in the courtroom. Just do the best you can to control yourself or else I will have to ask you to leave the courtroom. This is no picnic, you know. These are serious lawsuits.

Such "serious lawsuits" will, no doubt, continue, but they are not the only routes to change. There are others to be initiated by school systems themselves.

One route lies through the analysis of texts and attitudes. So long as those responsible for the education of children believe in the stereotypes as givens, rather than as hypothetical constructs that a patriarchal society has established as desired norms — so long as the belief continues, so will the condition. These beliefs are transmitted in the forms we call literature and history, either on the printed page or in other media.

Elementary school readers are meant for both sexes. Primers used in the first three grades offer children a view of a "typical" American family: a mother who does not work, a father who does, two children — a brother who is always older than a sister — and two pets — a dog and sometimes a cat — whose sexes and ages mirror those of the brother and sister. In these books, boys build or paint things; they also pull girls in wagons and push merry-go-rounds. Girls carry purses when they go shopping; they help mother cook or pretend that they are cooking; and they play with their dolls. When they are not making messes, they are cleaning up their rooms or other people's messes. Plots in which girls are involved usually depend on their inability to do something — to manage their own roller skates or to ride a pony. Or in another typical role, a girl named Sue admires a parachute jumper: "What a jump!" said Sue. "What a jump for a man to make!" When her brother puts on a show for the rest of the neighborhood, Sue, whose name appears as the title of the chapter, is part of his admiring audience.

The absence of adventurous heroines may shock the innocent; the absence of even a few stories about women doctors, lawyers, or professors thwarts reality; but the consistent presence of one female stereotype is the most troublesome matter:

> Primrose was playing house. Just as she finished pouring tea for her dolls she began to think. She thought and thought and she thought some more: "Whom shall I marry? Whomever shall I marry?
>
> "I think I shall marry a mailman. Then I could go over to everybody's house and give them their mail.
>
> "Or I might marry a policeman. I could help him take the children across the street."

Primrose thinks her way through ten more categories of employment and concludes, "But now that I think it over, maybe I'll just marry somebody I love." Love is the opiate designated to help Primrose forget to think about what she would like to do or be. With love as reinforcer, she can imagine herself helping some man in his work. In another children's book, Johnny says, "I think I will be a dentist when I grow up," and later, to Betsy, he offers generously, "You can be a dentist's nurse." And, of course, Betsy accepts gratefully, since girls are not expected to have work identity other than as servants or helpers. In short, the books that schoolgirls read prepare them early for the goal of marriage, hardly ever for work, and never for independence.

If a child's reader can be pardoned for stereotyping because it is "only" fiction, a social studies text has no excuse for denying reality to its readers. After all, social studies texts ought to describe "what is," if not "what should be." And yet, such texts for the youngest grades are no different from readers. They focus on families and hence on sex roles and work. Sisters are still younger than brothers; brothers remain the doers, questioners, and knowers who explain things to their poor, timid sisters. In a study of five widely used texts, Jamie Kelem Frisof finds that energetic boys think about "working on a train or in a broom factory" or about being President. They grow up to be doctors or factory workers or (in five texts combined) to do some hundred different jobs, as opposed to thirty for women.

Consider for a moment the real work world of women. Most women (at least for some portion of their lives) work, and if we include "token" women — the occasional engineer, for instance — they probably do as many different kinds of work as men. Even without improving the status of working women, the reality is distinctly different from the content of school texts and literature written for children. Schools usually at least reflect the society they serve; but the treatment of working women is one clear instance in which the reflection is distorted by a patriarchal attitude about who *should* work and the maleness of work. For example, there are women doctors — there have been women doctors in this country, in fact, for a hundred years or so. And yet, until the publication this month of two new children's books by the Feminist Press (Box 334, Old Westbury, N.Y. 11568), there were no children's books about women doctors.

In a novel experiment conducted recently by an undergraduate at Towson State College in Maryland, fourth-grade students answered "yes" or "no" to a series of twenty questions, eight of which asked, in various ways, whether "girls were smarter than boys" or whether "daddies were smarter than mommies." The results indicated that boys and girls were agreed that 1) boys were not smarter than girls, nor girls smarter than boys; but 2) that daddies were indeed smarter than mommies! One possible explanation of this finding depends on the knowledge that daddies, in school texts and on television (as well as in real life), work, and that people who work know things. Mommies, on the other hand, in books and on television, rarely stir out of the house except to go to the store — and how can someone like that know anything? Of course, *we* know that half of all mothers in the United States work at some kind of job, but children whose mommies do work can only assume — on the basis of evidence offered in school books and on television — that their mommies must be "different," perhaps even not quite "real" mommies.

If children's readers deny the reality of working women, high school history texts deny women their full historical role. A re-

cent study by Janice Law Trecker of thirteen popular texts concludes with what by now must seem a refrain: Women in such texts are "passive, incapable of sustained organization or work, satisfied with [their] role in society, and well supplied with material blessings." Women, in the grip of economic and political forces, rarely fighting for anything, occasionally receive some "rights," especially suffrage in 1920, which, of course, solves all *their* problems. There is no discussion of the struggle by women to gain entrance into higher education, of their efforts to organize or join labor unions, of other battles for working rights, or of the many different aspects of the hundred-year-long multi-issue effort that ended, temporarily, in the suffrage act of 1920. Here is Dr. Thecker's summary of the history and contributions of American women as garnered from the thirteen texts combined:

> Women arrived in 1619 (a curious choice if meant to be their first acquaintance with the New World). They held the Seneca Falls Convention on Women's Rights in 1848. During the rest of the nineteenth century, they participated in reform movements, chiefly temperance, and were exploited in factories. In 1920, they were given the vote. They joined the armed forces for the first time during the Second World War and thereafter have enjoyed the good life in America. Add the names of the women who are invariably mentioned: Harriet Beecher Stowe, Jane Addams, Dorothea Dix, and Frances Perkins, with perhaps Susan B. Anthony, Elizabeth Cady Stanton . . . [and you have the story].

Where efforts have been made in recent years to incorporate black history, again it is without attention to black women, either with respect to their role in abolitionist or civil rights movements, for example, or with respect to intellectual or cultural achievements.

Just as high school history texts rely on male spokesmen and rarely quote female leaders of the feminist movement — even when they were also articulate writers such as Charlotte Perkins Gilman, or speakers such as Sojourner Truth — so, too, literary anthologies will include Henry James or Stephen Crane rather than Edith Wharton or Kate Chopin. Students are offered James Joyce's *Portrait of the Artist as a Young Man* or the *Autobiography of Malcolm X*, rather than Doris Lessing's *Martha Quest* or Anne Moody's *Coming of Age in Mississippi.* As a number of studies have indicated, the literary curriculum, both in high school and college, is a male-centered one. That is, either male authors dominate the syllabus or the central characters of the books are consistently male. There is also usually no compensating effort to test the fictional portraits — of women and men — against the reality of life experience. Allegedly "relevant" textbooks for senior high school or freshman college composition courses continue to appear, such as Macmillan's *Representative Men: Heroes of Our Time.* There are two women featured in this book: Elizabeth Taylor, the actress, and Jacqueline Onassis, the Existential Heroine. Thirty-five or forty men — representing a range of racial, political, occupational, and intellectual interests — fill the bulk of a book meant, of course, for both men and women. And some teachers are still ordering such texts.

It's not a question of malice, I assume, but of thoughtlessness or ignorance. Six or seven years ago I too was teaching from a standard male-dominated curriculum — and at a women's college at that. But I speak from more than my own experience. Last fall at this time I knew of some fifty college courses in what has come to be known as women's studies. This fall, I know of more than 500, about half of which are in literature and history. I know also of many high

school teachers who have already begun to invent comparable courses.

School systems can and should begin to encourage new curricular developments, especially in literature and social studies, and at the elementary as well as the high school level. Such changes, of course, must include the education and re-education of teachers, and I know of no better way to re-educate them than to ask for analyses of the texts they use, as well as of their assumptions and attitudes. The images we pick up, consciously or unconsciously, from literature and history significantly control our sense of identity, and our identity — our sense of ourselves as powerful or powerless, for example — controls our behavior. As teachers read new materials and organize and teach new courses, they will change their views. That is the story of most of the women I know who, like me, have become involved in women's studies. The images we have in our heads about ourselves come out of literature and history; before we can change those images, we must see them clearly enough to exorcise them and, in the process, to raise others from the past we are learning to see.

That is why black educators have grown insistent upon their students' learning black history — slave history, in fact. That is also why some religious groups, Jews for example, emphasize their history as a people, even though part of that history is also slave history. For slave history has two virtues: Not only does it offer a picture of servitude against which one can measure the present; it offers also a vision of struggle and courage. When I asked a group of young women at the University of Pittsburgh last year whether they were depressed by the early nineteenth-century women's history they were studying, their replies were instructive: "Certainly not," one woman said, "we're angry that we had to wait until now — after so many years of U.S. history in high school — to learn the truth about some things." And another added, "But it makes you feel good to read about those tremendous women way back then. They felt some of the same things we do now."

Will public education begin to change the images of women in texts and the lives of women students in schools? There will probably be some movement in this direction, at least in response to the pressures from students, parents, and individual teachers. I expect that parents, for example, will continue to win legal battles for their daughters' equal rights and opportunities. I expect that indi-vidual teachers will alter their courses and texts and grow more sensitive to stereotypic expectations and behavior in the classroom. But so far there are no signs of larger, more inclusive reforms: no remedial program for counselors, no major effort to destereotype vocational programs or kindergarten class-rooms, no centers for curricular reform. Frankly, I don't expect this to happen without a struggle. I don't expect that public school systems will take the initiative here. There is too much at stake in a society as patriarchal as this one. And schools, after all, tend to follow society, not lead it.

RESTORING WOMEN TO HISTORY

RENATE BRIDENTHAL AND CLAUDIA KOONZ

Renate Bridenthal was born in Leipzig, Germany, in 1935, and was educated in New York at City College and Columbia University. She now teaches history and coordinates the Women's Studies program at Brooklyn College. With Claudia Koonz she edited *Becoming Visible: Women in European History* (1977), and her articles have appeared in *Radical America, Central European History,* and *Feminist Studies.* She credits the women's movement for changing her life and directing and inspiring her historical scholarship.

Claudia Koonz took her degrees at Rutgers, Columbia, and the University of Wisconsin and is now an associate professor of history at Holy Cross College, Worcester, Massachusetts. She has been active in groups concerned with women's history and women in history.

In this discussion, from the Introduction to *Becoming Visible,* Bridenthal and Koonz show how new, more accurate understanding of women's experience (in this case, history) proceeds from research with a feminist perspective. It serves both to erase distorted and derogatory information and to construct better models within which to analyze the information we have.

A chronicle of women's history points inevitably to a new feminist perspective. We depart from male-centered models and lit-

erally bring to our study a new point of view, although theorizing about women's history itself is not new. In *The Second Sex* (1949), Simone de Beauvoir constructed a general theory to explain women's chronic power-lessness. Passive onlookers in the historical drama of great events, women have, in her theory, acted in the service of patriarchy. Therefore, they have created no history of their own. Others have disagreed. Mary Beard, in *Woman as Force in History* (1946), called attention to the fact that women, despite formidable obstacles, have made far greater contributions to human history than is commonly recognized. They have been active, not merely passive; independent, not just ancillary. Both Beard's and de Beauvoir's categories are important, but they are too crude to aid us in interpreting the complexity of women's history.

Other analytic approaches attempt to depict women's history as an upward or downward curve, moving relentlessly toward liberation or more intensive oppression. The liberal tradition of Mary Wollstonecraft, Condorcet, John Stuart Mill, and Harriet Taylor Mill argues that history shows a steady progress of women from slavery to emancipation. Marxists see precisely the opposite development: from relative sexual equality under conditions of primitive society to relatively greater exploitation under capitalism. But again these notions of linear improvement or decline are too simple. A highly technological capitalist society differs so fundamentally from a nonliterate, communal one that relations of power, family, and the economy defy simple comparisons. Yesterday's abbess is not today's woman priest; the medieval alewife is not the modern barmaid; and the preindustrial wife is not the alienated drudge described by Betty Friedan....

Where can we find the lost women of earlier cultures? Central to our search is the discovery of new sources and the reevaluation of traditional ones. The primary and secondary materials most commonly available to historians have been written by men. Often these sources tell us more about male needs and attitudes than women's realities.

Starting with the very earliest written records, we find a bifurcated female image. Men have seen women as either passive and good or evil and powerful. The pedestal and the stake represent the polarities of men's views of women's place. Such a stereotypic vision masks the real women of the past and deprives them of their ordinary human strengths and frailties. The ensuing distortion serves several purposes: it rationalizes inequality, limits competition for wealth, power, and status, and displaces responsibility for social malfunctions. The polarized image of women makes it difficult for us to understand the complex realities of past societies and last, but not least, it prevents women from perceiving themselves as whole human beings capable of acting in and upon their environment. The stereotype is a self-fulfilling prophecy: women have rarely written their own history.

Now that we have begun, we have to decide how properly to use conventional, male-centered sources, which, despite their bias, contain valuable clues. Rather than discounting this material, we can reinterpret it. Many misogynistic accounts, for example, are merely symbolic; they may be pseudo-explanations of other conflicts perceived in social relations. We are learning to decode such accounts by placing them in their appropriate setting. For example, changing literary images of women in classical and Renaissance Europe provide us with a fresh perspective on changing relations between the sexes and concomitant transformations in the political and economic structures. We ask not only what the image of woman was and whether it corresponded to reality, but who created it and what function it served in a larger social setting.

Just as we have begun to reevaluate old sources, we find that we must redefine the categories within which we analyze history. Past politics, for example, that most traditional of all forms of history, appears at first glance to be an almost totally male preserve. On the rare occasions when women did actively participate in politics, historians have tended to perceive them as disruptive. To many observers, the very presence of women in politics provides an index of social decay. This view is rooted in a narrow definition of politics as the overt and recorded activity of officially recognized leaders operating in the public arena. But women rarely have a place in the formal organizations of power, particularly not at its highest levels. When they do, by accident of birth and circumstance, they are "exceptional" women, who managed to survive and flourish in a male world. Historians have been fascinated by these women because of their pseudo-maleness. Thus, they attract special scrutiny for being unnatural: men in women's bodies at best, monsters at worst. In no case are they considered representative of women generically. This is a realistic assessment. The "exceptional" women viewed themselves as atypical; frequently they rejected or ignored contemporaneous efforts to advance women's status. Their lives remain exceptions that prove the rule and do not help us to understand the common experience of women in politics.

Politics more broadly and correctly defined, however, extends beyond the activity of a few dazzling personalities or the agreements made by a handful of leaders. It is a complex set of conflictual power relations between classes, regions, and religious systems struggling for control over scarce resources. Such a conceptual framework greatly expands the nature of the sources we have to draw upon. The letters, diaries, and memoirs of aristocratic and bourgeois women show their intense involvement in the affairs of their family, property, and class. Their strength waxes and wanes in relation to the degree of independent control they exert over property and the size and centralization of the state. This influence can be traced through firsthand reports, changes in family and property law, church history, and women's recorded political activity.

The political expression of peasant and working-class women, like that of all historically inarticulate classes, must be sought in other sources. Absent or underrepresented in formal organizations of power, frequently illiterate, these classes usually are noticed only when they protest. Women's role in rebellion, religious upheavals, or political revolutions can be traced through eyewitness accounts, police records, newspapers, pamphlets and broadsides, minutes of meetings, and organizational records. Women's revolutionary demands included both proposals for change and complaints about the status quo. Interestingly, the latter often reveal important material losses over time, not merely nostalgia for a glorified past. Further, the study of political activities by women in revolutionary situations provides us with a new perspective on the revolutionary process itself. Women's participation in protest movements follows a recurrent pattern. In the early stages of a movement, women are welcomed for their selfless dedication. But at the moment of victory, their enthusiasm is rechanneled from disruptive to stabilizing activities, consigning them once more to the home. Revolutionary men attempting to establish a liberated new order have clung to patriarchal values and traditional domestic arrangements. The social relation between the sexes appears to resist change unless women organize among themselves, even within revolutionary movements.

In the nineteenth century, women began to organize themselves somewhat independently of kin networks. Only then do we see sustained female political activity. This movement began among middle-class women, whose leisure, affluence, and social position permitted them partially to escape the confines of their homes. Beginning with charitable and religious causes, they gradually progressed to more self-oriented activities. This first wave of feminism deserves the attention given it for its major achievements: the expansion of women's education, property-law reform, and the suffrage victory. Yet these accomplishments must also be evaluated in their total historical context. Suffrage, for example, is more important when it is limited and linked to property ownership. It carries less weight in highly developed political systems than in loosely structured, decentralized ones. With massive, bureaucratized parties on the one hand and manipulation by corporate interests on the other, the modern voter lacks the real political power wielded by the landed aristocrats and merchants who selected representatives in nineteenth-century parliaments. At the legislative level, women's voice grows feebler still. The "club" system of parliamentary bargaining remains largely a male preserve and the proportion of female leaders remains insignificant. One might hypothesize that the general expansion of the political base has produced a decline in women's political influence relative to their male counterparts. We do not intend to imply that women have achieved no political gains, but only that we must assess these achievements in context rather than as absolutes. We ask, also, if these gains translate into practical, economic benefits.

A recurrent theme . . . suggests that while formal political action has won major advances, women's lives have been more profoundly affected by structural changes in society. Economic and social institutions appear to develop according to their own dynamic, relatively inaccessible to political manipulation. To discover the sources of change in women's roles and status, we are drawn to the study of the family.

In preindustrial society the most common mode of political activity for women has been family strategy for social mobility, an important nexus between politics and economics. The changing nature of such a nexus is itself a historical problem. Preliterate societies exhibit no clear division between political and economic, public and domestic spheres. "Domestic" activities (involving the home, its space, its members, and its work) were "public" and shared by the entire community. The clan was at once an economic and political entity, whose members shared its wealth and governance on a remarkably egalitarian basis. With the development of private property and political institutions to safeguard it, inequalities developed inside the clan, between families and along sex lines. The development of commercial classes, capitalism, and concomitant changes in production and social relations further widened the gap between public and domestic functions. Responsibilities formerly assumed by the family were surrendered to specialized public institutions. The consolidation of capital wealth by a few eroded the economic and political power of the average family, and women's role within the family declined commensurately. The political significance of the family contracted.

This erosion of women's familial power was paralleled in economic areas as well. In preindustrial society, the major concern of every generation was to preserve, augment, and transmit to future generations family property and status. More fundamentally, the family, often through the efforts of its women, provided its own subsistence. As economic and technological developments transformed society, the structure and functions of the family gradually shifted. The family in industrial society became a non-producing collectivity of consumers, whose major responsibility was to provide emotional security for its members.

In both the producing and consuming forms of the family, women have played an active part. They have contributed to family income, allocated it, transformed it into consumable goods. They have influenced family inheritance and social mobility through birth control, the education of their children, selection of marriage partners for their children, and maintenance of kin networks. These functions, however, are not traceable in official chronicles or codified laws. One source of information on women's role in the family is demographic data, which note changes in age at marriage, criteria for selection of marriage partners, numbers of children born and surviving infancy, methods of birth control from infanticide through contraception, changing family life cycles, and migration statistics. Our best sources for demographic change are recent, since census data were not collected regularly until the nineteenth century. For earlier periods we must research indirect reports like baptismal certificates, hospital and asylum records, indices of nutrition and health such as harvest and butchering records, deeds, wills, tax registers, marriage contracts, and burial records. Using such sources, supplemented by first- or second-person reports, we can trace women's impact on family economy and, conversely, the effect of broader social patterns on women's experiential reality.

The search for women's role in past societies leads us to still other problems when we try to assess women's control over property and over their own labor. The sexual division of labor becomes more exaggerated with the accumulation of property in the hands of a new business elite. Not only does women's work become more distinct from men's, but it changes in a way that reduces women's ability to accumulate property and wield power. We ask therefore: What kind of work have women done? How was it evaluated? How did it fit into the total mode of production? of reproduction? How did women's expectations of work affect mechanization and specialization in specific industries? How did women's work relate to technological innovations, capitalization of manufacturing and trade, and the organization of production?

By focusing on these questions we add a new dimension to the debate on the Industrial Revolution. Although the impact of industrialization on women was uneven and depended on a multitude of variables, it now appears that the Industrial Revolution seriously reduced women's effective participation in production. An overview shows that women often predominate in stagnating industries while modernizing sectors engage men in new skills. If women do enter a new area of manufacturing, they do so at the bottom of its hierarchy. Thus, during the early stages of industrialization, women were eagerly recruited into the work force because their labor was so cheap. But male factory workers steadily replaced women even in the "women's" trades of spinning and weaving. An analysis of the impact of industrialization on women, however, cannot be limited to a study of factory women. Recent scholarship makes it clear that factory work occupied only a tiny fraction of all women. Far more important were changes that occurred in those sectors that traditionally employed large numbers of women: domestic service, agriculture, and the "sweated trades."

A lively debate continues over the ultimate benefits of industrialization for women. Single women, it seems, did enjoy expanded economic opportunities. This, in turn, gave them at least the potential to increase their leverage within their families, save money for their own dowries, and choose husbands more independently. Working-class women generally also gained the opportunity to join together in extrafamilial alliances. Some women mobilized for collective action by establishing their own unions or cooperative societies. Others joined predominantly male unions — although women's low wages made them objects of considerable resentment by male workers. Still other women responded to the appeal of socialism, not only by joining the rank and file but also by participating actively as organizers and intellectuals in the international movement.

These opportunities for working-class single women must be balanced against new difficulties created for married women. Because the workplace moved away from the household and into the factory, married women with children found it nearly impossible to harmonize their domestic duties with gainful employment. Moreover, the scope of women's responsibilities in their households diminished. The wife no longer produced her family's food and clothing but instead purchased it with the wages earned by other members of her family. The caricature of the spendthrift woman arises from this shift in women's functions — as does our contemporary ambivalence about the value of homemaking.

The technological and social changes that swept through nineteenth-century Europe affected the atmosphere and internal politics of the middle-class home. While bourgeois women found themselves increasingly relegated to the domestic sphere, they also discovered new outlets for their energy and idealism. Nowhere is this double trend better illustrated than in the areas of charity and social work. Middle-class women, liberated from the more menial tasks of homemaking, ministered to the larger family of humanity. In so doing they created an escape for themselves and their daughters. In the twentieth century this area of social caring became a state-run occupation whose policies were determined by men. Again, a modernizing influence opened up new opportunities for women in its initial stages and then pushed them out of responsible positions. Yet in the long run, the impact of an expanding public-service sector on middle-class women paralleled the effect of industrialization on working-class women. Both developments provided some women with paid occupations, giving them the possibility of greater bargaining power in family decision making and the option of living independently of the traditional family altogether. However limited, new career options did encourage more permanent employment patterns and sponsored women's adherence to unions and professional associations. The second wave of feminism can be attributed in large measure to this heightened consciousness.

We are interested, however, in assessing the trends of women's work not only in relation to its own linear development and in relation to men's but also in relation to other aspects of women's lives. More questions crowd in: How does change in women's work patterns affect the internal dynamics of their families and their other social behavior and attitudes? Does it affect their wish to bear and care for children? their feelings about sexuality? their relations with each other? the development of their wider abilities and interests?

In the area of reproduction, we see first that as the total economic context changed, so did family economy, the contributions of family members to it, and, therefore, women's life cycles. Thus, in preindustrial times, work and family life were relatively integrated. Production and reproduction meshed, and women's lives suffered little hiatus from childbearing. With the development of the factory system, the home was eventually displaced as the workplace, so work and family life *dis*integrated.

For bourgeois women, the split tended to relegate them to the home, for which there developed a "science of domestic economy" enhanced by the "cult of true womanhood." For working-class women, the split was mirrored in the double burden of wage labor and housework, which could be assumed simultaneously or serially. Typically, the working woman dropped out of the work force during her childbearing years. For both middle- and working-class women, the social ideal now emphasized childrearing over childbearing. This shift from quantity to quality occurred for several reasons. For one, family size decreased with urbanization. With the decline in child labor required by an agricultural society, multitudes of children became liabilities rather than assets — mouths to feed rather than extra hands for work. The spread of public education further limited children's contribution to the family economy. Besides these incentives to reduce family size, more children survived infancy, guaranteeing family continuity with fewer pregnancies.

These demographic changes, plus women's restriction to the home, resulted in major emotional reorientations. As earning became the responsibility of the father, parenting became increasingly the task of the mother. She became the emotional facilitator for her family and the repository and guardian of society's morality. Bourgeois mothers had the time and standard of living to aspire to such a role and gradually the middle-class ideology of motherhood became the norm for the working class. This process was accomplished through various media, including the social work of the very women whose time had been freed by their exclusion from productive work and their own rejection of a purely domestic role. Although

they themselves chose to leave the confines of their homes, these social workers still preached bourgeois values — which included a glorification of the home. Ironically, they became an important factor in the dissemination of the cult of domesticity to the working classes.

Similar contradictions have produced the recent crisis of identity experienced by women. The public assumption of functions that earlier were considered domestic and feminine has deprived the housewife of many traditional responsibilities. As "mother's work" is taken over by institutionalized education, health care, social work, and psychological counseling, women experience diminishing status within the home. Conflict is inevitable. Women who have opted for public roles will view the family as the source of potential oppression for all women; women who choose to remain identified with domestic responsibilities will resent institutional encroachments on their sphere. They will view feminist criticism of the family as endangering their feminine identity and role integrity.

Even more basic is the conflict women find within themselves as they confront their own feelings about these dual sources of identity. Self-doubt is inevitable whichever response women choose. Some will retreat from the problem by entrenching themselves even more firmly within the renewed mystique of homemaking and wifehood — seeking to escape the conflict by reaffirming their belief in their traditional role. These women may join the backlash against feminism. Yet at the same time an increasing number of women and men have begun to question the usefulness of a sexual division of labor and of personality traits. Why at this time have people begun to doubt the age-old stereotypes? Most obviously, the brute strength that traditionally defined masculinity loses its importance as machines assume most tasks requiring heavy labor or warfare. An increasingly managerial society requires socialization and skills once labeled "feminine," such as tact and the ability to empathize with and manipulate others. Whether closing a corporate merger, dealing with protesting workers, or lobbying for legislative proposals, psychological finesse is decisive. Society is forced to define masculinity along more androgynous lines. A similar androgynous movement has resulted from women's struggles to fashion a new identity. Besides learning to value themselves for their feminine attributes, women have adapted traits previously ascribed to men: ambition, competitiveness, and leadership. Even when women enter occupations and professions closely related to traditional female concerns (such as health care, social work, and education) they need "masculine"

detachment and goal orientation in order to succeed. As a result of this integrative process, polarities of masculine and feminine traits dissolve and woman's bifurcated image likewise merges into a single human personality.

The gains of previous struggles — education, suffrage, increased civil equality — have helped to create a new woman, restive with her remaining disabilities and appalled by her historical losses. We, the "new women," are searching for a new identity with freer attitudes toward work, sexuality, family relationships, individual development, and sisterhood. We are trying to create a new social matrix that will allow, even nurture, realization of this identity. In this quest, we need to understand what brought us to this place.

INTERNATIONAL WOMEN'S YEAR
MEDIA GUIDELINES

Recognizing the power of the media to create and reinforce derogatory images of women, the women's movement has long focused its attention on those industries. As early as the mid-1960s, feminists were making concerted efforts to challenge television networks, magazine publishers, newspapers, and others for their advertising and programming. In 1976 President Ford's Commission on International Women's Year presented to him these ten specific guidelines for the media. They were reaffirmed in Houston at the National Women's Conference. Delegates there also pointed out that since change would come only when women were in a position to express their own views of themselves, and since so few women held any power at all in media industries, the media should redouble their efforts to place women in policy-making positions.

1. The media should establish as an ultimate goal the employment of women in policymaking positions in proportion to their

participation in the labor force. The media should make special efforts to employ women who are knowledgeable about and sensitive to women's changing roles.

2. Women in media should be employed at all job levels — and, in accordance with the

Reprinted from *The Bulletin* of the American Society of Newspaper Editors, September 1976.

law, should be paid equally for work of equal value and be given equal opportunity for training and promotion.

3. The present definition of news should be expanded to include more coverage of women's activities, locally, nationally, and internationally. In addition, general news stories should be reported to show their effect on women. For example, the impact of foreign aid on women in recipient countries is often overlooked, as is the effect of public transportation on women's mobility, safety, and ability to take jobs.

4. The media should make special, sustained efforts to seek out news of women. Women now figure in less than 10 percent of the stories currently defined as news.

5. Placement of news should be decided by subject matter, not by sex. The practice of segregating material thought to be of interest only to women into certain sections of a newspaper or broadcast implies that news of women is not real news. However, it is important to recognize and offset an alarming trend wherein such news, when no longer segregated, is not covered at all. Wherever news of women is placed, it should be treated with the same dignity, scope, and accuracy as is news of men. Women's activities should not be located in the last 30–60 seconds of a broadcast or used as fillers in certain sections or back pages of a newspaper or magazine.

6. Women's bodies should not be used in an exploitive way to add irrelevant sexual interest in any medium. This includes news and feature coverage by both the press and television, movie and movie promotion, "skin" magazines, and advertising messages of all sorts. The public violation of a woman's physical privacy tends to violate the individual integrity of all women.

7. The presentation of personal details when irrelevant to a story — sex, sexual preference, age, marital status, physical appearance, dress, religious or political orientation — should be eliminated for both women and men.

8. It is to be hoped that one day all titles will be unnecessary. But in the meantime, a person's right to determine her (or his) own title should be respected without slurs or innuendoes. If men are called Doctor or Reverend, the same titles should be used for women. And a woman should be able to choose Ms., Miss, or Mrs.

9. Gender designations are a rapidly changing area of the language, and a decision to use or not to use a specific word should be subject to periodic review. Terms incorporating gender reference should be avoided. Use firefighter instead of fireman, business executive instead of businessman, letter carrier instead of mailman. In addition, women from at least the age of 16, should be called women, not girls. And at no time should a female be referred to as "broad," "chick," or the like.

10. Women's activities and organizations should be treated with the same respect accorded men's activities and organizations. The women's movement should be reported as seriously as any other civil rights movement; it should not be made fun of, ridiculed, or belittled. Just as the terms "black libbers" or "Palestine libbers" are not used, the term "women's libbers" should not be used. Just as jokes at the expense of blacks are no longer made, jokes should not be made at women's expense. The news of women should not be sensationalized. Too often news media have reported conflict among women and ignored unity. Coverage of women's conferences is often limited solely to so-called "splits" or fights. These same disputes at conferences attended by men would be considered serious policy debates.

THE SYMBOLIC ANNIHILATION OF WOMEN
BY THE MASS MEDIA

GAYE TUCHMAN

Sociologist Gaye Tuchman has studied at the State University of New York at Buffalo and at Brandeis University and has taught at Queens College, Columbia University, and the New School for Social Research in New York. She has written several papers on the sociology of knowledge, with particular reference to the mass media and TV news, and she has done considerable work in the media's treatment of sexual stereotyping. In addition to *Hearth and Home* (1978), she has edited *The TV Establishment: Programming for Power and Profit* (1974) and is the author of *Making News: A Study in the Construction of Reality* (1978).

Here Tuchman shows in concrete detail how women are "erased" from view by media treatment. So far as television is concerned, women "don't count for much"; in magazines women are depicted as creatures whose identities rest on their male relationships; and even in the news, women are tolerated at best. Tuchman's conclusion: Women are symbolically annihilated in the public view by being ignored or trivialized.

Television: Symbolic Annihilation of Women

To say television is the dominant medium in American life is a vast understatement. In the average American household, television sets are turned on more than six hours each winter day. More American homes have television sets than have private bathrooms, according to the 1970 census. Ninety-six percent of all American homes are equipped with television, and most have more than one set. As Sprafkin and Liebert note, by the time an American child is fifteen years old, she has watched more hours of television than she has spent in the classroom. And since she continues watching as she grows older, the amount of time spent in school can never hope to equal the time invested viewing television.

The use of television by children is en-couraged because of parental use. The average adult spends five hours a day with the mass media, almost as much time as she or he spends at work. Of these five hours, four are occupied by the electronic media (radio and television). The other hour is taken up with reading newspapers, magazines, and books. Television consumes forty percent of the leisure time of adult Americans. To be sure, despite increased economic concentration there are still 1,741 daily newspapers in this country. And studies indicate that 63,353,000 papers are sold each day. But the nation's nine hundred-odd television stations reach millions more on a daily basis. In 1976, over seventy-five million people watched one event via television, football's annual Super Bowl spectacular (Hirsch, 1978); and when "All in the Family" first appeared on Saturday night, it had a weekly audience of over 100,000,000, more than half the people in the nation. Each year, Americans spend trillions of hours watching television.

What are the portrayals of women to which Americans are exposed during these long hours? What can the preschool girl and the school girl learn about being and becoming a woman?

From children's shows to commercials to prime-time adventures and situation comedies, television proclaims that women don't count for much. They are underrepresented in television's fictional life — they are "symbolically annihilated." From 1954, the date of the earliest systematic analysis of television's content, through 1975, researchers have found that males dominated the television screen. With the exception of soap operas where men make up a "mere majority" of the fictional population, television has shown and continues to show two men for every woman. Figure 1 indicates that proportion has been relatively constant. The little variation that exists, occurs between types of programs. In 1952 sixty-eight percent of the characters in prime-time drama were male. In 1973, seventy-four percent of those characters were male. Women were concentrated in comedies where men make up "only" sixty percent of the fictional world. Children's cartoons include even fewer women or female characters (such as anthropomorphized foxes or pussycats) than adult's prime-time programs do. The paucity of women on American television tells viewers that women don't matter much in American society.

That message is reinforced by the treatment of those women who do appear on the television screen. As seen in Figure 2, when television shows reveal someone's occupation, the worker is most likely to be male. Someone might object that the pattern is inevitable, because men constitute a larger share of the pool of people who can be professionals. But that objection is invalidated by the evidence presented by soap operas, where women are more numerous. But the invariant pattern holds there too, despite the fact that men have been found to be only about fifty percent of the characters on the "soaps" (see Downing, 1974; Katzman, 1972).

Additionally, those few working women included in television plots are symbolically denigrated by being portrayed as incompetent or as inferior to male workers. Pepper, the "Policewoman" on the show of the same name (Angie Dickinson) is continually rescued from dire and deadly situations by her male colleagues. Soap operas provide even more powerful evidence for the portrayal of women as incompetents and inferiors. Although Turow (1974) finds that soap operas present the most favorable image of female workers, there too they are subservient to competent men. On "The Doctors," surgical procedures are performed by male physicians, and although the female M.D.'s are said to be competent at their work, they are primarily shown pulling case histories from file cabinets or filling out forms. On other soap operas, male lawyers try cases and female lawyers research briefs for them. More generally, women do not appear in the same professions as men: men are doctors, women, nurses; men are lawyers, women, secretaries; men work in corporations, women tend boutiques.

The portrayal of incompetence extends from denigration through victimization and trivialization. When television women are involved in violence, unlike males, they are more likely to be victims than aggressors (Gerbner, 1972a). Equally important, the pattern of women's involvement with television violence reveals approval of married women and condemnation of single and working women. As Gerbner demonstrates, single women are more likely to be victims of violence than married women, and working women are more likely to be villains than housewives. Conversely, married women who do not work for money outside the home are most likely to escape television's mayhem and to be treated sympathetically.

Figure 1 Percentage of males in TV programs, 1952–1974.

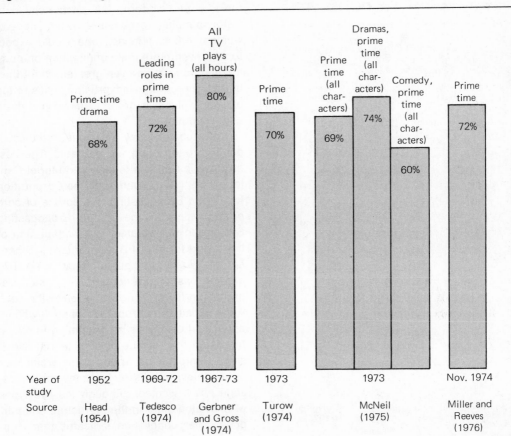

Year of study	1952	1969-72	1967-73	1973	1973		Nov. 1974
Source	Head (1954)	Tedesco (1974)	Gerbner and Gross (1974)	Turow (1974)	McNeil (1975)		Miller and Reeves (1976)

More generally, television most approves those women who are presented in a sexual context or within a romantic or family role (Gerbner, 1972a; cf. Liebert *et al.*, 1973). Two out of three television-women are married, were married, or are engaged to be married. By way of contrast, most television men are single and have always been single. Also, men are seen outside the home and women within it, but even here, one finds trivialization of women's role within the home.

According to sociological analyses of traditional sex roles (such as Parsons, 1949), men are "instrumental" leaders, active workers and decision makers outside the home; women are "affective" or emotional leaders in solving personal problems within the home. But television trivializes women in their traditional role by assigning this task to men too. The nation's soap operas deal with the personal and emotional, yet Turow finds that on the soap operas, the male sex is so dominant that men also lead the way to the solution of emotional problems. In sum, following the reasoning of the reflection hypothesis, we may tentatively conclude

Figure 2 Percentage of males among those portrayed as employed on TV, 1963–1973.

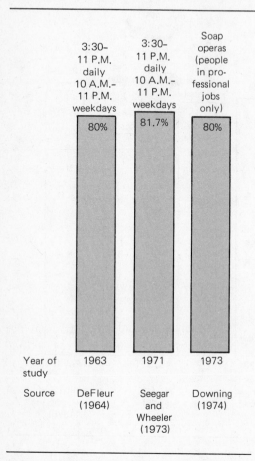

	3:30–11 P.M. daily 10 A.M.–11 P.M. weekdays	3:30–11 P.M. daily 10 A.M.–11 P.M. weekdays	Soap operas (people in professional jobs only)
	80%	81.7%	80%
Year of study	1963	1971	1973
Source	DeFleur (1964)	Seegar and Wheeler (1973)	Downing (1974)

that for commercial reasons (building audiences to sell to advertisers) network television engages in the symbolic annihilation of women.

Two additional tests of this tentative conclusion are possible. One examines noncommercial American television; the other analyzes the portrayal of women in television commercials. If the commercial structure of television is mainly responsible for the symbolic annihilation of women, one would expect to find more women on public

than on commercial television. Conversely if the structure of corporate commercial television is mainly responsible for the image of women that is telecast, one would expect to find even more male domination on commercial ads. To an even greater extent than is true of programs, advertising seeks to tap existing values in order to move people to buy a product.

Unfortunately, few systematic studies of public broadcasting are available. The best of these is Caroline Isber's and Muriel Cantor's work (1975), funded by the Corporation for Public Broadcasting, the source of core programming in the Public Broadcasting System. In this volume, in an adaptation of her report for the CPB, Cantor asks, "Where are the women in public television?" Her answer, based on a content analysis of programming is "in front of the television set." Although a higher proportion of adult women appear on children's programming in public television than is true of commercial television, Cantor finds "both commercial and public television disseminate the same message about women, although the two types of television differ in their structure and purpose." Her conclusion indicates that commercialism is not solely responsible for television's symbolic annihilation of women and its portrayal of stereotyped sex roles. Rather, television captures societal ideas even when programming is partially divorced from the profit motive.

Male domination has not been measured as directly for television commercials, the other kind of televised image that may be used to test the reflection hypothesis. Since so many of the advertised products are directed toward women, one could not expect to find women neglected by commercials. Given the sex roles commercials play upon, it would be bad business to show two women discussing the relative merits of power lawn mowers or two men chatting about waxy buildup on a kitchen floor. However, two indirect measures of male dominance are possible: (1) the number of commercials in which only men or only women appear; and (2) the use of males and females in voice-overs. (A "voice-over" is an unseen person speaking about a product while an image is shown on the television screen; an unseen person proclaims "two out of three doctors recommend" or "on sale now at your local. . . .")

On the first indirect measure, all-male or all-female commercials, the findings are unanimous. Schuetz and Sprafkin (1978), Silverstein and Silverstein (1974) and Bardwick and Schumann (1967), find a ratio of almost three all-male ads to each all-female ad. The second indirect measure, the use of voice-overs in commercials, presents more compelling evidence for the acceptance of the reflection hypothesis. Echoing the findings of others, Dominick and Rauch (1972) report that of 946 ads with voice-overs, "only six percent used a female voice; a male voice was heard on eighty-seven percent." The remainder use one male and one female voice.

The commercials themselves strongly encourage sex-role stereotypes. Although research findings are not strictly comparable to those on television programs because of the dissimilar "plots," the portrayals of women are even more limited than those presented on television dramas and comedies. Linda Busby (1975) summarized the findings of four major studies of television ads. In one study,

- 37.5% of the ads showed women as men's domestic adjuncts
- 33.9% showed women as dependent on men
- 24.3% showed women as submissive
- 16.7% showed women as sex objects
- 17.1% showed women as unintelligent
- 42.6% showed women as household functionaries.

Busby's summary of Dominick and Rauch's work reveals a similar concentration of women as homemakers rather than as active members of the labor force:

- Women were seven times more likely to appear in ads for personal hygiene products than not to appear [in those ads]
- 75% of all ads using females were for products found in the kitchen or in the bathroom
- 38% of all females in the television ads were shown inside the home, compared to 14% of the males
- Men were significantly more likely to be shown outdoors or in business settings than were women
- Twice as many women were shown with children [than] were men
- 56% of the women in the ads were judged to be [only] housewives
- 43% different occupations were coded for men, 18 for women.

As Busby notes, reviews of the major studies of ads (such as Courtney and Whipple, 1974) emphasize their strong "face validity" (the result of real patterns rather than any bias produced by researchers' methods), although the studies use different coding categories and some of the researchers were avowed feminist activists.

In sum, then, analyses of television commercials support the reflection hypothesis. In voice-overs and one-sex (all male or all female) ads, commercials neglect or rigidly stereotype women. In their portrayal of women, the ads banish females to the role of housewife, mother, homemaker, and sex object, limiting the roles women may play in society.

What can the preschool girl, the school girl, the adolescent female and the woman learn about a woman's role by watching television? The answer is simple. Women are not important in American society, except *perhaps* within the home. And even within the home, men know best, as the dominance of male advice on soap operas and the use of male voice-overs for female products, suggests. To be a woman is to have a limited life divorced from the economic productivity of the labor force.

Women's Magazines: Marry, Don't Work

As the American girl grows to womanhood, she, like her counterpart elsewhere in industrialized nations, has magazines available designed especially for her use. Some, like *Seventeen,* whose readers tend to be young adolescents, instruct on contemporary fashions and dating styles. Others, like *Cosmopolitan* and *Redbook,* teach about survival as a young woman — whether as a single woman hunting a mate in the city or a young married coping with hearth and home.

This section reviews portrayals of sex roles in women's magazines, seeking to learn how often they too promulgate stereotypes about the role their female readers may take — how much they too engage in the symbolic annihilation of women by limiting and trivializing them. Unfortunately, our analyses of images of women in magazines cannot be as extensive as our discussion of television. Because of researchers' past neglect of women's issues and problems, few published materials are available for review.

Like the television programs just discussed, from the earliest content analyses of magazine fiction (Johns-Heine and Gerth, 1949) to analyses of magazine fiction published in the early 1970s, researchers have found an emphasis on hearth and home and a denigration of the working woman. The ideal woman, according to these magazines, is passive and dependent. Her fate and her happiness rest with a man, not with partici-

pation in the labor force. There are two exceptions to this generalization: (1) The female characters in magazines aimed at working-class women are a bit more spirited than their middle-class sisters. (2) In the mid-1970s, middle-class magazines seemed less hostile toward working women. Using the reflection hypothesis, particularly its emphasis upon attracting readers to sell advertisements, we will seek to explain the general rule and these interesting exceptions to it.

Like other media, women's magazines are interested in building their audience or readership. For a magazine, attracting more readers is *indirectly* profitable. Each additional reader does not increase the magazine's profit margin by buying a copy or taking out a subscription, because the cost of publication and distribution per copy far exceeds the price of the individual copy — whether it is purchased on the newsstand, in a supermarket, or through subscription. Instead a magazine realizes its profit by selling advertisements and charging its advertisers a rate adjusted to its known circulation. Appealing to advertisers, the magazine specifies known demographic characteristics of its readership. For instance, a magazine may inform the manufacturer of a product intended for housewives that a vast proportion of its readership are homemakers, while another magazine may appeal to the producer of merchandise for young working women by lauding its readership as members of that target group. Women's magazines differentiate themselves from one another by specifying their intended readers, as well as the size of their mass circulation. Additionally, they all compete with other media to draw advertisers. (For example, *Life* and *Look* folded because their advertisers could reach a larger group of potential buyers at a lower price per person through television commercials.) Both daytime television and women's magazines present potential advertisers with particularly appealing audiences, because women are the primary purchasers of goods intended for the home.

Historically, middle-class women have been less likely to be members of the labor force than lower-class women. At the turn of the century, those married women who worked were invariably from working-class families that required an additional income to assure adequate food, clothing, and shelter (Oppenheimer, 1970). The importance of this economic impetus for working is indicated by the general adherence of working-class families to more traditional definitions of male and female sex roles (Rubin, 1976). Although middle-class families subscribe to a more flexible ideology of sex roles than working-class families, both groups of women tend to insist that the man should be the breadwinner. The fiction in women's magazines reflects this ideology.

Particularly in middle-class magazines, fiction depicts women "as creatures ... defined by the men in their lives" (Franzwa, 1974a, p. 106; see also Franzwa, 1974b, 1975). Studying a random sample of issues of *Ladies' Home Journal, McCall's,* and *Good Housekeeping* between the years 1940 and 1970, Helen Franzwa found four roles for women: "single and looking for a husband, housewife-mother, spinster, and widowed or divorced — soon to remarry." All the women were defined by the men in their lives, or by their absence. Flora (1971) confirms this finding in her study of middle-class (*Redbook* and *Cosmopolitan*) and working-class (*True Story* and *Modern Romances*) fiction. Female dependence and passivity are lauded; on the rare occasions that male dependence is portrayed, it is seen as undesirable.

As might be expected of characterizations that define women in terms of men, American magazine fiction denigrates the working woman. Franzwa says that work is shown to play "a distinctly secondary part in women's lives. When work is portrayed as important to them, there is a concomitant disintegration of their lives" (1974a, p. 106). Of the 155 major female characters depicted in Franzwa's sample of magazine stories, only 65 or forty-one percent were employed outside the home. Seven of the 65 held high-status positions. Of these seven, only two were married. Three others were "spinsters" whose "failure to marry was of far greater importance to the story-line than their apparent success in their careers." One single woman with a high status career was lauded: She gave up her career to marry.

From 1940 through 1950, Franzwa found, working mothers and working wives were condemned. Instead, the magazines emphasized that husbands should support their spouses. One story summary symbolizes the magazines' viewpoint: "In a 1940 story, a young couple realized that they couldn't live on his salary. She offered to work; he replied, 'I don't think that's so good. I know some fellows whose wives work and they might just as well not be married.'" Magazines after 1950 are even less positive about work. In 1955, 1960, 1965, and 1970 not one married woman who worked appeared in the stories Franzwa sampled. (Franzwa selected stories from magazines using five-year intervals to enhance the possibility of finding changes.)

Since middle-class American wives are less likely to be employed than their working-class counterparts, this finding makes sociological sense. Editors and writers may believe that readers of middle-class magazines, who are less likely to be employed, are also more likely to buy magazines approving this life-style. More likely to work and to be in families either economically insecure or facing downward mobility, working-class women might be expected to applaud effective women. For them, female dependence might be an undesirable trait. Their magazines could be expected to cater to such preferences, especially since those preferences flow from the readers' life situations. Such, indeed, are Flora's findings, presented in Table 1.

However, this pattern does not mean that the literature for the working-class woman avoids defining women in terms of men. All the women in middle-class magazines dropped from the labor force when they had a man present; only six percent of the women in the working-class fiction continued to work when they had a man and children. And Flora explained that for both groups "The plot of the majority of stories centered upon the female achieving the proper dependent status, either by marrying or manipulating existing dependency relationships to reaffirm the heroine's subordinate position. The male support — monetary, social, and psychological — which the heroine gains was generally seen as well worth any independence or selfhood given up in the process" (1971, p. 441).

Such differences as do exist between working-class and middle-class magazines remain interesting, though. For they indicate how much more the women's magazines may be responsive to their audience than television can be. Because it is the dominant mass medium, television is designed to appeal to hundreds of millions of people. In 1970, the circulation of *True Story* was "only" 5,347,000 and of *Redbook,* a "mere" 8,173,000. Drawing a smaller audience and by definition, one more specialized, the women's magazines can be more responsive to changes in the position of women in American society. If a magazine believes its audience is changing, it may alter the content to maintain its readership. The contradictions inherent in being women's magazines may free them to respond to change.

A woman's magazine is sex-typed in a way that is not true of men's magazines (Davis, 1976). *Esquire* and *Playboy* are for men, but the content of these magazines, is, broadly speaking, American culture. Both men's magazines feature stories by major American writers, directed toward all sophisticated Americans, not merely to men. Both feature articles on the state of male culture as American culture or of male politics as American politics. Women's magazines are designed in opposition to these "male magazines." For instance, "sports" are women's sports or news of women breaking into "men's sports." A clear distinction is drawn between what is "male" and what is "female."

Paradoxically, though, this very limitation can be turned to an advantage. Addressing women, women's magazines may suppose that some in their audience are concerned about changes in the status of women and the greater participation of women in the labor force. As early as 1966, before the growth of the modern women's movement, women who were graduated from high school or college assumed they would work until the birth of their first child. Clarke and Esposito (1966) found that magazines published in the 1950s and addressed to these women (*Glamour, Mademoiselle,* and *Cosmopolitan*) stressed the joys of achievement and power when describing working roles for women and identifying desirable jobs. Magazines addressed to working women were optimistic about these women's ability to combine work and home, a message that women who felt that they should or must work would be receptive to. Indeed, in 1958 Marya and David Hatch criticized *Mademoiselle, Glamour,* and *Charm* as "unduly optimistic" in their "evaluation of physical and emotional strains upon working women." Combining work and family responsibilities may be very difficult, particularly

Table 1 Female dependence and ineffectuality by class, by percentage of stories*

	Female dependence			Female ineffectuality		
	Undesirable	Desirable	Neutral	Undesirable	Desirable	Neutral
Working class	22	30	48	38	4	58
Middle class	18	51	31	18	33	49
Total	20	41	40	28	19	53

* Adapted from Flora (1971).

in working-class homes, since working-class husbands refuse to help with housework (Rubin, 1976). But even working-class women prefer work outside the home to housework (Rubin, 1976, Vanek, forthcoming) since it broadens their horizons. Wanting to please and to attract a special audience of working women, magazine editors and writers may be freed to be somewhat responsive to new conditions, even as these same writers and editors feature stereotyped sex roles in other sections of their magazines.

Additional evidence of the albeit limited responsiveness of women's magazines to the changing status of women in the labor force is provided by their treatment of sex-role stereotypes since the advent of the women's movement. The modern women's movement is usually said to begin in the mid-1960s with the founding of the National Organization for Women. The date is of consequence for the study of sex roles in women's magazines because of Betty Friedan's involvement in the National Organization for Women. Her book, *The Feminine Mystique*, published in 1963, provided much of the ideology for the young movement. And, its analysis of sexism ("the problem with no name") was based in part on an analysis of the portrayal of sex roles in women's magazines. In an undated manuscript cited in Busby (1975), Stolz and her colleagues compared the image of women in magazines be-

fore and after the advent of the women's movement. Like others, they found no changes between 1940 and 1972. However, a time lag ("culture lag") is probably operating since nonmaterial conditions (ideas and attitudes) change more slowly than do material conditions (such as participation in the labor force).

Several very recent studies affirm that women's magazines may be introducing new conceptions of women's sex roles that are more conducive to supporting the increased participation of women in the labor force. Butler and Paisley* note that at the instigation of an editor of *Redbook,* twenty-eight women's magazines published articles on the arguments for and against the Equal Rights Amendment, a constitutional change prompted by the women's movement and the increased participation of women in the labor force. Franzwa's impression of the women's magazines she had analyzed earlier is that they revealed more sympathy with working women in 1975.† Sheila Silver (1976) indicates that a "gentle support" for the aims of the women's movement and a "quiet concern" for working women may now be found in *McCall's.* By the terms "gentle support" and "quiet concern," she

* Matilda Butler and William Paisley. Personal communication, Fall 1976.

† 1976, personal communication.

means to indicate that the magazine approves equal pay for equal work and other movement aims, although it does not approve of the women's movement itself. That magazine and others, such as the *Ladies' Home Journal,* continue to concentrate upon helping women as housewives: They still provide advice on hearth and home. The women's magazines continue to assume that every woman will marry, bear children and "make a home." They do not assume that every woman will work some time in her life.

In sum, the image of women in the women's magazines is more responsive to change than is television's symbolic annihilation and rigid typecasting of women. The sex roles presented are less stereotyped, but a woman's role is still limited. A female child is always an eventual mother, not a future productive participant in the labor force.

Newspapers and Women: Food, Fashion, and Society

Following the argument developed thus far, one might expect the nation's newspapers to be even more responsive than magazines to the changing status of women in American society. With smaller circulations than the magazines and supposedly more responsive to a local population rather than a national one, newspapers might cater to their female readers in order to maintain or even increase the base of their circulation. Such an expectation seems particularly plausible because contemporary newspapers face increased costs and are suffering from the economic competition of the electronic media. But this expectation flies in the face of the actual organization of newswork, for newspapers are *not, strictly speaking, local media.* Rather, local newspapers' dependence upon national news services is

sufficiently great for them to be considered *components of a national medium,* designed to appeal to as many Americans as possible. As we have just seen, such a design encourages a rigid treatment of sex roles. An historical review of newspapers' treatment of news about women makes this result clearer.

Unlike the women's magazines, newspapers seek to appeal to an entire family. Historically, they have sought to attract female readers by treating them as a specialized audience, given attention in a segregated women's page, an autonomous or semi-autonomous department whose mandate precludes coverage of the "hard news" of the day. Although women's magazines have been published in the United States since the early nineteenth century, it took the newspaper circulation wars of the 1880s to produce the notion of "women's news." At that time, it appeared that every man who would buy a newspaper was already doing so. To build circulation by robbing each other of readers and attracting new readers, newspapers hired female reporters to write about society and fashion, as well as to expand "news" to include sports and comic strips. Items of potential interest to women were placed near advertisements of goods that women might purchase for their families. The origin of women's news reveals how long newspapers have traditionally defined women's interests as different from men's and how items of concern to women have become non-news, almost oddities. That view continues today. The budget for women's pages rarely provides for updating those pages from edition to edition, as is done for the general news, sports, and financial pages, sections held to be of interest to men. Finally, as is true of other departments as well, women's page budgets are sufficiently restricted to force that department's dependence upon the wire services.

During the nineteenth century's circulation wars, newspapers banded into cooperative services intended to decrease the costs of total coverage for each participating newspaper. A reporter would cover a story for newspapers in different cities, decreasing the need for scattered newspapers to maintain extensive bureaus in a variety of cities, such as Washington and New York. Furthermore, a newspaper in a small out-of-the-way town could be requested to share its story about an important event with newspapers from distant places that would not, under normal circumstances, have a reporter on hand. Aside from playing a limited role in the development of journalistic objectivity (Schudson, 1976), since stories were designed to meet the political-editorial requirements of diverse news organizations, the news services encouraged the expansion of definitions of news. Some provided features, such as comics and crossword puzzles. Others provided sports items, financial stories, and features of concern to women, as well as "hard news." Sometimes the women's items were scandalous revelations of the activities of "Society." More often, they were advice for the homemaker, such as recipes and articles about rearing children. In this century, syndicated and wire-service features include gossip columns about the celebrated and the notorious and advice to the lovelorn, such as that fictionalized in Nathanael West's *Miss Lonelyhearts* or that represented by "Dear Abby."

For women's pages, items like these represent more than an economic investment purchased by a newspaper on behalf of its women's department. They are also an investment of space in the paper. Expected by readers to appear on a Monday, the column inches set aside for advice or gossip cannot be withdrawn for news of the women's movement. Similarly, it may be difficult to turn aside essentially prepaid feature stories about clothing and fashions supplied by the Associated Press or some other news syndicate in order to hire additional women's page staff interested in covering the changing status of women in American society. Commitments like these "nationalize" the local media, because the news syndicate or wire service reaches virtually every daily newspaper in the United States. Because the wire services *as businesses* are necessarily committed to pleasing all (or as many as possible) of their subscribing newspapers, they must shrink from advocating vast social changes. As in the case of television, what goes in New York may not go in Peoria, Illinois or Norman, Oklahoma. National in scope, syndicated and wire-service items for the women's pages must seek an American common denominator. For the sex stereotyping of the women's pages to cease, the leadership of the Associated Press and the syndicates would have to be convinced that most of their subscribing papers wanted a different kind of story for their women's pages. Only then, it seems safe to say, would the papers serviced by the syndicates run the kinds of news about changes in the status of women that may be found in the *New York Times* and the *Los Angeles Times,* whose women's pages develop their own stories through independent staffs.

For now, a characterization of women's pages provided by Lindsay Van Gelder (1974) seems apt. She speculates thus: Suppose a Martian came to earth and sought to learn about American culture by reading the women's pages. Bombarded by pictures of wedding dresses, the Martian might suppose that American women marry at least once a week. After all, a Martian might reason that newspapers and their women's pages reflect daily life. That view, we might add, would seem justified by the women's pages' intense involvement with the social life of the upper class, because upper-class power is a daily aspect of American life. Women's pages feed upon the parties, marriages, engagements, and clothing and food preferences of the wealthy and the celebrated. In this, like newspapers in general (Lazarsfeld and Merton, 1948), the women's pages encourage all citizens to emulate the upper class and to chase after positions of high status and institutionalized importance.

Newspapers' very emphasis upon established institutions and those with institutionalized power may account in part for their denigration of women and the women's movement (Morris, 1974). Most information in the general sections of newspapers concerns people in power, and newspapers justify this emphasis by stressing that such people work in or head societal institutions that regulate social intercourse. But communications researchers view the matter somewhat differently. They argue that newspapers exercise social control: By telling stories about such people, newspapers lend status to approved institutions and chastise lawbreakers. Historically, those few women mentioned in the general news pages belonged to the powerful groups in society. Gladys Engel Lang suggests "the most admired woman" list probably reflects the publicity given to specific women. They are mainly wives of the powerful, celebrities and stars, and the few women who are heads of state. But women are mainly seen as the consorts of famous men, not as subjects of political and social concern in their own right.

This situation appears to be changing. Once ignored or ridiculed (Morris, 1974), the women's movement has received increasing coverage as it has passed through the stages characteristic of any social movement. As the women's movement became sufficiently routinized to open offices with normal business hours, some newspapers established a "women's movement beat" that required a reporter to provide at least periodic coverage of new developments. When increased legitimation brought more volunteers and more funds to wage successful law suits against major corporations and to lobby for the introduction of new laws, newspapers concerned with major institutions were forced to cover those topics. In turn, these successes increased the movement's legitimation. Legitimation also brought support of sympathizers within other organizations who were not movement members (Carden, 1973). Reporters having those other organizations as their beats are being forced to write about the ideas of the women's movement and women's changing status. For instance, the position of women and minorities in the labor force is becoming a required topic for labor reporters and those who write about changing personnel in the corporate world.

On the whole, though, despite coverage of women forcibly induced by the legitimation of the women's movement, newspapers continue to view women in the news as occasional oddities that must be tolerated. Attention to women is segregated and found on the women's page. As a recent survey of women's pages demonstrates (Guenin, 1975), most women's pages continue to cater to a traditional view of women's interests. They emphasize home and family, only occasionally introducing items about women at work. And those items are more likely to concern methods of coping with home and office tasks than they are with highlighting problems of sex discrimination and what the modern women's movement has done in combatting it. Like the television industry, appealing to a common denominator encourages newspapers to engage in the symbolic annihilation of women by ignoring women at work and trivializing women through banishment to hearth and home.

References

Bardwick, Judith and Suzanne Schumann. 1967. "Portrait of American Men and Women in TV Commercials." *Psychology.* 4(4):18–23.

Busby, Linda J. 1975. "Sex-role research on the mass media." *Journal of Communication.* 25(4):107–31.

Carden, Maren Lockwood. 1973. *The New Feminist Movement.* New York: Russel Sage.

Clarke, P. and V. Esposito. 1966. "A study of occupational advice for women in magazines." *Journalism Quarterly.* 43:477–85.

Courtney, A. E. and T. W. Whipple. 1974. "Women in TV commercials." *Journal of Communication.* 24(2):110–18.

Davis, Margaret. 1976. "The *Ladies' Home Journal* and *Esquire:* A comparison." Unpublished manuscript. Stanford University, Dept. of Sociology.

DeFleur, Melvin L. 1964. "Occupational roles as portrayed on television." *Public Opinion Quarterly.* 28(Spring):57–74.

Dominick, Joseph and Gail Rauch. 1972. "The image of women in network TV commercials." *Journal of Broadcasting.* 16(3):259–65.

Downing, Mildred. 1974. "Heroine of the daytime serial." *Journal of Communication.* 24(2):130–37.

Flora, Cornelia. 1971. "The passive female: Her comparative image by class and culture in women's magazine fiction." *Journal of Marriage and the Family.* 33(August):435–44.

Franzwa, Helen. 1974a. "Working women in fact and fiction." *Journal of Communication.* 24(2):104–9.

————. 1974b. "Pronatalism in women's magazine fiction." In Ellen Peale and Judith Senderowitz (eds.), *Pronatalism: The Myth of Motherhood and Apple Pie.* New York: T. Y. Crowell, pp. 68–77.

————. 1975. "Female roles in women's magazine fiction, 1940–1970." In R. K. Unger and F. L. Denmark (eds.), *Woman: Dependent or Independent Variable.* New York: Psychological Dimensions, pp. 42–53.

Gerbner, George. 1972a. "Violence in television drama: Trends and symbolic functions." In G. A. Comstock and E. A. Rubinstein (eds.), *Media Content and Control.* Television and Social Behavior, vol. 1. Washington, D.C.: U.S. Government Printing Office, pp. 28–187.

————. 1972b. "Communications and social environment." *Scientific American.* 227(3):153–60.

————, and Larry Gross. 1974a. "Cultural indicators: The social reality of television drama." Unpublished manuscript. Annenberg School of Communications, University of Pennsylvania.

————, with Michael F. Eleey, Nancy Tedesco, and Suzanne Jeffries-Fox. 1974b. "Violence profile no. 6: Trends in network television drama and viewer conception of social reality, 1967–1973." Unpublished research report. Annenberg School of Communications, University of Pennsylvania.

Guenin, Zena B. 1975. "Women's pages in contemporary newspapers: Missing out on contemporary content." *Journalism Quarterly.* 52(Spring):66–69, 75.

Hatch, Marya G. and David L. Hatch. 1958. "Problems of married and working women as presented by three popular working women's magazines." *Social Forces.* 37:148–53.

Head, Sydney W. 1954. "Content analysis of television drama programs." *Quarterly of Film, Radio and Television.* 9:175–94.

Hirsch, Paul. 1978. "Television as a national medium: Its cultural and political role in American society." In David Street (ed.), *Handbook of Urban Life.* San Francisco: Jossey-Bass.

Isber, Caroline and Muriel Cantor. 1975. *Report of the Task Force on Women in Public Broadcasting.* Washington: Corporation for Public Broadcasting.

Johns-Heine, P. and H. Gerth. 1949. "Values in mass periodical fiction, 1921–1940." *Public Opinion Quarterly.* 13(Spring):105–13.

Katzman, N. 1972. "Television soap operas: What's been going on anyway?" *Public Opinion Quarterly.* 35:200–12.

Lazarsfeld, Paul F. and Robert K. Merton. 1948. "Mass communication, popular taste and organized social action." In L. Bryson (ed.), *The Communication of Ideas.* New York: Harper Brothers, pp. 95–118.

Liebert, R. M., J. M. Neale, and E. S. Davidson. 1973. *The Early Window: Effects of Television on Children and Youth.* New York: Pergamon.

McNeil, Jean C. 1975. "Feminism, femininity, and the television series: A content analysis." *Journal of Broadcasting.* 19:259–69.

Miller, M. Mark and Byron Reeves. 1976. "Dramatic TV content and children's sex-role stereotypes." *Journal of Broadcasting.* 20(1):35–50.

Morris, Monica B. 1974. "The public definition of a social movement: Women's liberation." *Sociology and Social Research.* 57:526–43.

Oppenheimer, Valerie Kincaid. 1970. *The Female Labor Force in the United States: Demographic and Economic Factors Governing Its Growth and Changing Composition.* Population Monograph Series No. 5. Berkeley: University of California, Institute of International Studies.

Parsons, Talcott. 1949. "Age and sex in the social structure of the United States." *Essays in Sociological Theory.* New York: The Free Press.

Rubin, Lillian. 1976. *Worlds of Pain. Life in the Working-Class Family.* New York: Basic Books.

Schudson, Michael. 1976. "Origins of the ideal of objectivity in the professions: Studies in the history of American journalism and American law, 1830–1940." Ph.D. dissertation. Harvard University, Cambridge, Mass.

Shuetz, Stephen and Joyce N. Sprafkin. 1978. "Spot messages appearing within Saturday morning television programs." In Tuchman et al. (eds.), *Hearth and Home: Images of Women in Mass Media.* New York: Oxford University Press.

Seegar, J. F. and P. Wheeler. 1973. "World of work on TV: Ethnic and sex representation in TV drama." *Journal of Broadcasting.* 17:210–14.

Silver, Sheila. 1976. "Then and now — content analysis of *McCall's* magazine." Paper presented at the annual meetings of Association for Education in Journalism. College Park, Maryland, August.

Silverstein, Arthur Jay and Rebecca Silverstein. 1974. "The portrayal of women in television advertising." *FCC Bar Journal.* (1):71–98.

Sprafkin, Joyce N. and Robert M. Liebert. 1976. "Sex and sex-roles as determinants of children's television program selections and attention." Unpublished manuscript. State University of New York at Stony Brook.

Tedesco, Nancy S. 1974. "Patterns in prime time." *Journal of Communication.* 24(2):119–24.

Turow, Joseph. 1974. "Advising and ordering: Daytime, prime time." *Journal of Communication.* 24(2):138–41.

Vanek, Joann. Forthcoming. *Married Women and the Work Day: Time Trends.* Baltimore, Md.: Johns Hopkins University Press, chapter 4.

Van Gelder, Lindsay. 1974. "Women's pages: You can't make news out of a silk purse." *Ms.* (November):112–16.

POWER, PRESENTATIONS, AND THE PRESENTABLE

CATHARINE R. STIMPSON

Catharine R. Stimpson teaches English at Barnard College, writes both fiction and non-fiction, and is the editor of one of the finest journals in the field of Women's Studies, *Signs: Journal of Women in Culture and Society.* In this essay Stimpson analyzes how art is itself sexist — in its presentations and images — and how it promotes sexism by controlling arenas of consciousness formation, by discriminating against the female artist and critic, by reinforcing sexual stereotypes in its depictions, and by other means as well.

My premises, meant to have the austerity of axioms, are these: First, the ability to control consciousness, one's own or that of another, is a source of power. Next, to exercise such power entails shaping: (a) the raw process of thought and feeling; (b) the production of works of art, intellect, and the media; and (c) the institutionalization of the criteria of both truth and aesthetic excellence. Finally, though the agents of hegemony of consciousness vary from class to class, race to race, and time to time, they have persistently been men. One sex has had comparatively more power than another to present life, to play the role of presentor, and to define the presentable. My purpose now is to talk about this process, particularly in American arts and letters.

The legendary artists of Western culture — Daedalus, Icarus, Orpheus — have been male. The phrase, *homo faber,* has been taken literally. Behind such figures is an ideology that frankly sexualizes creativity.[1] According to its tenets, men do the intellectual and imaginative work of our society. They bring forth sermons, theories of relativity, and epic novels. They may even create women. So Pygmalion, the legendary but grumpy king of Cyprus, devised Galatea, with some aid from Aphrodite. The symbol of male fertility is the hand or the pen. Women do the biological work of society. They bring forth children. The symbol of female fertility is the womb. Certain rituals and clusters of imagery even suggest that "willed" male creativity is perceived as a compensation for or a substitute for "natural" female creativity. Writers, for example, often speak of being "pregnant" with an idea.[2] An anthropologist, Sherry B. Ortner, boldly speculates that the rough equation of males with the creative process of culture, which represents the operation of consciousness, and of females with the given process of nature, which represents the operation of unmediated biological life, characterizes nearly every society, not simply America.

Reprinted with permission from Dana V. Hiller and Robin A. Sheets, eds., *Women and Men: The Consequences of Power* (Cincinnati: Univ. of Cincinnati Women's Studies Office, 1977).

That equation may help to explain the common devaluation of women, their secondary status. Ortner writes:

> . . . my point is . . . that every culture implicitly recognizes and asserts a distinction between the operation of nature and the operation of culture (human consciousness and its products); and further, that the distinctiveness of culture rests precisely on the fact that it can under most circumstances transcend natural conditions and turn them to its purposes. Thus culture (i.e. every culture) at some level of awareness asserts itself to be not only distinct from but superior to nature, and that sense of distinctiveness and superiority rests precisely on the ability to transform — to "socialize" and "culturize" nature.
>
> Returning now to the issue of women, their pan-cultural second-class status could be accounted for, quite simply, by postulating that women are being identified or symbolically associated with nature, as opposed to men, who are identified with culture. Since it is always culture's project to subsume and transcend nature, then culture would find it "natural" to subordinate, not to say oppress, them . . . women are seen "merely" as being *closer* to nature than men.[3]

In the twentieth century, three non-Americans have helped to modernize the masculinization of the recording of "human thought and experience" that Americans have inherited and enhanced. Freud (1856–1939) asserted that male and female psychosexual development differed radically. Boys, because they are forced to generate a superego, become capable of the sublimation necessary for creative accomplishment. Girls, because they are relieved of that particular psychic pressure, do not. Joyce (1882–1939) wrote the novel many think the paradigmatic narrative of the artist-coming-of-age: *Portrait of the Artist as a Young Man.* In a crucial scene, Joyce's hero, Stephen Daedalus, a symbolic name, wakes up and fantasizes making love to a woman. As he does so, he constructs a poem. Describing Stephen, Joyce fuses male sexuality and creativity, semen and aesthetic speech.

> ...like a cloud of vapour or like waters circumfluent in space the liquid letters of speech, symbols of the element of mystery, flowed forth over his brain.[4]

Unlike Freud and Joyce, Shaw (1856–1950) believed in women's rights. His dissections of sex roles, social conventions, capitalism, marriage, and the family are glitteringly, savagely fastidious. Yet even he affirms that the task of women is to perpetuate life and what he calls the "Life Force," an energy of existence that exerts itself through sexual attraction, conception, and birth. The human race will "perish without (woman's) travail." The woman of genius will bear the infant superman. The man of genius will be a philosopher or an artist. In 1903, Shaw declared there are

> ...men selected by Nature to carry on the work of building up an intellectual consciousness of her own instinctive purpose.... Here Woman meets a purpose as impersonal, as irresistible as her own.

He did add, "When it is complicated by the genius being a woman, then the game is one for a king of critics."[5]

Empirical evidence suggests that America still conforms to and sustains the ideology that masculinizes the creation of the arts. Census data (1970) show that men are 68% of the total number of "writers, artists, and entertainers" in the "experienced civilian labor force." They are 58% of the actors; 69% of the authors; 18% of the dancers; 66% of the musicians; 63% of the painters and sculptors; 87% of the photographers. Though women work about the same number of median weeks, though women have

about the same amount of education, their earnings are 42% of men.[6]

Men also appear to have a stronger internalized sense of artistic vocation. In a recent survey, students in the San Francisco Art Institute were asked if they thought of themselves as artists: 66% of the men said yes; 67% of the women said no. The students were then asked if they thought of their work as better or worse than that of their colleagues: 40% of the men thought their work superior; 14% thought it inferior; 17% of the women thought their work superior; almost 40% thought it inferior. Men also stated a commitment to their career more often and more firmly.[7]

The more reputable, financially stable, professional and powerful the art, the more masculinized it tends to become. If an art is problematic, new, risky, despised, or weak, women may be there, but if the art establishes itself, men will tend to squeeze women out. Take the films.

> ...in 1928, out of 239 scenarists, 52 were female; by 1935 the total number had risen to 583; only 88 women, however, were working. In 1940 out of 608 screenplay writers, a mere 64 were women. As for directors, only one female managed to secure a steady position once the golden years of the thirties had arrived: Dorothy Arzner.[8]

In 1970, though 60% of the students in art schools were women, only 5% of the gallery shows were given to them.[9] In 1969–1970, 38% of the graduate students in music at the University of Oregon were women. Only 8% of the professorial ranks were [women].[10]

Moreover, the more "masculine" a particular job is within an art (the more authority over others it entails, for example), the more apt men are to fulfill it. The Director of the Barnard College Theatre Program once tabulated the number of men and the number of women who held positions in the summer stock companies in the 1974 season that sent advertising folders to the College.[11] They were:

Position	Number of men	Number of women
Director	49	5
Costume designer	2	3
Scene designer	3	0
Teacher of drama	18	12
Manager	13	4

What is true of the creation of art seems to be true of the administration of the arts as well. Grace Glueck, the journalist and critic, calls the proportion of women in "top" administrative positions in cultural agencies "dismally low." She says:

> ... of seven hundred fifty colleges surveyed in 1970 by the College Art Association ... only five percent had women as chairwomen of their Fine Arts Departments; of seventy-odd big museum members of the Association of Art Museum Directors which takes in museums with budgets of over $100,000, only two are women. Museums, of course, *employ* women — there are large numbers with the rank of curator, but they rarely have wide decision-making powers. There are also lots of women members of boards of trustees, chosen mostly for their money and social clout. But generally they tend to let the men on the board make their decisions for them.[12]

The media more than mimic the bureaucratic pattern of the arts. In 1973, for example, the CBS work force was 51% female, but of 400 managers, 15.2% were women; of 379 directors of various ranks, 5.5% were women; of 85 vice-presidents, one was a woman.[13]

The mechanisms through which the ideology of man as artist are enforced and reinforced are, in part, the same that perpetu-

ate sex roles in culture and society at large. In part, they take on the special features of the world of the arts. Many of them are personal and psychological. That is, they apparently tell men to their faces that they can create and tell women to their faces that they cannot. In a brief, tough essay, the critic Lucy R. Lippard lists many of them, especially in the fine arts.

> ... discrimination against women in the art world consists of: 1) disregarding women and stripping them of their self-confidence from art school on; 2) refusing to consider a married woman or mother a serious artist no matter how hard she works or what she produces; 3) labelling women unfeminine and abnormally assertive if they persist in maintaining the value of their art and protest their treatment; 4) treating women artists as sex objects and using this as an excuse not to visit their studios or show their work ...; 5) using fear of social or professional rejection to turn successful women against unsuccessful women, and vice versa; 6) ripping off women if they participate in the unfortunately influential social life of the art world (if she comes to the bar with a man she's a sexual appendage and is ignored as such; if she comes with a woman, she's gay; if she comes alone, she's on the make); 7) identifying women artists with their men ("That's so-and-so's wife; I think she paints too"); 8) exploiting women's inherent sensitivity and upbringing as nonviolent creatures by resorting to personal insults, shouting down, art-world clout, in order to avoid confrontation or to subdue and discourage women who may be more articulate and intelligent, or better artists than their male company; 9) galleries turning an artist away, saying, "Sorry, we already have a woman," or refusing to have any women in their stable because women are "too difficult." ... And so forth.[14]

A mechanism Lippard does not mention is the buddy system. To be more exact, there are two overlapping buddy systems:

(1) a group of persons who like similar persons, men who like men, women who like women, M. & M eaters who like M & M eaters, whether they have actually met each other or not. Members of such a group are willing to work actively for their mirror reflections, (2) a group of persons who support others who have also been a part of their favorite institution — be it a university, a ship, a club, or a job. Common sense insists that buddy systems, which may operate as much out of friends' mutual esteem as out of hostility for non-buddies, both buttress bias and maintain power relationships. One study of television provides confirming witness. News directors, largely male, were asked if they thought their audience would prefer men or women newscasters: 83% said the audience would prefer a man; 1% said it would prefer a woman; 16% said there would be no preference. But when audiences themselves were polled, the majority had no preference. If there was a tilt, it was men towards men; women often towards women. Some results were:[15]

Audience	Male preference	Female preference	No preference
University students			
M	36%	14%	56%
F	32%	23%	45%
4th and 5th graders			
M	42%	3%	55%
F	23%	15%	62%
Small-town parents			
M	48%	2%	50%
F	40%	0%	60%

However, a second theory in America has frequently undercut that of the masculinization of the artist and arts administrator. It postulates that high culture — arts, letters, learning — is feminine, if not foreign. Such a notion has classical roots in the figure of the Muse or in the figures of the Nine Muses. Daughters of either Zeus and Mneomosyne (Memory) or of Uranus and Gaea, they were goddesses of song. They also sponsored the arts and crafts. A poet's invocation of the Muse, at once prayer and demand for inspiration, is a standard literary device. Its tone may range from robust confidence to the bravura of a child trying to be strong in the night. Because the artist is so often male and the Muse is always female, his address to her may resemble one of a number of heterosexual advances: husband to wife, lover to beloved, son to mother, brother to sister.

In America itself, at least three forces have aided the sense of the feminization of culture. A more or less literate female audience has been able to consume works designed for them, which women themselves could often produce. Next, for a number of reasons, not always attractive, women have crowded into two occupations — primary school teaching and librarianship — that mediate between large numbers of people and the culture they appear to discuss and guard.[16] Finally, a post-Civil War bifurcation of life assigned public success to men and domestic refinement to women, many of whom, ironically, were protesting their exclusion from such public carriers of culture as the university. Richard Hofstadter writes:

> It was business, finally, that isolated and feminized culture by establishing the masculine legend that men are not concerned with the events of the intellectual and cultural world. Such matters were to be left to women — all too often to the type of women of whom Edith Wharton said that they were so afraid to meet culture alone that they hunted it in packs.[17]

However, even a feminization of culture fails to endorse the woman creator enthusiastically. The "true woman," for example, was neither professional performer nor artist.[18] Rather, women both embody and symbolize beauty. They adorn and ornament.[19] They may also nurture, transmit, and sustain culture, adapting traditional female roles. As patrons, in theory or practice, they may play several roles. First, they may provide psychic support for the artist himself. In nineteenth-century American fiction, ". . . the influence of a mother or sister was crucial to the blossoming of his genius. Women possessed the ability to perceive true talent; and like artists their special insights and moral purity exempted them from other conventions."[20] Next, they offer institutional support. Women, though not always sympathetic to female artists, have run some powerful modern galleries.[21] Presidents' wives have brought musicians to the White House for concerts that presidents attended. Finally, women may give financial support, if they have wealth and if they control it. For example, female donors are nearly as numerous as male donors to the National Endowment for the Arts.[22] A recent scholarly report on the economics of the performing arts also shows substantial monetary contributions from women that tend to be greater than those from men for the arts at which female attendance is greater than that of males.[23]

Though a feminization of culture may not breed genuine women artists, it may feminize the male artist. That male artists, intellectuals, or gifted souls might exhibit feminine virtues or traits is an old idea. Coleridge, for example, briefly speculated that the artist might be androgynous. Whether biologically female or male, the artist would partake of both feminine and masculine traits.[24] Such a notion may glorify the artist and his capabilities. However, if a society either devalues or constricts the feminine, it will disdain the man, be he artist or athlete, who exhibits the taint of "womanly" features. Male "femininity" will be less a sign of psychological flexibility and scope than of a nasty effeminacy.

The composer Gian-Carlo Menotti claims that the American alienation from the arts is inseparable from such a prejudice. Fathers get upset if their sons want to become artists. They consider it soft, "unmanly . . . un-American."[25] The financial instability of the arts is one reason why they seem emasculated. Certainly, as I have said before, the more profitable an art is, the more acceptably masculine it becomes. Supporting Menotti is the fact that dance, the art most "feminine" in reputation and the most female in proportion of its participants, is the least remunerative. Census data in 1960 showed that for males in "professional/technical" occupations, only religious workers had a lower median annual income than dancers and dance teachers.[26] Though Menotti's argument has the plausibility of truisms, his casual masculinizing of the family drama of the artist as a conflict between father and son inadvertently reveals another endorsement of the ideology of creative consciousness as a male function.

It is a sign of the low estimate of "the feminine" as depreciated currency that American artists and intellectuals have themselves assaulted the feminization of culture, in myth or in milieu. In 1911, for example, in a famous speech in Berkeley, George Santayana, a philosopher of Spanish descent raised in America, wittily and relentlessly attacked what he named the "genteel tradition" in American culture. He declared it a harmful separation of experience and thought, present and past, man and capacity.

The American Will inhabits the sky-scraper; the American Intellect inhabits the colonial mansion. The one is the sphere of the American man; the other, at least predominantly, of the American woman. The one is all aggressive enterprise; the other is all genteel tradition.[27]

In 1915, he again deployed a female/feminine image to picture a tendency he disliked. He said of antebellum American poetry:

It was a simple, sweet humane, Protestant literature, grandmotherly in that sedate spectacled wonder with which it gazed at this terrible world and said how beautiful and how interesting it all was.[28]

One wonders how much of the aggressive masculinity of twentieth-century male American artists has been, in part, a defensive mechanism against fears that to be an artist is to be womanly.

Of course, there have been women artists, more than we know, many of them brilliant, vigorously industrious, and innovative.[29] In the West, Sappho symbolizes the beginning of a tradition, which convents deepen; salons secularize; a Madame deStael energizes; a George Sand romanticizes; a Doris Humphrey, Martha Graham, Gertrude Stein, or Louise Nevelson modernizes. The private identity of such women is inseparable from their public identity as performer or creator. This serious and active professionalism dissociates them from both the male patron of the arts and the female amateur. Moreover, a tendency of current criticism is to broaden and to democratize the definitions of art, the criteria of an acceptable art object. As a result, the work of women, such as quilts, are now being granted aesthetic as well as utilitarian value. In the future other creations, such as certain speech patterns, may attain a similar status. To start to work, the woman artist must benefit from at least *one* of the following conditions: a social structure flexible enough to permit women to act in public, be it in a ritual, on stage, or in a drawing room; a shift in taste or custom to accommodate female players of female parts;[30] a

family skillful enough to train her, or affluent enough to educate her; a female audience prosperous enough to purchase her work, as readers of the novel did; a fledgling art fragile enough to discourage ordinary men from entering it; or a labor shortage severe enough to make the sex of a worker less important than ability. In America, symphony orchestras, particularly the less affluent and reputable, hired women when they could not find the men they needed.[31]

Curiously, women, when they do work, may have been more successful in the arts than in other professions. In nineteenth-century America, some women writers prospered nicely. Students of the 1960 census data for the "experienced civilian labor force" concluded, though with several qualifications:

While a negligible proportion (nearly zero percent!) of all professional women received at least $15,000, this income level was attained by 9 percent of all actresses, 6 percent of all authors and 1 percent of artists and art teachers.[32]

In part, this supports the romantic claims of art that it rises above such ugly, commonplace phenomena as sex discrimination. In greater part, it shows that we do not always take the arts seriously. They are marginal enterprises, outbuildings to the central fortress in which men wield and protect political and economic power. A female presence cannot fundamentally threaten the existing order. Moreover, the female presence in the arts itself may take reassuring forms. Many arts, such as writing poetry, may be performed in isolation or alone. They demand neither immediate collaboration nor command; women may take them on without challenging male prerogatives or groups.[33] Roles that involve control over other people — orchestra conductors, theatrical directors — have excluded all but the most exceptional women. Moreover, performing artists, during the performance itself, may be playing parts that enhance our most traditional concepts of sex and gender. A dancer, as Odette/Odile in *Swan Lake,* incarnates a dualistic notion of femininity. An actress, as Mary Stuart, reminds us of the arrogant fragility of women of power.

In brief, women must still surmount a double ideological burden. A feminization of culture, if it occurs, permits her to love the arts, but not to love herself as authentic artist. A masculinization of the role of the artist tends to exclude her.[34] The actual apparatus of the arts in America today, though it grants women access to them, favors men. The National Endowment for the Arts, NEA, can serve as a microcosm for the nation. Created on September 29, 1965, when President Lyndon B. Johnson signed into law a bill setting up a National Foundation on the Arts and Humanities, NEA may even be too sophisticated and tolerant to be a microcosm. A national agency, it can evade the severities of local bias. A government agency, on the other hand, it can be responsive to pressures from groups that seek change. It has a record of support for racial and ethnic activities. Nor is it a bastion of grim male chauvinism. In its first year of grant giving, it awarded the Radcliffe Institute money to aid women writers. Since 1969 it has had a woman head. In 1972, it put $1,000 into the New York Foundation for the Arts, Inc., in support of the Women's Interart Center, a feminist group. It increased the amount to $10,000 in 1973, a year in which it also gave $2,500 to the It's All Right to be a Woman Theater.

Yet men pervade, if they do not head, administrative operations. The first national council consisted of 29 males, 8 females; the first staff of 11 males, 6 females. State agencies follow the pattern. NEA's annual report for fiscal year 1973 listed 59 male chairmen

of state arts agencies, 20 female; 41 male executive directors, 13 female.[35] In fiscal year 1969, NEA appointed advisory panels and consultants for the various arts: 67 males, 12 females. To categorize advisers and consultants by sex is to find the same high ratio of men to women in subsequent years. To tabulate two sample years:

Fiscal Year 1970

Panel	Panel members		Consultants	
	Male	Female	Male	Female
Architecture, planning and design	9	0	1	0
Dance	6	5	0	0
Literature	13	4	1	1
Music	18	2	1	0
State and community operations	4	0	3	3
Theater	8	1	0	0
Visual arts	12	0	0	0
Education	0	0	5	0
Public media	0	0	1	0
Totals	70	12	12	4

Fiscal Year 1972

Dance	7	10	0	0
Expansion arts*	4	3	0	1
Literature	8	1	2	1
Museum	16	0	1	0
Music	21	3	0	0
Public media	9	0	0	0
State and community special projects	9	2	1	1
Theater	13	3	2	0
Architecture and environmental arts	0	0	4	0
Visual arts	10	2	0	0
Education	0	0	3	0
Totals	97	24	13	3

* In 1972, Panel Members, Sex Unknown: 2.

No vulgar cause-and-effect relationship should be inferred, but the sex distribution of awards and grants resembles that of administrators. To complicate interpretation is the fact that NEA gives money to institutions as well as to individuals. The annual reports rarely tell if men or women supervise the spending of institutional monies, if men or women profit most locally. In the 1970s the number of institutional grants increased. Nevertheless, to tabulate grants for three sample years is to find:

Fiscal Year 1968

Panel and total amount of grants	Number of institutional grants	Number of individual grants	
		Male	Female
Architecture planning and design[a]: $814,550	4	0	0
Dance: $623,699	18	2	1
Education: $181,595	3	4	0
Literature[b]: $578,915	12	62	21
Music: $1,154,969	16	1	0
Public media[c]: $2,903,805	5	0	0
Theatre: $1,393,719	38	2	0
Variety of art forms: $601,265	6	0	0
Visual arts: $596,200	25	32	1
Totals	127	103	23

[a] Number of Individual Grants, sex unknown: 1.
[b] Number of Individual Grants, sex unknown: 1.
[c] The NEA set up the American Film Institute.

Fiscal Year 1970

Panel and total amount of grants	Number of institutional grants	Number of individual grants	
		Male	Female
Architecture planning and design: $347,750	13	136	21
Dance: $1,751,350	27	0	0
Education: $1,240,000	39	0	0
Literature[a]: $513,121	29	27	10
Music: $2,525,195	56	19	0
Public media: $195,000	3	0	0
Theatre: $2,891,000	64	0	0
Visual arts: $970,294	47	0	0
Co-ordinated programs: $505,711	39	0	1
Totals	317	182	32

[a] In 1970 NEA continued to give a number of literary prizes, but did not name the winners. Number of Individual Grants, sex unknown: 113. In 1969, however, of a total of 81 equivalent prizes, 69 went to males, 12 to females.

Fiscal Year 1972

Panel and total amount of grants	Number of institutional grants	Number of individual grants	
		Male	Female
Architecture and environmental arts[a]: $785,162	46	49	6
Dance[b]: $2,267,741	65	23	21
Education: $1,750,736	123	0	0
Expansion arts: $1,137,088	82	0	0
Literature[c]: $636,050	31	28	10
Museums: $4,149,273	288	24	20
Music: $9,745,797.36	287	74	10
Public media: $1,979,877	49	7	1
Special projects: $656,228	61	0	0
Theatre: $2,696,000	79	0	0
Visual arts: $940,504.95	101	9	6
Totals	1,207	214	74

[a] Number of Individual Grants, sex unknown: 1.
[b] Number of Individual Grants, sex unknown: 1.
[c] Number of Individual Grants, sex unknown: 1.

In 1972, just under 26% of individual awards that could be sex-categorized went to women. On the surface, this barely conforms to 1970 census data about the proportion of professional women artists. However, in individual arts the record is hardly consistent. If census data show 66% of musicians are male, 88% of individual NEA grants are to men. On the other hand, if census data show 63% of painters and sculptors are male, they got but 60% of the individual grants. Of the three sample years, 1972 was the best for women as a whole, which may show an effect of the women's movement and the new consciousness about sex roles. For in 1970, women took just under 15% of the individual awards, in 1968 about 18%. A preliminary conclusion that might be drawn is that NEA has not only reflected, but sustained, a masculinized ideology of the working artist. Microcosm may nurture macrocosm.

Inevitably, the conditions under which art is created help to shape the work itself. Poems, dances, rock-and-roll songs — all originate from a palpable set of historical, psychological, aesthetic circumstances, not *ex nihilo.* Though men have treated gender brilliantly; though men have treated women sympathetically and accurately; though each work of art has its own internal integrity, the fact that male perspectives have dominated the arts has distorted and deformed our visions of sex and gender. I am not saying that men and women have innately different structures of consciousness. Surely the synapses and the cerebellum have escaped the trap of genderization. However, men and women have tended to have some dissimilar experiences. This has influenced their perceptions of themselves and of each other.

The dramatization of rape is but one example. With suspicious frequency, the rape scenes that (many) men create show a woman submitting to psychic and phallic violence and finding out that it is fun. Leda thrills to the swan. One perceptive male critic writes:

> Rape itself, traditionally the perquisite of victorious invaders, is one of the most insidiously fascinating, if least discussed, of the more unpleasant human activities.... More often than not, rape episodes arouse the discreditable suspicion that women end by getting pleasure from the experience.... This fantasy has revealed itself in a wide variety of works ... best-sellers ... cartoons in men's magazines ... straight thrillers ... and highbrow ones.... In other words, the dice have been loaded where rape is concerned....[36]

Another case can be made from the materials of the media. In 1973 and 1974 a group of women systematically observed sixteen popular television programs. The Americans they saw were both absurdly conventional and conventionally absurd. More males than females appeared in all shows, particularly adventures. The men, Mary Tyler Moore not withstanding, had twice as much variety of occupation. Both men and women persistently demonstrated negative behavior, but women did twice as often. If women were active, they were bungling and incompetent.[37] A bitter parody of the ideology of active men, passive women apparently takes place in prime time drama. There, among major characters, male killers outnumber killed mates at a rate of two to one. Killed females outnumber killed males at a rate of three to one.[38] American culture asks an implicit question of the sexes: which is better, to be a member of a set that kills, or of a set that gets killed?

However, it would be an error to believe that the distortions appear in precisely the same way for all women. Fiction, for example, written for working-class audiences is more apt to show active women, who head households, take care of themselves, and participate in the labor market, than does that designed for other audiences.[39] Such stories are both descriptive, i.e., they reflect social realities, and normative, i.e., they encourage certain kinds of behavior. In perhaps sinister ways, they encourage working-class women to hold tedious, but necessary, jobs. They encourage middle- and upper-middle class women to assist, but not to compete with, men in more prestigious work.

Fairness alone demands that men and women have equal access to expressions of consciousness in general and to the artist's life in particular, be it Bohemian or stolid. Moreover, to give women entry to the arts and media would restore fullness and accuracy to our pictures of experience.[40] It would also expand the range of the arts; increase their richness and playfulness; deepen their complexities; create an aesthetic, imaginative universe at once grander and more fissured, if only because more varied in origins.[41] In "Pygmalion," the poet Kathryn Ruby asks, "What would happen to the world, if Galatea created herself." Her question waits for an answer. To help generate it, feminists are now demanding equal access to both money and such arenas of display as galleries and museums. In 1973, to take but one instance, Women for Equality in the Media asked that women get 52% representation in film industry projects that the National Endowment for the Arts was helping to fund. Such demands ought to be made, not simply by feminists, but by anyone who believes that the arts ought to have less to do with the ideology and reality of man as primary creator and more to do with psychic and social equity.

Any call for a degenderizing of the apparatus of the arts and of the media is itself insufficient. The arts and media are instruments of consciousness, but they cannot reflect, though they may anticipate and prophesy, a new reality about sex and gender unless that new reality is there. When schools, the work force, the family, the military, government, and economic structures change, the arts will change. Until then, some of the time, in their anticipatory mode, they will allow their audience a chance to apprehend new forms of sex and gender, to experience them vicariously, to rehearse for the new reality. In the present and the future, they will also, one hopes, continue to reassure us that there can be a chance for some meaning and order at the end of chaos. . . .

Notes

1. Judith H. Montgomery traces this theme in American culture in "The American Galatea," *College English*, 32, No. 8 (May 1971), 890–99. I disagree, however, with some of her specific points.
2. For an acerbic commentary on such tendencies, see Mary Ellmann, *Thinking About Women* (New York: Harcourt, Brace, Jovanovich, 1968), esp. pp. 1–54.
3. Sherry B. Ortner, "Is Female to Male as Nature Is to Culture?" in the extremely good anthology, *Woman, Culture, and Society.* Ed. Michelle Zimbalist Rosaldo and Louise Lamphere (Stanford: University Press, 1974), pp. 72–73.
4. Viking Critical Edition. Ed. Chester G. Anderson (New York: Viking Press, 1968; original copyright, 1916), p. 223. Another paradigmatic fictive narrative about an aesthetic young man, D. H. Lawrence's *Sons and Lovers,* was published about the same time, in 1913.
5. *Man and Superman* (Baltimore: Penguin Books, 1957), pp. xx–xxi. I am using Freud, Joyce, and Shaw as internationally influential writers and as representative figures. See also Maurice Z. Schroder, *Icarus: The Image of the Artist in French Romanticism* (Cambridge: Harvard University Press, 1961).

6. *1970 Census of the Population* (Washington, D.C.: U.S. Department of Commerce, Social and Economic Statistics Administration, Bureau of the Census, 1973), PC (2)–7A, Table 1, Page 2. I calculated my percentages using census categories and figures. I am grateful to Shirley Lanz, Economics Department, Vassar College, for warning that census data may be unreliable in the field of the arts in terms of declaration of profession, and for reading an earlier draft of this paper.

7. Ravenna Helson, "Inner Reality of Women," *Women and the Arts,* special issue of *Arts in Society,* II, I (Spring–Summer 1974), 27. Unfortunately Helson does not say how many students were sampled. Helson also writes about the psychology of male and female artists and its projection into literature itself. See, for example, her "Heroic and Tender Modes in Women Authors of Fantasy," *Journal of Personality,* 41, No. 4 (December 1973), 493–511. Because she is dependent upon the theories of C. G. Jung and Otto Rank, as well as upon her empirical data, her findings are probably about as valuable as those theories.

8. Marjorie Rosen, *Popcorn Venus: Women, Movies and the American Dream* (New York: Coward McCann and Geoghegan, 1973), p. 374. See also Molly Haskell, *From Reverence to Rape* (Baltimore: Penguin Books, 1974); Joan Mellen, *Women and Their Sexuality in the New Film* (New York: Horizon Press, 1973); and Sharon Smith, *Women Who Make Movies* (New York: Hopkinson and Blake, 1975).

9. Testimony of Marjorie deFazio, *Women's Role in Contemporary Society: The Report of the New York City Commission on Human Rights, September 21–25, 1970* (New York: Avon Books, 1972), p. 727.

10. Nancy Barnes and Carol Neuls-Bates, "Women in Music: A Preliminary Report," *College Music Symposium: Journal of the College Music Society, 14* (Fall 1974), 69.

11. Kenneth Janes, Information memo to the Barnard Women's Center, May 20, 1974.

12. "Making Cultural Institutions More Responsive to Social Needs," *Women and the Arts,* 53.

13. Media Women's Association, compiler; Ethel Strainchamps, ed., *Rooms With No View: A Woman's Guide to the Man's World of the Media* (New York: Harper and Row, 1974), p. 303. The book consists of personal statements, often anonymous, and documentation.

14. "Sexual Politics, Art Style," *Art in America,* 59, No. 5 (September–October 1971), 19.

15. Cited in *Media Report to Women,* June 1, 1975, p. 15.

16. For a reliable and yet adventurous scholar about the female audience and writers, see Ann Douglas (Wood), e.g. her essay "The 'Scribbling Woman' and Fanny Fern: Why Women Wrote," *American Quarterly,* 23 (1971), 2–24. See also, Henry Nash Smith, "The Scribbling Women and The Cosmic Success Story," *Critical Inquiry,* 1, No. 1 (September 1974), 47–70. A full account is Ellen Moers, *Literary Women* (Garden City, N.Y.: Doubleday and Co., Inc., 1976). A good account of women librarians is Dee Garrison, "The Tender Technicians: The Feminization of Public Librarianship, 1876–1905," *Clio's Consciousness Raised,* ed. Mary S. Hartman and Lois W. Banner (New York: Harper and Row, 1974), pp. 137–57.

17. Richard Hofstadter, *Anti-Intellectualism in American Life* (New York: Vintage Book, 1963), p. 50. See, also, pp. 233–52. Even if Hofstadter's general point is well-taken, his tone is unnecessarily snide. A recent, jaunty journalistic account of financial support for the arts continues the cliché; see Alvin H. Reiss, *Culture and Company* (New York: Twayne Publishers, 1972), p. 11. But, currently respectable opinion has it, the war between business and the arts, with its attendant conflict between the masculine and the feminine, is over. See *The Performing Arts: Problems and Prospects* (New York: McGraw-Hill Book Co., 1965); Herbert Gans, *Popular Culture and High Culture: An Analysis and Evaluation of Taste* (New York: Basic Books, 1974); and Gideon Chagy, *The New Patrons of the Arts* (New York: Harry N. Abrams, n.d. but approximately 1973).

18. Welter, "The Cult of True Womanhood," *American Quarterly, XVIII* (Summer 1966), 165–68, describes some of the constraints placed upon the exercise of consciousness.

19. Written in 1899, now old-fashioned in the belief that the sexes have innate temperamental differences, Thorstein Veblen's *The Theory of the Leisure Class* is nevertheless among the boldest, most trenchant analyses of the role of the ornamental woman in capitalist society.

20. Neil Harris, *The Artist in American Society* (New York: George Braziller, 1966), p. 226. See also Judy Chicago, *Through the Flower: My Struggle as a Woman Artist* (Garden City, N.Y., 1975) and Linda Nochlin, "Why Have There Been No Great Women Artists?" in *Woman in Sexist Society*. Ed. Vivian Gornick and B. K. Moran (New York: Basic Books, 1971).

21. Thomas B. Hess and Elizabeth C. Baker, ed. *Art and Sexual Politics: Why Have There Been No Great Woman Artists?* (New York: Collier Books, Art News Series, 1973, 2nd printing 1974), pp. 56–57, 112–13. The book consists of a shortened version of Nochlin's essay; comments on it by women artists, some of whom attack Nochlin, some of whom confirm her thesis that there have been good, but no "great" women artists, for institutional and historical reasons related to sexism; and other essays.

22. A breakdown of donations for two sample years shows:

	Fiscal year 1972	Fiscal year 1973
Male donors	223	250
Female donors	206	242
Couples (married)	109	148
Corporations/firms	103	120
Trusts/foundations/ funds	139	135
Miscellaneous clubs, schools, unions	51	49
Unidentifiable	8	1

The lists from which I tabulated these figures are in National Endowment for the Arts and National Council on the Arts, *Annual Report* for fiscal year 1972, pp. 27–44; *Annual Report* for fiscal year 1973, pp. 27–38. The reports name donors, but not dollar amounts.

23. William J. Baumol and William G. Bowen, *Performing Arts — The Economic Dilemma: A Study of Problems Common to Theater, Drama, Music and Dance*, a Twentieth Century Fund Study (Cambridge, Mass.: M.I.T. Press, 1966, paperback, 1968), p. 532. Baumol and Bowen provide invaluable data about female/male characteristics of various audiences, pp. 75–76, 84, 453–67.

24. *Specimens of the Table Talk of Samuel Taylor Coleridge*, Vol. II (New York: Harper and Brothers, 1835), pp. 15–16, 51. Harris talks about the feminine male artist figure before the most acute feminization of culture when the male-feminine artist might show affinities with the Romantic movement. See *Artist in American Society*, pp. 224–26, 237.

25. "A Plea for the Creative Artist," *7 Arts*, ed. Fernando Puma (Garden City, New York: Doubleday and Co., Inc., 1953), p. 40. Menotti suggests that foundations have assumed the role of benign surrogate fathers. Key, *Male/Female Language* (Metuchen, N.J.: Scarecrow Press, 1975), p. 104, cites evidence that American males avoid cultivated speech to prove masculinity, that American females pursue it to compensate for their secondary status.

26. Baumol and Bowen, *Performing Arts*, p. 105.

27. "The Genteel Tradition in American Philosophy," in *The Genteel Tradition: Nine Essays by George Santayana*. Ed. Douglas L. Wilson (Cambridge: Harvard University Press, 1967), p. 40.

28. "Genteel American Poetry," Ibid., p. 73. John Tomsich, *A Genteel Endeavor: American Culture and Politics in the Gilded Age* (Stanford, Cal.: Stanford University Press, 1971), pp. 136–66 studies the attitudes of male writers who might be considered upholders of the genteel tradition towards sex, women and the arts.

29. For a comprehensive, highly intelligent ac-

count of the conditions of their work, see Gaye Tuchman, "Women and the Creation of Culture," *Another Voice: Feminist Perspectives on Social Life and Social Science.* Ed. Marcia Millman and Rosabeth Moss Kanter (Garden City: Anchor Books, 1975), pp. 171–202. One difficulty in tracing the work of women artists is that their accomplishments have often been assigned to men: Colette's early novels to her first husband; some of Fanny Mendelssohn's songs to her brother Felix. In another famous case, in 1917 a portrait attributed to David, was given to the Metropolitan Museum in New York. Several decades later it was re-attributed, to one of David's pupils, Constance-Marie Charpentier. Another pattern of confusion that exists is women deliberately taking the names of men: George Eliot, George Sand, Currer, Acton and Ellis Bell. In the recent twentieth century, the American painter Grace Hartigan first exhibited under the name George Hartigan. Asked if she had done so in order not to be dismissed because she was a woman, Hartigan said:

> I will never be able to correct that misunderstanding. It had absolutely nothing to do with the feeling that I was going to be discriminated against as a woman. It had to do with a romantic identification with George Sand and George Eliot. George Eliot is a great writer. I don't think of George Sand as a great writer but she certainly was a great force historically. I wanted to identify myself with these two great women.

See Cindy Nemser, *Arttalk: Conversations with Twelve Women Artists* (New York: Charles Scribner's Sons, 1975), p. 151.

30. An interesting account of one such change is Jane W. Stedman, "From Dame to Woman: W. S. Gilbert and Theatrical Transvestism." *Suffer and Be Still.* Ed. Martha Vicinus (Bloomington, Ind. and London: Indiana University Press, 1972, 2nd printing 1973), pp. 20–37.
31. Baumol and Bowen, *Performing Arts,* pp. 228–29.
32. Ibid., pp. 106, 469.
33. Cynthia Epstein, writing about all professional women, suggests that "women are less likely to succeed in fields which require the professional to operate as one of a team of equals rather than alone." *Woman's Place: Options and Limits in Professional Careers* (Berkeley: University of California Press, 1971), p. 175.
34. For more detail, see Elaine Showalter, "Women Writers and the Double Standard," *Woman in Sexist Society,* pp. 323–43.
35. National Endowment for the Arts, Fiscal Year 1973, pp. 120–22. Because a number of state agencies have co-chair-persons or co-executive directors, they add up to more than the actual number of states. My source for all my statements about the NEA is their annual reports. My method of tabulating the number of men and women in various functions, a simple hand count, is obviously crude, but it has the virtue of showing gross patterns of distribution of money and authority along sex lines. A more serious methodological weakness is that I cannot compare the number of job applicants to job holders, grant applicants to grant recipients. It is impossible, as a result, to show bias towards men, towards women, or objectivity in the actual process of deciding who will get jobs or money.
36. John Fraser, *Violence in the Arts* (Cambridge: Cambridge University Press, 1974), pp. 17–19. My excisions have been of his examples. Haskell, *From Reverence to Rape,* p. 25, claims that she can think of only three films, "glorious exceptions," in which a male director has given equal time and sympathy to male and female points-of-view of a situation.
37. Women on Words and Images, *Channeling Children: Sex Stereotyping in Prime-time TV* (Princeton, New Jersey: Women on Words and Images, 1975), pp. 17–25.
38. Nancy Tedesco, "Patterns in Prime Time," *Journal of Communications,* 24, No. 2 (Spring, 1974), 120.
39. Cornelia Butler Flora, "The Passive Female: Her Comparative Image by Class and Culture in Women's Magazine Fiction," *Journal of Marriage and the Family,* 33, No. 3 (August 1971), reprinted in a longer version in *Female and Male in Latin America.* Ed. Ann

Pescatello (Pittsburgh: University of Pittsburgh Press, 1973), pp. 59–85.

40. See Georgia Dullea, "The Women in TV: A Changing Image, A Growing Impact," *New York Times* (September 28, 1974), p. 18, for an account of the way in which the presence of women in TV production and programs helps to shatter sex role stereotypes.

41. The most substantial modern scholarship concludes that in tests of creativity, girls may be more verbal than boys, but neither sex is inherently more creative than the other. Eleanor Emmons Maccoby and Carol Nagy Jacklin, *The Psychology of Sex Differences* (Stanford, Cal.: Stanford University Press, 1974), pp. 113–14.

III

Women Move

"Gradually, the hot, persistent flame of anger, with which most feminists sustain their dedication, began to burn within me."

— Jo Freeman, *The Politics of Women's Liberation*

As we look at some of the past and present activities of women in behalf of women, it is worthwhile to consider afresh a point made earlier — that the "history of history" has been prevailingly male. Given the masculist emphasis on political and national power and the masculist contempt for things female, it is clear why women are by and large absent from history books and why the few appearances women do make are trivialized or distorted. If, as in this final chapter, we conceive of the women's movement as primarily a centuries-old process of women coming to awareness of themselves as women, we can recognize that it is not enough to have learned about the past within the context of masculist perspectives. The women's movement of traditional history is hardly the tip of the iceberg. To know and to understand the women's movement requires of us all to do at another time and in another place what can only be suggested here: to search for the totality of women's experience throughout history, to seek out previously hidden facts, to look at old information in new ways, to keep our minds open to reinterpretations of traditional recountings, and to be ready for surprises from the lost past of women on the move.

9

Feminist Activism:
Issues and Events

When Did the Women's Movement Begin?

It is often asked: When did the women's movement begin? Many discussions attempt to fix origins in relatively recent expressions of sociopolitical activity, specifically in the Enlightenment and the French Revolution, in the drive for the abolition of slavery, or in the American civil rights and war resistance movements. These attempts have a certain logic, but they can be misleading. They tend to focus attention not on one movement but on many: on eighteenth-, nineteenth-, or twentieth-century movements, each with a discernible starting point, each built around distinct needs and goals, and each with separate and characteristic political attitudes, personalities, and strategies. A traditional reading in this vein of pinpointed origins might be summed up as follows:

> The first stirrings of the women's movement were felt with the publication of Mary Wollstonecraft's *A Vindication of the Rights of Woman* in 1792. The Women's Rights Movement in the United States was born during the drive for abolition, particularly in the activities and writings of the Grimké sisters in the 1830s. It culminated in the winning of the vote in 1920; and then, because women had exhausted themselves in the fight for suffrage, it died, until Betty Friedan's *The Feminine Mystique* brought it back to life in 1963.

A conceptualization of the women's movement that strikes me as more helpful and more constructive is simply that of *women moving toward greater strength and freedom both in their awareness and in their sociopolitical position*. Development in this direction has been happening through the centuries, often for individuals, sometimes collectively. It has progressed, and it has receded; it is sometimes subterranean and sometimes crests into waves of activism. It has expressed itself in many ways — in the writing of poetry, in marches on courthouses, or in the quieter but sturdy resistance of the women of the household. It has been conceptualized and communicated in varying contexts — political, economic, psychological, or even physical — and it is not easily confined to one model. From this perspective, there is no discernible "beginning" or cutoff point to the women's movement. We do not need to exclude from consideration the Roman women demonstrating in the forum in 195 B.C. for repeal of the antifemale Oppian laws; or to exclude the poems of Sappho, or the struggles for survival of a thirteenth-century group of women called the Beguines (who chose to abjure marriage, live and work together, help the poor in the name of Christianity, but remain independent of the control of the male church). We can include in our understanding of the women's movement the egalitarian ideals of the Quakers, of Anne Hutchinson, or of "Constantia."

The value of such an approach is manifold. It reveals the universality across time and space of the nature of women's concern and awareness. It emphasizes the sisterhood of *all* women. It reveals the startling continuity of feminist issues, values, goals, and challenges and in so doing allows us to see that each wave of activism is not separate and anomalous, destined like the others for failure or for limited achievement at best, but rather an integral part of an ongoing and progressive development. Finally, it affords us a context for evaluating challenges not only to feminist goals but to the very legitimacy of feminism as a world movement of liberation.

Key Themes of Women's Movement

A perusal of the historical artifacts of women's activism, expressed through literature, politics, or other areas, brings to light the fact that for centuries, in groups and as individuals, women have spoken out consistently on certain key themes and issues. Although they may reflect the character of the times, the attitudes and issues prominent in their age, the products of feminist women's efforts have been remarkably consistent in their direction: They have to do with the *quality* of life for women and for the entire human community.

It is interesting to note also that opponents' reactions have been consistent as well. Adversaries generally attack feminists' "femaleness," good sense, and morality, and they charge activism in women's behalf with triviality or destructiveness or both (however inconsistent that may seem).

Major Issues for Women

It is a revelation to read, "The time has come to take this world muddle that men have created and strive to turn it into an ordered, peaceful, happy abiding place for humanity," [1] and discover that those words, which sound so like the women's liberation movement of the 1970s, were spoken by Alva Belmont in 1922. Mary Wollstonecraft chides the affectations and destructive results of traditional "femininity," and were it not for the habits of language current in her time, she would sound quite like Lucy Komisar or Kate Millett.

Again and again in poetry, political treatises, personal letters, speeches, and social analyses we see these themes reiterated: the folly of grossly distorting women's physical, emotional, and intellectual development; the

[1] *Ladies' Home Journal,* September 1922, p. 7; quoted in Judith Papachristou, ed., *Women Together* (New York: Knopf, 1976), p. 203.

injustice of denying to half the world's population their rights, opportunities, and contributions; the great need for humanitarian treatment of the young, the sick, and the powerless in the face of the insensitive and selfish values of traditional masculist institutions; the unlikeliness of peace and harmony in a world suffused with the aggressiveness and arrogance of Martial power values.

The consistency of themes and purposes in our history underscores the continuity of the movement, the character of feminist concerns, and, it would appear, the legitimacy of our claims. Feminist analysis is not transitory and culture-bound, but is part of the mainstream of ongoing sociopolitical thought and liberation philosophy, although it has not been perceived that way.

Charges and Countercharges

Feminist women call to the masculists: You misunderstand and malign us; you thwart us; you deny to the world our abilities and contributions; you distort the quality of life; you cause war and unrest; you are arrogant, foolish, and mean. Opponents answer: You, feminists, are misled and confused; your goals are contrary to reason, nature, and order; your behavior is unnatural and unseemly; you are either ill (unfeminine) or evil; your actions will cause your own downfall and that of your family, *the* family, the nation, and the world; you are unable to see this, or you don't care.

It crystallizes one's own sense of place and helps to resolve some personal conflicts to realize that activist women in any age have met the same misogynist accusations. Cato exclaimed of the Roman women, "It is complete liberty, or rather complete license they desire. If they win in this, what will they not attempt? The moment they begin to be your equals, they will be your superiors." [2] Doesn't that sound like: Give them an inch and they'll take a mile; they want to dominate men? Mary Wollstonecraft commented in 1792: "From every quarter have I heard exclamations against masculine women." [3] The same charge of "masculinity" was made against nineteenth-century activists, and what contemporary feminist has not been called masculine, or "queer"? Lucy Stone reported in 1855: "The last speaker [at the National Convention, Cincinnati] alluded to this movement as being that of a few disappointed women." [4] How modern! Feminists today are called "disappointed" (that is, frigid, jilted, or crabby) and are always taken to task for being "in the minority," not in the mainstream of female life.

Just a Disappointed Few

The contention that feminists are not of the majority of women or are not like "normal" women bears looking at, first because it is an attack so often made, and second because it raises the question of how accurately feminists may claim to represent women's concern. The argument is phrased in various ways: " 'Libbers' are just a bunch of losers who couldn't make it in the man/woman world." "Women's liberation is just a white middle-class movement." "Feminists are just bored women trying to get their own when there is *real* oppression in the world that affects millions of people." Let us consider those charges one by one.

A BUNCH OF LOSERS To the charge that her movement was that of a few disappointed women, Lucy Stone answered, "In education, in marriage, in religion, in everything, disappointment is the lot of woman! It shall be the business of my life to deepen this disappointment in every woman's heart until she bows down to it no longer." [5] That, of course, is the proper answer. Women *are* losers in a patriarchal society, not losers in ourselves, as the epithet implies, not losers because of some personal inadequacy, but losers in a game where the rules and the rewards are so heavily stacked against us. It is the business of the movement to clarify to all women that we are losing and to help us understand that we are the victims and not the perpetrators of loss.

A WHITE MIDDLE-CLASS MOVEMENT To a movement that proposes to speak to all women, a movement in which the term *sisterhood* is of first priority, the charge that we are composed of and concerned with only a small part of the female community, and that part the more privileged segment, would be a serious matter. Yet most feminists believe the charge to be false.

There was a period in feminism in the early part of the twentieth century when, in seeking the vote, activist groups put aside their original convictions and exploited in their favor themes of ethnic, racial, and class bigotry. Although it was a period that bears scrutiny for the lessons it reveals, it does not represent the greatest part of feminist history and thought, but the smallest. Eighteenth-century analysis, growing as it did out of the Enlightenment, was strongly egalitarian. The next wave of activism, in the nineteenth century, developed out of abolition and the theory of human rights. The first contemporary

[2] Quoted in Vern L. and Bonnie Bullough, *The Subordinate Sex* (Baltimore: Penguin, 1974), p. 88.

[3] Author's Introduction to Mary Wollstonecraft, *A Vindication of the Rights of Woman* (New York: Dutton, Everyman Library, 1929), p. 3.

[4] Quoted in Papachristou, *Women Together*, p. 32.

[5] Ibid.

feminists came out of the civil rights and antiwar movements of the 1950s and 1960s. Their work is clearly egalitarian in the treatment of class, sex, and race, and is internationalistic as well.

Certainly we do see a great deal of writing and activism that originated with middle-class or educated women (some from working-class backgrounds). An examination of history reveals, however, that almost all movements for liberation and change have originated among those people who would appear privileged beyond the means of those most sorely oppressed. It was they who had the education and training to see beyond their condition to reasons and alternatives, to articulate issues and instigate strategies for change; it was they who had the time and the wherewithal to act. The themes of *liberté, egalité* and *fraternité* of the French Revolution originated among the well-educated, well-placed philosophers of the Enlightenment, not among the wretched poor who suffered the most, needed change the most, and to whom help eventually flowed. Marx and Lenin were intellectuals, and although they hoped for a rising of the masses, Lenin ultimately came to believe in the necessity of an educated vanguard of leadership.

Although the movement may appear to have been articulated by the white middle class (and even this appearance is misleading), it is not a movement *of* the white middle class. That is, it is not about only the white middle class. The drive for jobs and occupational equity certainly concerns working-class and poor women as much as it does middle-class women. Opening skilled and semiskilled unions to women, reforming clerical and secretarial occupations, and expanding women's place in government-funded job-training projects are all goals of the feminist movement. Securing the right of women to control our own bodies affects poor women even more than it does the affluent. Welfare reform has long been a feminist goal. Borne out by political action and the activities of Houston, the extinction of racism is a major feminist target.

There has been tension over strategies and issues between black and white, gay and straight, moderate and radical feminists, but diversity and interchange are creative, and the ultimate values have stood.

A DIVERSION FROM "REAL" OPPRESSION Feminists have been told that the movement, only about "peripheral" and "trivial" matters, dangerously diverts resources away from "real" problems, far more serious than ours. That charge is neither new nor unique to our times. In 1776, Abigail Adams, then a young wife of the newly forming republic, wrote to her husband, John, that he should "remember the ladies."

> In the new code of laws which I suppose it will be necessary for you to make, I desire you would remember the ladies and be more generous and favorable to them than your ancestors. Do not put such unlimited power into the hands of the husbands. Remember, all men would be tyrants if they could. If particular care and attention is not paid to the ladies, we are determined to foment a rebellion, and will not hold ourselves bound by any laws in which we have no voice or representation.[6]

Husband John, at that time a young firebrand in the cause of liberty, but eventually to be the second president of the United States, cautioned her to be patient, for more important matters were at stake. In a letter to his compatriot James Sullivan, Adams revealed that although there were good reasons

[6] C. F. Adams, ed., *Familiar Letters of John Adams and His Wife Abigail Adams* (New York, 1876), pp. 149–150, quoted in Alice S. Rossi, ed., *The Feminist Papers: From Adams to De Beauvoir,* New York: Bantam, 1974, pp. 10–11.

to consider the rights of "the ladies," it was "dangerous to open so fruitful a source of controversy and altercation as would be opened by attempting to alter the qualifications of voters; there will be no end of it." [7] That is, the egalitarian founders of the new republic were too busy to open such a messy can of worms as women's rights. After the Civil War, when Congress forged the new constitutional amendments for human rights, feminists who had worked tirelessly for abolition asked that women be included among the newly protected persons. They were denied their request, being told that it was the Negro's day. Paradoxically, only black men, not black women, were guaranteed their rights. You will see in the debate over ERA that the omission of women from those civil rights amendments (13–15) continues to haunt us into the present. During the early 1920s, the new government of the USSR revoked all the gains made by women in the 1918 revolution on the grounds that Russia was under siege and other needs must take priority over women's rights. Last, women always come last.

Today, feminists are chided for "muscling in" to affirmative action, federal programs, and educational opportunities; female activists of the sixties were ridiculed for harping on "trivia" (women's issues) while the men worried about important things like the Cuban revolution or world war.

The charge of triviality is a constant in women's history. It should not surprise us. Reducing women's suffering to trivia is not only an enduring masculist perspective but a misogynist strategy as well. To the sane and right-minded, it is self-evident that denial of autonomy and freedom, denial of political, economic, and educational equity, and daily

exploitation are as destructive in women's lives as in men's. A revolution that advanced the position only of men could not justly be called a revolution for human rights. Similarly, "affirmative action" that guarantees jobs for men but not for women cannot claim to be a program for "equal" human rights. When political activists demand parity for the poor, the colonialized, and the oppressed, they must remember that more than half of those poor, colonialized, and oppressed are female, and that women are doubly tyrannized in being exploited even within their own subgroups, _as women,_ by men. History shows that, when all is said and done, women's liberation has been a drive for the liberation of all women from the tyranny of misogyny, of all humanity from the tyranny of masculism. Hardly a trivial matter.

Earlier Sisters, Ongoing Themes

The widest treatment of history and anthropology is required to begin to construct accurate images of women's movement toward awareness of ourselves as women and of our position in the society. There are cave paintings in France believed to have been executed by women recording their social organization, poems by ancient Sumerian and African mothers, letters written by a Renaissance woman to her daughter entering marriage, speeches attributed to condemned witches (practitioners of the "old religion"), psychological tracts and social treatises, all with powerful political messages and implications. By rights, a student of women's experience should see them all. Space, however, precludes so wide a sample. What is presented in this chapter is just a tiny segment of women's material, limited for the most part to the United States and to the last two centuries, selected primarily for its representativeness, in period or attitude, and for its fame.

[7] John Adams, _Works,_ IX (Boston, 1854), p. 378, quoted in Rossi, _The Feminist Papers,_ p. 15.

As you sample the writings of earlier sisters at the end of this chapter, notice how the analyses and arguments of each woman reflect the currents and ideas of her time yet maintain that continuity of concern discussed above. Many of the arguments are still powerful and timely today. Consider, too, how drives for progress in women's affairs have often emanated from human liberation movements, economic or racial, and how necessary it has been for women in every age to remind (male) society that its altruistic analyses must be extended to include women in its understanding of "humanity."

Enlightenment Themes

The eighteenth century was a period of tremendous upheaval and change, both in the character of its social organization and in the philosophical themes that developed out of it. Major issues of consideration flowed around the concept of rights that human beings could be said to have vis-à-vis society and government. Certain ideals, although hotly debated and often maintained more in principle than in fact, came to occupy a central position in political philosophy. For a variety of reasons, new importance was given to the notion of *natural* human worth, individual value, which was held to be somehow cosmic in its source and prior to any privilege or status that could be bestowed by "civilized" society. Men were said to be equal in that value, brothers to one another, rational and good. Education, free opportunity, and the exercise of reason were seen as supplying the major ingredients of progress and harmonious community. Privilege, hereditary wealth and power, and unearned status were represented as villainous. Authority unchecked and exercised without consent was tyranny. Human excellence was composed of rationality, responsibility, emotional and physical health, independence, and

tolerance. These were the major ideals of that segment of sociopolitical thought that came to be known as the Enlightenment. Although there was great diversity regarding the manner in which these ideals could be instituted, the values themselves were taken as fundamental by a very large portion of the intelligentsia.

Note that *men* were said to be equal in worth. "All *men* are created equal." Not women. It was left to thinkers like Mary Wollstonecraft to remind the great liberal egalitarians that all they had said regarding worth, rights, opportunity, and freedom, as well as the condition and potential of the poor and oppressed, the uneducated and unwashed, could and should be applied to women also. Although Abigail Adams's letter to her husband (quoted earlier) may have been, in her own words, "saucy," it revealed an important truth. The framers of the great experiment in political rights were guilty themselves of the same crime of tyranny against which they had so recently rebelled in righteous indignation.

Human Rights and Abolition

There was a saying and a belief among radical activists of the 1960s that the best way to attract people to the New Left movement was not to preach or cajole but to let them just once confront the police; establishment barbarity would radicalize them. That indeed in large measure was what happened to women activists in the nineteenth century. Incensed by the injustice of slavery, they moved to correct that social sin; finding themselves equally sinned against, they were radicalized in their own behalf.

The women learned much from their work in the abolition movement. It was the Enlightenment commitment to human rights that they brought against slavery, and it was not a far distance from the rights of blacks to the rights of women. (The black-female analogy runs frequently through feminist analysis right into the twentieth century.) Women learned about the effectiveness of organization and experienced for the first time the potential and the joy of female unity and assertiveness. They learned to say openly, "me too." As women came to see in sharp detail the hypocrisy and cruelty of black oppression, they gained the insight to recognize it in their own lives and the strength to reject the absurdity and meanness of masculist values, behavior, and rules.

Representing very well the relationship of black and female oppression and of black and female liberation is the speech of Sojourner Truth at a rights convention in Ohio in 1851. An ex-slave woman who had become a lecturer and preacher, Truth was described by the convention's president, Frances Gage, as an "almost Amazon form, which stood nearly six feet high, head erect, and eyes piercing the upper air like one in a dream." Truth's speech is probably one of the most powerful and stirring statements of masculist irrationality that the movement has:

"Dat man ober dar say dat womin needs to be helped into carriages, and lifted ober ditches, and to hab de best place everywhar. Nobody eber helps me into carriages, or ober mud-puddles, or gibs me any best place!" And raising herself to her full height, and her voice to a pitch like rolling thunder, she asked, "And a'n't I a woman? Look at me! Look at my arm!" (and she bared her right arm to the shoulder, showing her tremendous muscular power). "I have ploughed, and planted, and gathered into barns, and no man could head me! And a'n't I a woman? I could work as much and eat as much as a man — when I could get it — and bear de lash as well! And a'n't I a woman? I have borne thirteen chilern, and seen 'em mos' all sold off to slavery, and when I cried out with my mother's grief, none but Jesus heard me! And a'n't I a woman?" [8]

Themes of the First Half of the Twentieth Century

The first half of the twentieth century saw the people of the world drawing closer together, albeit painfully. The rise of industrialism, the need for increased trade, the Great War, the rise of Marxism, and yet other factors brought internationalistic questions to the foreground and forced re-examination of many questions. People had to place themselves in a wider context and reconsider the limits of authority, the sources of government, the uses of knowledge, the concepts of community, social responsibility, and freedom, and even the nature of happiness. During this period the social sciences were evolving — sociology, psychology, anthropology — and they too were creating new ideas and questions for consideration: the proper limits of science, new forms for the study and control of human behavior, or radically altered possibilities for the future of life and society.

The debate over women's issues did not go unaffected by the emerging intellectual models. There is a belief, prevalent among many feminists and nonfeminists alike, that the women's movement simply died in 1920 with the passage of the Nineteenth Amendment. It is claimed that since the movement narrowed in the latter part of the nineteenth century from very wide-ranging concerns to a total involvement in suffrage, and since the winning of that goal required a Herculean effort, when it was won activists simply folded in exhaustion. There is some basis to this argument. Certainly political activity on an organized scale like that of the preceding

[8] Quoted in Papachristou, *Women Together*, p. 36.

seven decades did diminish. One could look for reasons in the Depression of the 1930s, in the political turmoil of the entire world during that decade, and in the vast engagement of energy in World War II during the 1940s. Such monumental events coupled with the belief that the vote created the opportunity to cure all women's ills might indeed lead to a decrease in organized activism.

Yet the idea that the movement died (or even went to sleep) might be brought into different focus by placing it in the context of the events of the wider intellectual and cultural scene. As general political activism and dialogue in the thirties centered mainly in socialism and Marxism, so did feminism. Many of the questions raised by the original American feminists in the nineteenth century were debated by female socialists of this time — the isolation of housework, the opportunity for work, the right to an independent identity, the oppressive elements of marriage and romance. (In fact, feminist groups of all kinds during these years were accused of Bolshevist tendencies.)

Just as the impetus for general social change during this time often arose from within the newly developing social sciences, so too speculation about new possibilities for women's personal lives centered there. In the 1920s Freud's hypotheses regarding female sexuality (among others, that females *had* sexuality) touched off a whole set of issues that were carried into the thirties and forties by psychologists like Karen Horney and her contemporaries. Reinforced by the research of various feministically inclined anthropologists, like Margaret Mead and Ruth Benedict, more positive attitudes toward women's sexuality occasioned lively activism on behalf of biological freedom. The birth control and planned parenthood movement was born and flourished between the 1920s and the 1950s.

In the 1920s, the suffragist Alice Paul and her coworkers of the radical Congressional Union introduced the Equal Rights Amendment and lobbied for its passage. The National Council of Women, the Women's International League for Peace and Freedom, the League of Women Voters, and other organizations like these, each with its own political purpose and agenda, came into existence during this period, and many still function today.

In the first half of the twentieth century, America's economic system underwent tremendous change as did women's participation in it. After World War I women moved into the public work place in growing numbers on every level. Frequently, as they grew in numbers, they organized. Women were particularly active in the trade union movement. In the professions, organizations such as Business and Professional Women (BPW) not only supported women in gaining better educational and business opportunities, but they lobbied for other women's issues in the legislatures and with presidential commissions.

Given all this activity, it seems shortsighted to insist that exhausted women let their movement die. It seems more accurate and more constructive to point out that many suffrage activists moved into divergent areas of activity, that new feminist women expressed their values through these different models. The movement, less organized or centralized, less political, less visible in some ways, even less numerous, was nonetheless alive.

The Second Half and the Second Wave

Although women's issues as a major item of public discussion receded in importance during the 1940s, conditions that would give rise to change continued to develop. The Depression had had a negative effect on women's position in the economy. What jobs there were had gone to men, and women lost ground in education, professional status, work rights, and salary. During World War II, however, conditions changed. Positions left empty by men gone to war and jobs in the burgeoning industrial sector had to be filled by women. In factories, offices, and industry, managing small businesses, running farms, teaching college, and building tanks, women did very well. Situations until then deemed "for men only" were effectively accommodated by women, and they learned an unforgettable lesson: There is no masculine or feminine occupation.

From 1945 on, even after the war, when many women lost their jobs to returning veterans, there was a dramatic increase in the number and percentage of working women of all kinds — married and unmarried, young and mature, parent and nonparent. Their numbers grew, and the realities of women's lives expanded and changed. What did not change, and what eventually was to cause much of the conflict that crystallized in the fifties and exploded in the sixties, was the cultural mythology, the projected ideals of femininity. Except for the brief wartime appearance of the patriotic Rosie the Riveter, America's dream girl image never adjusted to women's new realities and changing needs. In fact, the gap between the myth and the reality widened. In the late forties and fifties, popular culture stressed the visions of the virginal, naive girl-next-door and the softly pliant housewife in cotton dress and three-inch spikes tending singlemindedly to family and home. On the surface, at least, it was a time of traditional values and "togetherness."

Betty Friedan, in *The Feminine Mystique,* credits the wars, especially the Korean War, for this period of retrenchment. Disillusioned and emotionally exhausted, people (particularly men) craved the security and succorance

of a stable family and home, and they retreated to the familiar and comforting arrangements of marriage, or at least the image of it, and to the concept of the nurturing, tender wife-mother. This is at least partly true.

Again, however, one must be careful not to oversimplify, and one must seek explanations for women's situation with an eye to events in the wider culture. Although the fifties was a period of apparent quiescence, it held within it the seeds of turmoil. Although the decade was known for a kind of apathy toward political and national events, it also saw the cold war, the second "red scare," McCarthy and McCarthyism. It saw "the corporation man" and the man in gray flannel, but it also saw Jack Kerouac and the anticonformist Beatniks. It saw a day in 1955 when Rosa Parks refused to go to the back of the bus and touched off the civil rights movement, the true beginnings of the New Left. These events and others like them were as much a part of the personal history of the new feminist women of the sixties as were the TV images of Superwife.

Somewhere between the opposing realities, between prom gowns and Rosa Parks, between affluence and Vietnam, between maternal admonitions of purity and displaced homemakers, the feminist of the Second Wave came into being.

The Women's Liberation Movement:
Themes and Theories

Although there are issues on which there is a high degree of consensus among feminists, there are also some on which there is great divergence in general philosophic orientation, strategy, or treatment. These issues, which can generate tension or conflict, are internal themes of contemporary feminism that have developed during and since the early sixties. Because they have a strong effect on the strategies and actions chosen by movement leaders, because they often determine how we articulate our concerns, and because they are often seized upon by opponents of feminism to split unity among women, these issues deserve careful attention.

In the introduction to their book, *Feminist Frameworks,* Alison Jaggar and Paula Rothenberg Struhl outline four basic feminist frameworks or theoretical orientations: *Liberal* feminism (some call it *moderate* feminism), which essentially seeks opportunities for women's advancement in the existent society through institutional changes in education and the workplace; *Marxist* feminism, which locates the source of women's oppression in the general problems of a capitalist society and the remedy, therefore, in its dissolution; *Radical* feminism, which locates the source of women's oppression not in any particular economic system, but in the nature and implications of gender (perhaps even sex) itself; and *Socialist* feminism, an amalgam of the last two, which holds both economic and gender/sex factors equally responsible.[9]

Jaggar and Struhl offer one viable classification; others are possible. Some feminists believe that it is better not to classify, arguing that labels are misleading, restrictive, difficult to apply, and thus counterproductive. There is merit in this view, for categorization is always risky. And yet configurations do present themselves, and distinctions are possible that can be helpful in placing ideas into perspective and rendering them more understandable.

[9] Alison M. Jaggar and Paula Rothenberg Struhl, eds., *Feminist Frameworks* (New York: McGraw-Hill, 1978), pp. xii–xiii.

Differences in Orientation: Moderate versus Radical Feminism

To be sure, the word *radical* is a relative term. Where anyone is placed on the radical-to-conservative spectrum is probably at least as much a function of the one who describes as it is of the one who is described. Yet there have been strong differences of opinion and splits among feminists regarding general approach: choices of strategy (for example, militancy, demonstrations, guerrilla theater, and strikes versus painstaking political-legal activism), procedural rules (for example, complete separatism versus male participation), and even language and conceptualization (for example, reform versus revolution).

Some commentators on the movement have associated moderation or conservatism with the women's rights organizations aimed basically at institutional reform. They have reserved the term *women's liberation* for the more radically inclined feminists and groups, those determined to go beyond institutional reform, which would create *equality* for women, to far-reaching cultural redefinition involving profound changes for both women and men in the entire construction of society. It has been said that moderate feminists want to secure for women a piece of the pie; radical feminists want to change the pie. Even this characterization, however, must be used with care, for clearly there must be some overlap of these perspectives. Radical feminists usually support institutional reform, and moderate or conservative activists realize that even small changes in social arrangements and institutions engender profound alterations and adjustments in the patterns of social and private life.

The differences between radicals and moderates are based in general philosophical orientation, in ethical priorities, in interpretation of causes, in cultural vision, and even in temperament. Compare, for example, the sharp differences in the tone, attitudes, explanatory constructs, strategies, and goals of the following documents.

Radical feminism recognizes the oppression of women as a fundamental political oppression wherein women are categorized as an inferior class based upon their sex. It is the aim of radical feminism to organize politically to destroy this sex class system.

As radical feminists we recognize that we are engaged in a power struggle with men, and that the agent of our oppression is man insofar as he identifies with and carries out the supremacy privileges of the male role. For while we realize that the liberation of women will ultimately mean the liberation of men from their destructive role as oppressor, we have no illusion that men will welcome this liberation without a struggle.

Radical feminism is political because it recognizes that a group of individuals (men) have organized together for power over women, and that they have set up institutions throughout society to maintain this power.

A political power institution is set up for a purpose. We believe that the purpose of male chauvinism is primarily to obtain psychological ego satisfaction, and that only secondarily does this manifest itself in economic relationships. For this reason we do not believe that capitalism, or any other economic system, is the cause of female oppression, nor do we believe that female oppression will disappear as a result of a purely economic revolution. The political oppression of women has its own class dynamic; and that dynamic must be understood in terms previously called "non-political" — namely the politics of the ego.*

> — from Anne Koedt's *Politics of the Ego,* a manifesto for New York Radical Feminists, 1969 [10]

We, men and women who hereby constitute ourselves as the National Organization for Women, believe that the time has come for a new movement toward true equality for all women in America, and toward a fully equal partnership of the sexes, as part of the worldwide revolution of human rights now taking place within and beyond our national borders.

The purpose of NOW is to take action to bring women into full participation in the mainstream of American society now, exercising all the privileges and responsibilities thereof in truly equal partnership with men.

We believe the time has come to move beyond the abstract argument, discussion and symposia over the status and special nature of women which has raged in America in recent years; the time has come to confront, with concrete action, the conditions that now prevent women from enjoying the equality of opportunity and freedom of choice which is their right, as individual Americans, and as human beings.

NOW is dedicated to the proposition that women, first and foremost, are human beings, who, like all other people in our society, must have the chance to develop their fullest human potential. We believe that women can achieve such equality only by accepting to the full the challenges and responsibilities they share with all other people in our society, as part of the decision-making mainstream of American political, economic and social life....

We realize that women's problems are linked to many broader questions of social justice; their solution will require concerted action by many groups. Therefore, convinced that human rights for all are indivisible, we expect to give active support to the common cause of equal rights for all those who suffer discrimination and deprivation, and we call upon other organizations committed to such

---

* ego: We are using the classical definition rather than the Freudian: that is, the sense of individual self as distinct from others. [Footnote in original source]

[10] "Politics of the Ego" was written by Anne Koedt for and adopted as the manifesto of New York Radical Feminists at its founding meeting in December 1969.

goals to support our efforts toward equality for women.

—from the National Organization for Women's *Statement of Purpose,* 1966.[11]

Differences in Organizational Values and Strategies

In their newly developed sensitivity to the destructiveness of domination, feminist women have been much concerned with the structure of women's groups and with the notions of authority, leadership, and alliance. Wanting to avoid the worst offenses of power, early groups set themselves against "personality" control, elitism, and hierarchy and favored democratic decision making. Personalities and leaders did, of course, emerge, since there were differences in ability and interests. Elites formed, some of them oppressive, and accomplishment was sometimes sacrificed unnecessarily to egalitarianism. But to a large extent, time has helped resolve the confusion surrounding the matter of leadership.

The questions of alliance, however, are still open. It is still asked, for example, given the male's predilection to precedence and women's conditioned tendency to defer, how much voice and participation men ought to be allowed in women's groups. May they be members, may they be only observers, or should they be encouraged to participate fully, even to hold office? There are those who welcome male participation without reservations; others who accept support but not leadership; and still others, called *separatists,* who eschew masculine assistance as counterproductive (regardless of whether or not they themselves maintain personal male relationships).

Another open question is the matter of

relationships with movements dominated by men and male concerns, as the abolitionist, socialist, and black civil rights movements have been, or the various national drives for colonial liberation. Given the historical tendency of male-identified movements to ignore women's needs, how should feminists relate to them? Those feminists who choose to remain within such organizations (for example, the Socialist party or the Weathermen) have been called *politicos,* although this issue seems to be fading. They work toward raising the consciousness of the men within their organization and attempt to attack both economic and sexual oppression at the same time.[12]

Radical feminists, however, have rejected such an association, often on two grounds. First, they argue that as long as women spend their energies in male organizations and/or for male causes, women's needs will continue to be ignored and trivialized. Yet other feminists argue that male-defined political organizations are insufficient to the problem, for sexual oppression and domination is the paradigm of all oppression, patriarchal consciousness the primary cause of all other political ills. Mary Daly,[13] for example, argues that the rape of women, of the poor, of the races, of smaller nations, and of natural resources are all subsets of the masculist worship of power. The end of sexism is logically and chronologically prior to the end of the other social problems.

The Scope and Extent of Participation

Feminists must not only confront the matter of *what* the women's movement is about, but

---

[11] Reprinted in Aileen S. Kraditor, ed., *Up From the Pedestal* (Chicago: Quadrangle, 1968), pp. 363ff.

[12] For an interesting discussion and a bibliography on feminism and socialism, see M. Jane Slaughter, "Women and Socialism: The Case of Angelica Balabanoff," *Social Science Journal,* 14, No. 2 (April 1977).

[13] Mary Daly, *Beyond God the Father* (Boston: Beacon Press, 1973), especially chap. 4.

must also consider *who* it is about. Women's liberationists have contended that the movement embraces all women and all women's issues. Yet even from within, certain groups have charged the majority with discrimination, bigotry, or insensitivity. Older women, black and third-world women, gay women, poor women, and housewives each in their turn have expressed alienation, distrust, or outright hostility for the mainstream of the movement. Although the opinion is controversial, it is my perception that many of these conflicts are coming to resolution. The movement is widening, growing in sophistication and awareness, expanding to articulate and treat the needs of greater numbers of women. At the same time, particular groups are becoming more assertive of their perspectives, more unified in action.

On the other hand, although feminists have applied strong and effective pressure to several social issues and have made progress, in a very real way the movement is not fully defined. We have no unified general program, no clear statement of ultimate goals, no far-reaching pragmatic strategy. Some have pointed out that there is advantage in fluidity; premature hardening might blind us to existing possibilities and directions, and there is time to test many strategies while pursuing those ends that are clear to us.

Yet for serious feminists there are tough questions that should be asked and kept ever in mind as we go about our business. As we grow in sophistication and influence, we need a better sense of our ultimate direction, sharper strategies, more unity. We need themes and constructs more carefully defined and strongly supported in order both to communicate with one another and to persuade the outsider. Perhaps the time has come to turn our attention to theory so long as we continue to anchor it firmly in events and action.

Selections

A VINDICATION OF THE RIGHTS OF WOMAN

MARY WOLLSTONECRAFT

It is not uncommon to begin the history of the nineteenth-century wave of feminism and women's rights movements with the work of the eighteenth-century British writer and radical thinker, Mary Wollstonecraft. After all, her work had great influence in Europe and the United States, and *The Rights of Woman* was read as inspiration by the founders of Seneca Falls, Lucretia Mott, Elizabeth Cady Stanton, and others.

Born in Spitalfields, a poor district near London, in 1759, Wollstonecraft was destined to live a hard and extraordinary life for women of her time, and to learn at first hand both the value and the elusiveness of strength and independence in the lives of women. Her father became a drunkard after financial failure, given periodically to beating his wife and family and trifling away their remaining money. Her sister Eliza, to escape conditions at home, had married badly while still in her teens, and Wollstonecraft believed she had to spirit Eliza away to safety. On their own, the two sisters found it very hard to earn a living. All but two or three occupations were closed to them as women, and Eliza was not well. With a friend, Fanny Blood, they opened a school for girls; but, ill prepared and untrained, they failed financially and the school closed.

Having educated herself, Wollstonecraft moved to London and began earning a living at writing — at first, books about educating girls and stories for children. But through her publisher she began to move in intellectual and radical circles and to grow in insight and awareness. In 1792 she published the *Vindication of the Rights of Woman,* which was well read and earned her some fame. Later in that year, to observe at first hand the revolution in France, she moved to Paris. There she began a history of the French Revolution, later published, and met the American, Gilbert Imlay, with whom she lived and had a daughter, Fanny. After Imlay left her in 1795, she returned to London, depressed and heartbroken, to rebuild her life and move in once again with the friends she had known. Soon she met the radical philosopher William Godwin, whom she agreed to marry when she became pregnant. In 1797, shortly after the birth of her daughter Mary, she died at the age of 38.

The following excerpts from *The Rights of Woman* are from the Introduction and the Dedication, in which Wollstonecraft sets forth her main principles: Women are turned into weak, petty creatures — mere "alluring objects" (sex objects?) — by neglected education, by manners and morals (what we today would probably call sex-role socialization), and by flattery and dependence. She chides M. Talleyrand-Périgord, and with him the nation of men, to apply to women the same concern and commitment for "human" rights and freedom that they hold for men.

Author's Introduction

After considering the historic page, and viewing the living world with anxious solicitude, the most melancholy emotions of sorrowful indignation have depressed my spirits, and I have sighed when obliged to confess that either Nature has made a great difference between man and man, or that the civilisation which has hitherto taken place in the world has been very partial. I have turned over various books written on the subject of education, and patiently observed the conduct of parents and the management of schools; but what has been the result? — a profound conviction that the neglected education of my fellow-creatures is the grand source of the misery I deplore, and that women, in particular, are rendered weak and wretched by a variety of concurring causes, originating from one hasty conclusion. The conduct and manners of women, in fact, evidently prove that their minds are not in a healthy state; for, like the flowers which are planted in too rich a soil, strength and usefulness are sacrificed to beauty; and the flaunting leaves, after having pleased a fastidious eye, fade, disregarded on the stalk, long before the season when they ought to have arrived at maturity. One cause of this barren blooming I attribute to a false system of education, gathered from the books written on this subject by men who, considering females rather as women than human creatures, have been more anxious to make them alluring mistresses than affectionate wives and rational mothers; and the understanding of the sex has been so bubbled by this specious homage, that the civilised women of

From *The Rights of Woman,* by Mary Wollstonecraft. An Everyman's Library Edition. Published in the United States by E. P. Dutton and in Canada by J. M. Dent.

the present century, with a few exceptions, are only anxious to inspire love, when they ought to cherish a nobler ambition, and by their abilities and virtues exact respect.

In a treatise, therefore, on female rights and manners, the works which have been particularly written for their improvement must not be overlooked, especially when it is asserted, in direct terms, that the minds of women are enfeebled by false refinement; that the books of instruction, written by men of genius, have had the same tendency as more frivolous productions; and that, in the true style of Mahometanism, they are treated as a kind of subordinate beings, and not as a part of the human species, when improvable reason is allowed to be the dignified distinction which raises men above the brute creation, and puts a natural sceptre in a feeble hand.

Yet, because I am a woman, I would not lead my readers to suppose that I mean violently to agitate the contested question respecting the quality or inferiority of the sex; but as the subject lies in my way, and I cannot pass it over without subjecting the main tendency of my reasoning to misconstruction, I shall stop a moment to deliver, in a few words, my opinion. In the government of the physical world it is observable that the female in point of strength is, in general, inferior to the male. This is the law of Nature; and it does not appear to be suspended or abrogated in favour of woman. A degree of physical superiority cannot, therefore, be denied, and it is a noble prerogative! But not content with this natural preeminence, men endeavour to sink us still lower, merely to render us alluring objects for a moment; and women, intoxicated by the adoration which men, under the influence of their senses, pay them, do not seek to obtain a durable interest in their hearts, or to become the friends of the fellow-creatures who find amusement in their society.

I am aware of an obvious inference. From every quarter have I heard exclamations against masculine women, but where are they to be found? If by this appellation men mean to inveigh against their ardour in hunting, shooting, and gaming, I shall most cordially join in the cry; but if it be against the imitation of manly virtues, or, more properly speaking, the attainment of those talents and virtues, the exercise of which ennobles the human character, and which raises females in the scale of animal being, when they are comprehensively termed mankind, all those who view them with a philosophic eye must, I should think, wish with me, that they may every day grow more and more masculine.

This discussion naturally divides the subject. I shall first consider women in the grand light of human creatures, who, in common with men, are placed on this earth to unfold their faculties; and afterwards I shall more particularly point out their peculiar designation.

I wish also to steer clear of an error which many respectable writers have fallen into; for the instruction which has hitherto been addressed to women, has rather been applicable to *ladies,* if the little indirect advice that is scattered through "Sandford and Merton" be excepted; but, addressing my sex in a firmer tone, I pay particular attention to those in the middle class, because they appear to be in the most natural state. Perhaps the seeds of false refinement, immorality, and vanity, have ever been shed by the great. Weak, artificial beings, raised above the common wants and affections of their race, in a premature unnatural manner, undermine the very foundation of virtue, and spread corruption through the whole mass of society! As a class of mankind they have the strongest claim to pity; the education of the rich tends to render them vain and helpless, and the unfolding mind is not strengthened by the practice of those duties which dignify the human character. They only live to amuse themselves, and by the same law which in Nature invariably produces certain effects, they soon only afford barren amusement.

But as I purpose taking a separate view of the different ranks of society, and of the moral character of women in each, this hint is for the present sufficient; and I have only alluded to the subject because it appears to me to be the very essence of an introduction to give a cursory account of the contents of the work it introduces.

My own sex, I hope, will excuse me, if I treat them like rational creatures, instead of flattering their *fascinating* graces, and viewing them as if they were in a state of perpetual childhood, unable to stand alone. I earnestly wish to point out in what true dignity and human happiness consists. I wish to persuade women to endeavour to acquire strength, both of mind and body, and to convince them that the soft phrases, susceptibility of heart, delicacy of sentiment, and refinement of taste, are almost synonymous with epithets of weakness, and that those beings who are only the objects of pity, and that kind of love which has been termed its sister, will soon become objects of contempt.

Dismissing, then, those pretty feminine phrases, which the men condescendingly use to soften our slavish dependence, and despising that weak elegancy of mind, exquisite sensibility, and sweet docility of manners, supposed to be the sexual characteristics of the weaker vessel, I wish to show that elegance is inferior to virtue, that the first object of laudable ambition is to obtain a character as a human being, regardless of the distinction of sex, and that secondary views should be brought to this simple touch-stone. . . .

The education of women has of late been more attended to than formerly; yet they are still reckoned a frivolous sex, and ridiculed or pitied by the writers who endeavour by satire or instruction to improve them. It is acknowledged that they spend many of the first years of their lives in acquiring a smattering of accomplishments; meanwhile strength of body and mind are sacrificed to libertine notions of beauty, to the desire of establishing themselves — the only way women can rise in the world — by marriage. And this desire making mere animals of them, when they marry they act as such children may be expected to act, — they dress, they paint, and nickname God's creatures. Surely these weak beings are only fit for a seraglio! Can they be expected to govern a family with judgment, or take care of the poor babes whom they bring into the world?

If, then, it can be fairly deduced from the present conduct of the sex, from the prevalent fondness for pleasure which takes place of ambition and those nobler passions that open and enlarge the soul, that the instruction which women have hitherto received has only tended, with the constitution of civil society, to render them insignificant objects of desire — mere propagators of fools! — if it can be proved that in aiming to accomplish them without cultivating their understandings, they are taken out of their sphere of duties, and made ridiculous and useless when the short-lived bloom of beauty is over,* I presume that *rational* men will excuse me for endeavouring to persuade them to become more masculine and respectable.

Indeed the word masculine is only a bugbear; there is little reason to fear that women will acquire too much courage or fortitude, for their apparent inferiority with respect to bodily strength must render them in some degree dependent on men in the various relations of life; but why should it be increased by prejudices that give a sex to virtue, and confound simple truths with sensual reveries?

Women are, in fact, so much degraded by mistaken notions of female excellence, that I do not mean to add a paradox when I assert that this artificial weakness produces a propensity to tyrannise, and gives birth to cunning, the natural opponent of strength, which leads them to play off those contemptible infantine airs that undermine esteem even whilst they excite desire. Let men become more chaste and modest, and if women do not grow wiser in the same ratio, it will be clear that they have weaker understandings. It seems scarcely necessary to say that I now speak of the sex in general. Many individuals have more sense than their male relatives; and, as nothing preponderates where there is a constant struggle for an equilibrium without it has naturally more gravity, some women govern their husbands without degrading themselves, because intellect will always govern.

To: M. Talleyrand-Périgord
Late Bishop of Autun

SIR, — Having read with great pleasure a pamphlet which you have lately published, I dedicate this volume to you — the first dedication that I have ever written, to induce you to read it with attention; and, because I think that you will understand me, which I do not suppose many pert witlings will, who may ridicule the arguments they are unable to answer. But, sir, I carry my respect for your understanding still farther; so far that I am confident you will not throw my work aside, and hastily conclude that I am in the

* A lively writer (I cannot recollect his name) asks what business women turned of forty have to do in the world?

wrong, because you did not view the subject in the same light yourself. And, pardon my frankness, but I must observe, that you treated it in too cursory a manner, contented to consider it as it had been considered formerly, when the rights of man, not to advert to woman, were trampled on as chimerical — I call upon you, therefore, now to weigh what I have advanced respecting the rights of woman and national education; and I call with the firm tone of humanity, for my arguments, sir, are dictated by a disinterested spirit — I plead for my sex, not for myself. Independence I have long considered as the grand blessing of life, the basis of every virtue; and independence I will ever secure by contracting my wants, though I were to live on a barren heath.

It is then an affection for the whole human race that makes my pen dart rapidly along to support what I believe to be the cause of virtue; and the same motive leads me earnestly to wish to see woman placed in a station in which she would advance, instead of retarding, the progress of those glorious principles that give a substance to morality. My opinion, indeed, respecting the rights and duties of woman seems to flow so naturally from these simple principles, that I think it scarcely possible but that some of the enlarged minds who formed your admirable constitution will coincide with me.

In France there is undoubtedly a more general diffusion of knowledge than in any part of the European world, and I attribute it, in a great measure, to the social intercourse which has long subsisted between the sexes. It is true — I utter my sentiments with freedom — that in France the very essence of sensuality has been extracted to regale the voluptuary, and a kind of sentimental lust has prevailed, which, together with the system of duplicity that the whole tenor of their political and civil government taught, have given a sinister sort of sagacity

to the French character, properly termed *finesse,* from which naturally flow a polish of manners that injures the substance by hunting sincerity out of society. And modesty, the fairest garb of virtue! has been more grossly insulted in France than even in England, till their women have treated as *prudish* that attention to decency which brutes instinctively observe.

Manners and morals are so nearly allied that they have often been confounded; but, though the former should only be the natural reflection of the latter, yet, when various causes have produced factitious and corrupt manners, which are very early caught, morality becomes an empty name. The personal reserve, and sacred respect for cleanliness and delicacy in domestic life, which French women almost despise, are the graceful pillars of modesty; but, far from despising them, if the pure flame of patriotism have reached their bosoms, they should labour to improve the morals of their fellow-citizens, by teaching men, not only to respect modesty in women, but to acquire it themselves, as the only way to merit their esteem.

Contending for the rights of women, my main argument is built on this simple principle, that if she be not prepared by education to become the companion of man, she will stop the progress of knowledge and virtue; for truth must be common to all, or it will be inefficacious with respect to its influence on general practice. And how can woman be expected to co-operate unless she knows why she ought to be virtuous? unless freedom strengthens her reason till she comprehends her duty, and see in what manner it is connected with her real good. If children are to be educated to understand the true principle of patriotism, their mother must be a patriot; and the love of mankind, from which an orderly train of virtues spring, can only be produced by considering the moral and civil interest of mankind; but the education and situation of woman at present shuts her out from such investigations.

In this work I have produced many arguments, which to me were conclusive, to prove that the prevailing notion respecting a sexual character was subversive of morality, and I have contended, that to render the human body and mind more perfect, chastity must more universally prevail, and that chastity will never be respected in the male world till the person of a woman is not, as it were, idolised, when little virtue or sense embellish it with the grand traces of mental beauty, or the interesting simplicity of affection.

Consider, sir, dispassionately these observations, for a glimpse of this truth seemed to open before you when you observed, "that to see one-half of the human race excluded by the other from all participation of government was a political phenomenon that, according to abstract principles, it was impossible to explain." If so, on what does your constitution rest? If the abstract rights of man will bear discussion and explanation, those of woman, by a parity of reasoning, will not shrink from the same test; though a different opinion prevails in this country, built on the very arguments which you use to justify the oppression of woman — prescription.

Consider — I address you as a legislator — whether, when men contend for their freedom, and to be allowed to judge for themselves respecting their own happiness, it be not inconsistent and unjust to subjugate women, even though you firmly believe that you are acting in the manner best calculated to promote their happiness? Who made man the exclusive judge, if woman partake with him of the gift of reason?

In this style argue tyrants of every denomination, from the weak king to the weak father of a family; they are all eager to crush reason, yet always assert that they usurp its throne only to be useful. Do you not act a similar part when you *force* all women, by denying them civil and political rights, to remain immured in their families groping in the dark? for surely, sir, you will not assert that a duty can be binding which is not founded on reason? If, indeed, this be their destination, arguments may be drawn from reason; and thus augustly supported, the more understanding women acquire, the more they will be attached to their duty — comprehending it — for unless they comprehend it, unless their morals be fixed on the same immutable principle as those of man, no authority can make them discharge it in a virtuous manner. They may be convenient slaves, but slavery will have its constant effect, degrading the master and the abject dependent.

But if women are to be excluded, without having a voice, from a participation of the natural rights of mankind, prove first, to ward off the charge of injustice and inconsistency, that they want reason, else this flaw in your NEW CONSTITUTION will ever show that man must, in some shape, act like a tyrant, and tyranny, in whatever part of society it rears its brazen front, will ever undermine morality.

I have repeatedly asserted, and produced what appeared to me irrefragable arguments drawn from matters of fact to prove my assertion, that women cannot by force be confined to domestic concerns; for they will, however ignorant, intermeddle with more weighty affairs, neglecting private duties only to disturb, by cunning tricks, the orderly plans of reason which rise above their comprehension.

Besides, whilst they are only made to acquire personal accomplishments, men will seek for pleasure in variety, and faithless husbands will make faithless wives; such ignorant beings, indeed, will be very excusable when, not taught to respect public good, nor allowed any civil rights, they attempt to do themselves justice by retaliation.

The box of mischief thus opened in society, what is to preserve private virtue, the only security of public freedom and universal happiness?

Let there be then no coercion *established* in society, and the common law of gravity prevailing, the sexes will fall into their proper places. And now that more equitable laws are forming your citizens, marriage may become more sacred; your young men may choose wives from motives of affection, and your maidens allow love to root out vanity.

The father of a family will not then weaken his constitution and debase his sentiments by visiting the harlot, nor forget, in obeying the call of appetite, the purpose for which it was implanted. And the mother will not neglect her children to practise the arts of coquetry, when sense and modesty secure her the friendship of her husband.

But, till men become attentive to the duty of a father, it is vain to expect women to spend that time in their nursery which they, "wise in their generation," choose to spend at their glass; for this exertion of cunning is only an instinct of nature to enable them to obtain indirectly a little of that power of which they are unjustly denied a share; for, if women are not permitted to enjoy legitimate rights, they will render both men and themselves vicious to obtain illicit privileges.

I wish, sir, to set some investigations of this kind afloat in France; and should they lead to a confirmation of my principles when your constitution is revised, the Rights of Woman may be respected, if it be fully proved that reason calls for this respect, and loudly demands JUSTICE for one-half of the human race.

I am, Sir,
Yours respectfully,
M. W.

HISTORICAL PRECEDENT:
NINETEENTH-CENTURY FEMINISTS

JUDITH HOLE AND ELLEN LEVINE

Judith Hole is a producer for CBS television news. Her credits include shows on the value of homemaking, stepparents, mother-daughter profiles, and the politics of cancer. Ellen Levine is a writer, photographer, and lawyer. She participated in the publication of *Notes from the Third Year* and the anthology *Radical Feminism*. She has also published a book of her feminist cartoons, *All She Needs*. Here Hole and Levine introduce us briefly to the characters and events of the nineteenth-century movement for suffrage and women's rights.

Introduction: Historical Precedent

The contemporary women's movement is not the first such movement in American history to offer a wide-ranging feminist critique of society. In fact, much of what seems "radical" in contemporary feminist analysis paral-

Reprinted with permission of the authors from *Rebirth of Feminism*, by Judith Hole and Ellen Levine, Quadrangle/ N.Y. Times, 1971. Copyright © 1971 by the authors.

lels the critique made by the feminists of the 19th century. Both the early and the contemporary feminists have engaged in a fundamental re-examination of the role of women in all spheres of life, and of the relationships of men and women in all social, political, economic and cultural institutions. Both have defined women as an oppressed group and have traced the origin of women's subjugation to male-defined and male-dominated social institutions and value-systems.

When the early feminist movement emerged in the 19th century, the "woman issue" was extensively debated in the national press, in political gatherings, and from Church pulpits. The women's groups, their platforms, and their leaders, although not always well received or understood, were extremely well known. Until recently, however, that early feminist movement has been only cursorily discussed in American history textbooks, and then only in terms of the drive for suffrage. Even a brief reading of early feminist writings and of the few histories that have dealt specifically with the woman's movement (as it was called then) reveals that the drive for suffrage became the single focus of the movement only after several decades of a more multi-issued campaign for women's equality.

The woman's movement emerged during the 1800's. It was a time of geographic expansion, industrial development, growth of social reform movements, and a general intellectual ferment with a philosophical emphasis on individual freedom, the "rights of man" and universal education. In fact, some of the earliest efforts to extend opportunities to women were made in the field of education. In 1833, Oberlin became the first college to open its doors to both men and women. Although female education at Oberlin was regarded as necessary to ensure the development of good and proper wives and mothers, the open admission policy paved

the way for the founding of other schools, some devoted entirely to women's education.[1] Much of the ground-breaking work in education was done by Emma Willard, who had campaigned vigorously for educational facilities for women beginning in the early 1820's. Frances Wright, one of the first women orators, was also a strong advocate of education for women. She viewed women as an oppressed group and argued that, "Until women assume the place in society which good sense and good feeling alike assign to them, human improvement must advance but feebly."[2] Central to her discussion of the inequalities between the sexes was a particular concern with the need for equal educational training for women.

It was in the abolition movement of the 1830's, however, that the woman's rights movement as such had its political origins. When women began working in earnest for the abolition of slavery, they quickly learned that they could not function as political equals with their male abolitionist friends. Not only were they barred from membership in some organizations, but they had to wage an uphill battle for the right simply to speak in public. Sarah and Angelina Grimké, daughters of a South Carolina slaveholding family, were among the first to fight this battle. Early in their lives the sisters left South Carolina, moved North, and began to speak out publicly on the abolition issue. Within a short time they drew the wrath of different sectors of society. A Pastoral letter from the Council of the Congregationalist Ministers of Massachusetts typified the attack:

> The appropriate duties and influence of woman are clearly stated in the New Testament.... The power of woman is her dependence, flowing from the consciousness of that weakness which God has given her for her protection.... When she assumes the place and tone of man as a public reformer

...she yields the power which God has given her ... and her character becomes unnatural.[3]

The brutal and unceasing attacks (sometimes physical) on the women convinced the Grimkés that the issues of freedom for slaves and freedom for women were inextricably linked. The women began to speak about both issues, but because of the objections from male abolitionists who were afraid that discussions of woman's rights would "muddy the waters," they often spoke about the "woman question" as a separate issue. (In fact, Lucy Stone, an early feminist and abolitionist, lectured on abolition on Saturdays and Sundays and on women's rights during the week.)

In an 1837 letter to the President of the Boston Female Anti-Slavery Society — by that time many female anti-slavery societies had been established in response to the exclusionary policy of the male abolitionist groups — Sarah Grimké addressed herself directly to the question of woman's status:

All history attests that man has subjugated woman to his will, used her as a means to promote his selfish gratification, to minister to his sensual pleasures, to be instrumental in promoting his comfort; but never has he desired to elevate her to that rank she was created to fill. He has done all he could to debase and enslave her mind; and now he looks triumphantly on the ruin he has wrought, and says, the being he has thus deeply injured is his inferior.... But I ask no favors for my sex.... All I ask of our brethren is, that they will take their feet from off our necks and permit us to stand upright on that ground which God designed us to occupy.[4]

The Grimkés challenged both the assumption of the "natural superiority of man" and the social institutions predicated on that assumption. For example, in her "Letters on the Equality of the Sexes," Sarah Grimké argued against both religious dogma and the institution of marriage. Two brief examples are indicative:

...Adam's ready acquiescence with his wife's proposal does not savor much of that superiority *in strength of mind,* which is arrogated by man.[5]

...man has exercised the most unlimited and brutal power over woman, in the peculiar character of husband — a word in most countries synonymous with tyrant.... Woman, instead of being elevated by her union with man, which might be expected from an alliance with a superior being, is in reality lowered. She generally loses her individuality, her independent character, her moral being. She becomes absorbed into him, and henceforth is looked at, and acts through the medium of her husband.[6]

They attacked as well the manifestations of "male superiority" in the employment market. In a letter "On the Condition of Women in the United States" Sarah Grimké wrote of:

...the disproportionate value set on the time and labor of men and of women. A man who is engaged in teaching, can always, I believe, command a higher price for tuition than a woman — even when he teaches the same branches, and is not in any respect superior to the woman.... [Or] for example, in tailoring, a man has twice, or three times as much for making a waistcoat or pantaloons as a woman, although the work done by each may be equally good.[7]

The abolition movement continued to expand, and in 1840 a World Anti-Slavery Convention was held in London. The American delegation included a group of women, among them Lucretia Mott and Elizabeth Cady Stanton. In Volume I of the *History of Woman Suffrage,* written and edited by Stanton, Susan B. Anthony and Matilda Joslyn Gage, the authors note that the mere presence of women delegates produced an ". . . excitement and vehemence of protest and denunciation [that] could not have been greater, if the news had come that the French were about to invade England." [8] The women were relegated to the galleries and prohibited from participating in any of the proceedings. That society at large frowned upon women participating in political activities was one thing; that the leading male radicals, those most concerned with social inequalities, should also discriminate against women was quite another. The events at the world conference reinforced the women's growing awareness that the battle for the abolition of Negro slavery could never be won without a battle for the abolition of woman's slavery:

> As Lucretia Mott and Elizabeth Cady Stanton wended their way arm in arm down Great Queen Street that night, reviewing the exciting scenes of the day, they agreed to hold a woman's rights convention on their return to America, as the men to whom they had just listened had manifested their great need of some education on that question.[9]

Mott and Stanton returned to America and continued their abolitionist work as well as pressing for state legislative reforms on woman's property and family rights. Although the women had discussed the idea of calling a public meeting on woman's rights, the possibility did not materialize until eight years after the London Convention. On July 14, 1848, they placed a small notice in the *Seneca* (New York) *County Courier* announcing a "Woman's Rights Convention." Five days later, on July 19 and 20, some three hundred interested women and men, coming from as far as fifty miles, crowded into the small Wesleyan Chapel (now a gas station) and approved a Declaration of Sentiments (modeled on the Declaration of Independence) and twelve Resolutions. The delineation of issues in the Declaration bears a startling resemblance to contemporary feminist writings. . . . Included in the list of twelve resolutions was one which read: "*Resolved,* That it is the duty of the women of this country to secure to themselves their sacred right to the elective franchise."

Although the Seneca Falls Convention is considered the official beginning of the woman's suffrage movement, it is important to reiterate that the goal of the early woman's rights movement was not limited to the demand for suffrage. In fact, the suffrage resolution was included only after lengthy debate, and was the only resolution not accepted unanimously. Those participants at the Convention who actively opposed the inclusion of the suffrage resolution:

> . . . feared a demand for the right to vote would defeat others they deemed more rational, and make the whole movement ridiculous. But Mrs. Stanton and Frederick Douglass seeing that the power to choose rulers and make law, was the right by which all others could be secured, persistently advocated the resolution. . . .[10]

Far more important to most of the women at the Convention was their desire to gain control of their property and earnings, guardianship of their children, rights to divorce, etc. Notwithstanding the disagreements at the Convention, the Seneca Falls meeting was of great historical significance. As Flexner has noted:

> . . . [The women] themselves were fully aware of the nature of the step they were taking; today's debt to them has been inadequately acknowledged. . . . Beginning in 1848 it was possible for women who rebelled against the circumstances of their lives, to know that they were not alone — although often the news reached them only through a vitriolic sermon or an abusive newspaper editorial. But a

movement had been launched which they could either join, or ignore, that would leave its imprint on the lives of their daughters and of women throughout the world.[11]

From 1848 until the beginning of the Civil War, Woman's Rights Conventions were held nearly every year in different cities in the East and Midwest. The 1850 Convention in Salem, Ohio:

> . . . had one peculiar characteristic. It was officered entirely by women; not a man was allowed to sit on the platform, to speak, or vote. *Never did men so suffer.* They implored just to say a word; but no; the President was inflexible — no man should be heard. If one meekly arose to make a suggestion he was at once ruled out of order. For the first time in the world's history, men learned how it felt to sit in silence when questions in which they were interested were under discussion.[12]

As the woman's movement gained in strength, attacks upon it became more vitriolic. In newspaper editorials and church sermons anti-feminists argued vociferously that the public arena was not the proper place for women. In response to such criticism, Stanton wrote in an article in the Rochester, New York *National Reformer*:

> If God has assigned a sphere to man and one to woman, we claim the right to judge ourselves of His design in reference to *us,* and we accord to man the same privilege. . . . We have all seen a man making a jackass of himself in the pulpit, at the bar, or in our legislative halls. . . . Now, is it to be wondered at that woman has some doubts about the present position assigned her being the true one, when her every-day experience shows her that man makes such fatal mistakes in regard to himself?[13]

It was abundantly clear to the women that they could not rely on the pulpit or the "establishment" press for either factual or sympathetic reportage; nor could they use the press as a means to disseminate their ideas. As a result they depended on the abolitionist papers of the day, and in addition founded a number of independent women's journals including *The Lily, The Una, Woman's Advocate, Pittsburgh Visiter* [sic], etc.

One of the many issues with which the women activists were concerned was dress reform. Some began to wear the "bloomer" costume (a misnomer since Amelia Bloomer, although an advocate of the loose-fitting dress, was neither its originator nor the first to wear it) in protest against the tight-fitting and singularly uncomfortable cinched-waisted stays and layers of petticoats. However, as Flexner has noted, "The attempt at dress reform, although badly needed, was not only unsuccessful, but boomeranged and had to be abandoned."[14] Women's rights advocates became known as "bloomers" and the movement for equal rights as well as the individual women were subjected to increasing ridicule. Elizabeth Cady Stanton, one of the earliest to wear the more comfortable outfit, was one of the first to suggest its rejection. In a letter to Susan B. Anthony she wrote:

> We put the dress on for greater freedom, but what is physical freedom compared with mental bondage? . . . It is not wise, Susan, to use up so much energy and feeling that way. You can put them to better use. I speak from experience.[15]

When the Civil War began in 1861, woman's rights advocates were urged to abandon their cause and support the war effort. Although Anthony and Stanton continued arguing that any battle for freedom must include woman's freedom, the woman's movement activities essentially stopped for the duration of the War. After the War and the ratification of the 13th Amendment abolishing slavery (for which the women activists had campaigned vigorously), the abolitionists began to press for passage of a 14th Amendment to secure the rights, privileges and immunities of citizens (the new freedmen) under the law. In the second section of the proposed Amendment, however, the word "male" appeared, introducing a sex distinction into the Constitution for the first time. Shocked and enraged by the introduction of the word "male," the women activists mounted an extensive campaign to eliminate it. They were dismayed to find no one, neither the Republican Administration nor their old abolitionists allies, had any intention of "complicating" the campaign for Negroes' rights by advocating women's rights as well. Over and over again the women were told, "This is the Negroes' hour." The authors of *History of Woman Suffrage* analyzed the women's situation:

> During the six years they held their own claims in abeyance to the slaves of the South, and labored to inspire the people with enthusiasm for the great measures of the Republican party, they were highly honored as "wise, loyal, and clear-sighted." But again when the slaves were emancipated and they asked that women should be recognized in the reconstruction as citizens of the Republic, equal before the law, all these transcendent virtues vanished like dew before the morning sun. And thus it ever is so long as woman labors to second man's endeavors and exalt *his sex* above her own, her virtues pass unquestioned; but when she dares to demand rights and privileges for herself, her motives, manners, dress, personal appearance, character, are subjects for ridicule and detraction.[16]

The women met with the same response when they campaigned to get the word "sex" added to the proposed 15th Amendment which would prohibit the denial of suffrage on account of race.[17]

As a result of these setbacks, the woman's movement assumed as its first priority the drive for woman's suffrage. It must be noted, however, that while nearly all the women activists agreed on the need for suffrage, in 1869 the movement split into two major factions over ideological and tactical questions. In May of that year, Susan B. Anthony and Elizabeth Cady Stanton organized the National Woman Suffrage Association. Six months later, Lucy Stone and others organized the American Woman Suffrage Association. The American, in an attempt to make the idea of woman's suffrage "respectable," limited its activities to that issue, and refused to address itself to any of the more "controversial" subjects such as marriage or the Church. The National, on the other hand, embraced the broad cause of woman's rights of which the vote was seen primarily as a *means* of achieving those rights. During this time Anthony and Stanton founded *The Revolution* which became one of the best known of the independent women's newspapers. The weekly journal began in January, 1868, and took as its motto, "Men, their rights and nothing more; women, their rights and nothing less." In addition to discussions of suffrage, *The Revolution* examined the institutions of marriage, the law, organized religion, etc. Moreover, the newspaper touched on ". . . such incendiary topics as the double standard and prostitution."[18] Flexner describes the paper:

> . . . [It] made a contribution to the women's cause out of all proportion to either its size, brief lifespan, or modest circulation. . . . Here was news not to be found elsewhere — of the organization of women typesetters, tailoresses, and laundry workers, of the first women's clubs, of pioneers in the professions, of women abroad. But *The Revolution* did more

than just carry news, or set a new standard of professionalism for papers edited by and for women. It gave their movement a forum, focus, and direction. It pointed, it led, and it fought, with vigor and vehemence.[19]

The two suffrage organizations coexisted for over twenty years and used some of the same tactics in their campaigns for suffrage: lecture tours, lobbying activities, petition campaigns, etc. The American, however, focused exclusively on state-by-state action, while the National in addition pushed for a woman suffrage Amendment to the federal Constitution. Susan B. Anthony and others also attempted to gain the vote through court decisions. The Supreme Court, however, held in 1875[20] that suffrage was not necessarily one of the privileges and immunities of citizens protected by the 14th Amendment. Thus, although women were *citizens* it was nonetheless permissible, according to the Court, to constitutionally limit the right to vote to males.

During this same period, a strong temperance movement had also emerged. Large numbers of women, including some suffragists, became actively involved in the temperance cause. It is important to note that one of the main reasons women became involved in pressing for laws restricting the sale and consumption of alcohol was that their legal status as married women offered them no protection under the law against either physical abuse or abandonment by a drunken husband. It might be added that the reason separate women's temperance organizations were formed was that women were not permitted to participate in the men's groups. In spite of the fact that temperance was in "women's interests," the growth of the women's temperance movement solidified the liquor and brewing industries' opposition to woman suffrage. As a result, suffrage leaders became convinced

of the necessity of keeping the two issues separate.

As the campaign for woman suffrage grew, more and more sympathizers were attracted to the conservative and "respectable" American Association which, as noted above, deliberately limited its work to the single issue of suffrage. After two decades "respectability" won out, and the broad-ranging issues of the earlier movement had been largely subsumed by suffrage. (Even the Stanton-Anthony forces had somewhat redefined their goals and were focusing primarily on suffrage.) By 1890, when the American and the National merged to become the National American Woman Suffrage Association, the woman's movement had, in fact, been transformed into the single-issue suffrage movement. Moreover, although Elizabeth Cady Stanton, NAWSA's first president, was succeeded two years later by Susan B. Anthony, the first women activists with their catholic range of concerns were slowly being replaced by a second group far more limited in their political analysis. It should be noted that Stanton herself, after her two-year term as president of the new organization, withdrew from active work in the suffrage campaign. Although one of the earliest feminist leaders to understand the need for woman suffrage, by this time Stanton believed that the main obstacle to woman's equality was the church and organized religion.

During the entire development of the woman's movement perhaps the argument most often used by anti-feminists was that the subjugation of women was divinely ordained as written in the Bible. Stanton attacked the argument head-on. She and a group of twenty-three women, including three ordained ministers, produced *The Woman's Bible*,[21] which presented a systematic feminist critique of woman's role and image in the Bible. Some Biblical chapters were presented as proof that the Scripture itself was the source of woman's subjugation; others to show that, if reinterpreted, men and women were indeed equals in the Bible, not superior and inferior beings. "We have made a fetish [sic] of the Bible long enough. The time has come to read it as we do all other books, accepting the good and rejecting the evil it teaches." [22] Dismissing the "rib story" as a "petty surgical operation," Stanton argued further that the entire structure of the Bible was predicated on the notion of Eve's (woman's) corruption:

> Take the snake, the fruit-tree and the woman from the tableau, and we have no fall, nor frowning Judge, no Inferno, no everlasting punishment, — hence no need of a Savior. Thus the bottom falls out of the whole Christian theology. Here is the reason why in all the Biblical researches and higher criticisms, the scholars never touch the position of women.[23]

Not surprisingly, *The Woman's Bible* was considered by most scandalous and sacrilegious. The Suffrage Association members themselves, with the exception of Anthony and a few others, publicly disavowed Stanton and her work. They feared that the image of the already controversial suffrage movement would be irreparably damaged if the public were to associate it with Stanton's radical tract.

Shortly after the turn of the century, the second generation of woman suffragists came of age and new leaders replaced the old. Carrie Chapman Catt is perhaps the best known; she succeeded Anthony as president of the National American Woman Suffrage Association, which by then had become a large and somewhat unwieldy organization. Although limited gains were achieved (a number of western states had enfranchised women) no major progress was made in the campaign for suffrage until Alice Paul, a young and extremely militant suffragist, became active in the movement. In April, 1913, she formed a small radical group known as the Congressional Union (later reorganized as the Woman's Party) to work exclusively on a campaign for a *federal* woman's suffrage Amendment using any tactical means necessary no matter how unorthodox. Her group organized parades, mass demonstrations, hunger strikes, and its members were on several occasions arrested and jailed.[24] Although many suffragists rejected both the militant style and tactics of the Congressional Union, they nonetheless did consider Paul and her followers in large part responsible for "shocking" the languishing movement into actively pressuring for the federal Amendment. The woman suffrage Amendment (known as the "Anthony Amendment"), introduced into every session of Congress from 1878 on, was finally ratified on August 26, 1920.

Nearly three-quarters of a century had passed since the demand for woman suffrage had first been made at the Seneca Falls Convention. By 1920, so much energy had been expended in achieving the right to vote, that the woman's movement virtually collapsed from exhaustion. To achieve the vote alone, as Carrie Chapman Catt had computed, took:

> . . . fifty-two years of pauseless campaign. . . . fifty-six campaigns of referenda to male voters; 480 campaigns to get Legislatures to submit suffrage amendments to voters; 47 campaigns to get State constitutional conventions to write woman suffrage into state constitutions; 277 campaigns to get State party conventions to include woman suffrage planks; 30 campaigns to get presidential party conventions to adopt woman suffrage planks in

party platforms, and 19 campaigns with 19 successive Congresses.[25]

With the passage of the 19th Amendment the majority of women activists as well as the public at large assumed that having gained the vote woman's complete equality had been virtually obtained.

It must be remembered, however, that for most of the period that the woman's movement existed, suffrage had not been seen as an all-inclusive goal, but as a means of achieving equality — suffrage was only one element in the wide-ranging feminist critique questioning the fundamental organization of society. Historians, however, have for the most part ignored this radical critique and focused exclusively on the suffrage campaign. By virtue of this omission they have, to all intents and purposes, denied the political significance of the early feminist analysis. Moreover, the summary treatment by historians of the 19th and 20th century drive for woman's suffrage has made that campaign almost a footnote to the abolitionist movement and the campaign for Negro suffrage. In addition, the traditional textbook image of the early feminists — if not wild-eyed women waving placards for the vote, then wild-eyed women swinging axes at saloon doors — has further demeaned the importance of their philosophical analysis. . . .

Notes

1. Mount Holyoke opened in 1837; Vassar, 1865; Smith and Wellesley, 1875; Radcliffe, 1879; Bryn Mawr, 1885.
2. Quoted in Eleanor Flexner, *Century of Struggle: The Woman's Rights Movement in the United States* (Cambridge, Mass.: The Belknap Press of Harvard University Press, 1959), p. 27.
3. *History of Woman Suffrage* (Republished by Arno Press and *The New York Times,* New York, 1969). Vol. I, p. 81. Hereafter cited as *HWS*. Volumes I to III were edited by Elizabeth Cady Stanton, Susan B. Anthony and Matilda Joslyn Gage. The first two volumes were published in 1881, the third in 1886. Volume IV was edited by Susan B. Anthony and Ida Husted Harper and was published in 1902. Volumes V and VI were edited by Ida Husted Harper and published in 1922.
4. Sarah M. Grimké, *Letters on the Equality of the Sexes and the Condition of Woman* (Boston: Isaac Kanapp, 1838, reprinted by Source Book Press, New York, 1970), p. 10 ff.
5. *Ibid.,* pp. 9–10.
6. *Ibid.,* pp. 85–86.
7. *Ibid.,* p. 51.
8. *HWS,* p. 54.
9. *HWS,* p. 61.
10. *HWS,* p. 73.
11. Flexner, p. 77.
12. *HWS,* p. 110.
13. *Ibid.,* p. 806.
14. Flexner, p. 83.
15. *Ibid.,* p. 84.
16. *HWS,* Vol. 2, p. 51.
17. The 13th Amendment was ratified in 1865; the 14th in 1868; the 15th in 1870.
18. Flexner, p. 151.
19. *Loc. cit.*
20. *Minor v. Happersett,* 21 Wall. 162, 22 L. Ed. 627 (1875).
21. New York, European Publishing Company, 1895 and 1898. Two Parts.
22. *Ibid.,* II, pp. 7–8.
23. Stanton, letter to the editor of *The Critic* (New York), March 28, 1896, quoted from Aileen S. Kraditor, *The Ideas of the Woman Suffrage Movement, 1890–1920* (New York: Columbia University Press, 1965), n. 11, p. 81.
24. A total of 218 women from 26 states were arrested during the first session of the 65th Congress (1917). Ninety-seven went to prison.
25. Carrier Chapman Catt and Nettie Rogers Shuler, *Woman Suffrage and Politics* (New York, 1923), p. 107. Quoted from Flexner, p. 173.

DECLARATION OF SENTIMENTS AND RESOLUTIONS, SENECA FALLS CONVENTION OF 1848

The "woman question" had been bubbling heatedly among the intelligentsia, the great reformers of the times, and in the press at least since women had begun to emerge as strong and active movers in the antislavery societies. A major precipitating factor of clearly feminist activism occurred in 1840 in London at the World Anti-Slavery Convention attended by many Americans, among them Lucretia Mott, a strong, intelligent Quaker minister, delegate of the American Anti-Slavery Society, and Elizabeth Cady Stanton, then the bride of Henry Stanton, delegate of the American and Foreign Anti-Slavery Society. Although debate over the issue of women's participation in the abolition movement had been sharp in the United States, women had gained some degree of tolerance, if not wholehearted acceptance. Furthermore, the women involved here were educated, spirited women, accustomed to speaking out. They were not prepared for their reception in London: After a full day of debate on the question, on the grounds of morality and propriety (not to mention incompetence) women were finally allowed only to attend, not to participate actively in discussion. Barred from the central gathering, they were required to sit in a separate curtained gallery, hidden from view, forbidden to speak. Humiliated and furious at the hypocrisy of liberals who could see one brand of oppression but not another, the American women determined to call their own convention on their own issue upon their return home.

Although diverted for nearly eight years, they made good their plan on July 19, 1848, at Seneca Falls, New York. The convention brought forth the following document, written primarily by Stanton, and ultimately adopted by the gathering. The decision to use the language of the Declaration of Independence was pointedly made to remind all that women had been omitted from the concerns and safeguards of the original U.S. Constitution. The arguments are clearly in the tradition of eighteenth-century Enlightenment liberalism and nineteenth-century reformism. Notice the breadth of concerns voiced here, suffrage being only a part (and not a well-supported one!) of the commitment. Notice, too, the parallels between these ideas and those of today's women's liberation movement.

Declaration of Sentiments

When, in the course of human events, it becomes necessary for one portion of the family of man to assume among the people of the earth a position different from that which they have hitherto occupied, but one to which the laws of nature and of nature's God entitle them, a decent respect to the opinions of mankind requires that they should declare the causes that impel them to such a course.

We hold these truths to be self-evident: that all men and women are created equal; that they are endowed by their Creator with certain inalienable rights; that among these are life, liberty, and the pursuit of happiness; that to secure these rights governments are instituted, deriving their just powers from the consent of the governed. Whenever any form of government becomes destructive of these ends, it is the right of those who suffer from it to refuse allegiance to it, and to insist upon the institution of a new government, laying its foundation on such principles, and organizing its powers in such form, as to them shall seem most likely to effect their safety and happiness. Prudence indeed, will dictate that governments long established should not be changed for light and transient causes; and accordingly all experience hath shown that mankind are more disposed to suffer, while evils are sufferable, than to right themselves by abolishing the forms to which they were accustomed. But when a long train of abuses and usurpations, pursuing invariably the same object evinces a design to reduce them under absolute despotism, it is their duty to throw off such government, and to provide new guards for their future security. Such has been the patient sufferance of the women under this government, and such is now the necessity which constrains them to demand the equal station to which they are entitled.

The history of mankind is a history of repeated injuries and usurpations on the part of man toward woman, having in direct object the establishment of an absolute tyranny over her. To prove this, let facts be submitted to a candid world.

He has never permitted her to exercise her inalienable right to the elective franchise.

He has compelled her to submit to laws, in the formation of which she had no voice.

He has withheld from her rights which are given to the most ignorant and degraded men — both natives and foreigners.

Having deprived her of this first right of a citizen, the elective franchise, thereby leaving her without representation in the halls of legislation, he has oppressed her on all sides.

He has made her, if married, in the eye of the law, civilly dead.

He has taken from her all right in property, even to the wages she earns.

He has made her, morally, an irresponsible being, as she can commit many crimes with impunity, provided they be done in the presence of her husband. In the covenant of marriage, she is compelled to promise obedience to her husband, he becoming, to all intents and purposes, her master — the law giving him power to deprive her of her liberty, and to administer chastisement.

He has so framed the laws of divorce, as to what shall be the proper causes, and in case of separation, to whom the guardianship of the children shall be given, as to be wholly regardless of the happiness of women — the law, in all cases, going upon a false supposition of the supremacy of man, and giving all power into his hands.

After depriving her of all rights as a married woman, if single, and the owner of property, he has taxed her to support a government which recignizes her only when her property can be made profitable to it.

He has monopolized nearly all the profitable employments, and from those she is permitted to follow, she receives but a scanty remuneration. He closes against her all the avenues to wealth and distinction which he considers most honorable to himself. As a teacher of theology, medicine, or law, she is not known.

He has denied her the facilities for obtaining a thorough education, all colleges being closed against her.

He allows her in Church, as well as State, but a subordinate position, claiming Apostolic authority for her exclusion from the ministry, and, with some exceptions, from any public participation in the affairs of the Church.

He has created a false public sentiment by giving to the world a different code of morals for men and women, by which moral delinquencies which exclude women from society, are not only tolerated, but deemed of little account in man.

He has usurped the prerogative of Jehovah himself, claiming it as his right to assign for her a sphere of action, when that belongs to her conscience and to her God.

He has endeavored, in every way that he could, to destroy her confidence in her own powers, to lessen her self-respect, and to make her willing to lead a dependent and abject life.

Now, in view of this entire disfranchisement of one-half the people of this country, their social and religious degradation — in view of the unjust laws above mentioned, and because women do feel themselves aggrieved, oppressed, and fraudulently deprived of their most sacred rights, we insist that they have immediate admission to all the rights and privileges which belong to them as citizens of the United States.

In entering upon the great work before us, we anticipate no small amount of misconception, misrepresentation, and ridicule; but we shall use every instrumentality within our power to effect our object. We shall employ agents, circulate tracts, petition the State and National legislatures, and endeavor to enlist the pulpit and the press in our behalf. We hope this Convention will be followed by a series of Conventions embracing every part of the country.

Seneca Falls Resolutions

Whereas, The great precept of nature is conceded to be, that "man shall pursue his own true and substantial happiness." Blackstone in his Commentaries remarks, that this law of Nature being coeval with mankind, and dictated by God himself, is of course superior in obligation to any other. It is binding over all the globe, in all countries and at all times; no human laws are of any validity if contrary to this, and such of them as are valid, derive all their force, and all their validity, and all their authority, mediately and immediately, from this original; therefore;

Resolved, That such laws as conflict, in any way, with the true and substantial hap-

piness of woman, are contrary to the great precept of nature and of no validity, for this is "superior in obligation to any other."

Resolved, That all laws which prevent woman from occupying such a station in society as her conscience shall dictate, or which place her in a position inferior to that of man, are contrary to the great precept of nature, and therefore of no force or authority.

Resolved, That woman is man's equal — was intended to be so by the Creator, and the highest good of the race demands that she should be recognized as such.

Resolved, That the women of this country ought to be enlightened in regard to the laws under which they live, that they may no longer publish their degradation by declaring themselves satisfied with their present position, nor their ignorance, by asserting that they have all the rights they want.

Resolved, That inasmuch as man, while claiming for himself intellectual superiority, does accord to woman moral superiority, it is pre-eminently his duty to encourage her to speak and teach, as she has an opportunity, in all religious assemblies.

Resolved, That the same amount of virtue, delicacy, and refinement of behavior that is required of woman in the social state, should also be required of man, and the same transgressions should be visited with equal severity on both man and woman.

Resolved, That the objection of indelicacy and impropriety, which is so often brought against woman when she addresses a public audience, comes with a very ill-grace from those who encourage, by their attendance, her appearance on the stage, in the concert, or in feats of the circus.

Resolved, That woman has too long rested satisfied in the circumscribed limits which corrupt customs and a perverted application of the Scriptures have marked out for her, and that it is time she should move in the enlarged sphere which her great Creator has assigned her.

Resolved, That it is the duty of the women of this country to secure to themselves their sacred right to the elective franchise.

Resolved, That the equality of human rights results necessarily from the fact of the identity of the race in capabilities and responsibilities.

Resolved, therefore, That, being invested by the Creator with the same capabilities, and the same consciousness of responsibility for their exercise, it is demonstrably the right and duty of woman, equally with man, to promote every righteous cause by every righteous means; and especially in regard to the great subjects of morals and religion, it is self-evidently her right to partici-pate with her brother in teaching them, both in private and in public, by writing and by speaking, by any instrumentalities proper to be used, and in any assemblies proper to be held; and this being a self-evident truth growing out of the divinely implanted principles of human nature, any custom or authority adverse to it, whether modern or wearing the hoary sanction of antiquity, is to be regarded as a self-evident falsehood, and at war with mankind.

Resolved, That the speedy success of our cause depends upon the zealous and untiring efforts of both men and women, for the overthrow of the monopoly of the pulpit, and for the securing to woman an equal participation with men in the various trades, professions, and commerce.

SPEECH BEFORE THE LEGISLATURE, 1860

ELIZABETH CADY STANTON

Elizabeth Cady was born in Johnstown, New York, in 1815. As the daughter of a judge of comfortable means, she encountered people and situations that afforded her more than the usual opportunities for education allowed girls of her time. Having displayed an earnest zest and ability for learning, she was granted special permission to attend the Boys Academy in Johnstown. Prevented by her sex from attending college, she was graduated from the rather conservative Emma Willard Seminary in Troy, New York. Afterward she studied law with her father but, again because of her sex, was prevented from gaining admission to the bar. She had learned, however, precisely how the law burdened women and wives.

Elizabeth's family and friends included many of the brightest thinkers of the Northeast, all of whom taught and influenced her. Her marriage to the activist Henry Stanton in 1840, their trip to the World Anti-Slavery Convention in London, and their move in 1842 to Boston further developed her social sensitivities, knowledge, and thirst for intellectual stimulation. After the family returned from Boston in 1846 to settle in Seneca Falls, New York, Elizabeth became isolated from friends and society. She became immersed in the duties and experiences of a housewife and mother of seven. It suffocated her. Only her visits to her friend Lucretia Mott in Waterloo, New York, revived her. There, with Lucretia and her sister Martha Wright, with Jane Hunt and Mary Ann McClintock, in what could only be called consciousness-raising sessions, seated around a table for tea, the women talked, vented their frustration, and finally planned the convention at Seneca Falls.

After that time Elizabeth Cady Stanton worked determinedly for the whole range of women's freedoms — from discrimination in marriage and divorce, to freedom from the misogyny of traditional religion (she published the *Woman's Bible* in 1895), to suffrage, and more. In 1851 she met Susan B. Anthony, with whom she worked until the end. They founded a radical magazine, *The Revolution,* in 1868, and in 1869 Stanton was elected president of the National Woman's Suffrage Association, on which she served for over twenty years. Stanton was always brave, outspoken, often ahead of her time, sometimes considered too radical even for many of the feminists. She died still at work in New York City in 1902.

Early in 1860, Stanton was invited to address the New York state legislature on a pending bill (subsequently passed) for an enlargement of women's property rights. Her speech, presented here, expressed the themes of natural human rights, the necessary limits of authority, and the parallels between blacks and females. Here is introduced, furthermore, yet another extremely important concept, one that should be carried into the present, woman as citizen. We are, after all, citizens of the United States, and our inalienable right is full participation in all the opportunities of the country.

GENTLEMEN OF THE JUDICIARY: — There are certain natural rights as inalienable to civilization as are the rights of air and motion to the savage in the wilderness. The natural rights of the civilized man and woman are government, property, the harmonious development of all their powers, and the gratification of their desires. There are a few people we now and then meet who, like Jeremy Bentham, scout the idea of natural rights in civilization, and pronounce them mere metaphors, declaring that there are no rights aside from those the law confers. If the law made man too, that might do, for then he could be made to order to fit the particular niche he was designed to fill. But inasmuch as God made man in His own image, with capacities and powers as boundless as the universe, whose exigencies no mere human law can meet, it is evident that the man must ever stand first; the law but the creature of his wants; the law giver but the mouthpiece of humanity. If, then, the nature of a being decides its rights, every individual comes into this world with rights that are not transferable. He does not bring them like a pack on his back, that may be stolen from him, but they are a component part of himself, the laws which insure his growth and development. The individual may be put in the stocks, body and soul, he may be dwarfed, crippled, killed, but his rights no man can get; they live and die with him.

Though the atmosphere is forty miles deep all around the globe, no man can do more than fill his own lungs. No man can see, hear, or smell but just so far; and though hundreds are deprived of these senses, his are not the more acute. Though rights have been abundantly supplied by the good Father, no man can appropriate to himself those that belong to another. A citizen can have but one vote, fill but one office, though thousands are not permitted to do either. These axioms prove that woman's poverty does not add to man's wealth, and if, in the plenitude of his power, he should secure to her the exercise of all her God-given rights, her wealth could not bring poverty to him. There is a kind of nervous unrest always manifested by those in power, whenever new claims are started by those out of their own immediate class. The philosophy of this is very plain. They imagine that if the rights of

Reprinted from Elizabeth Cady Stanton, Susan B. Anthony, and Matilda Joslyn Gage, eds., *History of Woman Suffrage,* vol. I (New York: Fowler and Wells, 1881). This work was reprinted by Arno Press, Inc., New York, in 1969.

this new class be granted, they must, of necessity, sacrifice something of what they already possess. They can not divest themselves of the idea that rights are very much like lands, stocks, bonds, and mortgages, and that if every new claimant be satisfied, the supply of human rights must in time run low. You might as well carp at the birth of every child, lest there should not be enough air left to inflate your lungs; at the success of every scholar, for fear that your draughts at the fountain of knowledge could not be so long and deep; at the glory of every hero, lest there be no glory left for you. . . .

If the object of government is to protect the weak against the strong, how unwise to place the power wholly in the hands of the strong. Yet that is the history of all governments, even the model republic of these United States. You who have read the history of nations, from Moses down to our last election, where have you ever seen one class looking after the interests of another? Any of you can readily see the defects in other governments, and pronounce sentence against those who have sacrificed the masses to themselves; but when we come to our own case, we are blinded by custom and self-interest. Some of you who have no capital can see the injustice which the laborer suffers; some you who have no slaves, can see the cruelty of his oppression; but who of you appreciate the galling humiliation, the refinements of degradation, to which women (the mothers, wives, sisters, and daughters of freemen) are subject, in this the last half of the nineteenth century? How many of you have ever read even the laws concerning them that now disgrace your statute-books? In cruelty and tyranny, they are not surpassed by any slaveholding code in the Southern States; in fact they are worse, by just so far as woman, from her social position, refinement, and education, is on a more equal ground with the oppressor.

Allow me just here to call the attention of that party now so much interested in the slave of the Carolinas, to the similarity in his condition and that of the mothers, wives, and daughters of the Empire State. The negro has no name. He is Cuffy Douglas or Cuffy Brooks, just whose Cuffy he may chance to be. The woman has no name. She is Mrs. Richard Roe or Mrs. John Doe, just whose Mrs. she may chance to be. Cuffy has no right to his earnings; he can not buy or sell, or lay up anything that he can call his own. Mrs. Roe has no right to her earnings; she can neither buy nor sell, make contracts, nor lay up anything that she can call her own. Cuffy has no right to his children; they can be sold from him at any time. Mrs. Roe has no right to her children; they may be bound out to cancel a father's debts of honor. The unborn child, even by the last will of the father, may be placed under the guardianship of a stranger and a foreigner. Cuffy has no legal existence; he is subject to restraint and moderate chastisement. Mrs. Roe has no legal existence; she has not the best right to her own person. The husband has the power to restrain, and administer moderate chastisement.

Blackstone declares that the husband and wife are one, and learned commentators have decided that that one is the husband. In all civil codes, you will find them classified as one. Certain rights and immunities, such and such privileges are to be secured to white male citizens. What have women and negroes to do with rights? What know they of government, war, or glory?

The prejudice against color, of which we hear so much, is no stronger than that against sex. It is produced by the same cause, and manifested very much in the same way. The negro's skin and the woman's sex are both *prima facie* evidence that they were intended to be in subjection to the white Saxon man. The few social privileges which the man gives the woman, he makes up to the negro in civil rights. The woman may sit at the same table and eat with the white man; the free negro may hold property and vote. The woman may sit in the same pew with the white man in church; the free negro may enter the pulpit and preach. Now, with the black man's right to suffrage, the right unquestioned, even by Paul, to minister at the altar, it is evident that the prejudice against sex is more deeply rooted and more unreasonably maintained than that against color. As citizens of a republic, which should we most highly prize, social privileges or civil rights? The latter, most certainly.

To those who do not feel the injustice and degradation of the condition, there is something inexpressibly comical in man's "citizen woman." It reminds me of those monsters I used to see in the old world, head and shoulders woman, and the rest of the body sometimes fish and sometimes beast. I used to think, What a strange conceit! but now I see how perfectly it represents man's idea! Look over all his laws concerning us, and you will see just enough of woman to tell of her existence; all the rest is submerged, or made to crawl upon the earth. Just imagine an inhabitant of another planet entertaining himself some pleasant evening in searching over our great national compact, our Declaration of Independence, our Constitutions, or some of our statute-books; what would he think of those "women and negroes" that must be so fenced in, so guarded against? Why, he would certainly suppose we were monsters, like those fabulous giants or Brobdignagians of olden times, so dangerous to civilized man, from our size, ferocity, and power. Then let him take up our poets, from Pope down to Dana; let him listen to our Fourth of July toasts, and some of the sentimental adulations of social life, and no logic could convince him that this creature of the law, and this angel of the family altar, could be one and the same being. Man is in such a labyrinth of contradictions with his marital and property rights; he is so befogged on the whole question of maidens, wives, and mothers, that from pure benevolence we should relieve him from this troublesome branch of legislation. We should vote, and make laws for ourselves. Do not be alarmed, dear ladies! You need spend no time reading Grotius, Coke, Puffendorf, Blackstone, Bentham, Kent, and Story to find out what you need. We may safely trust the shrewd selfishness of the white man, and consent to live under the same broad code where he has so comfortably ensconced himself. Any legislation that will do for man, we may abide by most cheerfully. . . .

But, say you, we would not have woman exposed to the grossness and vulgarity of public life, or encounter what she must at the polls. When you talk, gentlemen, of sheltering woman from the rough winds and revolting scenes of real life, you must be either talking for effect, or wholly ignorant of what the facts of life are. The man, whatever he is, is known to the woman. She is the companion, not only of the accomplished statesman, the orator, and the scholar; but the vile, vulgar, brutal man has his mother, his wife, his sister, his daughter. Yes, delicate, refined, educated women are in daily life with the drunkard, the gambler, the licentious man, the rogue, and the villain; and if man shows out what he is anywhere, it is at his own hearthstone. There are over forty thousand drunkards in this State. All these are bound by the ties of family to some woman. Allow but a mother and a wife to each, and you have over eighty thousand women. All these have seen their fathers, brothers, husbands, sons, in the lowest and most debased stages of obscenity and degradation. In your own circle of friends, do you not know refined women, whose whole lives are darkened and saddened by gross and brutal associations? Now, gentlemen, do you talk to woman of a rude jest or jostle at the polls, where noble, virtuous men stand ready to protect her person and her rights, when, alone in the darkness and solitude and gloom of night, she has trembled on her own threshold, awaiting the return of a husband from his midnight revels? — when, stepping from her chamber, she has beheld her royal monarch, her lord and master — her legal representative — the protector of her property, her home, her children, and her person, down on his hands and knees slowly crawling up the stairs? Behold him in her chamber — in her bed! The fairy tale of "Beauty and the Beast" is far too often realized in life. Gentlemen, such scenes as woman has witnessed at her own fireside, where no eye save Omnipotence could pity, no strong arm could help, can never be realized at the polls, never equaled elsewhere, this side the bottomless pit. No, woman has not hitherto lived in the clouds, surrounded by an atmosphere of purity and peace — but she has been the companion of man in health, in sickness, and in death, in his highest and in his lowest moments. She has worshiped him as a saint and an orator, and pitied him as madman or a fool. In Paradise, man and woman were placed together, and so they must ever be. They must sink or rise together. If man is low and wretched and vile, woman can not escape the contagion, and any atmosphere that is unfit for woman to breathe is not fit for man. Verily, the sins of the fathers shall be visited upon the children to the third and fourth generation. You, by your unwise legislation, have crippled and dwarfed womanhood, by closing to her all honorable and lucrative means of employment, have driven her into the garrets and dens of our cities, where she now revenges herself on your innocent sons, sapping the very foundations of national virtue and strength. Alas! for the young men just

coming on the stage of action, who soon shall fill your vacant places — our future Senators, our Presidents, the expounders of our constitutional law! Terrible are the penalties we are now suffering for the ages of injustice done to woman.

Again, it is said that the majority of women do not ask for any change in the laws; that it is time enough to give them the elective franchise when they, as a class, demand it.

Wise statesmen legislate for the best interests of the nation; the State, for the highest good of its citizens; the Christian, for the conversion of the world. Where would have been our railroads, our telegraphs, our ocean steamers, our canals and harbors, our arts and sciences, if government had withheld the means from the far-seeing minority? This State established our present system of common schools, fully believing that educated men and women would make better citizens than ignorant ones. In making this provision for the education of its children, had they waited for a majority of the urchins of this State to petition for schools, how many, think you, would have asked to be transplanted from the street to the school-house? Does the State wait for the criminal to ask for his prison-house? the insane, the idiot, the deaf and dumb for his asylum? Does the Christian, in his love to all mankind, wait for the majority of the benighted heathen to ask him for the gospel? No; unasked and unwelcomed, he crosses the trackless ocean, rolls off the mountain of superstition that oppresses the human mind, proclaims the immortality of the soul, the dignity of manhood, the right of all to be free and happy.

No, gentlemen, if there is but one woman in this State who feels the injustice of her position, she should not be denied her inalienable rights, because the common household drudge and the silly butterfly of fashion are ignorant of all laws, both human and Divine. Because they know nothing of governments, or rights, and therefore ask nothing, shall my petitions be unheard? I stand before you the rightful representative of woman, claiming a share in the halo of glory that has gathered round her in the ages, and by the wisdom of her past words and works, her peerless heroism and self-sacrifice, I challenge your admiration; and, moreover, claiming, as I do, a share in all her outrages and sufferings, in the cruel injustice, contempt, and ridicule now heaped upon her, in her deep degradation, hopeless wretchedness, by all that is helpless in her present condition, that is false in law and public sentiment, I urge your generous consideration; for as my heart swells with pride to behold woman in the highest walks of literature and art, it grows big enough to take in those who are bleeding in the dust.

Now do not think, gentlemen, we wish you to do a great many troublesome things for us. We do not ask our legislators to spend a whole session in fixing up a code of laws to satisfy a class of most unreasonable women. We ask no more than the poor devils in the Scripture asked, "Let us alone." In mercy, let us take care of ourselves, our property, our children, and our homes. True, we are not so strong, so wise, so crafty as you are, but if any kind friend leaves us a little money, or we can by great industry earn fifty cents a day, we would rather buy bread and clothes for our children than cigars and champagne for our legal protectors. There has been a great deal written and said about protection. We, as a class, are tired of one kind of protection, that which leaves us everything to do, to dare, and to suffer, and strips us of all means for its accomplishment. We would not tax man to take care of us. No, the Great Father has endowed all his creatures with the necessary powers for self-support, self-defense,

and protection. We do not ask man to represent us; it is hard enough in times like these for man to carry backbone enough to represent himself. So long as the mass of men spend most of their time on the fence, not knowing which way to jump, they are surely in no condition to tell us where we had better stand. In pity for man, we would no longer hang like a millstone round his neck. Undo what man did for us in the dark ages, and strike out all special legislation for us; strike the words "white male" from all your constitutions, and then, with fair sailing, let us sink or swim, live or die, survive or perish together.

At Athens, an ancient apologue tells us, on the completion of the temple of Minerva, a statue of the goddess was wanted to occupy the crowning point of the edifice. Two of the greatest artists produced what each deemed his masterpiece. One of these figures was the size of life, admirably designed, exquisitely finished, softly rounded, and beautifully refined. The other was of Amazonian stature, and so boldly chiselled that it looked more like masonry than sculpture. The eyes of all were attracted by the first, and turned away in contempt from the second. That, therefore, was adopted, and the other rejected, almost with resentment, as though an insult had been offered to a discerning public. The favored statue was accordingly borne in triumph to the place for which it was designed, in the presence of applauding thousands, but as it receded from their upturned eyes, all at once agaze upon it, the thunders of applause unaccountably died away — a general misgiving ran through every bosom — the mob themselves stood like statues, as silent and as petrified, for as it slowly went up, and up, the soft expression of those chiselled features, the delicate curves and outlines of the limbs and figure, became gradually fainter and fainter, and when at last it reached the place for which it was intended, it was a shapeless ball, enveloped in mist. Of course, the idol of the hour was now clamored down as rationally as it had been cried up, and its dishonored rival, with no good will and no good looks on the part of the chagrined populace, was reared in its stead. As it ascended, the sharp angles faded away, the rough points became smooth, the features full of expression, the whole figure radiant with majesty and beauty. The rude hewn mass, that before had scarcely appeared to bear even the human form, assumed at once the divinity which it represented, being so perfectly proportioned to the dimensions of the building, and to the elevation on which it stood, that it seemed as though Pallas herself had alighted upon the pinnacle of the temple in person, to receive the homage of her worshippers.

The woman of the nineteenth century is the shapeless ball in the lofty position which she was designed fully and nobly to fill. The place is not too high, too large, too sacred for woman, but the type that you have chosen is far too small for it. The woman we declare unto you is the rude, misshapen, unpolished object of the successful artist. From your stand-point, you are absorbed with the defects alone. The true artist sees the harmony between the object and its destination. Man, the sculptor, has carved out his ideal, and applauding thousands welcome his success. He has made a woman that from his low stand-point looks fair and beautiful, a being without rights, or hopes, or fears but in him — neither noble, virtuous, nor independent. Where do we see, in Church or State, in school-house or at the fireside, the much talked-of moral power of woman? Like those Athenians, we have bowed down and worshiped in woman, beauty, grace, the exquisite proportions, the soft and beautifully rounded outline, her delicacy, refinement, and silent helplessness — all well when she is viewed simply as an object of sight, never to rise one foot above the dust from which she sprung. But if she is to be raised up to adorn a temple, or represent a divinity — if she is to fill the niche of wife and counsellor to true and noble men, if she is to be the mother, the educator of a race of heroes or martyrs, of a Napoleon, or a Jesus — then must the type of womanhood be on a larger scale than that yet carved by man.

In vain would the rejected artist have reasoned with the Athenians as to the superiority of his production; nothing short of the experiment they made could have satisfied them. And what of your experiment, what of your wives, your homes? Alas! for the folly and vacancy that meet you there! But for your club-houses and newspapers, what would social life be to you? Where are your beautiful women? your frail ones, taught to lean lovingly and confidingly on man? Where are the crowds of educated dependents — where the long line of pensioners on man's bounty? Where all the young girls, taught to believe that marriage is the only legitimate object of a woman's pursuit — they who stand listlessly on life's shores, waiting, year after year, like the sick man at the pool of Bethesda, for some one to come and put them in? These are they who by their ignorance and folly curse almost every fireside with some human specimen of deformity or imbecility. These are they who fill the gloomy abodes of poverty and vice in our vast metropolis. These are they who patrol the streets of our cities, to give our sons their first lessons in infamy. These are they who fill our asylums, and make night hideous with their cries and groans.

The women who are called masculine, who are brave, courageous, self-reliant and independent, are they who in the face of adverse winds have kept one steady course upward and onward in the paths of virtue and peace — they who have taken their gauge of womanhood from their own native strength and dignity — they who have learned for themselves the will of God concerning them. This is our type of womanhood. Will you help us raise it up, that you too may see its beautiful proportions — that you may behold the outline of the goddess who is yet to adorn your temple of Freedom? We are building a model republic; our edifice will one day need a crowning glory.

Let the artists be wisely chosen. Let them begin their work. Here is a temple of Liberty, to human rights, on whose portals behold the glorious declaration, "All men are created equal." The sun has never yet shone upon any of man's creations that can compare with this. The artist who can mold a statue worthy to crown magnificence like this, must be godlike in his conceptions, grand in his comprehensions, sublimely beautiful in his power of execution. The woman — the crowning glory of the model republic among the nations of the earth — what must she not be? (Loud applause)

CONSTITUTIONAL ARGUMENT

SUSAN B. ANTHONY

Susan B. Anthony was born in Adams, Massachusetts, in 1820. Her father, a Quaker steeped in that religion's historic principle of sexual equality, held Susan in high regard. He educated her as he would a son, taught her responsibility and self-reliance, entrusted her with the management of his farm, and introduced her to the people and ideas of the liberal reform movements current in Rochester, New York, where they had come to live about 1839. In her teens, Susan taught at the Canajoharie Institute, but teaching was not a sufficient challenge for her. Later, having returned to Rochester, she became active in a reform movement to which several of her friends belonged — temperance. It was through the Rochester Daughters of Temperance that she met Amelia Bloomer of Seneca Falls who, in 1851, introduced her to Elizabeth Cady Stanton.

The women became friends very quickly. Anthony was soon invited to Stanton's home to discuss ideas, and Anthony's views developed rapidly to coalesce with Stanton's. The two lectured and worked together and founded *The Revolution,* a radical magazine. In 1872, to bring to the test of the Supreme Court her conviction that as a citizen she was guaranteed by the Fourteenth Amendment the right to vote, Anthony "knowingly, wrongfully, and unlawfully" cast a vote in the election in Rochester. Arrested, convicted, and fined, she refused to pay, hoping for an appeal path, but the fine was not pursued. Nonetheless, she brought her principle into view and gained considerable sympathy. Later she was to lecture on co-education (deemed very radical at the time) and on all the various women's issues, and to serve on the National American Woman's Suffrage Association and the International Council of Women. In 1902, shortly after her retirement, she died.

Like Stanton, Anthony was one of the strongest models in feminist history. The following selection is from a speech delivered during a tour of New York State prior to her trial in 1873. In it Anthony argued her thesis that both the original conception and the current law of the U.S. Constitution guaranteed her a citizen's right to vote.

FRIENDS AND FELLOW-CITIZENS: — I stand before you under indictment for the alleged crime of having voted at the last presidential election, without having a lawful right to vote. It shall be my work this evening to prove to you that in thus doing, I not only committed no crime, but instead simply exercised my citizen's right, guaranteed to me and all United States citizens by the National Constitution beyond the power of any State to deny.

Our democratic-republican government is based on the idea of the natural right of every individual member thereof to a voice and a vote in making and executing the laws. We assert the province of government to be to secure the people in the enjoyment of their inalienable rights. We throw to the winds the old dogma that government can give rights. No one denies that before governments were organized each individual possessed the right to protect his own life, liberty and property. When 100 or 1,000,000 people enter into a free government, they do not barter away their natural rights; they simply pledge themselves to protect each other in the enjoyment of them through prescribed judicial and legislative tribunals. They agree to abandon the methods of brute force in the adjustment of their differences and adopt those of civilization. Nor can you find a word in any of the grand documents left us by the fathers which assumes for government the power to create or to confer rights. The Declaration of Independence, the United States Constitution, the constitutions of the several States and the organic laws of the Territories, all alike propose to *protect* the people in the exercise of their God-given rights. Not one of them pretends to bestow rights.

Reprinted from Ida H. Harper, *Life and Work of Susan B. Anthony,* vol. II (Indianapolis: Bowen-Merrill, 1898).

All men are created equal, and endowed by their Creator with certain inalienable rights. Among these are life, liberty and the pursuit of happiness. To secure these, governments are instituted among men, deriving their just powers from the consent of the governed.

Here is no shadow of government authority over rights, or exclusion of any class from their full and equal enjoyment. Here is pronounced the right of all men, and "consequently," as the Quaker preacher said, "of all women," to a voice in the government. And here, in this first paragraph of the Declaration, is the assertion of the natural right of all to the ballot; for how can "the consent of the governed" be given, if the right to vote be denied? Again:

> Whenever any form of government becomes destructive of these ends, it is the right of the people to alter or abolish it, and to institute a new government, laying its foundations on such principles, and organizing its powers in such form, as to them shall seem most likely to effect their safety and happiness.

Surely the right of the whole people to vote is here clearly implied; for however destructive to their happiness this government might become, a disfranchised class could neither alter nor abolish it, nor institute a new one, except by the old brute force method of insurrection and rebellion. One-half of the people of this nation today are utterly powerless to blot from the statute books an unjust law, or to write there a new and a just one. The women, dissatisfied as they are with this form of government, that enforces taxation without representation — that compels them to obey laws to which they never have given their consent — that imprisons and hangs them without a trial by a jury of their peers — that robs them, in marriage, of the custody of their own persons, wages and children — are this half of the people who are left wholly at the mercy of the other half, in direct violation of the spirit and letter of the declarations of the framers of this government, every one of which was based on the immutable principle of equal rights to all. By these declarations, kings, popes, priests, aristocrats, all were alike dethroned and placed on a common level, politically, with the lowliest born subject or serf. By them, too, men, as such, were deprived of their divine right to rule and placed on a political level with women. By the practice of these declarations all class and caste distinctions would be abolished, and slave, serf, plebeian, wife, woman, all alike rise from their subject position to the broader platform of equality.

The preamble of the Federal Constitution says:

> We, the people of the United States, in order to form a more perfect union, establish justice, insure domestic tranquillity, provide for the common defence, promote the general welfare and secure the blessings of liberty to ourselves and our posterity, do ordain and establish this Constitution for the United States of America.

It was we, the people, not we, the white male citizens, nor we, the male citizens; but we, the whole people, who formed this Union. We formed it not to give the blessings of liberty but to secure them; not to the half of ourselves and the half of our posterity, but to the whole people — women as well as men. It is downright mockery to talk to women of their enjoyment of the blessings of liberty while they are denied the only means of securing them provided by this democratic-republican government — the ballot. . . .

But I submit that in view of the explicit assertions of the equal right of the whole people, both in the preamble and previous article of the constitution, this omission of the adjective "female" should not be construed into a denial; but instead should be considered as of no effect. Mark the direct prohibition, "No member of this State shall be disfranchised, unless by the law of the land, or the judgment of his peers." "The law of the land" is the United States Constitution; and there is no provision in that document which can be fairly construed into a permission to the States to deprive any class of citizens of their right to vote. Hence New York can get no power from that source to disfranchise one entire half of her members. Nor has "the judgment of their peers" been pronounced against women exercising their right to vote; no disfranchised person is allowed to be judge or juror — and none but disfranchised persons can be women's peers. Nor has the legislature passed laws excluding women as a class on account of idiocy or lunacy; nor have the courts convicted them of bribery, larceny or any infamous crime. Clearly, then, there is no constitutional ground for the exclusion of women from the ballot-box in the State of New York. No barriers whatever stand today between women and the exercise of their right to vote save those of precedent and prejudice, which refuse to expunge the word "male" from the constitution. . . .

For any State to make sex a qualification, which must ever result in the disfranchisement of one entire half of the people, is to pass a bill of attainder, an ex post facto law, and is therefore a violation of the supreme law of the land. By it the blessings of liberty are forever withheld from women and their female posterity. For them, this government has no just powers derived from the consent of the governed. For them this government is not a democracy; it is not a republic. It is the most odious aristocracy ever established on the face of the globe. An oligarchy of wealth, where the rich govern the poor;

an oligarchy of learning, where the educated govern the ignorant; or even an oligarchy of race, where the Saxon rules the African, might be endured; but this oligarchy of sex which makes father, brothers, husband, sons, the oligarchs over the mother and sisters, the wife and daughters of every household; which ordains all men sovereigns, all women subjects — carries discord and rebellion into every home of the nation. This most odious aristocracy exists, too, in the face of Section 4, Article IV, which says: "The United States shall guarantee to every State in the Union a republican form of government."

What, I ask you, is the distinctive difference between the inhabitants of a monarchical and those of a republican form of government, save that in the monarchical the people are subjects, helpless, powerless, bound to obey laws made by political superiors; while in the republican the people are citizens, individual sovereigns, all clothed with equal power to make and unmake both their laws and law-makers? The moment you deprive a person of his right to a voice in the government, you degrade him from the status of a citizen of the republic to that of a subject. It matters very little to him whether his monarch be an individual tyrant, as is the Czar of Russia, or a 15,000,000 headed monster, as here in the United States; he is a powerless subject, serf or slave; not in any sense a free and independent citizen.

It is urged that the use of the masculine pronouns *he, his* and *him* in all the constitutions and laws, is proof that only men were meant to be included in their provisions. If you insist on this version of the letter of the law, we shall insist that you be consistent and accept the other horn of the dilemma, which would compel you to exempt women from taxation for the support of the government and from penalties for the violation of laws. There is no *she* or *her* or *hers* in the tax laws, and this is equally true of all the criminal laws.

Take for example the civil rights law which I am charged with having violated; not only are all the pronouns in it masculine, but everybody knows that it was intended expressly to hinder the rebel men from voting. It reads, "If any person shall knowingly vote without *his* having a lawful right." It was precisely so with all the papers served on me — the United States marshal's warrant, the bail-bond, the petition for habeas corpus, the bill of indictment — not one of them had a feminine pronoun; but to make them applicable to me, the clerk of the court prefixed an "s" to the "he" and made "her" out of "his" and "him"; and I insist if government officials may thus manipulate the pronouns to tax, fine, imprison and hang women, it is their duty to thus change them in order to protect us in our right to vote.

So long as any classes of men were denied this right, the government made a show of consistency by exempting them from taxation. When a property qualification of $250 was required of black men in New York, they were not compelled to pay taxes so long as they were content to report themselves worth less than that sum; but the moment the black man died and his property fell to his widow or daughter, the black woman's name was put on the assessor's list and she was compelled to pay taxes on this same property. This also is true of ministers in New York. So long as the minister lives, he is exempted from taxation on $1,500 of property, but the moment the breath leaves his body, his widow's name goes on the assessor's list and she has to pay taxes on the $1,500. So much for special legislation in favor of women! . . .

The only question left to be settled now is: Are women persons? I scarcely believe any of our opponents will have the hardihood to say they are not. Being persons, then, women are citizens, and no State has a right to make any new law, or to enforce any old law, which shall abridge their privileges or immunities. Hence, every discrimination against women in the constitutions and laws of the several States is today null and void, precisely as is every one against negroes. . . .

If once we establish the false principle that United States citizenship does not carry with it the right to vote in every State in this Union, there is no end to the petty tricks and cunning devices which will be attempted to exclude one and another class of citizens from the right of suffrage. It will not always be the men combining to disfranchise all women; native born men combining to abridge the rights of all naturalized citizens, as in Rhode Island. It will not always be the rich and educated who may combine to cut off the poor and ignorant; but we may live to see the hard-working, uncultivated day laborers, foreign and native born, learning the power of the ballot and their vast majority of numbers, combine and amend State constitutions so as to disfranchise the Vanderbilts, the Stewarts, the Conklings and the Fentons. It is a poor rule that won't work more ways than one. Establish this precedent, admit the State's right to deny suffrage, and there is no limit to the confusion, discord and disruption that may await us. There is and can be but one safe principle of government — equal rights to all. Discrimination against any class on account of color, race, nativity, sex, property, culture, can but embitter and disaffect that class, and thereby endanger the safety of the whole people. Clearly, then, the national government not only must define the rights of citizens, but must stretch out its powerful hand and protect them in every State in this Union.

If, however, you will insist that the Fifteenth Amendment's emphatic interdiction against robbing United States citizens of their suffrage "on account of race, color or previous condition of servitude," is a recognition of the right of either the United States or any State to deprive them of the ballot for any or all other reasons, I will prove to you that the class of citizens for whom I now plead are, by all the principles of our government and many of the laws of the States, included under the term "previous condition of servitude."

Consider first married women and their legal status. What is servitude? "The condition of a slave." What is a slave? "A person who is robbed of the proceeds of his labor; a person who is subject to the will of another." By the laws of Georgia, South Carolina and all the States of the South, the negro had no right to the custody and control of his person. He belonged to his master. If he were disobedient, the master had the right to use correction. If the negro did not like the correction and ran away, the master had the right to use coercion to bring him back. By the laws of almost every State in this Union today, North as well as South, the married woman has no right to the custody and control of her person. The wife belongs to the husband; and if she refuse obedience he may use moderate correction, and if she do not like his moderate correction and leave his "bed and board," the husband may use moderate coercion to bring her back. The little word "moderate," you see, is the saving clause for the wife, and would doubtless be overstepped should her offended husband administer his correction with the "cat-o'-nine-tails," or accomplish his coercion with blood-hounds.

Again the slave had no right to the earnings of his hands, they belonged to his master; no right to the custody of his children, they belonged to his master; no right to sue or be sued, or to testify in the courts. If he committed a crime, it was the master who must sue or be sued. In many of the States there has been special legislation, giving married women the right to property inherited or received by bequest, or earned by the pursuit of any avocation outside the home; also giving them the right to sue and be sued in matters pertaining to such separate property; but not a single State of this Union has ever secured the wife in the enjoyment of her right to equal ownership of the joint earnings of the marriage copartnership. And since, in the nature of things, the vast majority of married women never earn a dollar by work outside their families, or inherit a dollar from their fathers, it follows that from the day of their marriage to the day of the death of their husbands not one of them ever has a dollar, except it shall please her husband to let her have it.

In some of the States, also, laws have been passed giving to the mother a joint right with the father in the guardianship of the children. Twenty-five years ago, when our woman's rights movement commenced, by the laws of all the States the father had the sole custody and control of the children. No matter if he were a brutal, drunken libertine, he had the legal right, without the mother's consent, to apprentice her sons to rumsellers or her daughters to brothel-keepers. He even could will away an unborn child from the mother. In most of the States this law still prevails, and the mothers are utterly powerless.

I doubt if there is, today, a State in this Union where a married woman can sue or be sued for slander of character, and until recently there was not one where she could sue or be sued for injury of person. However damaging to the wife's reputation any slander may be, she is wholly powerless to institute legal proceedings against her accuser unless her husband shall join with her; and how often have we heard of the husband conspiring with some outside barbarian to blast the good name of his wife?

A married woman can not testify in courts in cases of joint interest with her husband. . . .

I submit the question, if the deprivation by law of the ownership of one's own person, wages, property, children, the denial of the right as an individual to sue and be sued and testify in the courts, is not a condition of servitude most bitter and absolute, even though under the sacred name of marriage? Does any lawyer doubt my statement of the legal status of married women? I will remind him of the fact that the common law of England prevails in every State but two in this Union, except where the legislature has enacted special laws annulling it. I am ashamed that not one of the States yet has blotted from its statute books the old law of marriage, which, summed up in the fewest words possible, is in effect "husband and wife are one, and that one the husband."

Thus may all married women and widows, by the laws of the several States, be technically included in the Fifteenth Amendment's specification of "condition of servitude," present or previous. The facts also prove that, by all the great fundamental principles of our free government, not only married women but the entire womanhood of the nation are in a "condition of servitude" as surely as were our Revolutionary fathers when they rebelled against King George. Women are taxed without representation, governed without their consent, tried, convicted and punished without a jury of their peers. Is all this tyranny any less humiliating and degrading to women under our democratic-republican government today than it was to men under their aristocratic, monarchial government one hundred years ago? . . .

Is anything further needed to prove woman's condition of servitude sufficient to entitle her to the guarantees of the Fifteenth Amendment? Is there a man who will not agree with me that to talk of freedom without the ballot is mockery to the women of this republic, precisely as New England's orator, Wendell Phillips, at the close of the late war declared it to be to the newly emancipated black man? I admit that, prior to the rebellion, by common consent, the right to enslave, as well as to disfranchise both native and foreign born persons, was conceded to the States. But the one grand principle settled by the war and the reconstruction legislation, is the supremacy of the national government to protect the citizens of the United States in their right to freedom and the elective franchise, against any and every interference on the part of the several States; and again and again have the American people asserted the triumph of this principle by their overwhelming majorities for Lincoln and Grant. . . .

It is upon this just interpretation of the United States Constitution that our National Woman Suffrage Association, which celebrates the twenty-fifth anniversary of the woman's rights movement next May in New York City, has based all its arguments and action since the passage of these amendments. We no longer petition legislature or Congress to give us the right to vote, but appeal to women everywhere to exercise their too long neglected "citizen's right." . . .

CLASS ROOTS OF FEMINISM

KAREN SACKS

Karen Sacks teaches anthropology and Women's Studies, currently at the Center for the Study of Family and the State at Duke University. She is the author of several articles on women and class struggle and of a forthcoming book, *Sisters and Wives*.

Generally speaking, we tend to hear most about the political and psycho-social issues raised during the nineteenth century and carried into the twentieth. One ought not to forget that economic issues were also at the heart of both the abolition and the women's rights movements. Karen Sacks traces those issues in the following article. She describes the separate trends in the women's movement: black women's drive for legal and economic equality, middle-class women's push for educational opportunity and full legal membership in their class, and working-class women's drive for economic progress. Sacks's discussion reveals some of the sources of tension among these groups today, in their differing needs and priorities, but she demonstrates the fallacy of identifying the entire movement as a "white middle-class movement."

During the nineteenth century (say from 1820 to 1920) the women's movement in the United States was not a single movement, but rather three movements which were consciously movements for the rights of women.

There was an industrial-working-class women's movement for economic improvement

This article is a revised version of a paper read at the University of Connecticut Anthropology Department and at the 1973 meetings of the American Anthropological Association. The following people gave various kinds of assistance and very helpful criticism: Mary Clark, Soon Young Yoon, Bill Derman, Bobbye Ortiz, Rayna Reiter, Susan Reverby, the N.Y. Women's Anthropology Conference, and the librarians at the Archives of Labor History and Urban Affairs at Wayne State University. [K. Sacks' note] and equality which began with the earliest factories in the United States, the New England textile mills of the 1830s. Second, there was a black women's movement made up of working- and middle-class black women against racism and for both economic improvement and legal equality with whites. This also had its roots in the 1830s, in the black convention movements.* And finally, there was the white middle-class movement for legal equality which had its beginnings in women's attempts to become full legal members of their class, also in the 1830s.

While two well-known histories of the women's movement[1] show clearly that the white middle-class movement did not speak for all women, they do not examine the demands, priorities, and alliances of all three movements from the viewpoint of class roots and class interests. I would like to sketch such an analysis.

Class is the key, in the sense that the material conditions of black and working-class women, as well as the social ideology regarding them, have been very different from the material conditions of white middle-class women and their corresponding social ideologies. In both the colonial period and after independence, the only woman whose place was in the home was the woman of property. Neither slave women nor free propertyless women "belonged" there. Before the growth of industry, the United States had a domestic and agrarian economy in which men and women both could play a productive role "at home," so to speak — provided they owned or leased or otherwise had access to a home with farm (means of production), which most whites and some free blacks did. But those without their own household means of production, both men and women, had to work for someone else. Puritan religion and law in the North and slavery in the South were in agreement that those without property, free or slave, male or female, had an obligation to work for those with property. The terrible stigma attached to idleness by the Puritan religion largely served the interests of employers of labor. Efforts to stimulate a cloth-making industry, dating from the colonial period, emphasize the labor of "our own women and children who are now in a great measure idle."[2] Propertyless people who were not working for a master were a "public nuisance," the "public" in this phrase meaning, of course, people with property (especially manufacturing interests). Several New England states had laws compelling the binding out of children of the poor until the age of marriage. Adult poor, female as well as male, could be punished for "idleness." Thus for free as well as slave women, work outside the home was not looked down upon as unfeminine; rather, it was demanded as the only virtuous activity of propertyless women.

Propertied women, on the other hand, were virtuous and productive mistresses of households — until factories operated by propertyless women began to transform the domestic economy into an industrial one. Then they became ladies ("of leisure" being implicit in the word). The Southern transformation from domestic to industrial economy lay earlier, in the development of plantation slavery, with cotton grown partly by black women and a household run by the labor of

* I could find very little information on the class composition of black women's organizations, or on the organizations and struggles of working-class black women. Thus there is a data bias of which the reader should be aware. Though there were national black conventions from 1830, the earliest specific mention of women's rights, support for the Seneca Falls Declaration, is in 1848 (R. E. Paulson, *Women's Suffrage and Prohibition* [Glenview: Scott Foresman, 1973], p. 34). The 1848 convention in Cleveland resolved for equality for women with men and for full citizenship, including the vote for black men and women (H. H. Bell, ed., *Minutes and Proceedings of the National Negro Conventions 1830–1864* [New York: Arno Press and the *New York Times*, 1969]).

black women. Thus, a double standard based on class came into being for women.

The self-consciously feminist movements and groups which developed — chiefly in the North during the nineteenth century — reflect the different circumstances of middle- and working-class women in the pre-Civil War years. Goals and tactics differed by class. Working-class women fought for more wages, equal wages with men, shorter hours, health, safety, and protective legislation. These were clearly class demands, and collective action was used to get them: strikes and unions mainly, but electoral pressure too (even without the vote). But working-class women also formed protective societies which got together for the purpose of self-"improvement" or of coping with various facets of a difficult life, rather than for the purpose of fighting to change social conditions.

The middle-class movement used analogous tactics, but in different proportions. Here, struggles of women to obtain and provide professional education and professional jobs for women, and to speak in public as full members of the anti-slavery movement, were, by and large, waged individually by women, rather than as part of a collective movement. It was the Abolition movement which gave birth to a self-conscious women's movement in the middle class, one which engaged in collective action, largely in the form of legislative petitions.

The pre-Civil War struggles were more social and thus collective among working-class women, and more self-help among middle-class women. This was due largely to the nature of the demands themselves and to the identity of the enemy, or obstacle. Education involved attacking no enemies. Likewise, both black and white women's improvement or protective societies were self-help ventures and did not identify enemies. The economic demands of women factory workers, on the other hand, were pursued solely by collective action directed against both mill owners and legislators.

Along with mill work, teaching school was a widespread women's occupation throughout this period. Not only were teachers and mill girls from the same background (farm families), but some women did both, alternating teaching and mill work. Though mill work paid badly, teaching paid worse. Schools were tiny affairs with few teachers, but factories often had several thousand workers. Despite the relatively better pay, it was the collective situation which allowed women to define "relatively better" as absolutely unsatisfactory by forming their own organization. Teachers, isolated and scattered, seem to have suffered in silence.

In the middle-class movement, collective action focused on those aspects of domestic law which prevented married women from having an independent economic status. Women's right to own inherited property was petitioned for and won without much opposition. But such a law had little relevance to working-class women. The situation in New York, the first state to pass such a law (1848), is illuminating. Its moving force was largely propertied males: "Fathers who had estates to bequeath to their daughters," and "husbands in extensive business operations [who could] see the advantage of allowing the wife the right to hold separate property." [3]

Middle-class women led two other important struggles in the legal realm of household affairs which did have relevance to working-class women: for the right of the woman to her own wages and to custody of children. By 1880 these were won in most states. New York was again the first state in which public sentiment for these changes was organized, beginning in 1854 via a petition campaign throughout the state. Middle-class feminists organized a delegation of working-class women to present this petition to the legislature and argue for it.[4] When it failed to move the legislature, Susan B. Anthony campaigned again throughout the state. Precisely what happened between 1855 and 1860 is not clear. But in 1860 the legislature passed a bill giving women property ownership, the right to collect their own wages, to sue in court, and to inherit the husband's property. It seems, though, that the majority of advances in civil law pertained to property law and thus to the middle and upper classes. While legislatures may have had to be persuaded, there were solid class interests for such reforms among propertied males and females.

As regards working-class women, the middle-class women who gathered at the Rochester women's convention in 1848 seem to have been both conscious of their own class and divided on class vs. sex interests. While all other resolutions passed clearly stated beliefs and principles, this one hedged: Resolved *"that those who* believe the laboring classes of women are oppressed, ought to do all in their power to raise their wages, beginning with their own household servants."[5]

Collective action by textile-mill women preceded that of middle-class women. Textile mills, centered in New England and staffed almost totally by women, were the nuclei of pre-Civil War U.S. industry. The first factory strike took place in 1824, just after the birth of the factories themselves, and involved both men and women. The 1830s saw a large number of strikes and the beginnings of many labor organizations, labor parties and papers, all short-lived. In this context, the record is full of male-female labor cooperation and independent women's actions and organizations. One of these labor parties, the Association of Working People of New Castle, Delaware, demanded the vote for women in 1831.[6]

Women were in the forefront and leadership of trade-union development in the 1840s and the focus was in the textile industry. The mills of the 1830s had been staffed by single women, largely daughters of farmers, who worked for a short time or a specific purpose. In the crisis of 1837 many farms were wiped out, and the workers in the mills during the forties and fifties were, by and large, landless native-born and Irish immigrants who could no longer quit if wages and hours were unsatisfactory. Out of this milieu came a whole host of factory-worker papers and organizations. The New England Female Labor Reform Association (FLRA) under its president, Sarah Bagley, a Lowell factory worker, became the main group for factory women. In addition to organizing in New England, this group stimulated and kept in contact with branches of women textile-worker groups in New York and western Pennsylvania. Though officially an affiliate of the New England Working-men's Association (NEWA), in reality it was the center of it and provided much of its leadership, particularly in the fight for the ten-hour day. The FLRA argued for a ten-hour law in the Massachusetts legislature and, despite the fact that women could not vote, ran a successful campaign to defeat the re-election of Lowell's state representative, a mill owners' man who opposed the ten-hour bill.

Though women workers were centered in New England, the biggest women's struggle took place in the western Pennsylvania textile mills. Here the workers struck in 1845 for a ten-hour day. After a month, some workers began returning to the mills. But women strikers, aided by a "men's auxiliary," stormed the gates of one factory and threw out the strikebreakers. Despite this militancy, the strikers were told that they would get a ten-hour day only when New England workers did. They then appealed to the NEWA and the FLRA for help. Apparently only the women in New England were ready to call a general strike. In the face of the NEWA's hopelessness, they gave it up. Again in 1848 the Pennsylvania workers went out on strike, and again it looked like defeat. This time, the women, armed with axes, stormed the factory, took on a company of police, captured the strikebreakers, and then closed it down again. The leaders were arrested, but the strike continued. Though they finally won a ten-hour day only by accepting a wage cut, it is not clear whether they soon increased their wages to what they had been for twelve hours' work.[7] In any case, these early textile battles show the militance and leadership women gave to the early labor movement.

Though largely separate, the working-class and middle-class movements had a common ground in the anti-slavery movement. Abolition joined white well-to-do and professional people with free black men and women, and in the 1840s with a growing number of white workers, particularly from the New England textile mills. In Abolition one finds the seeds of class and race conflicts which pitted the women's movements against each other. In the 1830s the anti-slavery movement had split over women's participation, with particularly strong objections coming from the clergy. Middle-class women saw Abolition and women's rights as part of a single movement for extending democracy. In 1832 Lowell factory women formed a Female Anti-Slavery Society, and by 1845 they were fund-raising and circulating anti-slavery petitions, despite hostility on the part of the mill owners.[8] But their reasons for favoring Abolition differed from those of middle-class women. The mill women argued that a labor force in slavery degraded free labor as well as slave labor, and that all labor had a two-faced enemy:

"the lord of the loom and the lord of the lash."

Abolition, whether spoken by middle- or working-class people, faced much more organized opposition than women's rights. Mobs in the North were "organized and led by prominent, respected members of the community." And, according to R. B. Nye, the major root of pro-slavery force was economic: fear of displeasing the Southern planter on whom much of New York commerce and rising New England textiles depended.[9] Indeed, H. Josephson has shown how assiduously the New England magnates of the 1840s and 1850s courted the planters and reviled the Abolitionists.[10]

Yet the anti-slavery movement contained much of the racism and class antagonisms which led to three separate and generally antagonistic women's movements after the Civil War. Many white middle-class Abolitionists were violently anti-labor, and most crafts excluded free black workers. While many Abolitionist groups spoke out against job discrimination against black workers in the North, some of their members were at the same time also practicing this same discrimination. In 1852 a number of black men applied for jobs at the businesses of members of the American and Foreign Anti-Slavery Society. Some were rejected outright; others got only menial jobs.[11] The widespread exclusion of black men and women from craft and factory jobs is well known. What has not received adequate treatment is the extent to which employers and workers were responsible for it.

These class and race antagonisms among the Abolitionists (important divisions to be inherited by the women's movement) were deepened by pro-slavery forces. Before the 1830s its defenders rationalized slavery as a necessary evil. To counter anti-slavery forces they developed a whole pseudo-science of white supremacy. Together with nativist corollaries, this became a cornerstone of post-Civil War bourgeois ideology. The war itself gave birth to accelerated industrialization and thus to the development of an industrial working class as well as a more powerful bourgeoisie. The latter took governmental power from the Southern agrarian bourgeoisie. Once in power, the Northern industrialists re-allied themselves with the Southern planters to defeat Reconstruction and entrench their common position against the black and white working class. Economic, political, and legal discrimination against black people was made a virtue through the newly developed national policy of white supremacy; at the same time an anti-foreignism was directed against white working-class immigrants in the North. Racism and nativism were important to the new capitalists because neither black nor white workers passively accepted the conditions of industrial wage slavery. Against this general background, we may better understand the divisions in the developing women's movement.

From the end of the Civil War until 1920, when it collapsed, the white middle-class women's movement defined itself as middle class by excluding black and working-class women. As such women moved from the liberalism of the Reconstruction period to the racist and anti-working-class mainstream of the "progressive era," they took for granted this status quo — a status quo with a sharp division between middle and working classes and with hierarchical divisions within the working class based on race, nationality, and sex. Black men and women were to be confined to agrarian and domestic work; native-born and immigrant white men and women would make up the industrial working class, with skilled crafts largely excluding all save native-born white men.

The Civil War itself led to middle-class women's widespread involvement in a variety of service and professional positions — from nursing and teaching to office work. By and large, the new war opportunities were important for middle-class kinds of jobs, mainly for whites, but some black women also entered, particularly in teaching, through the Freedmen's Bureau. Opportunities were there, but they were not equal. For example, the federal government was delighted to have women replace male office workers, not least because they worked for half pay. Black women received even less for their work — if they received anything at all. Harriet Tubman had to fight almost until her death before the government would pay her for her very considerable services, both military and civilian, during and after the war. Even then she received a pittance, and that as a pension for her husband. Tubman was nationally famous. It is thus probable that the thousands of less famous black women were treated much worse.

Postwar years, then, saw the growth in numbers of middle-class women as independent earners in largely professional or so-called semi-professional occupations. Materially, they were members of a growing middle class. As such (and like the women factory workers of prewar years) they began developing a stronger class identity. They began to see themselves less as a socially excluded and oppressed segment of humanity and more as second-class members of the white middle class. Black middle-class women were largely prevented from claiming *class* rights by the practice of segregation and white supremacy. As black women they struggled against racial oppression, including the ideological stereotyping of black women as immoral.

The Civil War affected working-class

women in some basically different ways than it affected middle-class women, even though there were some superficial similarities. While groups of middle-class women might get together to sew uniforms for the Union army as their patriotic duty, for working-class women taking in sewing of uniforms was wage work for survival in a period of inflation. However, they were often not paid for this work. Apparently the government felt that since middle-class women did not need to be paid, neither did working-class women. The war and postwar years saw working-class women developing their own unions and protective associations, at least in part to combat situations like the above. By and large, these were localized efforts. To some extent, though, they were integrated into the National Labor Union (NLU). Thus, in 1863, women collar workers in Troy, New York, formed a local union and struck successfully for higher wages. Kate Mullaney, their president, became assistant secretary of the NLU. But this women's local disbanded with the demise of the NLU.

To some extent, women's locals were joined with men's local or national organizations in the same industry. The men and women weavers in Fall River exemplify this pattern. In the face of a pay cut in 1875, the men's union voted to acquiesce; the women, knowing the results of the men's meeting, held their own and voted to strike three mills. The men then followed their lead and they won.[12]

Women workers did form one national organization. The Daughters of St. Crispin, begun by women shoe-stitchers in Lynn, Massachusetts, was an organization parallel to the men's Knights of St. Crispin. New England shoe workers, particularly women, had organized before the Civil War. In 1860 they had gone on strike throughout New England in the most extensive pre-Civil War strike.[13] The Daughters of St. Crispin, formed in 1869, had 24 chapters, most of which were in New England — the center of the shoe industry — and in six other states as well. They demanded equal pay for equal work. Though they affiliated with the NLU, they managed to outlast it, staying in existence through much of the 1873 depression, and continuing in New England until 1876. For those days it was a long-lived organization.

The Knights of Labor, the first enduring national labor organization in the United States, saw women and black people as important parts of the working class, and on this basis supported equality within the organization and demanded it of employers. At its first national convention in 1878, they voted for equal pay for equal work, and began from the outset to include women workers in separate locals as well as in male-female locals. The first all-women local, of Philadelphia shoe workers, joined in 1878. By 1886, at the peak of the Knights of Labor, there were about 194 women's locals and about 50,000 women members (8–9 percent of the total). In Massachusetts the proportion was higher: 1 in 7 members were women.[14] The Knights followed the same direction with regard to black workers, organizing them in the South and the North into both black-white and separate black locals. In 1886 there were about 60,000 black Knights out of about 700,000; in 1887 some 90,000 out of about half a million.[15] The Knights did seem to try in practice as well as rhetoric to fight for equal rights for all workers.

By contrast, the newly formed American Federation of Labor, an association of craft unions, supported few working-class women's issues, even though its membership included male-female as well as all-female locals, especially in the United Garment Workers (UGW). But if the UGW is any example of female participation, the AFL did not take the needs of its women members seriously.[16] The AFL did have some unofficial women organizers in the early years. Hannah Morgan organized some 23 women's locals in a variety of jobs; she also built the Illinois Women's Alliance, which led mass campaigns for protective legislation for women and children (and she organized secondarily for suffrage). Also under the AFL, the collar and shirt workers of Troy pulled together again, struck and won in 1891. The leader of the Working Women's Society of New York City unofficially organized women into the AFL, while the society organized support for strikes and for factory legislation.[17]

Meanwhile, the middle-class movement had become mainly a suffrage movement. But it too was divided. The National Women's Suffrage Association (NWSA) Stanton-Anthony wing), though biased in favor of the middle class by its suffrage focus, was willing to join with labor. Anthony and other suffrage leaders organized women's protective societies, supported and helped organize women's unions. For a time Susan Anthony was a member of the Knights of Labor (which favored suffrage). The rival group of suffragists, the American Women's Suffrage Association (AWSA), was anti-labor, narrowly suffragist, and drew its support from professional and leisured middle-class women, mainly through women's clubs.

Until 1890, then, there was a strong organization in the Knights of Labor fighting for equal rights for all labor, as well as a middle-class organization willing to join its main fight for suffrage with the economic demands of working women. Class determined the priorities, but on these issues there was no necessary conflict between them.

But the balance of forces favoring such inter-class cooperation changed in the 1890s. With the demise of the Knights, the AFL faced no competition and freely moved

to organize skilled crafts only, largely the province of white, native-born men. Not only by focusing on skilled labor but also by deliberately excluding black and female skilled and semi-skilled workers, the AFL spread racism and sexism during its long-term domination of trade unionism.* Women continued to form unions, some independent, which had a hard time, and some affiliated with the AFL, which seem to have faced almost equal difficulties.[18] At the same time that the unity of labor was weakened by this organizational practice, the ruling class stepped up its propaganda to cultivate and fix black-white, native-immigrant divisions and conflicts. The suffrage movement, represented by the National American Women's Suffrage Association (NAWSA, the merger of the two suffrage groups), fell solidly into line with them, abandoning even the divided support they had given working-class women in the 1860s.

In 1892, when the Homestead Steel workers struck and were embroiled in a nearly full-scale war to save job and union from Carnegie, the Pinkertons, and federal troops, Lucy Stone wanted to know why the workers didn't start their own businesses if they didn't like their jobs.[19] And Susan Anthony went to labor asking for suffrage support, but refused to do anything about working women's demands until the vote was won. Likewise, she raised her influential voice to argue that NAWSA should do nothing to fight Jim Crow laws barring black people (including black women) from decent railroad seats.

Their arguments for suffrage, as Kraditor has clearly shown,[20] came explicitly to be arguments for enfranchising white, American-born, and educated women as allies

* It seems to me that modern-day notions about working-class racism and sexism are based heavily on the AFL's practice.

with their male counterparts against black and immigrant workers.

> This government is menaced with great danger.... That danger lies in the votes possessed by the males in the slums of the cities, and the ignorant foreign vote which was sought to be brought up by each party, to make political success.... In the mining districts, the danger has already reached this point — miners are supplied with arms, watching with greedy eyes for the moment when they can get in their deadly work of despoiling the wealth of the country.... There is but one way to avert the danger — cut off the vote of the slums and give to woman, who is bound to suffer all, and more than man can, of the evils his legislation has brought upon the nation, the power of protecting herself that man has secured for himself — the ballot.[21]

NAWSA closed ranks against working-class women, not so much by the demand for suffrage itself as by their arguments claiming it should be granted and by their hostility to more pressing needs of women workers and black women of both classes. Thus the 1893 convention of NAWSA passed the following resolution directed against black people in the same way that Catt's speech attacked immigrants and the working class:

> *Resolved,* that without expressing any opinion on the proper qualifications for voting, we call attention to the significant facts that in every State there are more women who can read and write than all negro [*sic*] voters; more American women who can read and write than all foreign voters; so that the enfranchisement of such women would settle the vexed question of rule by illiteracy, whether of home-grown or foreign-born production.[22]

They lashed out at "foreigners" not only for being "ignorant" in general, but for being a major force in opposing women's rights.

Kraditor summed up suffrage explanations of why voting in wards with large immigrant populations went against suffrage: "Foreign-born men had been brought up in a culture in which women were inferior [here the suffragists forgot earlier arguments and proudly pointed to the respected position of women in their own society]; ... the ignorance of the foreign born disqualified them from voting wisely; ... the new voters generally used alcoholic beverages and feared that woman suffrage would bring prohibition; ... foreign-born workers in cities voted as dictated by saloonkeepers, rich employers, or party machines."[23] Ironically, when New York finally passed its suffrage referendum in 1917, it was working-class and immigrant New York City which carried it over the opposition from non-worker, native-born upstate! By this time, though, some members of NAWSA had begun to overcome their aversion to the working class, and to campaign in working-class districts. As late as 1916, however, NAWSA had made little effort to communicate across class lines.

While the overt anti-working-class, racist, and nativist arguments remained until the end, there were growing numbers of NAWSA members after the turn of the century who believed it important to speak to the working class. Thus Florence Kelley worked hard to fight the exploitation of workers in the sweatshops and to obtain protective legislation for women workers. She even criticized the anti-foreign mouthings of NAWSA. Yet she too resented being forced to campaign among workers: "[It was] an ignominious way to treat us, to send us to the Chinamen [*sic*] in San Francisco, to the enfranchised Indians of other western states, to the negroes [*sic*], Italians, Hungarians, Poles, Bohemians and innumerable Slavic immigrants in Pennsylvania and other mining States to obtain our rights of suffrage."[24]

Jessie Ashley, treasurer of NAWSA and a

socialist, also criticized the association for its anti-worker attitudes, in particular for not addressing its campaigns to the real needs of working-class women — economic needs. But she did accept some very middle-class stereotypes of working-class women. Remarking on the contrast made in another article between the "handsome ladies" at a suffrage parade and the working girls getting onto the subway, Ashley wrote,

> For it is those "handsome ladies," and they alone, who have begun to see that women must stand and think and work together, and they, alas, are not the ones whose need to do so is the greatest.... For the most part the handsome ladies are well satisfied with their personal lot, but they want the vote as a matter of justice, while the fluttering, jammed-in subway girls are terribly blind to the whole question of class oppression and of sex oppression. Only the women of the working class are really oppressed, but it is not only the working-class women to whom injustice is done. Women of the leisure class need freedom, too.[25]

Considering that this was written less than two years after the massive women's garment strike in New York (where Ashley lived), her talk of working-class women being blind to class oppression flies in the face of reality, as does her notion that only the "handsome ladies" know they must work together. Essentially, Ashley is reflecting the stereotype of the ignorant and docile working girl.

Along with the general racist stereotyping of black people, which NAWSA accepted and propagated, there existed the stigmatizing of black women as "loose" and "immoral." Sometimes this stereotyping was done "sympathetically":

> The negro [sic] women of the South are subject to temptations, of which their white sisters of the North have no appreciation, and which come to them from the days of their race enslavement. They are still the victims of the white man under a system tacitly recognized, which deprives them of the sympathy and help of the Southern white women, and to meet such temptations the negro [sic] woman can only offer the resistance of a low moral standard, an inheritance from the system of slavery, made still lower from a life-long residence in a one-roomed cabin.[26]

But it propagates the same false stereotype of the immoral black woman, adding another kind of fuel to racist propaganda.

Black women, led by black middle-class and professional women, had long before formed their own clubs and expressed a desire to work with the white clubs, which in general the latter refused to do. To combat this racism they formed the National Association of Colored Women. The conditions facing black women differed in many ways from those facing white middle-class women. Black women's clubs organized around providing a particular social service, since public facilities were even less available in black communities than in white working-class communities. They also exposed and organized against lynching and terror campaigns directed against black men and women. At least one club maintained a settlement house and served the poor and working-class neighborhoods through militant action as well as services. Moreover, the membership, if not the leadership, of black women's clubs differed from their white counterparts. While the white clubs were middle class and professional, black club members were often workers, tenant farmers, or poor women.[27]

Even though the suffrage movement somewhat weakened its anti-worker attitude and to some extent its anti-immigrant posture, it never publicly mitigated its racism. This was largely due to the strategy of allying with Southern white middle-class women, who wanted the vote at least as much to maintain white supremacy as to have the vote. As a result of this "Southern strategy," black women were all but kept out of the association.[28] While support for racial equality was ruled out of order as an extraneous issue, the numerous white-supremacy speeches never met any such objection, or any other kind of public objection, for that matter.

What little amelioration there was of NAWSA's anti-worker and anti-immigrant stance came about largely because of the growth of city-wide women's strikes, notably in the garment and textile industries, in 1909 in New York, 1910 in Chicago, and 1912 in Lawrence. Prior to that time a number of white middle-class women — radicals, reformers, and socialists like Jessie Ashley, Ella Reeve Bloor, etc. — had urged concentration on working women's needs. But they were mainly rebuffed by NAWSA.

It was largely through the National Women's Trade Union League (NWTUL), formed in 1903, that the suffrage movement saw possible allies in working-class women. Made up of women trade unionists, but run mainly by middle-class reformers, many of whom were active suffragists, the NWTUL tried to serve two functions. First, in the face of AFL indifference to women workers, it organized women to improve their working conditions through trade unionism. Specifically, it organized women into AFL locals and supported AFL strikes. Its second role was to make trade unionism "respectable" through publicity and by winning middle-class support for strikes. It did succeed in organizing women into the AFL and in making *certain kinds* of unions "respectable." But it did not reform the AFL, which sold out the Chicago clothing strike in 1911. And the following year, despite anger over Chicago, the NWTUL actually helped the AFL break a strike, in Lawrence, Massachusetts.

In this case, the AFL had organized only among skilled (white, male, native-born) workers. But the vast majority were unskilled female, as well as male and immigrant, workers. The IWW [International Workers of the World] represented these workers; and when they walked out, it was the IWW that led this Lawrence strike. Together with the AFL, the Boston TUL set up a relief council which aided only those who pledged to go back to work.[29]

So while they did unionize women and ameliorate some of the anti-worker attitudes in the middle class, their role within the working-class movement was to be in the midst of things, to see that events did not get out of control, and to make sure women workers stayed respectable in bourgeois eyes.

Many women in the Boston TUL were disgusted with the role of their own organization in Lawrence. "Are we, the NWTUL, to ally ourselves inflexibly with the 'stand-patters' of the Labor Movement or are we to hold ourselves ready to aid the 'insurgents,' those who are freely fighting the fight of the exploited, the oppressed, and the weak among the workers?"[30] While this may have been a widespread feeling among NWTUL members, publicly they stood pat with the stand-patters of the AFL. Their official stance appeared in *Life and Labor,* the NWTUL paper:[31] the AFL "refused to take any action during the first fortnight of the strike while it was being led by enemies of organized labor [the IWW], but now that it shows every symptom of collapse they do not propose to allow the misled workers to suffer or lose any opportunity to bring them into recognized trade organizations."[32]

Working-class women, the IWW, and radicals reacted to this suffragist and middle-class bias. One working woman wrote to Leonora O'Reilly of her experience at a New York suffrage conference:

I feel as if I have butted in where I was not wanted. Miss Hay gave me a badge and was very nice to me but you know they had a school teacher represent the Industrial workers if you ever herd her it was like trying to fill a barrell with water that had no bottom not a word of labor spoken at this convention so far . . . after the hole thing was over some people came to me and said I had a right to speak for labor but they kept away until it was over. . . . I am not goying to wait for sunday meeting I am goying home saturday.[33]

In the New York shirtwaist strike, two upper-class women rented the Hippodrome for a strike-support rally, attended by approximately 8,000 people. Though much has been made of rich women's generosity, Theresa Malkiel, a striker, wrote another side to it in her diary:

The most of our girls had to walk both ways in order to save their car fare. Many came without dinner, but the collection baskets had more pennies than anything else in them — it was our girls themselves who helped make it up, and yet there were so many rich women present. And I'm sure the speakers made it plain to them how badly the money was needed, then how comes it that out of the $300 collected there should be $70 in pennies?[34]

The IWW saw the vote as irrelevant and the suffrage movement as making working women "the tail of a suffrage kite in the hands of women of the very class driving the girls to lives of misery and shame."[35] Yet Elizabeth Gurley Flynn, then an IWW organizer, speaks approvingly of socialists in 1904 organizing working-class women to demand the vote so they can vote on labor issues.[36] Emma Goldman saw suffrage as a "modern fetish" of women who swore loyalty to every institution which oppresses them. "Else how is one to account for the tremen-

dous, truly gigantic effort set in motion by those valiant fighters for a wretched little bill which will benefit a handful of propertied ladies, with absolutely no provision for the vast mass of working women?"[37]

Through the efforts of middle-class NWTUL women, and to some degree those of the militant suffragists' Women's Party, Wage Earners' Suffrage Leagues did come into being and working-class women did march in suffrage demonstrations. But even where working-class women participated in suffrage demands, they did so separately from the middle-class organizations, in a labor-based organization. Suffrage in this context never had a high priority for working-class women as a whole.

The years 1909–1912 marked a huge upsurge in working-class women's activity. The 1909 New York dressmakers' strike, or the "Uprising of 20,000," was the largest women's strike in history. It was followed by many large and small garment and textile strikes and the formation of enduring unions, steps toward the elimination of sweatshops, cutting hours, and increasing pay for women workers. By and large, women won these victories without the ballot.

As a rule, next to nothing is said of black working-class women in these struggles. Though black women were largely excluded from industry before the First World War, and hence from unions, there were black women working in the packinghouses of Chicago, in tobacco warehouses in the South, and as pressers in the garment industry in New York. In 1902 two packinghouse women organized a women's local which included black women. But more significant is a white garment worker and organizer's account of the beginning of the 1909 New York strike. She writes of her anxiety as to whether the women of the shop would walk out at the appointed time. They did, fifteen minutes early, when the fifty-three black women of the pressing department dropped their work and led the whole shop out.[38] Even where black women were employed during and after the First World War, they were largely in the worst jobs, with little or no chance for advancement, and often paid one half or one third what white women received. For example, pressers in the garment industry had the most physically difficult job in that industry. This was the job given to black women.[39]

Whom the women's movements perceived as the enemy illuminates the primacy of class lines over sex. In the working-class movement it was clearly the employer. The suffragists saw their enemies mainly as the liquor interests and, to some extent, big-business interests. Only the Women's Party actually saw the President and much of Congress as real enemies of women. For this breach of class loyalty they got the same treatment as working-class women strikers: jail, police brutality, etc.

The working-class women's movement, rather than dying in 1920, continued in the drives of the 1920s and 1930s to organize in Southern textile and tobacco shops. Here, black and white working-class women not only struggled to overcome racism, but had to take on the AFL[40] directly. Neither before nor since 1920 have women won equal pay for equal work, one of the two long-standing working-class women's demands. However, to the extent that women have won union representation, male-female pay scales have made moves in that direction. The other demand, for unionization itself, also continues. As middle-class women's jobs have become collectivized (teaching, white-collar, health, social work, clerical), middle-class women have also moved into union situations, which at least provide a material basis for middle-class women to join working-class women rather than the ruling class.

Notes

1. A. Kraditor, *The Ideas of the Woman Suffrage Movement, 1890–1920* (New York: Columbia University Press, 1965); E. Flexner, *Century of Struggle* (New York: Atheneum, 1968).
2. E. Abbott, *Women in Industry* (New York: Appleton and Company, 1913), pp. 21–22.
3. E. C. Stanton, S. B. Anthony, and M. J. Gage, *History of Women's Suffrage,* vol. 1 (Rochester: Chas. Mann), p. 16.
4. A. Henry, *The Trade Union Woman* (New York: Appleton and Company, 1915), p. 254.
5. Stanton, Anthony, and Gage, p. 809. Italics added.
6. On early struggles by women the major source is J. B. Andrews and W. D. P. Bliss, *History of Women in Trade Unions* (vol. 10 of *Report on Conditions of Women and Child Wage Earners in the U.S.,* in 19 vols., U.S. Senate Doc. 645, 61st Cong., 2d Sess.); see also Flexner; Abbott; P. Foner, *History of the Labor Movement in the United States,* vol. 1 (New York: International, 1947); Henry, 1915; and A. Henry, *Women and the Labor Movement* (New York: Doran, 1923). Flexner claims men feared women's competition but gives no specifics. For this early period, only the printers and cigarmakers manifested the conservative stance, though it was later a strong position among conservative skilled trades unions. The instances of early cooperation between men's and women's unions are more impressive: in 1834 the Lady Shoe Binders of Lynn struck for higher wages and were supported by the men's cordwainers union in the form of money, a pledge not to work for any manufacturer who refused the women's demands, and an attempt to organize a boycott of such (Foner, pp. 108–111). In 1833 the Baltimore seamstresses and tailoresses were supported by the men journeymen tailors (Henry 1923, p. 41). In 1835 the Philadelphia Journeymen Cigarmakers opposed the low wages paid to women and recommended a joint strike. In this city, too, the men cordwainers and Ladies Shoe Binders Society waged a joint strike. In 1831 the New England Farmers, Mechanics and Other Workingmen

tried, though without success, to spread unionism from skilled workers to factory women (Foner, pp. 105, 108–111).

7. For differing accounts see Andrews and Bliss, p. 65; Foner, p. 212; Flexner, p. 56.

8. Foner, p. 267.

9. R. B. Nye, *Fettered Freedom: Civil Liberties and the Slave Controversy, 1830–1860* (East Lansing: Michigan State University Press, 1963), p. 194.

10. H. Josephson, *Golden Threads: New England's Mill Girls and Magnates* (New York: Duell, Sloan and Pearce, 1949), pp. 300–303.

11. C. H. Wesley, *Negro Labor in the United States, 1850–1925* (New York: Russell and Russell, 1967), pp. 78–79.

12. In addition to Andrews and Bliss, pt. 2, see Abbott, p. 131; and Henry, 1923, p. 48.

13. Foner, p. 241; Henry, 1923, p. 47.

14. Foner, vol. 2, p. 61; Flexner, p. 194.

15. R. Logan, *The Betrayal of the Negro* (New York: Macmillan, 1970), pp. 150–151.

16. M. H. Willett, *The Employment of Women in the Clothing Trade* (New York: AMS Press, 1968).

17. Foner, vol. 2, pp. 189–193.

18. *Ibid.,* pp. 364–366; Foner, vol. 3, pp. 724–727.

19. Kraditor, p. 159.

20. *Ibid.,* chap. 6.

21. Carrie Chapman Catt, in *The Woman's Journal,* 1894; quoted in Flexner, p. 125.

22. *Ibid.,* p. 131.

23. *Ibid.,* p. 128.

24. *Ibid.,* p. 139.

25. *The Woman's Journal,* 1911; quoted in Flexner, p. 157.

26. *Ibid.,* p. 187.

27. G. Lerner, *Black Women in White America* (New York: Pantheon, 1972), pp. 198, 437.

28. Kraditor, pp. 170, 212–214; Logan, pp. 239–241.

29. Foner, vol. 4, pp. 338–339.

30. Letter from Mrs. Clark to Mrs. Robins; quoted in G. Boone, *The Women's Trade Union Leagues in Great Britain and the United States of America* (New York: AMS Press, 1968), p. 106.

31. *Life and Labor,* vol. 2, pp. 73, 77, 196.

32. *Ibid.,* p. 77.

33. Quoted in Kraditor, p. 160.

34. Quoted in R. Jacoby, "Feminism and Class Consciousness in the British and American Women's Trade Union Leagues, 1890–1925." Unpublished ms. (History Dept., University of Michigan, 1973), p. 21.

35. Quoted in Foner, vol. 4, p. 168.

36. E. G. Flynn, *I Speak My Own Piece* (New York: Masses and Mainstream, 1955), p. 46.

37. E. Goldman, *Anarchism and Other Essays* (New York: Mother Earth Publishing Association, 1917), p. 212.

38. A. Hourwich, *I Am a Woman Worker: A Scrapbook of Autobiographies* (New York: Affiliated Schools for Workers, Inc., 1936), p. 110.

39. On pressers' work: J. Laslett, *Labor and the Left* (New York: Basic Books, 1970), p. 103. On discrimination against black women: Henry 1923, pp. 203–206.

40. Supported again by a dying NWTUL. See *Life and Labor Bulletin* (July 1928 and January 1931).

MARRIAGE AND LOVE

EMMA GOLDMAN

Anarchist author, lecturer, and activist, Emma Goldman was born in Lithuania in 1869 and emigrated to the United States in 1886, settling in Rochester, New York. After a brief period working in a factory there, she moved to New York City and began her lifelong participation in radical political activity. Militantly involved in the labor movement, accused of complicity in the assassination of President McKinley, and active in the antidraft-antiwar movement of World War I, she was jailed twice, was deported to Russia in 1919, and spent the rest of her life traveling, writing, lecturing, and agitating on a variety of social issues. From 1906 to 1917 she co-published a radical American journal, *Mother Earth,* and she wrote several books, among them *Anarchism and Other Essays* (1910), excerpted here, and *Living My Life* (1934), an autobiography. She died in Toronto, Canada, in 1940.

As an anarchist, Goldman opposed any state interference in personal life. As a feminist, therefore, she opposed institutional marriage, the dependency it fostered, and laws relating to contraception and abortion. The following essay considers the relationship of love, sex, marriage, and parenthood, and calls for the freeing of women from the "insurance pact" of state-sanctioned wedlock. Goldman's issues are classic in the women's movement, although she treats them in the context of her own particular political beliefs. She is an excellent example of the twentieth-century shift in feminist activism from a purely women's movement to more comprehensive organizations or models.

The popular notion about marriage and love is that they are synonymous, that they spring from the same motives, and cover the same human needs. Like most popular notions this also rests not on actual facts, but on superstition.

Marriage and love have nothing in common; they are as far apart as the poles; are, in fact, antagonistic to each other. No doubt some marriages have been the result of love. Not, however, because love could assert itself only in marriage; much rather is it because few people can completely outgrow a convention. There are today large numbers of men and women to whom marriage is naught but a farce, but who submit to it for the sake of public opinion. At any rate, while it is true that some marriages are based on love, and while it is equally true that in some cases love continues in married life, I maintain that it does so regardless of marriage, and not because of it.

On the other hand, it is utterly false that love results from marriage. On rare occasions one does hear of a miraculous case of a married couple falling in love after marriage, but on close examination it will be

found that it is a mere adjustment to the inevitable. Certainly the growing-used to each other is far away from the spontaneity, the intensity, and beauty of love, without which the intimacy of marriage must prove degrading to both the woman and the man.

Marriage is primarily an economic arrangement, an insurance pact. It differs from the ordinary life insurance agreement only in that it is more binding, more exacting. Its returns are insignificantly small compared with the investments. In taking out an insurance policy one pays for it in dollars and cents, always at liberty to discontinue payments. If, however, woman's premium is a husband, she pays for it with her name, her privacy, her self-respect, her very life, "until death doth part." Moreover, the marriage insurance condemns her to life-long dependency, to parasitism, to complete uselessness, individual as well as social. Man, too, pays his toll, but as his sphere is wider, marriage does not limit him as much as woman. He feels his chains more in an economic sense. . . .

Perchance the poor quality of the material whence woman comes is responsible for her inferiority. At any rate, woman has no soul — what is there to know about her? Besides, the less soul a woman has the greater her asset as a wife, the more readily

Reprinted from Emma Goldman, *Anarchism and Other Essays* (1910; Port Washington, N.Y.: Kennikat Press, 1969).

will she absorb herself in her husband. It is this slavish acquiescence to man's superiority that has kept the marriage institution seemingly intact for so long a period. Now that woman is coming into her own, now that she is actually growing aware of herself as a being outside of the master's grace, the sacred institution of marriage is gradually being undermined, and no amount of sentimental lamentation can stay it.

From infancy, almost, the average girl is told that marriage is her ultimate goal; therefore her training and education must be directed towards that end. Like the mute beast fattened for slaughter, she is prepared for that. Yet, strange to say, she is allowed to know much less about her function as wife and mother than the ordinary artisan of his trade. It is indecent and filthy for a respectable girl to know anything of the marital relation. Oh, for the inconsistency of respectability, that needs the marriage vow to turn something which is filthy into the purest and most sacred arrangement that none dare question or criticize. Yet that is exactly the attitude of the average upholder of marriage. The prospective wife and mother is kept in complete ignorance of her only asset in the competitive field — sex. Thus she enters into life-long relations with a man only to find herself shocked, repelled, outraged beyond measure by the most natural and healthy instinct, sex. It is safe to say that a large percentage of the unhappiness, misery, distress, and physical suffering of matrimony is due to the criminal ignorance in sex matters that is being extolled as a great virtue. Nor is it at all an exaggeration when I say that more than one home has been broken up because of this deplorable fact.

If, however, woman is free and big enough to learn the mystery of sex without the sanction of State or Church, she will stand condemned as utterly unfit to become the wife of a "good" man, his goodness consisting of an empty brain and plenty of money. Can there be anything more outrageous than the idea that a healthy, grown woman, full of life and passion, must deny nature's demand, must subdue her most intense craving, undermine her health and break her spirit, must stunt her vision, abstain from the depth and glory of sex experience until a "good" man comes along to take her unto himself as a wife? That is precisely what marriage means. How can such an arrangement end except in failure? This is one, though not the least important, factor of marriage, which differentiates it from love.

Ours is a practical age. The time when Romeo and Juliet risked the wrath of their fathers for love, when Gretchen exposed herself to the gossip of her neighbors for love, is no more. If, on rare occasions, young people allow themselves the luxury of romance, they are taken in care by the elders, drilled and pounded until they become "sensible."

The moral lesson instilled in the girl is not whether the man has aroused her love, but rather is it, "How much?" The important and only God of practical American life: Can the man make a living? can he support a wife? That is the only thing that justifies marriage. Gradually this saturates every thought of the girl; her dreams are not of moonlight and kisses, of laughter and tears; she dreams of shopping tours and bargain counters. This soul poverty and sordidness are the elements inherent in the marriage institution. The State and the Church approve of no other ideal, simply because it is the one that necessitates the State and Church control of men and women.

Doubtless there are people who continue to consider love above dollars and cents. Particularly is this true of that class whom economic necessity has forced to become self-supporting. The tremendous change in woman's position, wrought by that mighty factor, is indeed phenomenal when we reflect that it is but a short time since she has entered the industrial arena. Six million women wage workers; six million women, who have the equal right with men to be exploited, to be robbed, to go on strike; aye, to starve even. Anything more, my lord? Yes, six million wage workers in every walk of life, from the highest brain work to the mines and railroad tracks; yes, even detectives and policemen. Surely the emancipation is complete.

Yet with all that, but a very small number of the vast army of women wage workers look upon work as a permanent issue, in the same light as does man. No matter how decrepit the latter, he has been taught to be independent, self-supporting. Oh, I know that no one is really independent in our economic treadmill; still, the poorest specimen of a man hates to be a parasite; to be known as such, at any rate.

The woman considers her position as worker transitory, to be thrown aside for the first bidder. That is why it is infinitely harder to organize women than men. "Why should I join a union? I am going to get married, to have a home." Has she not been taught from infancy to look upon that as her ultimate calling? She learns soon enough that the home, though not so large a prison as the factory, has more solid doors and bars. It has a keeper so faithful that naught can escape him. The most tragic part, however, is that the home no longer frees her from wage slavery; it only increases her task.

According to the latest statistics submitted before a Committee "on labor and wages, and congestion of population," ten per cent of the wage workers in New York City alone are married, yet they must continue to work at the most poorly paid labor in the world. Add to this horrible aspect the

drudgery of housework, and what remains of the protection and glory of the home? As a matter of fact, even the middle-class girl in marriage can not speak of her home, since it is the man who creates her sphere. It is not important whether the husband is a brute or a darling. What I wish to prove is that marriage guarantees woman a home only by the grace of her husband. There she moves about in *his* home, year after year, until her aspect of life and human affairs becomes as flat, narrow, and drab as her surroundings. Small wonder if she becomes a nag, petty, quarrelsome, gossipy, unbearable, thus driving the man from the house. She could not go, if she wanted to; there is no place to go. Besides, a short period of married life, of complete surrender of all faculties, absolutely incapacitates the average woman for the outside world. She becomes reckless in appearance, clumsy in her movements, dependent in her decisions, cowardly in her judgment, a weight and a bore, which most men grow to hate and despise. Wonderfully inspiring atmosphere for the bearing of life, is it not?

But the child, how is it to be protected, if not for marriage? After all, is not that the most important consideration? The sham, the hypocrisy of it! Marriage protecting the child, yet thousands of children destitute and homeless. Marriage protecting the child, yet orphan asylums and reformatories overcrowded, the Society for the Prevention of Cruelty to Children keeping busy in rescuing the little victims from "loving" parents, to place them under more loving care, the Gerry Society. Oh, the mockery of it!

Marriage may have the power to bring the horse to water, but has it ever made him drink? The law will place the father under arrest, and put him in convict's clothes; but has that ever stilled the hunger of the child? If the parent has no work, or if he hides his identity, what does marriage do then? It invokes the law to bring the man to "justice," to put him safely behind closed doors; his labor, however, goes not to the child, but to the State. The child receives but a blighted memory of its father's stripes.

As to the protection of the woman, — therein lies the curse of marriage. Not that it really protects her, but the very idea is so revolting, such an outrage and insult on life, so degrading to human dignity, as to forever condemn this parasitic institution.

It is like that other paternal arrangement — capitalism. It robs man of his birthright, stunts his growth, poisons his body, keeps him in ignorance, in poverty, and dependence, and then institutes charities that thrive on the last vestige of man's self-respect.

The institution of marriage makes a parasite of woman, an absolute dependent. It incapacitates her for life's struggle, annihilates her social consciousness, paralyzes her imagination, and then imposes its gracious protection, which is in reality a snare, a travesty on human character.

If motherhood is the highest fulfillment of woman's nature, what other protection does it need, save love and freedom? Marriage but defiles, outrages, and corrupts her fulfillment. Does it not say to woman, Only when you follow me shall you bring forth life? Does it not condemn her to the block, does it not degrade and shame her if she refuses to buy her right to motherhood by selling herself? Does not marriage only sanction motherhood, even though conceived in hatred, in compulsion? Yet, if motherhood be of free choice, of love, of ecstasy, of defiant passion, does it not place a crown of thorns upon an innocent head and carve in letters of blood the hideous epithet, Bastard? Were marriage to contain all the virtues claimed for it, its crimes against motherhood would exclude it forever from the realm of love.

Love, the strongest and deepest element in all life, the harbinger of hope, of joy, of ecstasy; love, the defier of all laws, of all conventions; love, the freest, the most powerful moulder of human destiny; how can such an all-compelling force be synonymous with that poor little State and Church-begotten weed, marriage?

Free love? As if love is anything but free! Man has bought brains, but all the millions in the world have failed to buy love. Man has subdued bodies, but all the power on earth has been unable to subdue love. Man has conquered whole nations, but all his armies could not conquer love. Man has chained and fettered the spirit, but he has been utterly helpless before love. High on a throne, with all the splendor and pomp his gold can command, man is yet poor and desolate, if love passes him by. And if it stays, the poorest hovel is radiant with warmth, with life and color. Thus love has the magic power to make of a beggar a king. Yes, love is free; it can dwell in no other atmosphere. In freedom it gives itself unreservedly, abundantly, completely. All the laws on the statutes, all the courts in the universe, cannot tear it from the soil, once love has taken root. If, however, the soil is sterile, how can marriage make it bear fruit? It is like the last desperate struggle of fleeting life against death. . . .

WOMAN AND THE NEW RACE

MARGARET SANGER

Nothing has contributed so much to women's growing liberation as the increasing control women can exercise over their reproductive capacities. Although some forms of birth control had been practiced back into antiquity, it did not become a major force in the lives of masses of women, especially poor women, until the twentieth century. In this country, into the 1930s, the so-called Comstock Laws of 1873 forbade the distribution of birth control information through the mails, and many states had laws prohibiting the use and sale of contraceptives until the efforts of the Birth Control League and particularly Margaret Sanger resulted in the social acceptance of "planned parenthood."

Sanger was born in Corning, New York, in 1883. She studied nursing in White Plains and New York City, and early in her first marriage worked as an obstetrical nurse on New York's very poor Lower East Side, where she witnessed the destructive burdens of unchecked reproduction among the poor and underprivileged. After studying contraception in Europe in 1913, she returned to New York, founded the magazine *Women Rebel,* and in 1916 opened her first clinic with her sister, Ethel Byrne, and a friend, Fania Mindell. All were arrested, and Byrne was subsequently jailed and mistreated. The episode brought the rarely discussed issue into public view, and 1917 saw the founding of the National Birth Control League, with a growing membership.

Although it did not have the support of many of the established women's rights organizations, who feared the controversy, the birth control campaign was pressed vehemently by various reform groups (including some trade unions) and by women activists, many from the suffrage movement. Circumstances were in many ways analogous to today's abortion debate. Then as now, opposition was highly charged and well organized, in both religious and political circles; the poor were in even greater need of the reform than were the more affluent; and issues centered on matters of morality and "nature." Sanger ultimately won her fight. In 1952 in Bombay, well respected, she was named first president of the International Planned Parenthood Federation. She died in Arizona in 1966. She had founded various journals and leagues and had written six books, including *Woman and the New Race* (1920). In the section reprinted here, Sanger argues the claims of women's right to personal freedom and autonomy in procreative decisions, the implications for the world community of unchecked reproduction, and the centrality of woman alone in the burdens and responsibility of childbearing and childrearing, all contemporary themes.

Chapter I

Woman's Error and Her Debt

The most far-reaching social development of modern times is the revolt of woman against sex servitude. The most important force in

the remaking of the world is a free motherhood. Beside this force, the elaborate international programmes of modern statesmen are weak and superficial. Diplomats may formulate leagues of nations and nations may pledge their utmost strength to maintain them, statesmen may dream of reconstructing the world out of alliances, hegemonies and spheres of influence, but woman, continuing to produce explosive populations, will convert these pledges into the proverbial scraps of paper; or she may, by controlling birth, lift motherhood to the plane of a voluntary, intelligent function, and remake the world. When the world is thus remade, it will exceed the dream of statesman, reformer and revolutionist.

Only in recent years has woman's position as the gentler and weaker half of the human family been emphatically and generally questioned. Men assumed that this was woman's place; woman herself accepted it. It seldom occurred to anyone to ask whether she would go on occupying it forever.

Upon the mere surface of woman's organized protests there were no indications that she was desirous of achieving a fundamental change in her position. She claimed the right of suffrage and legislative regulation of her working hours, and asked that her property rights be equal to those of the man. None of these demands, however, affected directly the most vital factors of her existence. Whether she won her point or failed to win it, she remained a dominated weakling in a society controlled by men.

Woman's acceptance of her inferior status was the more real because it was unconscious. She had chained herself to her place in society and the family through the maternal functions of her nature, and only chains thus strong could have bound her to her lot as a brood animal for the masculine civilizations of the world. In accepting her rôle as the "weaker and gentler half," she accepted that function. In turn, the acceptance of that function fixed the more firmly her rank as an inferior.

Caught in this "vicious circle," woman has, through her reproductive ability, founded and perpetuated the tyrannies of the Earth. Whether it was the tyranny of a monarchy, an oligarchy or a republic, the one indispensable factor of its existence was, as it is now, hordes of human beings — human beings so plentiful as to be cheap, and so cheap that ignorance was their natural lot. Upon the rock of an unenlightened, submissive maternity have these been founded; upon the product of such a maternity have they flourished.

No despot ever flung forth his legions to die in foreign conquest, no privilege-ruled nation ever erupted across its borders, to lock in death embrace with another, but behind them loomed the driving power of a population too large for its boundaries and its natural resources.

No period of low wages or of idleness with their want among the workers, no peonage or sweatshop, no child-labor factory, ever came into being, save from the same source. Nor have famine and plague been as much "acts of God" as acts of too prolific mothers. They, also, as all students know, have their basic causes in over-population.

The creators of over-population are the women, who, while wringing their hands over each fresh horror, submit anew to their task of producing the multitudes who will bring about the *next* tragedy of civilization.

While unknowingly laying the foundations of tyrannies and providing the human tinder for racial conflagrations, woman was also unknowingly creating slums, filling asylums with insane, and institutions with other defectives. She was replenishing the ranks of the prostitutes, furnishing grist for the criminal courts and inmates for prisons. Had she planned deliberately to achieve this tragic total of human waste and misery, she could hardly have done it more effectively.

Woman's passivity under the burden of her disastrous task was almost altogether that of ignorant resignation. She knew virtually nothing about her reproductive nature and less about the consequences of her excessive childbearing. It is true that, obeying the inner urge of their natures, *some* women revolted. They went even to the extreme of

infanticide and abortion. Usually their re-
volts were not general enough. They fought
as individuals, not as a mass. In the mass
they sank back into blind and hopeless subjection. They went on breeding with staggering rapidity those numberless, undesired
children who become the clogs and the de-
stroyers of civilizations.

To-day, however, woman is rising in fundamental revolt. Even her efforts at mere reform are, as we shall see later, steps in that
direction. Underneath each of them is the
feminine urge to complete freedom. Millions
of women are asserting their right to voluntary motherhood. They are determined to
decide for themselves whether they shall
become mothers, under what conditions and
when. This is the fundamental revolt referred to. It is for woman the key to the
temple of liberty.

Even as birth control is the means by
which woman attains basic freedom, so it is
the means by which she must and will up-
root the evil she has wrought through her
submission. As she has unconsciously and
ignorantly brought about social disaster, so
must and will she consciously and intelli-
gently *undo* that disaster and create a new
and a better order.

The task is hers. It cannot be avoided by
excuses, nor can it be delegated. It is not
enough for woman to point to the self-
evident domination of man. Nor does it avail
to plead the guilt of rulers and the exploiters
of labor. It makes no difference that she does
not formulate industrial systems nor that she
is an instinctive believer in social justice. In
her submission lies her error and her guilt.
By her failure to withhold the multitudes of
children who have made inevitable the most
flagrant of our social evils, she incurred a
debt to society. Regardless of her own
wrongs, regardless of her lack of opportunity and regardless of all other considerations, *she* must pay that debt.

She must not think to pay this debt in any
superficial way. She cannot pay it with palli-
atives — with child-labor laws, prohibition,
regulation of prostitution and agitation
against war. Political nostrums and social
panaceas are but incidentally and superficially useful. They do not touch the source
of the social disease.

War, famine, poverty and oppression of
the workers will continue while woman
makes life cheap. They will cease only when
she limits her reproductivity and human life
is no longer a thing to be wasted.

Two chief obstacles hinder the discharge
of this tremendous obligation. The first and
the lesser is the legal barrier. Dark-Age laws
would still deny to her the knowledge of
her reproductive nature. Such knowledge is
indispensable to intelligent motherhood and
she must achieve it, despite absurd statutes
and equally absurd moral canons.

The second and more serious barrier is
her own ignorance of the extent and effect
of her submission. Until she knows the evil
her subjection has wrought to herself, to her
progeny and to the world at large, she cannot wipe out that evil.

To get rid of these obstacles is to invite
attack from the forces of reaction which are
so strongly entrenched in our present-day
society. It means warfare in every phase of
her life. Nevertheless, at whatever cost, she
must emerge from her ignorance and assume her responsibility.

She can do this only when she has awakened to a knowledge of herself and of the
consequences of her ignorance. The first
step is birth control. Through birth control
she will attain to voluntary motherhood. Having attained this, the basic freedom of her
sex, she will cease to enslave herself and
the mass of humanity. Then, through the understanding of the intuitive forward urge
within her, she will not stop at patching up
the world; she will remake it.

Chapter VIII

Birth Control — a Parents'
Problem or Woman's?

The problem of birth control has arisen directly from the effort of the feminine spirit to free itself from bondage. Woman herself has wrought that bondage through her reproductive powers and while enslaving herself has enslaved the world. The physical suffering to be relieved is chiefly woman's. Hers, too, is the love life that dies first under the blight of too prolific breeding. Within her is wrapped up the future of the race — it is hers to make or mar. All of these considerations point unmistakably to one fact — it is woman's duty as well as her privilege to lay hold of the means of freedom. Whatever men may do, she cannot escape the responsibility. For ages she has been deprived of the opportunity to meet this obligation. She is now emerging from her helplessness. Even as no one can share the suffering of the overburdened mother, so no one can do this work for her. Others may help, but she and she alone can free herself.

The basic freedom of the world is woman's freedom. A free race cannot be born of slave mothers. A woman enchained cannot choose but give a measure of that bondage to her sons and daughters. No woman can call herself free who does not own and control her body. No woman can call herself free until she can choose consciously whether she will or will not be a mother.

It does not greatly alter the case that some women call themselves free because they earn their own livings, while others profess freedom because they defy the conventions of sex relationship. She who earns her own living gains a sort of freedom that is not to be undervalued, but in quality and in quantity it is of little account beside the untrammeled choice of mating or not mating, of being a mother or not being a mother. She gains food and clothing and shelter, at least, without submitting to the charity of her companion, but the earning of her own living does not give her the development of her inner sex urge, far deeper and more powerful in its outworkings than any of these externals. In order to have that development, she must still meet and solve the problem of motherhood.

With the so-called "free" woman, who chooses a mate in defiance of convention, freedom is largely a question of character and audacity. If she does attain to an unrestricted choice of a mate, she is still in a position to be enslaved through her reproductive powers. Indeed, the pressure of law and custom upon the woman not legally married is likely to make her more of a slave than the woman fortunate enough to marry the man of her choice.

Look at it from any standpoint you will, suggest any solution you will, conventional or unconventional, sanctioned by law or in defiance of law, woman is in the same position, fundamentally, until she is able to determine for herself whether she will be a mother and to fix the number of her offspring. This unavoidable situation is alone enough to make birth control, first of all, a woman's problem. On the very face of the matter, voluntary motherhood is chiefly the concern of the woman.

It is persistently urged, however, that since sex expression is the act of two, the responsibility of controlling the results should not be placed upon woman alone. Is it fair, it is asked, to give her, instead of the man, the task of protecting herself when she is, perhaps, less rugged in physique than her mate, and has, at all events, the normal, periodic inconveniences of her sex?

We must examine this phase of her problem in two lights — that of the ideal, and of the conditions working toward the ideal. In an ideal society, no doubt, birth control would become the concern of the man as well as the woman. The hard, inescapable fact which we encounter to-day is that man has not only refused any such responsibility, but has individually and collectively sought to prevent woman from obtaining knowledge by which she could assume this responsibility for herself. She is still in the position of a dependent to-day because her mate has refused to consider her as an individual apart from his needs. She is still bound because she has in the past left the solution of the problem to him. Having left it to him, she finds that instead of rights, she has only such privileges as she has gained by petitioning, coaxing and cozening. Having left it to him, she is exploited, driven and enslaved to his desires.

While it is true that he suffers many evils as the consequence of this situation, she suffers vastly more. While it is true that he should be awakened to the cause of these evils, we know that they come home to her with crushing force every day. It is she who has the long burden of carrying, bearing and rearing the unwanted children. It is she who must watch beside the beds of pain where lie the babies who suffer because they have come into overcrowded homes. It is her heart that the sight of the deformed, the subnormal, the undernourished, the overworked child smites first and oftenest and hardest. It is *her* love life that dies first in the fear of undesired pregnancy. It is her opportunity for self expression that perishes first and most hopelessly because of it.

Conditions, rather than theories, facts, rather than dreams, govern the problem. They place it squarely upon the shoulders of woman. She has learned that whatever the moral responsibility of the man in this direction may be, he does not discharge it. She has learned that, lovable and considerate as the individual husband may be, she

has nothing to expect from men in the mass, when they make laws and decree customs. She knows that regardless of what ought to be, the brutal, unavoidable fact is that she will never receive her freedom until she takes it for herself.

Having learned this much, she has yet something more to learn. Women are too much inclined to follow in the footsteps of men, to try to think as men think, to try to solve the general problems of life as men solve them. If after attaining their freedom, women accept conditions in the spheres of government, industry, art, morals and religion as they find them, they will be but taking a leaf out of man's book. The woman is not needed to do man's work. She is not needed to think man's thoughts. She need not fear that the masculine mind, almost universally dominant, will fail to take care of its own. Her mission is not to enhance the masculine spirit, but to express the feminine; hers is not to preserve a man-made world, but to create a human world by the infusion of the feminine element into all of its activities.

Woman must not accept; she must challenge. She must not be awed by that which has been built up around her; she must reverence that within her which struggles for expression. Her eyes must be less upon what is and more clearly upon what should be. She must listen only with a frankly questioning attitude to the dogmatized opinions of man-made society. When she chooses her new, free course of action, it must be in the light of her own opinion — of her own intuition. Only so can she give play to the feminine spirit. Only thus can she free her mate from the bondage which he wrought for himself when he wrought hers. Only thus can she restore to him that of which he robbed himself in restricting her. Only thus can she remake the world.

The world is, indeed, hers to remake, it is

hers to build and to recreate. Even as she has permitted the suppression of her own feminine element and the consequent impoverishment of industry, art, letters, science, morals, religions and social intercourse, so it is hers to enrich all these.

Woman must have her freedom — the fundamental freedom of choosing whether or not she shall be a mother and how many children she will have. Regardless of what man's attitude may be, that problem is hers — and before it can be his, it is hers alone.

She goes through the vale of death alone, each time a babe is born. As it is the right neither of man nor the state to coerce her into this ordeal, so it is her right to decide whether she will endure it. That right to decide imposes upon her the duty of clearing the way to knowledge by which she may make and carry out the decision.

Birth control is woman's problem. The quicker she accepts it as hers and hers alone, the quicker will society respect motherhood. The quicker, too, will the world be made a fit place for her children to live.

THE ROOTS OF REVOLT

JO FREEMAN

Political scientist Jo Freeman has long been involved in the women's movement, both as an activist and as a theoretician. She has taught Women's Studies and political science and has lectured and written widely on feminism. In addition to several articles, she is the author of a book entitled *The Politics of Women's Liberation* (1975) and editor of *Women: A Feminist Perspective,* 2nd ed. (1978). In the article reprinted here, Freeman describes the origins of the contemporary movement, from the conflicts and growing awareness of the 1960s to its crystallization in institutionally oriented organizations like NOW and in individual groups and societies.

During the early 1960s a great number of books and articles appeared about women:[1] women's history, economics and women, women's work, women in literature, the psychology of women, and the social position of women in general. Most of these works concluded that not only was women's position pretty bad, but that women were not likely to do anything about it. Women, they said, were content in their place.

There was a touch of irony in this conclusion. For not only did these new works contribute considerably to the consciousness necessary for a woman's liberation movement to develop in the last half of the decade, but they were also indicative of its imminence. Most social and political movements advertise their coming long before any but the most perceptive recognize their potential existence. One way this is done is through the printed word. More articles and books concerning women were printed outside of established women's publications in the five years that preceded the present women's movement than had been printed in the previous twenty years.

Discontent also manifests itself patho-

Excerpted from "Women on the Move: The Roots of Revolt," by Jo Freeman, in *Academic Women on the Move,* edited by Alice S. Rossi and Ann Calderwood, © 1973 by Russell Sage Foundation, New York.

logically. The 1940s and 1950s witnessed the phenomenon of "momism." [2] Everything was mom's fault — she was trying to run her husband and was ruining her children. No one noticed that this happened at the same time women were being encouraged to return to the home and devote their lives to husband and family. Such women lived at the height of the "feminine mystique." They were told to live through others, and they did, to the dismay of everyone concerned.

Another pathology was the divorce rate. One out of every three first marriages ended in court. Alcoholism and drug addiction were on the increase among housewives, particularly among those with few financial worries. But the most common sign of anxiety was a growing sense that there must be more to life than marriage and children. It was this vague unspecified malaise that Friedan called "the problem that has no name" (Friedan 1963). One West Coast psychologist called it a "great reservoir of rage in women — just under the surface" (Farson 1969). What these people lacked — the ones who wrote the books, took the drugs and felt the rage — was a unifying idea to explain their feelings and a structure through which to communicate with each other. Instead, most women attributed their distress to personal inadequacy. . . .

In the 1960s, two networks of communication were created in which women played prominent roles that allowed, even forced, an awakened interest in the old feminist ideas. Thus the movement has two different origins and the resulting branches differ in style, orientation, values, and forms of organization. The first of these will be called the older branch of the movement, in part because it began first, and in part because the median age of its activists has been higher. Its most prominent organization is the National Organization for Women (NOW),

but it also contains such groups as the Professional Women's Caucus (PWC), Federally Employed Women (FEW), and the self-defined "right wing" of the movement, the Women's Equity Action League (WEAL). These groups are made up largely of employed women and have been primarily concerned with the problems of working women. Their style of organization tends to be formal, with elected officers, boards of directors, bylaws and the other trappings of democratic structure and procedure. They all started as top-down organizations lacking a mass base. Some have subsequently developed that base, some have not yet done so, and others do not want to develop one.

The younger branch of the movement is all mass base and no national organization. It consists of innumerable small groups engaged in a variety of activities, whose contact with each other is at best tenuous. Its composition, like that of the older branch, tends to be predominantly white, middle class, and college educated, but much more homogeneously so.

It is a common mistake to try to place the various feminist organizations on the traditional left/right spectrum. The terms "reformist" and "radical" are convenient and fit into our preconceived notions about the nature of political organization, but feminism cuts through the usual categories and demands new perspectives in order to be understood. Some groups often called "reformist" have a platform which would so completely change our society it would be unrecognizable. Other groups called "radical" concentrate on the traditional female concerns of love, sex, children, and interpersonal relationships (although with non-traditional views). The activities of the organizations are similarly incongruous. The most typical division of labor is, ironically, that those groups labeled "radical" engage primarily in educational work while the so-called reformist groups are the activists. Structure and style rather than ideology more accurately differentiate the various groups, and even here there has been much borrowing on both sides. In general the older branch has used the traditional forms of political action while the younger branch has been experimental.

As will be seen, the different style and organization of the two branches of the movement were largely derived from the different kind of political education and experiences of the women involved. Women in the older branch were trained and experienced in traditional forms of political action, while the younger branch inherited the loose, flexible, person-oriented attitude of the youth and student movements. The different structures that have evolved have been in turn the primary determinant of the strategy of the two branches. These differences often are perceived as conflicting, but in reality their essential complementarity has been one of the strengths of the movement.

The Formation of the National Organization for Women

The National Organization for Women is the oldest, largest, and best known of the organizations in the older branch of the women's movement. The forces which led to its formation were set in motion in 1961 when President Kennedy established the President's Commission on the Status of Women, at the behest of Esther Peterson, then director of the Women's Bureau.[3] The 1963 commission report, *American Women,* and subsequent committee publications documented just how thoroughly women still were denied many rights and opportunities in American society.

The major response to the President's Commission was the creation of state commissions — eventually in all fifty states. While many governors saw them as an easy opportunity to pay off political favors, many women saw the state commissions as opportunities to turn attention to their concerns. These commissions in turn researched and wrote their own reports, which varied widely in quality and depth.

The federal and state commission activity laid the ground for the future movement by providing ample evidence of women's unequal status and creating among many politically active women a climate of expectation that something should and could be done. During this time, two other events of significance occurred. The first was the publication of Betty Friedan's book, *The Feminine Mystique,* in 1963. An immediate best seller, it stimulated many women to question the status quo and some women suggested to Friedan that a new organization should be formed to attack their problems. The second event was the addition of "sex" to Title VII of the 1964 Civil Rights Act.

Many thought the "sex" provision was a joke — its initiator, Representative Howard W. Smith of Virginia, only wanted to make the employment section of the bill look silly and sufficiently divide the liberals to prevent its passage. However, the provision was taken very seriously by most of the female members of the House, regardless of party or politics. Representative Martha Griffiths of Michigan, the leading feminist of the House, claims she intended to sponsor the amendment, but held off when she learned of Smith's intentions as she knew he would bring another 100 votes with him. Most of the House liberals opposed the provision, arguing that it would weaken the bill, and Representative Griffiths knew it needed every vote it could get. Despite their many disagreements, both Smith and the liberal opponents played the provision for all the laughs it was worth and the ensuing uproar went down in congressional history as "Ladies Day in the House." [4]

Thanks to determined leadership by the congresswomen and concerted lobbying by the provision's supporters, "sex" was added to the bill, only to be aborted by the very agency set up to administer it. The first executive director of the Equal Employment Opportunity Commission (EEOC), Herman Edelsberg, publicly stated that the provision was a "fluke conceived . . . out of wedlock" (Edelsberg 1965). This attitude caused Griffiths to blast the agency in a speech on the House floor. She declared that the EEOC had "started out by casting disrespect and ridicule on the law" and that their "wholly negative attitude had changed — for the worse" (Griffiths 1966).

Not everyone within the EEOC was opposed to the "sex" provision. There was a feminist coterie that argued that "sex" would be taken more seriously if there were "some sort of NAACP for women" to put pressure on the government. As government employees they could not organize such a group, but they hoped someone would and spoke to several people about this idea.

Ten days after Griffith's speech, the three strands of incipient feminism were tied together and NOW was formed from the knot. On June 30, 1966 the Third National Conference of Commissions on the Status of Women, ironically titled "Targets for Action," forbade the presentation of a resolution calling for the EEOC to treat sex discrimination as seriously as race discrimination; officials said one government agency could not be allowed to pressure another. The small group of women sponsoring the resolution had met the night before with Betty Friedan, in town researching her second book, to discuss the possibility of a civil rights organization for women. Not convinced of its need, they chose instead to propose the resolution. When the conference

officials vetoed it, these women held a whispered conversation over lunch and agreed to form an action organization independent of government. The time for conferences was over, they felt. Now was the time to fight, and when word leaked out, twenty-eight women paid $5.00 to join the new organization (Friedan 1967). NOW's purpose was "to bring women into full participation in the mainstream of American society now, assuming all the privileges and responsibilities thereof in truly equal partnership with men."

By the time the organizing conference of NOW was held on October 29 and 30, 1966, more than 300 women and men had become charter members of the new organization. They were primarily from the professions, labor, government, and communications fields, and were between the ages of 25 and 45. Although special efforts were made to recruit academic women, and the temporary "office" of NOW was located at the Center for Continuing Education at the University of Wisconsin, very few academic women were among these charter members. According to Kathryn Clarenbach, NOW's first board chairperson, "they were scared to death — even though NOW had no reputation." [5] Nonetheless there were eight college professors and administrators among the original twenty-six board members and officers of NOW. Though few in number, they were very influential.[6]

At the organizing meeting in Washington, a statement of purpose and a national structure were hammered out.[7] The statement articulated a general philosophy of equality and justice under law, rather than specific areas for action. It also emphasized that "women's problems are linked to many broader questions of social justice; their solution will require concerned action by many groups." To research the need for specific actions, seven task forces were set up on discrimination against women in employment, education, and religion; the family; women's image in the mass media; women's political rights and responsibilities; and the problems of poor women. To handle NOW's administrative needs the office was moved to Detroit where it was run by Caroline Davis out of the United Auto Worker's Women's Committee.

NOW's activities for the following year reflected its limited origins more than its broad goals. Its main target was the executive branch where it sought to bend the might of federal power to the benefit of women. . . .

By NOW's second conference in November 1967, the organization had grown to 1,200 members and lines of tension were already apparent. As the only action organization concerned with women's rights, it had attracted many different kinds of people with many different views on what and how to proceed. With only a national structure and at this point no broad base, it was difficult for individuals to pursue their particular concerns on a local level; they had to persuade the whole organization to support them. Given NOW's top-down structure and limited resources, this placed severe limits on diversity, and in turn, severe strains on the organization.

Conflict came to a head when the 1967 conference proposed a Bill of Rights for Women to be presented to candidates and parties in the 1968 elections. Five points called for enforcement of laws banning sex discrimination in employment; maternity leave rights in employment and in social security benefits; a tax deduction for home and child-care expenses for working parents; child-care centers; equal and unsegregated education; and equal job training opportunities and allowances for women in poverty. These five points presented no problem to the organization, but when some women proposed that support for the Equal Rights Amendment and repeal of all abortion laws be added, several members threatened to walk out.

Women from the United Auto Workers (UAW) opposed inclusion of the ERA not on personal grounds but because their union was against it. They said they would be forced out of NOW if the organization took a stand on the issue. Another group said they would walk out if NOW did *not* speak out. When the ERA was added to the NOW Bill of Rights, the UAW women did not resign, but they did withdraw from active participation. This action cost NOW the use of the UAW office and clerical services, compelling relocation of the national office to Washington, D.C. and creating administrative chaos in the process. Two years later the UAW reversed their stand on the ERA and the members of their Women's Committee resumed active participation in NOW.

The second major disagreement in 1967 was over the inclusion of "reproductive issues." Several women viewed NOW as an "NAACP type organization" and thought it should stick to economic and legal issues. At this time abortion repeal was not a national issue and public discussion was considered controversial. Some NOW members thought that abortion was not a women's rights issue and that support for repeal of abortion laws would only scare off potential financial contributors. Nevertheless NOW supported abortion law repeal, making it the first time "control of one's body" was stated as a woman's right. This action cost NOW its "conservative" wing a year later (Hole and Levine 1971:67–68).

In the fall of 1968 the many disagreements erupted and NOW fissioned off several new organizations. The "conservatives" announced the formation of the Women's Equity Action League which would concentrate on legal and economic issues, especially in the area of employment and education. Initially, it was concentrated in Ohio and consisted primarily of the former Ohio NOW chapters; but it would eventually make the biggest impact on academe of all the groups.

The "radicals" left because of disagreements on structure, not program. By now the younger branch of the movement was becoming publicly known as was its disavowal of traditional structure. The "radicals," most of whom were from New York, wanted to replace what they felt was NOW's "elitist" structure with decision-making positions chosen by lot. NOW's rejections of this proposal represented not only a preference for traditional forms of structure, but a certain amount of fear of the New York chapter since it had over half the national membership, and was the most active and best known of all the chapters. To many, the New York chapter *was* NOW. Chapters in other cities had gone through many false starts, forming and then collapsing in confusion and inactivity. Unlike New York City, which had easy access to the national media and many people skilled at using it, the other chapters had difficulty developing programs not dependent on the media. As the national program focused almost exclusively on legal cases or federal lobbying, the regional chapters could not easily fit into that either. By the fall of 1968, two years after NOW's founding, the chapters were beginning to get on their feet with local programs. They did not want to see the national organization taken over by New York.

As it turned out, New York did not like the proposed structural changes either and a month later rejected a move to use them in the New York chapter. At this time the three strongest proponents of these changes walked out and formed the October 17th Movement (commemorating the day they left), a group eventually known as The Feminists. Although The Feminists started as a split-off from NOW, most of their new members came from the younger branch of the movement and the group has grown to be one of the more prolific sources of radical feminist ideas.

If the conservatives walked out over programs and the radicals over structure, the third group to leave that fall departed from impatience. Since 1966, NOW had been trying to form a tax-exempt sister organization to handle legal cases modeled on the NAACP Legal Defense and Education Fund. In 1968, it was running into numerous problems and three of the lawyers — Mary Eastwood, Caruthers Berger, and Sylvia Ellison — walked out in disgust. With them they took NOW's most important legal cases, on which they had been working.[8] Eventually these lawyers formed Human Rights for Women (HRW), a nonprofit, tax-exempt corporation to support sex discrimination cases. . . .

The next two years were spent putting together a grass-roots organization, and forming liaisons with the younger branch of the movement. In November 1969, the first Congress to Unite Women was held in New York and several others were held elsewhere during the following year. They were largely unsuccessful. Fraught with dissension, backbiting, and namecalling, they did not result in any umbrella organization to speak for the interests of all feminists. But this very failure portended some success, as feminists from both branches — but particularly from NOW — began to realize that a diverse movement might be more valuable than a united one. The multitude of different groups reached out to different kinds of women, served different functions within the movement, and presented a wide variety of feminist ideas. Although they made coordinated action difficult, they allowed an individual woman to relate to the movement in the way most appropriate to her life. Fission began to seem creative as it broadened the scope of the movement without weakening its impact. The groups agreed to disagree and to work together where possible. When NOW organized the August 26 strike to commemorate the fiftieth anniversary of the Nineteenth Amendment, it was supported by virtually every feminist group in some manner or other.

This strike marked a turning point for the women's liberation movement. It was the first time that the potential power of the movement became publicly apparent, and with this the movement came of age. It was also the first time the press gave a women's demonstration straight coverage. Weeks before they had given it a good deal of publicity, but mostly because it was a slow summer for news and this appeared to be the most entertaining event of the season. Whether encouraged by the amount of publicity or angered by its tone of wry amusement, women turned out by the thousands in cities all over the country and in two European countries. The sheer numbers shocked everyone — including the organizers — and made it clear that the movement would now have to be taken seriously. . . .

The August 26 strike also compelled the movement to define its goals narrowly for the first time. The entire history of the movement has been one of broadening its scope and narrowing its immediate goals — a very necessary process for any social movement. The strike was centered around three central demands — abortion on demand, twenty-four hour child-care centers and equal opportunity in employment and education. These were not viewed as the sole goals of the movement, but merely the first steps on the road to liberation. As such, they provided a programmatic structure that gave sympathizers something *to do* rather than just talk about oppression.

At the same time, NOW gained a broader

conception of just how interrelated are all social phenomena and the contextual nature of women's situation. At its convention in the fall of 1971, numerous resolutions were passed establishing a feminist position on a multitude of subjects not directly related to women. This move was anticipated by NOW's original Statement of Purpose, its early support of the guaranteed annual income, and its concern with women in poverty. Nonetheless, it was a major break with the past. . . .

The Growth of the Small Groups

During the mid-1960s, unaware and unknown to NOW, the EEOC, and the state commissions, younger women began forming their own movement. Contrary to popular myth, it did not begin on the campus, nor was it started by Students for a Democratic Society (SDS). While few of its activators were students, all were "under 30," and they had obtained their political education as participants or concerned observers of the social action projects of the sixties. These projects, particularly the civil rights movement, attracted a large number of women. Many were to say later that one of the major appeals of this movement was that the social role if not the economic condition of blacks was similar to that of women. But this observation was a retrospective one. At the time most women would not have expressed these thoughts even if they could have articulated them. The few who did were quickly put down.

Whether as participants in civil rights groups, the New Left, peace groups, or in the free universities, women found themselves quickly shunted into traditional roles. One early pamphlet described these roles as those of "workers" and "wives": the "workers" serviced the radical organizations with their typing and clerical skills and the "wives" serviced the radical men with their homemaking and sexual skills. Those few women who refused these roles and insisted on being accepted in the "realm of the mind" found themselves desexed and often isolated by their comrades (Bernstein et al. 1966).

The situation in which these women found themselves unavoidably conflicted with the ideologies of "participatory democracy," "freedom," and "justice" that they were expressing. They were working in a "freedom movement" but were not very free. Nor did their male colleagues tolerate any dissent. Generally, the men followed the example of Stokeley Carmichael, who cut off all debate on a woman's resolution at a 1964 Student Nonviolent Coordinating Committee conference by saying, "The only position for women in SNCC is prone." The problems for women in the radical movement were raised again and again over the next three years. In Seattle, members of the Socialist Workers Party (SWP) defected and formed the independent Freedom Socialist Club in 1964. The refusal of the SWP to consider "the woman question" was a major cause. Civil rights workers, housewives, and students in New Orleans formed a summer free school discussion group in 1965. Women on the 1966 Meredith Mississippi march held secret nightly meetings after they were ordered to walk on the inside of the march line and be accompanied by a man at all times.

The idea of women's "liberation" was first raised at an SDS convention in December 1965. It was laughed off the floor by the male radicals. Undaunted, some New Left women circulated papers on the issue[9] and tried to interest SDS women in organizing themselves. Although they largely failed, the workshops on women in SDS regional conferences attracted many women who were later to be instrumental in the formation of feminist groups. At the summer 1967 national conference, SDS women finally succeeded in passing a resolution calling for the full participation of women in SDS. Generalizing from their experiences (and unknowingly paralleling the developing NOW program) they also suggested that SDS work on behalf of all women for communal child care, wide dissemination of contraceptives, easily available abortions, and equal sharing of housework. More specifically, they requested that SDS print relevant literature and that the SDS paper solicit articles on women. These requests were largely ignored. Instead, the SDS organ, *New Left Notes,* decorated the page on which the women's resolution appeared with a freehand drawing of a girl in a baby-doll dress holding a picket sign and petulantly declaring "We want our rights and we want them now!" (*New Left Notes,* July 10, 1967).

No single group or organization among these protest movements directly stimulated the formation of independent women's liberation groups. But together they created a "radical community" in which like-minded women continually interacted or were made aware of each other. This community provided the necessary network of communication and its radical ideas provided the framework of analysis which "explained" the dismal situation in which radical women found themselves. In this fertile field, the younger branch of the women's movement took root in 1967 and 1968. At least five groups in five different cities (Chicago, Toronto, Seattle, Detroit, and Gainesville, Florida) formed spontaneously and independently of each other. They came at a very auspicious moment: 1967 was the year in which the blacks expelled the whites from the civil rights movement, student power had been discredited by SDS, and the organized New Left was on the wane. Only draft resistance activities were on the increase, and this movement more than any other exemplified the social inequities of the sexes. Men could resist the draft. Women could only counsel resistance. For months women met quietly to analyze their perpetual secondary roles in the radical movement, to assimilate the lessons learned in free university study groups, or to reflect on their treatment in the civil rights movement. They were constantly ridiculed by the men they worked with and told that their meetings with other women were "counterrevolutionary" because it would further splinter an already badly factioned movement. In many ways this very ridicule served to increase their growing rage.

A typical example was the August 1967 National Conference on New Politics convention held in Chicago. Although a women's caucus met for days, it was told its resolution was not significant enough to merit a floor discussion. By threatening to tie up the convention with procedural motions, the women succeeded in having their statement tacked to the end of the agenda. It was never discussed. The chair refused to recognize any of the women standing by the microphones, their hands straining upward. When he instead called on someone to speak on "the forgotten American, the American Indian," five women rushed the podium to demand an explanation. But the chairman just patted one of the women on the head and told her "cool down, little girl, we have more important things to talk about than women's problems."

This was only the beginning. At the 1969 demonstrations at Nixon's inauguration, women asked and received time for two short speeches at the rally, after many objections from the men. When they tried to speak they were hooted down with cries of "take her off the stage and fuck her." This was only one among many such incidents. Despite this friction, women still continued to work within the radical community, and to use the underground press and the free universities to disseminate women's liberation ideas. Many women traveled widely to Left conferences and demonstrations, using the opportunity to talk with other women about the new movement. In spite of public derision by movement men, or perhaps because of it, young women steadily formed new groups around the country.

Although women were quick to use the underground media, they took longer to form their own. Moreover, they had great difficulty articulating their grievances in specific terms. The early Chicago women produced the first Statement of Principles of eight points only after months of work and ended by lamenting that they knew their statement was reformist, but it was the best they could do at the time (*New Left Notes* November 13, 1967). By the time the first national women's liberation gathering took place in August 1968, only five pamphlets had been written.[10]

The three-day meeting in Sandy Springs, Maryland, was limited to twenty women from six cities (Boston, Washington, D.C., Baltimore, New York, Chicago, and Gainesville, Florida) and was to be focused on clarifying the issues that were developing in the embryonic movement. The main question was whether there was a movement at all: should it remain a branch of the radical Left or become an independent women's movement? There was a rough correlation between people's political background and their initial stand on this issue. Those from the New Left favored remaining within the radical fold and those from civil rights and related experiences favored independence. Proponents of the former became known as "politicos" and the latter as "feminists." They traded arguments about whether capitalism or male-dominated social institutions and values were the enemy. The only major agreement to come out of the Sandy Springs meeting was to hold an open national conference in Chicago the following Thanksgiving, and four women from four cities volunteered to arrange it. Although notices were sent out only a month in advance, over 200 women attended from twenty states and Canada. The diversity and rapid growth of the movement were apparent at this convention and the participants returned home turned on by the *idea* of women's liberation and began to organize more and more small groups.

The influx of large numbers of previously apolitical women eventually shifted the balance of power from politicos to feminists, and an independent, autonomous women's liberation movement developed. The continuing hostility of radical men also convinced many politicos to shift to a primarily feminist position. Nonetheless the basic differences in orientation remained. The former politicos continued to see women's issues within a broader political context while the original feminists focused almost exclusively on women's concerns.

Another early disagreement centered on what to call the new women's groups. These discussions occurred primarily in New York and Chicago and revolved around a choice of "radical women" or "women's liberation." The former was favored by most because their identities were tied up with the idea of "radicalism" and they wanted to develop the concept of being radical as a woman, not just of a woman who was a radical. Since many feminists in New York also thought that the term "women's liberation" was too much an imitation of politico jargon, both factions agreed to call themselves New York Radical Women. Women in Seattle likewise adopted the name Radical Women as did several groups elsewhere.

The advocates of "women's liberation" liked the term not so much because of its implied identification with third world and black liberation movements, but because they wanted to define the terms of debate in what they saw as a potentially significant movement. They had been educated by the misunderstandings created by the referent, "the Negro problem," which inevitably structured people's thinking in terms of "the problem with Negroes" rather than racism and what to do about it. They were also aware of the historical "woman question" and "Jewish question" which had led to the same mistake. The problem, they felt, was not women but women's liberation, and the best way to get people to think of the problem in those terms was to label it as such from the very beginning.[11]

Women's Liberationists started the first national newsletter for the minuscule movement. The first issue came out in March 1968 as three untitled mimeographed sheets with the tag line "The voice of the women's liberation movement." By the second issue three months later, it had grown to four offset sheets and the label became the name. Under a different editor each issue, *The Voice of the Women's Liberation Movement* (*VWLM*) served as the main vehicle of communication for the growing movement for the next sixteen months. The publication came to represent the national movement to most women who read it, and the term "women's liberation" came to be used more and more frequently.

Initially, the term "women's liberation" applied only to the younger branch of the movement. Organizations such as NOW considered themselves part of a women's movement, but not a women's liberation movement. Gradually, however, more and more NOW people and other women not associated with any particular group adopted the name. Some feminists still do not like to be thought of as part of women's liberation and some of the latter do not like the term feminist, but for most the two terms are synonymous. . . .

In the fall of 1969, the major news media simultaneously decided to carry stories on women's liberation, and they appeared steadily for the next six months. Quickly discovering that only women could cover the movement, editors tried to pick reporters known for their objectivity and nonfeminist views. The results were not unexpected: their female staff became politicized by what they learned. Women writers, researchers, and secretaries became conscious of their secondary role on their own publications, formed their own small groups, and began protesting for better working conditions.[12]

In setting up such groups, feminists developed certain organizing principles. The basic unit of the younger branch of the movement is the small group of from five to twenty women. The groups have a variety of functions but a very consistent style, which deemphasizes structure and damns the idea of leadership. The thousands of groups around the country are virtually independent of each other, linked only by numerous publications, personal correspondence and cross country travelers. Some cities have a coordinating committee which attempts to maintain communication among the local groups and to channel newcomers into appropriate ones. Other cities have women's centers which provide places for meetings, classes, informal gatherings, and emergency assistance to individual women. Neither centers nor coordinating committees have any real power over group activities, let alone group ideas, and most small groups are not formally associated with them.

One result of this style is a very broad-based, creative movement, to which individuals can relate pretty much as they desire, with no concern for orthodoxy or doctrine. Another result is a kind of political impotency. It is virtually impossible to coordinate a national action, assuming there could be any agreement on issues around which to coordinate one. Fortunately, the older branch of the movement does have the structure necessary to coordinate such actions, and is usually the one to initiate them as well, as NOW did for the August 26, 1970 national strike.

Common characteristics of the small groups include a conscious lack of formal structure, an emphasis on participation by everyone, a sharing of tasks, and the exclusion of men. This latter policy has been, to observers, one of the most controversial aspects of the movement, but it was and is one of the least controversial issues within the movement itself. There was virtually no debate on this policy in any city at any time. Originally the idea was borrowed from the black power movement, which was much in the public consciousness when the women's liberation movement began. It was reinforced by the unremitting hostility of most of the New Left men. Even when such hostility was not present, women in virtually every group in the United States and Canada soon discovered that the traditional sex roles reasserted themselves in mixed groups regardless of the good intentions of the participants. Men inevitably dominated the discussions, and usually would talk only about how women's liberation related to men, or how men themselves were oppressed by sex roles. In all-female groups women found the discussions were more open, honest, and extensive, and gave them the opportunity they wanted and needed to learn to relate to other women.

The policy of male exclusion was continued because women felt men were largely irrelevant to the development of their movement. Their goal was to reach women, and it was both frustrating and a waste of time to have men present. Women also discovered a tactical advantage to the policy: their activities were taken much more seriously when they insisted that they only wanted to speak with women. The tactic had shock value, as it had in the early insistence that their activities be reported by women. Another result was that men formed groups of their own around the problems of the male sex role.

The basic form of political education of women came not through movement literature, but through "rap groups." In such groups, women explore personal questions of feminist relevance by "rapping" to each other about their individual experiences and analyzing them communally.[13] Unlike the male exclusion policy, the concept of rap groups did not develop spontaneously or without a struggle. The political background of many of the early feminists predisposed them against the rap group as "unpolitical" and they condemned discussion meetings which "degenerated" into "bitch sessions." Other feminists saw that the rap session met a basic need. They seized upon it and created a new institution. From a sociological perspective the rap group is probably the most valuable contribution the women's liberation movement has made so far to the tools for social change. . . .

This laissez-faire philosophy of organization has allowed the talents of many women to develop spontaneously and allowed others to learn new skills. It has also created some major problems for the movement. Most women come into the movement via the rap group and most go out from there. There is no easy way to move from a rap group to a project; women either stumble onto one or start their own. Most do neither. Once involved in a project, participation often consumes enormous amounts of time. Moreover, most groups are unwilling to change their structure when they change their tasks. They have accepted the ideology of "structurelessness" without realizing its limitations. The rap group style encourages participation in discussion and its supportive atmos-

phere elicits personal insight, but neither the style nor the tone of the rap group is very efficient to handle specific tasks. Essentially, this means that the movement is run on a local level by women who can work at it full-time.

Nationally, the movement is not run by anyone, and no public figure commands obedience from any part of it. But because the movement has not chosen women to speak for it, believing that no one could, the media has done the choosing instead. This has created a tremendous amount of animosity between local movement "leaders" — who would deny that they are leaders — and those labeled "leaders" by the media. The movement did not give them their platform, and it cannot take it away from them; so instead it deplores the fact that a platform exists at all.

The problem of "structurelessness" is causing several organizational crises within the movement as a whole.[14] For one, the formation of rap groups as a major movement function has become obsolete. Due to the intense press publicity that began in the fall of 1969, and the numerous "overground" books and articles now being circulated, women's liberation has become a household word. Its issues are discussed and informal rap groups emerge among people who are not formally associated with a movement group. Ironically, this subtle, silent, and subversive spread of feminist consciousness is causing a situation of political unemployment. Educational work is no longer such an overwhelming need. The younger branch of the movement has never had ways of channeling participants into other areas; now that it so desperately needs to develop those areas, it does not even know who are its participants.

The need for a program and the inability of most younger branch movement groups to formulate it has driven young women into other feminist and nonfeminist organizations. Quite a few are joining NOW, despite their original hostility to the older group. Many others are starting and joining a plethora of new organizations. All are now searching for some way to constructively act on the problems of which they have become so aware.

Notes

1. A cursory examination of the card catalog of any large library and the indexes of major journals for books and articles on women discloses a striking decrease in their number after the mid-1920s that curves up again only in the 1960s. The years 1927 and 1959 appear to be the inflexion points.
2. Wylie who created and popularized the term, almost gave his "subspecies" a feminist interpretation in his commentary on the twentieth edition (1955) of his infamous book. He said: "When we and our culture and our religions agreed to hold woman the inferior sex, cursed, unclean, and sinful – we made her mom. And when we agreed upon the American Ideal Woman, the Dream Girl of National Adolescence, the Queen of Bedpan Week, the Pin-up, the Glamour Puss — we insulted women and . . . thus made mom. The hen-harpy is but the Cinderella chick come home to roost; the taloned, crackling residue of burnt-out puberty in a land that has no use for mature men or women" (Wylie 1955:197).
3. The Women's Bureau was created in 1920 as a result of feminist activity at that time. Although its main concern has been with women workers, it has done an excellent job of producing reports and pamphlets on many aspects of women's situation. (Single copies of all materials are free upon request from regional bureaus.) Its *Handbook on Women Workers* is the movement's main source book on legal and economic discrimination.
4. For a thorough documentation of this event, see Bird 1968, Chapter I. For a blow-by-blow account of the floor happenings, see *Congressional Record,* House, February 8, 1964.
5. Personal interview, September 22, 1971.
6. The employment background of the national board and officers was as follows: Board — labor, three; academe, seven; church related, one; government, two; law, two; communications two; miscellaneous, three. Officers — labor, academe, church, and communications, one each; government, two. Most recent occupation was used as the criterion for classification, and potential cross-filing was arbitrarily eliminated. For example, two academic nuns were counted under "academe" rather than "church."
7. The first officers accurately reflected NOW's origins. Friedan was elected as president, two former EEOC commissioners as vice-presidents, a representative of the United Auto Workers as secretary-treasurer, and seven past and present members of state commissions on the status of women were appointed to the twenty-member national board. Of the charter members, 126 were Wisconsin residents, and Wisconsin had the most active state commission.
8. These were *Bowe* v. *Colgate Palmolive* and *Menglekock* v. *State of California.* The former has been settled favorably and the latter is still in court. The Legal Defense Fund did not begin operation until 1971.
9. "A Kind of Memo" by Casey Hayden and Mary King was circulated in mimeograph form for many months prior to the 1965 SDS convention and largely stimulated the discussion there. The essay was later published in *Liberation.*
10. These pamphlets were "Towards a female liberation movement" by Judith Brown and Beverly Jones; "Position paper on radical women in the professions" by Marlene Dixon; "Towards a radical women's movement" by Marilyn Salzman Webb; "Women in the radical movement: A reply to *Ramparts*" by Evelyn Goldfield, Heather Booth and Sue Munaker; and "The look is you: Towards a strategy for radical women" by Naomi Jaffe and Bernadine Dohrn.
11. Unfortunately they did not anticipate that

"liberation" would be caricatured as "lib," "libbie," and "libbest" and contribute to the women's movement not being taken seriously.

12. *Newsweek,* in particular, illustrated all these phenomena. The person originally assigned to the story was a young writer being "given her chance." Her piece was criticized for lack of objectivity, rewritten by the male editors every week for two months, and finally dropped. In her place a free-lancer who happened to be the wife of one of *Newsweek's* senior editors was hired. She was paid in advance, specified no undue editing, and wrote the most personal report of all. Despite the fact that it was quite different from *Newsweek's* usual style, it was printed. In the meantime, women staffers watched these developments with great interest and made plans of their own to commemorate the occasion. They chose the day of the special issue's publication to announce that their complaint of discrimination had been filed with the EEOC.

13. For a thorough elaboration on the function and operation of the rap group see Allen 1970.

14. For a more thorough examination of why and how this problem has occurred see Joreen 1972.

References

Allen, Pamela. 1970. *Free space: A perspective on the small group in women's liberation.* New York: Times Change Press.

Bernstein, Judi et al. 1966. Sisters, brothers, lovers . . . listen. . . . Boston: The New England Free Press.

Bird, Caroline. 1968. *Born female: The high cost of keeping women down.* New York: David McKay Co.

Congressional Record, House of Representatives. February 8, 1964, pp. 2577–2584.

Edelsberg, Herman. August 25, 1965. N.Y.U. eighteenth conference on labor. *Labor Relations Reporter,* 61:253–255.

Farson, Richard. December 16, 1969. The rage of women. *Look,* 33:21–23.

Freeman, Jo. February 24, 1969. The new feminists. *Nation,* 208(8):243.

Freeman, Jo. January 1973. The origins of the women's liberation movement. *American Journal of Sociology.* 78(4):792–811.

Friedan, Betty. 1963. *The feminine mystique.* New York: Dell Publishing Co.

Friedan, Betty. April 1967. N.O.W., how it began. *Women Speaking,* 10:4.

Griffiths, Martha. June 20, 1966. Speech in the House of Representatives. *Congressional Record,* 89th Congress, 2d Session.

Hayden, Casey, and King, Mary. April 1966. Sex and caste: A kind of memo. *Liberation,* 11(2):35.

Hole, Judith and Levine, Ellen. 1971. *Rebirth of feminism.* New York: Quadrangle.

Joreen. 1972. The tyranny of structurelessness. *The Second Wave,* 2(1):20.

New Left Notes. July 10, 1967. 2(26):4.

New Left Notes. November 13, 1967. 2(39):2.

Wylie, Philip. 1955. *Generation of vipers.* New York: Rinehart.

THEORY OF SEXUAL POLITICS

KATE MILLETT

Kate Millett, feminist author and sculptor, was born in 1934 in St. Paul, Minnesota. She studied English at the University of Minnesota and at Oxford University, and finished a doctorate at Columbia University with a dissertation that became the book *Sexual Politics.* Millett has taught English and Women's Studies, worked as a sculptor, and co-directed a film, *Three Lives.* An activist early in her career, she served in CORE (Congress of Racial Equality) in the 1950s, supported student strikes while teaching at Barnard, and served in NOW as Chair of the Education Committee. In addition to *Sexual Politics,* her books include *Flying* (1974), *The Prostitution Papers* (1976), and *Sita* (1977).

The publication of *Sexual Politics* (1970) was an important development in the current movement. It received wide attention in the press, focused public attention on women's liberation, and was one of the first books to articulate a broad theoretical base for the ideas of the growing movement. Millett has widened the term *politics* (which traditionally means simply "that which pertains to the *polis,* or city") to refer to "power-structured relationships . . . whereby one group of persons is controlled by another," and then shows how this concept captures the essence of male-female arrangements. Using literary and historical models to support her thesis, she argues that social and sexual relations between women and men are not-so-nice power arrangements, grounded in misogyny, expressing themselves as a life view (patriarchy) and resulting in the worldwide oppression of women on both an institutional and a personal level.

. . . In introducing the term "sexual politics," one must first answer the inevitable question "Can the relationship between the sexes be viewed in a political light at all?" The answer depends on how one defines politics.[1] This essay does not define the political as that relatively narrow and exclusive world of meetings, chairmen, and parties. The term "politics" shall refer to power-structured relationships, arrangements whereby one group of persons is controlled by another. By way of parenthesis one might add that although an ideal politics might simply be conceived of as the arrangement of human life on agreeable and rational principles from whence the entire notion of power *over* others should be banished, one must confess that this is not what constitutes the political as we know it, and it is to this that we must address ourselves.

The following sketch, which might be described as "notes toward a theory of patriarchy," will attempt to prove that sex is a status category with political implications. Something of a pioneering effort, it must

perforce be both tentative and imperfect. Because the intention is to provide an overall description, statements must be generalized, exceptions neglected, and subheadings overlapping and, to some degree, arbitrary as well.

The word "politics" is enlisted here when speaking of the sexes primarily because such a word is eminently useful in outlining the real nature of their relative status, historically and at the present. It is opportune, perhaps today even mandatory, that we develop a more relevant psychology and philosophy of power relationships beyond the simple conceptual framework provided by our traditional formal politics. Indeed, it may be imperative that we give some attention to defining a theory of politics which treats of power relationships on grounds less conventional than those to which we are accustomed.[2] I have therefore found it pertinent to define them on grounds of personal contact and interaction between members of well-defined and coherent groups: races, castes, classes, and sexes. For it is precisely because certain groups have no representation in a number of recognized political structures that their position tends to be so stable, their oppression so continuous.

In America, recent events have forced us to acknowledge at last that the relationship between the races is indeed a political one which involves the general control of one collectivity, defined by birth, over another collectivity, also defined by birth. Groups who rule by birthright are fast disappearing, yet there remains one ancient and universal scheme for the domination of one birth group by another — the scheme that prevails in the area of sex. The study of racism has convinced us that a truly political state of affairs operates between the races to perpetuate a series of oppressive circumstances. The subordinated group has inadequate redress through existing political institutions, and is deterred thereby from organizing into conventional political struggle and opposition.

Quite in the same manner, a disinterested examination of our system of sexual relationship must point out that the situation between the sexes now, and throughout history, is a case of that phenomenon Max Weber defined as *herrschaft,* a relationship of dominance and subordinance.[3] What goes largely unexamined, often even unacknowledged (yet is institutionalized nonetheless) in our social order, is the birthright priority whereby males rule females. Through this system a most ingenious form of "interior colonization" has been achieved. It is one which tends moreover to be sturdier than any form of segregation, and more rigorous than class stratification, more uniform, certainly more enduring. However muted its present appearance may be, sexual dominion obtains nevertheless as perhaps the most pervasive ideology of our culture and provides its most fundamental concept of power.

This is so because our society, like all other historical civilizations, is a patriarchy.[4] The fact is evident at once if one recalls that the military, industry, technology, universities, science, political office, and finance — in short, every avenue of power within the society, including the coercive force of the police, is entirely in male hands. As the essence of politics is power, such realization cannot fail to carry impact. What lingers of supernatural authority, the Deity, "His" ministry, together with the ethics and values, the philosophy and art of our culture — its very civilization — as T. S. Eliot once observed, is of male manufacture.

If one takes patriarchal government to be the institution whereby that half of the populace which is female is controlled by that half which is male, the principles of patriarchy appear to be twofold: male shall dominate female, elder male shall dominate younger. However, just as with any human institution, there is frequently a distance between the real and the ideal; contradictions and exceptions do exist within the system. While patriarchy as an institution is a social constant so deeply entrenched as to run through all other political, social, or economic forms, whether of caste or class, feudality or bureaucracy, just as it pervades all major religions, it also exhibits great variety in history and locale. In democracies,[5] for example, females have often held no office or do so (as now) in such minuscule numbers as to be below even token representation. Aristocracy, on the other hand, with its emphasis upon the magic and dynastic properties of blood, may at times permit women to hold power. The principle of rule by elder males is violated even more frequently. Bearing in mind the variation and degree in patriarchy — as say between Saudi Arabia and Sweden, Indonesia and Red China — we also recognize our own form in the U.S. and Europe to be much altered and attenuated by the reforms described in the next chapter.

I Ideological

Hannah Arendt[6] has observed that government is upheld by power supported either through consent or imposed through violence. Conditioning to an ideology amounts to the former. Sexual politics obtains consent through the "socialization" of both sexes to basic patriarchal polities with regard to temperament, role, and status. As to status, a pervasive assent to the prejudice of male superiority guarantees superior status in the male, inferior in the female. The first item, temperament, involves the formation of human personality along stereotyped lines of sex category ("masculine" and "feminine"), based on the needs and values of the dominant group and dictated by what its members cherish in themselves and find convenient in subordinates: aggression, intelligence, force, and efficacy in the male; passivity, ignorance, docility, "virtue," and ineffectuality in the female. This is complemented by a second factor, sex role, which decrees a consonant and highly elaborate code of conduct, gesture and attitude for each sex. In terms of activity, sex role assigns domestic service and attendance upon infants to the female, the rest of human achievement, interest, and ambition to the male. The limited role allotted the female tends to arrest her at the level of biological experience. Therefore, nearly all that can be described as distinctly human rather than animal activity (in their own way animals also give birth and care for their young) is largely reserved for the male. Of course, status again follows from such an assignment. Were one to analyze the three categories one might designate status as the political component, role as the sociological, and temperament as the psychological — yet their interdependence is unquestionable and they form a chain. Those awarded higher status tend to adopt roles of mastery, largely because they are first encouraged to develop temperaments of dominance. That this is true of caste and class as well is self-evident.

.   .   .

IV Class

It is in the area of class that the castelike status of the female within patriarchy is most liable to confusion, for sexual status often operates in a superficially confusing way within the variable of class. In a society where status is dependent upon the economic, social, and educational circumstances of class, it is possible for certain females to appear to stand higher than some males. Yet not when one looks more closely at the subject. This is perhaps easier to see by means of analogy: a black doctor or lawyer has higher social status than a poor white sharecropper. But race, itself a caste system which subsumes class, persuades the latter citizen that he belongs to a higher order of life, just as it oppresses the black professional in spirit, whatever his material success may be. In much the same manner, a truck driver or butcher has always his "manhood" to fall back upon. Should this final vanity be offended, he may contemplate more violent methods. The literature of the past thirty years provides a staggering number of incidents in which the caste of virility triumphs over the social status of wealthy or even educated women. In literary contexts one has to deal here with wish-fulfillment. Incidents from life (bullying, obscene, or hostile remarks) are probably another sort of psychological gesture of ascendancy. Both convey more hope than reality, for class divisions are generally quite impervious to the hostility of individuals. And yet while the existence of class division is not seriously threatened by such expressions of enmity, the existence of sexual hierarchy has been re-affirmed and mobilized to "punish" the female quite effectively.

The function of class or ethnic mores in patriarchy is largely a matter of how overtly displayed or how loudly enunciated the general ethic of masculine supremacy allows itself to become. Here one is confronted by what appears to be a paradox: while in the lower social strata, the male is more likely to claim authority on the strength of his sex rank alone, he is actually obliged more often to share power with the women of his class who are economically productive; whereas in the middle and upper classes, there is less tendency to assert a blunt patriarchal dominance, as men who enjoy such status have more power in any case. . . .

One of the chief effects of class within patriarchy is to set one woman against another, in the past creating a lively antagonism between whore and matron, and in the present between career woman and housewife. One envies the other her "security" and prestige, while the envied yearns beyond the confines of respectability for what she takes to be the other's freedom, adventure, and contact with the great world. Through the multiple advantages of the double standard, the male participates in both worlds, empowered by his superior social and economic resources to play the estranged women against each other as rivals. One might also recognize subsidiary status categories among women: not only is virtue class, but beauty and age as well.

Perhaps, in the final analysis, it is possible to argue that women tend to transcend the usual class stratifications in patriarchy, for whatever the class of her birth and education, the female has fewer permanent class associations than does the male. Economic dependency renders her affiliations with any class a tangential, vicarious, and temporary matter. Aristotle observed that the only slave to whom a commoner might lay claim was his woman, and the service of an unpaid domestic still provides working-class males with a "cushion" against the buffets of the class system which incidentally provides them with some of the psychic luxuries of the leisure class. Thrown upon their own resources, few women rise above working class in personal prestige and economic power, and women as a group do not enjoy many of the interests and benefits any class may offer its male members. Women have therefore less of an investment in the class system. But it is important to understand that as with any group whose existence is parasitic to its rulers, women are a dependency class who live on surplus. And their marginal life frequently renders them conservative, for like all persons in their situation (slaves are a classic example here) they identify their own survival with the prosperity of those who feed them. The hope of seeking liberating radical solutions of their own seems too remote for the majority to dare contemplate and remains so until consciousness on the subject is raised.

As race is emerging as one of the final variables in sexual politics, it is pertinent, especially in a discussion of modern literature, to devote a few words to it as well. Traditionally, the white male has been accustomed to concede the female of his own race, in her capacity as "his woman" a higher status than that ascribed to the black male. Yet as white racist ideology is exposed and begins to erode, racism's older protective attitudes toward (white) women also begin to give way. And the priorities of maintaining male supremacy might outweigh even those of white supremacy; sexism may be more endemic in our own society than racism. For example, one notes in authors whom we would now term overtly racist, such as D. H. Lawrence — whose contempt for what he so often designates as inferior breeds is unabashed — instances where the lower-caste male is brought on to master or humiliate the white man's own insubordinate mate. Needless to say, the female of the non-white races does not figure in such tales save as an exemplum of "true" womanhood's servility, worthy of imitation by other less carefully instructed females. Contemporary white sociology often operates under a similar patriarchal bias when its rhetoric inclines toward the assertion that the "matriarchal" (e.g. matrifocal) aspect of black society and the "castration" of the black male are the most deplorable symptoms of black oppression in white racist society, with the implication that racial inequity is capable of solution by a restoration of masculine authority. Whatever the facts of the matter may be, it can also be suggested that analysis of this kind presupposes patriarchal values without questioning them, and tends to obscure both the true character of and the responsibility for racist injustice toward black humanity of both sexes.

.   .   .

VI Force

We are not accustomed to associate patriarchy with force. So perfect is its system of socialization, so complete the general assent to its values, so long and so universally has it prevailed in human society, that it scarcely seems to require violent implementation. Customarily, we view its brutalities in the past as exotic or "primitive" custom. Those of the present are regarded as the product of individual deviance, confined to pathological or exceptional behavior, and without general import. And yet, just as under other total ideologies (racism and colonialism are somewhat analogous in this re-

spect) control in patriarchal society would be imperfect, even inoperable, unless it had the rule of force to rely upon, both in emergencies and as an ever-present instrument of intimidation.

Historically, most patriarchies have institutionalized force through their legal systems. For example, strict patriarchies such as that of Islam, have implemented the prohibition against illegitimacy or sexual autonomy with a death sentence. In Afghanistan and Saudi Arabia the adulteress is still stoned to death with a mullah presiding at the execution. Execution by stoning was once common practice through the Near East. It is still condoned in Sicily. Needless to say there was and is no penalty imposed upon the male corespondent. Save in recent times or exceptional cases, adultery was not generally recognized in males except as an offense one male might commit against another's property interest. In Tokugawa, Japan, for example, an elaborate set of legal distinctions were made according to class. A samurai was entitled, and in the face of public knowledge, even obliged, to execute an adulterous wife, whereas a chōnin (common citizen) or peasant might respond as he pleased. In cases of cross-class adultery, the lower-class male convicted of sexual intimacy with his employer's wife would, because he had violated taboos of class and property, be beheaded together with her. Upper-strata males had, of course, the same license to seduce lower-class women as we are familiar with in Western societies.

Indirectly, one form of "death penalty" still obtains even in America today. Patriarchal legal systems in depriving women of control over their own bodies drive them to illegal abortions; it is estimated that between two and five thousand women die each year from this cause.[7]

Excepting a social license to physical abuse among certain class and ethnic groups, force is diffuse and generalized in most contemporary patriarchies. Significantly, force itself is restricted to the male who alone is psychologically and technically equipped to perpetuate physical violence.[8] Where differences in physical strength have become immaterial through the use of arms, the female is rendered innocuous by her socialization. Before assault she is almost universally defenseless both by her physical and emotional training. Needless to say, this has the most far-reaching effects on the social and psychological behavior of both sexes.

Patriarchal force also relies on a form of violence particularly sexual in character and realized most completely in the act of rape. The figures of rapes reported represent only a fraction of those which occur,[9] as the "shame" of the event is sufficient to deter women from the notion of civil prosecution under the public circumstances of a trial. Traditionally rape has been viewed as an offense one male commits upon another — a matter of abusing "his woman." Vendetta, such as occurs in the American South, is carried out for masculine satisfaction, the exhilarations of race hatred, and the interests of property and vanity (honor). In rape, the emotions of aggression, hatred, contempt, and the desire to break or violate personality, take a form consummately appropriate to sexual politics. In the passages analyzed at the outset of this study, such emotions were present at a barely sublimated level and were a key factor in explaining the attitude behind the author's use of language and tone.[10]

Patriarchal societies typically link feelings of cruelty with sexuality, the latter often equated both with evil and with power. This is apparent both in the sexual fantasy reported by psychoanalysis and that reported by pornography. The rule here associates sadism with the male ("the masculine role") and victimization with the female ("the feminine role").[11] Emotional response to violence against women in patriarchy is often curiously ambivalent; references to wife-beating, for example, invariably produce laughter and some embarrassment. Exemplary atrocity, such as the mass murders committed by Richard Speck, greeted at one level with a certain scandalized, possibly hypocritical indignation, is capable of eliciting a mass response of titillation at another level. At such times one even hears from men occasional expressions of envy or amusement. In view of the sadistic character of such public fantasy as caters to male audiences in pornography or semi-pornographic media, one might expect that a certain element of identification is by no means absent from the general response. Probably a similar collective *frisson* sweeps through racist society when its more "logical" members have perpetrated a lynching. Unconsciously, both crimes may serve the larger group as a ritual act, cathartic in effect.

Hostility is expressed in a number of ways. One is laughter. Misogynist literature, the primary vehicle of masculine hostility, is both an hortatory and comic genre. Of all artistic forms in patriarchy it is the most frankly propagandistic. Its aim is to reinforce both sexual factions in their status. Ancient, Medieval, and Renaissance literature in the West has each had a large element of misogyny.[12] Nor is the East without a strong tradition here, notably in the Confucian strain which held sway in Japan as well as China. The Western tradition was indeed moderated somewhat by the introduction of courtly love. But the old diatribes and attacks were coterminous with the new idealization of woman. In the case of Petrarch, Boccaccio, and some others, one can find both attitudes fully expressed, presumably as evidence of different moods, a courtly pose adopted for the ephemeral needs of the vernacular, a grave animosity for sober and eternal Latin.[13] As courtly love was transformed to romantic love, literary misogyny grew somewhat out of fashion. In some places in the eighteenth century it declined into ridicule and exhortative satire. In the nineteenth century its more acrimonious forms almost disappeared in English. Its resurrection in twentieth-century attitudes and literature is the result of a resentment over patriarchal reform, aided by the growing permissiveness in expression which has taken place at an increasing rate in the last fifty years.

Since the abatement of censorship, masculine hostility (psychological or physical) in specifically *sexual* contexts has become far more apparent. Yet as masculine hostility has been fairly continuous, one deals here probably less with a matter of increase than with a new frankness in expressing hostility in specifically sexual contexts. It is a matter of release and freedom to express what was once forbidden expression outside of pornography or other "underground" productions, such as those of De Sade. As one recalls both the euphemism and the idealism of descriptions of coitus in the Romantic poets (Keats's *Eve of St. Agnes*), or the Victorian novelists (Hardy, for example) and contrasts it with Miller or William Burroughs, one has an idea of how contemporary literature has absorbed not only the truthful explicitness of pornography, but its anti-social character as well. Since this tendency to hurt or insult has been given free expression, it has become far easier to assess sexual antagonism in the male.

The history of patriarchy presents a variety of cruelties and barbarities: the suttee execution in India, the crippling deformity of footbinding in China, the lifelong ignominy of the veil in Islam, or the widespread persecution of sequestration, the gynacium, and purdah. Phenomena such as clitoroidec-tomy, clitoral incision, the sale and enslavement of women under one guise or another, involuntary and child marriages, concubinage and prostitution, still take place — the first in Africa, the latter in the Near and Far East, the last generally. The rationale which accompanies that imposition of male authority euphemistically referred to as "the battle of the sexes" bears a certain resemblance to the formulas of nations at war, where any heinousness is justified on the grounds that the enemy is either an inferior species or really not human at all. The patriarchal mentality has concocted a whole series of rationales about women which accomplish this purpose tolerably well. And these traditional beliefs still invade our consciousness and affect our thinking to an extent few of us would be willing to admit.

Notes

1. The American Heritage Dictionary's fourth definition is fairly approximate: "methods or tactics involved in managing a state or government." *American Heritage Dictionary* (New York: American Heritage and Houghton Mifflin, 1969). One might expand this to a set of stratagems designed to maintain a system. If one understands patriarchy to be an institution perpetuated by such techniques of control, one has a working definition of how politics is conceived in this essay.

2. I am indebted here to Ronald V. Samson's *The Psychology of Power* (New York: Random House, 1968) for his intelligent investigation of the connection between formal power structures and the family and for his analysis of how power corrupts basic human relationships.

3. "Domination in the quite general sense of power, i.e. the possibility of imposing one's will upon the behavior of other persons, can emerge in the most diverse forms." In this central passage of *Wirtschaft und Gesellschaft* Weber is particularly interested in two

such forms: control through social authority ("patriarchal, magisterial, or princely") and control through economic force. In patriarchy as in other forms of domination "that control over economic goods, i.e. economic power, is a frequent, often purposively willed, consequence of domination as well as one of its most important instruments." Quoted from Max Rheinstein's and Edward Shil's translation of portions of *Wirtschaft und Gesellschaft* entitled *Max Weber on Law in Economy and Society* (New York: Simon and Schuster, 1967), pp. 323–24.

4. No matriarchal societies are known to exist at present. Matrilineality, which may be, as some anthropologists have held, a residue or a transitional stage of matriarchy, does not constitute an exception to patriarchal rule, it simply channels the power held by males through female descent — e.g., the Avunculate.

5. Radical democracy would, of course, preclude patriarchy. One might find evidence of a general satisfaction with a less than perfect democracy in the fact that women have so rarely held power within modern "democracies."

6. Hannah Arendt, "Speculations on Violence," *The New York Review of Books,* Vol. XII No. 4, February 27, 1969, p. 24.

7. Since abortion is extralegal, figures are difficult to obtain. This figure is based on the estimates of abortionists and referral services. Suicides in pregnancy are not officially reported either.

8. Vivid exceptions come to mind in the wars of liberation conducted by Vietnam, China, etc. But through most of history, women have been unarmed and forbidden to exhibit any defense of their own.

9. They are still high. The number of rapes reported in the city of New York in 1967 was 2432. Figure supplied by Police Department.

10. It is interesting that male victims of rape at the hands of other males often feel twice imposed upon, as they have not only been subjected to forcible and painful intercourse, but further abused in being reduced to the status of a female. Much of this is evident in Genet and in the contempt homosexual society reserves for its "passive" or "female" partners.

11. Masculine masochism is regarded as exceptional and often explained as latently homosexual, or a matter of the subject playing "the female role" — e.g., victim.

12. The literature of misogyny is so vast that no summary of sensible proportions could do it justice. The best reference on the subject is Katherine M. Rogers, *The Troublesome Helpmate, A History of Misogyny in Literature* (Seattle, University of Washington Press, 1966).

13. As well as the exquisite sonnets of love, Petrarch composed satires on women as the "De Remediis utriusque Fortunae" and *Epistolae Seniles.* Boccaccio too could balance the chivalry of romances (Filostrato, Ameto, and Fiammetta) with the vituperance of Corbaccio, a splenetic attack on women more than medieval in violence.

A RESPONSE TO INEQUALITY:
BLACK WOMEN, RACISM, AND SEXISM

DIANE K. LEWIS

Diane Lewis is professor of anthropology at the University of California at Santa Cruz. She was born in Los Angeles, did her undergraduate work at UCLA, and received her doctorate at Cornell University. She has done field work in Malaysia and in an American black community. Her writings include "Anthropology and Colonialism" (*Current Anthropology,*

1973); "The Black Family: Socialization and Sex Roles" (*Phylon,* 1975); and "Rules for Agrarian Change: Negri Sembilan Malys and Agricultural Innovation" (*Journal of Southeast Asian Studies,* 1976). Her current work focuses on issues of race, sex, and class inequality. She is at present conducting research on the educational and vocational needs of women in a local jail.

Since its earliest days, women's liberation has been strongly committed to sisterhood, to embracing all women across ethnic, racial, and class lines and across choices of sexual preference. The goal has yet to be met, however. Conflicts and misunderstanding between groups have been difficult to resolve, but it is safe to say that progress is being made. With regard to race, many white feminists are developing sensitivity to their own ethnocentricity, and black women are growing in their feminist consciousness. In the following selection, Lewis describes some of the factors responsible for the growing participation and assertiveness of black women in the feminist movement.

Introduction

The women's liberation movement has generated a number of theories about female inequality. Because the models usually focus exclusively upon the effects of sexism, they have been of limited applicability to minority women subjected to the constraints of both racism and sexism.[1] In addition, black women have tended both to see racism as a more powerful cause of their subordinate position than sexism and to view the women's liberation movement with considerable mistrust.[2]

Yet there are recent indications that a growing number of black women have become more responsive to the issue of women's rights.[3] During the past few years black women's organizations have emerged whose specific aim is to combat both sexism and racism. In January 1973 fifteen women formed the San Francisco–based Black Women Organized for Action (BWOA). It now has between 300 and 400 members.[4]

From *Signs: Journal of Women in Culture and Society,* 3, No. 2 (Winter 1977). © 1977 by The University of Chicago. Reprinted by permission of The University of Chicago Press and Diane K. Lewis.

I am indebted to Oscar Berland and Naomi Katz for comments on an earlier draft of this paper. [D. K. Lewis' note]

In December 1973 the first conference of the National Black Feminist Organization (NBFO) met on the east coast in New York. It attracted 400 women. Though its leadership acknowledged difficulties in organizing black women around feminist issues,[5] the group stressed that many goals central to the women's liberation movement — day care, abortions, maternity leaves — were of critical importance to black women. Indeed, some were of greater intrinsic concern to them than to white women because of their more severe economic disadvantage.

This paper attempts to explain the initial rejection and then more favorable reaction to the women's movement on the part of black women. To do so, it develops a model of inequality which may illuminate the situation of women in complex societies who experience discrimination because of race and sex. A trend toward a greater acceptance of feminism may be due to changes in black women's perception of oppression, which in turn reflects changes in the social order. In the 1960s the black liberation movement began to generate important structural shifts in the relationship between blacks and whites in America. Blacks began to participate more fully in public activities previously reserved for whites. In such domains they encountered patterns of sexual discrimination. As the bulk of the higher-status, authoritative positions meted to blacks went to black men, a number of black women, particularly in the middle class, became more sensitive to the obstacle of sexism and to the relevance of the women's movement.[6]

Structural Inequality and Black Americans

Michelle Rosaldo has offered a model of female inequality. It proposes that (a) women are universally subordinate to men, (b) men are dominant due to their participation in public life and their relegation of women to the domestic sphere, and (c) the differential participation of men and women in public life gives rise not only to universal male authority over women but to a higher valuation of male over female roles.[7] The point that female inequality is inseparable from differential male/female activity in the public sphere is well taken. Nevertheless, a careful look at the relationship between black men and women and between blacks and whites in this society casts doubt on the full validity of Rosaldo's model.

Historically, black men, like black women, have been excluded from participation in the dominant society's politico-jural sphere and denied access to authority. Moreover, special measures have been needed to reaffirm black male inferiority. Since slavery coexisted with male dominance in the wider society, black men, as men, constituted a potential threat to the established order of white superiority. Laws were formulated that specifically denied black men normal adult prerogatives.[8] Such covertly sanctioned acts as lynchings and the rape and sexual exploitation of black women further intensified black male powerlessness.

Stringent institutionalized barriers to male participation continued for almost 100 years after slavery. These included the refusal of membership in national trade unions, which effectively barred black men from the job market;[9] prejudicial welfare laws, which undermined the man's status as husband and father;[10] and vigorous tactics to block black participation in the political process.[11] The systematic exclusion of black men from the public sphere suggests that black sex-role relationships cannot be adequately explained by the notion of a structural opposition between the domestic and public spheres or the differential participation of men and women in the public sphere.[12]

Rosaldo also suggests that egalitarian sex relationships can only develop in a society at a time when both sexes share equal participation in the public and domestic spheres.[13] There is growing evidence of strong egalitarianism in black sex-role relationships.[14] However, black men and women shared equal exclusion from, rather than equal participation in, the public sphere. What the black experience suggests is that differential participation in the public sphere is a symptom rather than a cause of structural inequality. While inequality is *manifested* in the exclusion of a group from public life, it is actually *generated* in the group's unequal access to power and resources in a hierarchically arranged social order. Relationships of dominance and subordination, therefore, emerge from a basic structural opposition between groups which is reflected in exclusion of the subordinate group from public life. This process may be further accentuated by increasing differentiation between the public and domestic spheres.[15] Members of a subordinate group, moreover, constitute a potential common-interest group whose interests derive from their shared powerlessness.[16] Their interests remain latent, however, until the power relations between themselves and a dominant group begin to shift and the structural opposition between them erupts into conflict.

Black women, due to their membership in two subordinate groups that lack access to authority and resources in society, are in structural opposition with a dominant racial and a dominant sexual group. In each subordinate group they share potential common interests with group comembers, black men on the one hand and white women on the other. Ironically, each of these is a member of the dominant group: black men as men, white women as whites. Thus, the interests which bind black women together with and pull them into opposition against comembers crosscut one another in a manner which often obscures one set of interests over another. Historically, their interests as blacks have taken precedence over their interests as women. A shift in the power relations between the races had to come before changes in the structural relationship between the sexes.

It has been noted that the latent interests shared by members of a subordinate group become manifest when they have been formulated into a conscious ideology.[17] Ideology, I suggest, articulates increasing discontent, which emerges as a group's members perceive that their legitimate expectations are being frustrated. Frustration arises as they experience a sense of relative deprivation vis-à-vis other groups, a process occurring when (1) members of a subordinate group perceive the possibility of their own improved, more equitable position in the social system by comparing themselves with another group of structurally equivalent status whose members are improving their positions, and (2) members of a dominant group continue to frustrate their legitimate expectations for improved position while granting privileges and resources to members of the other subordinate group. The set of potential interests most clearly perceived

as illegitimately blocked will become manifest first through the process of structural conflict. The black women's reactions to the black liberation and feminist movements described below reflect, I feel, their changing interests as they have become manifest through shifts in power relations between the races and between the sexes. Their response suggests that, as a subordinate group's interests change, the lines of conflict and structural opposition between groups tend to shift correspondingly.

The Structural Position of Black Women and White Women in America

Both white and black women in America have been excluded from the politico-jural domain and from positions of authority and prestige which have been reserved mainly for white men. Their joint exclusion as women would place them structurally in the same subordinate group, sharing potential common interests. Yet, due to racism, black women have occupied a structural position subordinate to white women in society.[18] They have had less access to deference, power, and authority. Sanday, noting the difference between deference and power as a basis of women's position, finds that Western women may receive deference in their "often highly valued roles as helpmate, sex object, the 'driving force behind every successful man,' etc." She contrasts this with women who, playing important economic roles in other societies, may have power over critical resources but who lack deference and may be resented and feared by their husbands.[19] Black women, on account of male exclusion from the job market, have been forced to share with black men marginal participation in the public work world of the dominant society through menial and ill-paying jobs. Their economic contributions have often been essential to their families. Their important economic role has assured them power over the limited resources available to a racially excluded group. On the basis of power over crucial resources, black women have held a relatively high position within a dominated society.[20] This contrasts with the deference accorded white women in the dominant society. For, unlike white women, black women have lacked deference in the dominant society principally because of the stigma of race. Within the dominated society, their source of power has become one basis of denial of deference. Black writers have noted that black men, unable to get and keep jobs, display resentment toward black women who assume the role of "provider."[21] Concomitantly, the roles played by white women which are highly valued, that is, "the driving force behind every successful man," the valued sex object, are frequently denied black women: the first because of the exclusion of black men from the public world, and the second because of the impossibility of attaining a white standard of beauty.

White women have not only been given deference. They have also had some access to power and authority.[22] While they themselves lacked authority in the dominant society, they have had a route to power through their kinship and marital ties with men (e.g., fathers, husbands, and sons) who do exercise authority in the public sphere. Moreover, white women, as members of the dominant group, formerly held both considerable authority and power vis-à-vis the subordinate racial group.

The variance in deference and access to power and authority between black and white women have proven to be critical factors underlying the black woman's perception of common group interests with black men and distrust of white women. During

the long period of male exclusion from the public sphere, black women shared the experience of racial oppression with black men. From their perspective as members of a subordinate and powerless racial group, white women wielded greater power and garnered more respect than black men and far more than black women. In fact, attributes of the white woman's status currently criticized by many feminists as examples of sexism were seen (and are still seen) by many black women as representative of the unique privileges of women of the dominant group. For example, women who were forced to take menial jobs (often, in the past, and still to some extent in the present, as domestics in white women's homes) and who were unable to care for their own children or to rely on men for economic support contrasted themselves with white women who were not required to work outside their own homes and who were well provided for by their husbands.

A Response to Inequality

During the protest political movements of the sixties, radical white women became discontented at the subordinate position assigned them by white male activists. They formulated an ideology of female liberation to express their common interests as members of a powerless group in conflict with men, whom they perceived as blocking their legitimate aspirations to authority and resources in society.[23] Significantly, their sense of deprivation grew as they saw black people demanding and acquiring an improved and more equitable position in the wider society. The women's liberation movement emerged, in part, to acquire for women the same access to authority and resources that the civil rights movement was fighting to obtain for blacks.[24]

The reaction of white women to traditional female subordination did not go unnoticed by black women. They, however, initially began to crystallize their interests as women at the same time that they continued to perceive obstacles to their most legitimate interests primarily in racial terms. In the remarkable anthology edited by Toni Cade, black women warn that the patterning of sex roles in white society offers a dangerous and stultifying model for blacks.[25] They note the detrimental effect of the dominant society on black man-woman relations.[26] They clearly establish that their aim is not so much to demand rights as women as to clarify issues or to "demand rights as Blacks first, women second." [27] In fact, the shared interests of black women seem to have little in common with white women. Cade asks: "How relevant are the truths, the experiences, the findings of White women to Black women? I don't know that our priorities are the same, that our concerns and methods are the same." [28]

Three years after publication of the Cade anthology, however, black women began clearly to formulate their interests as women concomitantly with their interests as members of an oppressed racial group. At the NBFO conference in 1973 a participant stated: "While we share with our men a history of toil and dignity, it is categorically different to be Black and a woman in this society than it has been to be Black and male." [29] The emergence of a feminist movement among black women, signaled by formation of the NBFO, the BWOA, and other organizations concerned with the special problems of being female and black,[30] indicates that some contemporary black women have begun to perceive the way both sex inequality and race inequality affect their lives.

In order to understand the structural factors which account for the black women's growing responsiveness to feminism it is necessary to analyze the effect of the race struggle on the position of black women. The worldwide black struggle against oppression heightened the discontent of American blacks at their subordinate position. As African countries gained independence from European colonizers, Afro-Americans experienced a growing sense of relative deprivation and perceived the possibility of changing power relationships between whites and blacks in the United States. While for many years the conflict between black and white was waged at the covert level and expressed in an ideology of gradual "race" advancement, black Americans became increasingly impatient at obstacles to their legitimately perceived expectations. Their interests became manifest, their ideology "militant." Civil rights activity in the 1950s spawned the "Black Power" movement, aimed at direct black participation in the political process, and the "Black Is Beautiful" movement, focused on a legitimation of black standards of beauty and physical worth. While black women easily perceived their own interests expressed in these political and cultural ideologies, and while they played a critical role in civil rights activities,[31] these movements, significantly, were seen as primarily male inspired and male led. According to some, the black woman's alleged place was "a step behind" the man's, and her proper role was the bearing and rearing of warriors for the struggle. Many women activists interpreted this attitude as an understandable reaction by black men, who had been duped by proposed white models of black matriarchy and male castration. They counseled patience and conciliation at what they perceived as deliberate divisive tactics by the dominant society.[32] Consequently, Pauli Murray noted, in spite of the black women's broad participation in the civil rights movement "... the aspirations of the black community have been articulated almost exclusively by black males. There has been very little public discussion of the problems, objectives or concerns of black women." [33] The black liberation movement resulted in the passage of such federal laws as the Civil Rights Act of 1964 and the Voting Rights Act of 1965. They were to provide institutional support for the termination of black exclusion from the public sphere. The laws, which had a dominoes effect, began to knock down barriers in many American institutions. Education, direct political participation, and jobs began to become more accessible to "upwardly mobile" blacks. However, as blacks began to participate in the wider society they moved into a public arena sharply characterized by sex inequality. This situation, together with male domination of the black movement, signaled a significant differentiation in the participation of black men and women in the public sphere. Observing this situation, another black woman, corroborating Murray, notes: "It is clear that when translated into actual opportunities for employment and promotional and educational benefits the civil rights movement really meant rights for black men...." [34]

This differentiation is apparent in a comparison of the relative educational levels of black men and women. Education for blacks appears to have shifted in favor of men during the past few years, preceding apace with greater black inclusion in institutions of higher learning. Formerly, sociological studies of black communities showed that black women had higher rates of literacy and more years of schooling than males.[35] They were expected to go into higher education more often than men and had different aspirations,[36] which were linked primarily to the job market for adult

blacks in the past. For example, in the South in the 1940s black men aspired to some independence through working their own farms or learning a skilled trade like bricklaying, plastering, or painting, skills transmitted from father to son. Black women, however, were offered higher education so they could become schoolteachers in the segregated school systems of the South and thereby get "out of the white folk's kitchen," the only other job possibility for black females.[37]

In the past, black women were also given greater educational opportunities than men by their families because "educational achievement for black men did not mean the opening up of economic opportunities." [38] Census data show that black women have more median years of schooling and more often graduate from high school than black men. The median years of formal education for black women and men twenty-five years of age and older between 1940 and 1970 are given in table 1.

In 1966, for blacks between twenty-five and thirty-four years of age women more often had a college degree than men; 5.2 percent of the men and 6.1 percent of the women had completed four or more years of college. However, by 1974 the situation had reversed, and 8.8 percent of the men and 7.6 percent of the women had achieved that level of education.[39] Recent figures also show a sharp rise in the numbers of black men currently enrolled in college. While in 1970 16 percent of black men and 15 percent of black women between eighteen and twenty-four years of age were enrolled in college, by 1974 the figures were 20 percent and 16 percent, respectively.[40] The data indicate a decided shift in favor of black men in higher education over the past few years.[41]

Even in the late 1960s, however, when black women were enrolled in college in

Table 1 Median years of schooling for ages 25 and over

Year	Black women	Black men
1940	6.1	5.3
1960	8.5	7.9
1970	10.0	9.3

Sources: Figures for 1940 are from U.S. Department of Commerce, Bureau of the Census, *Sixteenth Census of the United States: 1940. Population: Characteristics of the Nonwhite Population by Race* (Washington, D.C.: Government Printing Office, 1943), table 6, p. 34; for 1960 are for "nonwhite" and are from U.S. Bureau of the Census, *U.S. Census of Population: 1960. Educational Attainment of the Population of the United States: 1960.* Supplementary Reports PC (S1)-37. (Washington, D.C.: Government Printing Office, 1972), table 173, p. 6; for 1970 are from U.S. Bureau of the Census, *Census of Population: 1970. Subject Reports. Educational Attainment.* Final Report PC(2)-5B (Washington, D.C.: Government Printing Office, 1973), table 1, pp. 3, 6.

Table 2 Median earnings year-round full-time workers ($)

Group	1963	1970	1974
White males	6,245	9,447	12,434
Black males	4,019	6,435	8,705
White females	3,687	5,536	7,021
Black females	2,280	4,536	6,371

Sources: Figures for 1963 are from U.S. Bureau of the Census, *Income of Families and Persons in the United States, 1963,* Current Population Reports, Series P-60, No. 43 (Washington, D.C.: Government Printing Office, 1964), table 18, p. 34 (the table compares whites and nonwhites; the latter are predominantly black); for 1970 are from U.S. Bureau of the Census, *Money Income in 1973 of Families and Persons in the United States,* Current Population Reports, Series P-60, No. 97 (Washington, D.C.: Government Printing Office, 1975), table F, p. 12; for 1974 are from U.S. Bureau of the Census, *Money Income in 1974 of Families and Persons in the United States,* Current Population Reports, Series P-60, No. 101 (Washington, D.C.: Government Printing Office, 1975), pp. 106–7.

somewhat greater proportions than black men, black men were more likely to obtain graduate degrees beyond the M.A. than black women.[42] Jackson's 1968 study of black institutions found that 91 percent of the professional degrees granted in the combined fields of medicine, dentistry, law, veterinary medicine, and theology went to black men and only 9 percent to black women.[43] Two surveys of blacks with doctorates in all fields from all institutions in 1969 and 1970 suggest that black women hold roughly 21 percent of these advanced degrees.[44] Moreover, black men attend more prestigious institutions than black women, and this factor, along with their greater monopoly of advanced professional degrees, affects occupational patterns.[45]

For, according to figures of the U.S. Census Bureau, black women are the poorest paid in the occupational structure. Black men earn more than both black women and white women. The median earnings for year-round, full-time workers in 1963, 1970, and 1974 show an interesting trend over the eleven-year span (see table 2). Note that the wage differential between black women's and black men's salaries went from $1,739 in 1963 to $2,334 in 1974. Although the gap between the dollar earnings of black women and black men widened, there was some improvement in the ratio of female to male income, black women earning 57 percent of the income of black men in 1963 and 74 percent in 1974. In the past, the low pay of black women was related to their frequent employment as domestics. In 1963, as shown in table 3, one out of three black women was a private household worker, but by 1974 only 11 percent of black women were domestics. However, a comparison of jobs held by black women with those held by black men in 1974 shows that while black women have been moving out of domestic work 37 percent or over one-third were still in low-paying service and household jobs not covered by the federal minimum wage, as compared with only 15 percent of black

Table 3 Occupation of men and women, 1963, 1970, 1974 (annual averages, in percentages)

	1963				1970				1974			
	Women		Men		Women		Men		Women		Men	
	White	Negro and other races*	White	Negro and other races*	White	Negro and other races*	White	Negro and other races*	White	Negro and other races*	White	Negro and other races*
White-collar workers:	61	21	41	15	64	36	43	22	64	42	42	24
Professional and technical	14	8	13	5	15	11	15	8	15	12	15	9
Managers and administrators except farm	5	2	15	4	5	2	15	5	5	2	15	5
Sales workers	8	2	6	2	8	3	6	2	7	3	6	2
Clerical workers	34	10	7	5	36	21	7	7	36	25	6	7
Blue-collar workers:	17	15	46	57	16	19	46	60	15	20	46	57
Craft and kindred workers	1	0.5	20	11	1	1	21	14	2	1	21	16
Operatives, including transport	15	14	20	25	14	17	19	28	13	17	18	26
Non-farm laborers	0.3	0.7	6	21	...	1	6	18	1	1	7	15
Service workers	15	22	6	16	15	26	6	13	17	26	7	15
Private household workers	5	34	...	...	3	18	...	...	3	11	...	...
Farm workers	3	7	8	11	2	2	5	6	2	1	5	4

Sources: Figures for 1963 taken from U.S. Bureau of the Census, *The Social and Economic Status of the Black Population in the United States, 1973,* Current Population Reports. Special Studies Series P-23, No. 48 (Washington, D.C.: Government Printing Office, 1974), table 38, p. 54 and table 39, p. 55; for 1970 and 1974 taken from U.S. Bureau of the Census, *The Social and Economic Status of the Black Population in the United States, 1974,* Current Population Reports, Series P-23, No. 54 (Washington, D.C.: Government Printing Office, 1975), table 48, p. 73, and table 49, p. 74.

* Nearly 90 percent are Negro.

men. Moreover, while black women white-collar workers relative to black men have been highly represented in teaching, nursing, and social work—occupations which are extensions of their domestic roles and traditional careers for women—black men, as they have moved into the public sphere, have been more often found than women in the more prestigious and better-paid professions of medicine, law, science, and college teaching.[46]

Figures showing gradual black inclusion in the field of higher education clearly indicate that black women are either poorly represented or relegated to the lower-status and lower-paid jobs. For example, Carroll found that at the University of Pittsburgh in 1970 black and white women were disproportionately represented in nontenured academic positions and that black men, as well as white men, in relationship to their total numbers, monopolized the higher and tenured ranks (see table 4). Carroll notes that for the University of Pitts-

Table 4 Full-time professional staff at University of Pittsburgh, 1970

Rank	White men	White women	Minority men	Minority women
Full professor	420	25	21	0
Associate professor	355	42	17	1
Nontenured	792	268	83	31

Source: Figures compiled from Constance M. Carroll, "Three's a Crowd: The Dilemma of the Black Woman in Higher Education," in *Academic Women on the Move*, ed. Alice Rossi and Ann Calderwood (New York: Russell Sage Foundation, 1973), table 9.3, p. 175.

Note: "Minority" refers to predominantly black.

burgh, "Clearly, sex is more of a handicap than race ... and the disproportion between the sexes is far greater for blacks than for whites."[47] Five years later, the occupational profile of the University of California, one of the largest educational complexes in the United States, shows that continued recruitment of blacks and other minorities has resulted in a marked sex inequality in high-level positions. The figures for April 1975 show employment in administration and in tenured and nontenured ladder-faculty positions for black men and women in the nine-campus system (see table 5).[48]

Information on black law-faculty members, nationwide, shows a similar skewing in favor of black men. The 1976 directory of minority law professors reveals that there are 226 blacks and thirty-eight non-white women out of a total of 282 minority professors. A check of the directory turned [up] thirty-seven women who could be identified by name and judging by surname the majority of these were probably black (see table 6).

The situation in institutions of higher learning is paralleled in government jobs and in the business world generally. In 1974 black women were 19.8 percent of all women and 63.7 percent of all blacks working full time as GS-graded federal employees. While they were generally underrepresented among women in the higher-level jobs, among blacks they were both markedly overrepresented in the lower-ranking jobs and underrepresented in the higher-ranking jobs, as shown in table 7.

Similarly, the 1975 California State Personnel Board's report to the governor and legislature on state employees, which gave monthly salary by sex and race, showed that while the percentages of black men and women were approximately the same (i.e., 3.7 and 3.4 percent, respectively, of the total numbers employed) black men were more highly represented than black

Table 5 Total minorities at the University of California, October 1975

Rank	Black men	Black women	Other minority men	Other minority women	Total men	Total women
Deans and provosts	6	1	1	2	155	16
Full professors	24	3	126	...	2,947	124
Associate professors	21	3	82	10	1,398	135
Nontenured ladder faculty	47	15	91	23	1,146	290

Source: University of California Computer printout, PER 1023, "Summary of Ethnic and Sex Employment, Academic Group/Rank, All Campuses, as of October 31, 1975," pp. 1–3.

Table 6 Minority Law-faculty members

Rank	Total blacks	Minority women
Professor	37	4
Associate professor	39	6
Assistant professor	51	8
Administrator	24	6
Teacher/administrator	22	5
Part time	49	6
Teaching fellow	4	2
Total	226	37

Source: *1976 Directory of Minority Law Faculty Members,* Section on Minority Groups, Association of American Law Schools, pp. 9, 25–48.

Table 7 Full-time federal employment of black women

General schedule grade grouping	Total black	Black women N	Black women All blacks (%)	Black women All women (%)
GS-1–4	66,999	50,143	74.8	12.7
GS-5–8	67,316	45,147	67.1	19.5
GS-9–11	20,772	8,591	41.4	15.8
GS-12–15	11,429	2,206	19.3	12.2
GS-16–18	149	16	10.7	13.3
Total	166,665	106,103	63.7	19.8

Source: From U.S. Bureau of the Census, *The Social and Economic Status of the Black Population in the United States, 1974* (see table 3 above), table 53, p. 78.

women at the higher salary ranges (see table 8). A recent survey of minorities in the mass-media industry indicates that 82 percent were males.[49] In the business-management training field as well, men, regardless of race, have been given a decided preference over women.[50]

Direct black participation in the political process through election to office has increased over the past five years. While

Table 8 California state employees: Percentage distribution of monthly salary for black workers, March 1975

Monthly salary rate ($)	Black men	Black women
Under 500	3.6	12.5
500–699	2.6	7.9
700–899	5.2	5.3
900–1,099	5.7	2.8
1,100–1,299	2.9	1.1
1,300–1,599	2.4	0.9
1,600–2,099	2.4	0.7
Over 2,099	1.8	0.2

Source: "Minority Women: Triple Discrimination," *Affirmative Action in Progress* 2 (April 1976): 6.

blacks are still woefully underrepresented in government, they moved from 1,230 to 2,630 elected officials between 1969 and 1974. However, movement of blacks into politics, as into higher-paying jobs generally, replicates the wider societal pattern of unequal female inclusion in the politico-jural domain. In 1974, while 2,293 black men were elected officials only 337 black women held that position.[51] This is a significant shift toward disparity, given the tradition of egalitarianism between the sexes and the former importance of women in black public life.[52]

If, as an aftermath of the 1960s, a number of black men were recruited into higher-paying, more authoritative, and prestigious positions, black women generally moved into the lower-status and lower-paying jobs traditionally reserved for women in the dominant society. During this process they made significant strides relative to white women. Although the difference in earnings between black men and women has widened, the income gap between black women and white women has tended to narrow (see table 9). Black women earned 62 percent of the median income of white women in 1963; this increased to 90 percent in 1974.[53] Similarly, recent census data indicate that the overall occupational distribution of black women has improved relative to white women. Since 1963 black women have moved out of domestic work and into clerical positions in greater numbers. Thus, in 1963, 34 percent of black women were domestics, and only 10 percent were clerical workers; in 1974, 11 percent were domestics and 25 percent were clerical workers. Since the percentages for white women clerical workers have remained relatively stable between 1963 and 1974 (34 percent and 36 percent, respectively), black women appear to be moving toward parity with white women in that occupation (see table 3). Although the position of black women has improved in relationship to white women, the data show that for women as a whole sexism continues to constitute a major barrier in the wider society. In fact, the ratio of white female to white male earnings has *decreased* slightly between 1963 and 1974, women earning 59 percent of the male's median income in 1963 and only 56 percent in 1975 (computed from table 3). The existence of sex bias in the wider society explains the observation that the civil rights movement elicited active efforts to provide career opportunities for black men, while little attention was paid to the employment needs of black women.[54]

Class and Sexism

The black liberation movement began to generate important structural changes in the relationship between blacks and whites in American society. For black women, these changes serve to heighten their perception of sexism, since they experience

Table 9 Wage differential between black women, black men and white women ($)

	1963	1970	1974
Between black women and black men	1,739	1,899	2,334
Between black women and white women	1,407	1,000	650

deep-seated sex discrimination as they engage in increased participation in the public sphere. Middle-class black women, in particular, are becoming more sensitive to the obstacle of sexism as racial barriers begin to fall and as the bulk of the higher-status, authoritative positions reserved for blacks have gone to black men. Nevertheless, if the leadership of black organizations recently formed to combat both racism and sexism appears to be middle class, the membership in these black women's groups seems to crosscut class lines. Thus the BWOA notes that its members include welfare recipients, maids, and the unemployed as well as high-income earners. In recognition of this diversity, the organization has adopted a flexible membership policy.[55] Similarly, the NBFO conference attracted domestic workers, welfare mothers, and other poor black women as well as students, housewives, and professionals. As one participant put it, "We were able to do what white feminists have failed to do: transcend class lines and eradicate labels." [56]

A further examination of the structural position of black women suggests why not only upwardly mobile black women but also poor black women will become more responsive to feminist issues. They, along with middle-class black women, are seriously affected by sex discrimination on the job. For example, Dietrich and Greiser in a study of black blue-collar workers found sexism to be an important factor in black poverty.[57] Furthermore, demographic and occupational trends, which affect all black women, should also elicit among them a sense of common interest which crosscuts class lines. There has been a steadily declining sex ratio from 95.0 in 1940 to 90.8 in 1970.[58] This probably contributes to the fact that black women are more often single than white women, more often work, and are more often heads of household. Thus, in 1974 about one half of minority women worked compared with 44 percent of white women.[59] In 1973, while 77 percent of white women who were fourteen years old and over and ever married were married and living with their husbands, only 54 percent of black women in the same category were married and residing with their spouses.[60] In 1975, while only 11 percent of white families were female headed, 35 percent of black families were supported by women.[61] Black women with preschool-aged children were also more likely to work than white mothers; in 1973, 49 percent of black women as compared with 32 percent of white women with small children were in the labor force.[62]

Black women, then, are more often self-supporting than white women and far more likely to carry single-handedly responsibilities for dependent children. These factors, together with their continued greater concentration in lower-paying service-related jobs than either white women or black men, cause poor black women, particularly, to be vitally affected by matters of inadequate income and child-care facilities, both major issues in the women's movement. For poor women, as a black welfare mother notes, women's liberation is "a matter of survival," a perception increasingly held by such groups devoted to removing obstacles to the legitimate interests of poor black

women as the National Welfare Rights Organization.[63]

Since both poor and middle-class black women participate in and have been aware of some of the successes of the black liberation movement, their expectations of greater access to resources have been raised. As these expectations have been frustrated, a sense of common interest is beginning to emerge which may increasingly include all classes of black women. A study of race and class factors affecting women's attitudes toward the women's liberation movement in Cleveland found that white working-class women were far less likely than white middle-class women to be interested in women's rights, while black working-class women were somewhat *more* receptive than black middle-class women to efforts to change women's status[64] (see table 10).

The shared experience of racism has also tended to blur class lines among blacks. This, too, probably will contribute to a greater tendency for both poor and middle-class black women to agree regarding women's rights. For example, middle-class black families are in a more precarious position than middle-class white families because of racism. Especially in times of economic recession and high unemployment, they may find themselves in economic straits similar to lower-class blacks.[65]

Whether black women develop a sense of common interests that is manifested more in opposition to sexism or to racism will depend upon the structural relationship between the sexes and between the races. With growing black participation in the wider society some black women, experiencing frustration of their interests primarily as women, now probably share the viewpoint a member of NBFO expressed. "White women are our natural allies; we can't take on the system alone." [66] Middle-class black women will increasingly feel their interests as women illegitimately frustrated if a combination of factors continues: (1) the income gap between themselves and white women narrows even more, (2) the overall position of women remains low, and (3) the white male hierarchy persists in admitting minority males but excluding minority females from equitable participation in the wider society. Middle-class black women, even more than middle-class white women, occupy a structural position likely to generate a pervasive sense of relative deprivation and an ideology of discontent.

However, on the other hand, black women may see that racism still affects a considerable number of blacks, including black men. Jessie Bernard, analyzing occupations and earnings for black and white men and women for the period 1939–70, concluded: ". . . racism tends to be more serious for black men than black women . . . (and) sexism tends to be more serious for black women than racism." [67] While some middle-class black men have made significant advances, a careful inspection of the trends of the ratio of black to white earnings shows that black men, as a whole, are making much slower headway in closing the income gap between them and white men than are black women relative to white women. Black men earned 64 percent of the median income of white men in 1967; 67 percent of the income of white men in 1973. [68] This would appear to matter to black women. For example, if they marry, there will probably be more pressure on them to work in order to supplement the family income than on married white women. Indeed, now black married women are more likely to work outside the home than their white counterparts. [69]

Perpetuation of a situation in which all

Table 10 Percentage of black and white women manifesting a high or low degree of interest in women's rights

Degree of interest	Black women		White women	
	Middle class	Working class	Middle class	Working class
High	44	48	54	27
Low	56	52	46	73

Source: From Willa Mae Hemmons, "Toward an Understanding of Attitudes Held by Black Women on the Women's Liberation Movement" (Ph.D. diss., Case Western Reserve University, 1973), tables 7 and 8, p. 101.

black men, irrespective of their socioeconomic status, are subject to racism, might well propel increasing numbers of black women, irrespective of their class backgrounds into overt opposition to both sexism and racism. Their way of doing so, however, might involve organizations concerned with women's rights, but limited to blacks and strongly racially oriented. [70] The concern with racism would preclude too exclusive a concern with sexism.

Notes

1. For example, *Women, Culture and Society*, ed. Michelle Z. Rosaldo and Louise Lamphere (Stanford, Calif.: Stanford University Press, 1974), proposes several models of female subordination, but none considers fully the structural position and theoretical implications of women subject to both racism and sexism.
2. See Linda J. M. LaRue, "Black Liberation and Women's Lib," *Transaction* 8 (November–December 1970): 59–64; Nathan and Julia Hare, "Black Women 1970," ibid., pp. 68, 90; Jean Cooper, "Women's Liberation and the

Black Woman," *Journal of Home Economics* 63 (October 1971): 521–23; Toni Cade, ed., *The Black Woman* (New York: New American Library, Signet Books, 1970); Mae C. King, "The Politics of Sexual Stereotypes," *Black Scholar* 4 (March–April 1973): 12; Inez Smith Reid, *"Together" Black Women* (New York: Third Press, 1972).

3. A 1972 poll showed that black women were more sympathetic than white women to efforts to upgrade women's status in society (62 percent to 45 percent, respectively) and that black women were also more supportive than white women of the attempts by women's liberation groups to do so (67 percent and 35 percent, respectively) (see Louis Harris & Associates, *The 1972 Virginia Slims American Women's Opinion Poll: A Survey of the Attitudes of Women on Their Roles in Politics and the Economy*, pp. 2, 4). Interestingly, Lucy Komisar notes that black organizations such as the Urban League and the National Association for the Advancement of Colored People, which formerly had little interest in feminist issues, have, in recent years, worked jointly with the National Organization of Women to further both minority and women's rights (see Lucy Komisar, "Where Feminism Will Lead," *Civil Rights Digest* 6 [Spring 1974]: 9).

4. Patsy G. Fulcher, Aileen C. Hernandez, and Eleanor R. Spikes, "Sharing the Power and the Glory," *Contact* 4 (Fall, 1974): 52. Eleanor Spikes, a cofounder of the organization, gave the recent estimate of membership (personal communication, April 1976) (see also, *What It Is,* the BWOA Newsletter which can be obtained from P.O. Box 10572, San Francisco, California 94115). Other black women's groups recently organized to eliminate both racism and sexism are League of Black Women (in Chicago), Black Women Concerned (in Baltimore), National Black Women's Political Leadership Caucus (in Detroit), and Sisters Getting Ourselves Together (in Davis, Calif.). (List compiled by Hernandez Associates, 4444 Geary Boulevard, San Francisco, California 94118). The BWOA is dedicated to involving black women in the

political process, to helping them get jobs, and to supporting them in business, the arts, and all areas where they face discrimination and exclusion.

5. For example, when Eleanor Holmes Norton, Commissioner of Human Rights for New York City and a NBFO board member stated, "Five years ago you couldn't have gotten five women to come here," a welfare mother said, "Five years ago! . . . We tried to start a consciousness raising group four months ago and nobody was interested" (see "Feminism: 'The Black Nuance,'" *Newsweek* [December 17, 1973], p. 89).

6. Eudora Pettigrew concluded more bluntly: "The black man grapples to achieve social justice and parity with the white male — essentially to attain white male power, privilege and status — while black women are shoved to the back of the bus." Quoted in Geraldine Rickman, "A Natural Alliance: The New Role for Black Women," *Civil Rights Digest* 6 (Spring 1974): 62 (see also Pauli Murray, "The Liberation of Black Women," in *Women: A Feminist Perspective,* ed. Jo Freeman [Palo Alto, Calif.: Mayfield Publishing Co., 1975], p. 354).

7. Rosaldo, "Women, Culture and Society: A Theoretical Overview," in Rosaldo and Lamphere, pp. 17–42.

8. Even Moynihan notes that black exclusionary laws were aimed primarily at defining and keeping the black *man* in his place (see Daniel Moynihan, *The Negro Family: The Case for National Action* [Washington, D.C.: Department of Labor, 1965], p. 62; Lerone Bennett, Jr., *Before the Mayflower* [Baltimore: Pelican Books, 1968], pp. 70–71, 92–93).

9. Andrew Billingsley, *Black Families in White America* (Englewood Cliffs, N.J.: Prentice-Hall, Inc., 1968), pp. 85–90.

10. For a discussion of how modern public welfare functions to replace the male in low-income families, a process which affects a still-sizable number of blacks on welfare, see Helen Icken Safa, "The Female-based Household in Public Housing," *Human Organization* 24 (Summer 1965): 135–39 (see also Johnnie Tillmon, "Welfare Is a Woman's Issue," in

Marriage and the Family: A Critical Analysis and Proposals for Change, ed. Carolyn C. Perrucci and Dena B. Targ [New York: David McKay Co., 1974], p. 109).

11. In the past, this took the form of intimidation and poll tax laws in the South and gerrymandering and cooptation in the North. For an analysis of other establishment bars to effective black political participation, see Stokely Carmichael and Charles V. Hamilton, *Black Power: The Politics of Liberation in America* (New York: Random House, Vintage Books, 1967).

12. Among racially oppressed groups it is important to distinguish between the public life of the dominant and the dominated societies. Using this framework, we recognize a range of male participation from token admittance to the public life of the dominant society to its attempts to destroy the public life within a dominated society. Mexican-American men, for example, have played strong public roles in their own dominated society, and, in fact, as Mexican-Americans have become more assimilated to the dominant society, sex roles have become less hierarchical (see Leo Grebler, Joan W. Moore, and Ralph C. Guzman, *The Mexican American People: The Nation's Second Largest Minority* [New York: Free Press, 1970], pp. 361–72). On the other hand, Afro-American men historically faced attempts at exclusion, enforced by the dominant society, from participation in a public life even among their own people (see Bennett, pp. 70–71, 92–93, and also Robert Staples, "The Myth of the Impotent Black Male," *Black Scholar* 2 [June 1971]: 3).

13. Rosaldo, pp. 40–42.

14. Virginia Heyer Young, "Family and Childhood in a Southern Negro Community," *American Anthropologist* 72 (April 1970): 269–88; Peter Kunkel and Sara Sue Kennard, *Spout Spring: A Black Community* (New York: Holt, Rinehart & Winston, 1971); Diane K. Lewis, "The Black Family: Socialization and Sex Roles," *Phylon* 36 (September 1975): 221–37; Robert B. Hill, *The Strengths of Black Families* (New York: Emerson Hall, 1972), p. 18. It has been pointed out that the notion of women's universal inferiority may be a reflection of our own Western cultural bias (see Nancy Tanner, "Matrifocality in Indonesia and Africa and among Black Americans," in Rosaldo and Lamphere, pp. 129–56, and Ruby Rohrlich Leavitt, *Peaceable Primates and Gentle People: Anthropological Approaches to Women's Studies* [New York: Harper & Row, 1975]). After developing most of the ideas in this paper, I was interested to see further critiques of the thesis of worldwide female inequality by the contributors to *Women Cross-culturally: Change and Challenge,* ed. Ruby Rohrlich Leavitt (The Hague: Mouton & Co., 1975), particularly the articles "Women, Knowledge and Power," by Constance Sutton, Susan Makiesky, Daisy Dwyer, and Laura Klein (pp. 581–600), and "Class, Commodity, and the Status of Women," by Eleanor Leacock (pp. 601–16).

15. See Louise Lamphere, "Strategies, Cooperation and Conflict among Women in Domestic Groups," in Rosaldo and Lamphere, p. 100; and Leacock, pp. 610–11. Lamphere notes the relationship between sex egalitarianism and the merging of public and private spheres, and Leacock suggests that it is the imposition of hierarchical social forms that give rise to a division between public and domestic domains.

16. This model derives from ideas in Ralf Dahrendorf, "Toward a Theory of Social Conflict" in *Social Change: Sources, Patterns, Consequences,* ed. Amitai Etzioni and Eva Etzioni (New York: Basic Books, 1964), pp. 98–111, and in Denton E. Morrison, "Some Notes toward Theory on Relative Deprivation, Social Movements, and Social Change," *American Behavioral Scientist* 14 (May 1971): 675–90. "Power" here refers to "having great influence or control over others" (*The American Heritage Dictionary* [New York: Houghton Mifflin Co., 1969], p. 1027); "interests" refers to common values, objectives, and definitions of a situation.

17. See Dahrendorf, p. 107.

18. Class, a third mitigating factor, is purposely omitted from this section in order to highlight the contrasts between white and black

women which stem from racism. That white women represent on the whole a far more privileged group than black women is shown in census data which reveal that 64 percent of employed white women but only 42 percent of black and other minority women hold professional, clerical, or sales jobs, while 19 percent of white women and 37 percent of black and other minority women work in low-paying service-related and domestic occupations (see U.S. Bureau of the Census, *The Social and Economic Status of the Black Population in the United States, 1974,* Current Population Reports, Series P-23, No. 54 [Washington, D.C.: Government Printing Office, 1975], table 49, p. 74). Thus, while poor white women occupy a subordinate position, a greater percentage of black women are poor, and their inequality is compounded by race as well as class and sex.

19. Peggy R. Sanday, "Female Status in the Public Domain," in Rosaldo and Lamphere (n. 1 above), p. 191.

20. See Clyde W. Franklin, Jr., and Laurel R. Walum, "Toward a Paradigm of Substructural Relations: An Application to Sex and Race in the United States," *Phylon* 33 (Fall 1972): 249.

21. For example, William A. Blakey, a black man who is Director of Congressional Liaison for the U.S. Commission on Civil Rights, writes that the attitude of many black men toward black women is one of disrespect and a desire to dominate. He suggests that black men feel they must persecute black women in order to repudiate the myth of the " 'castrating' black matriarch" (see William A. Blakey, "Everybody Makes the Revolution: Some Thoughts on Racism and Sexism," *Civil Rights Digest* 6 [Spring 1974]: 19). Alice Walker also noted the prevailing antagonism of black men when she stated: "Black women are called matriarchs, called castraters of the men, and all kinds of things by black men. . . . [However black women] don't [*sic*] realize that they were all these ugly things that people said they were. They thought they were just providing for their families, that

they were just surviving" (see Alice Walker, quoted in "Women on Women," *American Scholar* 972 [Autumn 1972]: 601–2. See also Frances Beale, "Double Jeopardy: To Be Black and Female," in Cade (n. 2 above), p. 92; Toni Cade, "On the Issue of Roles," ibid., p. 106; W. H. Grier and Price M. Cobb, *Black Rage* (New York: Basic Books, 1968). The contrast between female power over resources and male attitudes toward women that vary from resentment to lack of deferential treatment, which is characteristic not only of black Americans but of a number of other societies as well (e.g., Nupe, Iroquois; see Sanday, p. 191), suggests the complex factors involved in assessing sex-role relationships. Thus, structural egalitarianism may or may not be paralleled by mutual respect and deference just as male dominance may coexist with female deference or with women's fear and resentment toward men.

22. Authority can be defined as the legitimate right to make decisions and command obedience. It contrasts with power where influence and control over others are not institutionalized but rest informally with individuals or their roles (see Rosaldo, p. 21, n. 2).

23. Jo Freeman, "The Origins of the Women's Liberation Movement," in *Changing Women in a Changing Society,* ed. Joan Huber (Chicago: University of Chicago Press, 1973), pp. 37–39.

24. Catharine Stimpson, " 'Thy Neighbor's Wife, Thy Neighbor's Servants': Women's Liberation and Black Civil Rights," in *Women in Sexist Society,* ed. Vivian Gornick and Barbara K. Moran (New York: New American Library, Signet Books, 1971), pp. 622–57.

25. E.g., Cade, "On the Issue of Roles," pp. 102–3.

26. Beale, pp. 90–92.

27. "Preface," in Cade, *The Black Woman,* p. 10.

28. Ibid., p. 9.

29. Eleanor H. Norton, quoted on p. 86 in Bernette Golden, "Black Women's Liberation," *Essence* 4 (February 1974): 35–36, 75–76, 86.

30. Patricia Bell Scott, "Black Female Liberation and Family Action Programs: Some Consid-

erations" (unpublished paper, n.d., p. 4), suggests that most black women's organizations are now concerned with the issue of black feminism, that is, the plight of the black women who are oppressed by both sexism and racism. Among groups she cites, in addition to the NBFO, are the National Welfare Rights Organization, the National Committee on Household Employment, Domestics United of North Carolina, and the Black Women's Community Development Foundation.

31. For a discussion of some of the significant contributions of black women to the black liberation movement, see Phyl Garland, "Builders of a New South," *Ebony* 21 (August 1966): 27–30, 34–37.

32. See Beale, p. 93; Cade, "On the Issues of Roles," pp. 107–8; Jean Carey Bond and Patricia Perry, "Is the Black Male Castrated," in Cade, *The Black Woman,* pp. 113–18; and Gwen Patton, "Black People and the Victorian Ethos," ibid., pp. 143–48. Francis Beale in a 1970 newspaper interview noted: "Often, as a way of escape . . . black men have turned their hostility toward their women. But this is what we have to understand about him . . . as black women we have to have a conciliatory attitude" (see Charlayne Hunter, "Many Blacks Wary of Women's Liberation Movement in U.S.," *New York Times* [November 17, 1970], p. 47).

33. Murray (n. 6 above), p. 354.

34. Constance M. Carroll, "Three's a Crowd: The Dilemma of the Black Woman in Higher Education," in *Academic Women on the Move,* ed. Alice Rossi and Ann Calderwood (New York: Russell Sage Foundation, 1973), p. 177.

35. Charles Johnson, *Shadow of the Plantation* (Chicago: University of Chicago Press, 1969), pp. 129–30.

36. Hylan Lewis, *Blackways of Kent* (New Haven, Conn.: College and University Press, 1964), pp. 105–6.

37. Ibid.

38. Gerda Lerner, ed., *Black Women in White America: A Documentary History* (New York: Random House, Pantheon Books, 1972), p. 220.

39. U.S. Bureau of the Census (n. 18 above), table 68, p. 97.

40. Ibid., table 65, p. 94.

41. See Cynthia Fuchs Epstein, "Positive Effects of the Multiple Negative: Explaining the Success of Black Professional Women," in Huber (n. 23 above), pp. 152–53. See also a study by Elias Blake, Linda Jackson Lambert, and Joseph L. Martin, "Degrees Granted and Enrollment Trends in Historically Black Colleges: An Eight Year Study" (Washington, D.C.: Institute for Services to Education, 1974), table 9a, p. 31, which shows that in black four-year colleges, as well, black male enrollment has gradually increased from 45.4 percent in 1966 to 47.8 percent in 1973.

42. Carroll, pp. 174–75.

43. Jacqueline J. Jackson, "Black Women and Higher Education" (unpublished paper, 1973), cited ibid., table 9.1, p. 174. Jackson's figures show that 62 percent of these professional degrees were in the fields of medicine and law and that 85.6 percent of the M.D.'s and 90.4 percent of the LL.B.'s were granted to black men.

44. See Kent G. Mommsen, "Career Patterns of Black American Doctorates" (Ph.D. diss., Florida State University, 1970), table 1, p. 41.

45. Jacqueline J. Jackson, "But Where Are the Men?" *Black Scholar* 3 (December 1971): 30–41.

46. See Epstein, pp. 153–54, and Jackson, "But Where Are the Men?" p. 32.

47. Carroll, pp. 174–75 (see also William Moore, Jr., and Lonnie H. Wagstaff, *Black Educators in White Colleges* [San Francisco: Jossey-Bass, Inc., 1974], pp. 154–77).

48. It should be stressed that blacks and other minorities (Asian/Asian-Americans, American Indians and Mexican/Spanish-Americans) are still greatly underrepresented in higher education. The point here is that their gradual inclusion into the system has been proceeding along sex discriminatory lines. This was especially evident in the employment figures for April 1974 (see the table below for figures for April 1974). Comparison with table 5 shows that there has been some improve-

ment for minority women over the ensuing eighteen months. A total of twelve additional black women were hired while seven "other minority" women were added.

	Black men	Black women	Other minority men	Other minority women
Deans and provosts	5	1	1	. . .
Tenured faculty	41	. . .	178	7
Nontenured ladder faculty	51	9	84	21

Source: University of California computer printout, PER 1096, "Summary of Ethnic and Sex Employment, as of April 30, 1974," pp. 1–3.

49. Abigail Jones Nash, Marilyn Jackson-Beeck, Leverne Tracy Regan, and Vernon A. Stone, "Minorities and Women in Broadcast News: Two National Surveys" (paper presented at the annual convention of the Association for Education in Journalism, San Diego, 1974), p. 7.
50. See Bird McCord, "Identifying and Developing Women for Management Positions," *Training and Development Journal* 25 (November 1971): 2.
51. U.S. Bureau of the Census, *The Social and Economic Status of the Black Population in the United States, 1973,* Current Population Reports, Special Studies Series P-23, No. 48, (Washington, D.C.: Government Printing Office, 1974), table 74, p. 103. In 1974 blacks held 0.5 of 1 percent of the elective offices (see Herrington J. Bryce and Alan E. Warrick, "Black Women in Elective Offices," *Black Scholar* 6 [October 1974]: 17–20).
52. Lerner (n. 38 above), pp. 319–22, shows that in the past black women, although not holders of elective office, were active in politics.
53. For a comparison of increases in the ratio of black to white median income from 1967 to 1973 for men and women, see U.S. Bureau of the Census, *Money Income in 1973 of Families and Persons in the United States,* Current Population Reports, Series P-60, No. 97 (Washington, D.C.: Government Printing Office, 1975), table E, p. 19.
54. See Pauli Murray, "Jim Crow and Jane Crow," in Lerner, p. 596.
55. Dues are computed on a sliding scale from $5.00 to $25.00 a year, but members pay when and what they can. Moreover, a woman can become a member *either* by paying dues *or* attending meetings *or* working on a committee (see Fulcher et al. [n. 4 above], pp. 52, 63).
56. Ashaki Habiba Taha, letter *MS* 3 (August 1974): 12 (see also Golden [n. 29 above], p. 36).
57. Kathryn Dietrich and Lee Greiser, "The Influence of Sex on Wage-Income of Black, Blue-Collar Workers in Selected Non-metropolitan and Metropolitan Areas of Texas" (paper presented at the annual meeting of the Southern Association of Agricultural Scientists, Memphis, Tennessee, February 1974).
58. Jackson, "But Where Are the Men?" table 3, p. 39. The sex ratio among whites has also declined steadily but in 1970 was, at 95.3, far more favorable for whites.
59. U.S. Bureau of the Census, *The Social and Economic Status of the Black Population in the United States, 1973,* p. 93.
60. Ibid., table 64, p. 90.
61. U.S. Bureau of the Census, *The Social and Economic Status of the Black Population in the United States, 1974,* table 72, p. 107.
62. U.S. Bureau of the Census, *The Social and Economic Status of the Black Population in the United States, 1973,* table 68, p. 95.
63. Tillmon (n. 10 above), pp. 108, 109, 111.
64. Willa Mae Hemmons, "Toward an Understanding of Attitudes Held by Black Women on the Women's Liberation Movement" (Ph.D. diss., Case Western Reserve University, 1973). Her sample for this exploratory study was a purposive one, including eighty-three women, forty-five black and thirty-seven white. She notes that she sought women from different classes and residential and occupational

areas; however the size of her sample makes her results more suggestive than conclusive (see her discussion of the sample, pp. 80–86).

65. Cf. Billingsley (n. 9 above), pp. 10–15.
66. Eleanor H. Norton, quoted in Golden, p. 86.
67. Jessie Bernard, "The Impact of Sexism and Racism on Employment Status and Earnings, with Addendum," Module 25 (New York: MSS Modular Publications, Inc., 1974), p. 5.
68. U.S. Bureau of the Census, *Money Income in 1973 of Families and Persons in the United States,* table F, p. 12. This was similar to the rate of growth of black female income to the black male's, i.e., black women earned 67 percent of the income of black men in 1967 and 70 percent of the income of black men in 1973.
69. U.S. Bureau of the Census, *The Social and Economic Status of the Black Population in the United States, 1973,* table 67, p. 95.
70. For an alternate thesis on the possible direction of change in the relationship between blacks and whites, males and females, see Franklin and Walum (n. 20 above), pp. 247–52. See also Rickman (n. 6 above), pp. 57–65, for an interesting discussion of the black professional woman's structural position which enables her to act as catalyst for change in the position of both women and blacks.

LEARNING FROM LESBIAN SEPARATISM

CHARLOTTE BUNCH

Charlotte Bunch, a feminist activist, theorist, organizer, and teacher since 1968, is an editor of *Quest: A Feminist Quarterly* and has edited five anthologies of feminist writings, the most recent of which is *Not by Degrees: Essays in Feminist Education.* She serves on the board of directors of the National Gay Task Force, was a delegate to the International Women's Year Conference, where she spoke on behalf of the sexual preference plank, and is now a director of the Public Resource Center in Washington, D.C. In her essay here, Bunch describes her own perception of the alienation between gay and straight feminists, of the special insights lesbian feminists have to offer the movement, and of the gains to be made for both groups by achieving greater integration and awareness.

It was December, when I first slept with a woman: I was married, it was snowing outside, and my days were filled with the unceasing events of Women's Liberation. Six months later, my four-year-old marriage was finished, my life with women was entire, and the sweltering summer heat of Washington, D.C., had replaced the snow. I sat on a mattress in a back room with 11 other women planning what to do now: we had just declared ourselves *lesbian-feminist separatists* and had dissociated ourselves from all Women's Movement activities. It was 1971. We realized, as similar groups did in other cities during that early fast-moving spread of lesbianism through the Women's Movement, that we had to figure out what had happened to us, and why. A few members of our group had been lesbians for years, some had previous experience in the gay liberation movement; but the majority of us — for a variety of reasons — had come out within the context of feminism. The movement had been our family — our mother and our child. When we began to proclaim our love for one another in ways that went beyond the boundaries of "familial love," most of us did not realize how savagely we would be disinherited by our "sisters."

We had to ask the difficult question: Why? Why was a movement devoted to women's freedom of choice so afraid of women who chose to love women — instead of men? We could tell ourselves that such organizations as the National Organization for Women were frightened of losing their acceptance in the male world, but that didn't seem enough of an answer. Furthermore, most of our own experience had not been in reformist structures like NOW, but in the radical feminist movement: that loose network of consciousness-raising, theoretical and activist groups talking about a deep and revolutionary change in every part of society, not just reforms that left basic patriarchy intact. Yet our experiences as lesbians in radical feminist groups had been no less painful than those of other lesbians in NOW.

Coletta Reid was a feminist who had also recently left her husband, found her identity as a lesbian, and then chosen a lesbian-separatist stance. In an article called "Coming Out in the Women's Movement" (*Lesbianism and the Women's Movement,* Diana Press, 1975), she later describes an incident that helps to explain why we became separatists:

> The full range of attitudes and prejudices came out in the course of a meeting of a day-care center I had helped found and worked in for nine months. One woman expressed misgivings about me or my friends being around her daughter since I had become a lesbian. She evidently thought I would molest her little precious; she had no similar qualms about my being around her son when I was heterosexual. Nor had she any qualms about the heterosexual men being around her daughter, which is strange since 100 percent of the child molestation cases reported in the District of Columbia last year were committed by men. Another woman said she thought lesbians were too hostile, angry, and man-hating to be around children who needed love and good vibes. . . . Some of the men at the daycare center were outrageously piggy toward the children, but they were never called on the carpet at a meeting or put in the position of having to defend themselves as I was.

The lesbians who had been gay prior to the existence of the feminist movement were less surprised by our rejection than those of us newly gay and full of enthusiasm for our recent self-discoveries. The "older" lesbians knew something that we had just begun to learn: lesbianism is not only a threat to men, but also to many heterosexual women. It suggests that women do not inevitably have to love men, or to love them at any cost.

Of course, challenging heterosexuality in any form is seen as threatening by some women. We are sometimes accused by "straight" feminists of guilt-tripping them about their personal lives; of implying that sexual dependence on men made them somehow less feminist. In fact, we were less concerned about an individual woman's personal choice than about the institution of heterosexuality; less concerned with sex-roles than with sex-power. Furthermore, challenging almost any issue impacting women — marriage, motherhood, and so on — necessarily raises questions about women's lives. We cannot abandon our insights into these institutions of male supremacy in order to avoid making each other uncomfortable.

As separatists, we stopped trying to justify our lives to straight society and instead concentrated on ourselves. We began to analyze our experiences and our perceptions of the world in the relative isolation of a collective of 12 white lesbians from varying class backgrounds. In January of 1972, we began a newspaper, *The Furies,* dedicated to lesbian-feminist political analysis and ideology.

For the first time in our lives, our reality was the dominant one, and we were able to begin to understand how it differed from the heterosexual reality that dominated everywhere else. We had become separatists for many reasons, but one was to learn about ourselves as a people — and learn we did. We discovered the strengths of women who have to live on their own. Heterosexuality, in providing some of us with a buffer zone in a man's world, had stunted our growth. We also encountered acute class and race conflict in our own midst, made all the more clear by the absence of men and male influence. We experienced the pain and the exhilaration of developing relationships where society gave us no models; relationships among equals, not based on preset male and female roles. Most of all we saw that lesbians are indeed a people, similar to other women, but also different.

Thanks in part to this time of separatism by lesbian groups in many cities, lesbian communities can now exist openly and proudly throughout the nation as the backbone of many feminist political, cultural, and economic activities. Most women's groups now recognize the "legitimacy" of lesbians' civil rights in society, as well as our right to exist openly in their midst.

Lesbian-feminism, however, is far more than civil rights for queers or lesbian communities and culture. It is a political perspective on a crucial aspect of male supremacy — heterosexism, the ideological and institutional domination of heterosexuality. The development of this political perspective was one of the most important results of lesbian separatism.

The first public statement of lesbian-feminist politics can be dated, at least symbolically, from a paper called "The Woman-Identified Woman," issued by Radicalesbians in New York City on May 1, 1970. It begins:

> What is a lesbian? A lesbian is the rage of all women condensed to the point of explosion. She is the woman who, often beginning at an extremely early age, acts in accordance with her inner compulsion to be a more complete and freer human being than her society — perhaps then, but certainly later — cares to allow her.... On some level she has not been able to accept the limitations and oppressions laid on her by the most basic role of her society — the female role.

The paper went on to analyze the nascent political power and consciousness in the personal act of being a lesbian in a male-supremacist society; of putting women first in defiance of a culture that has structured the female life around the male. It discussed how the word, the label, "lesbian," has been used to keep women divided: "When a woman hears this word tossed her way, she knows she is stepping out of line ... for a woman to be independent means she *can't* be a woman — she must be a dyke.... As long as the label 'dyke' can be used to frighten women into a less militant stand, keep her separate from her sisters, keep her from giving primacy to anything other than men and family — then to that extent she is controlled by the male culture."

The statement expanded the definition of lesbianism by developing the idea of woman-identification as an act of self-affirmation and love for all women; primary identification with women that gives energy through a positive sense of self, developed with reference to ourselves, and not in relation to men. As Rita Mae Brown, one of the founders of both Radicalesbians and *The Furies,* explained:

> Women who love women are lesbians. Men, because they can only think of women in sexual terms, define lesbian as sex between women. However, lesbians know that it is far more than that, it is a different way of life. It is a life determined by a woman for her own benefit and the benefit of other women. It is a life that draws its strength, support, and direction from women.... You refuse to limit yourself by the male definitions of women. You free yourself from male concepts of "feminine" behavior.

Since all traditionally defined lesbians were not women-identified in their heads and hearts, this definition might not apply to some of them. Yet potentially, any woman could become woman-identified. The original paper concluded with a call for woman-identification and suggested that this was the central importance of lesbianism to the Women's Movement.

The heart of the woman-identified-woman statement and of all lesbian-feminist politics is the recognition that, in a male-supremacist society, heterosexuality is a political institution. Both lesbianism and heterosexuality are therefore political forces as well as personal lifestyles.

Recognition of the political significance of lesbianism led us to an analysis of exactly how heterosexuality functions to support male supremacy. Every institution that feminists have shown to be oppressive to women — the workplace, schools, the family, the media, organized religion — is also based on heterosexism, on the assumption that every woman either is or wishes to be bonded to a man both economically and emotionally. In order to effectively challenge our oppression in those institutions, we must also challenge the ideology of heterosexism.

Granted, this challenge must seem initially difficult for women whose sexual life is bound up with men; but less difficult as we understand that heterosexuality is more than sex. In our society, heterosexuality goes hand in hand with the sexist assumption that each woman exists for a man — her body, her children, and her services are his property. If a woman does not accept that definition of heterosexuality and of herself, she is queer — no matter who she sleeps with. Heterosexism depends on the idea that heterosexuality is both the only natural and the superior form of human sexuality, thus providing ideological support to male supremacy. Heterosexism is basic to women's oppression in the family and to discrimination against single or other women who live outside the nuclear family.

Heterosexism also supports male supremacy in the workplace. Women are defined and exploited as secondary and marginal workers on the assumption that work is not our primary vocation; even if we work all our lives, we are assumed to be primarily committed to home and to have a second (major) breadwinner supporting us. No matter how false this is for most women, especially gay, black, and lower-class women, the ideology of heterosexuality continues to justify the mythology, and thus the discrimination against women at work.

One of the things that keeps heterosexual domination going is heterosexual privilege; those actual or promised benefits for a woman who stays in line: legitimacy, economic security, social acceptance, legal and physical protection. Through these privileges, a woman is given a stake in behaving properly and in maintaining her own oppression. She works against her own self-interest by becoming dependent on a man and on male privileges and undermines her self-respect. She also separates herself from her sisters — in particular her lesbian sisters —

who have no such privileges. Unless a woman, no matter what her personal connection to men, realizes that her own survival is tied more to that of all women than it is to one man, the "privileges" she receives are not lasting benefits but links in the chain of oppression.

Feminists, whatever their sexual orientation, have to understand that heterosexual privilege is a small and short-term bribe in return for giving up lasting self-discovery and collective power. I have seen countless instances when women gave up their long-term interests and power in exchange for such a "benefit." For example, one woman actively involved in a fight against female job discrimination at a university deserted her position when the battle closed in on her man's job privileges and thus indirectly on her heterosexual privileges.

Straight feminists sometimes ask me how they can fight heterosexism if they do not choose to live a lesbian lifestyle. This is a crucial question in bridging the gay-straight gap. Heterosexual women can, for example, challenge the assumptions and privileges of heterosexuality as they encounter them daily, in every area from the denial of spousal benefits for lesbians in various health, life insurance, and pension policies to social attitudes about correct behavior at a party. (For example, why must people come in pairs, or be seated alternately "boy-girl" no matter what their interests?)

One of the ways to understand better what I am saying — and what anyone can do — is to "think queer," no matter what your sexuality. By "think queer," I mean imagine life as a lesbian for a week. Announce to everyone — family, roommate, on the job, everywhere you go — that you are a lesbian. Walk in the street and go out only with women, especially at night. Imagine your life, economically and emotionally, with women instead of men. For a whole week,

experience life as if you were a lesbian, and you will learn quickly what heterosexual privileges and assumptions are, and how they function to keep male supremacy working.

You will also see, as lesbians have learned, that it is *not* okay to be a lesbian in America. And it is not okay for a reason that goes beyond individual attitudes or bigotry. It is not okay because self-loving and independent women are a challenge to the idea that men are superior, an idea that social institutions strengthen and enshrine. Most men know that, even though women have often been slow to realize it. The more any woman steps outside of society's assumptions, the more "lesbian" she becomes and the more clearly she sees exactly how those heterosexist assumptions confine her as an individual and women as a group.

One week of pretending will show you why the life of a lesbian is not the same as that of a straight woman. This does not necessarily make lesbians better or worse feminists; but it does make our perspective on male society different. That difference, like differences of race and class, can be the basis of division among women or it can be an opportunity for broader feminist analysis and action. To deny these differences is to deny both our particular oppression and our particular strength. True unity is grounded not on a false notion of sameness, but on understanding and utilizing diversity to gain the greatest possible scope and power.

In the past couple of years, many lesbian-feminist separatists have begun to work again with straight feminists. My own move away from complete separatism began in 1973. I had learned, changed, and grown during those years as a separatist, but I felt that I was becoming too isolated. Since the core of a lesbian-feminist politics and community had been developed, it seemed important that we become involved with other feminist projects and analytical developments. (In reporting my own experiences, I do not mean to imply that separatism is dead. In some places it is still performing that first task of uniting lesbians. Separatism is a dynamic strategy to be moved in and out of whenever a minority feels that its interests are being overlooked by the majority, or that its insights need more space to be developed.)

Unless lesbian-feminist politics is incorporated into feminist analysis and action, however, we will reexperience the old and destructive gay-straight split. Furthermore, we will ultimately lose the battle against male supremacy, for no woman is truly free to be anything until she is also free to be a lesbian.

Lesbian-feminist separatism, whether chosen or enforced, has produced not only a political analysis vital to all women, but structural innovations as well. After all, lesbians must create new institutions for survival, particularly once we have come out publicly, because we do not fit anywhere, whether it's the family or church, schools or nightclubs. Of necessity, we must challenge those structures to change or create alternatives.

Lesbians have played a leading role in the creation of women's art, media, and other cultural institutions, as well as in feminist economic ventures such as credit unions, bookstores, and restaurants. Our enforced economic independence has led to a growing class-consciousness and an emphasis on the economic problems of women. When lesbians come out and actively pursue the meaning of woman-identification, survival questions must immediately be faced.

If I return to the women whose story started this article — for instance — the women who formed *The Furies* collective, the life-force of lesbian feminism becomes very clear. Most of the women in that group have continued to be involved in the development of feminist theory, communications, economic and cultural strategies. *The Furies* ceased publication in 1973, and many of us went on to found and sustain a variety of projects, all national in scope. Rita Mae Brown and I became part of the group that started *Quest: a feminist quarterly*; Coletta Reid and Nancy Myron helped develop and expand Diana Press into one of the major feminist presses; Joan Biren is one of the founders of Moonforce Media, a national women's film company. Several other *Furies* members helped to conceive and develop Olivia Records, a women's recording company, and later, Women in Distribution (WIND), a national distribution service for women's media.

Our time as lesbian-feminist separatists, like that of lesbians in other cities, was less a period of being "out" of the Women's Movement than of being profoundly "in" the heart of its matter. It was a time that allowed us to develop both political insights and concrete projects that now aid women's survival and strength. We learned that change is a process. And in that process, becoming women-identified women may be the only way that women, whatever our sexual identity, can begin to see our potential for change.

THE POLITICAL IMPLICATIONS OF FEMINISM: A PLEA FOR POLITICAL THEORY

SUZANNE JACOBITTI

Suzanne Duvall Jacobitti was born in Washington, D.C., in 1940 and raised in Arlington, Virginia. She received her B.A. from Swarthmore and her M.S. and Ph.D. from the University of Wisconsin, all in political science. Currently an associate professor in government at Southern Illinois University at Edwardsville, she teaches courses and publishes in political theory and the philosophy of social science. As a political theorist, Jacobitti poses some hard questions for the women's movement. Essentially she prompts us to look at our claims and beliefs in a critical and tough-minded way, to separate some of our utopian ideals from our practical agenda, and to develop a workable and working theory of feminism in politics.

Many feminist writings contain an implicit — and sometimes explicit — political utopianism: that is, they suggest an image of a radically better political or social order, a society that would be innocent of war and violence; would not suffer from the domination of one person by another; perhaps would even be free of the need for government and political power. Such utopianism may seem to follow logically from a feminist analysis of society. If it is the case that all human beings are shaped from birth by the social norms and role expectations prevailing in the society in which they are raised, and if it is further the case that the "patriarchal" or typically male virtues have constituted an important part of the norms or role expectations into which men are socialized in America and indeed in virtually all advanced societies, then surely political behavior has been deeply influenced by this situation. If men are trained to be dominant, aggressive, competitive, and otherwise typically "macho," then one may well suppose that a society composed of such men and of women who admire them or submit to them would itself be warlike, aggressive, violent, and power-loving.

But if it is the case that the macho virtues may be a cause of war and violence, does it follow that they are *the only* cause of war and violence? If the male virtues may cause competitiveness and conflict, are they the only causes of competitiveness and conflict? And if the acceptance of the male virtues provides a motive for men (and women) in our society to seek positions of power and to enjoy exercising power or dominion over others, is this the only reason power relations exist? And does it really follow that if matriarchy — or some form of society in which the female virtues prevailed over the male virtues — were to replace patriarchy, then war, violence, conflict, power, and domination would disappear? Feminists who tend to accept such utopian conclusions tend also to express disregard for contemporary political institutions, contempt for the military establishment, and impatience with practical problems of politics, defense, and the control of power. This utopianism, it seems to me, requires serious examination, for if it is falsely based — as I believe it is — it is distracting feminists from thinking seriously about the very difficult and important question of separating out, among those evils of contemporary society, those that *can* be eliminated or ameliorated by moving away from macho attitudes and values, and those that cannot.

It is my purpose here to ask feminists to think clearly and realistically about their own political assumptions. I will argue that in any future society one can reasonably imagine — even one in which macho attitudes have been replaced — there would continue to be power, government, conflict, and the threat of war, and that this would be true because of certain characteristics of *human* nature and the *human* condition that will not change no matter how successful feminists may otherwise be in achieving their objectives. If my argument is persuasive, then it follows that feminists need to take seriously the traditional questions of political theory: questions of how political power may be controlled, how conflict may be limited, how government and politics may be improved and war prevented.

What is it then about human nature and the human condition that leads me to believe that government, the threat of war, and so on, will always be present? First, it is a part of human nature (female and male) to be more self-interested than altruistic. This is not to say that everyone is always out for herself or himself at the expense of everyone else; rather it is to say that it is only natural for people to care more about the health, welfare, and security of themselves, their immediate families, and their close friends than about the needs of humanity or society as a whole. Indeed it can be argued that only because of such a natural caring for things close to us do we ever learn to care at all for people and things that are more removed.[1]

Second, the human condition has always been and in the foreseeable future always will be characterized by a scarcity of things that are desired and hence by conflict and the threat of war over such things. In no foreseeable future is it realistic to imagine that there would be such an abundance of the things people want as to obviate the need for some system of allocation of scarce goods. At the very least, rising populations — or even zero population growth coupled with modest increases in standards of living in third-world countries — will create a demand for food and energy in excess of supply. But even if the shortages of these basic needs were miraculously overcome, it still seems inevitable that people would want more things than would be easily available.

These two assumptions about human nature and the human condition provide the basis of the modern liberal tradition of political theory, according to which government will always be necessary. Government, in this theory, is the powerful agent of an organized community, which has the authority to use force when necessary to protect the community as a whole and individuals within it. The key problem for liberal political theorists has therefore been to develop means (such as constitutional checks and balances) by which this necessary evil of government may be controlled and limited so that individual liberty may be protected from its abuse.

That government, however great the potential for its abuse, is necessary and is the only alternative to a chronic state of war or insecurity follows from the above assumptions about human nature and the human condition for several reasons.

1. Conflict over scarce goods makes government necessary. At the most basic level, there will, in the foreseeable future, be less food and less energy resources than people will demand. But even beyond that, in any future society that permits personal possessions, there will be a distribution of goods in which possessions are either equally or unequally divided. Whether there is equality (in which case those who have greater needs

or desires or work harder will be unhappy) or inequality (in which case those who have less will be unhappy), self-interested people will be unlikely to accept passively what they consider to be an unjust distribution of goods. Indeed even if most people did accept the existing distribution, the fact that a few would not would make all possessions insecure. In the absence of government with the legitimate authority to protect life and property and to provide for peaceful means by which disputes over the distribution of goods may be resolved, individuals would inevitably arm themselves and take "justice" into their own hands. And, as Locke pointed out, individuals — being only human and hence self-interested — would tend to assume that the wrong done them was greater than it objectively was and hence demand more than a "just" retribution. Thus any society without government would quickly degenerate into an armed camp and would almost certainly create a government that preferred security of life and property to chronic insecurity.[2] Of course there have always been anarchists and utopian socialists who have believed that the complete elimination of private property would put an end to conflict over scarce resources and hence to this argument for government. Perhaps some feminists are in fact also anarchists or utopian socialists, but then they must make it clear that it is not merely patriarchy they oppose but also private property, and they should prepare themselves to respond to the formidable arguments that have been put forth over the ages in defense of private property.

2. Cooperation beyond the immediate family and circle of friends requires an organization with the authority to use coercion when necessary. It follows from the assumption that people care more about what is close to them than about society as a whole that one cannot expect individuals to give up their valuable time, energy, or money for common objectives unless each one has reasonable assurances that all of the others will do so. Rousseau, in his "Discourse on the Origin and Foundations of Inequality," makes this point in a simple way. He imagines primitive men living separately in a forest without government. They are hungry and agree to cooperate to hunt a stag which, if they catch it, will provide food for them all. In the course of the hunt, however, one of the men sees a hare. He abandons the stag hunt, catches the hare and satisfies his own hunger. The stag escapes and his former companions go hungry. Though such behavior may appear shortsighted, it is not at all irrational for the man to go after the hare since he cannot be certain that one of the others will not do the same. The solution would be for the group to have the power to punish anyone who did not cooperate.[3]

This kind of need for central authority does not, however, exist merely in such desperate and primitive situations. It is true of almost any form of cooperation in a large society. As the economist Mancur Olson has pointed out, it is frequently quite rational for an individual not to participate with time or money in a collective venture (for example, paying dues to a consumer organization or voting in a democratic election) even if he or she would benefit greatly from the success of the venture. This is especially true if (a) the venture is on such a large scale that the participation of any one individual alone will not make much difference in the outcome; and (b) if the benefits of the venture are collective in the sense that the individual will benefit from its success whether she or he has contributed or not. This is a problem familiar to labor union leaders who know that most workers, even if they want the benefits of unionization, will not give their time and energies to the organizing drive and that many will not voluntarily pay their dues even if the benefits are forthcoming. Hence the union tries to obtain a clause in the contract (which is *legally enforceable*) requiring dues payment by all workers.[4] One of the reasons for relying on government to solve so many social problems is that, in a large society, only the government, through taxation that people are *compelled* to pay, has the means to act. In any imaginable future society, the problems will continue to be large scale and solutions will involve, if not always government, then at least large-scale bureaucratic organizations in which superiors have authority over subordinates and can enforce cooperation. To deny or disregard the fact that such organizations will exist is again to fail to pay attention to the great need of preventing abuses of their power.

3. Defense of the society requires government, including police and a military establishment. Even if one remains skeptical of the arguments above and convinced that the scarcity of food and energy can be overcome and that human nature can be made sufficiently altruistic to avoid the need for government to control conflict and enforce cooperation, there would be another problem. It is inconceivable that the new feminist society would be achieved everywhere on earth all at once. Assuming this did not happen, there would be the recalcitrants at home and abroad who would be ready and eager to use force to destroy the new society. The new feminist society thus would have to defend itself against internal and external enemies. This means that, at least temporarily, it would have to have police and a defense establishment — hence an army, a navy, an air force, nuclear weapons, defensive satellites; it would have to consider the "national interest," "national security," and "balance of power." There is nothing inherently male, then, about such weapons or such considerations; they are made nec-essary by certain situations. One can wish these situations did not exist; one can even believe that at some point in the future they will not exist. But until that time, one has to recognize that they do exist and that even an ideal society must have a government and a military establishment to defend it. This is a problem the Russian Bolsheviks had to face when they came to power in 1917. Even though the Marxist society was not supposed to have a government or to be militaristic, the new Russian leaders found themselves surrounded by hostile countries who were actively assisting their internal enemies. Even had men less evil than Stalin come to power, they still would have had to build a government and a military establishment.

The mention of Marxism at this point is not accidental. There are important parallels between Marxist utopianism and feminist utopianism that suggest some lessons for the feminist movement. Like many feminists, Marx believed that war and social conflict had a single cause that lay deep in the structure of a society. For Marx, this cause was economic and had to do with the mode of production and the social classes that derived from it; for feminists, of course, the cause lies in the very basic social roles that shape the attitudes and relationships of men and women. For Marx, once the basic structural problem was removed — that is, once class conflict and economic exploitation had been overcome in the historical process — the "superstructure" too would change radically. The need for domination, for conflict and war would disappear and hence government would no longer be necessary. In the new Communist society, peace and brotherhood would prevail. Feminists, as we have seen, have suggested similar hopes.

The parallel goes further. Just as feminist utopians have tended to avoid political theory, so did Marx and his followers. The experience of the Marxists without political principles to guide them is instructive. Where Marxists have found themselves in control of a government, they have either been unabashedly authoritarian and imperialistic (as in the Soviet Union) or have uneasily and usually uncritically adopted prevailing liberal ideas (as in the case of West German and Italian Social Democrats). Where Marxists have constituted powerful political parties but have not yet held positions in government, their political principles remain mysterious. For example, Communist party leaders in France and Italy frequently criticize "bourgeois" liberty and "bourgeois" democracy, but they also frequently insist that they are committed to liberty and to the principle of democratic elections. Thus no one (including perhaps themselves) knows what to expect from them. Although feminists do not constitute a political party seeking to control the reins of government, they do seek political influence and radical social change. The Marxist experience suggests that it is simply irresponsible for the leaders and leading intellectuals of any important social movement to avoid answering basic questions of political theory.

What then are the questions of political theory to which feminists should address themselves and where should their inquiry begin? First of all — given that government will be necessary, and will also, in our large society, be large and powerful — how can government be limited, how can its great power be controlled? For this question, the best place to begin is surely with the classical liberals — that is, with the thought of Locke, Montesquieu, Madison, and John Stuart Mill — amending that theory where necessary to ensure that the liberties, equalities, and rights that are protected apply to all individuals — women as well as men.

Feminists then need to inquire further

whether they would want government to take on major welfare functions in addition to the merely protective functions assigned it by the classical liberals. If so, they must seriously examine the experience of the United States, England, Sweden, and other countries to consider how this additional governmental power — and the large-scale bureaucracy associated with it — can be managed.

Feminists must also consider problems related to national defense and the prevention of war. Perhaps a good point at which to begin would be to trace the philosophical discussions over the nature of a "just war" that go back to Aristotle. In a more contemporary vein, there is a real need to attempt to distinguish carefully between arguments about the national defense that are based on realistic considerations of national interest and those that are based on "macho" reactions — for example, arguments of the form: "If we give back the Panama Canal, we lose our national manhood."

All of the above questions or problems belong to the liberal-socialist tradition that began in the seventeenth century (or some would say with Machiavelli). But this tradition may not be sufficient. With all its stress on rights and liberties, it has had perhaps too little to say about responsibilities. And after all, though women have won a good many rights in contemporary liberal states, we are not merely concerned with what women are *permitted* to do if they want, but with what women as well as men *should be expected to do* in order to take their full share in making decisions affecting our common future. Here one might well turn to the ancient Greek concept of political virtue, which was "the art of ruling and being ruled," the art of good citizenship, of knowing how to take one's turn in governing the community. To the Greeks, political virtue was an essential part of human excellence;

a person who lacked the ability or the opportunity to take political responsibility was less than fully human. Feminists could well endorse this vision of human excellence.[5] In this regard, I refer the reader to the works of Hannah Arendt, a superb political theorist, who happened, incidentally, to have been a woman.[6]

In sum, then, feminists have a responsibility to engage in political theory. In the short run, this might of necessity be an avowedly *feminist* political theory; but in the long run one would hope that feminists would help to shape what is simply a better and more humane political theory without qualification.

Notes

1. Aristotle argues, against the recommendation in Plato's *Republic* that private property and private family be abolished, that if you take away this natural incentive to care for people and things, care for the larger society will never develop at all. (*The Politics,* Book II, 4.)
2. Whether rational individuals would prefer any kind of government at all — even dictatorship and loss of liberty — to the anarchy of a "state of nature," as Hobbes thought, or whether they would only prefer limited constitutional government to the state of nature, as Locke maintained, is an important question for political theory.
3. Lest the point of the story be missed — it is quite incidental that the hunters are men. Suppose they were women; or suppose they were men and women each with a hungry family at home. In the latter case, the situation is more realistic and the stakes are higher; hence the pressure to abandon the stag hunt and feed one's family on the hare is even greater. Cited in K. Waltz, *Man, The State and War* (New York: Columbia University Press, 1954), pp. 167–68. For the original, see Jean-Jacques Rousseau, *The First and Second Discourses* (New York: St. Martin's Press, 1964), p. 145.
4. Feminists sometimes argue that the sort of rational calculation of costs and benefits that the above argument assumes is typically human is really a male trait and would itself disappear in a feminist society. But there seems little reason to believe that desire to choose the most efficient — that is, easiest, least costly means — to achieve goals is peculiarly male. See Mancur Olson, *The Logic of Collective Action* (Cambridge, Mass.: Harvard University Press, 1965).
5. And give credit to Plato, who, unlike most of his contemporaries, believed that women were not necessarily unfit by nature to share in human excellence.
6. See especially Hannah Arendt, *The Human Condition* (Chicago: University of Chicago Press, 1958).

Rediscovering American Women

A Chronology Highlighting Women's History
in the United States

1587 Virginia Dare, a girl, was the first baby born to English colonists in the New World. The daughter of Elenor White Dare and Ananias Dare, she was born on August 18 in Roanoke Island, Virginia.

circa 1600 The Constitution of the Iroquois Confederation of Nations guaranteed women the sole right and power to regulate war and peace. The women also selected tribal leaders.

1607 Princess Pocahantas saved the life of Captain John Smith, one of the founders of the Jamestown Colony, by interceding with her father, king of the Powhatan Confederacy.

1620 The Mayflower Compact was signed aboard ship by 39 men and male servants among the 102 passengers aboard the Pilgrim vessel. Women, who were not considered free agents, were not asked to sign. Only five of the 18 wives who arrived in Plymouth on the *Mayflower* survived the first harsh winter in the new land.

1638 Anne Hutchinson was excommunicated by the Puritan church in Boston for challenging its religious doctrines. One of her followers, Mary Dwyer, later became a Quaker and was hanged in 1660 in Boston for refusing to accept a sentence of banishment. Another woman who fought for freedom of conscience was Lady Deborah Moody, who moved from Massachusetts to Gravesend, Long Island where she and her companions established a community based on religious tolerance and self-government.

1648 The first attempt by a white woman to obtain political power in America originated with Margaret Brent. In a petition to the Colony of Maryland House of Delegates she requested two votes in the Assembly. She believed she merited one vote as a landowner, a vote a man would have obtained without question, and one vote as the executrix for the deceased brother of Lord Baltimore. Her request was denied.

1652 Elizabeth Poole formed a joint stock company in Taunton, Massachusetts to manufacture iron bars. This was one of the first successful iron production plants in the colonies.

1717 Twenty young women sent by King Louis XIV aboard a "brides' ship" to Louisiana to marry French settlers there refused to do so when they arrived in the primitive colony. Their revolt became known as the "petticoat rebellion."

1735 During the eight months that printer Peter Zenger was in jail in New York awaiting trial on charges of printing seditious materials, his wife, Catherine, kept his printshop running. She set type, read proof, wrote, and continued publication of his *New York Weekly Journal*. After her husband's death in 1746, Catherine Zenger continued to publish the newspaper.

Reprinted from *The Spirit of Houston: The First National Women's Conference. An Official Report to the President, the Congress and the People of the United States*, March, 1978. Washington, D.C.: National Commission on the Observance of International Women's Year, U.S. Department of State, 1978.

The first woman publisher in the Colonies was believed to be Elizabeth Timothy, who took over her late husband's paper, the weekly *South Carolina Gazette,* in Charleston, South Carolina. An estimated 30 women were newspaper publishers in the 18th century Colonies.

1761 The first black poet whose work was to be preserved arrived in Boston harbor on a slave ship from western Africa. Then seven years old, Phyllis Wheatley was taught to read and write English and Latin, and her poetry became a focus for antislavery forces.

American Revolution Women's groups, such as the Daughters of Liberty, organized to boycott tea and later to provide clothing and supplies for the Army. Deborah Sampson served as a soldier, for which she received a military pension, and Molly Pitcher assisted in the battlefield.

Groups of New Jersey women took vigorous action against husbands who abused their wives. Entering the home of a known wife-beater in the evening, they stripped the man and spanked him with sticks, shouting, "Woe to the men that beat their wives."

1777 Abigail Adams wrote to her husband, John Adams, and suggested, "... in the code of laws ... I desire you to remember the ladies and be more generous and favorable to them than your ancestors. Do not put such unlimited power into the hands of the husbands. Remember all men would be tyrants if they could. If particular care and attention is not paid to the ladies, we are determined to foment a rebellion and will not hold ourselves bound by any laws in which we have no voice or representation." The future President replied: "Depend upon it, we know better than to repeal our Masculine systems."

In the years immediately following the American Revolution, women had the right to vote in some parts of Virginia and New Jersey. Later, the adoption of State constitutions limited the franchise to white males and excluded women.

1788 Mercy Otis Warren, the first American woman historian, a political satirist and playwright, wrote her *Observations on the New Constitution* in which she deplored the absence of a Bill of Rights. The first 10 Amendments (the Bill of Rights) were added to the Constitution in 1791.

1800–1820 Deborah Skinner operated the first power loom. In the first two decades of the 19th century, factories were established employing large numbers of women and children, particularly in the New England textile industry.

1804 Sacajawea, a young Indian woman, accompanied the Lewis and Clark expedition to the West. Her skill and courage were credited with helping to make the exploration a success.

1805 Mercy Otis Warren published a three-volume history of the American Revolution which is still used by historians.

1810 Mother Elizabeth Bayley Seton founded and became head of the first sisterhood in America, the Sisters of Charity of St. Joseph's. She was canonized as the Catholic Church's first U.S.-born Saint by Pope Paul VI in 1975.

1821 Emma Willard founded a female seminary at Troy, N.Y., the first effort to provide secondary education for women. In 1837 Mary Lyon founded Mt. Holyoke Seminary (later College), which provided education similar to that offered to men at the better men's colleges.

1828 The first known strike of women workers over wages took place in Dover, N.H. Similar strikes were waged in Lowell, Mass. in 1834 and 1836 by women textile workers protesting reduced real wages.

1833 Prudence Crandall opened a school for black girls in her Connecticut home. She was arrested, persecuted, and forced to give up the school to protect her pupils from violence.

1837 First national Anti-Slavery Convention of American Women met in New York City. This was the first national gathering of women organized for action without the assistance or supervision of men.

1839 After this time, most states began to recognize through legislation the right of married women to hold property. In New York State, Ernestine Rose and Susan B. Anthony led a petition campaign for women's rights. Mrs. Rose,

Polish-born daughter of a rabbi, addressed the New York state legislature on at least five occasions until the body enacted a married women's property law in 1848.

1841 The first woman graduated from Oberlin College, having completed an easier "literary" course. At Oberlin, female students were required to wash male students' clothing, clean their rooms, serve them at meals, and were not permitted to recite in public or work in the fields with male students.

1845 *Woman in the Nineteenth Century,* written by Margaret Fuller, was an early and influential publication urging women's rights. Fuller wrote: "We would have every path laid open to Woman as freely as to Man."

1847 Trained by her father as an astronomer, Maria Mitchell at age 29 discovered a comet while standing on a rooftop scanning the sky with a telescope. In 1848 she became the first woman elected to the American Academy of Arts and Sciences in Boston.

1848 The first Women's Rights Convention was held in Seneca Falls, N.Y., led by Lucretia Mott and Elizabeth Cady Stanton. Its Declaration of Sentiments, paraphrased from the Declaration of Independence, stated that "all men and women are created equal." Eleven resolutions were approved, including equality in education, employment, and the law. A resolution advocating the right to suffrage passed by a narrow margin, with some delegates feeling that it was too daring a proposal.

The first issue of *The Lily,* a temperance paper, appeared with an editorial by Amelia Bloomer, later known for her experiment in clothing reform.

1849 Elizabeth Blackwell received her medical degree at Geneva, N.Y., becoming the first woman doctor in the United States.

1851 Sojourner Truth, ex-slave, electrified an audience in Akron, Ohio by drawing a parallel between the struggle for women's rights and the struggle to abolish slavery. In answer to arguments that women were delicate creatures who necessarily led sheltered lives, she described the hard physical labor she had done as a black woman slave and demanded, "And ain't I a Woman?"

1854 The first American day nursery opened in New York City for children of poor working mothers. In later years, licensing standards were established, but only minimal Federal funding was provided, except during the Depression and World War II.

1860 Elizabeth Peabody, a teacher, writer, and associate of the Transcendentalists, organized in Boston the first formal kindergarten in the United States. It was modeled on the Froebel kindergarten system in Germany.

Civil War Women were responsible for the establishment of the U.S. Sanitary Commission. Dorothea Dix, Clara Barton, and Mother Bickerdyke served as nurses and trained others. Dr. Mary Walker was one of several women who served as doctors and surgeons at the front.

Susan B. Anthony organized the National Women's Loyal League to collect signatures for passage of the 13th amendment abolishing slavery. Women's rights leaders were prominent in the struggle to end slavery.

Women entered government offices to replace clerks who went to war. This established women not only in Government service but in clerical work. After the invention of the typewriter in 1867, women flocked to white collar office work, which began to be considered a women's specialty.

1864 Working Women's Protective Union was founded in New York to ensure fair treatment for women wage earners. Thousands of women were working in factories.

1865 Vassar College opened, offering the first college-level curriculum for women. Five years later, Wellesley and Smith Colleges were founded. Although women were admitted to some coeducational institutions, their opportunities to study with men were limited until the University of Michigan admitted women in 1870 and Cornell University became coeducational in 1872.

1866 Elizabeth Cady Stanton became the first woman candidate for Congress, although women could not vote. She received 24 votes.

1868 The first women's suffrage amendment to the Constitution was introduced by Senator S. C. Pomeroy of Kansas. In 1878 another proposal for woman suffrage, which came to be known as the Anthony Amendment, was introduced.

1869 After passage of the 14th and 15th amendments granting suffrage to all males, both black and white, leaders of the women's movement determined to press their own claims more vigorously. Because of differences over strategy, two organizations were formed. The National Woman Suffrage Association was led by Elizabeth Cady Stanton and Susan B. Anthony while the more conservative American Women Suffrage Association was directed by Lucy Stone and Julia Ward Howe. Unification of these two groups was not achieved until 1890.

1870 Women gained the right to vote and to serve on juries in the Territory of Wyoming.

1872 Susan B. Anthony attempted to vote in Rochester, N.Y. She was tried and convicted of voting illegally but refused to pay the $100 fine.

1873 Belva Lockwood was admitted to the bar of the District of Columbia and in 1879 won passage of a law granting women lawyers the right to practice law before the U.S. Supreme Court. She ran for President in 1884 as candidate of the National Equal Rights Party and got 4,149 votes.

1874 Under the leadership of Frances Willard, the Women's Christian Temperance Union became the largest women's organization in the Nation. During this same period, the Young Women's Christian Association evolved to meet the needs of working women away from home. Other women organized for cultural purposes and by 1890 the General Federation of Women's Clubs was formed. The Association of Collegiate Alumnae, organized in 1882 to investigate the health of college women, eventually became the American Association of University Women.

1878 The Knights of Labor advocated equal pay for equal work, the abolition of child labor under age 14, and in 1881 opened their membership to working women. By 1886, 50,000 women were members.

1880's Lucy Gonzalez Parson, a labor organizer, traveled in 16 states to raise funds to help organize women garment workers and others. She founded *The Alarm* newspaper and edited *The Liberator.*

1890 Elizabeth Cady Stanton was elected first president of the unified suffrage organization, the National American Woman Suffrage Association. She also studied organized religion as a major source of women's inferior status and in 1895 published *The Woman's Bible.*

1893 Rebelling against an invitation to organize a Jewish women's committee to serve at receptions during Chicago's big Columbian Exposition, Hannah Greenbaum Solomon invited Jewish women from all over the country to attend a conference at the same time as the Exposition. The result was formation of the National Council of Jewish Women, dedicated to education, social reform, and issues of concern to women.

1896 The National Association for Colored Women, the first national organization of black women, was established, and Mary Church Terrell served as first president.

1898 Charlotte Perkins Gilman published *Women and Economics,* in which she decried the wasted efforts and the low economic status of the housewife. Gilman advocated the industrialization of housework and the socialization of child care.

1899 Florence Kelley became general secretary of the National Consumers League and worked for legislation in behalf of working women and children.

1900 The first decade of the 20th century showed the greatest increase in the female labor force of any period prior to 1940. New groups were formed to protect women and children from exploitation by industry. Several unions were organized at this time composed largely of women in the garment trades. Mother Jones, a labor organizer, led a march of children who worked in the Pennsylvania textile mills to the home of President Roosevelt in Oyster Bay, Long Island to call public attention to their plight.

1902 Carrie Chapman Catt organized the International Suffrage Alliance to help establish effective women's groups in other countries.

1904 Mary McLeod Bethune founded Bethune-Cookman College in Daytona Beach, Florida.

1907 The landmark case, *Muller* v. *Oregon,* established sex as a valid classification for protective legislation. The sociological type of evidence assembled by Florence Kelley and Josephine Goldmark to convince the court that overlong hours were harmful to the future of the race provided a model brief for later laws. While labor laws applying only to women were on the whole beneficial to women in the early part of the century, when jobs were largely sex segregated, the laws did result in loss of job opportunities for those seeking "male" jobs.

1908 A poem, "The New Colossus," written by Emma Lazarus, a poet who had died in 1887, was inscribed on a tablet in the pedestal of the Statue of Liberty in New York harbor. Its most famous lines: "Give me your tired, your poor, Your huddled masses yearning to be free..."

1909 The first significant strike of working women, "The Uprising of the 20,000," was conducted by shirtwaist makers in New York to protest low wages and long working hours. The National Women's Trade Union League (founded in 1903) mobilized public opinion and financial support for the strikers.

1911 The Triangle fire on March 25, in which 146 women shirtwaist operators were killed, dramatized the poor working conditions of immigrant women. A report of the Senate Investigation of the Condition of Women and Child Wage Earners led to establishment of the Children's Bureau (1912) and later the Women's Bureau of the Department of Labor (1920).

Liga Feminil Mexicanista was founded in Laredo, Texas to insure that the Mexican American culture and heritage would be preserved and transmitted.

1913 Harriet Tubman, ex-slave and most famous "conductor" on the Underground Railroad, died in poverty. Before the Civil War, she made 19 rescue trips to save hundreds of slaves. During the war, she served as a nurse, spy, and scout and led daring raids into the South.

1914 The Alaska Native Sisterhood was formed as an auxiliary of the Alaska Native Brotherhood, the most powerful union of native peoples in Alaska.

1915 Jane Addams, "the angel of Hull House," Carrie Chapman Catt, and other women leaders held a meeting of 3,000 women in Washington, D.C. on January 10 which organized the Women's Peace Party. They called for the abolition of war.

Margaret Sanger, having studied birth control clinics abroad, returned home to campaign against the legal barriers to the dissemination of contraceptive information. She and other women, including Emma Goldman, were jailed for their efforts.

1916 Impatient with the slow pace of the woman suffrage campaign, Alice Paul organized the National Woman's Party to conduct a more militant strategy. Its followers organized suffrage parades, picketed the White House, and chained themselves to its fence. Repeatedly arrested and imprisoned, the women protested their illegal and harsh confinement by going on hunger strikes. They were force-fed by prison authorities. Their suffering aroused widespread public outrage and was credited with hastening ratification of the suffrage amendment.

1917 Jeannette Rankin, a Republican from Montana, was the first woman elected to serve in Congress. The first vote she cast opposed American entry into World War I. She was the only woman to serve in Congress before adoption of the Federal suffrage amendment.

1919 An outgrowth of women suffrage organizations, the League of Women Voters was set up to educate women for their new political and social responsibilities. The National Federation of Business and Professional Women's Clubs was also organized.

1919 Jane Addams led a delegation of American women to a Women's Conference in Zurich, which paralleled the official peace conference in Paris. They formed the Women's International

League for Peace and Freedom, with Jane Addams as president and Emily Green Balch as secretary-treasurer.

1920 On August 26, the 19th amendment was ratified and 26 million women of voting age finally gained the right to vote.

1923 The Equal Rights Amendment, advocated by Alice Paul and the National Woman's Party, was introduced in Congress for the first time. Most women did not support this effort because they feared it would threaten protective legislation for women workers who labored in sweatshop conditions.

In the following years, the momentum of women's campaigns for access to equal education, employment, and professional achievement waned. Discrimination against women intensified. From 1925 to 1945 medical schools placed a quota of five percent on female admissions. Columbia and Harvard law schools refused to consider women applicants.

1928 Doris Stevens became the first president of the Inter-American Commission of Women, the Organization of American States.

1930 The Depression encouraged reaction against any change in women's traditional domestic role. Legislation restricted the employment of married women, and there was strong public disapproval of women working when men were unable to find employment. Nevertheless, many women performed low-paid labor to support their families. Opportunities for women to obtain college educations and graduate training were limited by lack of financial support.

1931 Suma Sugi, the first Nisei lobbyist (American born of Japanese ancestry), succeeded in amending the Cable Act of 1922 to permit American-born Asian women to regain their American citizenship upon termination of their marriage to an alien.

1933 Frances Perkins, the first woman to hold a Cabinet post, was appointed to head the Department of Labor by President Roosevelt and served in his cabinet for 12 years.

Eleanor Roosevelt turned her 12 years in the White House into a model of activism and humanitarian concern for future First Ladies.

1935 The National Council of Negro Women was founded in New York, with Mary McLeod Bethune as its first president.

1940 The percentage of working women was almost the same as it had been in 1900, when one of every five women worked for wages. After the U.S. entered World War II, wartime needs required the employment of large numbers of women. "Rosie the Riveter" became a national symbol. After the war, many women remained in the labor force, although many were displaced by returning veterans. Between 1940–60, the number of working women and the proportion of working wives doubled. More women over 35 were employed in rapidly expanding business and industry. Inequities in pay and advancement opportunities became more obvious limitations affecting large numbers of women. Economic conditions produced a favorable environment for the increasing demands for equity voiced by the women of the 1960's.

1950 A repressive decade for Chicana activists. Several were deported for their attempts to organize communities. Also deported was film actress Rosaura Revueltas, featured in the film, "Salt of the Earth," about striking miners in the Southwest.

1952 The Constitution of the Commonwealth of Puerto Rico was enacted, embodying the Equal Rights Amendment.

1953 Simone de Beauvoir's *The Second Sex,* a scholarly and historical analysis of the inferior status of women, was published in the United States.

1956 Rosa Parks, a black seamstress, refused to give up her bus seat to a white man and was arrested, touching off the Montgomery, Alabama bus boycott.

1957 Daisy Bates, coeditor with her husband of a black newspaper and president of the Arkansas National Association for the Advancement of Colored People, acted as spokesperson and counselor for the nine black youths who desegregated Little Rock Central High School.

1960 Women Strike for Peace was formed as an outgrowth of protests against resumption of nuclear testing by the Soviet Union and United States.

1961 The President's Commission on the Status of Women, chaired by Eleanor Roosevelt, was established by Executive Order 10980, with a charge to study seven areas: education, private and Federal employment, social insurance and tax laws, protective labor laws, civil and political rights and family law, and home and community. Esther Peterson, Director of the Women's Bureau, was the moving force in its establishment, with the assistance of then Vice President Lyndon Johnson.

1962 In Michigan, the Governor's Commission on the Status of Women became the first State commission. Union women Mildred Jeffrey and Myra Wolfgang were the leaders in obtaining its establishment.

1962 Acting on a recommendation of his Commission on the Status of Women, President Kennedy issued an order requiring Federal employees to be hired and promoted without regard to sex. Prior to this order, Federal managers could restrict consideration to men or women.

1963 The National Federation of Business and Professional Women's Clubs adopted as its top priority the nationwide establishment of State commissions on the status of women. By June 1964 when the first national conference was held, there were 24 commissions, and by the end of the year there were 33.

The Equal Pay Act was passed in June, effective June 1964, after formation of a coalition of women's organizations and unions to support it in Congress.

The Feminine Mystique by Betty Friedan was published. Describing social pressures that sought to limit women to roles as wives and mothers, it became a national and influential best seller.

The Interdepartmental Committee on the Status of Women and Citizens Advisory Council on the Status of Women were established by Executive Order 11126, with Margaret Hickey as its first chairperson. The Committee and Council sponsored national meetings of the State commissions, issued annual reports on issues affecting women, and made legislative and administrative recommendations. Subsequent chairpersons were Maurine Neuberger and Jacqueline Gutwillig. (The Council was terminated on August 22, 1977 by Executive Order 12007.)

1964 The Spring issue of *Daedalus,* Journal of the American Academy of Arts and Sciences, devoted an entire issue to "The Woman in America," enhancing the academic respectability of the subject. Alice Rossi's "Equality Between the Sexes: An Immodest Proposal," probably the most widely reproduced article in the women's movement, first appeared here.

Title 7 of the Civil Rights Act, enacted in 1964, prohibited discrimination in employment because of sex, race, color, religion, and national origin.

The first meeting of the First National Institute on Girls' Sports was held "to increase the depth of experience and expand opportunities for women."

1965 The U.S. Supreme Court found that a Connecticut law banning contraceptives was unconstitutional because it violated the right to privacy. *Griswold* v. *State of Connecticut,* 381 U.S.C. 479.

1966 A Federal court declared that an Alabama law excluding women from State juries was in violation of the equal protection clause of the 14th amendment, the first time in modern times a Federal court had found a law making sex distinctions unconstitutional. *White* v. *Crook,* 251 F. Supp. 401.

The National Organization for Women (NOW) was organized at the Third National Conference of Governors' Commissions on the Status of Women as a culmination of dissatisfaction with the failure to enforce Title 7 of the Civil Rights Act. Among the 28 women who founded NOW were: Betty Friedan, Aileen Hernandez, Dr. Kathryn Clarenbach, Dr. Pauli Murray, Marguerite Rawalt, Catherine Conroy, Dorothy Haener, and Dr. Nancy Knaak.

1967 The first "women's liberation" group was formed in Chicago, partially in rebellion against the low status of young women in civil rights and "new left" campus movements. Similar groups were independently organized in New York, Toronto, Detroit, Seattle, San Francisco, and other cities. Initially concerned with analyzing the origins, nature, and extent of women's subservient status in society, some groups used the technique of "consciousness-raising" sessions to help women liberate themselves from restricting inferior roles. Most of the groups were small, egalitarian and opposed to elitism. They called for far-reaching and radical change in almost all aspects of American society.

Executive Order 11246, prohibiting discrimination by Federal contractors, was amended to include sex discrimination, with an effective date of October 1968.

A law repealing arbitrary restrictions on military rank held by women was signed by the President.

1968 *The Church and the Second Sex* by Dr. Mary Daly, a scholarly critique of Catholic Church doctrine, influenced Protestant as well as Catholic women. The first stirrings of Catholic feminist dissent occurred at the Second Vatican Council. The American branch of St. Joan's Alliance, an international Catholic feminist organization, had been formed in 1965 by Frances McGillicuddy.

Beginning in 1968, a number of distinguished Native American women, including Lucy Covington (Colville), Ramona Bennett (Puyallup), Joy Sundberg (Yurok), and Ada Deer (Menominee), were elected as tribal chairs.

Federally Employed Women was organized in September to press for equality in Federal employment, with Allie Weedon, a black attorney, as first president.

The Women's Equity Action League was organized in December by Dr. Elizabeth Boyer and other members of the National Organization for Women and concentrated on attacking sexism in higher education.

Women liberationists picketed the Miss America beauty pageant in Atlantic City. Contrary to myth, they did not burn bras. They carried signs that said: Women Are People, Not Livestock.

1969 Shirley Chisholm, Democrat of New York City, was the first black woman elected to Congress.

Weeks v. *Southern Bell Telephone Co.*, 408 F. 2d 228, was the first appeals court decision interpreting sex provisions of Title 7 of the Civil Rights Act of 1964. The lawsuit was brought by a blue collar union woman protesting discriminatory effects of State labor laws applying only to women. Marguerite Rawalt, NOW legal counsel, located a Louisiana lawyer, Sylvia Roberts, to represent Mrs. Weeks, and NOW paid court costs. The excellent decision, the great courage of the plaintiff, and the important victory of a volunteer woman lawyer and a women's organization over highly paid corporation lawyers were a great boost to the women's movement.

An equally important Title 7 case was decided by the Seventh Circuit Court of Appeals, *Bowe* v. *Colgate Palmolive*, 416 F. 2d 711. Union women and volunteer women attorneys were the pattern in this case, too. These and later Title 7 cases illustrated the real effects of State labor laws applying only to women and led to their early demise and broadened support for the Equal Rights Amendment.

The first Commission on the Status of Women appointed by a professional association began to function inside the Modern Language Association. In its early years, that Commission assumed responsibility for collecting and disseminating data on women's studies courses and programs. In December 1970 the Commission published a list of 110 women's studies courses taught at 47 colleges and universities. There were by then two Women's Studies Programs at Cornell University and San Diego State University.

In Fall 1972, the *Women's Studies Newsletter*, edited by Florence Howe, began to appear quarterly on the SUNY College at Old Westbury campus, published by The Feminist Press. Annually, the newsletter lists Women's Studies Programs; in 1977, there were 276. There are also groups of women's studies courses on more than 1,000 other campuses. The total number of courses now offered exceeds 15,000.

A women's caucus was organized at the Chicano Liberation Conference held in Denver.

The Boston Women's Health Collective was organized, one of a number of women's self-help groups that emerged in various parts of the country. The group researched and wrote *Our Bodies, Ourselves,* which later became a worldwide bestseller.

The four Republican Congresswomen — Florence Dwyer, Margaret Heckler, Catherine May, and Charlotte Reid — asked for an unprecedented audience with President Nixon to discuss women's issues. They presented a letter which outlined a proposed administration program and provided data on discrimination. Their program became the agenda of the President's Task Force on Women's Rights and Responsibilities, which the President later established with Virginia Allan as chair.

Women in the American Sociological Association formed the first caucus within a professional association, after presentation of a survey by Dr. Alice Rossi on the status of women in graduate departments of sociology. By the end of 1971 every professional association had an activist women's caucus or official commission to study the status of women.

1970 Women's Equity Action League officer, Dr. Bernice Sandler, filed the first formal charges of sex discrimination under Executive Order No. 11246 against the University of Maryland. The charges were well documented. By the end of 1971 women professors had filed formal charges of sex discrimination against more than 300 colleges, largely through the efforts of Dr. Sandler and WEAL.

The first statewide meeting of AFL-CIO women was held in Wisconsin in March. The women endorsed the ERA, opposing AFL-CIO national policy. The next month the United Auto Workers became the first major national union to endorse ERA. Later the AFL-CIO executive council changed its position and announced its support for the ERA.

The Subcommittee on Constitutional Amendments of the Senate Judiciary Committee, chaired by Senator Birch Bayh, held three days of hearings on the ERA in May. Leaders of women's organizations and unions, women lawyers, and Members of Congress testified.

The NAACP adopted a women's rights platform at its annual national convention in June.

The first national commercial newsletters to serve the women's movement — *Women Today,* published in Washington by Myra and Lester Barrer, and *Spokeswoman,* published in Chicago by Susan Davis — were issued.

The Interstate Association of Commissions on the Status of Women was organized to provide a national voice and greater autonomy for the State commissions. Elizabeth Duncan Koontz, newly appointed Director of the Women's Bureau, arranged the organized meetings, and Dr. Kathryn Clarenbach was elected first president.

The Women's Bureau held its 50th anniversary conference, attended by more than 1,000 women. The Conference endorsed the ERA and other recommendations of the President's Task Force on Women's Rights and Responsibilities.

On the first day of the Women's Bureau Conference, Congresswoman Martha Griffiths filed a petition to discharge the ERA from the House Judiciary Committee, where it had rested without hearings since 1948. The petition was successful, and the ERA was debated in the House on August 10, passing overwhelmingly. It was then defeated in the Senate by the addition of unacceptable amendments.

Hearings on discrimination in education were held in June and July by Congresswoman Edith Green, chairing a special House Subcommittee on Education. The two-volume report is a classic in documenting discrimination against women in education.

The Women's Affairs Division of the League of United Latin American Citizens was organized at the convention in Beaumont, Texas, with Julia Zozoya and Ada Pena in the forefront.

The National Conference of Commissioners on Uniform State Laws published the Uniform Marriage and Divorce Act, based on the assumption that marriage is an economic partnership and recognizing homemakers' contributions as having economic value.

A nationwide celebration of the 50th anniversary of the suffrage amendment, including a mammoth parade in New York City, was held in all major cities on August 26 by a wide spectrum of organizations and individual women. The parade became an annual event.

Sixty-three Native American women from 43 tribes and 23 States met at Colorado State University to discuss their common concerns. They organized the North American Indian Women's Association.

Patsy Mink, Democrat of Hawaii, was the first and only Asian woman elected to Congress. In New York City, Democrat Bella Abzug was the first woman elected to Congress on a women's rights platform. They were among only 11 women in the 435-member House of Representatives.

The Women's Action Organization of State, AID and ICA, the first women's caucus in the federal government, was formed to eliminate discrimination and promote equality of opportunity for women in the foreign affairs agencies.

1971 The National Women's Political Caucus was organized at a meeting in Washington in July, with Congresswoman Bella Abzug, Gloria Steinem, Aileen Hernandez, Fannie Lou Hamer, Edith Van Horn, Liz Carpenter, Koryne Horbal, Congresswoman Shirley Chisholm, Brownie Ledbetter, Betty Friedan, Bobby Kilberg, Jo Ann Gardner, LaDonna Harris, and Virginia Allan among the early leaders.

The U.S. Supreme Court held in *Reed* v. *Reed* that an Idaho law giving preference to males as executors of estates was invalid under the 14th amendment, the first in a series of Supreme Court cases expanding the application of the 5th and 14th amendments to sex discrimination, 404 U.S. 71, 1971.

A preview issue of *Ms.* magazine was published in December with Gloria Steinem as editor. Established to give voice to the ideas of the women's movement, it was an immediate success.

The Women's National Abortion Coalition was organized to work for repeal of anti-abortion laws.

1972 The Equal Rights Amendment was overwhelmingly approved by the Congress and submitted to the States for ratification. Hawaii was the first State to ratify.

The Equal Employment Opportunity Act of 1972, extending coverage and giving the EEOC enforcement authority, passed. The EEOC issued greatly improved sex discrimination guidelines.

Title 9 of the Education Amendments of 1972 was passed, prohibiting discrimination on account of sex in most Federally assisted educational programs. The Equal Pay Act was extended to cover administrative, professional, and executive employees, and the Civil Rights Commission was given jurisdiction over sex discrimination.

The Democratic and Republican Party platforms endorsed the ERA and vigorous enforcement of anti-discrimination laws. As a result of campaigns by the National Women's Political Caucus, the participation of women as convention delegates was higher than in previous conventions. At the Democratic convention, women were 40 percent of the delegates; at the Republican convention, 30 percent.

The National Conference of Puerto Rican Women was organized in Washington, with Carmen Maymi and Paquito Viva in leading roles.

The November elections brought more women into elective office. The number of women elected to State legislatures was 28.2 percent higher than those serving in the preceding year. In the House of Representatives, the number of Congresswomen increased to 16, but with the retirement of Margaret Chase Smith, the U.S. Senate once again became all-male.

Members of the National Council of Jewish Women conducted a study of day-care facilities in 176 areas. The NCJW report, written by Mary Keyserling, concluded that while the need for day-care centers was enormous, facilities were nonexistent in most places or were of poor quality, underfunded, and understaffed.

1973 AT&T signed an agreement with the EEOC and the Labor Department providing goals and timetables for increasing utilization of women and minorities. About $15 million in back pay was paid to some 15,000 employees.

In a historic decision on January 22, the U.S. Supreme Court held that during the first trimester of pregnancy, the decision to have an abortion must be left solely to a woman and her physician. The only restriction a State may impose is the requirement that the abortion be performed by a physician licensed by the State. In the second and third trimesters, the Court held, the States may impose increasingly stringent requirements. Lawyers for the plaintiffs were Sarah Weddington and Marjorie Hames. *Doe* v. *Bolton* and *Roe* v. *Wade,* 93 S. Ct. 739 and 755.

The National Black Feminists Organization was formed. Eleanor Holmes Norton, leading attorney and head of the New York City Human Rights Commission, was one of the leaders.

The Foreign Assistance Act (Public Law 93–189, 87 Stat. 714) included the Percy Amendment providing that in administering financial aid, particular attention be given to "programs, projects, and activities which tend to integrate women into the national status and assisting the total development effort." Dr. Irene Tinker and the Federation of Organizations for Professional Women were leading proponents.

Billie Jean King beat Bobby Riggs in straight sets in their "Battle of the Sexes" tennis match.

1974 The Coalition of Labor Union Women was organized in Chicago with over 3,000 women in attendance. Olga Madar, former UAW vice president, was elected president.

More than 1.5 million domestic service workers were brought under the coverage of the Fair Labor Standards Act by Public Law 93–259, approved April 8. A rate of $1.90 per hour was effective May 1, 1974, with increases slated for later periods.

The Wisconsin Commission on the Status of Women, chaired by Dr. Kathryn Clarenbach, inaugurated a series of six regional conferences to examine the status of the homemaker.

A national newsletter, *Marriage, Divorce and the Family,* edited by Betty Blaisdell Berry, began publication.

The Mexican American Women's Association (MAWA) was founded.

A study by Dr. Constance Uri, a Cherokee/Choctaw physician, revealed the widespread use and abuse of sterilization of Native American women in Indian health care facilities. The exposé led to the investigation of excessive sterilization of poor and minority women and to the 1977 revision of the Department of Health, Education, and Welfare's guidelines on sterilization.

Congresswoman Bella Abzug's bill to designate August 26 "Women's Equality Day" in honor of the adoption of the Suffrage Amendment became Public Law 93–392.

The Housing and Community Development Act of 1974, Public Law 93–383, prohibited sex discrimination in carrying out community development programs and in making federally related mortgage loans. The Civil Rights Act of 1968 was also amended to prohibit sex discrimination in financing, sale or rental of housing, or the provision of brokerage services.

The Equal Credit Opportunity Act became Public Law 93–495 after Congresswomen Bella Abzug, Margaret Heckler, and Leonor Sullivan led the fight for it in the House. It prohibited discrimination in credit on the basis of sex or marital status. Later, Congresswoman Abzug led a delegation of women members of Congress to meet with Chairman Arthur Burns of the Federal Reserve Board to protest unsatisfactory regulations designed to implement the new law. The regulations were revised.

The Screen Actors Guild reported a nationwide survey of 10,000 viewers on their opinions of women in the media. The majority wanted a more positive image of women, wanted to see women appearing on TV in positions of authority and in leading roles, and felt the media did not encourage young girls to aspire to a useful and meaningful role in society.

Following a "Win With Women" campaign by the National Women's Political Caucus, 18 women were elected to the 94th Congress. A 19th member was elected in a special election in early 1975. In the State legislatures there was a 29.5 percent increase in the numbers of women (465 to 604). The first woman governor to be elected in her own right, Ella Grasso, was elected Governor of Connecticut. Mary Anne Krupsak was elected Lieutenant Governor of New York, and many more women were elected to statewide offices.

1975 The U.S. Supreme Court held in *Wiesenfeld* v. *Wineberger* that a widower with minor children whose deceased wife was covered by social security is entitled to a social security benefit under the same circumstances as a widow would be. The Court held unanimously that the fifth amendment prohibited the present difference in treatment. 43 USLW 4393.

The Supreme Court also held that, in the context of child support, a Utah statute providing that the period of minority extending for males to age 21 and for females to age 18 denies equal protection of the laws guaranteed by the 14th amendment. *Stanton* v. *Stanton,* 43 USLW 4167.

Ms. magazine published a petition for sexual freedom signed by 100 prominent women. They pledged to work for repeal of all laws and regulations that discriminate against homosexuals and lesbians.

The National Commission on the Observance of International Women's Year, 1975, was appointed by President Ford with Jill Ruckelshaus as presiding officer. Elizabeth Athanasakos became presiding officer in 1976. Members of the Commission represented the United States at the United Nations International Women's Year Conference in Mexico City in June.

The First American Indian Women's Leadership Conference met in New York City, sponsored by the International Treaty Council in conjunction with IWY.

A bill introduced by Congresswoman Bella Abzug directed the National Commission to organize and convene a National Women's Conference, preceded by State meetings. The bill was passed by both Houses, was signed by President Ford and became Public Law 94–167.

1976 The number of women delegates to the political party conventions rose to 31.4 percent at the Republican convention and declined to 34 percent at the Democratic convention. A large and effective women's caucus at the Democratic convention in New York met with Presidential nominee Jimmy Carter and obtained pledges from him to appoint significant numbers of women to his administration, to take other steps to improve the position of women, and to campaign for ratification of the ERA.

The major parties nominated 52 women for the House of Representatives, eight more than in 1974, but 31 ran against incumbents. Eighteen were elected, one less than in the previous Congress. Although women won seats in Maryland and Ohio and all incumbents won reelection, Congresswomen Bella Abzug and Patsy Mink gave up their seats to make unsuccessful campaigns for the Senate, and Congresswoman Leonor Sullivan retired. The number of women in State legislatures increased to 685, representing nine percent of legislative seats.

1977 President Carter named a new National Commission on the Observance of IWY and appointed Bella Abzug presiding officer. He named two women, Patricia Harris and Juanita Kreps, to his Cabinet and made other major appointments of women. An analysis of the Presidential personnel plum file appointments list in October, however, showed that of 526 top positions in the Carter administration, only 60 (11 percent) were held by women.

The drive for final ratification of ERA was stalled at 35 States, with three more States needed to meet the 1979 deadline for ratification.

The National Women's Conference met in Houston, Texas, November 18–21, attracted almost 20,000 people, including 2,005 delegates, adopted a National Plan of Action, and was acclaimed a success.

Editor's Note: In highlighting some of the notable women and events affecting women in American history, this chronology makes no pretense to being complete or even comprehensive. It is intended rather to remind readers that the role of women in America has too often been overlooked and that the struggle for equality for women is as old as our Nation.

Among the books which the editors found particularly useful in compiling this chronology were:

Chafe, William. The American Woman: Her

Changing Social, Economic and Political Roles, 1920–1970. *Oxford University Press.*

DePauw, Linda Grant. Fortunes of War, New Jersey Women and the American Revolution. *New Jersey Historical Commission.*

Flexner, Eleanor. Century of Struggle. *Atheneum.*

Freeman, Jo. Women: A Feminist Perspective. *Mayfield.*

Hole, Judith, and Ellen Levine. Rebirth of Feminism. *Quadrangle.*

Lerner, Gerda. "The Lady and the Mill Girl: Changes in the Status of Women in the Age of Jackson." American Studies Journal, *Spring 1969.*

Lerner, Gerda. Black Women in White America. *Vintage.*

O'Neill, William. Everyone Was Brave. *Quadrangle.*

Papachristou, Judith. Women Together, A History in Documents of the Women's Movement in the United States. A *Ms.* Book.

Wertheimer, Barbara. We Were There: The Story of Working Women in America. *Pantheon.*

Special thanks to Catherine East for compiling the original chronology on which this is based, which appeared as an IWY publication in 1975.

For Further Reading

Chapter 1

Women's Studies

Ahlum, Carol, and Jacqueline Fralley, eds. *High School Feminist Studies.* Old Westbury, N.Y.: Feminist Press, 1974.

Berkowitz, Tamar, Jean Mangi, and Jane Williamson, eds. *Who's Who and Where in Women's Studies.* Old Westbury, N.Y.: Feminist Press, 1974.

Brush, Lorelei R., Alice Ross Gold, and Marni Goldstein White. "The Paradox of Intention and Effect: A Women's Studies Course," *Signs,* 3, No. 4 (Summer 1978).

Chmaj, Betty E. *American Women and American Studies.* Pittsburgh: Know, Inc., 1971.

——. *Feminist Resources for Schools and Colleges: A Guide to Curricular Materials.* Old Westbury, N.Y.: Feminist Press, 1973.

Daly, Mary. *Beyond God the Father.* Boston: Beacon Press, 1973. Introduction.

——. *Gyn/Ecology: The Metaethics of Radical Feminism.* Boston: Beacon Press, 1978.

Female Studies. Vols. I–X. Old Westbury, N.Y.: Feminist Press. (A collection of resources by various editors covering bibliographies, syllabi, guides, and faculty.)

Howe, Florence, ed. *Women and the Power to Change.* New York: McGraw-Hill, 1975.

Rossi, Alice, and Ann Calderwood, eds. *Academic Women on the Move.* New York: Russell Sage, 1973.

"Women's Studies: Awakening Academe." A symposium issue of *The Social Science Journal,* 14, No. 2 (April 1977).

The Biology of Sex Difference

Bleier, Ruth H. "Brain, Body, and Behavior." In *Beyond Intellectual Sexism.* Ed. Joan I. Roberts. New York: David McKay, 1976.

Frieze, Irene H., et al. *Women and Sex Roles.* New York: Norton, 1978.

Maccoby, E. E., ed. *The Development of Sex Differences.* Stanford, Calif.: Stanford University Press, 1966.

Maccoby, E. E., and C. N. Jacklin. *The Psychology of Sex Differences.* Stanford, Calif.: Stanford University Press, 1974.

Money, J., and A. A. Ehrhardt. *Man and Woman, Boy and Girl.* Baltimore: Johns Hopkins Press, 1972.

Stoll, Clarice Stasy. *Female and Male.* Dubuque, Iowa: Wm. C. Brown, 1974.

Chapter 2

Barker-Benfield, G. J. *The Horrors of the Half-known Life.* New York: Harper Colophon, 1976.

David, Deborah S., and Robert Brannon, eds. *The Forty-Nine Percent Majority: The Male Sex Role.* Reading, Mass.: Addison-Wesley, 1976.

Davis, Elizabeth Gould. *The First Sex.* New York: Putnam, 1971.

Dworkin, Andrea. *Our Blood.* New York: Harper & Row, 1976.

Fasteau, Marc Feigen. *The Male Machine.* New York: McGraw-Hill, 1974.

Figes, Eva. *Patriarchal Attitudes.* Greenwich, Conn.: Fawcett, 1971.

Iglitzin, Lynne B., and Ruth Ross, eds. *Women in*

the World: A Comparative Study. Santa Barbara, Calif.: Clio Press, 1976.

Johnson, Robert A. *He.* New York: Perennial Library, 1977.

Komarovsky, Mirra. *Dilemmas of Masculinity.* New York: Norton, 1976.

Korda, Michael. *Male Chauvinism! How It Works.* New York: Random House, 1972.

Mailer, Norman. *The Prisoner of Sex.* Boston: Little, Brown, 1971.

Marine, Gene. *A Male Guide to Women's Liberation.* New York: Avon, 1972.

Millett, Kate. *Sexual Politics.* New York: Doubleday, 1970.

Money, J., and A. A. Ehrhardt. *Man and Woman, Boy and Girl.* Baltimore: Johns Hopkins University Press, 1972.

Pleck, J. H., and J. Sawyer. *Men and Masculinity.* Englewood Cliffs, N.J.: Prentice-Hall, 1974.

Sumner, William Graham. *Folkways.* Boston: Ginn, 1907.

Thornburg, Hershel D. *Punt, Pop.* Tucson, Ariz.: HELP Books, 1977.

Chapter 3

Adams, Elsie, and Mary Louise Briscoe, eds. *Up Against the Wall, Mother.* Beverly Hills, Calif.: Glencoe Press, 1971.

Agonito, Rosemary, ed. *History of Ideas on Woman: A Source Book.* New York: Capricorn, 1977.

Andelin, Helen B. *Fascinating Womanhood.* New York: Bantam, 1975.

Barker-Benfield, G. J. *The Horrors of the Half-known Life.* New York: Harper Colophon, 1976.

Bengis, Ingrid. *Combat in the Erogenous Zone.* New York: Knopf, 1972.

Bullough, Vern L., and Bonnie Bullough. *The Subordinate Sex.* Baltimore: Penguin, 1974.

Campbell, Joseph. *The Masks of God.* New York: Viking, 1961.

Cleaver, Eldridge. "White Woman, Black Man." In *Soul on Ice.* New York: Delta Books, 1968.

Daly, Mary. *Beyond God the Father.* Boston: Beacon Press, 1973.

———. *The Church and the Second Sex.* New York: Harper Colophon, 1975.

———. *Gyn/Ecology.* Boston: Beacon Press, 1978.

Davis, Elizabeth Gould. *The First Sex.* New York: Putnam, 1971.

Dworkin, Andrea. *Our Blood.* New York: Harper & Row, 1976.

———. *Woman-Hating.* New York: E. P. Dutton, 1974.

Ellmann, Mary. *Thinking About Women.* New York: Harcourt Brace Jovanovich, 1968.

Erikson, Erik H. "Inner and Outer Space: Reflexions on Womanhood." *Daedalus,* 93 (1964), 582–606.

Figes, Eva. *Patriarchal Attitudes.* Greenwich, Conn.: Fawcett, 1971.

Frieze, Irene H., et al. *Women and Sex Roles.* New York: Norton, 1978.

Greer, Germaine. *The Female Eunuch.* New York: McGraw-Hill, 1971.

Hays, H. R. *The Dangerous Sex.* New York: Putnam, 1964.

Janeway, Elizabeth. *Man's World, Woman's Place.* New York: Delta Books, 1971.

Levin, Ira. *The Stepford Wives.* Greenwich, Conn.: Fawcett, 1972.

Lerner, Gerda. *The Female Experience.* Indianapolis: Bobbs, Merrill, 1977.

Mahowald, Mary B., ed. *Philosophy of Woman: Classical to Current Concepts.* Indianapolis: Hackett, 1978.

Millett, Kate. *Sexual Politics.* New York: Doubleday, 1970.

Mitchell, Juliet. *Woman's Estate.* New York: Vintage, 1973.

Moynihan, Patrick. *The Negro Family: The Case for National Action.* Washington, D.C.: U.S. Department of Labor, 1965.

Reid, Inez Smith. *"Together" Black Women.* New York: Third Press, 1975.

Rowbotham, Sheila. *Woman's Consciousness, Man's World.* Baltimore: Penguin, 1973.

Welter, Barbara. "The Cult of True Womanhood: 1820–1860," *American Quarterly,* 18, No. 2, Pt. 1 (1966), 151–174.

Whitbeck, Caroline. "Theories of Sex Difference." In *Women and Philosophy: Toward a Theory of Liberation.* Ed. Carol C. Gould and Marx W. Wartofsky. New York: Putnam, 1976.

Yorburg, Betty. *Sexual Identity.* New York: Wiley, 1974.

Chapter 4

Adams, Elsie, and Mary Louise Briscoe, eds. *Up Against the Wall, Mother.* Beverly Hills, Calif.: Glencoe, 1971.

Amundsen, Kirsten. *The Silenced Majority: Women and American Democracy.* Englewood Cliffs, N.J.: Prentice-Hall, 1971.

Angelou, Maya. *I Know Why the Caged Bird Sings.* New York: Bantam, 1971.

Bengis, Ingrid. *Combat in the Erogenous Zone.* New York: Knopf, 1972.

Bird, Caroline. *Born Female. The High Cost of Keeping Women Down.* New York: David McKay, 1968.

Chmaj, Betty E. *Image, Myth, and Beyond.* Pittsburgh: Know, Inc., 1972.

Cooke, Joanne, Charlotte Bunch-Weeks, and Robin Morgan, eds. *The New Women.* Greenwich, Conn.: Fawcett, 1970.

Daly, Mary. *Beyond God the Father.* Boston: Beacon Press, 1973.

————. *The Church and the Second Sex.* New York: Harper Colophon, 1975.

————. *Gyn/Ecology.* Boston: Beacon Press, 1978.

Dworkin, Andrea. *Our Blood.* New York: Harper & Row, 1976.

————. *Woman-Hating.* New York: Dutton, 1974.

Ellmann, Mary. *Thinking About Women.* New York: Harcourt Brace Jovanovich, 1968.

Ferguson, Mary Anne, ed. *Images of Women in Literature.* 2nd ed. Boston: Houghton Mifflin, 1977.

Freeman, Jo, ed. *Women: A Feminist Perspective.* 2nd ed. Palo Alto, Calif.: Mayfield, 1979.

Friedan, Betty. *The Feminine Mystique.* New York: Dell, 1963.

Gornick, Vivian, and Barbara E. Moran, eds. *Women in Sexist Society.* New York: Basic Books, 1971.

Greer, Germaine. *The Female Eunuch.* New York: McGraw-Hill, 1971.

Haskell, Molly. *From Reverence to Rape: The Treatment of Women in the Movies.* New York: Holt, Rinehart and Winston, 1973.

Hole, Judith, and Ellen Levine. *Rebirth of Feminism.* New York: Quadrangle Books, 1971.

Iglitzen, Lynne B., and Ruth Ross, eds. *Women in the World: A Comparative Study.* Santa Barbara, Calif.: Clio Press, 1976.

Kaplan, Alexandra G., and Joan P. Bean, eds. *Beyond Sex-Role Stereotypes.* Boston: Little, Brown, 1976.

Korda, Michael. *Male Chauvinism! How It Works.* New York: Random House, 1972.

Lerner, Gerda. *The Female Experience.* Indianapolis: Bobbs-Merrill, 1977.

Levin, Ira. *The Stepford Wives.* Greenwich, Conn.: Fawcett, 1972.

Millett, Kate. *Sexual Politics.* New York: Doubleday, 1970.

Mitchell, Juliet. *Woman's Estate.* New York: Vintage, 1973.

Morgan, Robin, ed. *Sisterhood Is Powerful.* New York: Vintage, 1970.

O'Leary, Virginia E. *Toward Understanding Women.* Belmont, Calif.: Brooks-Cole, 1977.

Reed, Evelyn. *Problems of Women's Liberation.* New York: Pathfinder Press, 1971.

Reid, Inez Smith. *"Together" Black Women.* New York: Third Press, 1975.

Seaman, Barbara. *Free and Female.* New York: Coward McCann & Geoghegan, 1972.

Shulman, Alix Kates. *Memoirs of an Ex-Prom Queen.* New York: Knopf, 1972.

Tanner, Leslie B., ed. *Voices from Women's Liberation.* New York: Signet, 1970.

Tavris, Carol, and Carole Offir. *The Longest War.* Part I. New York: Harcourt Brace Jovanovich, 1977.

Thompson, Mary Lou, ed. *Voices of the New Feminism.* Boston: Beacon Press, 1970.

Tuchman, Gaye, Arlene K. Daniels, and James Benét, eds. *Hearth and Home: Images of Women in the Mass Media.* New York: Oxford University Press, 1978.

Wittig, Monique. *Les Guérillères.* Trans. David Le Vay. New York: Avon, 1973.

Chapter 5

Ardrey, Robert. *The Territorial Imperative.* New York: Atheneum, 1966.

Davis, Elizabeth Gould. *The First Sex.* New York: Putnam, 1971.

Firestone, Shulamith. *The Dialectic of Sex.* New York: Bantam, 1971.

Frazer, Sir James George. *The New Golden Bough.* Ed. Theodor H. Gaster. New York: S. G. Phillips, 1959.

Goldberg, Steven. *The Inevitability of Patriarchy.* New York: Morrow, 1974.

Hoch-Smith, Judith, and Anita Spring, eds. *Women in Ritual and Symbolic Roles.* New York: Plenum, 1978.

Iglitzin, Lynne B., and Ruth Ross, eds. *Women in the World: A Comparative Study.* Santa Barbara, Calif.: Clio Books, 1976.

Lamphere, Louise. "Anthropology." *Signs,* 2, No. 3 (Spring 1977), 612–627.

Lederer, Wolfgang. *The Fear of Women.* New York: Grune & Stratton, 1968.

Martin, M. Kay, and Barbara Voorhies. *Female of the Species.* New York: Columbia University Press, 1975.

Mead, Margaret. *Coming of Age in Samoa.* New York: Morrow, 1928.

———. *Male and Female.* New York: Dell, 1949.

———. *Sex and Temperament in Three Primitive Societies.* New York: Morrow, 1935.

Mitchell, Juliet. *Psychoanalysis and Feminism.* New York: Vintage, 1975.

Montague, Ashley. *The Natural Superiority of Women.* New York: Collier Books, 1974.

Morgan, Elaine. *The Descent of Woman.* New York: Stein & Day, 1972.

Morris, Desmond. *The Naked Ape.* New York: McGraw-Hill, 1968.

Reed, Evelyn. *Problems of Women's Liberation.* New York: Pathfinder Press, 1970.

———. *Woman's Evolution.* New York: Pathfinder Press, 1975.

Reiter, Rayna, ed. *Toward an Anthropology of Women.* New York: Monthly Review Press, 1975.

Rohrlich-Leavitt, Ruby, ed. *Women Cross-Culturally.* The Hague, the Netherlands: Mouton Press, 1975.

Rosaldo, Michelle Z., and Louise Lamphere, eds. *Women, Culture, and Society.* Stanford, Calif.: Stanford University Press, 1974.

Stone, Merlin. *When God Was a Woman.* New York: Harcourt Brace Jovanovich, 1978.

Tanner, Nancy, and Adrienne Zihlman. "Women in Evolution, Part I: Innovation and Selection in Human Origins." *Signs,* 1, No. 3, Pt. 1 (Spring 1976), 585–608.

Tavris, Carol, and Carole Offir. *The Longest War.* New York: Harcourt Brace Jovanovich, 1977.

Tiger, Lionel. *Men in Groups.* New York: Random House, 1969.

Tiger, Lionel, and Robin Fox. *The Imperial Animal.* New York: Holt, Rinehart and Winston, 1971.

Wilson, Edward O. *Sociobiology: The New Synthesis.* Cambridge, Mass.: Harvard University Press, 1975.

Zihlman, Adrienne L. "Women in Evolution, Part II: Subsistence and Social Organization among Early Hominids." *Signs,* 4, No. 1 (Autumn 1978), 4–20.

Chapter 6

Abbott, Sidney, and Barbara Love. *Sappho Was a Right-on Woman.* New York: Stein & Day, 1973.

Ashley, Jo Ann. *Hospitals, Paternalism, and the Role of the Nurse.* New York: Teachers College Press, 1976.

Barker, Diana Leonard, and Sheila Allen. *Dependence and Exploitation in Work and Marriage.* New York: Longman, 1976.

Barrett, Carol J. "Women in Widowhood." *Signs,* 2, No. 4 (Summer 1977), 856–868.

Bell, Ange Powell. "The Double Standard: Age." In *Women: A Feminist Perspective.* Ed. Jo Freeman. Palo Alto, Calif.: Mayfield, 1975.

Bengis, Ingrid. *Combat in the Erogenous Zone.* New York: Knopf, 1972.

Bernard, Jessie. *American Family Behavior.* New York: Russell & Russell, 1973.

———. *The Future of Marriage.* New York: Bantam, 1973.

———. *The Future of Motherhood.* New York: Dial, 1974.

———. *Remarriage.* New York: Russell & Russell, 1971.

———. *Sex Games: Communication Between the Sexes.* New York: Atheneum, 1972.

————. *Women in the Public Interest.* Chicago: Aldine, 1971.

————. *Women, Wives, Mothers: Values and Options.* Chicago: Aldine, 1975.

Billings, Victoria. *The Womansbook.* Los Angeles: Wollstonecraft, 1974.

Boston Women's Health Collective. *Our Bodies, Ourselves.* New York: Simon & Schuster, 1973.

Brownmiller, Susan. *Against Our Will: Men, Women, and Rape.* New York: Simon & Schuster, 1975.

Caine, Lynn. *Widow.* New York: Morrow, 1974.

Chafetz, Janet Saltzman. *Masculine/Feminine or Human?* Ithasca, Ill.: Peacock, 1974.

Ditzion, Sidney. *Marriage, Morals, and Sex in America: A History of Ideas.* New York: Norton, 1978.

Dworkin, Andrea. *Our Blood.* New York: Harper & Row, 1976.

————. *Woman-Hating.* New York: E. P. Dutton, 1974.

Erickson, Pat, and Mary Stewart. "The Sociology of Birth: A Critical Assessment of Theory and Research." *Social Science Journal,* 14, No. 2 (April 1977), 33–47.

Falk, Ruth. *Women Loving.* New York: Random House, 1975.

Feinberg, Joel, ed. *The Problem of Abortion.* Belmont, Calif.: Wadsworth, 1973.

Firestone, Shulamith. *The Dialectic of Sex.* New York: Bantam, 1971.

Frankfort, Ellen. *Vaginal Politics.* New York: Quadrangle, 1972.

Friedan, Betty. *The Feminine Mystique.* New York: Dell, 1963.

————. *It Changed My Life: Writings on the Women's Movement.* New York: Random House, 1976.

Frieze, Irene H., et al. *Women and Sex Roles.* New York: Norton, 1978.

Glazer, Nona, and Helen Youngelson Waehrer, eds. *Woman in a Man-Made World: A Socioeconomic Handbook.* Chicago: Rand McNally, 1977.

Greer, Germaine. *The Female Eunuch.* New York: McGraw-Hill, 1971.

Griffen, Joyce. "A Cross-Cultural Investigation of Behavioral Changes at Menopause." *Social Science Journal,* 14, No. 2 (April 1977), 49–65.

Griffin, Susan. *Rape: The Power of Consciousness.* San Francisco: Harper & Row, 1979.

Hite, Shere. *Sexual Honesty.* New York: Warner, 1974.

Hunt, Morton. *Sexual Behavior in the 1970's.* New York: Dell, 1975.

————. *The World of the Formerly Married.* New York: McGraw-Hill, 1966.

Jong, Erica. *Fear of Flying.* New York: Signet, 1973.

————. *Loveroot.* New York: Holt, Rinehart and Winston, 1976.

Kammeyer, Kenneth C. W., ed. *Confronting the Issues: Sex Roles, Marriage, and the Family.* Boston: Allyn & Bacon, 1975.

Levin, Ira. *The Stepford Wives.* Greenwich, Conn.: Fawcett, 1972.

McBride, Angela Barron. *Living with Contradictions: A Married Feminist.* New York: Harper Colophon, 1977.

Martin, Del, and Phyllis Lyon. *Lesbian/Woman.* New York: Bantam, 1972.

Millett, Kate. *Sexual Politics.* New York: Doubleday, 1970.

Mitchell, Juliet. *Woman's Estate.* New York: Vintage, 1973.

————. *Psychoanalysis and Feminism.* New York: Vintage, 1975.

Oakley, Ann. *Woman's Work: The Housewife Past and Present.* New York: Vintage, 1976.

O'Leary, Virginia E. "Female Sexuality." In *Toward Understanding Women.* Belmont, Calif.: Brooks-Cole, 1977.

Pizzey, Erin. *Scream Quietly or the Neighbors Will Hear.* Baltimore: Penguin, 1974.

Réage, Pauline. *Story of O.* Trans. Sabine d'Estrée. New York: Grove Press, 1965.

Rich, Adrienne. *Adrienne Rich's Poetry.* New York: Norton, 1975.

Russell, Bertrand. *Marriage and Morals.* New York: Liveright, 1929.

Sarton, May. *Journal of a Solitude.* New York: Norton, 1973.

Scanzoni, John. *Sexual Bargaining: Power Politics in the American Marriage.* Englewood Cliffs, N.J.: Prentice-Hall, 1972.

Seaman, Barbara. *Free and Female.* New York: Coward, McCann & Geoghegan, 1972.

Sheehy, Gail. *Passages.* New York: Dutton, 1976.

Shulman, Alix Kates. *Memoirs of an Ex-Prom Queen.* New York: Knopf, 1972.

Stannard, Una. *Mrs. Man.* San Francisco: Germain Books, 1977.

Wittig, Monique. *Les Guérillères.* Trans. David Le Vay. New York: Avon, 1973.

Chapter 7

Ahern, Dee Dee, and Betsy Bliss. *The Economics of Being a Woman.* New York: Macmillan, 1976.

Almquist, Elizabeth M. "Women in the Labor Force." *Signs,* 2, No. 4 (Summer 1977).

Auerbach, Sylvia. *A Woman's Book of Money: A Guide to Financial Independence.* New York: Doubleday, 1976.

Bell, Carolyn Shaw. "Social Security: Society's Last Discrimination." *Business and Society Review,* No. 3 (Autumn 1972).

Bird, Caroline. *Born Female: The High Cost of Keeping Women Down.* New York: David McKay, 1968.

Boserup, Ester. *Women's Role in Economic Development.* London: Allen and Unwin, 1970.

Brownlee, W. Elliot, and Mary H. Brownlee. *Women in the American Economy.* New Haven: Yale University Press, 1976.

Cassell, Kay Ann. "The Legal Status of Women." *Library Journal,* 96 (September 1971), 2600–2603.

DeCrow, Karen. *Sexist Justice.* New York: Vintage, 1975.

Diamond, Irene. *Sex Roles in the State House.* New Haven: Yale University Press, 1976.

Eastwood, Mary. "The Double Standard of Justice: Women's Rights Under the Constitution." *Valparaiso University Law Review,* 5, No. 2 (1971).

"Economy," *Fact Sheets on Institutional Sexism.* New York: Council on Interracial Books for Children, March 1976.

English, Jane, ed. *Sex Equality.* Englewood Cliffs, N.J.: Prentice-Hall, 1977.

Epstein, Cynthia Fuchs. *Woman's Place.* Berkeley, Calif.: University of California Press, 1970.

"E.R.A.: A Constitutional Basis for Equal Rights for Women." *Yale Law Journal,* Special Issue, 80, No. 5 (April 1971).

Fraser, Donald M. "Equity in Social Security for Individuals and Families." *Congressional Record,* 122, No. 82 (June 1976).

Freeman, Jo, ed. *Women: A Feminist Perspective.* 2nd ed. Palo Alto, Calif.: Mayfield, 1979.

Ginsberg, Ruth Bader. "The Equal Rights Amendment Is the Way." *Harvard Women's Law Journal,* 1, No. 1 (Spring 1978), 19–26.

————. "The Need for the Equal Rights Amendment." *American Bar Association Journal,* 59 (September 1973), 1013–1019.

Githens, Marianne, and Jewel L. Prestage, eds. *A Portrait of Marginality: The Political Behavior of the American Woman.* New York: David McKay, 1977.

Glazer, Nona, and Helen Youngelson Waehrer, eds. *Woman in a Man-Made World: A Socioeconomic Handbook.* Chicago: Rand McNally, 1977.

Goldberg, Marilyn Power. "The Economic Exploitation of Women." *Review of Radical Political Economics,* 2, No. 1 (Spring 1970).

Handbook on Women Workers — 1975. Washington, D.C.: Department of Labor, Women's Bureau.

"Hard Facts About Retirement for Women." *Changing Times,* June 1978, pp. 13–15.

Hennig, Margaret, and Anne Jardim. *The Managerial Woman.* New York: Doubleday, Anchor, 1977.

Hiller, Dana V., and Robin Ann Sheets, eds. *Women and Men: The Consequences of Power.* Part III. Cincinnati: University of Cincinnati, Office of Women's Studies, 1977.

Howe, Louise Kapp. *Pink Collar Workers.* New York: Putnam, 1977.

Jongeward, Dorothy, and Dru Scott. *Affirmative Action for Women: A Practical Guide for Women and Management.* Reading, Mass.: Addison-Wesley, 1975.

Joreen. "The 51 Percent Minority: A Statistical Essay." In *Sisterhood Is Powerful.* Ed. Robin Morgan. New York: Vintage, 1970.

Kanowitz, Leo. *Women and the Law: The Unfinished Revolution.* Albuquerque, N.M.: University of New Mexico Press, 1969.

Kerr, James R. "Why We Need a Woman on the

Supreme Court." *Alumnus,* Southern Illinois University at Edwardsville, Alumni Association Publication, 5, No. 3 (June 1977).

Keys, Hon. Martha. "Treatment of Women Under Social Security." *Congressional Record,* 124, No. 160 (October 1978).

Korda, Michael. *Male Chauvinism! How It Works.* New York: Random House, 1972.

Kreps, Juanita. *Sex in the Marketplace: American Women at Work.* Baltimore: Johns Hopkins Press, 1971.

Leo, Andre. "ADC: Marriage to the State." In *Notes from the Third Year.* Eds. Anne Koedt, and Shulamith Firestone. New York, 1971.

Macmanus, Susan A., and Nikki R. Van Hightower. "The Impacts of Local Government Tax Structures on Women: Inefficiencies and Inequalities." *Social Science Journal,* 14, No. 2 (April 1977).

A Matter of Simple Justice. Report of the President's Task Force on Women's Rights and Responsibilities. Washington, D.C.: Government Printing Office, 1970.

National Commission on the Observance of International Women's Year. *"To Form a More Perfect Union...": Justice for American Women.* Washington, D.C.: U.S. Department of State, 1976.

Oakley, Ann. *The Sociology of Housework.* New York: Pantheon, 1974.

Oppenheimer, Valerie K. *The Female Labor Force in the United States.* Population Monograph Series, no. 5. Berkeley: University of California, Institute of International Studies, 1970.

Porter, Sylvia. *Sylvia Porter's Money Book.* New York: Avon, 1976.

Ross, Heather L., and Isabel V. Sawhill. *Time of Transition.* Washington, D.C.: Urban Institute, 1975.

Self, Donnie J., ed. *Philosophy and Public Policy.* Norfolk, Virginia: Teagle and Little, 1977.

Stromberg, Ann H., and Shirley Harkess, eds. *Women Working.* Palo Alto: Mayfield, 1978.

Tavris, Carol, and Carole Offir. *The Longest War.* Chapter 7. New York: Harcourt Brace Jovanovich, 1977.

Tolchin, Susan. "The Exclusion of Women from the Judicial Process." *Signs,* 2, No. 4 (Summer 1977).

Tolchin, Susan, and Martin Tolchin. *Clout: Womanpower and Politics.* New York: Capricorn, 1976.

Underutilization of Women Workers. Washington, D.C.: U.S. Department of Labor, Women's Bureau, 1971.

U.S. Working Women: A Databook. Washington, D.C.: U.S. Department of Labor, Bureau of Labor Statistics, 1977.

Wallach, Aleta. "A View from the Law School." In *Women and the Power to Change.* Ed. Florence Howe. New York: McGraw-Hill, 1975.

"What's Social Security Got for You Now?" *Changing Times,* April 1978.

"Women and the Law: A Dialogue with Ruth Bader Ginsberg." *Women's Studies Newsletter,* 5, No. 4 (Fall 1977), 25–28.

"Women and Money: Beyond the Cookie Jar." *Monitor,* 3, No. 3 (May–June 1977).

Working Woman's Guide to Her Job Rights. Washington, D.C.: U.S. Department of Labor, Women's Bureau, 1974.

Chapter 8

Agonito, Rosemary, ed. *History of Ideas on Women: A Source Book.* New York: Capricorn, 1977.

Bardwick, Judith M., ed. *Readings on the Psychology of Women.* New York: Harper & Row, 1972.

Bullough, Vern L., and Bonnie Bullough. *The Subordinate Sex.* Baltimore: Penguin, 1974.

Chesler, Phyllis. *Women and Madness.* New York: Doubleday, 1972.

Chmaj, Betty E. *Image, Myth, and Beyond.* Pittsburgh: Know, Inc., 1972.

Christ, Carol P., and Judith Plaskow, eds. *Womanspirit Rising: A Feminist Reader in Religion.* San Francisco: Harper & Row, 1979.

Collins, Sheila D. *A Different Heaven and Earth.* Valley Forge, Pa.: Judson Press, 1974.

Daly, Mary. *Beyond God the Father.* Boston: Beacon Press, 1973.

————. *The Church and the Second Sex.* New York: Harper Colophon, 1975.

————. *Gyn/Ecology.* Boston: Beacon Press, 1978.

Davis, Elizabeth Gould. *The First Sex.* New York: Putnam, 1971.

Dworkin, Andrea. *Our Blood.* New York: Harper & Row, 1976.

———. *Woman-Hating.* New York: E. P. Dutton, 1974.

Ellmann, Mary. *Thinking About Women.* New York: Harcourt Brace Jovanovich, 1968.

Emswiler, Sharon Neufer, and Thomas Neufer Emswiler. *Women and Worship: A Guide to Non-Sexist Hymns, Prayers and Liturgies.* New York: Harper & Row, 1974.

Frieze, Irene H., et al. *Women and Sex Roles.* New York: Norton, 1978.

Gearhart, Sally, and William R. Johnson. *Loving Women — Loving Men: Gay Liberation and the Church.* San Francisco: Glide, 1974.

Griffin, Susan. *Woman and Nature: The Roaring Inside Her.* New York: Harper & Row, 1978.

Haskell, Molly. *From Reverence to Rape: The Treatment of Women in the Movies.* New York: Holt, Rinehart and Winston, 1973.

Hole, Judith, and Ellen Levine. *Rebirth of Feminism.* New York: Quadrangle, 1971.

Horner, Matina. "A Bright Woman Is Caught in a Double Bind." *Psychology Today,* 3, No. 6 (November 1969).

Iglehart, Hallie. "Unnatural Divorce of Spirituality and Politics." *Quest,* 14, No. 3 (Summer 1978).

Lerner, Gerda. *The Female Experience.* Indianapolis: Bobbs-Merrill, 1977.

Levin, Ira. *The Stepford Wives.* Greenwich, Conn.: Fawcett, 1972.

McBride, Angela Barron. *Living with Contradictions: A Married Feminist.* New York: Harper Colophon, 1977.

Mahowald, Mary B., ed. *Philosophy of Woman: Classical to Current Concepts.* Indianapolis: Hackett, 1978.

Mander, Anica V., and Anne K. Rush. *Feminism as Therapy.* New York: Random House, 1974.

Richardson, Betty. *Sexism in Higher Education.* New York: Seabury, 1974.

Rowbotham, Sheila. *Hidden from History.* New York: Vintage, 1976.

Ruether, Rosemary Radford, ed. *Religion and Sexism.* New York: Simon & Schuster, 1974.

Stacey, Judith, et al., eds. *And Jill Came Tumbling After: Sexism in American Education.* New York: Dell, 1974.

Stanton, Elizabeth Cady. *The Woman's Bible.* New York: Arno Press, 1972.

Stone, Merlin. *When God Was a Woman.* New York: Harcourt Brace Jovanovich, 1976.

Thorne, Barrie, and Nancy Henley, eds. *Language and Sex: Difference and Dominance.* Rowley, Mass.: Newbury House, 1975.

Tuchman, Gaye, Arlene K. Daniels, and James Benét, eds. *Hearth and Home: Images of Women in the Mass Media.* New York: Oxford University Press, 1978.

Chapter 9

Abbott, Sidney, and Barbara Love. *Sappho Was a Right-on Woman.* New York: Stein & Day, 1973.

Adelstein, Michael E., and Jean G. Pival, eds. *Women's Liberation.* New York: St. Martin's, 1972.

Altbach, Edith Hoshino, ed. *From Feminism to Liberation.* Cambridge, Mass.: Schenkman, 1971.

Amundsen, Kirsten. *The Silenced Majority: Women and American Democracy.* Englewood Cliffs, N.J.: Prentice-Hall, 1971.

Babcox, Deborah, and Madeline Belkin, comps. *Liberation Now!* New York: Dell, 1971.

Banner, Lois W. *Women in Modern America: A Brief History.* New York: Harcourt Brace Jovanovich, 1974.

Baxandall, Rosalyn, et al., eds. *America's Working Women.* New York: Random House, 1976.

Beal, Frances M. "Slave of a Slave No More: Black Women in Struggle." *The Black Scholar,* 6 (March 1975), 2–10.

Bunch, Charlotte. "Beyond Either/Or: Feminist Options." *Quest,* 3, No. 1 (Winter, 1977), 2–17.

Cade, Toni. *The Black Woman.* New York: Signet, 1970.

Chafe, William H. *The American Woman: Her Changing Social, Economic, and Political Roles, 1920–1970.* New York: Oxford University Press, 1974.

Chisholm, Shirley. "Race, Revolution, and Women." *The Black Scholar,* 2 (December 1971), 17–21.

————. *Unbought and Unbossed.* New York: Avon, 1971.

Cotera, Martha P. *The Chicana Feminist.* Austin, Tex.: Information Systems Development, 1977.

————. *Diosa y Hembra: The History and Heritage of Chicanas in the United States.* Austin, Texas: Information Systems Development, 1976.

Daly, Mary. *Beyond God the Father.* Boston: Beacon Press, 1973.

————. *The Church and the Second Sex.* New York: Harper Colophon, 1975.

————. *Gyn/Ecology.* Boston: Beacon Press, 1978.

Davis, Angela. "Reflections on the Black Woman's Role in the Community of Slaves." *The Black Scholar,* 3, No. 4 (December 1971), 2–16.

————. *With My Mind on Freedom: An Autobiography.* New York: Random House, 1974.

de Beauvoir, Simone. *The Second Sex.* Trans. and ed. H. M. Parshley. New York: Knopf, 1953.

Deckard, Barbara. *The Women's Movement.* 2nd ed. New York: Harper & Row, 1979.

Decter, Midge. *The New Chastity and Other Arguments Against Women's Liberation.* New York: Coward, McCann & Geoghegan, 1972.

Ellis, Julie. *Revolt of the Second Sex.* New York: Lancer, 1970.

English, Jane, ed. *Sex Equality.* Englewood Cliffs, N.J.: Prentice-Hall, 1977.

Firestone, Shulamith. *The Dialectic of Sex.* New York: Bantam, 1971.

Flexner, Eleanor. *Century of Struggle.* New York: Atheneum, 1973.

Freeman, Jo, ed. *Women: A Feminist Perspective.* 2nd ed. Palo Alto, Calif.: Mayfield, 1979.

Gonzales, Sylvia. "The White Feminist Movement: The Chicana Perspective." *Social Science Journal,* 14, No. 2 (April 1977), 67–76.

Gould, Carol C., and Marx W. Wartofsky, eds. *Women and Philosophy: Toward a Theory of Liberation.* New York: Putnam, 1976.

Gurko, Miriam. *The Ladies of Seneca Falls: The Birth of the Women's Rights Movement.* New York: Macmillan, 1974.

Hole, Judith, and Ellen Levine. *Rebirth of Feminism.* New York: Quadrangle, 1971.

Jacobs, Sue-Ellen, and Karen T. Hansen. *Anthropological Studies of Women: A Course for Independent Study.* Seattle: University of Washington, 1977.

Jagger, Alison M., and Paula R. Struhl, eds. *Feminist Frameworks.* New York: McGraw-Hill, 1978.

Janeway, Elizabeth. *Man's World, Woman's Place.* New York: Delta, 1971.

Johnston, Jill. *Lesbian Nation.* New York: Simon & Schuster, 1973.

Kraditor, Aileen S. *The Ideas of the Woman Suffrage Movement, 1890–1920.* New York: Columbia University Press, 1965.

————, ed. *Up from the Pedestal.* Chicago: Quadrangle, 1968.

Mahowald, Mary B., ed. *Philosophy of Woman: Classical to Current Concepts.* Indianapolis: Hackett, 1978.

Marine, Gene. *A Male Guide to Women's Liberation.* New York: Avon, 1972.

Martin, Del, and Phyllis Lyon. *Lesbian/Woman.* New York: Bantam, 1972.

Martin, Wendy, ed. *The American Sisterhood.* New York: Harper & Row, 1972.

Millman, Marcia, and Rosabeth M. Kanter, eds. *Another Voice: Feminist Perspectives on Social Science.* New York: Doubleday, 1975.

Mitchell, Juliet. *Woman's Estate.* New York: Vintage, 1973.

Morgan, Robin, ed. *Sisterhood Is Powerful.* New York: Vintage, 1972.

Myron, Nancy, and Charlotte Bunch, eds. *Lesbianism and the Women's Movement.* Oakland, Calif.: Diana Press, 1975.

Nieto, Consuelo. "The Chicana and the Women's Rights Movement." *Civil Rights Digest,* 6, No. 3 (Spring, 1974), 36–42.

Papachristou, Judith, ed. *Women Together: A History in Documents of the Women's Movement in the United States.* A *Ms.* book. New York: Knopf, 1976.

Reid, Inez Smith. *"Together" Black Women.* New York: Third Press, 1975.

Rosaldo, Michelle Z., and Louise Lamphere, eds. *Woman, Culture, and Society.* Stanford, Calif.: Stanford University Press, 1974.

Rossi, Alice S., ed. *The Feminist Papers.* New York: Bantam, 1973.

Rowbotham, Sheila. *Woman's Consciousness, Man's World.* Baltimore: Penguin, 1973.

———. *Women, Resistance and Revolution.* New York: Vintage, 1974.

Ryan, Mary P. *Womanhood in America: From Colonial Times to the Present.* New York: Franklin Watts, 1975.

Schneir, Miriam, ed. *Feminism: The Essential Historical Writings.* New York: Random House, 1971.

Sochen, June. *Herstory.* Sherman Oaks, Calif.: Alfred Publishing Co., 1974.

———. *Movers and Shakers: American Women Thinkers and Activists, 1900–1970.* New York: Quadrangle, 1974.

Spirit of Houston: The First National Women's Conference. Washington, D.C.: U.S. Department of State, National Commission on the Observance of Women's Year, 1978.

Stanton, Elizabeth Cady, Susan B. Anthony, and Matilda Joslyn Gage, eds. *History of Woman Suffrage.* 3 vols. New York: Fowler and Wells, 1881–1886.

Staples, Robert. *The Black Woman in America.* Chicago: Nelson Hall, 1973.

Tanner, Leslie B., ed. *Voices from Women's Liberation.* New York: Signet, 1970.

Tavris, Carol, and Carole Offir. *The Longest War.* New York: Harcourt Brace Jovanovich, 1977.

Thompson, Mary Lou, ed. *Voices of the New Feminism.* Boston: Beacon Press, 1970.

Current Periodicals

International Journal of Women's Studies. Eden Press, Box 51, St. Albans, Vermont 05478

Quest: A Feminist Quarterly. Box 8843, Washington, D.C.

Signs: Journal of Women in Culture and Society. University of Chicago Press, 11030 Langley Ave., Chicago, Illinois 60628

University of Michigan Papers in Women's Studies. 1058 LSA Bldg., University of Michigan, Ann Arbor, Michigan 48104

Womanspirit: A Quarterly Journal at Equinoxes and Solstices. Box 263, Wolf Creek, Oregon.

Women's Studies International Quarterly. Pergamon Press Ltd., Oxford, England

Women's Studies Newsletter. Feminist Press, Box 334, Old Westbury, N.Y. 11568

Index

Abolition
  and class, 490, 492
  and women's movement, 449–450,
    460–468, 472, 565
Abortion, 267, 287–300, 359, 515, 529
Abstinence. *See* Sexual abstinence
Achievement motivation, 170–175
Adams, Abigail, 447, 449, 564
Addams, Jane, 567–568
Adultery, 529. *See also* Prostitution
Advertising, 107–114, 385, 416–417
Affect, 52–53
Affirmative action, 411–412, 448
After-marriage, 260–264
Ageism, 346
Aggression, and testosterone, 208
Aid to Families with Dependent
    Children (AFDC), 319
Alaska Native Sisterhood, 567
Alimony and child support, 316, 361
Alterity. *See* Other, woman as
Ambivalence, toward women, 87–88
American Association of University
    Women, 566
American Bar Association, and ERA,
    369
American Federation of Labor
    (AFL), 494–495, 498, 500
American Revolution, 564
American Woman Suffrage Associa-
    tion (AWSA), 468, 495, 566
Amir, Menachem, 301–307 *passim*
Anatomy, as destiny, 91, 197
Androcentrism. *See* Masculism
Androgyne, splitting of, 155–157
Anthony, Susan B.
  and abolition, 465
  and labor movement, 495
  political action, 491, 565, 566
  and suffrage, 370, 467–470, 476,
    482
"Anthropological Approaches to the
    Subordination of Women," 195–
    204
Anthropology, 195–204
  sexism in, 195–196, 214–222
Anti-Semitism, 146

Anti-Slavery Convention of American
    Women, 564
Anxiety, 171, 172, 174–175
Appearance, 266. *See also* Attractive-
    ness
Aquinas, Saint Thomas, 3, 98
Arendt, Hannah, 527, 562
Aristotle, 3, 36
Arms race, 78–79
Art, origin of, 217
Art administration, 428–429, 433–
    435
Artists, 427–429, 431–434, 436
Arts and films, 386–387
  sex distribution in, 428–429, 433–
    434
Ashley, Jessie, 496–497
Association of Collegiate Alumnae,
    566
Atkinson, John, 171
Attractiveness, 161
Authenticity, 144
Autonomy, 4

Bachofen, J. J., 201, 223, 226, 231
Bagley, Sarah, 491
Balch, Emily Green, 568
Barre, Poulain de la, 144–145
Barton, Clara, 565
Bates, Daisy, 568
Battered wives, 362, 564
Baxandall, Rosalyn F., 347
Beard, Mary, 405
Beauty, 161
Beauvoir, Simone de, 139, 404–405,
    568
Belmont, Alva, 445
Berger, Caruthers, 516
Bernard, Jessie, 26–27, 252, 545
Bernard, Shirley, 319
Bethune, Mary McLeod, 567, 568
"Beyond Intellectual Sexism," 21–26
Bias, in education, 6–9. *See also*
    Discrimination; Oppression;
    Sexual asymmetry
Bickerdyke, Mother, 565
Binary mental structures, 200
Biology, 189–190, 197–199, 204–214

Bird, Caroline, 28
Biren, Joan, 556
Birth, first, 87, 194, 392
Birth control. *See* Contraception
Bisexuality 126, 127, 137
Blacks
  discrimination against and anti-
    feminism, 146, 307–308, 310–
    311, 528–529
  earnings and income, 541–543,
    545
  education among, 538–539
  female stereotype, 95–96
  occupational distribution among,
    539–543
  perception of oppression, 539–543
  sex roles for, 534
  See also Black women
Blackstone, Sir William, 325, 360
Blackwell, Elizabeth, 565
Black women, 95–96, 535–536
  and rape, 307–311
  See also Black women's move-
    ment; Racism
Black Women Organized for Action,
    533, 537, 543
Black women's movement, 489, 497,
    499–500, 532–551, 566, 568
Bloomer, Amelia, 467, 482, 565
Bodies
  as chattel, 265–269, 309–310
  control of, 508–511, 515
Bonding, 198, 204, 210–213
Bradwell v. *The State*, 357
Brent, Margaret, 563
Bride capture, 233–234
Bridenthal, Renate, 404
"Bright Woman Is Caught in a
    Double Bind, A," 170–175
Brown, Rita Mae, 553–556
Brownmiller, Susan, 232
Bunch, Charlotte, 551
Busby, Linda, 417
Business, 58–60
Business and Professional Women
    (BPW), 451
Bysiewicz, Shirley Raissi, 354

Student Evaluation Form for Issues in Feminism: A First Course in Women's Studies

Your comments on this book will help us in developing other new textbooks and future editions of this book. Please answer the following questions and mail this page to: **College Marketing Services, Houghton Mifflin Company, One Beacon Street, Boston, MA 02107**

1. What was your overall impression of the book? _____

_____

_____

2. Did you find the book interesting and readable? ___ Yes ___ No

If not, what problems did you have? _____

_____

3. How would you rate the following features of the text?

	Excellent	Very good	Good	Fair	Poor
Chapter organization: author's text followed by selections	—	—	—	—	—
Author's text	—	—	—	—	—
Introductory notes to selections	—	—	—	—	—
Length of selections	—	—	—	—	—
Variety of selections	—	—	—	—	—
Interest level	—	—	—	—	—

Feel free to comment on any of the above items. _____

_____

_____

4. Which chapters were required reading for your class? _____

_____

_____

5. Did you read any chapters on your own that were not required reading? _____

_____

_____

6. Are there any topics you think should have been covered in the text, but were not?

_____

_____

7. Did you find the book stimulating? Did you find yourself strongly agreeing or disagreeing with what you read? _____

_____

_____

8. Which selections were especially interesting to you? _____

_____

_____

9. Which selections would you omit from future editions of the book? _____

_____

_____

10. Did you find the bibliography useful for further reading and research? _____

_____

11. Do you have any suggestions that might make this a better textbook? _____

_____

_____

_____

Name of your school: _____

Course title: _____

Department offering the course: _____

Level: __ Freshman __ Sophomore __ Junior __ Senior __ Graduate

Number of students in the class: _____

Your major: _____